PERSONALITY, IDENTITY, AND CHARACTER

Moral notions are foundational questions that have commanded deep reflection since antiquity, reflection that psychological science cannot evade, because the moral formation of children is a central concern of parents, schools, and communities charged with educating the next generation. In this respect there are few domains of study more crucial than moral psychology, and few topics of greater importance than the development of moral self-identity, of moral character, and of the moral personality. Heretofore, the fragmented research on moral personality has been mostly a study of cognition without desires, rationality without brains, agents without contexts, selves without culture, traits without persons, persons without attachments, dispositions without development. This edited volume features the expertise of preeminent scholars in moral personality, self, and identity, such as moral philosophers, personality theorists, developmental psychologists, moral personality researchers, social psychologists, and neuroscientists. It brings together cutting-edge work in moral psychology that illustrates an impressive diversity of theoretical perspectives and methodologies, and simultaneously points the way toward promising integrative possibilities.

Darcia Narvaez is an Associate Professor in Psychology, specializing in moral development and character education, at the University of Notre Dame and directs the university's Collaborative for Ethical Education. She is coeditor of *The Handbook on Moral and Character Education* (with Larry Nucci), *Moral Development in the Professions: Psychology and Applied Ethics* (with James Rest), and coauthor or coeditor of the award-winning books *Postconventional Moral Thinking: A Neo-Kohlbergian Approach* (with James Rest, Muriel Bebeau, and Stephen Thoma) and *Moral Development, Self, and Identity* (with Daniel Lapsley). Narvaez was the leader of the design team for the Minnesota Community Voices and Character Education Project. She currently serves on the editorial boards of the *Journal of Educational Psychology* and the *Journal of Moral Education*.

Daniel K. Lapsley is the ACE Collegiate Professor of Psychology and Chair of the Department of Psychology at the University of Notre Dame. He is the author or editor of seven books, including *Moral Psychology*, and of numerous articles and chapters on various topics in child and adolescent development – particularly in the areas of social cognition, personality development, moral psychology, and moral education. He is coeditor of the award-winning book *Moral Development, Self, and Identity* (with Darcia Narvaez). He currently serves on the editorial boards of the *Journal of Educational Psychology* and the *Journal of Early Adolescence*.

For our parents,

MAXINE, RICHARD, CORRINE, THOMAS

Personality, Identity, and Character

EXPLORATIONS IN MORAL PSYCHOLOGY

Edited by

Darcia Narvaez
University of Notre Dame

Daniel K. Lapsley
University of Notre Dame

CAMBRIDGE
UNIVERSITY PRESS

University Printing House, Cambridge CB2 8BS, United Kingdom

One Liberty Plaza, 20th Floor, New York, NY 10006, USA

477 Williamstown Road, Port Melbourne, VIC 3207, Australia

314-321, 3rd Floor, Plot 3, Splendor Forum, Jasola District Centre, New Delhi - 110025, India

79 Anson Road, #06-04/06, Singapore 079906

Cambridge University Press is part of the University of Cambridge.

It furthers the University's mission by disseminating knowledge in the pursuit of education, learning and research at the highest international levels of excellence.

www.cambridge.org
Information on this title: www.cambridge.org/9780521719278

© Cambridge University Press 2009

This publication is in copyright. Subject to statutory exception
and to the provisions of relevant collective licensing agreements,
no reproduction of any part may take place without the written
permission of Cambridge University Press.

First published 2009

A catalogue record for this publication is available from the British Library

Library of Congress Cataloging in Publication data
    Personality, identity, and character : explorations in moral psychology / edited by Darcia Narvaez, Daniel K. Lapsley.
      p. cm.
    Includes bibliographical references and index.
    ISBN 978-0-521-89507-1 (hbk.) – ISBN 978-0-521-71927-8 (pbk.)
    1. Moral development.   2. Judgment (Ethics)   3. Psychology – Philosophy.
    I. Narvaez, Darcia.   II. Lapsley, Daniel K.   III. Title.
    BF723.M54P46 2009
    155.2'5–dc22   2009002830

ISBN 978-0-521-89507-1 Hardback
ISBN 978-0-521-71927-8 Paperback

Cambridge University Press has no responsibility for the persistence or accuracy of URLs for external or third-party internet websites referred to in this publication, and does not guarantee that any content on such websites is, or will remain, accurate or appropriate.

CONTENTS

Contributors		*page* vii
Introduction		1
1.	The Moral Personality *Dan P. McAdams*	11
2.	The Moral Functioning of the Person as a Whole: On Moral Psychology and Personality Science *Daniel Cervone and Ritu Tripathi*	30
3.	Moral Science? Still Metaphysical After All These Years *Owen Flanagan*	52
4.	Cultural Pluralism and Moral Identity *David B. Wong*	79
5.	Neuroscience and Morality: Moral Judgments, Sentiments, and Values *Jorge Moll, Ricardo de Oliveira-Souza, and Roland Zahn*	106
6.	Triune Ethics Theory and Moral Personality *Darcia Narvaez*	136
7.	Early Foundations: Conscience and the Development of Moral Character *Ross A. Thompson*	159
8.	The Development of the Moral Personality *Daniel K. Lapsley and Patrick L. Hill*	185

9. Urban Neighborhoods as Contexts for Moral Identity Development 214
Daniel Hart and M. Kyle Matsuba

10. Moral Personality Exemplified 232
Lawrence J. Walker and Jeremy A. Frimer

11. Greatest of the Virtues? Gratitude and the Grateful Personality 256
Robert A. Emmons

12. The Elusive Altruist: The Psychological Study of the Altruistic Personality 271
Gustavo Carlo, Lisa M. PytlikZillig, Scott C. Roesch, and Richard A. Dienstbier

13. Growing Toward Care: A Narrative Approach to Prosocial Moral Identity and Generativity of Personality in Emerging Adulthood 295
Michael W. Pratt, Mary Louise Arnold, and Heather Lawford

14. Moral Identity, Integrity, and Personal Responsibility 316
Barry R. Schlenker, Marisa L. Miller, and Ryan M. Johnson

15. The Dynamic Moral Self: A Social Psychological Perspective 341
Benoît Monin and Alexander H. Jordan

16. The Double-Edged Sword of a Moral State of Mind 355
Linda J. Skitka and G. Scott Morgan

17. Moral Identity in Business Situations: A Social-Cognitive Framework for Understanding Moral Functioning 375
Karl Aquino and Dan Freeman

18. The Moral Functioning of Mature Adults and the Possibility of Fair Moral Reasoning 396
Augusto Blasi

19. Moral Personality: Themes, Questions, Futures 441
Darcia Narvaez and Daniel K. Lapsley

Author Index 449
Subject Index 451

CONTRIBUTORS

KARL AQUINO
University of British Columbia

MARY LOUISE ARNOLD
Ontario Institute for Studies in Education

AUGUSTO BLASI
University of Massachusetts, Boston

GUSTAVO CARLO
University of Nebraska–Lincoln

DANIEL CERVONE
University of Illinois at Chicago

RICARDO DE OLIVEIRA-SOUZA
LABS-D'Or Hospital Network and Gaffree e Guinle University Hospital, Rio de Janeiro, Brazil

RICHARD A. DIENSTBIER
University of Nebraska–Lincoln

ROBERT A. EMMONS
University of California, Davis

OWEN FLANAGAN
Duke University

DAN FREEMAN
University of Delaware

JEREMY A. FRIMER
University of British Columbia

DANIEL HART
Rutgers University

PATRICK L. HILL
University of Notre Dame

RYAN M. JOHNSON
University of Florida

ALEXANDER H. JORDAN
Stanford University

DANIEL K. LAPSLEY
University of Notre Dame

HEATHER LAWFORD
Concordia University

M. KYLE MATSUBA
University of Missouri–St. Louis

DAN P. MCADAMS
Northwestern University

MARISA L. MILLER
U.S. Army Research Institute, Fort Benning, Georgia

JORGE MOLL
*LABS-D'Or Hospital Network,
Rio de Janeiro, Brazil*

BENOÎT MONIN
Stanford University

G. SCOTT MORGAN
University of Illinois at Chicago

DARCIA NARVAEZ
University of Notre Dame

MICHAEL W. PRATT
Wilfrid Laurier University

LISA M. PYTLIKZILLIG
University of Nebraska–Lincoln

SCOTT C. ROESCH
University of Nebraska–Lincoln

BARRY R. SCHLENKER
University of Florida

LINDA J. SKITKA
University of Illinois at Chicago

ROSS A. THOMPSON
University of California, Davis

RITU TRIPATHI
University of Illinois at Chicago

LAWRENCE J. WALKER
University of British Columbia

DAVID B. WONG
Duke University

ROLAND ZAHN
The University of Manchester

Introduction

In the last decade there has been a remarkable resurgence of interest in studying moral rationality within the broad context of personality, selfhood, and identity. Although a concern with the moral self was never entirely absent from the cognitive developmental approach to moral reasoning, it is fair to say that sustained preoccupation with the ontogenesis of justice reasoning did not leave much room for reflection on how moral cognition intersects with personological processes. Indeed, some topics, such as moral personality, moral selfhood and identity, and the study of virtues and of character were pushed to the margins for paradigmatic or strategic reasons, because, for example, such notions could not be reconciled to moral judgment stage-typing, or could not provide what was wanted most, which was a way to defeat ethical relativism on psychological grounds.

Yet the neglect of the moral dimensions of selfhood and personality could not endure for long, mostly because moral notions go to the very heart of what it means to be a person. Moral notions penetrate our conceptions of what it means to live well the life that is good for one to live. These are foundational questions that have commanded deep reflection since antiquity, reflection that psychological science cannot evade, not the least because the moral formation of children is the central concern of parents, schools, and communities who are charged with educating the next generation. It matters to us that we raise children to be persons of a certain kind. It matters to us that we become such persons. In this respect there are few domains of study more crucial than moral psychology, and few topics of greater importance than the development of moral self-identity, moral character, and moral personality.

Yet moral psychology is not a cohesive field of study, and, indeed, psychology is not a unified discipline. As a result, research that is relevant to moral psychology can be found in diverse literatures and fields of study that invariably invoke different theoretical traditions, methodologies, and terms of reference. Some of the best writings on moral psychology are not written by psychologists at all, in fact, but by philosophers, two of whom are contributors to this volume. Oftentimes researchers who study dispositions do so without the moral domain in mind. Or, those who study the dispositional aspects of moral functioning – under the headings, say, of moral self-identity, character, or personality – propose powerful and interesting models, albeit without developmental grounding, bypassing entirely relevant developmental literatures that might serve integrative purposes. In turn developmental research on moral self-identity would profit from the well-attested literatures of social and personality psychology that flesh out adult forms of moral psychological functioning. As it stands now, "moral personality" is like an orphan who wanders about developmental, personality, and social psychological neighborhoods, recognizing some commonplaces but getting lost all the same.

We would like to bring the study of moral personality home to an integrative field of study. The purpose of this edited volume is to provide a seedbed for the study of the moral self and the nature of moral identity, personality, and character. The impetus for this volume was the *2006 Notre Dame Symposium on Personality and Moral Character*, which brought together renowned scholars from diverse perspectives to wrestle with how best to understand the moral dimensions of personality, and what this might require by way of theory and methodology. To our knowledge this was the first time that nationally visible scholars representing developmental, social, personality, and cognitive psychology were assembled to address theoretical and empirical questions regarding moral selfhood, personality, and identity. A second *Notre Dame Symposium* in 2008, held under the auspices of Notre Dame's College of Arts and Letters Henkels Lecture Series, resulted in more voices being added to the ongoing conversation.

The aim of the two Notre Dame symposia, and now of this volume, is to carve out space for a new field of study on the moral self that is deeply integrative across the domains of psychology, philosophy, and neuroscience. Heretofore, the fragmented research on moral personality has been mostly a study of cognition without desires, rationality without brains, agents without contexts, selves without culture, traits without persons, persons without attachments, dispositions without development. We hope the present volume starts to change all that. One will find here diverse points of view and genuine disagreement about the meaning of foundational constructs, to be sure, but we are confident that the volume points the way to promising integrative futures.

OVERVIEW OF THE CHAPTERS

The volume includes contributions from philosophy, personality, neuroscience, and from social and developmental psychology. We were tempted to group this overview by discipline, but such an organizing scheme would only reinforce disciplinary boundaries and undermine the volume's thematic intention, which is that such boundaries are likely to get in the way of strong integrative theory building and research.

The first two chapters set the pace for the volume by presenting options for moral personality from the perspective of extant theory and research in personality science. In the first chapter, Dan McAdams explores the implications of his "new Big Five" perspective for the moral personality, while Daniel Cervone and Ritu Tripathi take up the social cognitive option in the second.

For McAdams, personality is (1) an individual's unique variation on general evolutionary design for human nature, which is (2) experienced as a pattern of dispositional traits, (3) characteristic adaptations, and (4) self-defining life narratives, which are (5) situated complexly in social contexts and culture. If one wants to ask about moral personality, one must first specify at what level the question is directed. Moral personality is a plural concept. Moral considerations are embedded at each level, although perhaps morality is of prime importance in the construction of self-defining life stories – the internalized and evolving narratives that people construct to make meaning and find purpose in life. In summarizing 15 years of research on life stories of generative adults, McAdams contends that life stories of personal redemption are particularly valued as a powerful narrative of virtue and goodness in American adult life, one that provides a script that motivates, sustains, and provides meaning for moral projects.

In Cervone and Tripathi's view, a more flexible approach to personality theory is available in the social-cognitive perspective. They emphasize a model that includes cognitive appraisal and the limits of working memory that can move us down the road in explaining the shifting behavior people exhibit. They show how the Knowledge-and-Appraisal Architecture (KAPA) model of personality best captures the distinction between affective and cognitive processes, and contextual variation, in disposition. KAPA provides a way to characterize the consistency in personality across situations by combining "enduring knowledge about the self" and "dynamic processes of meaning construction that occur within a given encounter," factors that vary idiosyncratically and are constrained by working memory limitations. In each situation, the individual appraises affordances based on self-efficacy (knowledge of self) in the context (beliefs about the situation). Appraisals operate continually as dynamic functions within situations, allowing the individual to select an appropriate course of action.

Owen Flanagan (Chapter 3) and David Wong (Chapter 4) each provide powerful philosophical perspectives on personality and identity. Flanagan defends the notion of personality against recent claims that character traits do not exist or, if they do exist, are trumped easily by the demand characteristics of situations. He also unpacks problematic metaphysical assumptions that underlie self-narratives, including the notion of "free will," and certain master-narratives ("hard work and effort pay") that function like heuristics, but are larded with descriptive and normative claims that do not bear analysis. His point here is that proper moral education requires the examination and critique of the metaphysical assumptions underlying moral precepts, especially in regards to master-narratives about the self or the good life.

In Chapter 4, Wong explores the interplay among culture, morality, and identity. In his naturalistic theory, moralities are part of culture. After sorting out various philosophical difficulties with respect to culture, Wong proposes that we think of culture as a kind of conversation that necessarily involves plural voices, and he works out the implications of this metaphor for understanding moral identity. For example, he points out the differences between a conversationalist view of culture – one that fluctuates, exhibits tensions, diversity, and contradictions – and an essentialist view that considers culture fixed and static. The conversationalist view allows the individual to select which aspects of a culture to adopt, to adapt, or reject. Within this conversation, one's moral identity may also fluctuate. Wong urges us to consider that such culturally flexible behavior may also apply to morality. Individuals may be not only linguistically bilingual but also morally bilingual.

The first four chapters, then, provide overviews and critiques of moral personality from psychological and philosophical perspectives. The next two chapters take up neuroscience and evolutionary perspectives on moral functioning. In Chapter 5, Jorge Moll, Ricardo de Oliveiros-Souza, and Roland Zahn review the research on moral cognitive neuroscience. They stress that human emotion and cognition functionally are not separate but intertwined, which is most evident in the experience of a moral dilemma when motivational significance is linked to abstract symbols and ideas. They note that the neurophysiology of attachment often underlies moral motivation. The brain systems that promote attachment enable humans to imbue other things with motivational abstract meaning, or what the authors' call "sophisticated moral sentiments." These allow an individual to embrace broader notions of "other" as understood by his culture, which Moll et al. term "extended attachment," at the same time "promoting altruistic behaviors within sociocultural groups" and "facilitating outgroup moralistic aggression."

The next chapter by Darcia Narvaez also builds on evolutionary neuroscience to suggest a dynamic view of moral personality, expressed as three ethics rooted in evolved strata of the brain. The three basic moral orientations – Security, Engagement, and Imagination – can be dispositional or situationally activated, influencing perceptual processing and goal salience. The most primitive and related to survival, Security, becomes the default ethic, if early experience is too far from the environment of evolutionary adaptedness. To develop sophistication, the other ethics require nurturing experience during sensitive periods. Narvaez challenges moral psychology to pay more attention to early development, sensitive periods, and their relation to moral functioning.

In Chapter 7, Ross Thompson reviews developmental literatures that speak to the development of moral character in early childhood. After reviewing classic moral developmental theories, he explores current research findings on the development achievements of infants and young children, including the ability to understand others' needs, awareness of intentionality and of normative behavioral standards. Although these literatures are not traditionally considered a contribution to moral development, they are clearly foundational to the emergence of the moral self. Thompson also reviews evidence regarding moral affect and on the development of conscience, which he regards as the foundation of the moral personality. Conscience can be defined as the cognitive, affective, and relational processes that influence how young children construct and act consistently with generalizable, internal standards of conduct. The burgeoning research on early conscience development shows that young children are developing moral orientations that are simpler, but fundamentally similar, to those of older children and adolescents, and that the moral capacities of youngsters have been underestimated. Thompson argues that the conceptual foundations of moral reasoning are well-established in early childhood; and that the development of cooperation and compliance and other features of the moral self are bound up with the dynamics of early relationships with caregivers.

Daniel Lapsley and Patrick Hill (Chapter 8) also take up developmental issues, but their starting point is modern personality theory. Lapsley and Hill begin by considering some broad issues concerning the basic units of personality, and recent advances in understanding the trait-structure and types of personality. They then extract five themes from the extant empirical literature on personality development – including temperament, persons, and contexts, continuity and consequence, the special status of early adulthood – and explore their implications for theory and research in the moral character development literature. After noting the two traditions of social cognitive development, Lapsley and Hill attempt to explicate a possible developmental course for the social cognitive mechanisms that seem to underlie moral self-identity, as well as prospects for future integrative research.

In Chapter 9, Daniel Hart and Kyle Matsuba present a distinctive model which claims that the contours of moral identity are constrained not only by stable aspects of personality but also by characteristics of family and neighborhood, a view that aligns with the best insights of developmental contextualism. By invoking two constituent layers to moral personality – enduring "dispositional traits" and "characteristic adaptations" – the model shares some affinity with the "new Big Five" framework of McAdams, "but it emphasizes the importance of broader contextual influences as well." Whereas moral identity includes self-awareness, a sense of self-integration, and continuity over time, a commitment to plans of action and an attachment to one's moral goals, moral identity is also a joint product of personal and contextual factors. They review evidence of factors that lead to moral commitment, including relationships that draw adolescents into moral activities and protect against "moral collapse." Community service is one such activity that promotes moral identity and civic engagement.

The new Big Five framework is also put to good use by Lawrence Walker and Jeremy Frimer (Chapter 10) who examined adult brave and caring exemplars. Walker and Frimer assessed moral personality at the levels of dispositional traits, characteristic adaptations, and integrative self-narratives, along with moral reasoning. Overall, caring and brave exemplars were distinguished in their personality profiles, with strong differences (favoring caring exemplars) evident in nurturance, generativity, and optimistic affective tone. Moreover, the caring exemplars' communal, generative, and affiliation/intimacy orientations were evident both at the levels of characteristic adaptations and in the life-story narratives. Differences between moral exemplars and non-exemplars were also examined and were best revealed, not so much at the level of dispositions and adaptations, but at the level of life-story narratives. Walker and Frimer identified a foundational core to the moral personality, which is characterized by (1) an orientation to agency and communion; (2) the tendency to reframe critical life events redemptively, that is, as leading to positive results; (3) the presence of mentors and helpers in early life; and (4) the quality of childhood attachments.

Robert Emmons (Chapter 11) describes the rich yield that result from explicating the features of a particular virtue – gratitude – and the role it plays in motivating moral action. For Emmons, gratitude serves as a moral barometer that provides one with an affective readout, which accompanies the perception that another has treated one prosocially, as well as with a moral motive. Reviewing evidence of the "moral motive hypothesis," Emmons shows that gratitude shapes prosocial responding, and that gratitude is a psychologically substantive experience, relevant to how people negotiate their moral and interpersonal lives.

From gratitude we move on to the dispositional basis of altruism. Is there such a thing as the "altruistic personality"? Gustavo Carlo, Lisa PytlikZillig, Scott Roesch, and Richard Dienstbier (Chapter 12) think there is. After reviewing the empirical basis of their claim, they describe a study on those who volunteer others to help victims, reporting that those with greater altruism were more likely to volunteer themselves, especially when trait distress was high. Moreover, sex differences were found for those volunteering others. Men with high distress and high prosocial traits were *more* likely to send others to help whereas women with these traits were *less* likely to do so. Carlo and his colleagues conclude with some fertile suggestions for future research.

In Chapter 13, Michal Pratt, Mary Louise Arnold, and Heather Lawford take up the relationship between prosocial moral identity and a sense of generativity in adulthood, using narrative strategies that build on McAdams's life-narratives approach. They articulate a refreshing theoretical perspective that cuts across traditional developmental psychology, personality theory, and family studies, integrating life-course and systems perspectives. Following Erikson, they consider identity and morality to be mutually sustaining, and identity to be a central motivation throughout the life span. Pratt, Arnold, and Lawford present evidence for the early construction of generative moral themes during adolescence and emergent adulthood. These themes are revealed in the stories that adolescents tell about their lives and, in particular, in their account of their commitment to moral ideals. Hence the authors show the usefulness of tracing themes of identity through the lifespan, but also that of generativity.

After considering the nature of gratitude (Chapter 11), altruism (Chapter 12), and generativity (Chapter 13), the volume next examines the problem of integrity, personal responsibility, and moral identity. Barry Schlenker, Marisa Miller, and Ryan Johnson (Chapter 14) argue that what determines the strength of the relationship between moral beliefs and moral behavior is a person's commitment to ethical ideologies. These ideologies function as a dominant schema that influences the appraisal of the social landscape and guides behavior. Some individuals have steadfast commitment to ethical ideologies ("integrity"), while others view the commitment as expedient and adaptable. The authors view the principled-expedient continuum because of its implications for moral identity, self-regulation, and moral behavior, and because it captures some of the great tensions in human affairs. Schlenker designed the Integrity Scale to measure steadfast commitment to ethical principles. Research using the scale indicates that integrity is accurately perceived by friends, is reflected in self-beliefs, affects social judgment, and predicts pro-social and anti-social activities. The authors conclude with an account of the "triangle model of responsibility," which explains when and why the self-system becomes engaged in moral action (or disengages from undesirable behavior).

Chapter 15, by Benoit Monin and Alex Jordan, takes up a social psychological account of the moral self. After challenging a self-consistency view of moral identity, the authors draw a distinction among three other possible meanings: moral identity as a normative ideal (a type of identity that has deeply integrated moral values and leads to an exemplary life); moral identity as a stable personality variable (how much one sees the self as a moral person); and moral identity as a dynamic and reflective self-image (a fluctuating sense of one's morality at any given moment). As social psychologists, they focused on the third meaning. They argue that everyday situations and behaviors affect our moral self-regard from moment to moment, and that this fluctuating self-regard in turn affects later behavior. They review empirical evidence to show that that when people are made secure about their morality – in the sense that they have already demonstrated their "moral credentials" – they sometimes act less morally. They also find that people sometimes boost their moral self-image to compensate for failure in other domains. When the behavior of moral exemplars is seen as an indictment of other people's choices, they are disliked rather than admired.

Linda Skitka and Scott Morgan argue in Chapter 16 that a moral frame of mind can cut both ways as a "double-edged sword." That is, the way that people's moral concerns play out in everyday social interaction may not always have normatively virtuous implications. For example, stronger moral conviction about specific issues is associated with more intolerance of attitudinally dissimilar others in both intimate (e.g., that of a friend) and distant (e.g., with the owner of a store one frequents) relationships; lower levels of goodwill and cooperativeness in attitudinally heterogeneous groups; and decreased ability to compromise on procedural solutions for conflict. People are also more likely to perceive vigilantism and other sacrifices of due process as fair when they achieve "moral" ends. This "double-edged sword" of moral perception shows that what can be described from the mindset of the actor as moral is nonetheless condemned as immoral from the mindset of the observer. Although primarily associated with prosocial and positive consequences, people's moral convictions, motives, and sentiments are sometimes associated with negative and antisocial consequences as well. As a result, the authors warn that efforts to increase the centrality of moral identity or of moral concerns could have paradoxical effects – and double-edged swords – that lead as much to negative as to positive consequences.

A social cognitive theory of moral identity is endorsed in Chapter 17 by Karl Aquino and Dan Freeman. What is prized about this line of research is its application to a specific context, which is the ecology of business settings. For the authors, moral identity is a self-regulatory mechanism that motivates choices, behaviors, and responsiveness to others, to the extent that identification with morality is judged as highly self-important. Indeed, whether moral identity influences moral behavior hinges on its salience, that is to say, its self-importance. Moral identity is motivational to the extent that one desires to maintain self-consistency. However, the authors point out that the salience of moral identity can be influenced by situational factors, including financial incentives, group norms, and role models. These factors may increase or decrease the salience of moral identity within one's working self-concept. Moral identity exerts greater regulatory control and motivational potency when situational factors elevate its salience. The authors review empirical evidence for the social-cognitive view of moral identity, along with certain moderators of moral identity, particularly as these apply to business settings.

The volume's final chapter (Chapter 18) is by Augusto Blasi, whose writings on moral self, identity, and personality are considered classic and foundational to the emerging discipline. In his chapter, Blasi seems to take a sharp turn from his usual emphasis on the moral self to an emphasis on the importance of reflective reasoning of the mature moral agent. He offers a masterful critique of the intuitionist shift in some areas of moral psychology, taking on in turn, Haidt (2001), Hauser (2006), and Gigerenzer (2008). Calling on evolutionary explanations, these theorists present rather fuzzy and unfalsifiable theories about the primacy of evolved heuristics and intuitions in moral judgment, despite the fact that they admit intuitions often lead us astray. Blasi is critical of their dismissal of the reality and importance of reasoned reflection in the way we live our moral lives. In emphasizing the dominance of intuition and heuristics in moral judgment, not only do they ignore everyday moral functioning, they ignore the great number of studies conducted showing how reasoning and reflection are normal parts of adult lives. Blasi presents sample types of skills adults need for optimal functioning, and advocates a shift in emphasis in the field toward understanding mature adult functioning.

The volume concludes with a brief reflection by the editors on some of the recurring themes and tensions that resonate throughout the volume, and with some ideas for an interdisciplinary field of moral personality studies.

We thank the University of Notre Dame for its generous support for hosting the two symposia around which this volume was developed. We thank everyone who attended the symposia, and the volume contributors for their inestimable scholarship. We thank Eric Schwartz for his efforts in getting the project off the ground and Simina Calin for seeing it through to completion. The first editor thanks the Spencer Foundation for its support during the completion of this project. We hope this volume has a galvanizing impact on a new, integrative field of study.

1

The Moral Personality

DAN P. MCADAMS

Going back to the ancient Hebrews and Greeks, Western writers have struggled to characterize morality and to define a moral life. Poets and storytellers have told moving tales of human virtue and evil, of how people have led moral lives or failed to live up to moral standards. Philosophers, theologians, and lawmakers have codified morality in terms of legal systems, moral imperatives, ethical standards, commandments, norms, rules, principles, and a vast array of codes and constructs designed to regulate, sanction, and affirm certain forms of human conduct. In the last 100 years, psychologists have gotten into the act. From William James to Lawrence Kohlberg, psychological theorists and researchers have proposed their own conceptions of moral life, typically couching their pronouncements in the language of science and backing up their claims with empirical data. Psychologists have invoked such terms as moral development, moral character, moral identity, moral schemas and values, altruism, cooperation, prosocial behavior, conscience, and the like. Until recently, however, few writers have explicitly discussed the prospects of a *moral personality*. Picking up the central theme in the current volume, this chapter makes a case for the viability of this new term and for the psychological and social complexity it brings to the fore.

What is a moral personality? The question implicitly assumes an answer to a more general question: What is *personality*? The author of the first authoritative textbook on personality psychology – Gordon Allport (1937) – proposed 49 different definitions of personality before he settled on his own. Personality has been defined as a set of traits that assure individual continuity, as the motivated core of human behavior, as a self-regulating system designed to maximize adaptation to life's challenges, and on and on. Shorn of its sexist language, Allport's (1937) definition is still one of the best: Personality is "the dynamic organization within the individual of those psychophysical systems that determine his [the individual's] unique adjustments to his environment" (p. 48). Like Allport's, most definitions envision personality as a broad and integrative thing that accounts for continuity in human behavior over time and across situations, and that captures some of the uniqueness of an individual life (McAdams, 1997). In the early and middle decades of the twentieth century, personality psychologists proposed and formulated a large number of grand theories aimed at capturing the breadth of the concept. Spelled out in exhaustive detail in textbooks on personality theory (Hall & Lindzey, 1957), these diverse and more or less irreconcilable systems were grouped into those espousing psychoanalysis (e.g., Freud, Jung, Adler, Horney, Fromm, Sullivan), humanism (Rogers, Maslow, May), behaviorism and social learning (Rotter, Bandura), personology (Murray, McClelland, White), traits and types (Eysenck, Guilford, Cattell), developmental stages (Erikson, Loevinger), and cognitive schemas (Kelly, Mischel).

Today the grand theories of personality are viewed mainly as historical set pieces. Contemporary perspectives on personality are typically much more limited, and more empirically grounded, than the grand theories ever were, as different researchers today carve out their own pieces of what Allport believed to be the "dynamic organization." Nonetheless, the urge to synthesize disparate findings remains strong in personality psychology. To that end, a growing number of personality psychologists today are coming around to an integrative framework for the field of personality studies that conceives of personality itself in terms of five basic concepts (Hooker, 2002; McAdams, 1995, 2009; McAdams & Adler, 2006; McAdams & Pals, 2006; Roberts & Wood, 2006; Sheldon, 2004; Singer, 2005). In a broad synthesis drawn selectively from traditional theories and contemporary research trends, McAdams and Pals (2006) recently articulated this five-point framework for an integrative science of personality. They described personality as (1) an individual's unique variation on the general evolutionary design for human nature, expressed as a developing pattern of (2) *dispositional traits*, (3) *characteristic adaptations*, and (4) *self-defining life narratives*, complexly and differentially situated in (5) culture and social context.

From the standpoint of McAdams and Pals (2006), each human life is an individual variation on a general design whose functional significance makes primary sense in terms of the human environment of evolutionary adaptedness (EEA). Variations on a small set of broad dispositional traits implicated in social life (both today and in the EEA) constitute the most stable and recognizable aspect of psychological individuality (McCrae & Costa, 1997). Beyond dispositional traits, however, human lives vary with respect to a wide range of motivational (Emmons, 1986; Little, 1999), social-cognitive

(Mischel & Shoda, 1995), and developmental (Elder, 1995; Erikson, 1963) adaptations, complexly contextualized in time, place, and/or social role. Beyond dispositional traits and characteristic adaptations, furthermore, human lives vary with respect to the integrative life stories, or personal narratives, that individuals construct to make meaning and identity in the modern world (McAdams, 1985, 2006, 2008; McLean, Pasupathi, & Pals, 2007; Sarbin, 1986; Tomkins, 1987). Culture exerts differential effects on different levels of personality: It exerts modest effects on the phenotypic expression of dispositional traits; it shows a stronger impact on the content and timing of characteristic adaptations; and it reveals its deepest and most profound influences on life stories, essentially providing a menu of themes, images, and plots for the psychosocial construction of narrative identity.

What then is a *moral* personality? It depends on what aspect of personality you are talking about – be it dispositional traits, characteristic adaptations, or life stories.

MORAL PERSONALITY AT THE LEVEL OF DISPOSITIONAL TRAITS

Personality begins with traits. From birth onward, psychological individuality may be observed with respect to broad dimensions of behavioral and emotional style that cut across situations and contexts and readily distinguish one individual from another (Caspi, Roberts, & Shiner, 2005). Through repeated and complex transactions between genes and environments over developmental time, early temperament differences morph into the broad traits of personality that may be observed in adulthood, and that go by such names as "extraversion," "dominance," and the tendency toward "depressiveness." Typically assessed via self-report scales, dispositional traits account for broad consistencies in behavior across situations and over time. A considerable body of research speaks to the longitudinal continuity of dispositional traits, their substantial heritability, and their ability to predict important life outcomes, such as psychological well-being, job success, and mortality (McAdams, 2009; Ozer & Benet-Martinez, 2006; Roberts & Pomerantz, 2004). Decades of factor-analytic studies conducted around the world suggest, furthermore, that the broad universe of trait dimensions may be organized into about five regions or clusters, now routinely called the Big Five (Goldberg, 1993; McCrae & Costa, 1997). The most well-known conception of the Big Five divides traits into the categories of extraversion (vs. introversion), neuroticism (vs. emotional stability), conscientiousness, agreeableness, and openness to experience.

The Big Five traits capture broad variations in human social behavior that human beings have evolved to take note of and to care about. It is not so much, then, that evolutionary forces have shaped levels of the Big Five traits (although this, in principle, could be true as well), as it is the fact that *humans have evolved to note variations in these kinds of traits*, for these variations have important bearing on adaptation to group life. As cognitively gifted and exquisitely social animals, living in groups and striving to get along and get ahead in the environment of evolutionary adaptedness, human beings have been designed by natural selection to detect differences in others with respect to such qualities as how sociable and dominant a person is (extraversion), the extent to which a person is caring and cooperative (agreeableness), a person's characteristic level of dependability and industriousness (conscientiousness), levels of emotional stability and dysfunction in other people (neuroticism), and the extent to which a person may be cognitively flexible or rigid in facing a range of adaptive problems (openness to experience) (Buss, 1996; Hogan, 1982). For human beings, relative success in meeting a wide range of adaptive problems – from raising viable progeny to building effective coalitions – may depend, in part, on the accurate perception and judicious assessment of such qualities of mind as dominance, friendliness, honesty, stability, and openness. Factor-analytic studies of trait ratings in societies the world over suggest that the Big Five structure, or something very close to it, emerges in many different cultures and language traditions (Church, 2000). The reason is clear: The Big Five implicitly encodes those broad and pervasive individual differences in personality that have tended to make a big difference in adaptation to group life over the course of human evolution, as they continue to make a difference today.

For human beings (and for certain other primates, too), group life is moral life (de Waal, 1996). Human beings have evolved to be moral animals, to detect cheating and other breaches of moral standards, to uphold codes of moral conduct, and to react with righteous indignation, and even murderous intent, when those codes are violated (Tooby & Cosmides, 1992; Wright, 1994). Considerations of morality infuse social life. Human beings have evolved to express strong moral feelings, to hold deep moral intuitions, and to develop elaborate moral codes with respect to at least five domains of social life, argues Haidt (2007): (1) harm and suffering, (2) reciprocity and fair exchange, (3) authority and the hierarchical structure of groups, (4) loyalty and commitment to others, and (5) sacredness/purity. It should not be surprising to learn, therefore, that the five basic traits identified by personality psychologists carry considerable moral meaning.

For example, agreeableness speaks to caring and altruistic tendencies, and the opposite qualities of mean-spiritedness, callousness, and cruelty. People high in agreeableness may be more sensitive to the suffering of others, may be more positively disposed toward fairness and reciprocity, and may prove more loyal to others with whom they feel close bonds (Matsuba & Walker, 2004).

Conscientiousness encompasses qualities such as honesty and dependability in interpersonal relationships. A recent meta-analysis shows that adults who are high on the trait of conscientiousness tend to invest more heavily in family and work roles, tend to be more religiously observant, and tend to be more involved in prosocial volunteer activities, compared to individuals low in conscientiousness (Lodi-Smith & Roberts, 2007). Low levels of conscientiousness predict a wide range of outcomes that carry negative moral meaning – from substance abuse to dishonesty in the workplace (Bogg & Roberts, 2004; Roberts & Hogan, 2001). Adult conscientiousness may be the end result of a long and complex developmental course through which early-childhood temperament dimensions, such as conscience (Kochanska & Aksan, 2006) and effortful control (Li-Grinning, 2007), combine with propitious environmental experiences to produce a well-socialized, rule-abiding, hardworking, and civically minded adult.

The personality trait that may be most closely associated with moral reasoning and thought is openness to experience. People who are dispositionally high on openness tend to be highly imaginative, reflective, intellectual, and broadminded. They welcome change and complexity in life, and they show high levels of tolerance for ambiguity. By contrast, individuals lower in openness tend to be more concrete, dogmatic, and traditional. Openness tends to be positively associated with both education level and intelligence. Individuals high in openness to experience tend to score higher on Loevinger's (1976) ego development (McCrae & Costa, 1980), which itself is closely associated with Kohlberg's (1969) stages of moral reasoning. Therefore, high openness tends to predict postconventional moral reasoning in adults; low openness is associated with conventional and preconventional moral reasoning. Extremely low scores on openness, furthermore, tend to predict right-wing authoritarianism (Jost, Glaser, Kruglanski, & Sulloway, 2003). A large empirical literature links authoritarianism to rigidity and intolerance in the moral and political realms, and to racism, sexism, and prejudice against outgroups (Altemeyer, 1996).

In sum, a number of broad dispositional traits appear to have implications for the moral personality. Certain dispositional profiles – high conscientiousness and agreeableness, and at least moderately high openness to experience – tend to be associated with patterns of behavior and thought indicative of high moral functioning. Most generally, conscientiousness and agreeableness tend to predict pro-social behavior whereas openness to experience tends to predict principled moral reasoning. These general tendencies begin to sketch a dispositional outline of the moral personality. But a more detailed portrait requires the move to more subtle and contextualized aspects of personality. Dispositional traits can take us only so far in understanding how personality relates to morality. To articulate a more nuanced understanding, one must move from the dispositional sketch provided by personality traits to a second level of personality.

CHARACTERISTIC ADAPTATIONS: MORAL GOALS AND SCHEMAS

From middle childhood onward, human beings build a second layer of personality upon the dispositional base, even as that base continues to develop thereafter. Residing at the second level are characteristic adaptations – a wide assortment of motivational, social-cognitive, and developmental constructs that are more specific than dispositional traits and that are contextualized in time, place, and/or social role (McAdams, 2009; McAdams & Pals, 2006). Included in this list are motives, goals, strivings, personal projects, values, interests, defense mechanisms, coping strategies, relational schemata, possible selves, developmental concerns, and other variables of psychological individuality that speak directly to what people *want and do not want* (e.g., fear) in life and how they think about and go about getting what they want and avoiding what they do not want in particular situations, during particular times in their lives, and with respect to particular social roles. Characteristic adaptations have typically been the constructs of choice for classic motivational (Deci & Ryan, 1991; Murray, 1938/2008), social-cognitive (Cervone & Shoda, 1999; Mischel & Shoda, 1995), and developmental (Erikson, 1963; Loevinger, 1976) theories of personality. Whereas broad personality traits provide a dispositional sketch for psychological individuality, characteristic adaptations fill in many of the details.

Among those characteristic adaptations that are most instrumental in shaping morality are personal goals and projects (Freund & Riediger, 2006; Little, 1999). Goals and projects are always about the future – the imagined ends for tomorrow that guide behavior today. Research has shown that personal goals focused on caring for others and making positive contributions to society in the future are often associated with greater psychological well-being and reports of higher life meaning (Bauer & McAdams,

2004; Emmons, 1999; Kasser & Ryan, 1996). Findings like these suggest that certain features of a moral personality benefit not only others, but also the self.

As situations change, as people grow older, as individuals move from one social role to the next, goals and projects change to meet new demands and constraints. For example, as people move into their thirties, forties and beyond, their goals may reflect the greater developmental urgency of what Erikson (1963) called *generativity*. Generativity is an adult's concern for, or commitment to, promoting the well-being of future generations, as evidenced in parenting, teaching, mentoring, leadership, and engaging in a wide range of activities aimed at leaving a positive legacy of the self for the future (McAdams & de St. Aubin, 1992). Erikson viewed generativity in highly moral terms (Browning, 2004; Wakefield, 1998). In their midlife years, adults face the moral challenge of providing care for the next generation and of contributing to the social good in ways that are congruent with and supportive of culture. Their efforts to do so may be bolstered or undermined by economic and psychological exigencies, by religious and political factors, and by the extent to which an adult is able to summon forth what Erikson (1963, p. 267) felicitously described as a "belief in the species" – a fundamental faith in the goodness and *worthwhileness* of the human enterprise.

Generative goals and inclinations wax and wane over the adult life course, as the social ecology of life changes to meet new developmental demands and the unpredictable contingencies of everyday life. At any given time, however, personalities can be compared and contrasted in terms of the extent to which generative goals and generative concerns predominate. A growing body of research shows that individual differences in generative goals and concerns predict a wide range of behaviors that have moral significance. For midlife adults, high scores on measures of generativity are positively associated with greater levels of involvement in children's education, patterns of parenting emphasizing both warmth and discipline, sustained efforts to pass on wisdom to the next generation, involvement in religious organizations, political participation, and volunteer work aimed at helping the poor (for reviews, see de St. Aubin, McAdams, & Kim, 2004; McAdams, 2001).

Another set of characteristic adaptations that bear directly on moral personality are value-laden cognitive schemas and personal ideologies. What are people's most cherished beliefs and values about what is good and true? How do they think through issues of morality in everyday life? Research in this domain ranges widely, from examinations of normative and humanistic ideological scripts (de St. Aubin, 1996, 1999) to the classic studies of moral reasoning pioneered by Kohlberg (1969) and his associates. Examples of the former prioritize the content of people's moral beliefs and values, whereas the latter examine the structure of moral reasoning itself. A related line of research examines the extent to which moral schemas are activated in daily life. Individuals for whom knowledge structures linked to morality are quickly and consistently activated show high levels of *moral chronicity* (Narvaez, Lapsley, Hagele, & Lasky, 2006). Compared to low moral chronics, these individuals may have greater access to moral schemas and may use those schemas more frequently as guides for processing social information.

Representing different approaches to conceptualizing cognitive schemas about morality, personal ideologies, stages of moral reasoning, and levels of moral chronicity are integral components of the moral personality – as important to personality itself as are the fundamental Big Five traits. What makes them different from traits is their circumscribed and contextual nature. Whereas dispositional traits of conscientiousness and agreeableness describe cross-situational and longitudinal continuities in broad patterns of behavior, thought, and feeling, the more circumscribed constructs at Level 2 in personality – moral goals, moral schemas – speak to the contextualized details of personal morality. Whereas dispositional traits may show impressive continuity over time, the contextualized details of personal morality are likely to show much greater variability and sensitivity to developmental and social contingencies. Generative goals, for example, may prove to be important features of the moral personality during certain periods of life (e.g., midlife) but not during others; stages of moral reasoning may shape how people think about certain issues in life (e.g., fairness, justice) but not others; moral chronics have greater access to knowledge structures about morality but not to other kinds of knowledge structures. A broad accounting of moral personality requires, at minimum, the dispositional sketch and the contextualized details. But even that is not quite enough.

THE LIFE NARRATIVE AS A MORAL CONSTRUCTION

Late adolescence and young adulthood bring to the fore of personality the psychological problem of establishing an *identity* (Erikson, 1963; McAdams, 1985). In his theory of psychosocial development, Erikson viewed identity to be a special arrangement of the self. The arrangement functions to integrate disparate roles, goals, needs, fears, skills, and inclinations into a coherent pattern, a pattern that specifies how the emerging adult will live, love, work, and believe in a complex and changing world. The virtue of the identity stage is *fidelity*, Erikson maintained. One must show fidelity to a particular arrangement of selfhood. One must commit oneself to a particular kind of meaningful life. At the very heart of identity, then, is the problem of meaning and purpose in life (McAdams, 1985). What does my life mean *in full*? Who am I today? How am I different today from what I was in my past? Who will I be in the future? These large questions regarding the meaning of one's life in full developmental time – past, present, and future – cannot be fully answered through dispositional traits and characteristic adaptations. Instead, they require a *story* of who I am, was, and will be. One way to read Erikson's idea of identity is to see it as an internalized and evolving story of the self that people begin to construct in the emerging adult years (Habermas & Bluck, 2000; McAdams, 1985). Beyond dispositional traits and characteristic adaptations, then, lies the realm of narrative identity.

Layered over the Big Five traits and the panoply of goals, motives, projects, fears, strategies, values, beliefs, and schemas that comprise the first two levels of personality is an emerging narrative identity – an internalized and evolving story of the reconstructed past and imagined future that aims to provide life with unity, coherence, and purpose. For both the self and others, the life story explains how I came to be, who I am today, where I am going in the future, and what I believe my life means within the psychosocial niche provided by family, friends, work, society, and the cultural and ideological resources of my environment. It is a story that distinguishes me from all others, and yet shows how I am connected to others as well. It is a story that narrates the evolution of a particular self, but it is a self in cultural context. Every life story says as much about the culture within which a person lives as it does about the person living it. In constructing a life story, people choose from the menu of images, themes, plots, and characters provided by the particular environments to which they are exposed (McAdams, 2006; Rosenwald & Ochberg, 1992). They make meaning within the milieu of meanings provided by culture.

What prompts the emergence of narrative identity in late adolescence and young adulthood? Cognitive factors are surely important. With the advent of what Piaget called formal operational thought, adolescents are now able to take their own lives as objects of systematic reflection (Breger, 1974; McAdams, 1985). Whereas young children can dream about what might someday be, adolescents can think through the possibilities in a hypothetico-deductive manner. They can now ask themselves questions such as: What is my life really about? Who might I be in the future? What if I decide to reject my parents' religion? What would it mean to live a *good life*? This newfound philosophical inclination requires a narrative frame for self-construction. The earliest drafts of narrative identity may take the form of what Elkind (1981) called the *personal fable* – fantastical stories of the self's greatness. But later drafts become more realistic and tempered, as reality testing improves and narrative skills become further refined. Habermas and Bluck (2000) have shown how adolescents gradually master the cognitive skills required for constructing a coherent narrative of the self. By the end of their teenaged years, they regularly engage in sophisticated forms of *autobiographical reasoning*. They can link together multiple autobiographical scenes in causal sequences to explain what they believe to be their own development in a given area of life. And they can extract underlying themes that they believe characterize unique aspects of their lives in full.

Social and cultural factors also help to bring narrative identity to the developmental fore at this time. Their peers and their parents expect adolescents to begin sorting out what their lives mean, both for the future and the past. Given what I have done up to this point in my life, where do I go now? What kind of life should I make for myself? Paralleling the cognitive and emotional changes taking place within the individual are shifts in society's expectations about what the individual, who was a child but who is now almost an adult, should be doing, thinking, and feeling. Erikson (1959) wrote, "It is of great relevance to the young individual's identity formation that he be responded to, and be given function and status as a person whose gradual growth and transformation make sense to those who begin to make sense to him" (p. 111). In general, modern societies expect their adolescents and young adults to examine occupational, ideological, and interpersonal opportunities around them and to begin to make some decisions about what their lives as adults are to be about. This is to say that both society and the emerging adult are ready for his or her explorations in narrative identity by the time he or she has, in fact, become an emerging adult. As Erikson described it:

> The period can be viewed as a psychosocial moratorium during which the individual through free role experimentation may find a niche in some section of his society, a niche which is firmly defined and yet seems to be uniquely made for him. In finding it the young adult gains an assured sense of inner continuity and social sameness which will bridge what he was as a child and what he is about to become, and will reconcile his conception of himself and his community's recognition of him. (Erikson, 1959, p. 111)

Moral meanings run through life narratives. MacIntyre (1981) has argued that all life stories speak from a moral perspective. Either explicitly or implicitly, the narrator takes a moral stand vis-à-vis the self and society, draws on moral understandings which frame the narrative, and justifies or condemns his or her own identity tale in moral terms. Furthermore, in any given culture some stories exhibit greater moral cachet than do others. For example, Cobly and Damon (1992) describe how men and women nominated as moral exemplars construct their own lives as tales of steadfast commitment to ideals and the progressive enlargement of one's moral mission over time. Walker and Frimer (2007) compared life-narrative accounts of Canadian adults awarded honors for either bravery or a lifetime of caring commitment, and they contrasted the accounts with the life stories of a matched control sample. Among their many informative findings, Walker and Frimer showed that the stories of brave and caring exemplars tended to underscore secure attachment experiences and the transformation of negative events into positive outcomes, to a greater degree than did the stories told by the matched controls.

Finding positive meanings in negative events is the central theme that runs through McAdams's (2006) conception of *the redemptive self*. In a series of nomothetic and idiographic studies conducted over the past 15 years, McAdams and colleagues have consistently found that midlife American adults who score especially high on self-report measures of generativity – suggesting a strong commitment to promoting the well-being of future generations and improving the world in which they live (Erikson, 1963) – tend to see their own lives as narratives of redemption (Mansfield & McAdams, 1996; McAdams & Bowman, 2001; McAdams, Diamond, de St. Aubin, & Mansfield, 1997; McAdams, Reynolds, Lewis, Patten, & Bowman, 2001). Compared to their less generative American counterparts, highly generative adults tend to construct life stories that feature redemption sequences, in which the protagonist is delivered from suffering to an enhanced status or state. In addition, highly generative American adults are more likely than their less generative peers to construct life stories in which the protagonist (a) enjoys a special advantage or blessing early in life; (b) expresses sensitivity to the suffering of others or societal injustice as a child; (c) establishes a clear and strong moral value system in adolescence that remains a source of unwavering conviction through the adult years; (d) experiences significant conflicts between desires for agency/power and desires for communion/love; and (e) looks to achieve goals to benefit society in the future. Taken together, these themes articulate a general script or narrative prototype that many highly generative American adults employ to make sense of their own lives. For highly productive and caring midlife American adults, the redemptive self is a narrative model of an especially good and morally enhanced life.

The redemptive self is a life-story prototype that serves to support the efforts of midlife men and women to make a positive contribution to society. Their redemptive life narratives tell how generative adults seek to give back to society in gratitude for the early advantages and blessings they feel they have received. In every life, generativity is tough and frustrating work, as every parent or community volunteer knows. But if an adult constructs a narrative identity in which the protagonist's suffering in the short run often gives way to reward later on, he or she may be better able to sustain the conviction that seemingly thankless investments today will pay off for future generations. Redemptive life stories support the kind of life strivings that a highly caring man or woman, deeply committed to moral principles, is likely to set forth.

At the same time, the redemptive self may say as much about American culture and tradition as it does about the highly generative American adults who tend to tell this kind of story about their lives. McAdams (2006) argued that the life-story themes expressed by highly generative American adults recapture and couch in a psychological language especially cherished, as well as hotly contested, ideas in American cultural history – ideas that appear prominently in spiritual accounts of the seventeenth-century Puritans, Benjamin Franklin's eighteenth-century autobiography, slave narratives and Horatio Alger stories from the nineteenth century, and the literature of self-help and American entrepreneurship from more recent times. Evolving from the Puritans to Emerson to Oprah, the redemptive self has morphed into many different storied forms in the past 300 years, as Americans have sought to narrate their lives as redemptive tales of atonement, emancipation, recovery, self-fulfillment, and upward social mobility. The stories speak of heroic individual protagonists – the *chosen people* – whose *manifest destiny* is to make a positive difference in a dangerous world, even when the world does not wish to be redeemed. The stories translate a deep and abiding script of American exceptionalism into the many contemporary narratives of success, recovery, development, liberation, and self-actualization that so pervade American talk, talk shows, therapy sessions, sermons, and commencement speeches. It is as if especially generative American adults, whose lives are dedicated to making the world a better place for future generations, are, for better and sometimes for worse, the most ardent narrators of a general life-story script as American as apple pie and the Super Bowl.

In their most recent studies, McAdams and colleagues have noted moral and political variations on the redemptive self as constructed by highly generative American Christians in their midlife years (McAdams, Albaugh, Farber, Daniels, Logan, & Olson, 2008). Most of the 128 men and women in this study believed they were leading exemplary moral lives. As a whole, the participants showed remarkably high engagement in pro-social behavior, charitable donations, volunteer work, and the like. Almost all of the participants, furthermore, were politically informed and regularly voted in municipal and state elections. Important variations in narrative identity appeared, however, with respect to political affiliation. In their self-narrations, Christian conservatives tended to underscore the moral values of respect for authority, commitment and loyalty, and the sacredness of the self (Haidt, 2007) to a much greater extent than did liberals. They also constructed self-defining scenes in their life stories that highlighted what Lakoff (2002) described as a *strict-father morality* – emphasizing societal rules and self-discipline. By contrast, Christian liberals tended to underscore the moral values of preventing harm and promoting fairness or reciprocity, and their salient life-story scenes tended to emphasize what Lakoff (2002) called a *nurturant caregiver morality*, highlighting autobiographical episodes in which characters showed care toward others and expressed openness and empathy. Both the Christian conservatives and Christian liberals narrated their moral lives in redemptive terms. Their redemptive life stories served to buttress their moral commitments and sustain their efforts to make positive contributions to their families, neighborhoods, churches, and society. But their stories reflected somewhat different moral agendas and different plots and guiding metaphors for what ultimately constitutes a good life.

CONCLUSION

Personality is an individual's unique variation on the general evolutionary design for human nature, expressed as a complex pattern of dispositional traits, characteristic adaptations, and self-defining life stories, situated in culture. By extension, a moral personality would consist of those traits, adaptations, and stories that best support and sustain a moral life in culture. What constitutes a moral life itself surely varies from one culture to the next, but certain common features – such as commitment to alleviating suffering, assuring fairness and reciprocity, respecting legitimate authority, manifesting loyalty and commitment to the common good, and valuing sacredness and purity (Haidt, 2007) – may be discerned across a wide range of cultures.

Personality research suggests that, at Level 1 of personality, dispositional traits linked to conscientiousness, agreeableness, and openness to experience have strong moral implications. High scores on conscientiousness and agreeableness have been linked to pro-social behavior, commitment to societal institutions, honesty, integrity, and fewer instances of violating moral norms. At least moderately high levels of openness to experience appear to be a prerequisite for valuing tolerance and diversity in society, for understanding multiple perspectives, and for principled moral reasoning. Of course, high scores on these traits do not guarantee these behavioral correlates for every case; empirical findings in psychology are almost always probabilistic. But all other things being equal, high levels of conscientiousness, agreeableness, and openness to experience lay the foundation for a moral personality.

At Level 2, the moral personality may be expressed through the characteristic adaptations that situate psychological individuality in time, place, and social role. Moral goals and schemas flesh out the details of the moral life. They spell out what moral aims people are trying to accomplish in their lives, how they take on moral roles in families and societies, what values they emphasize in pursuing moral ends, and how they think about moral dilemmas and choices in life. Unlike dispositional traits, moral goals and schemas show substantial change over time and across contexts, and they are often closely connected to developmental concerns. Among midlife adults, for example, goals and concerns linked to generativity have been shown to predict a wide range of morally significant behaviors, from conscientious parenting to civic engagement. Moral schemas are expressed in a wide range of forms, from personal ideologies (content) to stages of moral reasoning (structure).

Layered on top of traits and adaptations are the internalized and evolving stories people live by. At Level 3 of personality, people construct integrative life narratives to provide their lives with some measure of unity, purpose, and meaning. Narrative identities are profoundly shaped by culture. Culture provides a menu of images, metaphors, plots, characters, and envisioned endings for the narrative construction of the self. In late adolescence and early adulthood, people living in modern societies begin to put their lives together into self-defining stories, reconstructing the past and imagining the future in terms of a sensible and culturally valued narrative with beginning, middle, and end. Different kinds of life stories reflect different moral agendas. In American society, especially generative adults – those committed to promoting the well-being of future generations – tend to construct redemptive stories for their lives. Appropriating culturally cherished (and contested) narratives of atonement, upward mobility, recovery, and liberation in American culture and heritage, highly generative American adults repeatedly narrate the movement from suffering to enhancement in their life stories. Their narratives conceive of the moral life as a personal quest in which a gifted protagonist, equipped with moral steadfastness, journeys forth into a dangerous world, overcomes adversity, and ultimately gives back to society in gratitude for the blessings he or she has received. Constructing a redemptive narrative identity may support and reinforce a moral life for many American adults committed to making a positive difference in the world. The redemptive self, then, is a particular kind of narrative identity that provides the psychological resources that many Americans who aspire to live a morally exemplary life feel they need in order to live such a life.

But there are many ways to live a moral life, and many stories that might be told about it. Redemptive life narratives of the sort documented by McAdams (2006) illustrate one particularly powerful narrative form for living a good life in American society. But many Americans who believe they are living morally exemplary lives may reject this story as not true to their own lived experience – there are always exceptions to the narrative norms a culture provides. And it is quite likely that the life stories of moral exemplars in other societies do not resemble the redemptive self. At the end of the day, Level 3 in personality owes its very existence and constituents to the cultural menu for life narratives available to people living in a particular time and place. Culture provides a range of possibilities for life-story construction, and each culture provides its own characteristic range. It is, therefore, at the level of life narrative where the moral personality may show its greatest variation and cultural nuance. Certain basic traits – agreeableness and conscientiousness, for example – may provide a dispositional foundation for the moral personality. But what gets built upon that foundation may follow the architectural guidelines specified within a given moral community and culture.

REFERENCES

Allport, G. W. (1937). *Personality: A psychological interpretation*. New York: Holt, Rinehart & Winston.
Altemeyer, R. A. (1996). *The authoritarian specter*. Cambridge, MA: Harvard University Press.
Bauer, J. J., & McAdams, D. P. (2004). Growth goals, maturity, and well-being. *Developmental Psychology, 40*, 114–127.
Bogg, T., & Roberts, B. W. (2004). Conscientiousness and health-related behavior: A meta-analysis of the leading behavioral contributions to mortality. *Psychological Bulletin, 130*, 887–919.
Breger, L. (1974). *From instinct to identity: The development of personality*. Englewood Cliffs, NJ: Prentice-Hall.

Browning, D. (2004). An ethical analysis of Erikson's concept of generativity. In E. de St. Aubin, D. P. McAdams, & T. C. Kim (Eds.), *The generative society: Caring for future generations* (pp. 241–256). Washington, D.C.: American Psychological Association Press.

Buss, D. M. (1996). Social adaptation and the five factors of personality. In J. S. Wiggins (Ed.), *The five-factor model of personality: Theoretical perspectives* (pp. 180–207). New York: Guilford Press.

Caspi, A., Roberts, B. W., & Shiner, R. L. (2005). Personality development: Stability and change. In S. T. Fiske & D. Schacter (Eds.), *Annual Review of Psychology* 56, 453–484.

Cervone, D., & Shoda, Y. (1999). Social-cognitive theories and the coherence of personality. In D. Cervone & Y. Shoda (Eds.), *The coherence of personality* (pp. 3–33). New York: Guilford Press.

Church, A. T. (2000). Culture and personality: Toward an integrated cultural trait psychology. *Journal of Personality*, 68, 651–703.

Colby, A., & Damon, W. (1992). *Some do care: Contemporary lives of moral commitment.* New York: The Free Press.

de St. Aubin, E. (1996). Personal ideology polarity: Its emotional foundation and its manifestation in individual value systems, religiosity, political orientation, and assumptions concerning human nature. *Journal of Personality and Social Psychology*, 71, 152–165.

(1999). Personal ideology: The intersection of personality and religious beliefs. *Journal of Personality*, 67, 1105–1139.

de St. Aubin, E., McAdams, D. P., & Kim, T. C. (Eds.). (2004). *The generative society: Caring for future generations.* Washington, D.C.: American Psychological Association Press.

de Waal, F. (1996). *Good natured: The origins of right and wrong in humans and other animals.* Cambridge, MA: Harvard University Press.

Deci, E. L., & Ryan, R. M. (1991). A motivational approach to self: Integration in personality. In R. Dienstbier & R. M Ryan (Eds.), *Nebraska symposium on motivation: 1990* (pp. 237–288). Lincoln, NE: University of Nebraska Press.

Elder, G. H., Jr. (1995). The life course paradigm: Social change and individual development. In P. Moen, G. H. Elder, Jr., & K. Luscher (Eds.), *Examining lives in context: Perspectives on the ecology of human development* (pp. 101–139). Washington, D.C.: American Psychological Association Press.

Emmons, R. A. (1986). Personal strivings: An approach to personality and subjective well-being. *Journal of Personality and Social Psychology*, 51, 1058–1068.

(1999). *The psychology of ultimate concerns: Motivation and spirituality in personality.* New York: Guilford Press.

Erikson, E. H. (1959). Identity and the life cycle: Selected papers. *Psychological Issues*, 1, 5–165.

(1963). *Childhood and society (2nd Ed.).* New York: Norton.

Freund, A. M., & Riediger, M. (2006). Goals as building blocks of personality and development in adulthood. In D. K. Mroczek & T. D. Little (Eds.), *Handbook of personality development* (pp. 353–372). Mahwah, NJ: Lawrence Erlbaum Associates.

Goldberg, L. R. (1993). The structure of phenotypic personality traits. *American Psychologist*, 48, 26–34.

Habermas, T., & Bluck, S. (2000). Getting a life: The emergence of the life story in adolescence. *Psychological Bulletin, 126,* 748–769.
Haidt, J. (2007). The new synthesis in moral psychology. *Science, 316,* 998–1001.
Hall, C. S., & Lindzey, G. (1957). *Theories of personality.* New York: John Wiley & Sons.
Hogan, R. (1982). A socioanalytic theory of personality. In M. Page (Ed.), *Nebraska symposium on motivation: Vol. 30. Personality: Current theory and research* (pp. 55–89). Lincoln, NE: University of Nebraska Press.
Hooker, K. (2002). New directions for research in personality and aging: A comprehensive model linking levels, structures, and processes. *Journal of Research in Personality, 36,* 318–334.
Jost, J. T., Glaser, J., Kruglanski, A. W., & Sulloway, F. J. (2003). Political conservatism as motivated social cognition. *Psychological Bulletin, 129,* 339–375.
Kasser, T., & Ryan, R. M. (1996). Further examining the American dream: Well-being correlates of intrinsic and extrinsic goals. *Personality and Social Psychology Bulletin, 22,* 281–288.
Kochanska, G., & Aksan, N. (2006). Children's conscience and self-regulation. *Journal of Personality, 74,* 1587–1617.
Kohlberg, L. (1969). Stage and sequence: The cognitive-developmental approach to socialization. In D. A. Goslin (Ed.), *Handbook of socialization theory and research* (pp. 347–480). Skokie, IL: Rand McNally.
Lakoff, G. (2002). *Moral politics: How liberals and conservatives think* (2nd Ed.). Chicago, IL: University of Chicago Press.
Li-Grinning, C. P. (2007). Effortful control among low-income preschoolers in three cities: Stability, change, and individual differences. *Developmental Psychology, 43,* 208–221.
Little, B. R. (1999). Personality and motivation: Personal action and the conative evolution. In L. A. Pervin and O. John (Eds.), *Handbook of personality: Theory and research* (2nd ed., pp. 501–524). New York: Guilford Press.
Lodi-Smith, J., & Roberts, B. W. (2007). Social investment and personality: A meta-analysis of the relationship of personality traits to investment in work, family, religion, and volunteerism. *Personality and Social Psychology Review, 11,* 68–86.
Loevinger, J. (1976). *Ego development.* San Francisco: Jossey-Bass.
Mansfield, E. D., & McAdams, D. P. (1996). Generativity and themes of agency and communion in adult autobiography. *Personality and Social Psychology Bulletin, 22,* 721–731.
Matsuba, M. K., & Walker, L. J. (2004). Extraordinary moral commitment: Young adults working for social organizations. *Journal of Personality, 72,* 413–436.
McAdams, D. P. (1985). *Power, intimacy, and the life story: Personological inquiries into identity.* Homewood, IL: Dorsey Press.
——— (1995). What do we know when we know a person? *Journal of Personality, 63,* 365–396.
——— (1997). A conceptual history of personality psychology. In R. Hogan, J. Johnson, & S. Briggs (Eds.), *Handbook of personality psychology* (pp. 3–29). San Diego, CA: Academic Press.

(2001). Generativity in midlife. In M. E. Lachman (Ed.), *Handbook of midlife development* (pp. 395–443). New York: Wiley.

(2006). *The redemptive self: Stories Americans live by*. New York: Oxford University Press.

(2008). Personal narratives and the life story. In O. John, R. Robins, and L. Pervin (Eds.), *Handbook of personality: Theory and research* (3rd Ed., pp. 241–261). New York: Guilford Press.

(2009). *The person: An introduction to the science of personality psychology* (5th Ed.). New York: John Wiley.

McAdams, D. P., & Adler, J. M. (2006). How does personality develop? In D. Mroczek and T. Little (Eds.), *The handbook of personality development* (pp. 469–492). Mahwah, NJ: Lawrence Erlbaum Associates.

McAdams, D. P., Albaugh, M., Farber, E., Daniels, J., Logan, R. L., & Olson, B. (2008). Family metaphors and moral intuitions: How conservatives and liberals narrate their lives. *Journal of Personality and Social Psychology, 95*, 978–990.

McAdams, D. P., & Bowman, P. (2001). Narrating life's turning points: Redemption and contamination. In D. P. McAdams, R. Josselson, & A. Lieblich (Eds.), *Turns in the road: Narrative studies of lives in transition* (pp. 3–34). Washington, DC: American Psychological Association Press.

McAdams, D. P., & de St. Aubin, E. (1992). A theory of generativity and its assessment through self-report, behavioral acts, and narrative themes in autobiography. *Journal of Personality and Social Psychology, 62*, 1003–1015.

(Eds.). (1998). *Generativity and adult development: How and why we care for the next generation*. Washington, D.C.: American Psychological Association Press.

McAdams, D. P., Diamond, A., de St. Aubin, E., & Mansfield, E. D. (1997). Stories of commitment: The psychosocial construction of generative lives. *Journal of Personality and Social Psychology, 72*, 678–694.

McAdams, D. P., & Pals, J. L. (2006). A new Big Five: Fundamental principles for an integrative science of personality. *American Psychologist, 61*, 204–217.

McAdams, D. P., Reynolds, J., Lewis, M., Patten, A., & Bowman, P. J. (2001). When bad things turn good and good things turn bad: Sequences of redemption and contamination in life narrative, and their relation to psychosocial adaptation in midlife adults and in students. *Personality and Social Psychology Bulletin, 27*, 472–483.

McCrae, R. R., & Costa, P. T., Jr. (1980). Openness to experience and ego level in Loevinger's sentence-completion test: Dispositional contributions to developmental models of personality. *Journal of Personality and Social Psychology, 39*, 1179–1190.

(1997). Personality trait structure as a human universal. *American Psychologist, 52*, 509–516.

McLean, K. C., Pasupathi, M., & Pals, J. L. (2007). Selves creating stories creating selves: A process model of self-development. *Personality and Social Psychology Review, 11*, 262–278.

Mischel, W., & Shoda, Y. (1995). A cognitive-affective systems theory of personality: reconceptualizing situations, dispositions, dynamics, and invariance in personality structure. *Psychological Review, 102*, 246–268.

Murray, H. A. (1938/2008). *Explorations in personality*. New York: Oxford University Press.

Narvaez, D., Lapsley, D. K., Hagele, S., & Lasky, B. (2006). Moral chronicity and social information processing: Tests of a social-cognitive approach to the moral personality. *Journal of Research in Personality, 40*, 966–985.

Ozer, D. J., & Benet-Martinez, V. (2006). Personality and the prediction of consequential outcomes. In S. Fiske et al. (Eds.), *Annual Review of Psychology 57*, 401–421.

Roberts, B. W., & Hogan, R. (Eds.). (2001). *Personality psychology in the workplace*. Washington, D.C.: American Psychological Association Press.

Roberts, B. W., & Pomerantz, E. J. M. (2004). On traits, situations, and their integration: A developmental perspective. *Personality and Social Psychology Review, 8*, 402–416.

Roberts, B. W., & Wood, D. (2006). Personality development in the context of the neo-socioanalytic model of personality. In D. Mroczek & T. Little (Eds.), *The handbook of personality development* (pp. 11–39). Mahwah, NJ: Lawrence Erlbaum Associates.

Rosenwald, G., & Ochberg, R. L. (Eds.). (1992). *Storied lives: The cultural politics of self-understanding*. New Haven: Yale University Press.

Sarbin, T. (Ed.). (1986). *Narrative psychology: The storied nature of human conduct*. New York: Praeger.

Sheldon, K. M. (2004). *The psychology of ultimate being: An integrative, multi-level perspective*. Mahwah, NJ: Lawrence Erlbaum Associates.

Singer, J. A. (2005). *Personality and psychotherapy: Treating the whole person*. New York: Guilford Press.

Tomkins, S. S. (1987). Script theory. In J. Aronoff, A. I. Rabin, & R. A. Zucker (Eds.), *The emergence of personality* (pp. 147–216). New York: Springer.

Tooby, J., & Cosmides, L. (1992). The psychological foundations of culture. In J. H. Barkow, L. Cosmides, & J. Tooby (Eds.), *The adapted mind: Evolutionary psychology and the generation of culture* (pp. 19–136). New York: Oxford University Press.

Wakefield, J. C. (1998). Immortality and the externalization of the self: Plato's unrecognized theory of generativity. In D. P. McAdams & E. de St. Aubin (Eds.), *Generativity and adult development: How and why we care for the next generation* (pp. 133–174). Washington, D.C.: American Psychological Association Press.

Walker, L. J., & Frimer, J. A. (2007). Moral personality of brave and caring exemplars. *Journal of Personality and Social Psychology, 93*, 845–860.

Wright, R. (1994). *The moral animal*. New York: Pantheon.

2

The Moral Functioning of the Person as a Whole: On Moral Psychology and Personality Science

DANIEL CERVONE AND RITU TRIPATHI

Noun phrases such as "moral psychology" and the "moral domain" appear to refer to singularities. There apparently is a particular type of psychology that comes into play in a particular domain of life: the moral. And maybe there is. Yet even a quick glance at work in the field reveals multiplicities.

Consider the model presented by Rest (1984; also reviewed in Bergman, 2004). The components of moral functioning that are identified encompass psychological functions that are diverse: interpreting situations, formulating courses of action, contemplating and selecting among alternative values that bear on a given circumstance, executing courses of action. If one considers also the psychological structures and processes (declarative and procedural knowledge, affective systems, cognitive appraisal processes, etc.) that may come into play as individuals execute each of these four functions (interpreting, formulating, selecting, executing), the resulting set of psychological systems is so diverse that it becomes difficult to identify systems that are *not* involved in moral reasoning or action. The set of relevant psychological systems only expands when one considers theoretical views in which evolved, domain-specific mechanisms that may be localizable within specific regions of the brain underpin responses to moral dilemmas and violations of moral codes (Greene, Sommerville, Nystrom, Darley, & Cohen, 2001; Haidt, 2001; Hauser, 2006). When psychologists whose primary expertise is not in moral psychology – such as the present authors – look in on the field, they are tempted to ask: "What's the difference between moral psychology and psychology in general?"

There is a ready answer to that question, of course. The difference is the domain: moral psychology is distinguished by its focus on that set of encounters that bear on people's core values and convictions. Yet here, again, one finds diversity. The set of encounters that is moral, like most sets, exhibits fuzziness and family resemblance rather than clear-cut boundaries. Work by Shweder and colleagues indicates that some cultures view as violations of moral principles actions that, in Western culture, would be deemed mere violations of social convention (Shweder, Mahapatra, & Miller, 1987). Research by Skitka and colleagues indicates that, within a given culture, individuals differ in their reports of whether a given issue (e.g., physician-assisted suicide, gay marriage) is morally mandated – that is, whether the issue elicits deeply held feelings about universal codes of correct conduct (Skitka, Bauman, & Sargis, 2005; Skitka & Lytle, 2008). There exist individual differences, then, in beliefs about the exact domain that constitutes the moral; "the presence or absence of moral conviction about a specific issue," Skitka et al. (2005, p. 898) suggest, "is likely to be relatively idiosyncratic."

This leads one to a sequence of observation and conclusion. When one looks at the field of moral psychology, one observes theory and findings that reveal individual differences and some degree of idiosyncrasy in the domain, and observes also that a multiplicity of psychological systems contribute to moral reasoning and action. This observation leads to a conclusion reached already by Blasi (2004b): "Morality, psychologically, is not a self-subsistent entity served by autonomous processes but rather a specific mode of functioning of each person as a whole" (p. 336). The next observation is that, when one looks to the field of psychology as a whole, one finds that there already is a discipline that is devoted to study of the functioning of each person as a whole, and that endeavors to understand how multiple psychological systems contribute to social behavior, interindividual differences, and individual idiosyncrasy. It is the psychology of personality (Caprara & Cervone, 2000) – or, if one views the endeavor as an integrative, interdisciplinary enterprise, it is *personality science* (Cervone & Mischel, 2002). This latter observation leads us to the following conclusion. If one wishes to advance the field of moral psychology, there may be merit in "stepping outside" of that field to survey developments in personality science as a whole. One then can "step back into" the moral domain, per se, armed with whatever useful additional analytical tools one may find in the study of personality.

This, then, is our plan for the current chapter. We recognize that our plan is not entirely unique. Personality theorists have focused intently on questions of moral reasoning, emotion, and action ever since the work of Freud (1923). In the recent era, Blasi (2004b), Lapsley (1996), and others have called for analyses of moral functioning that are located within analyses of whole personality systems. The social-cognitive tradition in personality psychology already has endeavored to respond to such calls, in particular in theoretical and empirical analyses by Bandura and colleagues (1986, 1991; Bandura, Caprara, Barbaranelli, Pastorelli, & Regalia, 2001), as well as by Mischel (Mischel & Mischel, 1976). The works of these authors and others who have contributed to social-cognitive conceptions of personality structure and dynamics (see Cervone & Shoda, 1999) greatly inform the present contribution.

ON PERSONALITY SCIENCE

Dual Meaning of "Personality Structure"

One notable development in the study of personality in recent years is pretheoretical – that is, it concerns conceptual presuppositions that are logically prior to the formulation of theory and research on personality. The development is clarification regarding alternative referents for the word "personality" and the key phrase "personality structure" (Cervone, 2005).

When investigators in an area outside of personality psychology, per se – such as moral psychology – look to the personality psychology literature for insight, they face an obstacle. They must circumvent confusion that may arise from the fact that the term "personality structure" is used to refer to two entities that are quite distinct. In personality theories from Freud to the present day (reviewed in Cervone & Pervin, 2008), theorists have provided scientific models of mental systems that underlie individual consistency, coherence, and uniqueness. A personality "structure," in these theories, is a mental entity that is possessed enduringly by the individual. Theorists generally posit that all individuals possess the given mental entity, but its form, content, or functioning may vary significantly from one person to the next. Freud's superego, for example, is one such entity in psychoanalytic theory. Self-schemas are cognitive structures of personality in social-cognitive theories (Cervone, 2004).

In a second, quite different, usage, a "personality structure" is a model of interindividual differences in the population. The structure is a conceptual system for organizing differences *between* people. Investigators commonly employ factor analysis to identify primary dimensions of variation in ratings of observable personality tendencies; the resulting set of statistical dimensions is the personality structure. Recent findings in multiple languages suggest that six factors are necessary and reasonably sufficient to summarize these interindividual differences (reviewed in Ashton & Lee, 2007); investigators who previously posited five-factor models (Goldberg, 1981) now suggest that six factors (neuroticism, extraversion, conscientiousness, agreeableness, openness to experience, and honesty/humility) are needed to summarize interindividual differences sufficiently (Ashton et al., 2004). As investigators such as Ashton and Lee (2005) and Saucier, Hampson, and Goldberg (2002) make clear, investigators who construct these factor-analytical models commonly do *not* assume that the between-person factors correspond to mental entities in the head of the individual – an assumption that, were it made, would have no grounding in the statistical methods employed (Borsboom, Mellenberg, & van Heerden, 2003; Borsboom, Kievit, Cervone, & Hood, in press). In other words, there generally is no assumption that the between-person factors are structures in the sense in which the superego is a structure in psychodynamic theory.[1]

Personality psychology, then, has professionalized in such a way that it encompasses two classes of scientific activity that may be complementary, yet are distinct: the charting of interindividual differences in typical behavioral dispositions, and the exploration of intrapsychic cognitive and affective systems that underlie the coherence of psychological experience and social behavior (Cervone, 1991, 2005). When students of moral behavior turn to the personality psychology literature, then, they find two classes of theoretical variables: dispositional variables that function to describe between-person differences in typical behavioral tendencies, and intrapsychic variables that serve to model features of mental life, or "personality architecture" (Cervone, 2004).[2] The distinction is quite consequential; it bears on issues of direct relevance to questions of moral psychology and personality, as we see in the section ahead.

---

[1] In the mid-1990s, some writers did present theoretical work in which between-person factors were reified, that is, were posited to exist as within-person mental structures (McCrae & Costa, 1996). Our sense is that the absence of an evidentiary base for this position (see Borsboom et al., 2003; Cervone, 2005) has resulted in there being relatively few other investigators in the current field who would now hold it. The practical utility of identifying statistical factors that summarize major dimensions of interindividual difference in global traits is widely acknowledged; the reification of the constructs that correspond to these statistical dimensions is not.

[2] Some refer to these alternative classes of personality variables as different "levels" of personality. We find the spatial metaphor of "levels" here to be obfuscating rather than clarifying. Consider, by way of analogy, different constructs that can be used to describe cars. Cars vary in reliability and in the number of cylinders in their engines. Would one say that degree of reliability and number of cylinders both refer to different "levels" of cars? The term would seem to obscure the ontological differences between the constructs; the car does not "have cylinders" in the same sense that is "has reliability." The differences, in other words, are not different levels of analysis within a given ontology, as the term "levels" implies.

Personality Consistency and Hartshorne and May (1929)

Historically, a prominent intersection of personality psychology and moral psychology was the work of Hartshorne and May (1929). As has often been reviewed (Mischel, 1968), when these investigators directly observed the behavior of school children and measured, in a variety of situations, the degree to which the children displayed conduct indicative of high moral character, the primary finding was *in*consistency in conduct across situations. Correlations between in-classroom and out-of-classroom measures of moral character averaged < .20 (Mischel, 1968). As Nucci (2004) recently noted, these findings figured significantly in discourse in moral psychology, with the results leading investigators "to view personality as something one does in particular settings, rather than as something one has independent of context," and leading Kohlberg, in particular, to emphasize that "the application of virtues always occurs in context" (p. 114).

We applaud this attention to context in moral psychology. It dovetails with trends in personality science in general (Shoda, Cervone, & Downey, 2007) – trends evident both in cognitively and in biologically grounded analyses of personality and individual differences (see Kagan, 2007). Yet acknowledging the critical role of context is not equivalent to concluding that personality is "something one does" rather than "something one has independent of context." The subtle yet important lack of equivalence hinges on the question we raised above: To what is "personality" referring? Given the findings of Hartshorne and May, what exactly is it that one does or doesn't "have" independent of context?

If personality refers to between-person differences in average levels of behavior – as it does in factor-analytic models of interindividual differences – then the Hartshorne and May findings are quite consequential. Their work, and many similar findings (Mischel & Peake, 1982), indicates that the nature of the differences between people is something that itself differs across context. In some situations, Child X appears to have higher moral character than Child Y, whereas in other situations the opposite is true, yielding the low cross-situational consistency correlations Hartshorne and May report. Personality variables, one would conclude, are weak.

The conclusion changes, however, if personality variables refers to intra-psychic personality architecture. Depending on one's conceptual model of personality architecture, one might never have expected that personality structures would manifest themselves in high levels of cross-situational consistency in a paradigm such as that of Hartshorne and May. Work by one of us illustrates the point; we turn to that work now.

The KAPA model of personality architecture. The conceptual scheme guiding this work is a Knowledge-and-Appraisal Personality Architecture (KAPA; Cervone, 2004). The KAPA model is designed to characterize psychological systems that underlie cross-situational coherence and consistency in experience and action. It posits that personality consistency derives, to a significant degree, from a combination of two factors: (1) enduring knowledge about the self, or self-schemas; and (2) subjective beliefs about social situations, especially beliefs about the relevance of personal attributes to behavioral success in one versus another context. A key feature of the model is its anticipating that the content of the self-schemas and situational beliefs may vary idiosyncratically. Even people who share schematic beliefs about their personal attributes – for example, two people who both possess the belief that they are "shy" (see Cervone, 1997) – may differ entirely in their beliefs about the situations in which these attributes come into play. Our research thus employs idiographically tailored methods (Cervone, Shadel, & Jencius, 2001) to assess elements of personal knowledge. We use these measures to predict people's appraisals of self-efficacy (Bandura, 1997) – that is, their self-appraisals of whether they can cope with specific behavioral challenges in specified, everyday situations.

Findings reveal that idiographically tailored assessments of self-schemas and situational beliefs are highly predictive of cross-situational consistency in self-efficacy appraisals (Cervone, 1997, 2004a; Cervone, Orom, Artistico, Shadel, & Kassel, 2007; Cervone et al., 2008; also see Caldwell, Cervone, & Rubin, in press; Wise, 2007). Importantly, the patterns of personality consistency that are commonly observed are quite idiosyncratic. Individuals display consistency across sets of situations that are *not* the same from one person to another, and that often violate the structure of nomothetic trait categories (Orom & Cervone, in press).

What is the implication for Hartshorne and May (1929)? As others have noted (Bem & Allen, 1974), these investigators did not find that personality was relatively inconsequential. They found that personality *as construed by them, the experimenters,* was relatively inconsequential. The experimenters chose a personality construct (honesty), designated a set of situations and actions as manifestations of that construct, and found that children did not exhibit personality consistency when the litmus test for consistency was consistency across *these experimenter-designated situations.* The findings generated by the KAPA model raise questions that can be phrased simply: Who cares about these experimenter-designated situations? Why would anyone think that the personality of each and every individual would manifest itself consistently across the same set of situations? Attention to idiosyncrasy can reveal a powerful influence of personality characteristics that is obscured by generalized, nomothetic studies.

The KAPA Model of Personality Architecture: Two Implications for Moral Psychology

The KAPA model of personality architecture (Cervone, 2004) addresses two additional points of potential interest to the student of moral behavior. We spell them out briefly here; more extended discussions of related issues can be found elsewhere (Cervone, 2000, 2005, in press; Cervone, Caldwell, & Orom, in press; Cervone, Shadel, Smith, & Fiori, 2006).

Consistency between cognition and action. An enduring puzzle in the study of moral action is that people's actions often seem not to align with their cognitions (see Blasi, 1980, 1983). An individual's morally relevant beliefs and capacity for moral reasoning may endure over time, yet their morally relevant actions may vary across time and context. What conceptual tools from personality science might address this puzzle? One is a distinction in the KAPA model. Drawing on work by Lazarus (1991), the KAPA model distinguishes two qualitatively distinct aspects of cognition: knowledge and appraisal. Knowledge consists of enduring mental representations of persons or the physical or social world. Appraisals, in contrast, are not enduring, "static" elements of knowledge; they are dynamic processes of meaning construction that occur within a given encounter. People continually appraise the relevance of circumstances to their well-being, their capacity to cope with challenges in the environment, and the social and moral appropriateness of alternative courses of action.

This distinction addresses the question of consistency between action and cognition by dividing it in two: (1) Is action consistent with dynamic cognitive appraisal processes? (2) Is action consistent with enduring elements of knowledge? The KAPA model (as well as appraisal models of emotion, such as that of Lazarus (1991) do expect relatively consistent cognition-action relations when the cognitions at issue are cognitive appraisals; appraisals are viewed as a proximal determinant of emotional experience and self-regulated action. But the KAPA model explicitly does not expect uniformly consistent cognition-action relations when the cognitions at issue are elements of knowledge. As indicated by various models of knowledge and information processing in the field of social cognition (Higgins, 1990; Markus & Wurf, 1987), people possess a vast store of knowledge about the social world and the self, and only a small subset of that knowledge can possibly come into play at any given moment. Many elements of knowledge that might potentially bear on appraisals of a situation simply will be inactive; priming manipulations that are designed to activate one versus another element of knowledge support this general conception of the activation of beliefs (Cervone et al., 2008).

In the moral domain and elsewhere, then, the individual will possess numerous beliefs, goals, and standards for evaluating actions that are unconnected to action in a given encounter for a simple reason. In that encounter, they are mentally latent – like books on a shelf of a personal library that contain information that *might* inform a person's course of action if they had time to take the book off the shelf and remind themselves of its content.

Interpreting the ambiguous. The second point concerns a phenomenon that has been of central interest to researchers in personality and social psychology, yet that garners lesser attention in studies of moral reasoning and action. It is the interpretation of circumstances that are informationally complex and inherently ambiguous. In innumerable everyday circumstances – a consumer judging whether a salesperson is truly friendly or manipulative; a student judging whether a professor is being helpful or condescending; a citizen considering whether a government's plans (for military action, for economic development, etc.) are beneficial or morally objectionable – people's actions and their meanings may be ambiguous, and the number of factors that potentially bear on these meanings may be large. Consider, as a more elaborated example, a hypothetical small town in which a group of officials are considering plans for expanded business and housing. Some may focus entirely on the economic benefits of development. Others may focus on potential harm to wildlife and the natural environment and view those harms in moral terms. By virtue of their attention to different aspects of a complex issue, some individuals are "in the moral domain," and others are not.

The phenomena that require explanation, then, include not merely reasoning, motivation, and emotion that occur in circumstances that unambiguously are relevant to moral concerns. The phenomena also include processes of meaning construction that occur in circumstances that are complex or ambiguous – processes through which some individuals attend to moral concerns that others do not even notice. These processes are unaddressed by experimental paradigms that feature informationally simple scenarios depicting a single issue (physical harm, incest, etc.) that lies unambiguously in the moral domain.

Work by Zelli and colleagues illustrates how social-cognitive theory and research methods can address the question of whether people spontaneously detect morally relevant concerns in ambiguous circumstances (Zelli, Cervone, & Huesmann, 1996; Zelli, Huesmann, & Cervone, 1995). They explored spontaneous inferences of hostility and aggressive intent (inferences related to the moral domain, in that bodily harm is morally relevant). In a cued-recall paradigm, participants first read textual material that was ambiguous with respect to whether a person's actions (e.g., a policeman pushing someone out of the way) were intentionally hostile and aggressive. Participants subsequently tried to recall the material after exposure to verbal recall cues, some of which featured hostile content. Individuals who reported experiencing high levels of aggression in their everyday life were more likely to recall the sentence content when they were presented with hostile recall cues (Zelli et al., 1995, 1996). This suggests that, as a result of their experiences with aggression, these individuals developed highly accessible knowledge pertaining to aggression that, in turn, led them spontaneously to categorize ambiguous actions as aggressive. Research by Narvaez, Lapsley, Hagele, & Lasky (2006) speaks even more directly to spontaneous social-cognitive processing in the moral domain. They used a primacy-of-output method (participants list traits describing individuals they know, and the semantic content of traits enumerated at the outset of the lists is assessed) to identify individual differences in the possession of highly accessible knowledge in the moral domain. Subsequently, participants read sentences that were ambiguous with respect to whether depicted actions were morally virtuous. People with chronically accessible moral constructs recalled more sentence material when prompted with recall cues that referred to morally relevant personal dispositions. These and other findings supported a social-cognitive view of morality positing that "moral personality can be understood in terms of the chronic accessibility of moral schemas for construing social events" (Narvaez et al., 2006, p. 980).

Social-cognitive research exploring individual differences in people's construals of ambiguous information indirectly raises questions about theories in which moral functioning is explained by reference to universal, evolved psychological systems that are activated by eliciting cues and that automatically produce moral emotions and intuitions (Haidt, 2001; Hauser, 2006). Even if one were to presume that such models accurately characterize the nature of evolved systems, there is a limit to what they explain. If one wants to understand moral thought, emotion, and action that occur in complex, ambiguous social settings, one must identify psychological systems that determine whether people categorize ambiguous actions as morally relevant. These systems cannot be domain-specific moral mechanisms since, if an individual does not attend to moral violations or categorize actions as morally relevant, they are not, subjectively, in the moral domain in the first place (also see Cervone, 2000). Questions about the categorization of ambiguous actions are circumvented within laboratory paradigms that present to research participants vivid, unambiguous violations of moral codes. But such questions must be confronted if one wants to understand the experience of persons who are acting in naturally occurring environments that are complex or ambiguous.

MORAL IDENTITY, SELF-CONSISTENCY, AND SOCIAL-COGNITIVE PERSONALITY ARCHITECTURE

Having now reviewed developments in personality science, it is time for us to "step back into" the moral domain. We consider how conceptual and empirical tools found in social-cognitive analyses of personality architecture might speak to questions of ongoing discussion in moral psychology. We focus, in particular, on the moral identity theory of Blasi (1983, 1984; see also 2004a, 2004b). We do so because of its exceptional impact and continued promise, and also because it is a framework about which questions are raised in the literature (Nucci, 2004).

Self and Identity in Moral Functioning

Blasi (1983), following his provocative review (Blasi, 1980) indicating that relations between moral cognition and moral action are only moderate, proposed the Self Model of Moral Functioning. His analyses of self and moral identity (Blasi, 1983, 1984; see also 2004a, 2004b; Blasi & Glodis, 1995) are deservedly recognized as a major step forward in filling the conceptual gap between moral understanding and moral action (Bergman, 2004; Hardy & Carlo, 2005).

Blasi's (1984) theory focuses on the role, in moral functioning, of self, self-identity, and self-consistency. Of critical importance is the conception of self in his view. To Blasi, the self is not a collection of self-representations; it is not a simple mental enumeration of one's personal attributes. Instead, self "is an organization of self-related information in which the various elements are brought together according to certain principles of psychological consistency" (Blasi, 1984, p. 131). The organizing principle refers to the process of determining the order and hierarchy among the ideals or concerns included in the self, along "metaphorical" (p. 131) dimensions such as "centrality" and "importance." Those core values that are most central and are considered indispensable to the self constitute the "essential or the core self" (p. 131), and "identity is considered equivalent to the essential self" (p. 130). When identity comprises moral concerns or ideals, or when such concerns are seen as central and essential to one's self, one is said to have a moral identity. In this model, identity figures centrally in motivated action. It does so through a principle of self-consistency: "the motivational basis for moral action lies in the internal demand for psychological self-consistency" (p. 129). The person with a strong moral identity feels a sense of responsibility, or a compulsion, to act. Action reflects not on a rationalistic calculation of costs and benefits, but on "an extension of the essential self into the domain of the possible," an extension that must occur if the person is "to remain true to himself or herself" (p. 132). Failure to act triggers anxiety and guilt (Blasi, 1984; Blasi & Glodis, 1995). Blasi (2004a, 2004b), in essence, it emphasizes the subjective, agentic, and experiential aspects of the self – that is, of the whole, integrated person.

Self, Identity, and Self-Based Motives in Social-Cognitive Theory

How, then, does the moral identity model of Blasi relate to the social-cognitive models of Bandura, Mischel, and other social-cognitive investigators (Cervone & Shoda, 1999), including one of the present authors (Cervone, 2004)? We consider this question by addressing first the notion of self-consistency, and then the concepts of identity and self.

Self-consistency. In social-cognitive theory, motivation is explained by reference to a diverse set of socially grounded incentives for action, as well as a self of internal, cognitive motivators that also have foundations in social interaction (Bandura, 1986). A feature that distinguishes social-cognitive theories of personality from phenomenological personality theories such as that of Carl Rogers (1959), or from perspectives such as that of Blasi, is that social-cognitivists do not posit a self-consistency motive. Theorists such as Bandura recognize, of course, that people commonly are motivated to maintain a consistent sense of self and to regulate action according to consistent standards of self-evaluation. However, they do not feel that these processes are universal, and thus do not posit self-consistency as a universal motive.

There are at least two grounds for questioning whether self-consistency is a universal motive. One is the human capacity and tendency to reinvent oneself: to change plans, change pursuits, change one's social self.[3] Though

---

[3] The tendency may be particularly prevalent in the United States, where "reinventing oneself," a reviewer of the autobiography of Bob Dylan writes, "may be America's most important indigenous art form" (DeRogatis, 2004). Even Erikson (1963), who highlighted

people often appear to act as if they have an inner compass, they sometimes act as if they have decided to throw their compass in the trash and set out in directions unknown. Such potentialities for reinvention in personality functioning (Caprara & Cervone, 2000) lead many investigators to avoid the positing of consistency motives.

The second concern with self-consistency motives is that they may not be universal. Cultural psychologists instruct that the self, as construed by Western psychologists, may not be the lens through which all persons view their social world and their own personhood (Kitayama & Markus, 1999). Motives in some cultures may be distinctly more other-focused than they are in the West (Tripathi & Cervone, in press). The social-cognitivist, then, hesitates to posit a motive for self-consistency.

We note that Blasi, too, is keenly aware of the possibilities of cultural variation. The "type of self experience based on an attitude of care for the self, desire for integrity, and assiduous work on oneself, is not universal, but seems to depend on historical and economic conditions, culturally accepted ideas, and on individual development" (Blasi, 2004a, p. 7). Research in cultural psychology suggests that such awareness is critical in the psychology of self and intentional action (see Heine, Lehman, Markus, & Kitayama, 1999, for a review). In Japanese culture, Heine and colleagues (1999; see also Kitayama, Markus, Matsumoto, & Norasakkunkit, 1997) could not find consistent evidence of psychological strategies for maintenance of self-esteem (a construct that differs from Blasi's concept of self-identity, yet that still relates to the notion of people's "work on oneself"). Heine and Lehman (1999) report that in Japanese culture *self-criticism* is a more adaptive way of functioning, and is less strongly related to depression, than in American culture; self-criticism in Japan is a dominant mode of experiencing the self because it helps in self-improvement vis-à-vis the demands and expectations of others (Kitayama & Markus, 1999). In the moral domain, Miller and colleagues document qualitative variations in what constitutes personal choice or moral duty among Indians and Americans. Indians, compared to Americans, show a greater tendency to view meeting the needs of close others as a matter of moral duty rather than of personal choice (Miller, Bersoff, & Harwood, 1990; Miller & Bersoff, 1992); for example, Indians, more so than Americans, perceive helping behavior in moral terms when interpersonal reciprocity considerations are involved (Miller & Bersoff, 1994).

the continuity in the sense of self, noted that the American history of "contrasts and abrupt changes" fosters the recognition of "dynamic polarities" in development and the tendency "to leave [one's] choices open" (p. 286).

What does this mean in identity terms? Are Indians and Japanese, because of the demands of interpersonal obligations and responsibility, less agentic than their American counterparts and therefore less likely to recognize their essential self? The database of cultural psychology is still relatively sparse. One wise course of action may be to answer such questions after more evidence comes in. We thus turn to the second of the concerns in relating Blasi's work to that of social-cognitive theory, namely, phenomena of self and identity.

The self and identity in social-cognitive theories. Although one can't tell a book by its cover, one can tell something from a book's subject index. The most comprehensive volume in the history of the social-cognitive tradition is that of Bandura (1986). In its subject index, the number of page references one finds when searching for "identity" is zero.[4]

It would be superficial, and also incorrect (see Bandura, 1999), to conclude that this means that social-cognitivists are uninterested in identity. Yet one can conclude something. The absence of index entries, we think, reveals something about the way in which social-cognitive approaches treat the concept of identity. By comparison, imagine looking for "invisible hand" in the index of an economics textbook. One might find few entries, yet one could not conclude that the author was uninterested in the possibility that individual decision makers in a free market who are acting to maximize personal gain might, as Adam Smith suggested, end up acting so as to maximize the welfare of the overall community. The dearth of references would suggest the manner in which the book treated the phenomenon under consideration: not by explaining the market through the action of a hand (invisible or not), but in terms of a complex system of interlinked economic processes, with the system exhibiting emergent properties that include those that we describe with the term "invisible hand." Analogously, social-cognitive theory takes a systems perspective on personality and identity (Bandura, 1999; Cervone, 1997, 2004; Mischel & Morf, 2003; Morf, 2006). Personality is viewed "as an emergent property of self-relevant processes" (Morf, 2006, p. 1528), including "identity goals that [give] substance and meaning" (Morf, 2006, p. 1534) to cognitions about the self and to social activities. The phenomena that we call "identity" are thought to be explicable by reference to social-cognitive and affective processing dynamics that inherently function as coherent systems (Cervone & Shoda, 1999).

---

[4] The "identity theory" referenced in Bandura's (1986) index is an identity theory of mind in which mental states are posited to be identical to brain states, not a theory of identity that addresses questions about the consistent organization of self-relevant information.

This systems view is best construed as a meta-theory rather than as a specific theoretical formulation, as Mischel (2004) explains. At the level of theoretical formulation, a critical psychological structure in identity is posited to be the self-schema. Individuals are thought generally to develop a small number of domains of personal expertise (Cantor & Kihlstrom, 1980) in which their self-relevant knowledge is highly elaborated, or schematic (Markus, 1977). People display consistent patterns of thinking across social domains that may in some respects be diverse, yet that may relate to a given aspect of schematic knowledge (Cervone, 2004). In such a social-cognitive analysis, an individual who possessed an integrated system of self-schemas in a domain, who possessed personal goals that were linked to this self-knowledge, and who held related standards for evaluating the self in its pursuit of these goals would be said to have a strong identity in that domain. If someone, for example, saw herself as highly "athletic" and possessed elaborate self-schemas in the domain of athletics, enduringly possessed goals pertaining to athletic attainment, and maintained rigid standards for evaluating her training and athletic performance, the social-cognitivist would say, "That's it; she identifies with the domain of athletics; she has an athlete identity."

The question, then, is: Is that it? Even in principle, does this conception of interconnected beliefs, goals, and personal standards (Cervone, 2004) constitute identity, or is there something more – some additional, distinct psychological system that underlies the organization of self and the associated phenomenological experiences that we call "identity"? As we understand the writing of Blasi (2004), he would claim not only that there is something more, but that one cannot even get there (to a proper analysis of identity) from here (a social-cognitive model of self-representations): "It is very difficult to imagine, at least for me, how, starting from cognitive self-representations, one could *theoretically* explain the attitudes of care for the core self, and the active, responsible management of the self" (p. 8).

Here we wish to say two things: One can be seen to be in defense of the social-cognitive perspective and the other could be seen to be in defense of Blasi (not that he needs our defending). Blasi is correct in pointing out the difficulties encountered when trying to get from self-representations, which commonly are conceived in a manner that is static and decontextualized, to self-management, which involves a contextualized, dynamic, agentic self. Yet getting from "here" to "there" is precisely one of the tasks for which the KAPA model, reviewed earlier, was devised. The KAPA model recognizes that the way to account for experience and action is not through static mental representations, but through dynamic appraisal processes – processes that numerous emotions theorists (Scherer, Schorr, & Johnstone, 2001; Smith & Lazarus, 1990; Ellsworth & Scherer, 2003) contend are central to emotional experience and motivational dynamics. Schematic self-representations, then, are conceived not as immediate determinants of self-regulated action but as one factor that influences the appraisals the person forms in a given context. This conception reformulates the here-to-there problem as noted above by dividing it in two. Can one (1) start from dynamic cognitive appraisals through which individuals evaluate the self-relevance of encounters, their capacity for coping with encounters, and norms that constrain behavior in those encounters; and (2) get to an active, agentic, motivated-and-emotional self-regulating self? Quite a wealth of research on cognitive appraisal processes, emotions, the motivational implications of emotional states, and the self-regulation of emotions suggests so (in addition to references above, see Ochsner & Gross, 2004). Can one get from enduring mental representations to dynamic appraisal processes? Quite a wealth of research in social cognition (Moskowitz, 2005), including work that manipulates the accessibility of mental representations experimentally to determine their impact on self-appraisals (Cervone et al., 2008), suggests so.

However, the question that remains is whether this formulation addresses the phenomenology of selfhood and identity of interest to Blasi. Here we are inclined to say that it may not do so – certainly that it may not do so in full. Fully addressing the phenomenology of acting in a domain in which one is highly identified may, indeed, require an expansion of traditional social-cognitive formulations. One particularly sophisticated expansion is suggested by Kuhl and colleagues in their functional analyses of personality and self that is known as Personality-Systems Interaction (PSI) Theory (Kuhl & Koole, 2004). PSI theory distinguishes between two self-regulatory functions: self-control, which involves the inhibition of impulsive actions in order to maintain a focus on specific goals, and self-maintenance, which involves directing action toward activities that are intrinsically appealing or congruent with one's overall system of personal aims and values, yielding experiences that may be described as "flow" states (Csikszentmihalyi, 1990) or experiences of self-determination (Deci & Ryan, 1985). Importantly, PSI suggests that these different functions are subserved by qualitatively different types of self-systems. One is a system of self-representations similar to that envisioned in analyses deriving from the study of social cognition (Markus & Wurf, 1987); it subserves the function of self-control. The other, however, is a more holistic system of integrated beliefs, affects, and personal values in which self-representations are implicit rather than explicit (Kuhl & Koole, 2004); this holistic system underlies the capacity for self-maintenance. Kuhl and colleagues suggest that the holistic system that underlies self-maintenance and "flow" states can be modeled through parallel-processing architectures (Rumelhart & McClelland, 1986) and that, neuroanatomically, it entails right-hemispheric processing to a greater degree than does the system of propositionally represented goals and beliefs about the self. A great advantage of PSI analyses is that they begin to concretize, in the language of the contemporary psychological sciences, holistic processes that sometimes are described merely at a metaphorical level that is a less generative guide to research.

The inclusion in PSI theory of two self-referent mental systems can be seen as consistent with Blasi's contention that a model positing only propositionally represented beliefs is not sufficient to capture the psychology of identity and self-management. Yet, the PSI formulation is not damning of social-cognitive theory. It suggests merely a normal-science conceptual advance in which, based on empirical findings, one would differentiate two psychological systems that previously were conceived as one (cf. Mischel & Shoda, 1995; Metcalfe & Mischel, 1998). In principle, in an approach such as the KAPA model, one would differentiate systems of mental representation in the manner that PSI theory suggests.

We will not take a stand on this issue here at the close of this chapter. We will, however, take a stand on strategies for approaching it, and related issues we have discussed. As we have seen, discourse in moral psychology raises questions of general significance to psychological science: the difficulty of linking thought to action; the scope of explanations that reference evolved mental mechanisms rather than socially developed knowledge; the challenge of modeling mental systems that underlie the spectrum of human experiences. The best way to advance understanding of these topics surely is not through a compartmentalized discourse within moral psychology, per se, but through a generalized discourse involving moral psychology, personality science, and psychological science as a whole. The challenge for investigators in the social-cognitive tradition, as we have suggested, is to face squarely the phenomena of self and identity described by theorists such as Erikson (1963) and Blasi (1984). A challenge for students of self, identity, and moral action is to consider fully how the psychological analyses found in personality science and the cognitive sciences (see Bechtel & Abrahamsen, 2007) might inform their understanding of the psychological systems that enable persons to function as moral agents.

REFERENCES

Ashton, M. C., & Lee, K. (2005). A defence of the lexical approach to the study of personality structure. *European Journal of Personality, 19,* 5–24.

  (2007). Empirical, theoretical, and practical advantages of the HEXACO model of personality structure. *Personality and Social Psychology Review, 11,* 150–166.

Ashton, M. C., Lee, K., Perugini, M., Szarota, P., de Vries, R. E., Di Blas, L., Boies, K., & De Raad, B. (2004). A six-factor structure of personality-descriptive adjectives: Solutions from psycholexical studies in seven languages. *Journal of Personality and Social Psychology, 86,* 356–366.

Bandura, A. (1986). *Social foundations of thought and action.* Englewood Cliffs, NJ: Prentice Hall.

  (1991). Social cognitive theory of moral thought and action. In W. M. Kurtines & J. L. Gewirtz (Eds.), *Handbook of moral behavior and development. Theory, research and applications* (vol. 1 pp. 71–129). Hillsdale, NJ: Erlbaum.

  (1997). *Self-efficacy: The exercise of control.* New York: Freeman.

  (1999). Social-cognitive theory of personality. In D. Cervone & Y. Shoda (Eds.), *The coherence of personality: Social-cognitive bases of consistency, variability, and organization* (pp. 185–241). New York: Guilford Press.

Bandura, A., Caprara, G. V., Barbaranelli, C., Pastorelli, C., & Regalia, C. (2001). Sociocognitive self-regulatory mechanisms governing transgressive behavior. *Journal of Personality and Social Psychology, 80,* 125–135.

Bechtel, W., & Abrahamsen, A. (2007). Mental mechanisms, autonomous systems, and moral agency. *Proceedings of the 29th Annual Cognitive Science Society,* pp. 95–100.

Bem, D. J., & Allen, A. (1974). Predicting some of the people some of the time: The search for cross-situational consistencies in behavior. *Psychological Review, 81,* 506–520.

Bergman, R. (2004). Identity as motivation: Toward a theory of the moral self. In D. K. Lapsley & D. Narvaez (Eds.), *Moral development, self, and identity* (pp. 21–46). Mahwah, NJ: Erlbaum.

Blasi, A. (1980). Bridging moral cognition and moral action: A critical review of the literature. *Psychological Bulletin, 88,* 1–45.

  (1983). Moral cognition and moral action: A theoretical perspective. *Developmental Review, 3,* 178–210.

  (1984). Moral identity: Its role in moral functioning. In W. M. Kurtines & J. L. Gewirtz (Eds.), *Morality, moral behavior, and moral development* (pp. 129–139). New York: Wiley.

  (2004a). Neither personality nor cognition: An alternative approach to the nature of the self. In C. Lightfoot, C. Lalonde, & M. Chandler (Eds.), *Changing conceptions of psychological life* (pp. 3–25). Mahwah, NJ: Lawrence Erlbaum Associates.

  (2004b). Moral functioning: Moral understanding and personality. In D. K. Lapsley & D. Narvaez (Eds.), *Moral development, self, and identity* (pp. 189–212). Mahwah, NJ: Lawerence Erlbaum Associates.

Blasi, A., & Glodis, K. (1995). The development of identity: A critical analysis from the perspective of the self as subject. *Developmental Review, 15,* 404–433.

Borsboom, D., Kievit, R., Cervone, D., & Hood, S. B. (in press). The two disciplines of scientific psychology, or: The disunity of psychology as a working hypothesis. In J. Valsiner, P. C. M. Molenaar, M. C. D. P. Lyra, & N. Chaudary (Eds.), *Developmental process methodology in the social and developmental sciences*. New York: Springer.

Borsboom, D., Mellenbergh, G. J., & van Heerden, J. (2003). The theoretical status of latent variables. *Psychological Review, 110*, 203–219.

Caldwell, T. L., Cervone, D., & Rubin, L. H. (in press). Explaining intra-individual variability in social behavior through idiographic assessment: The case of humor. *Journal of Research in Personality, 42*, 1229–1242.

Cantor, N., & Kihlstrom, J. F. (1987). *Personality and social intelligence*. Englewood Cliffs, NJ: Prentice-Hall.

Caprara, G. V., & Cervone, D. (2000). *Personality: Determinants, dynamics, and potentials*. New York: Cambridge University Press.

Cervone, D. (1991). The two disciplines of personality psychology. *Psychological Science, 2*, 371–377.

(1997). Social-cognitive mechanisms and personality coherence: Self-knowledge, situational beliefs, and cross-situational coherence in perceived self-efficacy. *Psychological Science, 8*, 43–50.

(2000). Evolutionary psychology and explanation in personality psychology: How do we know which module to invoke? Special issue on Evolutionary Psychology (J. Heckhausen & P. Boyer, Eds.), *American Behavioral Scientist, 6*, 1001–1014.

(2004). The architecture of personality. *Psychological Review, 111*, 183–204.

(2005). Personality architecture: Within-person structures and processes. *Annual Review of Psychology, 56*, 423–452.

(in press). Explanatory models of personality: Social-cognitive theories and the knowledge-and-appraisal model of personality architecture. To appear in G. Boyle, G. Matthews, & D. Saklofske (Eds.), *Handbook of personality and testing*, London: Sage Publications.

Cervone, D., Caldwell, T. L., Fiori, M., Orom, H., Shadel, W. G., Kassel, J., & Artistico, D. (2008). What underlies appraisals?: Experimentally testing a knowledge-and-appraisal model of personality architecture among smokers contemplating high-risk situations. *Journal of Personality, 76*, 929–967.

Cervone, D., Caldwell, T. L., & Orom, H. (2008). Beyond person and situation effects: Intraindividual personality architecture and its implications for the study of personality and social behavior. In A. Kruglanski & J. Forgas (Series Eds.) & F. Rhodewalt (Volume Ed.), *Frontiers of social psychology: Personality and social behavior* (pp. 9–48). New York: Psychology Press.

Cervone, D., & Mischel, W. (Eds.) (2002). *Advances in personality science*. New York: Guilford Press.

Cervone, D., Orom, H., Artistico, D., Shadel, W. G., & Kassel, J. (2007). Using a knowledge-and-appraisal model of personality architecture to understand consistency and variability in smokers' self-efficacy appraisals in high-risk situations. *Psychology of Addictive Behaviors, 21*, 44–54.

Cervone, D., & Pervin, L. A. (2008). *Personality: Theory and research* (10th ed.). Hoboken, NJ: Wiley.

Cervone, D., Shadel, W. G., & Jencius, S. (2001). Social-cognitive theory of personality assessment. *Personality and Social Psychology Review, 5*, 33–51.

Cervone, D., Shadel, W. G., Smith, R. E., & Fiori, M. (2006). Self-regulation: Reminders and suggestions from personality science. *Applied Psychology: An International Review, 55*, 333–385.

Cervone, D., & Shoda, Y. (Eds.) (1999). *The coherence of personality: Social-cognitive bases of consistency, variability, and organization.* New York: Guilford Press.

Csikszentmihalyi, M. (1990). *Flow: The psychology of optimal experience.* New York: Harper & Row.

Deci, E., & Ryan, R. (1985). *Intrinsic motivation and self determination in human behavior.* New York: Plenum Press.

DeRogatis, J. (2004). *Reinventing Bobby Zimmerman.* Online at http://www.jimdero.com/News2004/Oct31DylanBook.htm, Accessed 1/15/08.

Ellsworth, P. C., and Scherer, K. R. (2003). Appraisal processes in emotion. In R. J. Davidson, K. R. Scherer, & H. H. Goldsmith (Eds.), *Handbook of the affective sciences* (pp. 572–595). New York and Oxford: Oxford University Press.

Erikson, E. H. (1963). *Childhood and society* (2nd ed.). New York: Norton.

Freud, S. (1923/1961). *The ego and the id.* London: Hogarth Press.

Greene, J. D., Sommerville, R. B., Nystrom, L. E., Darley, J. M., & Cohen, J. D. (2001). An fMRI investigation of emotional engagement in moral judgment. *Science, 293*, 2105–2108.

Haidt, J. (2001). The emotional dog and its rational tail: A social intuitionist approach to moral judgment. *Psychological Review, 108*, 814–834.

Hardy, S. A., & Carlo, G. (2005). Identity as a source of moral motivation. *Human Development, 48*, 232–256.

Hartshorn, H., & May, M. A. (1928). *Studies in the nature of character. Vol. 1: Studies in deceit.* New York: Macmillen.

Hauser, M. D. (2006). *Moral minds: How nature designed our universal sense of right and wrong.* New York: Harper Collins.

Heine, S. J., & Lehman, D. R. (1999). Culture, self-discrepancies, and self-satisfaction. *Personality and Social Psychology Bulletin, 25*, 915–925.

Heine, S. J., Lehman, D. R., Markus, H. R., & Kitayama, S. (1999). Is there a universal need for positive self-regard? *Psychological Review, 106*, 766–794.

Higgins, E. T. (1990). Personality, social psychology, and person-situation relations: Standards and knowledge activation as a common language. In L. A. Pervin (Ed.), *Handbook of personality: Theory and research* (pp. 301–338). New York: Guilford Press.

Kagan, J. (2007). The power of context. In Y. Shoda, D. Cervone, & G. Downey (Eds.), *Persons in context: Building a science of the individual* (pp. 43–61). New York: Guilford Press.

Kitayama, S., & Markus, H. R. (1999). Yin and yang of the Japanese self: The cultural psychology of personality coherence. In D. Cervone & Y. Shoda (Eds.), *The coherence of personality: Social-cognitive bases of consistency, variability, and organization* (pp. 242–302). New York: Guilford.

Kitayama, S., Markus, H. R., Matsumoto, H., & Norasakkunkit, V. (1997). Individual and collective processes in the construction of the self: Self-enhancement in the United States and self-criticism in Japan. *Journal of Personality and Social Psychology, 72*, 1245–1267.

Kuhl, J., & Koole, S. L. (2004). Workings of the will: A functional approach. In J. Greenberg, S. L. Koole, & T. Pyszczynski (Eds.), *Handbook of experimental existential psychology* (pp. 411–430). New York: Guilford.

Lapsley, D. K. (1996). *Moral psychology*. Boulder, CO: Westview Press.

Lazarus, R. S. (1991). *Emotion and adaptation*. New York: Oxford University Press.

Markus, H. (1977). Self-schemata and processing information about the self. *Journal of Personality and Social Psychology, 35*, 63–78.

Markus, H., & Wurf, E. (1987). The dynamic self-concept: A social psychological perspective. *Annual Review of Psychology, 38*, 299–337.

McCrae, R. R., & Costa, P. T. (1996). Toward a new generation of personality theories: Theoretical contexts for the five-factor model. In J. S. Wiggins (Ed.), *The five-factor model of personality: Theoretical perspectives* (pp. 51–87). New York: Guilford.

Metcalfe, J., & Mischel, W. (1999). A hot/cool-system analysis of delay of gratification: Dynamics of willpower. *Psychological Review, 106*, 3–19.

Miller, J. G., & Bersoff, D. M. (1992). Culture and moral judgment: How are conflicts between justice and interpersonal responsibilities resolved? *Journal of Personality and Social Psychology, 62*, 541–554.

——— (1994). Cultural influences on the moral status of reciprocity and the discounting of endogenous motivation. *Personality and Social Psychology Bulletin, 20*, 592–605.

Miller, J. G., Bersoff, D. M., & Harwood, R. L. (1990). Perceptions of social responsibilities in India and in the United States: Moral imperatives or personal decisions? *Journal of Personality and Social Psychology, 58*, 33–47.

Mischel, W. (1968). *Personality and assessment*. New York: Wiley.

——— (2004). Toward an integrative science of the person. *Annual Review of Psychology, 55*, 1–22.

Mischel, W., & Harriet, N. (1976). A cognitive social learning approach to morality and self-regulation. In T. Lickona (Ed.), *Moral development and behavior: Theory, research and social issues* (pp. 84–107). New York: Holt, Rinehart & Winston.

Mischel, W., & Morf, C. C. (2003). The self as a psycho-social dynamic processing system: A meta-perspective on a century of the self in psychology. In M. R. Leary & J. P. Tangney (Eds.), *Handbook of self and identity* (pp. 15–43). New York: Guilford.

Mischel, W., & Peake, P. K. (1982). Beyond deja vu in the search for cross-situational consistency. *Psychological Review, 89*, 730–755.

Mischel, W., & Shoda, Y. (1995). A cognitive-affective system theory of personality: Reconceptualizing situations, dispositions, dynamics, and invariance in personality structure. *Psychological Review, 102*, 246–286.

Morf, C. C. (2006). Personality reflected in a coherent idiosyncratic interplay of intra- and interpersonal self-regulatory processes. *Journal of Personality, 74*, 1527–1556.

Moskowitz, G. B. (2005). *Social cognition: Understanding self and others*. New York: Guilford Press.
Narvaez, D., Lapsley, D., Hagele, S., & Lasky, B. (2006). Moral chronicity and social information processing: Tests of a social cognitive approach to the moral personality. *Journal of Research in Personality, 40*, 966–985.
Nucci, L. P. (2004). Reflections on the moral self construct. In D. K. Lapsley & D. Narvaez (Eds.), *Moral development, self, and identity* (pp. 111–132). Mahwah, NJ: Lawrence Erlbaum Associates.
Ochsner, K. N., & Gross, J. J. (2004). Thinking makes it so: A social cognitive neuroscience approach to emotion regulation. In R. Baumeister & K. Vohs (Eds.), *The handbook of self-regulation: Research, theory and applications* (pp. 229–255). New York: Guilford Press.
Orom, H., & Cervone, D. (in press). Personality dynamics, meaning, and idiosyncrasy: Identifying cross-situational coherence by assessing personality architecture. *Journal of Research in Personality*.
Rest, J. R. (1984). The major components of morality. In W. M. Kurtines & J. L. Gewirtz (Eds.), *Morality, moral behavior, and moral development* (pp. 24–37). New York: Wiley.
Rogers, C. R. (1959). A theory of therapy, personality, and interpersonal relationships as developed in the client-centered framework. In S. Koch (Ed.), *Psychology: A study of science* (pp. 184–256). New York: McGraw-Hill.
Rumelhart, D. E., McClelland, J. L., & PDP Research Group (1986). *Parallel distributed processing: Explorations in the microstructure of cognition: Vol. 1. Foundations*. Cambridge, MA: MIT Press.
Saucier, G., Hampson, S. E., & Goldberg, L. R. (2000). Cross-language studies of lexical personality factors. In S. E. Hampson (Ed.), *Advances in personality psychology* (Vol. 1, pp. 1–36). East Sussex, England: Psychology Press Ltd.
Scherer, K. R., Schorr, A., & Johnstone, T. (Eds.) (2001). *Appraisal processes in emotion: Theory, methods, research*. New York: Oxford University Press.
Shoda, Y., Cervone, D., & Downey, G. (Eds.) (2007). *Persons in context: Building a science of the individual*. New York: Guilford Press.
Shweder, R. A., Mahapatra, M., & Miller, J. G. (1987). Culture and moral development. In J. Kagan & S. Lamb (Eds.), *The emergence of morality in young children* (pp. 1–90). Chicago, IL: University of Chicago Press.
Skitka, L. J., Bauman, C. W., & Sargis, E. G. (2005). Moral conviction: Attitude strength or something more? *Journal of Personality and Social Psychology, 88*, 895–917.
Skitka, L. J., & Lytle, B. L. (2008). *The relative effects of religiosity, values, and moral mandates on projected activism related to physician-assisted suicide*. Manuscript under editorial review.
Smith, C. A., & Lazarus, R. S. (1990). Emotion and adaptation. In L. A. Pervin (Ed.), *Handbook of personality: Theory and research* (pp. 609–637). New York: Guilford.
Tripathi, R., & Cervone, D. (in press). Cultural variations in achievement motivation despite equivalent motivational strength: Motivational concerns among Indian and American corporate professionals, *Journal of Research in Personality*.

Turiel, E. (1983). *The development of social knowledge: Morality and convention.* Cambridge: Cambridge University Press.

Wise, J. (2007). Testing a theory that explains how self-efficacy beliefs are formed: Predicting self-efficacy appraisals across recreational activities. *Journal of Social and Clinical Psychology, 26,* 841–848.

Zelli, A., Cervone, D., & Huesmann, L. R. (1996). Social inference and individual differences in aggression: Evidence for spontaneous judgments of hostility. *Social Cognition, 14,* 165–190.

Zelli, A., Huesmann, L. R., & Cervone, D. (1995). Social inference and individual differences in aggression: Evidence for spontaneous judgments of hostility. *Aggressive Behavior, 21,* 405–417.

3

Moral Science? Still Metaphysical After All These Years

OWEN FLANAGAN

VIRTUOUS INTERDEPENDENCY

At the end of the *Nicomachean Ethics,* the most influential secular ethics text in the West (a set of lecture notes dutifully copied by Aristotle's son Nicomachus), Aristotle wrote (or taught) that he would next take up politics, which in any case he ought to have done before the ethics. It would have been equally sensible if Aristotle had written (or taught) the *Politics* first, that he might have had the reverse afterthought – namely, that he should now turn to moral psychology and ethics, to providing a theory of individual flourishing (*eudaimonia*) as well as a theory of human agency, the virtues, moral development, moral education, and weakness of the will (*akrasia*), which in any case he ought to have done first, before providing a theory of social or political good.

So which really comes first (or what is different, should come first) ethics, including what we now call moral psychology – moral development, affective and cognitive components of moral competence, and so on – or politics, including what we now call the theories of justice and social good? The answer to both the descriptive and normative questions is that ethics, moral psychology, and a conception of social and political good typically coevolve and depend upon each other conceptually. Thus this messy feature of interdependency is as it should be, as it must be. In the domain of morality, as a lived phenomenon and as an area of inquiry, neither philosophy nor psychology nor social and political theory serves as the foundation for any other. There is instead massive, and necessary, interpenetration among psychology, ethics, and politics, between the descriptive and the normative, even, as we shall see, between the psychophysical and the metaphysical.

It follows that the only sensible aim of anyone seriously concerned with the good life, with questions of how we individually and collectively ought to live, is to maintain reflective equilibrium among our psychological theories of the nature and varieties of moral personality, and among these and our theories about the nature of individual flourishing – what I call *eudaimonics* (Flanagan, 2007): good character, a good society, how to develop and maintain these – as well as among our epistemic and metaphysical theories that can explain whether and how judgments of value can be something respectable, something objective; or if not objective, then at least something more than emotive power plays designed to advance the ways of being and acting that I and the members of my tribe favor.

Here I focus on two areas where the discipline of philosophy, including normative ethics and political philosophy, and the discipline of psychology are especially interactive:

(1) *The Ontology of Moral Personality*. What basic entities and basic events or processes are theories of moral personality committed to? Persons? Persons with personalities? Personalities constituted by character traits – for example, virtues and vices? Assuming that there are character traits, are these traits causally efficacious and "in" persons, like area V1, which is part of the visual system and is housed in the brain? Or are character traits dispositions, tendencies to express reliably certain patterns of perception, feeling, thinking, and behavior, similar perhaps to my know-how for bike riding, which is not in me as an area of my brain is in me, but is a disposition in me that is activated by bikes; and which is not possessed by my friends who don't know how to ride bikes? (See Cervone and Tripathi, this volume, and McAdams, this volume, for examples of psychologists who differ about how to conceptualize traits along something like the latter lines.) Or, more skeptically, could character trait ascriptions have predictive or some sort of instrumental value, but name nothing real, nothing that ought to be part of a philosophically respectable metaphysic? Consider: One can reliably orchestrate one's days around sunrises and sunsets, even though, since Copernicus, there are no such things. Or, consider: Is the part of physics committed to studying solids committed to their really being solids, as opposed to providing an analysis for how things that are mostly (80–90%) empty space might seem solid? Along these lines, one might wonder: What do the experts, in this case, psychologists, say about the commitments of every moral philosophy ever invented – yes, every single one – to the reality of some such apparatus as reliable traits of persons, commonly designated in the moral

sphere of life as "virtues"? Has psychology revealed that there are no such things? A couple of mischief-makers in philosophy say "yes." But they are mistaken. I'll explain.

(2) *Narrative Metaphysics.* The second zone of interest involves narrative self-construction. Many common modes of moral self-presentation and other-evaluation drip or ooze metaphysics – as William James might have put it – by making a mother lode of philosophically contentious assumptions about free will, causation, personal merit, blame, desert, and the role of luck or fate. I'll call the sort of narratives that are permitted, indeed favored, in America to ascribe moral decency or indecency to oneself or others, but that arguably rest on philosophical mistakes, *morally harmful master-narratives.* I'll explain by way of a familiar master-narrative that Americans use to speak about themselves, and about what they deserve as reward for conscientiousness and hard work. This *standard narrative of accomplishment and desert* might seem natural from the point of view of social psychology and may well ground feelings of self-esteem and judgments of self-respect. But upon analysis, it appears to rest on problematic philosophical assumptions about desert, luck, and agency. This case raises complex questions about whether there might be nonparochial psychological requirements for self-esteem and self-respect that involve making objective judgments of responsibility, credit, merit, desert, and their opposites when, from the point of view of metaphysics (so I say), it is exceedingly difficult – perhaps impossible – to make sense of these concepts as we intend them. The worry is that the demands of human psychology, and perhaps of sociopolitical-economic life, generally, require good record-keeping about what people have done, are up to, are likely to do next, as well as systems of doling out rewards and punishment, credit and blame, where doing so has an instrumental rationale, but utterly lacks any deep moral or metaphysical rationale. There continues to be – and there is no reason to be optimistic that it can be overcome – genuine conflict between the demands of practical life and what philosophical theory teaches, between the subjective and the objective, between the psychosocial needs of our kind of animal and what metaphysics teaches.

THE NONEXISTENCE OF CHARACTER TRAITS

It may surprise psychologists that this 1970s–early 80s debate (Mischel, 1968; Nisbett Ross, 1980) inside psychology about the ontology of traits, despite having reached a resolution in psychology – Mischel, for example, is a defender of a hybrid "social-cognitive" view – and which retains a place for judiciously depicted personality traits, survives nonetheless in philosophy. "The Nonexistence of Character Traits" is the title of a twenty-first century paper by an important philosopher, Gilbert Harman (2000). I take some responsibility for the fact that philosophers are carrying on in this way, since I was the first philosopher to call attention to the debate among psychologists about these matters, and to claim that the debates about persons and situations had important implications for ethics, especially virtue theories (Flanagan, 1991). It did, and it does. But this point – which was intended to be a complex one calling on moral theorists to speak more precisely about the nature and structure of the variety of components that comprise moral competence – opened the door to a playground where a small band of mischievous hyperbolists, really just two, have had their fun for too long making ontological mischief. So I will begin here to make my amends, and to try to quiet the cheerleaders within philosophy (Doris, 1998, 2002; Harman, 1999, 2000), who say that character traits are like phlogiston or unicorns, and thus that moral theories that depend on the positing of traits – virtue theories first and foremost (in fact, the criticism, if it were apt, would apply to all moral theories West and East) – are nonstarters.

In a recent encyclopedia piece on "Moral Psychology: Empirical Issues," Doris and Stich (2008) write: "Initially, philosophers interested in the empirical literature advanced views that were, in varying degrees, *skeptical* of the conceptions of character current in virtue ethics but this skepticism subsequently drew spirited replies from defenders of virtue ethics and character psychology." In the endnote attached, they write: "The issues were first broached in Flanagan's (1991) important discussion, but Flanagan did not advance the aggressive skepticism of later writers." This is true. I "did not advance the aggressive skepticism" that exactly two "initial" writers in the text, now (exactly two) "later" writers in the endnote, namely Doris and Harman, advanced aggressively, incredibly, and with much fanfare. The reason I did not claim there were no character traits is because there are character traits. This was obvious when I wrote *Varieties* in 1991, and it is obvious now almost two decades later. At that time, after examining the trait research as well as the situationist challenge to a trait ontology, I advocated a modest conclusion that both philosophers and psychologists ought to exercise care when speaking of virtues, and more generally when speaking about the nature and structure of the multifarious components of human moral psychology, precisely so that concerns of both ontological legitimacy and psychological realizability can be satisfied.

So when the "aggressively sceptical" conclusion was pressed with no important new psychological research or new philosophical arguments backing it, I expected the noise to abate amidst the variety of wise responses to the hyperbole – which included some "spirited replies from defenders of virtue ethics and character psychology" to the "no character traits" claim (e.g., Annas, forthcoming; Kamtekar, 2004; Merritt, 2000; Miller, 2003; Sabini & Silver, 2005; Vranas, 2005, Sreenivasan, 2002, 2008). But it hasn't. The claim that there are no character traits, and that psychology has shown this to be so, continues to be made despite my initial arguments (1991), and the latter able responses from defenders of various philosophical virtue theories on behalf of the specific conception of virtue advocated by different virtue theoretical traditions – e.g., Aristotle (Annas, Miller) or Hume (Merritt).

This topic of the ways philosophy and psychology interact makes this a perfect place to do what many have been asking for, namely, to provide my response to the "no character trait" thesis. Since I opened the door to the playground where its defenders play, I'll cut to the chase and try to make quick work of putting to rest the idea that there are no traits of character. Reference to virtues and vices, and to the aim of trying to equip agents with a good character comprised of virtues is psychologically, sociologically, and politically wise, as well as ontologically respectable.

Several claims must be distinguished: Are there any character traits at all? Are there virtues – "habits of the hearts and mind" that pertain to moral life – among the character traits that there are (like Dewey, I think that using a language of moral habits instead of virtues and vices is best, but I won't fuss over the linguistic matter here)? Are character trait attributions, specifically virtue attributions, just instrumental devices that third parties and first persons use to predict or, what is different, sum up, or describe and type, heterogeneous behaviors? So that, for example, saying "she is shy" is a way of telling you that you can expect from her some of the behaviors that we folk around here call "shy," but which doesn't name anything more than that, doesn't refer to anything psychological – the way, for example, "bad weather" names a practically informative heterogeneous kind, but not a meteorological kind. Or, finally, are virtues psychologically real and thus respectable members of the ontological table of elements? The answers are yes, yes, no, and yes.

The Aim of *Varieties of Moral Personality*

In philosophy, and in Britain, just as Kohlberg's program was being launched in Chicago, Elizabeth Anscombe (1958) argued that the enlightenment ideal of rule-abiding principled reasoners was distant from the way(s) good people, even the principled reasoners, normally operate, and she recommended a revival of ancient virtue theory, which was still, she thought, being deployed by moral teachers, even if not philosophically defended. Murdoch said that normative ethics might as well cease until we philosophers had a better and more credible idea of the equipment real people deploy in moral life. My overall aim in *Varieties* (1991) could be read (it wasn't consciously so) as an attempt to advance Murdoch's program by making the case for ethical theorizing that is *psychologically realistic*. I tried to reveal how much fertile, under-explored common ground there is between philosophers and psychologists, including on such issues as what good character is, what it consists in, and how predictively reliable it is. I was not aggressively skeptical of virtue talk, because whether or not virtue talk was problematic depended on what was being assumed by such talk. What I did say was this: if, or insofar, as virtues or moral character traits are reified as *things inside persons* or, what is different, are conceived to be *situationally insensitive*, there are problems. If you don't commit what Whitehead memorably called "the fallacy of misplaced concreteness" with respect to virtues, and if you don't think virtues make one's character immune to deficiency in the domain that the virtue is set up to cover, then you are off to a good start in proposing a psychologically and philosophically viable normative conception. I argued that philosophers, my main audience, who work in moral psychology ought to speak carefully about the psychological equipment involved in various types of moral competence in accordance with what a judicious interpretation of the psychological evidence requires.

What a Virtue Might Be

Simplistically, we can divide communities who speak about traits, moral habits, and virtues and vices into three: philosophers, psychologists, and ordinary people. I have no firm opinion about what ordinary people think about the metaphysics of traits or how they work psychologically, nor does it matter very much whether and how nonspecialists think, so long as they can acquire a morality and teach it to their charges. I understood the question of whether moral character traits exist to be a question about what the experts say are legitimate posits, not, in the first instance, what ordinary people assert or assume or imply by their talk of virtues and vices.

We better hope that morality can be taught without knowing what it is (just as we assume that kids can learn that night follows day and day follows night without knowing what night and day really are, or why they follow each other), or why exactly one should be moral, and certainly without knowing (because no one knows) how the multifarious components of moral competence are configured in the mind-brain world. In any case, what ordinary people think or are ontologically committed to is not really any of my business as a philosopher. I only want to know what kinds of ontological commitments talk of traits commits philosophers to, and how such talk fares in terms of what psychologists who pay attention to such matters say traits are or might be. It is these disciplines that have to make the world safe for character traits, and then only if there really are any.

So, what is a moral trait? In particular, what would a virtue (or a vice) be if there were any? First pass, and in the spirit of Aristotle, we can provide this schema:

> *A virtue is a disposition {to perceive, to feel, to think, to judge, to act} in a way that is appropriate to the situation.*

Philosophers who know the history of ethics (not even all ethicists do) know that not all these components are thought necessary for every virtue. How many of these five components are required or thought ideal is variable. It may depend on the particular person, the virtue, and the demands of the social world. On most every view, one at least needs to *perceive* that a situation is of a certain kind, and then to think, although perhaps not declaratively, that something ought to be done (not always by me). But some virtues, especially in an expert, may require little or no thought. So we can imagine the schema written this way, where **&v** = and/or:

> *A virtue is a disposition {to perceive &v to feel &v to think &v to judge &v to act} in a way that is appropriate to the situation.*

A moral habit or virtue so defined or characterized by this schema could be mainly, possibly purely, *behavioral*. A person sees a person in need and reliably helps (traits like being agreeable, or assertive, or being a hard worker might be better examples of traits that in some people are best described behaviorally). She gives helping no thought, nor does she get emotional about the situation. Another individual sees a person in need and reliably helps, but always *feels* for the person in need, perhaps before she helps, perhaps as she is helping, possibly after she helps. A third person is (or is thought to be) an extremely sensitive detector of neediness, and *perceives* a larger number of, or different, people as needy than do the first two.

The familiar, but different, ways that various philosophical traditions conceive of virtue tracks alleged differences among persons, and can be represented by the schema. Socrates and the Stoics did not think "feeling" was desirable in the activation of the virtues, whereas Plato and Aristotle think it is essential. Confucius and Mencius think we just need to grow the good seeds that are already inside us in order to become virtuous, whereas Mozi, who comes between the two, is said to think the mind is a moral *tabula rasa*, and thus that virtues like compassion and honesty will need to be built from scratch in the way my ability to play a musical instrument is (but see Flanagan, 2008). Hindus, Buddhists, and Jains all think that there are poisonous dispositions in our natures that require elimination in order for positive dispositions, the virtues, to take hold. Iris Murdoch, Simone Weil, Lawrence Blum (1994) emphasize acute, particularistic, perceptual sensitivity more than most ancients and, in part, because of the more complex requirements of modern social worlds. The virtues of the Buddhist bodhisattva or the Christian ascetic don't require much in the action department, but Confucian and Deweyean virtues do. And so on.

All this disagreement is possible and perfectly legitimate because ethical life requires decisions about how best to teach the youth, to maintain virtue and order, and to live satisfying, meaningful lives in different kinds of social worlds (Wong, 2006).

Everyone has a virtue theory. Even philosophers like Kant and Mill, who are thought to have alternatives to virtue theory, have elaborate theories of virtue. But, as expected, these "rule-theorists" think that one crucial virtue will be a cognitive meta-virtue, which (possibly orchestrated by an on-guard attentional mechanism) will kick some moral problem cases upstairs for cognitive testing by the categorical imperative or principle of utility, respectively. People who go to good schools know all this, otherwise not. The main point for now is that there is lots of disagreement among philosophers who advocate the virtues – and everyone does – about which, among the above aspects of virtues – perceiving, feeling, thinking, judging, and acting – and how, these ought normatively to be tuned up or down (Homiak, 1997, 2008; Sherman, 1989; Swanton, 2003). Furthermore, every moral tradition that works with and through virtues thinks that such tuning up or down, even building from scratch if necessary, is possible (you learn bike riding from scratch, why not the same – if necessary – for being honest?), and thus that the virtues are psychologically realizable.

On the schema for virtue provided above, and on the assumption that the perception of the situation as calling for moral attention (component 1) must occur with at least one other ingredient from the list, there are 15 combinations – disposition kinds – for a minimal virtue ascription. If we imagine adding "aptness conditions" on the degree to which other components can and should be expressed, so that turning off one aspect – feeling, say, for the Stoics – means 0 activation and that we can turn each aspect (of the four remaining) up (by 1s) to a maximum setting of 5 (say, feelings of sympathy or empathy in theories that favor such feelings), then the general ways possible of doing or activating each of the virtues would be on the order of 1,250.

Still, what kind of thing is a virtue? The answer is that virtues are dispositions (if there are any). But they are different kinds of dispositions. Virtues comprise a multiplicity of kinds: A virtue might involve all five of the elements or components in the schema above or it might only involve two – say, perceiving and doing. (In America it is common to emphasize these two elements as the most important.)

Much silliness can be avoided if we remind ourselves of this: if virtues exist at all, they exist as dispositions. Solubility and flammability are dispositions, and dispositions are cashed out in terms of subjunctive conditionals. To say that sugar is soluble means that, if sugar were put in water, it would dissolve. *Where* is the solubility when the sugar in not in the water? It might seem natural to say it is *in* the sugar. But that is not quite the right answer. And the problem is that asking *where* for dispositions is to ask a bad question. Virtues and vices, if they exist, and they do, are instantiated in neural networks. A virtue, if it is accurately ascribed, names a real and reliable pattern among relata (normally comprised of states or processes in things – in a person and the world), but they are not themselves things. They are also not ontologically spooky. Sugar will reliably dissolve in water, and we can explain why in terms of the chemical process that ensues when water and sugar come into contact. Sugar and water causally interact to cause sugary, nongranular, water. Likewise I have the ability to add numbers. If you ask me to add 57 and 34, I can do it. No one knows where and how this ability is housed when it is not being activated by arithmetic questions, but no one would be driven to skepticism about the reality of the ability to do addition and subtraction, and to think that this ability, in virtue of being nowhere, is nothing at all when not active. The ability we are pretty certain is real, and is housed somehow in neural networks.

Now one can start to see how a mistake might be made. We might think that a virtue is a causally efficacious thing inside a person, when it isn't that or not literally that. A virtue does play a causal role, and it is mostly inside the person. But it is not totally inside a person, and it is not a thing. Instead a virtue, like all other character traits (if there any), is a reliable habit of the heart-mind. It has characteristic activating conditions, so that tokens of a situation type activate a neural network, which has been trained-up to be activated by situations of that kind. In robust cases (according to the schema above), a situation that deserves moral attention activates a {perception – feeling – thought – judgment – action} sequence. The full sequence goes from a situation in the world to an action in the world, and thus there are at least two components that are not literally "in" the person – although both the perceiving and the action are done by the person with the virtue (or vice).

So, the ascription of a virtue or a vice is normally an ascription of a disposition that reliably activates the desired sequence. Although it is not quite right to say that the solubility is in the sugar or the honesty is in the person, it is acceptable to speak this way so long as one is careful. We say that the sugar *is* soluble or the person *is* honest or that the sugar cube or the person has such and such property because the disposition moves with the person (or sugar) across situations of a certain kind, and that is because the disposition is *instantiated* in the sugar chemically, and in the person neurophysiologically: it is activated only when the sugar or person come into contact with the right activating conditions. The activation of the virtue requires that the person with (or, who possesses the disposition to) the virtue be in a token (instance) of the type of situation that the virtue is (was designed to be) responsive to.

So virtue as defined, or better, as characterized, above is a disposition, not a thing. There is no reason for metaphysical anxiety. Reality is filled with many real "things" that are not really things. Days occur. They go by. But the days aren't things. Perhaps they are events. Love and friendship are among the most important things in life, despite not really being things. Tables and chairs and rocks are things, unless you are Heraclitean, in which case they are just slowly moving unfoldings, processes. In a world conceived along event or process lines, dispositions might seem less queer. But even if you think that most things are real substantial things, you'll still need to allow dispositions, causes, space, time, and the like to explain what happens among the things, and none of these are themselves things.

Dispositions – like solubility and flammability and honesty – have instantiations all over the place in things and in events in the world, and some things are prone to showing the disposition in active form and others not: gas is flammable, water is not, unless gas gets on top on the water; people but not rocks and turtles can be honest, and so on. A virtue does not *qua* virtue have location, although it, or better, its components are activated in space and time. If the virtue involves activation of a feeling, e.g., an empathic state, then this occurs at a place – in my body/brain – at a particular time. If a virtue involves an action, this requires place and time – but the action is hardly in me, although my actions are mine; they involve me doing things in the world. Finally virtues, according to the schema, are defined in terms of the characteristic situations that activate them, so they cannot be thought of as situationally insensitive. They are defined as dispositions that are active only in certain situations. The essence of a virtue is to be a disposition designed to be situationally sensitive.

The Phenomenology of Virtue (& Vice)

In my work in philosophy of mind (Flanagan, 1992, 1996, 2000, 2002, 2007), I have recommended using what I call "the natural method." In making decisions about the nature and function of conscious mental states, or states with conscious components, consult the phenomenology as well as the psychological and neuroscientific research. This is helpful in the case of virtues, because one of the many reasons to think that there are character traits and that they are psychological – unlike the disposition of my digestive system to digest food, which is a nonpsychological disposition – is because they possess phenomenal aspects. Indeed, the claim that some dispositions are more than behavioral is ancient. Before Socrates, Plato, and Aristotle made arguments for the psychological reality of virtuous dispositions, Confucius and Mencius provided phenomenological evidence for their reality. Mencius claims that everyone (even Hitler, we might say) will feel himself moved (emotionally and physically) to want to rescue a child falling into a well. This is a proto-moral disposition that is recognizable as psychologically real. If we wished, we could measure what is going on in the body and the brain of people who have the Mencian (pre)dispositon. To explain how or why this disposition to save the child is activated without training (assuming it is), we would need to go to evolutionary biology. In any case, the reason the phenomenology matters is that it adds credence to all the other evidence that character traits are real: it feels like something to have that child-saving urge that may be felt recognizably by simply hearing about it, just as it feels like something to be shy or to experience lust. Jimmy Carter once told a *Playboy* interviewer that he experienced "lust in his heart," and not just for his wife Rosalyn. Most normal people are familiar with the feel and the activation conditions of sexy thoughts and feelings. It does not require expertise in rocket science to explain why humans are reliably disposed to feel, think, and wish to act on these desires. Whether one's sexual disposition becomes a virtue or a vice depends on how the person and her moral community manage to (re)structure the natural psychological economy of the underlying disposition. In any case, the possibility that character trait descriptions are simply descriptively and/or predictively useful summary statements of behavioral tendencies is belied in many cases by the phenomenology. One doesn't just act honestly or compassionately or sexually. Activation of these dispositions normally involves a robust and distinctive phenomenology.

Numbers for Philosophers

So, the character trait skeptics cannot win on the metaphysics or the phenomenology. They sometimes act as if they can win based on the empirical evidence. But this is not so. Walter Mischel (1968) challenged the ability of personality psychology to reliably predict and, what is different, to explain behavior on the basis of trait ascriptions, citing a low *correlation coefficient*. A correlation coefficient is the statistic that describes the degree to which traits and behavior are correlated (and ranges from −1 to +1). The correlation coefficient is a measure of actual effect size, which is a different and stronger measure than statistical significance, which is a measure of how unlikely, relative to chance, a result is. Mischel claimed that the average value for the correlation coefficient between traits and behavior, using personality tests, was .30. Nisbett and Ross (1980) put the number at .40. The idea is that both numbers are pathetically low. But they aren't. They are quite high.

Suppose chance would yield 50% accuracy in guessing what person P will do in S, where S is a high stakes situation in which dishonesty will pay. A prediction of what P will do in S based on information about a trait – e.g., honest or dishonest – with a *correlation coefficient* .40 will improve one's accuracy by 20%. That is, using the trait information gathered by valid and reliable testing (not just any old person's opinion) will increase accuracy in prediction to the level of accuracy 70% of the time (Funder, 2001, p. 81; Hemphill, 2003).

A standard move is to say this: "Well, that still leaves 30% of the time that you won't predict correctly using trait ascriptions, and this missing 30% must be explained by the situation." But there is a misstep here. First, one cannot determine the power of situations, or whatever the main cause(s) is or might be, by subtraction. Second, it is incorrect to frame the debate so that it seems to be about the degree to which the situation or the trait (or set of traits) – in our case, a virtue or vice – does more of the explaining. Although it is commonplace to take the lesson of famous social psychological experiments to show that the situation overpowers the person and her traits, it is entirely possible that the so-called "missing variance" can be equally well explained by adverting to other personality traits, as to features of the situations. Third, no reasonable person would deny that situations might in fact overpower a disposition. There are abundant examples: Sugar is soluble means sugar dissolves in water; but sugar in ice (= water) doesn't display its solubility very well. Why not? Slow down the motion of the water molecules, and the dissolution doesn't happen normally. Fourth, when classic experiments (obedience to authority, bystander effects) are reanalyzed algebraically, converting the social psychologist statistics to a correlation coefficient, which measures the relation between features such as degree of isolation in Milgram-type experiments or the number of bystanders in Samaritan-type experiments, these features have a correlation coefficient of .40. So knowing about these aspects of the situations will yield the same sort of increase in predictive power as knowing about traits. That is, the predictive value of these specific features of these unusual situations is about the same as the average predictive value of trait attributions. I have heard no philosopher make these points. They matter, and thus I do so. Both situations and traits are real – they must be to get these real effects. And no one would be led to be a situation skeptic based on the fact that very refined analysis of the kinds of situations, or the aspects of situations (like the water that is ice), that produce unexpected results yields predictive accuracy with 30% misses; that is no one (happily) is led to be a situation skeptic based on a .40 correlation coefficient in cases where our intuitions are strong that the situation must be doing the mother lode of causal work.

The upshot is that debates about the relative causal efficacy of traits versus situations is a discussion about the relative causal power of two kinds of causes, where both exist. There are traits, and there are situations. They interact. End of story. Any questions about the phenomenology, robustness, globality, and causal efficacy of character traits are empirical questions that ought to be discussed and evaluated on a case-by-case basis. Such questions are not questions about which philosophers' opinions carry any weight. The upshot is this: The argument about the nonexistence of character traits is much ado about nothing. It fills a niche that (still) deserves to remain empty.

In *Varieties* I asked, What lessons should a defender of psychological realism draw from this research? I said this: "Traits are real and predictive, but no credible moral psychology can focus solely on traits, dispositions, and character. Good lives cannot be properly envisaged, nor can they be created and sustained, without paying attention to what goes on outside the agent – to the multifarious interactive relations between individual and the natural and social environments" (1991, p. 312). I (still) agree with my statement.

THE METAPHYSICS OF NARRATIVE

A second area where several disciplines – psychology and philosophy, but also anthropology, sociology, political theory, comparative literary studies – can engage each other profitably is on the topic of narrative self-presentation and self-comprehension. When I speak about myself (or you), especially if I tell part of my story (or yours), I stand on the shoulders of ancestral storytellers who have supplied what are now – but once were contested – commonsense categories and familiar plot lines in service of the interpretation of persons and their lives. These ancestral storytellers were themselves dependent on communities of predecessors who invented and/or stabilized the language we speak, parsed the universe, and introduced word linkages, word spans, that attempt to capture what we now think of as our kind of beings-in-time doing what our kind of beings-in-time do in time.

Many disciplines have a name for the method of taming unruly phenomena by imposition of master-narrative or mother-theoretical structure. There are scripts, frames, the background, heuristics, ideal types, tropes, themes, ways of world making, *Weltanschauung*, and even meta-narrative, the mother of all narratives, the narrative that ends all narratives by speaking the ultimate truth about us – if there could be such a thing. Each of these grand terms names or gestures at a (possibly, somewhat different) way in which, by way of a general thematic structure, we gain purchase on the patterns that are there, or that we impose on the incredible variety of persons and lives.

Normative Narratives

One important function of self-narration, for both first-personal and third-personal consumption, is to present oneself as morally decent, possibly as morally good, even virtuous (Fireman et al., 2003; Flanagan, 1991, 1992, 1996, 2002, 2007). One feels good about oneself, and social intercourse goes best, when social actors feel morally self-respecting, and are perceived by others as morally decent, or better, as truly good. The complexities of modern life suggest that narratives, as opposed to direct observation, and as told by oneself and others who have heard one's story(ies), provide much of the material for assessments of decency. The principle of charity in interpretation teaches that we ought to assume normally that extreme self-deception and social manipulation are not in play, and thus that most people speak truthfully when they tell their story (with a hefty dollop of self-serving spin), and thus that our stories are (self-)revealing of our moral personality, our character traits, and their complex situational sensitivities.

Because narratives are designed in part to efficiently play this role of situating us in social space as morally good agents, they incorporate all sorts of assumptions about the nature of persons and goodness, some of which I'll call *foundational* or *metaphysical*. An assumption is foundational or metaphysical if it articulates, without defense, what is taken to be a settled matter of philosophy – e.g., that persons exist; that there are multifarious character traits, many of which subserve moral life and can be used to predict and explain behavior; that some actions are voluntary, some are not; that responsibility tracks voluntariness; and so on. An assumption is foundational or metaphysical in a problematic way if it takes for granted a dubious stance about free will – e.g., that we are totally self-initiating causes; or that will itself has no prior causes; or if it underestimates fate or luck in life's circumstances. A familiar American narrative of accomplishment and desert (Clark, 1997) can serve as an example of a type of narrative that, despite being commonplace and widely accepted as a way of articulating legitimate grounds for self-esteem and self-respect, in fact makes philosophically questionable assumptions about agency, effort, luck, and desert.

The target mother-narrative is familiarly American. It is not itself universal (Gouda, 1995; MacIntyre, 1987), although it may be universal to make some sort of distinction between acts that merit credit and/or blame and those that don't. The narrative is built broadly around themes such as that "hard work and effort pay." It incorporates subsidiary tropes such as these: "People who work hard deserve to enjoy the fruits of their labor." "If one chooses to share these fruits that is nice; but it is entirely above and beyond the call of duty." "Individuals are responsible for their own fates." "Luck can be mitigated by conscientious planning and hard work." "Social safety nets are there for people who *would* work hard if they could but who, due to bad luck, can't."

The "hard work and effort pay" master-narrative typically exists in a web with some or all of these latter themes embedded in a taken for granted way. If one is a conscientious and successful worker, then the elements of the web work conceptually together to warrant positive self-assessment. The master-narrative that "hard work and effort pay" is of course intended to be both empirical or descriptive (normally hard work pays) and normative (hard work ought to pay), and thus action-guiding (one ought to work hard) (Sunstein, 2005).

The *narrative metaphysics thesis* says that this narrative, as well as many other common narratives (examples follow), incorporates philosophical assumptions. The *narrative metaphysics thesis* is stronger than the claims that narratives are pinned on socially attractive narrative hooks, and that which hooks appeal is culturally variable, both of which are also true (Fireman et al., 2003; Flanagan, 1991, 1992, 1996, 2002). The *narrative metaphysics thesis* says that at least in some important cases our modes of self-depiction incorporate assumptions that can be called normative or metaphysical in a distinctively philosophical sense – they involve assumptions about agency, free will, luck, fate, responsibility, desert, and the like.

The second point is a sequelae of the first. If the socially endorsed storylines about my (or your) self generally, and my (or your) moral self in particular, incorporate a metaphysic of morals, then moral education requires examination, critique, and endorsement or rejection of the metaphysic assumed. Call this the *moral education as metaphysical critique requirement*. Moral education, be it the work of moral self-improvement, moral self-cultivation, or teaching the youth to be better than we elders are, sometimes requires systematic and deliberate attention to our metaphysic of morals (Blum, 2002; MacIntyre, 1982, 1987). One reason is that the acquisition of morality involves education of the sentiments, e.g., building or refining feelings of compassion. But to do this, agents need to be taught who – what creatures even – deserve compassion (or moral consideration) and why they deserve compassion. If one believes, as Cartesians do, that animals do not actually have minds, and thus do not have experiences of pleasure and pain but only simulate them, there will be no reason to extend moral consideration to (other) animals. When there are false assumptions about such matters as sentience, and what oneself or others deserve, the moral educators have an obligation to set things straight. But the moral educators can't do this if they themselves buy into the problematic metaphysic. In this case they will be part of the problem, not the solution (MacIntyre, 1982).

Let us distinguish two kinds of *morally harmful master-narratives*. The first kind conceals or allows us to overlook a mistake, which, if we correct it, will lead us to better be able to abide the moral principles we already avow. So the moral educator who engages in critique might convince others that their principle of equal consideration of interests requires that the interests of other races, as well as of nonhuman animals, ought, by their own standards, to be taken into account. Making this correction might well require narrative adjustments in the way the space of "persons" or of "rights-bearing creatures" is conceptualized and spoken about. But the required correction is possible. The second kind of morally harmful master-narrative is weirder and more puzzling than the first. Here the harm, if there can be said to be harm, comes from the fact that practical life may demand that we apply moral concepts – like responsibility, credit, and blame – when metaphysics can make it seem as if these concepts name nothing real, and thus that it is unfair (in a moral sense) to apply such concepts to ourselves or others. I'll return to this worrisome matter at the end.

For now we can say this much in a clear vein: A major function of master-narrative structures is to situate persons and lives in moral space by depicting types of lives that are deemed decent, good, noble, virtuous, and the like. The patterns of familiar narratives allow us to quickly classify whether individuals are good or not, trustworthy or not, and what sort of karmic outcomes are likely to accrue in their vicinity.

Take the "rags to riches" motif, which is closely related to "the hard work and effort pay" motif. In Horatio Alger's *Ragged Dick*, and in most of Alger's other stories, the poor immigrant boy who is morally quite good (but naïve) makes it into the bottom rung of middle-class respectability. The character, the shoeshine boy ("blackboot") in this case, doesn't actually get rich in the story. But we are left to think that he will continue going up the ladder of economic success (if he is good, and he is good). In this way, the "rags to riches" master-narrative allows inferences, which are based upon other common American, Ben Franklin-style, tropes, e.g., "virtue and hard work (for men and boys) can overcome any adversity." It is an interesting question whether a narrative such as "rags to riches" is taken to describe how things normally work out, as opposed to how they ideally should work (and do sometimes). This matters since we also have tropes that say such things as "virtue is its own reward," which could be read as a runner-up promise, a sort a consolation prize in case the material success does not occur. If this is right, then the work "rags to riches" does is less predicting (as it might seem) that effort and work pay, as recommending that one ought to think so, which of course might arouse sensible worries about the opiating properties of such narratives.

Another familiar master-narrative trope that is related to the "rags to riches" and " hard work and effort pay" ones, is the "what goes up must go down" trope which tends to come with a karmic justice subtext – on the way up, fat cats especially, have to do bad stuff, and they will pay. The "robber baron" narrative, for example, enacts the way justice works out, and in that way allows the listener to have her vengeful reactive attitudes, some sort of *Schadenfreude*, toward exploiters satisfied. A very different, more recent, and cynical motif is familiar from twentieth-century drama, such as Beckett's "Waiting for Godot." Postmodernism, with help from existentialism and (scientific) chaos and complexity theory, has given us the "each life is an idiosyncratic absurd performance" storyline, which both permits and endorses stories (as "interesting," but perhaps only among a certain social and intellectual class) in which the moral, temporal, interpersonal chaos that is any individual person is a different kind of chaos from every other chaotic person-thingamajig. In this way, each person is a possible object of curiosity for the other members of the community of chaotic conscious beings who know about the person's life or read his story or hear about it. Some absurd beings – Sisyphus, Hamlet perhaps, the compassionate characters in Camus's *La Peste*, for example – are admirable amidst their absurd, chaotic situation, which doesn't reduce the absurd and chaotic quality of everything. It just makes it more poignant, and in that way possibly more absurd still. Here there is no pattern (in a life or among lives). But that nonpattern is the pattern. In this case, the narrative structure is overtly philosophical because it is endorsed, as it were, directly by a school of philosophy.

To sum up this section so far: we speak and make sense of ourselves and each other in terms of narratives, which deploy as part of their interpretive arsenal an ontology (there are characters, and they possess traits), as well as metaphysical assumptions about free will, fate, desert, the conditions of self-worth, which are domesticated in familiar storylines, what I am calling mother-theories or master-narrative structures. These are richly normative and give guidance and direction on how things will go from here, and on what is the likely trajectory, both empirically and normatively, of this life or these lives. Master-narrative structures provide interpretive shortcuts, heuristics, ways of indicating where in interpretive space, where in the space of possible storylines, I want you to orient your thought about the person, persons, or type of situation being thought about or talked about.

The Target Narrative of Accomplishment and Desert

In light of these points, consider a common, perhaps the dominant, American mother-theory about accomplishment and desert. According to the mother-theory that is my focus here, hard work and conscientious effort are good and ought to be rewarded. If an individual works hard, she deserves (to keep for use) the fruits of her labor. Hard work and conscientious effort are both caused by, and signs of, virtue, wisdom, and free rational choice. Conversely, people who have not suffered the slings and arrows of outrageous fortune, and who choose to slack off or worse, are responsible for their situation.

This familiar narrative about individual responsibility and desert ramifies into public policy debates. For example, proposals to uncap payroll taxes for the Social Security fund are politically unpopular, and they are unpopular (John Kerry's team told me this in 2004) because of dominant views among most Americans about their "right" to keep what they earn. The main rationale for changing the cap that might appeal to American voters would not appeal to fairness or social solidarity, but to prudence. For example, taxation for welfare makes the poor (or sick or both) less prone to commit crimes, and thus to endanger public safety. Without some such purely prudential rationale, taxation for welfare is a form of mandatory charity (which is no charity at all), or even worse, it is state theft.

Regarding desert within a political economy such as ours, a standard view is this:

> My pre-tax income and the wealth I already hold are mine. I made what I made, and own what I own, and I deserve to keep it. Any discussion of the right of the state to tax me and/or take some of my stuff starts from my presumptive ownership of my stuff, my money, my property.

Liam Murphy and Thomas Nagel (2002) call this idea "the myth of ownership," the idea that pretax income and wealth is mine in some "morally meaningful sense." Why is it a myth? Among other reasons, what I make is made possible by a preexisting set of political and economic practices, institutions, and principles. I am indebted to these institutions and practices for what I gross. My gross income and the property I have are not the first link in a link of possessions; they are late links. Why's that? Essentially there would be no secure economy in place, no property, no rights, and so on were it not for the existence of a state constituted to allow such things. So both my gross income and my "preexisting wealth" are outcomes of a complex scheme of distribution and redistribution that antedates my arrival on the planet. It is an utter cosmic coincidence – matter of luck, good or bad – that I have the gifts (or liabilities) I have, and live in a world to which they are suited or not.

The logic of the dominant mother-theory about accomplishment and desert (and its ramifications) can be analyzed in terms of assumptions it makes/assumes/floats on that (we might assume) are so well-grounded that they don't need mentioning, but which are not so well-grounded. Consider these three assumptions that might be taken for granted, but that ought not to be taken for granted because they are philosophically quite implausible.

(1) *A view of agent causation* or libertarian free will that many philosophers think is the dominant folk view (but see Nahmias et al., 2006), and which Roderick Chisholm (1976) endorsed this way: "each of us when we act, is a prime mover unmoved. In doing what we do, we cause certain things to happen, and nothing – or no one – causes us to cause those events to happen."

(2) *A Lockean view of property ownership and desert*: I deserve the income from my labor, and I deserve to keep it. In general, combining #2 with #1 we get: How I do my life, whether I choose good or bad, well or badly, is self-originating (in some deep sense) and thus I deserve credit or blame for what I do, how I live, what I make of things.

(3) *Luck denial*: A denial of the claim that all my general capacities (including – assuming I possess such things – my intelligence, wit, ingenuity, conscientiousness, desire to work hard, social skills, and so on), and all my specific desires and beliefs, are 100% contingent on causal antecedents over which I had no control, and thus that, from the point of view *sub specie eternitatis*, "luck swallows everything" (Strawson, 1998). Nietzsche said *amor fati* – love fate. Why? Because despite the eternal and heroic – sweet, dear, and laughable – human attempt to actually do something completely self-originating, it has never happened, nor will it ever happen. It takes a "strong poet" to say this, let alone to embrace the idea. The facts are that it may be true.

Luck's Logic

Before proceeding to explain briefly why #1–3 are problematic philosophical assumptions, I'll say a bit more about why it is credible to think that they are commonplace assumptions. Candace Clark (1997) has explored the deep structure of the logic of American attitudes about work, effort, desert, merit, and luck, which show up in our mother-narratives. Here are two key empirical findings:

- *Bimodalism*: Americans tend to have a bimodal rather than a continuum view of desert and luck. "The language Americans use to talk about problems places them *either* in the realm of responsibility *or* inevitability, chance, fate and luck *or* in the realm of intentionality, responsibility and blame" (p. 100). Outcomes of actions are either

deserved (if they are results of choice) or not (if they are matters of impersonal luck or fate).
- *Self-caused bad luck*: We give ourselves moral permission to ignore feeling compassion/sympathy if the victims of bad luck brought their misfortune on themselves – e.g., drug addiction, alcoholism, criminal behavior. "No matter how bad we consider a plight to be, however, if the sufferer, the social actor, has caused it others may not sympathize. A plight is *unlucky* when it is *not* the result of a person's willfulness, malfeasance, negligence, risk taking, or in some way "bringing it on him or herself" (p. 84).

These two guiding principles are either equivalent to, or conceptually enabled by, such theses as 1–3 above – to the effect that actions divide between those that are caused by my free agency and those that are not – i.e., tsunamis, neurological seizures, and the like (as in #1). Furthermore, and for similar reasons, *bimodalism* says that some actions are self-initiated and are not caused by features of the world outside an agent's control (#3), and that it is the products of these agent-initiated or agent-controlled actions for which credit and blame, ownership (I did it; it is mine) make sense (as in #2). When persons choose to do what is wrong or inconsiderate or lazy, they deserve to suffer the consequences. If I wish (because I am kind or generous) to help others who cause themselves grief to get back on track, I do what is optional (not required), albeit good.

Narratives of Free Agency

Since the seventeenth century, metaphysicians in the West (one rarely sees the idea of agent causation in China or India; Flanagan, 2008) have tried to make sense of the idea of agent causation. No one has been able to do so. The scientific image of persons, independently of the red herring of determinism v. indeterminism (as if indeterminacy in elementary particle physics would secure the respectability of agent causation), assumes – because there is great evidence for the view – that *ex nihilo nihil fit*, that everything that happens has a cause, and that the causes have causes. *Huis clos*. Call this the thesis of the *ubiquity of causation* (Flanagan, 2002). The problem this creates for the idea of agent-causation is not quite that there is no such thing as a self-initiated or self-controlling action, but rather that the state of my self, my will, my desires and preferences, themselves are caused. Indeed, the causes of who I am, and what I want, choose, and so on, are (always, they must be) antecedent to whatever choice I make.

The ubiquity of causation, once acknowledged as reasonable, not only calls #1 into question from a metaphysical perspective, but it also is what warrants, if anything does, a challenge to #3 and its replacement by the idea that *sub specie aeternitatis*, "luck swallows everything," in Galen Strawson's memorable phrase (the basic idea is old and has been discussed and sometimes endorsed by Stoics, Epicureans, in a famous Kantian antinomy, by Nietzsche, and many others).

This problem, or these two connected problems of agency, causation, and contingency (#1 and #3) might make it seem as if we are playing with that old disturbing problem of freedom and causation – we are – which one might claim is a notorious philosophical black hole and not, for that reason, worth discussing. True. So let's move on to #2 – *the Lockean view of property ownership and desert*. But first note that if the problems of agency, causation, and contingency (#1 and #3) take us into the vicinity of a philosophical black hole, it is not as if our standard self-locating moral narratives, including our target narrative of accomplishment and desert, are remotely neutral on its solution. The standard ways we speak morally involve some amount of conviction that the idea of genuinely self-initiated action makes sense, and that there is no need to "love fate" because we are not in its grip, and thus that # 1 and #3 are true even if they cannot be justified.

Narratives of Mixing Labor

A key feature of the dominant narrative of accomplishment and desert assumes that John Locke got things right, more or less, when he gave this argument, which I paraphrase:

1. God gave humans dominion over all of nature.
2. Nature is owned initially equally by all humans.
3. The exception to equal ownership is oneself, one's body, "every Man has a *Property* in his own *Person*. Thus no Body has any Right to any but himself" (God's plan).
4. God must "Of Necessity" have had a plan for how humans would interact with what is naturally possessed by all, so that His gift of earth's bounty could be enhanced, and so that humans could show themselves worthy of God's gift. It would be irrational (which is impossible) for God to have given man "The Earth, and all that is therein ... for the Support and Comfort of their being" and not (also and at the same time) to have given humans a way to interact morally (without sinning) with this gift.

5. God's plan must be this: Each person in virtue of his natural right to his own body (#3) is given at the same time a right to the products of "The *Labour* of his Body, and the *Work* of his Hands."
6. Thus, whenever a person mixes his *Labour* with what is initially owned by all (#2), he thereby makes it his *property*. "For this *Labour* being the unquestionable Property of the Labourer, no Man but he can have a right to what is once joyned to, at least where there is enough, and as good left in common for others" (John Locke, *The Second Treatise* "On Property," 26 & 27).

The Lockean story about the move from a state where there is no private ownership to one in which there is a just initial acquisition, and then justice in transfer, is widely accepted in America, despite many problems, some obvious – e.g., acquisition by theft from the original people, the phenomenon of the rich getting richer, etc. Indeed, most of the Lockean story (which is not just a history, it is a justificatory philosophical history) minus much (some or all) of the God talk, is part of common sense, and thus is part of our standard narrative of "just deserts." But it is a problem that we contemporary folk take the Lockean theory of property and desert seriously – indeed, take it for granted – without accepting the God talk that actually warrants, justifies, and rationalizes each premise in the argument.

The reason this is a problem is because the argument is a philosophical disaster unless the God warrants – or reasons that invoke God's plan – are epistemically credible. But they are not. First, the argument has no foundation, if we don't bring in the biblical story of God giving all of Nature to humans; and second, if we don't accept the principles of philosophical theology to the effect that there is a God and that he is perfect – that is, that God is the familiar all knowing, all loving God of the Abrahamic tradition. Without these assumptions there is no reason to think that there must be "Of Necessity" a divine plan for how we are to make the most of God's gift.

The upshot is that the Lockean view of property and desert may be commonsensical. But this is not because it is based on good arguments.

There are arguments in favor of doling out property rights in a Lockean manner (#2), and there are interesting arguments for why we should act as if agent causation is true (#1), and why we ought to treat ourselves and others *as if* we (not the Big Bang) are ultimately responsible for our actions (#3). But these "good" arguments are all practical, pragmatic, and political, not metaphysical.

This matters because, in my experience, people who morally self-locate inside a standard American narrative of accomplishment and desert, and are questioned about the legitimacy of the assignments of credit, merit, ownership, and desert that such narratives permit, commonly appeal to such ideas as #1–3 above, in which case they are, or seem to be, claiming metaphysical legitimacy for their practices, when they can't in fact remotely secure the metaphysical grounds that would justify the narratives they speak.

There is an exception: people will sometimes advert to rationales for changing our practices that are straightforwardly moral, not metaphysical: e.g., it would be good, fairer, more compassionate if Ψ. What are moral reasons? If moral reasons are, as Aristotle and many other naturalists have thought, one kind of practical reason, then the task of justification is easier, since we do know how to argue about practical matters. One problem with this view of ethics is that it will seem deflationary relative to expectations that morality is something really deep, and involves more (something transcendental perhaps) than making practical decisions about how to be, and how to conduct our affairs. If, however, moral reasons are truly supposed to be grounded on deep metaphysical truths about agency, merit, and desert, then the problem of justification we have been having repeats. We are left, after all these years, still wondering about what morality is, how it is possible, and why we ought to be moral.

My conclusion for this section on moral mother-narratives is tentative. The self-locating and self-presenting narratives we speak have both descriptive and normative functions. Psychology is able to explain how narrative self-construction is possible in memory and in language, how it works, and how master-narratives serve to mark in a shorthand manner moral merit or demerit, and/or encode moral lessons, and/or instruct on preferred moral trajectories, and/or equip self and other with useful predictive information. Philosophy, along with other critical disciplines, can help us examine what questionable factual, moral, or metaphysical assumptions our narratives make, embed, and enact. It is possible that there just are reasons deep in the biology and psychology of animals like ourselves that require us to live as if certain assumptions such as #1–3 are true, when the weight of the philosophical evidence is that they are false. It is possible that the psychology of self-esteem and self-respect, as well as practices that take advantage of our plasticity and responsiveness to social approval and disapproval, rest most naturally on strong convictions about the nature of the self and agency that are unwarranted. If one is a philosopher who relishes consistency this is a bad outcome. If, however, like Walt Whitman, we can relish contradiction, and the "containment of multitudes," then this tension between the objective and subjective points of view (Nagel, 1979) can be welcomed as a creative one, a source of motivation to keep paying attention, to keeping our eyes on how our practices, intellectual and social, are hanging together, or not.

CONCLUSION

I've looked at the interaction between psychology and philosophy as it pertains to two questions of ethics, broadly construed: (1) the ontology of moral personality, and (2) the metaphysics and epistemology of narratives of moral (self and other) location. With regard to (1), I provided an analysis of character traits, specifically of virtues, that satisfies three desiderata: they are psychologically realizable; they are psychologically realized; and they are what virtue theories claim must exist if human morality is possible. With regard to (2), I argued that one important function of some masternarratives is to present self and other as morally decent, or better, as virtuous. Narratives do so by providing a sort of shorthand code that marks oneself or others as good, virtuous, deserving, and so on. Some such narratives, specifically a standard American narrative of accomplishment and desert, ride on taken-for-granted philosophical assumptions about agency, merit, and desert that are dubious. I left the reader with a paradox: it may be that the demands of practical life, for example, the conditions of self-esteem and self-respect, as well as smooth coordination of social life, require, or go best, with assumptions about, for example, agent causation and immunity to bad luck, that don't bear up well under close metaphysical scrutiny. But, of course, there was no guarantee that our methods of interacting efficiently, and properly understanding ourselves, would be smoothly co-compatible. Knowing that our ideals and our psychologies are sometimes, possibly often, in tension, is the oldest problem in ethics. Knowing when, where, how, and why this is so might provide us with some methods to reduce the distance between the two, assuming, that is, that knowledge is power.

REFERENCES

Annas, J. (1993). *The morality of happiness*. New York and Oxford: Oxford University Press.
Anscombe, G. E. M. (1958). Modern moral philosophy. *Philosophy*, 33, 1–19.
Aristotle. (1984). *The complete works of Aristotle* (Ed. by J. Barnes). Princeton, NJ: Princeton University Press.
Baier, A. (1991). *A progress of sentiments*. Cambridge, MA: Harvard University Press.
Blum, L. (1994). *Moral perception and particularity*. New York: Cambridge University Press.
   (2002). *I'm not a racist, but...: The moral quandary of race*. Ithaca, NY: Cornell University Press.

Brandt, R. B. (1970). Traits of character: A conceptual analysis. *American Philosophical Quarterly, 7,* 23–37.
Cervone, D., & Tripathi, R. (2009). The moral functioning of the person as a whole: On moral psychology and personality science. (This Volume.)
Chisholm, R. (1976). *Person and object.* LaSalle, IL. Open Court.
Clark, C. (1997). *Misery and company: Sympathy in everyday life.* Chicago,IL: University of Chicago Press.
Doris, J. M. (1998). Persons, situations, and virtue ethics. *Noûs, 32,* 504–530.
   (2002). *Lack of character: Personality and moral behavior.* New York: Cambridge University Press.
Doris, J. M., & Stich, S. P. (2008). Moral psychology: Empirical issues. http://plato.stanford.edu/entries/moral-psych-emp.
Fireman, G. D., McVay, T. E., & Flanagan, O. (Eds.) (2003). *Narrative and consciousness: Literature, psychology, and the brain.* New York: Oxford University Press.
Flanagan, O. (1991a). *The science of the mind,* 2nd edition. Cambridge, MA: MIT Press.
   (1991b). *Varieties of moral personality: Ethics and psychological realism.* Cambridge, MA: Harvard University Press.
   (1992). *Consciousness reconsidered.* Cambridge, MA: MIT Press.
   (1996). *Self expressions: Mind, morals, and the meaning of life.* New York: Oxford University Press.
   (2000). *Dreaming souls: Sleep, dreams, and the evolution of the conscious mind.* New York: Oxford University Press.
   (2002). *The problem of the soul: Two visions of mind and how to reconcile them.* New York: Basic Books.
   (2007). *The really hard problem: Meaning in the material world.* Cambridge, MA: MIT Press.
   (2008 in press). Moral contagion and logical persuasion in the *Mozi. Journal of Chinese Philosophy.*
Funder, D. C. (2001). *The personality puzzle,* 2nd edition. New York: W.W. Norton.
Gouda, F. (1995). *Poverty and political culture: The rhetoric of social welfare in the Netherlands and France, 1815–1854.* Amsterdam: Amsterdam University Press. (Forward by Arjo Klamer.)
Harman, G. (1999). Moral philosophy meets social psychology: Virtue ethics and the fundamental attribution error. *Proceedings of the Aristotelian Society, 99,* 315–331.
   (2000). The nonexistence of character traits. *Proceedings of the Aristotelian Society, 100,* 223–226.
Hemphill, J. F. (2003). Interpreting the magnitude of correlation coefficients. *American Psychologist, 58,* 78–80.
Homiak, M. (1997). Aristotle on the soul's conflicts: Toward an understanding of virtue ethics. In A. Reath, B. Herman, & C. Korsgaard (Eds.), *Reclaiming the history of ethics: Essays for John Rawls.* Cambridge: Cambridge University Press.
   (2008). Character traits. http://plato.stanford.edu/entries/moral-character/
Hursthouse, R. (1999). *On virtue ethics.* Oxford and New York: Oxford University Press.

Kamtekar, R. (2004). Situationism and virtue ethics on the content of our character. *Ethics, 114*, 458–491.
Kupperman, J. J. (2001). The indispensability of character. *Philosophy, 76*, 239–250.
MacIntyre, A. (1982). *After virtue*. South Bend, IN: University of Notre Dame.
  (1987). *Whose justice? Which rationality?* South Bend, IN: University of Notre Dame.
McAdams, D. F. (2009). The moral personality. (This Volume.)
Merritt, M. (2000). Virtue ethics and Situationist personality psychology. *Ethical Theory and Moral Practice, 3*, 365–383.
Miller, C. (2003). Social psychology and virtue ethics. *The Journal of Ethics, 7*, 365–392.
Mischel, W. (1968). *Personality and assessment*. New York: John J. Wiley and Sons.
  (1999). Personality coherence and dispositions in a cognitive-affective personality system (CAPS) approach. In D. Cervone and Y. Shoda (Eds.), *The coherence of personality: Social-cognitive bases of consistency, variability, and organization*. New York and London: Guilford Press.
Murphy, L., & Nagel, T. (2002). *The myth of ownership: Taxes and justice*. Oxford: Oxford University Press.
Nagel, T. (1979). *Moral luck*. Cambridge: Cambridge University Press.
Nahmias, E., Morris, S., Nadelhoffer, T., & Turner, J. (2006). Is incompatibalism intuitive? *Philosophy and Phenomenological Research, LXXIII*(1), 28–53.
Nisbett, R. E., & Ross, L. (1980). *Human inference: Strategies and shortcomings of social judgment*. Englewood Cliffs, NJ: Prentice-Hall.
Nussbaum, M. C. (1999). Virtue ethics: A misleading category? *Journal of Ethics, 3*, 163–201.
Sabini, J., & Silver, M. (2005). Lack of character? Situationism critiqued. *Ethics, 115*, 535–562.
Sherman, N. (1989). *The fabric of character: Aristotle's theory of virtue*. New York: Oxford University Press.
Sreenivasan, G. (2002). Errors about errors: Virtue theory and trait attribution. *Mind, 111*, 47–68.
  (2008). Character and consistency: Still more errors. *Mind, 117*: 257–266.
Strawson, G. (1998). Luck swallows everything. *Times Literary Supplement*, July 26. http://www.naturalism.org/strawson.htm.
Sunstein, C. (2005). Moral heuristics. *Behavioral and Brain Sciences, 28*, 531–542.
Swanton, C. (2003). *Virtue ethics: A pluralistic view*. Oxford: Oxford University Press.
Vranas, P. B. M. (2005). The indeterminacy paradox: Character evaluations and human psychology. *Noûs, 39*, 1–42.
Watson, G. (1990). On the primacy of character. In O. Flanagan and A. O. Rorty (Eds.), *Identity, character, and morality: Essays in moral psychology*. Cambridge, MA: MIT Press.
Wong, D. B. (2006). *Natural moralities: A defense of pluralistic relativism*. Cambridge, MA: Cambridge University Press.

4

Cultural Pluralism and Moral Identity

DAVID B. WONG

Under the naturalistic theory of morality I have defended (Wong, 2006), moralities are parts of cultures. In this essay I give a brief introduction to the motivations for the theory, explain the sense in which it is relativistic, and address some of the difficulties that confront any theory that explains moralities in terms of cultures. In particular, these difficulties concern the internal diversity and contestation within cultures, as well as the fuzziness and variability of boundaries between cultures. The first section introduces the naturalistic explanation of moralities in terms of cultures. The second section surveys the ways in which difficulties for the concept of culture have been raised in recent anthropological and philosophical literature. The third section proposes a concept of culture as conversation that takes these difficulties into account. The fourth section traces implications of the concept of culture as conversation for the question of how cultures differ from one another, and for the question of the moral identity of the individual as a participant in cultural conversations. The proposed concept of culture, it will be argued, helps to defuse the problem of fuzziness and variability of boundaries between cultures, helps us to reconcile the autonomy with the cultural embedding of moral identity, and calls into question traditional understandings of healthy and developed moral identity as possessing the properties of consistency, integration, and stability.

Writing this essay was supported by a fellowship from the National Humanities Center. My thanks go to Amélie Rorty and Darcia Narvaez and Dan Lapsley for comments on a previous draft of this essay.

MORAL AMBIVALENCE AS A MOTIVATION FOR A NATURALISTIC APPROACH TO UNDERSTANDING MORALITY

Orthodox Anglophone moral philosophy assumes with very little argument that there is a single true morality, and the situation seems not much different in moral developmental psychology. One of the main reasons, and perhaps the main reason, for this universalist orthodoxy is the assumption that the only real alternative to it is an unrestricted moral relativism. "Moral relativism" is overwhelmingly used in the popular media as a term of condemnation, frequently of scorn or derision, and Anglophone moral philosophers play the same game in a more genteel fashion by defining and then dismissing the view as an extreme variety of subjectivism, or thoroughgoing conventionalism, which holds that a person's (or group's) accepting that something is right makes it right for that person (or group). Rarely does someone try to formulate a version of relativism that is nuanced and plausibly motivated.

The plausible motivation for a nuanced relativism is a form of moral disagreement that evokes the complex reaction of "moral ambivalence" (for the full discussion, see Wong, 2006, chapter 1). We experience this when we see that reasonable and knowledgeable people could have made different judgments than we make in the face of conflicts between values. We come to understand and appreciate the other side's viewpoint to the extent that our sense of the unique rightness of our own judgments gets destabilized. I do not claim that all intelligent and reasonably informed people experience this phenomenon. I only claim that some do, and that this requires explanation. Some who feel no moral ambivalence will claim they are right not to feel it. My position is that they overlook the complexity and plurality of moral truth.

An important value conflict that can give rise to moral ambivalence is between two types of moralities – one of them having at its center the rights persons have purely as individuals, and the other having at its center the duties arising from the value of community (which covers relationships to particular others as well as to groups of varying sizes). In the former type of morality, individuals are seen as having interests that need to be defended against others. Rights have come to be conceived in the West as owed to individuals independently of their potential contributions to any community. That is why a central kind of right protects against interference from others. In communally oriented moralities, however, duties arising from the individual's relationships occupy a central place (e.g., under Confucian morality, family relationships form a central portion of the good of individuals), and the interdependence of the individual's good and the community's good is stressed. This contrast is consistent with the fact that the value of community is a part of Western moral traditions. These traditions are distinct in the centrality they accord to notions of autonomy and individual rights, not by the absence of these other values. Reasonable and intelligent people who are rooted in either tradition can sometimes come to doubt that there is a single correct way to prioritize rights and community. This doubt is consistent with rejecting the extreme views that the protection of individual rights can justify any harm to the community and that any communal good can override individual rights.

Consider another form of value conflict between duties we have to others standing in some special relationship to us, such as family, and duties we have to others in virtue simply of their being persons. Most typically people devote a far greater proportion of their resources and energy to special relationships, but some reasonable and intelligent people experience profound ambivalence when they recognize that those resources could save the lives of many strangers or spare them from degradation and misery. They may come to doubt that there is a single correct way to balance such values in the face of circumstances that produce cruel conflicts between caring well for the few who are one's own and caring in the most basic ways for the many who are simply human beings.

Notice that moral ambivalence involves both agreement and disagreement. One cannot become ambivalent unless one can come to appreciate the reasons and values of the other side of the conflict. This complex phenomenon calls for a nuanced response that is not provided by a radical and simplistic form of moral relativism that assumes people live in different moral universes that have nothing in common with one another. Simplistic forms of moral relativism cannot recognize the commonalities that feed into moral ambivalence. But the simplistic forms of moral universalism cannot adequately recognize the fundamental differences that feed into moral ambivalence. One such form of universalism is premised on the assumption that moral goodness, badness, rights, and wrongs are part of the fabric of the universe in the way that Plato held the form of the Good to exist, or in the way that there are discoverable laws governing the mass and energy of particles. It is unclear how such a view could account for moral ambivalence. How do supposedly reliable perceivers of such moral properties arrive at clean and definitive resolutions of grave conflicts between values? If they do, how have those who disagree with these resolutions come to err in *their* perceptions? If these supposedly reliable perceivers arrive at uniquely correct resolutions to grave conflicts between special duties to family and duties to strangers in urgent need, for instance, the question is how they come to have this accurate perception when others err. On the other hand, if there is no single correct resolution, it is unclear why we should buy into the idea of *sui generis* properties.

Rather than taking moral properties as primitive givens, the naturalistic approach advocated here seeks to understand them in relation to our understanding of human beings and the role that morality plays in human life. Naturalism as a methodology for theory construction has many meanings (see Wong, 2006, chapter 2), but the ones accepted here include a rejection of any distinctive, *a priori* method for yielding substantive truths shielded from empirical testing, or from revision in response to new experience. What we claim to know cannot be regarded as permanently fixed or based solely on the deliverances of intuited self-evidence. Another meaning of naturalism as a methodology is that there is no sharp boundary between epistemology and the science of psychology. Our claims as to what we know should be integrated with a well-supported picture of what we could plausibly be expected to know, given that human beings are embodied organisms with certain perceptual and cognitive abilities. These two meanings of naturalism undermine the moral properties as *sui generis*, and that we somehow simply intuit as self-evident. What is the alternative?

MORALITY CONCEIVED AS A CULTURAL INVENTION WITH CERTAIN FUNCTIONS

The alternative is a naturalism that treats morality not as something just there, independently of human choice, but as arising from the decisions and actions of human beings striving to structure their lives together in response to the constraints imposed by their environments and by their own natural motivational propensities. Such propensities plausibly include instincts for self-preservation, capacities of care for kin, a willingness to engage in mutually beneficial practices of cooperation with others if they show a similar willingness, a willingness to punish those who violate the agreements and norms that make cooperative practices possible (even when the expenditure of resources to punish cannot be justified on the grounds of self-interest), and some degree of altruistic concern for non-related others. Human beings developed all these capacities because they were fitness enhancing in an inclusive sense, a conclusion that much of the latest work in evolutionary theory supports.[1] These diverse psychological

---

[1] On the selection mechanism for altruism toward kin, see Hamilton, 1964. On the mechanism for selecting a willingness to cooperate with others if they show willingness to

capacities also make human nature profoundly ambivalent and vulnerable to self-defeating motivational conflict. Cultural norms provide ways of managing such conflict. The long period of the Pleistocene during which human beings evolved social instincts overlapped considerably with the period in which people began living in social groups with cultural institutions. If culture was a partner in this biological evolution, then it is plausible to hypothesize that some of our biological traits, as anthropologists Robert Boyd and Peter Richerson (1985, 2003) have suggested, might prepare us to regulate ourselves through culture: for example, the disposition to follow the majority or to emulate the most successful members of one's group. Such traits could have conferred an evolutionary advantage on members of a group by enabling them to adopt satisfactory solutions to problems that were worked out by other members.

Moral norms culturally evolved to promote beneficial social cooperation, not simply through requiring behavior that is cooperative and considerate of the interests of others, and not just through constraining potentially destructive self-interest, but also through encouraging, strengthening, and directing the sorts of other-regarding emotions and desires that make people promising partners in social cooperation. Furthermore, effective moral norms provide outlets for the expression of self-interest that can be consistent with the expression of other-regarding motivations. Arrangements that generate some self-interested return to other-interested behavior can make such behavior less costly and increase the degree to which individuals feel they can afford to indulge their concerns for others. An effective morality often accomplishes a productive balance or reconciliation between self- and other-concern. Playing a crucial role in such reconciliation are norms of reciprocity that require a return of good for good received. The need to reconcile self- and other-concern appears first in family relationships. Across widely different cultures, there are duties to respect and to honor parents and others whose roles involve raising and nurturing the young. Performance of such duties constitutes a kind of return of good for good, though what is returned, of course, is not always the same kind of good as what was originally given. The benefit of being reciprocated for an act of helping need not be greater than the cost of helping in order to reinforce that initial act of helping. It need merely generate enough return so that

cooperate, see Trivers, 1971. For a theory of "group selection" as the mechanism behind concern for non-kin, see Sober and Wilson, 1998. For another theory emphasizing the role of sexual selection in altruism, see Miller, 2000. For evidence supporting the existence of non-self-interested willingness to punish and reward others who cooperate, see Gintis, 2000.

helpers feel they can afford to indulge whatever other-directed concerns they have.

Facilitating social cooperation is not the only function of morality. Some moral norms embody character ideals and conceptions of the good life, specifying what is worthwhile for the individual to become and to pursue. This function of morality comprehends what has been called the "ethical," as opposed to what might be called the "narrowly moral." The two functions of morality as broadly conceived are related. Even if a moral conception of right relations between people does not dictate a specific ideal of character or a specific set of ends, it will certainly limit the range of permissible ideals and sets of ends. From the other side, a moral conception of individual excellence of character will place limits on conceptions of justice and the right. Nevertheless, the intra-personal function emerges from a distinct set of human desires to identify and to aspire to a way of living that is worthwhile and that can be recommended to, or even required of, others as deserving of their aspiration or at least admiration. Most human beings have deeply social needs not only in the sense that personal relationships are among the most fulfilling things they can have, but also in the sense that they are strongly driven to share and to communicate with each other what we find most satisfying. This social nature also is reflected in our powerful influence on each other: our criteria for what is worthwhile gravitate toward the criteria others employ. What this suggests is that the human language of evaluation is such that we care about and strive to produce converging judgments, at least within certain rough, and sometimes fairly wide, boundaries.

Morality's functions, plus the nature of the beings it governs, constrain the content of its norms. Different moralities, in other words, must share certain general features (e.g., a norm of reciprocity) if they are to perform their functions of coordinating beings who have certain kinds of motivations. The shared general features account for the commonalities experienced in moral ambivalence. The diverging paths experienced in moral ambivalence arise from the fact that the constraints only *place boundaries on* the range of moralities that adequately fulfill the coordinating functions, but they do not select only one specific morality (e.g., they do not specify one correct way to prioritize between special duties toward family versus duties to treat strangers as human beings, or one correct way to prioritize community versus rights). Contrary to those who maintain that the denial of universalism leads to a radically permissive relativism, which holds that any morality is as good as any other, the approach defended here leads to a nuanced relativism that recognizes significant constraints on what could count as an adequate morality. Moralities can both be human inventions and subject to objective constraints. There are objective constraints on moralities as human inventions in a way analogous to there being objective constraints on bridges. There would be no bridges unless human beings conceived of structures that have the function of transporting people and vehicles across bodies of water or deep depressions in the terrain (this is analogous to the functions of moralities that were collectively established through cultural creation). However, given the materials available for building bridges (analogous to the "material" of widespread human motivational propensities), there are constraints on how an adequate bridge can be designed and built.

Having briefly set out some basic themes on the functions of moral norms as a subset of cultural norms (for a fuller discussion, see Wong, 2006, chapter 2), and how such a view of morality can help explain moral ambivalence while avoiding a radically permissive relativism, let me turn to the relation between moral norms and moral identity. I have defined a practical identity as those traits of character that fix a person's practical orientation toward the world (Wong, 2006, chapter 4). Such traits need not remain constant throughout an individual's lifetime. However, they typically make a systematic law-like difference to people's lives, to the habit-forming and action-guiding social categories in which they are placed, to the way that they act, react, and interact. Moral practical identity comprises the individual's orientation toward moral ends and requirements. Complex emotions such as compassion, shame, and guilt have cognitive dimensions: compassion can involve recognition of another's suffering as a reason to help; shame can involve seeing oneself as having failed to be the person one thinks he or she is or hopes to be; guilt can be felt over an action one has performed and sees as wrong. By providing norms and values that shape conceptions of *whose* suffering and under *what circumstances* counts as a reason to help, conceptions of ideals people aspire to realize, and conceptions of what counts as wrongful action, moralities shape some of the most powerful human emotions (Wong, 2006, chapter 7).

DIFFICULTIES FOR THE CONCEPT OF CULTURE

Given the conception of moral norms as cultural norms, and given the role that moral norms play in shaping moral identity, it is important to address certain difficulties that have been raised for the very concept of culture. These difficulties and how they are addressed have implications for how we should conceive of moral identities. Let me first note that the concept of culture can be specified at varying levels of abstraction. I begin with a very abstract concept of culture utilized by Boyd and Richerson (2003) in their argument that human biology and culture coevolved. Their concept is relatively uncontroversial because it is so abstract. Starting the discussion of culture with their concept allows us to identify controversial ways in which the concept is made more specific or "thickened." Boyd and Richerson characterize "culture" to be "information capable of affecting individuals' behavior that they acquire from other members of their species through teaching, imitation, and other forms of social transmission" (Boyd & Richerson, 2003, p. 5). By "information," they mean "any kind of mental state, conscious or not, that is acquired or modified by social learning, and affects behavior" (Boyd & Richerson, 2003, p. 5). Dan Sperber and Nicholas Claudière (2007) have argued that this concept of information is too broad in one sense – culture is better taken to include only *widely distributed* information – and that it is too narrow in another sense – the relevant kind of information can be implemented not only in the form of mental representations but also in the form of behaviors, artifacts, and institutions. Since I find these criticisms persuasive, let me adopt Boyd and Richerson's characterization of culture with Sperber and Claudière's suggested changes in the concept of socially transmitted information.

Call the resulting concept the "thin concept." The thin concept comprehends culture in the somewhat more familiar sense of shared and widely transmitted beliefs, values, and norms that enable groups to organize their experience and actions in meaningful patterns. The thin concept serves as a relatively uncontroversial starting point and enables discussion of what else needs to be said about culture. This concept does not tell us how to distinguish one particular culture from others. A thick concept of culture that embodies more assumptions about culture should enable us to distinguish one particular culture from other cultures. One particular thick concept of culture has been the most influential, but also the most controversial. It embodies four assumptions: that culture is shared by all members of the group possessing it (call this "consensuality"); that it is unchanging ("fixedness"); that its parts are logically consistent ("consistency"); and that many of these parts are linked by logical implication, as in the general entailing the more particular ("integration"). In looking to identify one particular culture as differentiated from others, this particular thick concept directs us to look for a fixed, consistent, and integrated set of beliefs, values, norms, and other carriers of socially transmitted information that is held by all members of a group. Call the particular thick concept of culture that takes on board all these assumptions the "essentialist concept."

The essentialist concept has come under forceful attack from two sources. Postmodernists criticize the concept of culture for ignoring power relations of dominance, contest, and struggle. Contest in a group with a culture often manifests itself in lack of universal consensus on beliefs, values, and norms, and hence lack of internal consistency and integration. Ongoing contest produces change in the items of culture. One major source of the postmodernist critique, Michel Foucault (1984, 1990), emphasizes the way that selves are socially constructed through cultural forms, discourses, and their related social and material conditions. Such constructed selves might be continually under construction and reconstruction as persons shift from this or that relationship of power. There might be acquiescence in one context (e.g., striving to produce significant academic work) and resistance in another (rejecting the role of an emotional woman who is not to be taken seriously) (see Holland, 1997 for a discussion of the effects of the postmodernist critique).

A particularly fascinating example of the ways in which selves might be socially constructed and yet mount resistance to prevailing power relationships is given by the anthropologist Saba Mahmood (2005) in her contemporary portrait of women who participated in religious study groups held in Egyptian mosques. The location of these study groups is significant in and of itself, since mosques previously constituted a male-dominated sphere. On the other hand, the language of religious piety used in the study groups emerged from religious discourse that has historically supported the subordination of women to male authority. For example, women's virtues, such as shyness, modesty, and humility, and ways to realize these virtues in the self are a major preoccupation within these study groups. Mahmood describes Amal, a woman who is naturally outspoken, but who created within herself through outward forms of "shy" behavior a way of being outspoken compatible with traditional Islamic reserve, restraint, and modesty. Mahmood rejects the interpretation of these women as displaying an obsequious deference to social norms. Rather it involves a kind of agency – creating an inner reality through outward forms of conduct.

Some of the most striking parts of Mahmood's study concern women's resistance to their husbands' insistence that they stop or curtail their activities in the mosque. Abir was not particularly observant as a young woman, but over time she becomes increasingly observant about her prayers, eventually donning a full body and face veil. Her husband Jamal wants a more worldly and stylish wife who would help him on his path to a higher class. He uses religious arguments to try to change Abir: in disobeying him, she was disobeying Islamic standards for proper wifely conduct, he said. Abir responds by cajoling and humoring him, and sometimes by taking the higher moral ground – playing tape-recorded sermons focusing on death and torture in hell and the final reckoning with God at full volume in the house. This prompts Jamal to dial back the pressure on Abir to abandon her religious studies. None of her tactics would have worked if Jamal had not regarded himself as a Muslim. But even within the context of their shared religious background, Abir's refusal of Jamal's wishes was daring. Study at the mosque is traditionally taken to be an optional, not a required, action according to most Muslim authorities, while obedience to one's husband is not optional. But Abir learned within the mosque a modern interpretation that makes it every individual Muslim's duty to take lessons, since in contemporary times there have been too many people, like her husband, who have lost knowledge of what it is to live as a Muslim. Abir exemplifies both acceptance of, and surprising resistance to, traditional Islamic norms concerning the status of women – and at times both in the very same act – as when she resists her husband's wishes in the name of restoring the place of Islam to contemporary Egyptian life. In place of consensuality, fixedness, consistency, and integration, there are disagreeing voices, change, tension, and contradiction.

The other source of the critique of the essentialist concept of culture is cosmopolitan political philosophy. Cosmopolitans are generally liberal theorists who stand in dialectical argument with communitarians and with liberal multiculturalists. Communitarians emphasize the importance of culture to the formation of the individual's sense of self and identity (MacIntyre, 1982, 1988; Sandel, 1998; Taylor, 1994; Walzer, 1987) and criticize forms of liberal political philosophy for assuming a concept of the individual as separable from culture. Liberal multiculturalists agree on the importance of culture to the individual, but attempt to incorporate that insight into a framework that affirms individual autonomy and liberty to choose a way of life (Kymlicka, 1995; Taylor, 1994[2]). Cosmopolitans do not necessarily deny the importance of culture to formation of individual self and identity, but dispute the idea of distinct cultures that need to have special consideration and in some cases protection. They argue that cultures typically absorb influences from all over the world, pointing to hybridity and fluidity of boundaries as constituting the standard situation for culture (Appiah, 2005; Waldron, 1991–1992). They question how one decides which culture, at which time, is to be protected. Cosmopolitans also emphasize the internal diversity of culture, and the likelihood that some members of

---

[2] Taylor's position is a hybrid of liberal multiculturalism and communitarianism.

a culture contest the beliefs, values, and norms of other members, even if these other members claim to represent the "traditional" or "authentic" culture of the group.[3] Cosmopolitans question the basis of any claim that any particular understanding is the "authentic" understanding, and warn of the oppressive uses to which such claims are often put (to undermine claims made by members whose interests are subordinated, for example).

Some targets of this criticism have acknowledged this problem. Will Kymlicka (1995, chapter 1), for example, grants that Quebec's societal culture has become liberalized such that people feel freer to question and reject traditional ways of life.[4] In the past, Quebecois generally shared a rural, Catholic, conservative, and patriarchal conception of the good. Today atheists live next door to Catholics, gays alongside heterosexuals, and urban yuppies alongside rural farmers. When pressed on what then distinguishes a liberalized, diverse societal culture such as Quebec's from Anglophone Canada, Kymlicka (2001, p. 25) tends to fall back on the idea of a shared language that is used in a variety of public and private institutions, such as schools, media, and government. But given that he disassociates a shared language from shared religious beliefs, family customs, and personal lifestyles, it is not clear that language and its use in social institutions is a sufficient basis for differentiating one societal culture from another, and for justifying the importance Kymlicka himself attaches to societal cultures (how could preservation of a particular language, divorced from distinctive values, norms, and practices, be necessary for enabling meaningful choices of the individual?).

Let me now address why the attack on the essentialist concept of culture poses challenges for the approach to morality as a form of culture. First, recognizing the phenomena of internal diversity and change prompts the question of how to draw the boundaries of a distinct culture and of a group that possesses a distinct culture. Second, recognizing internal diversity and change in moral values and norms prompts the question of what happens when culture is transmitted – horizontally between contemporaneous members of a group and vertically over time. The essentialist concept of culture conveys a picture of a fixed set of moral norms and values that is transmitted,

---

[3] For a perceptive argument emphasizing the contested nature of cultural identity, see Amélie Oksenberg Rorty, 1992.

[4] Kymlicka (1995, p. 76) defines a "societal culture" as "a culture which provides its members with meaningful ways of life across the full range of human activities including social, educational, religious, recreational, and economic life, encompassing both public and private spheres." It tends, he claims, to be territorially concentrated and based on a single language.

but if this picture seems entirely unrealistic, what is transmitted? Third, how are we to locate the individual and her moral identity in the midst of diversity and flux in moral culture? If her moral identity somehow embodies or is a product of her moral culture, does it embody the contradictions, and at the very least tensions and oppositions, that diversity and flux bring? Or do the moral identities of different individuals embody different parts of a culture, such that interpersonal disagreement and conflict embody the internal diversity and flux of the group's culture?

RECONSTRUCTING A THICKER NOTION OF CULTURE THAT IS NOT NAÏVE

This section proposes an alternative to the essentialist concept. It is necessary first to get clearer about what kind and degree of precision to expect in attempting to formulate a more adequate thick concept. Attempts to formulate a concept presuppose a normative model of what concepts are supposed to be like. Until relatively recently, philosophers and psychologists have assumed that a concept of a something X is constituted by a set of necessary and sufficient conditions for that something's being an X. The status of this model has badly eroded, partly because of philosophy's continuing failures to specify anything remotely resembling necessary and sufficient conditions for the classes and kinds that interest us (e.g., personhood, being the same person over time, knowledge, humor, pornography, and even what it is to be a set of necessary and sufficient conditions!).[5] As Wittgenstein observed, the concept of a game cannot be spelled out in terms of such a set, but rather covers a diverse array of activities and practices related through "a complicated network of similarities, overlapping and criss-crossing" (Wittgenstein, 1953, p. 66). Thus the critics of the essentialist concept of culture may be right to deny that cultures individuate by virtue of necessary and sufficient conditions for something's being culture X as opposed to any other culture. But this does not mean that talk of particular cultures fails to make sense simply because we cannot specify sharp and precise boundaries for them.

One of the proposed replacements for the classical model of concepts is prototype theory, according to which concepts include features possessed by their instances, the features embodying the average or most

---

[5] For the difficulties of spelling out what it is to be a set of necessary and sufficient conditions, see Brennan, 2003. Regarding pornography, Supreme Court Justice Potter Stewart (1964) famously remarked of hardcore pornography that it is hard to define but that "I know it when I see it." For knowledge, see Steup, 2006. For humor, see Smuts, 2006. For personhood and personal identity over time, see Olson, 2007.

typical instances. Take the concept of dogs. There are dogs that lack tails, have fewer than four legs, and do not bark. There may be no viable concept of dogs that can be spelled out in terms of necessary and sufficient conditions for an animal's being a dog. According to prototype theory (see Clark, 1998), the concept of dog includes features making up a kind of composite "everydog" (has four legs, a tail, emits barking sounds) and an object that is a candidate for falling under that concept is more likely to qualify the more it resembles the composite typical dog. This is compatible with vague or fuzzy boundaries of doghood, which seems right. Exemplar theory, alternatively, holds that having concepts involves the ability to call up particular instances that serve as the standards of comparison for candidate instances. Having the concept of a dog involves the ability to call up from memory particular dogs one has encountered, and one compares dog candidates to the closest exemplars to see if one gets a close-enough match. Concepts need not be limited to one structure (Prinz, 2003). Indeed some concepts might acquire prototypes that are constructed on the basis of exemplars. A child might acquire her prototype of "everydog" on the basis of encounters with particular dogs she knew while growing up. She might call up the dog prototype to categorize most dogs she encounters, but if she were to encounter a difficult case, she might recall an atypical dog exemplar that most closely resembles the present animal.

The concept of culture seems more amenable to treatment according to the exemplar or prototype models. When pressed for explanations of what a culture is, we tend to refer to examples. My parents came from Southern China, and while growing up in the American Midwest, I gradually became aware of some relatively systematic differences in the expectations and norms my parents applied to my sisters and me on the one hand, and on the other hand, the ones applied to my friends whose families had been in the U.S. for generations. My friends of recent Norwegian and Swedish heritage, on the other hand, fell into a third cultural category. Some people became aware of their own cultures only when they traveled to other places and encountered differences in expectations and norms for behavior and speech acts, such as greetings, polite excuses, and even the acceptable distance one can stand in relation to an acquaintance.

But what are these things of which we give examples and have no sharp and precise boundaries? They are beliefs, values, norms, and other kinds of socially transmitted information encoded in mental representations, behaviors, artifacts, and institutions. But how, in a given context, do we differentiate some of this information as belonging to one culture as opposed to other cultures? And how do we differentiate in ways that allow for people who hold the same culture to disagree on important beliefs, values, and norms, and that allow for change in a culture over time?

I propose that we think of cultures in analogy to conversations – usually with plural voices, and quite often with many voices. People in conversation with each other can differ over beliefs, values, and norms. Conversations are processes that change over the course of time: some voices can fall silent; voices that have been dominant can become recessive, and vice versa; new voices can enter and change the character of conversations. We can distinguish one conversation from another, even if the two conversations are about many of the same subjects and even if the voices articulate many of the same themes. Conversations can be different despite such similarities because we can hear some of the distinct voices differing *with each other*, i.e., addressing and responding to each other, arguing with each other. Even going through the motions of listening but not taking seriously the positions and reasons of others is a kind of conversational relation. Such a conversational relation may emerge from a power relation in which the one not seriously listening has the upper hand. A great advantage of the conversational model of culture is that it accommodates the cultural phenomena of internal diversity, power relations, and the accompanying changes.

People become participants in a conversation through originating, transmitting, and receiving beliefs, values, norms, behaviors, artifacts, and by playing roles in or resisting institutions (or both). Note here that the analogy to conversation should not be taken too narrowly. We may converse with others through our actions and our silences as well as our words. Analogously, acting according to values, norms, and roles does not require one to *articulate* those values, norms, and roles. Furthermore, the practical possibilities for action that one does not even consider performing (i.e., what is unthinkable for us), as well as the possibilities one enacts without having to decide upon them (i.e., the habitual or the spontaneous), can be ways of expressing values, norms, and roles.

Note furthermore something that Carol Worthman has put well: "As culture shapes persons, those persons shape culture" (1999, p. 53). Transmission of culture almost always involves significant variation. What is "received" at one end is not necessarily the same as what is transmitted on the other end. We teachers know this when we seek to discover what our students have learned from our lectures. Further, given that transmission of cultural items is accomplished very frequently through a kind of observational osmosis – seeing and hearing what other people appear to be doing, believing, and valuing – transmission is always subject to an individual's perception and interpretation of what is going on. Individual differences in temperament, which can have a basis in genetic inheritance and early experience, are also a primary source of variation in what is received by individuals. The fact that cultural entities are performed and enacted as ongoing conversations makes them subject to change through accidental and intentional permutations. Conceiving cultures as conversations leaves open the degree of logical consistency or integration to be found in a particular culture. Perhaps more important, it suggests that there are other kinds of coherence and integration. An *argument* can of course contain contradictory themes defended by different parties, but it can have a high degree of coherence in the sense that the parties *respond to each other*, and the flow of the conversation has the logic of an evolving response and counterresponse. To conceive of coherence and integration solely in terms of logical consistency between themes and relations of subsumption of the more specific under the general is to miss important ways in which cultural entities can fit together in a point-counterpoint relation even as they contradict or conflict with each other.

For example, within a culture there can be an argument between those who highly value liberty as freedom from interference with others and those who highly value relationship and membership in community. The argument need not be, and most often is not, between people who uphold one value and fail to recognize the other. The question is about value priorities. Noninterference and community often function as counterpoints to each other in the sense that one value is asserted against the other value because one addresses the liabilities of asserting the other value strongly. Collective responsiveness to individual need can be a great benefit of community, but when that responsiveness turns into oppressive suffocation or an alienating exclusion of those who fall from good standing, noninterference can be asserted against the value of community. On the other side, community gets asserted against barriers to intervention into the affairs of the individual when this benefit blocks responsiveness to the individual's need. The moral tradition that can be associated with the United States, I believe, exhibits this kind of dynamic between interference and community and, compared to many Asian traditions, gives far greater priority to noninterference, but the presence of the value of community is nevertheless real even if relatively recessive. There is an argument within American culture between those who highly value noninterference and those who highly value community, but there is a logic provided by our complex psychologies as to why these sides are in argument. The American argument between noninterference and community takes on a distinctive form given other cultural elements. The noninterference side, for example, is often supported by a robust optimism and hopefulness about the power of the individual to control his fate, combined with a pessimism about the competence of governmental structures, especially large ones, to accomplish good intentions.[6]

There is a similar point-counterpoint dynamic within traditional Chinese culture between Confucianism and Daoism. Confucianism is a deeply social ethic in which one finds one's highest fulfillment as a human being in certain kinds of human relationship, especially the family. Where it diverges most sharply from Confucianism, Daoism directs our attention most consistently to the human place in the natural world, and fosters a sense of identification with that which is conventionally construed as the nonhuman world. It deconstructs and lampoons the importance of humans judging other humans, and prizes acceptance of everyone and everything. Much of Confucianism's appeal lies in its fostering of responsiveness to the needs of those with whom one is in relationship. Yet that same strength can turn into a liability – into suffocating judgment and humiliating ostracism when the judgment is harsh and negative. In its stress on one's relationship to a larger whole that transcends the human and does not judge, Daoism functions as a response to this liability. At the same time, it cannot supply an answer to the human need for structure and support from the human community, which is precisely Confucianism's strength. There is a fit between these two ethics, even as they conflict.

A third example of a point-counterpoint conversation is one involving the value of harmony versus the value of individual rights. Harmony involves members of a community sharing and striving for common ends in such a way that their personal interests are conciliated with those common ends. Beginning in the nineteenth century, Chinese interest in the concept of individual rights grew, but often from the perspective that saw rights as a way of fostering individual energies and creativity so that they could be put to use for common ends (see Angle, 2002). This distinctive way of construing rights, which is different from seeing them as entitlements of the individual apart from their value for promoting shared ends of the community, is a fairly typical example of the way that influential concepts migrate across cultures. They not only contribute to transformation of the cultures to which they migrate, but often take on a form that is congenial to those cultures.[7] This does not mean that more individualistic concepts of rights

---

[6] For a summary of empirical work in cultural psychology that is related to the themes that cultural differences in morality are often differences in priorities given to shared values, see Miller, 2007.

[7] Hong, Wan, No, and Chiu (2007, 328) point out that "bicultural" individuals who are fluent in more than one cultural tradition have access to more of the ideas that help people

are absent in China. But they take their place in a conversation in which more communally oriented conceptions of rights have a strong voice, and in which skepticism about the ultimate compatibility of individual rights and social harmony is still a significant voice.

Whether there are any cultures that fit the essentialist rather than conversational model is ultimately an empirical question, but there are reasons to expect cultures to exhibit conversational characteristics. The diverse array of things that human beings value corresponds to the complexity of human need and desire. As just illustrated, the various human values are such that the emphasis on value often results in a contrapuntal emphasis on a value that exists in tension with the first. Furthermore, insofar as social cooperation is structured along the lines of differentiated social, economic, and political roles, there is likely to occur a diverse array of different character traits, dispositions to value certain styles of action, and norms for judging action. Different roles require of us different capabilities, different ways of perceiving and picking out what is most valuable in the world. Finally, intersocietal relations of trade, migration, and territorial aggression are likely to produce cultural hybridity.

Given the conversational concept of culture, what did cosmopolitans and postmodernists get right and what did they get wrong about culture? Cosmopolitans are right to point to the internal diversity of anything we could call a rich and vibrant culture. A culture is rich and vibrant only if it responds to the complexity of human need and the plurality of values that are often in tension with one another. But cosmopolitan attacks on communitarians and liberal multiculturalists tend to suggest that culture is a mélange all the way down, with no logic as to why the ingredients we find in a particular cultural conversation are there in a particular mix. Taken to an extreme, the cosmopolitan argument would have us reject the idea of distinct cultures and regard culture as one large pot of stew with every possible cultural ingredient indiscriminately mixed together. Jeremy Waldron, for example, celebrates "mongrelization" and "mélange" not only as sources of creativity, but as characteristic of the human condition (1991–1992, pp. 751–752). He describes the cosmopolitan in the following terms (1991–1992, p. 754):

> Though he may live in San Francisco and be of Irish ancestry, he does not take his identity to be compromised when he learns Spanish, eats

frame and interpret their situations. Enhanced creativity may result when the ideas of two traditions are juxtaposed and become a novel conceptual combination.

Chinese, wears clothes made in Korea, listens to arias by Verdi sung by a Maori princess on Japanese equipment, follows Ukrainian politics and practices Buddhist meditation techniques.

To present the cosmopolitan as typical of the general human condition, however, is mistaken. The cosmopolitan is rooted in a particular kind of culture that can be found in particular social strata of cities such as San Francisco, Paris, London, Mumbai, and Hong Kong. This kind of culture values consumption of the best the world has to offer, valorizes an international outlook and multilingual fluency (presupposing the material conditions to gain such fluency), and employs "techniques" abstracted from philosophies and religions, the overall teachings of which are inconsistent with certain features (e.g., consumption of fine things) of cosmopolitan lifestyles. The conversational concept of culture makes room for hybridity, of course, but the point is that cosmopolitan culture is a particular kind of hybridity that is made possible by special material conditions, and it is not simply an arbitrary mix.

Let me explain how I differ with the postmodernists, by explaining why I use the word "conversation" in contrast with another word that has become popular among postmodernists who have been influenced by Foucault: "discourse." Some anthropologists who reject the assumptions of consensuality, fixedness, consistency, and integration, and who equate the concept of culture with these assumptions, seek a word other than "culture" (Lutz & Abu-Lughod, 1990). However, Foucault's way of talking about discourse as an impersonal and omnipresent form of power that constructs the individual tends to obscure the causal role of personal agency in sustaining, interpreting, revising, and rejecting one's current culture. Foucault's influence can lead to another assumption that I want to avoid making: that beliefs, values, norms, and institutions are *solely* the instruments and structures of domination, or of acquiescing to or resisting domination. It is undeniable that power relationships are an ever-present dimension of what I want to call conversations, but the postmodernist assumption that there is nothing more to beliefs, values, norms, and institutions than domination, acquiescence, and resistance is as reductive and blind to diversity and individuality in its own way as is the essentialist thick concept of culture. It occludes the diversity of human motivations – such as the desire to seek truth despite its inevitable filtering and distortion through the lens of personal interest and power, and care for others that spans individual and group interest.

IMPLICATIONS FOR QUESTIONS OF A GROUP'S MORALITY

Having presented the conversational concept of culture, let me return to the challenges posed by criticisms of the essentialist concept. Recall that recognizing the phenomena of internal diversity and change in moral values and norms prompts the question of how to draw the boundaries of a distinct culture in general and, in particular, of a distinct moral culture and of the group that possesses that culture. As long as it is assumed that the boundaries have to be drawn around a fixed set of cultural items that constitute the necessary and sufficient conditions for being a particular culture, it seemed that the boundaries were impossible to draw. Once we see that a multiplicity of voices, even conflicting ones, does not undermine the idea of a common culture, drawing the boundaries becomes much less problematic. What we look for are patterns of assertion and counterassertion, question and response, that constitute conversation, and that by their very nature incorporate internal diversity and change.

Another implication of the conversational concept of culture is that the boundaries between cultures, and therefore of the groups that have cultures, are set contextually by interests and may be drawn differently accordingly to different contexts. Consider that a conversation, especially a complex one with many voices on different subjects, is subject to having its boundaries set according to the interests of the one who is judging whether there is one, or more than one, conversation. Consider several people seated at a dinner table and the way they might converse. At times everyone might discuss a common subject, but the people at one end might carry on the discussion in one direction, while the people at the other end carry it on in another direction. Then toward the end of the dinner, suppose that everyone joins together again in discussing another common subject. Is it all one conversation, or two or three or four? It depends on the interests of the one making the judgment. If my focus is on the way that being at the same table influenced everyone's discussion, I might say it was one conversation. If I want to focus on the way my end of the table discussed the beginning subject, I might say there were three or four.

Analogously, how cultures get individuated seems very much a contextual matter. Many of us had the experience as children of being told by our parents that our families had ways of doing things that weren't necessarily the same as the ways of others around us. It would not be an odd use of "culture" to say that our families had a culture different from others, but saying this is consistent with saying, in another context, that we might have shared a culture with those other families, say, of the South. In another context, it makes sense to differentiate the cultures of different parts of the South, or to talk about the hybrid culture of transplanted Northerners. Given the particular context, we have particular purposes that are served by broadening or narrowing our focus of attention and drawing the boundaries of culture in a certain way. If I am interested in the ways of my family, as opposed to the ways of other families in my neighborhood, I might draw the boundaries narrowly in this context. If I, as a transplanted Northerner, am interested in thinking about the values of the South in contrast to those of the North, I might draw the boundaries of culture relatively widely in this context. By modeling culture after conversation, I need not be drawn into the mistake of assuming that all Southerners share the same values or that all Northerners do, or even that they participate in the same set of conversations. I may instead be expressing my belief that certain voices speaking about values hold a more dominant place in one kind of cultural conversation in the South and that this differs in the North. Note, however, that saying we set the boundaries contextually does *not* imply that we make up the boundaries from thin air. The patterns of assertion and counterassertion, question and answer, are there, whether or not they serve as the basis for boundaries given our present focal points of interest.

Recall that recognizing internal diversity and change prompts the question of what is to be passed on if morality as a set of moral norms and values is passed on – horizontally between contemporaneous members of a group and vertically over time. In accordance with what was drawn above from the model of conversation, one must disambiguate the notion of cultural transmission: what is sent is not necessarily what is received. One's parents, teachers, and peers might teach or model certain norms, values, and behaviors with the intention of sending them. These cultural items might embody one or several voices in the cultural conversations into which one is being initiated. But one might not receive exactly the items they intended, and this might be due to "noise" in transmission, faulty or inattentive receiving equipment, or disagreement with the voice doing the sending, perhaps based on reflection on other voices whose transmissions one has received. So transmission typically does not occur from a single group as a whole to the individual. There are multiple lines of transmission with a group, and the individual receives transmissions from more than one group. A lot depends on what lines of communication go to the individual in question, and a lot depends on the individual in question and what she does with what is sent and "gets through." Consider another analogy to languages, dialects, and idiolects. National and regional differences between dialects of English can be substantial. A dialect corresponds to a "voice" of a subgroup that participates in a moral conversation. Within a dialect, there can be differences between the languages of individuals – idiolects – and these correspond to the individual's distinct voice, which can be different in certain details from any other individual's voice.

The last point leads to consideration of the challenge of how to locate the individual and her moral identity in the midst of diversity and flux in moral culture. I posed the question earlier of whether the individual's identity somehow embodies her moral culture, such that it embodies the contradictions and, at the very least, tensions and oppositions that diversity and flux bring; or whether moral identities of different individuals embody different parts of a culture, such that interpersonal disagreement and conflict embodies the internal diversity and flux of the group's culture. It now becomes clear that both and more possibilities can be realized. One can speak a moral "dialect" that aligns with a substantial subgroup within a cultural conversation; one can have an idiolect that is related to and overlaps with dialects, but that is also distinctive and may possibly influence others in the future. One can speak more than one moral dialect, or one may speak an idiolect that is a result of a fusion or synthesis of these dialects.

IMPLICATIONS FOR THE INDIVIDUAL'S MORAL IDENTITY

To conclude this essay, I want to briefly indicate how the conversational concept of culture can be brought to bear on some long-standing controversies over the relation between culture and moral identity. Consider the opposition between certain versions of communitarianism and certain versions of liberalism on the ideal of autonomy for moral agents. Autonomy can mean many things, but in the context of this opposition, the most salient meaning is roughly the ability to step back from the moral commitments one has received from others and to evaluate them so as to make one's commitments "one's own," and not merely those received from others. Communitarians such as Charles Taylor and Michael Sandel have criticized this ideal (at least as it appears in the most dominant versions of liberal thought) as presupposing an untenable separation between a person's most deeply held ideals, aims, and attachments on the one hand, and who that person is, on the other hand. Taylor (1985, pp. 29–30) has argued that a radical choice that presupposes no ideals, aims, and attachments at all is simply an arbitrary plumping for one thing or another. Sandel (1998, pp. 58–59) has argued, specifically against the John Rawls of *A Theory of Justice* (1971), that the liberal ideal of autonomy presupposes a metaphysically suspect notion of the person as stripped of all identifying aims and attachments, incapable of making meaningful choices. Only "situated" selves – whose identities incorporate aims and attachments that are not chosen – are capable of making meaningful choices.

By now, many liberals and communitarians have each accepted some part of the other side's positions. Liberals acknowledge the social and cultural sources of moral identities (Rawls, 2001, is a prominent example). One evaluates some of one's ends at any given time by taking as given certain other ends, but the latter are not permanently exempt from critical scrutiny at other times (Caney, 1992, p. 277). In response to the liberal charge that their philosophy endorses a conservative ethic that overlooks the claims of marginalized and oppressed groups, communitarians respond that they make room for heterogeneous subcommunities and for protests against dominant views of justice (Sandel, 1988, p. 22). The conversational concept of culture helps to explain how moral agents can be both situated and autonomous in the relevant senses. Communitarians are surely right to say that the self entirely liberated from its cultural inheritance is strangely empty and incapable of making a substantive decision. But moral identities that derive substance from the agents' cultures are liable to be internally diverse, just as the cultures are. The individual is not simply a passive recipient, but an enactor of culture who can interpret and transmit it to others. The degree to which individuals are self-consciously interpreting the norms of their cultures varies enormously, but one need not self-consciously interpret cultural norms in order to see and react to them (as these norms are embodied in the words, behaviors, practices of others) in ways that reflect one's particular life experience and character.

There is another interesting implication of the conversational concept of culture. One might think that the autonomy of the individual with an internally diverse cultural heritage lies in reflecting on that heritage, and then deciding on ways to order that heritage into a coherent practical orientation for herself. Where some parts of that heritage contradict each other, she might drop some parts or prioritize them so as to eliminate the contradiction. This conception of a desirable moral identity corresponds in some ways to the essentialist concept of culture (though it does not necessarily require a static or fixed identity), and is a possible option. One might reasonably hold that logical consistency among one's norms and values is of greater practical importance for the individual than for any culture of which she might be a member. Inconsistency, of course, can result in practical self-defeat through frustrating some of one's ends, and it can result in disturbing feelings of internal fragmentation and confusion. But I want to argue that there are and should be alternatives to a strict pursuit of a logically consistent moral identity, including the one of leaving in place unresolved contradictions. This is in effect to leave in place a divided moral identity, where one becomes, as it were, a moral bilingual. Here is one example of such an identity. A student born and raised in China remarked in one of my seminars that, when he sometimes expresses a normative opinion in Chinese, he says and believes one thing, and when he addresses the same matter in English, he says and believes a contradictory thing.

Is it necessarily a bad thing that the moral identity of my student embodies this contradiction? On the Chinese side of his identity, the more dominant voices of the conversation speak for the importance of social harmony, for the value of being in relationship, and having shared commitments and common ends. On the American side, the more dominant voices speak for the importance of providing options for the individual to choose from, and for protecting the individual's most important interests when they conflict with those of the group. Out of such conflicts there eventually can arise novel and hybrid voices, such as those that eventually arose in China when the notion of rights was introduced in the nineteenth century, voices (to which I referred earlier) that conceived the value of rights to lie in their enabling individuals to make greater contributions to the community. Such syntheses offer new ways of reconciling or balancing values that address present circumstances. Such syntheses may not arrive in time to help those with divided identities, but their identities play a role in personifying the dilemmas that motivate these syntheses over time. Does such a divided identity necessarily cause a harmful feeling of fragmentation or confusion? I submit that recognition of internal division can be a clear-headed acknowledgment of moral complexity. Furthermore, it can be accepted and preferred to shearing off one or the other half of the division. This is not confusion, and if it is division, it is not automatically harmful.

Here is another example involving a substantive conflict of values. Morality is often identified with the requirement to have impersonal concern. One must recognize that others have an equal moral status. Such an impersonal moral requirement seems to conflict with the claims generated by our moral ties to family members and particular others, such as friends. That is, what we are required to do for these particular others and with them can conflict with the requirements of having impersonal concern. We channel vastly disproportionate amounts of our time, energy, and resources toward those close to us rather than toward the vastly greater number of human beings in the world who have far greater needs than our own. Much philosophical literature strives to reconcile this conflict between our personal moral ties and impersonal concern, but whether it has succeeded is doubtful (see Wong, 2006, pp. 24–27). When, in such cases, value conflicts are not clearly resolved, is it better for the agent simply to drop one of the contradicting elements or to impose some sort of priority in order to eliminate the conflict? But it is arguably truer to our moral situation to acknowledge the conflict and its tragic nature. The conflicts between what we owe to those close to us on the one hand, and what we owe to strangers who are in great need and at great risk on the other hand, might leave us in a moral blind alley where no course of action is free from wrongdoing.[8]

It might be argued that such divided identities lead their possessors to self-defeating action, but this is not necessarily the case. One might, for example, decide to carry out one's duties to one's own, and acknowledge the wrongness (and the rightness) of doing so. This might not just serve the point of acknowledging what has occurred, but agents who embody the unresolved conflicts of their cultures can keep those conflicts alive as continuing problems that collective efforts might, over time, help to resolve, or at least mitigate the severity of their conflict. In the case of our duties to aid strangers in severe need, a major reason why individuals are caught in tragic conflicts of duties is that their governments have failed to direct the resources at their disposal toward these problems. Individual moral agents who carry within their identities this conflict have motivation to press these collective entities to redress their neglect.

The kind of acceptance advocated here of divided identities corresponds to what is usually said of the typical Chinese attitudes toward conflicts between Confucianism, Daoism, and Buddhism. A Chinese may think of herself as practicing all three kinds of teaching and not worry about the contradictions between and among them. Each kind of teaching may seem appropriate to some situation or other, and there is no particular concern about making the teachings consistent on a theoretical level. Of course, there are ways of doing so: one can truncate the scope of the requirements of one teaching in order to make it compatible with the requirements of another teaching. But to do so is to presume one knows in what manner they should be truncated – what indefinitely large class of cases to which the requirement present applies should now be ruled out as falling under the requirement. The problem is that this requires more knowledge than we typically have, or might ever have. So a perfectly rational solution is to leave

---

[8] For the concept of a moral blind alley, see Nagel, 1971. There can be disagreements within a culture, furthermore, over what must be done for a stranger and who counts as a stranger.

the requirements of both teachings in place, even though they contract with their present scope of application.

SUMMARY

In order to explain both the commonalities and differences in morality, a naturalistic approach rejects the understanding of morality as concerning *sui generis* properties. It holds that morality is to be explained as a cultural invention with the functions of promoting social cooperation and specifying worthwhile ends for the individual to pursue. These functions, and the fact that certain types of motivational propensities are powerful and widespread among human beings, limit the range of different types of moralities that could be adequate or true. An unrestricted moral relativism that treats any morality as good as any other is not the implication of approaching morality as a cultural invention, any more than is an unqualified universalism. Because all adequate moralities have certain functions and govern beings with certain motivational propensities, they will share values and norms, but they need not set the same priorities among these values and norms.

However, this approach to morality as part of culture requires a viable concept of culture. Actual cultures do not fit the essentialist paradigm of fixed and internally consistent entities that are shared by all their members. Based on prototype and exemplar theories of concepts, I have proposed a conversational model that allows cultures to be constituted by patterns of beliefs, norms, values, and practices that need not be logically consistent with each other or accepted by all their members. Just as conversations can be constituted by arguments between disagreeing voices, so too cultures can include patterns of point and counterpoint. Just as conversations can change because they are ongoing processes over time in which the participants help shape the course of the conversation, so also cultures can change because the participants can change patterns of point and counterpoint in the course of enacting and transmitting them. A moral culture, then, can provide its members with a kind of moral "language," within which there is plenty of room for different "dialects" or even "idiolects." Some individuals will have moral identities that include the oppositions and diversities of their cultures, these identities being the analogues to a person speaking two or more moral dialects or speaking an idiolect that is a novel fusion of dialects. I have argued that such identities are not necessarily unfortunate, but can reflect inevitable moral conflicts between the many and diverse things that are and should be prized by human beings. Besides being truer to a complex moral reality, internal diversity and division can motivate creative efforts to reconcile conflicting values.

REFERENCES

Angle, S. C. (2002). *Human rights and Chinese thought: A cross-cultural inquiry.* Cambridge: Cambridge University Press.

Appiah, K. A. (2005). *The ethics of identity.* Princeton, NJ: Princeton University Press.

Boyd, R., & Richerson, P. J. (1985). *Culture and the evolutionary process.* Chicago, IL: University of Chicago Press, 1985.

Boyd, R., & Richerson, P. J. (2003). *Not by genes alone: How culture transformed human evolution.* Chicago: University of Chicago Press.

Brennan, A. (2003). Necessary and sufficient conditions. In Edward N. Zalta (Ed.), *The Stanford Encyclopedia of Philosophy* (Fall 2003 Edition). Retrieved November 23, 2007, from http://plato.stanford.edu/archives/fall2003/entries/necessary-sufficient/.

Caney, S. (1992). Liberalism and communitarianism: A misconceived debate. *Political Studies, 40,* 273–289.

Clark, A. (1998). Connectionism, moral cognition, and collaborative problem solving. In L. May, M. Friedman, & A. Clark (Eds.), *Mind and morals: Essays on ethics and cognitive science* (pp. 109–113). Cambridge, MA: Bradford Books.

Foucault, M. (1984). *The Foucault reader* (Ed. Paul Rabinow). New York: Pantheon.

   (1990). *The history of sexuality: The use of pleasure.* New York: Vintage.

Gintis, H. (2000). *Game theory evolving.* Princeton, NJ: Princeton University Press.

Hamilton, W. D. (1964). The genetical evolution of social behavior. *Journal of Theoretical Biology, 7,* 1–52.

Holland, D. (1997). Selves as cultured: As told by an anthropologist who lacks a soul. In R. D. Ashmore & L. Jussim (Eds.), *Self and identity: Fundamental issues* (pp. 160–190). New York: Oxford University Press.

Hong, Y., Wan, C., No, S., & Chiu, C. (2007). Multicultural identities. In S. Kitayama and D. Cohen (Eds.), *Handbook of cultural psychology* (pp. 323–345). New York: Guilford Press.

Kymlicka, W. (1995). *Multicultural citizenship: A liberal theory of minority rights.* Oxford: Oxford University Press.

   (2001). *Politics in the vernacular: Nationalism, multiculturalism, and citizenship.* Oxford: Oxford University Press.

Lutz, C. A., & Abu-Lughod, L. (1990). Introduction. In C. A. Lutz & L. Abu-Lughod (Eds.), *Language and the politics of emotion* (pp. 1–23). Cambridge: Cambridge University Press.

MacIntyre, A. (1982). *After virtue.* Notre Dame, IN: University of Notre Dame Press.

   (1988). *Whose justice? Which rationality.* Notre Dame, IN: University of Notre Dame Press.

Mahmood, S. (2005). *Politics of piety: Islamic revival and the feminist subject*. Princeton, NJ: Princeton University Press.
Miller, G. (2000). *The mating mind*. New York: Anchor Books.
Miller, J. G. (2007). Cultural psychology of moral development. In S. Kitayama & D. Cohen (Eds.), *Handbook of cultural psychology* (pp. 477–499). New York: Guilford Press.
Nagel, T. (1972). War and Massacre. *Philosophy and Public Affairs, 1*, 123–144.
Olson, E. T. (2007). Personal identity. In E. N. Zalta (Ed.), *The Stanford Encyclopedia of Philosophy*. Retrieved November 23, 2007, from http://plato.stanford.edu/archives/spr2007/entries/identity-personal/.
Prinz, J. (2003). *Furnishing the mind*. Cambridge, MA: Bradford Books.
Rawls, J. (1971). *A theory of justice*. Cambridge, MA: Belknap Press of Harvard University Press.
 (2001). *The law of peoples*. Cambridge, MA: Harvard University Press.
Rorty, A. O. (1994). The hidden politics of cultural identification. *Political Theory, 22*, 152–166.
Sandel, M. (1988). Democrats and community: A public philosophy for our times. *New Republic, 198*(8), 20–23.
 (1998). *Liberalism and the limits of justice*. Cambridge: Cambridge University Press.
Smuts, A. (2006). Humor. *Internet Encyclopedia of Philosophy*. Retrieved November 23, 2007, from http://www.iep.utm.edu/h/humor.htm.
Sober, E., & Wilson, D. S. (1998). *Unto others: The evolution and psychology of unselfish behavior*. Cambridge, MA: Harvard University Press.
Sperber, D., & C. N. (2007). Defining and explaining culture. Forthcoming in *Biology and Philosophy*. Retrieved November 23, 2007, from http://www.dan.sperber.com/on%20Richerson%20&%20Boyd.htm#_ftn1.
Steup, M. (2006). The analysis of knowledge. In E. N. Zalta (Ed.), *The Stanford Encyclopedia of Philosophy* (Spring 2006 Edition). Retrieved November 23, 2007, from http://plato.stanford.edu/archives/spr2006/entries/knowledge-analysis/.
Stewart, P. (1964). Concurring opinion to *Jacobellis vs Ohio*. 378 U.S. 184; 84 S. Ct. 1676; 12 L. Ed. 2d 793; 1964 U.S. LEXIS 822; 28 Ohio Op. 2d 101.
Taylor, C. (1985). *Human agency and language: Philosophical papers I*. Cambridge: Cambridge University Press.
Trivers, R. (1971). The evolution of eciprocal altruism. *Quarterly Review of Biology, 46*, 35–56.
Waldron, J. (1991–1992). Minority cultures and the cosmopolitan alternative. *University of Michigan Review of Law Reform, 25*, 751–793.
Walzer, M. (1987). *Interpretation and social criticism*. Cambridge: MA: Harvard University Press.
Wittgenstein, L. (1953). *Philosophical investigations* (Ed. G. E. M. Anscombe & R. Rhees, trans. G.E.M. Anscombe). Oxford: Blackwell.
Wong, D. B. (2006). *Natural moralities: A defense of pluralistic relativism*. New York: Oxford.
Worthman, C. A. (1999). Emotions: You can feel the difference. In A. L. Hinton (Ed.), *Biocultural approaches to the emotions* (pp. 41–74). Cambridge: Cambridge University Press.

5

Neuroscience and Morality: Moral Judgments, Sentiments, and Values

JORGE MOLL, RICARDO DE OLIVEIRA-SOUZA, AND ROLAND ZAHN

What makes people recoil upon witnessing human tragedies, engage in costly helping behaviors, and violently protest against acts of injustice (Goodenough & Prehn, 2004; Zeki & Goodenough, 2004)? Strikingly, this inclination can go far beyond the interpersonal sphere, as humans often risk material resources, and even physical integrity, to uphold culturally shaped values in the form of societal causes, ideologies, or beliefs, for example. Moral and social values form the basis of personal and sociocultural identities, which is a core theme throughout this volume. It is thus not surprising that debates on the moral nature of humanity have occupied theologians, philosophers, and laymen for millennia. Here we will review how neuroscience is providing new insights on how the human brain enables complex moral cognition and behavior.

Defining morality is not a straightforward task, and any definition will suffer from shortcomings, especially when evaluated by scholars from different fields. The words "moral" (derived from the Latin *moralis*) and "ethical" (from the Greek *êthikos*) originally referred to the consensus of manners and customs (MacIntyre, 1985). This rather broad meaning of "moral," however, does not address a central question for the cognitive neuroscience of morality: What distinguishes moral cognition from other forms of socially relevant abilities? Most instances of social behavior are morally relevant because they have effects on others and are thus liable to be evaluated as "right" or "wrong" depending on socioculturally shaped norms. Therefore, one may argue that on the outside, any kind of social behavior is also moral in nature and that the neural and cognitive mechanisms guiding moral and social behavior should therefore be identical. From the perspective of the motivations behind social behavior, however, one can distinguish between social behavior motivated by complex moral motivations from behavior motivated by more basic reward and avoidance of punishment. Complex moral motivations guiding a subset of human social behavior have not been demonstrated in nonhuman primates to the same level of sophistication. Therefore, we propose that while moral cognition draws upon general cognitive and motivational abilities, its most distinctive feature is the ability to motivate social behaviors based on their impact on others and, in particular, behaviors which are costly for the agent or altruistic. As we will argue here, these "moral" motivations depend on the representation of complex moral sentiments and values.

Moral motivations have been claimed by virtue ethicists since antiquity (Casebeer, 2003). Aristotle stressed that living according to moral virtues leads to human flourishing (*eudaimonia*; Aristotle, 1926). Moral motivations lie at the core of moral values (i.e., "virtues"). Moral values, described by concepts such as "courage," contain the moral "ought" that can be tied to actions conforming to or opposing them. According to the notion of values proposed by British philosophers during the eighteenth century, "moral sentiments" determine whether we perceive something as a virtue or a vice, guiding our approval or disapproval accordingly (Hume, 1777b), a point of view which has gained recent support from moral psychology (Haidt, 2001). Hume emphasized the inextricable relation of actions as the objects of moral sentiments. He stated that the moral evaluation of such actions depends on whether these are caused internally or by external force (Hume, 1777a). When we are agents of social actions conforming to our values, we may feel pride, whereas when another person is perceived as the agent, we may feel gratitude. On the negative side, when we act counter to our values, we may feel guilt, and when another person acts in the same way toward us, we feel indignation or anger instead (Moll, Oliveira-Souza, Zahn, & Grafman, 2007). The anticipation of these moral sentiments evoked by particular social actions guides our behavior (Tangney, Stuewig, & Mashek, 2007).

Understanding the nature of human moral and, more specifically, altruistic inclinations is a challenging task, as these behaviors can be quite costly and do not confer clear material or survival advantages from the agent's perspective. While theoretical biology and experimental economics have strongly substantiated the validity of these "selfless" human behaviors (Fehr & Fischbacher, 2003; Fehr & Rockenbach, 2004; Maynard-Smith & Szathmary, 1997; Milinski, Semmann, & Krambeck, 2002; Trivers, 1971), the motivational sources of these inclinations have only recently started to be addressed by neuroscience. From a neurobiological perspective, it is reasonable to assume that without the engagement of motivational forces, the purely rational moral prescriptions ("oughts"), as defined by a sociocultural group or person, would not be translated into actual behaviors. On a more cautionary note, we would like to stress that this neurobiological perspective cannot replace the philosophical and societal debate about moral justification of behavior. While empirical neuroscience cannot determine what is morally justified, it can help to elucidate the neural bases of morally relevant behaviors and preferences and attempt to explain interactions between culture, individual learning, and neurobiological factors that create the large range of individual differences of morally motivated behavior.

Since the early reports of social behavioral changes following brain injury, functional neuroimaging and brain lesion analysis have espoused sophisticated cognitive models, fueling rapid advances in our neuroscientific understanding of human moral abilities (Moll, Zahn et al., 2005; Raine & Yang, 2006). Neuroscientific studies have addressed the neural underpinnings of moral judgments, emotions, and behavior (de Oliveira-Souza & Moll, 2000; Eslinger, Flaherty-Craig, & Benton, 2004; Greene, Nystrom, Engell, Darley, & Cohen, 2004; Heekeren, Wartenburger, Schmidt, Schwintowski, & Villringer, 2003; Koenigs et al., 2007; Moll, de Oliveira-Souza, Eslinger et al., 2002; Moll, Eslinger, & Oliveira-Souza, 2001), social concepts (Zahn et al., 2007), and attitudes (Cunningham, Raye, & Johnson, 2004; Luo et al., 2006; Ochsner et al., 2004). A picture that emerges from these recent studies is that there is large agreement about the brain regions supporting moral cognition, pointing to a reliable involvement of cortical (anterior and medial prefrontal and anterior temporal cortex) and subcortical limbic (ventral striatum, hypothalamus, amygdala, basal forebrain) structures in morality (Moll, Zahn et al., 2005) (*Figure 5.1*). Key issues now stand out as sources of debate in moral cognition, however: (1) How do cognition and emotion interact to produce moral judgments and decisions? (2) Do sophisticated, typically human moral capacities rely on evolutionarily ancient motivational systems? (3) Which are the neural bases of moral knowledge, moral sentiments, and moral values? Here, we will shortly review the evidence on the neural bases of moral cognition, with a special focus on new evidence on the neural representation of moral motivations and their relationships with moral knowledge.

LESION AND NEUROIMAGING EVIDENCE FOR THE NEURAL BASES OF MORAL ABILITIES

Since the initial demonstrations that moral behavior could be impaired by brain damage (Macmillan, 2000; Welt, 1888), systematic studies of acquired personality changes due to brain lesions, mostly to the frontal lobes, have

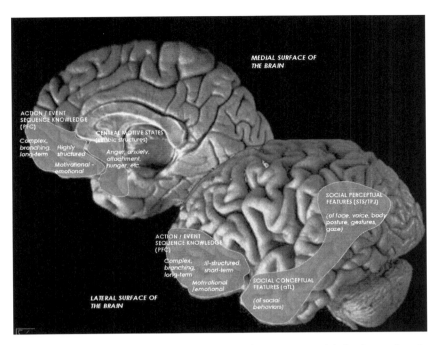

FIGURE 5.1. Brain regions implicated in moral cognition and behavior and main putative neurocognitive components of the event-feature-emotion complex (EFEC) model (Moll et al., 2005). Within the prefrontal cortex (PFC), cortical structures include the anterior prefrontal cortex (mainly the frontopolar cortex), the medial and lateral orbitofrontal cortex, right dorsolateral prefrontal cortex and additional frontal ventromedial sectors, involved in representing sequential knowledge of actions and complex motivations (Eslinger et al., 2004; Moll et al., 2003; Stone, Cosmides, Tooby, Kroll, & Knight, 2002). Within the temporal lobe, the anterior temporal cortex (aTL) and the superior temporal sulcus/temporo-parietal junction (STS/TPJ) are involved respectively in social conceptual knowledge and knowledge of complex perceptual features (Moll et al., 2005; Zahn et al., 2007). Subcortical limbic structures (Moll et al., 2003; Moll, de Oliveira-Souza, Eslinger et al., 2002; Weissenberger et al., 2001) include the amygdala, hypothalamus, ventral striatum-pallidum, basal forebrain (especially the septum and extended amygdala) and rostral brainstem tegmentum. These regions are responsible for basic central motive states, such as the experience of affiliation and anxiety. Integration across these components is believed to give rise to complex moral phenomena, such as moral values and sentiments (Moll et al., 2005; Zahn et al., 2008).

strongly lent support to the notion that selective neurological impairments could lead to disturbances of moral behavior, while leaving general intelligence and judgment intact (Eslinger & Damasio, 1985; Saver & Damasio, 1991; Tranel, Bechara, & Denburg, 2002). Damage to the ventromedial

(VMPFC) and frontopolar sectors (FPC) of the prefrontal cortex (PFC) at an early age may lead to even more severe impairments in moral behavior, suggesting that moral development can be arrested by early PFC damage (Anderson, Bechara, Damasio, Tranel, & Damasio, 1999; Eslinger, Grattan, Damasio, & Damasio, 1992).

Given the similarities with developmental psychopathy (Cleckley, 1976; Hare, 2003) – which includes an inability to sustain a steady job and to build constructive interpersonal relationships, irresponsible lifestyle, lack of regret, and frequent violation of the rights of others – such impairments in social conduct were dubbed "acquired sociopathy" (Saver & Damasio, 1991), although the complex constellation of behavioral abnormalities observed in developmental psychopathy can rarely, if at all, be produced by acquired brain lesions. Accordingly, a review of lesion studies of patients with acquired sociopathy and preserved general cognitive abilities showed that current models of normal social conduct have privileged the PFC at the expense of other brain regions, whose damage can also lead to impairments of moral conduct, including unprovoked physical assaults, paraphilias, inappropriate sexual advances, and teasing behavior (Moll, de Oliveira-Souza, & Eslinger, 2003). Recent evidence from volumetric (magnetic resonance imaging) MRI in developmental psychopathy points to the conjunction of subtle abnormalities in key areas within the moral cognition network (frontopolar, medial orbitofrontal/subgenual prefrontal and posterior superior temporal sulcus regions) as the correlate of callousness in psychopathic individuals (de Oliveira-Souza et al., 2008).

Evidence from studies on patients with neurodegenerative disorders, such as frontotemporal dementia, shows that the anterior temporal lobe also plays important roles in moral cognition and behavior (Bozeat, Gregory, Ralph, & Hodges, 2000; Liu et al., 2004; Mendez, Chow, Ringman, Twitchell, & Hinkin, 2000). Furthermore, abnormalities compatible with dysfunction of abstract conceptual knowledge in this brain region have been described in psychopathy (Kiehl et al., 2004). Another sector of the temporal cortex, the posterior superior temporal sulcus region (STS), is critical for decoding social cues, including inferences on agency and intentionality and social perception (Allison, Puce, & McCarthy, 2000; Decety & Jackson, 2004). Furthermore, lesions to limbic and paralimbic structures can impair basic motivational mechanisms – including feeding, sex, social attachment, and aggression – which can result in severe impairments of moral conduct (Burns & Swerdlow, 2003; Daigneault, Braun, & Montes, 1999; Weissenberger et al., 2001).

A number of functional magnetic resonance imaging (fMRI) studies conducted in recent years have provided important contributions to our understanding of the neural bases of moral cognition in the normally functioning brain. In an early experiment of the neural basis of moral judgment, normal volunteers were scanned during the auditory presentation of short statements and instructed to silently make categorical judgments (right versus wrong) on each (de Oliveira-Souza & Moll, 2000; Moll et al., 2001). Some statements had an explicit moral content ("The judge condemned an innocent man"), while others were factual statements without moral content ("Telephones never ring"). When the moral condition was contrasted to the factual one, the medial frontal gyrus and medial and lateral sectors of the FPC, cortical regions that are especially evolved in humans as compared to other primates (Allman, Hakeem, & Watson, 2002), were strongly activated. Robust effects were also observed in the right anterior temporal lobe (aTL) and the left angular gyrus/STS region. These effects could not be explained on the basis of overall degree of emotionality of stimuli.

Subsequently, Greene and colleagues (Greene, Sommerville, Nystrom, Darley, & Cohen, 2001) addressed another important aspect of the moral domain with fMRI. Normal subjects were exposed to moral and nonmoral dilemmas that were structurally more complex than the simple statements described above, which were associated with a higher load of reasoning and conflict. Moral dilemmas were divided into moral-personal (the agent personally inflicts an injury to another person to avoid a worse disaster – such as pushing an innocent to death on the tracks of a runaway trolley, in order to stop it and save five other individuals who would be killed otherwise) and moral-impersonal ones (the agent acts in an "impersonal" way, such as by pressing a button that will divert the trolley, thereby killing one innocent instead of five others). The moral-personal condition evoked similar activations in the FPC and angular gyrus, as compared to Oliveira-Souza and Moll's study.

Other studies followed, which addressed the contribution of general emotional arousal, bodily harm, response times, semantic content, cognitive load, conflict, intention, consequences, and emotional regulation (Berthoz, Armony, Blair, & Dolan, 2002; Greene et al., 2004; Harenski & Hamann, 2006; Heekeren et al., 2003; Heekeren et al., 2005; Moll, de Oliveira-Souza, Bramati, & Grafman, 2002; Schaich Borg, Hynes, Van Horn, Grafton, & Sinnott-Armstrong, 2006). Collectively, these studies have confirmed the role of lateral and medial sectors of the OFC, FPC, STS, and aTL in various aspects of moral judgment and moral sentiments.

These studies on moral judgment raised an important question: To what degree are these brain regions recruited by requirements of the task (semantic judgments, preference judgments, emotional judgments), or by the moral contents of moral scenarios (presence of written or visual stimuli having moral saliency, i.e., stimuli associated with moral values, rights, responsibilities, moral sentiments)? This issue was addressed in another fMRI study by passively exposing participants to pictures that varied in their moral content and emotional salience (Moll, de Oliveira-Souza, Eslinger et al., 2002). Activation of the anterior insula, amygdala, and subcortical structures were observed for both moral and nonmoral unpleasant stimuli. The FPC, medial OFC, and posterior STS regions, however, were selectively activated by moral appraisals. The engagement of the same brain networks by moral appraisals independently of task demands originated the idea of moral sensitivity as a mechanism by which moral significance is automatically attributed to ordinary events (Moll, de Oliveira-Souza, Eslinger et al., 2002). Moral sensitivity allows humans to quickly apprehend the moral implications of a social situation depending on context, agency, and consequences of one's choices, and crucially depends on specific moral sentiments.

Moral sentiments have long been claimed as the key in guiding our social behaviors (Hume, 1739/1984; Smith, 1759/1966) and are culturally ubiquitous (Ehrlich, 2000; Fessler, 1999). Both anticipated and actual violations of one's own principles and beliefs automatically trigger aversive sentiments such as guilt and shame (Eisenberg, 2000). Contrariwise, standing up for one's core values triggers positive sentiments, such as pride and awe (Baumeister, 2005). Nevertheless, it was not until very recently that their neural representations began to be scrutinized. Guilt, embarrassment, compassion, pride, and other sentiments were investigated using neuroimaging (Moll et al., 2007; Shin et al., 2000; Takahashi et al., 2004) and lesion studies (Beer, Heerey, Keltner, Scabini, & Knight, 2003). Moral sentiments are strong motivators for compliance with cultural norms and values, which carry intrinsic motivational force (Moll, Zahn et al., 2005).

MORAL CONFLICTS, REASON, AND EMOTION: FRIENDS OR FOES?

In Renaissance philosophical psychology, emotive functions of the "sensitive soul" resided in the heart, while cognition and voluntary motion had their seat in the brain (Park, 2000). While today such beliefs might sound amusing, it should be noted that modern science has tacitly retained the same dualistic principle when dealing with the relationships between mental processes and regional brain function. Different qualities of introspective experience – in this instance feeling and reasoning – are often assumed to "reside" in different anatomical loci (MacLean, 1973), with feelings occupying the limbic system and reasoning the isocortex (especially the PFC).

Although there is now little question of the importance of reasoning and feeling in human morality (Narvaez, 2005), the neural basis of these introspectively different ways of reaching moral decisions is hotly debated. One view is that reasoning (often assumed to be purely "cognitive"), and emotion (often equated with feeling), rely on anatomically separable systems (cognition in the PFC and parietal areas, and emotion in limbic regions), and that cognition and emotion can be placed in conflict and compete with each other during choice behavior (McClure, Botvinick, Yeung, Greene, & Cohen, in press). In the context of difficult moral choices, such as when one must decide whether it would be appropriate to push an innocent man to death on the tracks of a runaway trolley to save five other individuals (as illustrated above), the emotional system would tell the decision maker "Don't do it!!" the prepotent response; whereas the cognitive system would recommend the "utilitarian" choice, the one that leads to the maximum overall benefit, the rational choice (Greene et al., 2004). According to this "dual-process theory," choosing to push the man means that cognitive brain areas were successful in overcoming or suppressing the emotional bias of not doing it – an extension of the influential cognitive control model (Miller & Cohen, 2001) to the sphere of moral judgment.

We have proposed an alternative view that moral reasoning and feeling both arise by activation of associatively linked representations within fronto-temporo-limbic networks (Moll, Zahn et al., 2005), which is in line with some recent approaches in the field of moral psychology and moral philosophy (Narvaez, 2005; Narvaez & Gleason, 2007; Nichols, 2002; Prinz, 2006). Whereas both views agree that limbic regions are primarily responsible for emotional and motivational states, and that isocortical regions enable complex cognitive functions, they disagree on how information in limbic and isocortical systems interact to produce moral decisions.

Activation in the limbic system, according to the cortico-limbic integration view, would not be sufficient in itself to produce the subjective experience of an emotion. The experience of an emotion corresponds to integrated activation of cortical and limbic regions. We will refer to this subjectively experienced emotion as "feeling" or "sentiment" in order to contrast this more clearly from the crude basic "free-floating" emotional or motivation state (such as undirected anger, anxiety, etc.), which we hypothesized to be represented in limbic structures and associated subcortical areas (Moll, Zahn et al., 2005). When describing the cognitive control model, we will use the terms "emotion" and "cognition" as most authors working in that field do: "cognition" will refer mostly to explicit, rational mental processes, whereas "emotion" will refer to more implicit and behaviorally arousing ("hot") mental processes. Throughout the chapter, however, we will implicitly refer to both complex emotional experiences (i.e., feelings) and to more basic emotional states by using the term "emotion." Similarly, we will indiscriminately refer to complex conscious reasoning, as well as to more basic cognitive functions, as "cognition," since "emotion" and "cognition" are not mutually exclusive.

The cognitive control approach is intuitive, and builds on the classical distinction of cognition and emotion. Cognition is understood to be more explicit, effortful, and conscious, and supports cost-benefit analyses (Miller & Cohen, 2001). Emotion-based processes, on the other hand, are thought to be automatic, "hot," quick, and prepotent, and, to a great extent, operate unconsciously. Together with cognitive mechanisms, they help guide decisions toward the appropriate behavioral choices. Reasoning is based on cognitive operations residing in isocortical regions (mainly the PFC), whereas emotions are produced by limbic regions.

Cognition and emotion, this view poses, rely on broadly separable brain systems, but information processing taking place in these two systems do not always point to the same behavioral direction. According to the cognitive control view, cognitive and emotional systems can compete for behavioral output, when prepotent responses arising from "emotional brain regions" favor one type of outcome while "cognitive brain regions" point to another outcome. When faced with difficult choices – say, staying in shape or eating chocolate fudge, or admitting a mistake instead of getting away without being caught – we vividly experience a feeling of conflict. Indulging in the chocolate fudge or failing to admit a mistake can thus be seen as a failure of this control mechanism over emotions. Neural theories on the workings of the frontal lobes have largely embraced this view. In fact, it has been consistently demonstrated that PFC lesions indeed lead to poor choices and impaired decision making (Grafman, 1995). This led to the concept of the "central executive," an overarching controller of our behaviors, which is able to supervise and steer our choices according to performance criteria (Shallice & Burgess, 1996).

Executive abilities subserved by the PFC have been variously described as tapping on diverse cognitive functions, such as behavioral inhibition, selective attention, working memory, and cognitive control (Miller & Cohen,

2001). PFC function is thought to be particularly important for novel situations, mainly when multiple behavioral options are present at the same time. According to this view, the PFC exerts top-down control over other brain areas. In the field of moral cognition and decision making, this approach is represented by the cognitive conflict and control model of moral cognition (Greene et al., 2004). Greene at al. proposed a division between cognitive and emotional brain regions. Cognitive regions, in this model, would include the (dorsolateral prefrontal cortex) DLPFC and FPC and some posterior cortical areas. These areas are believed to exert inhibitory influence or control over emotional regions. Rational judgments in morally conflicting settings would therefore result from successful inhibition of emotional responses, whereas emotion-based choices (when a more "rationally appropriate" option is available) would represent a failure of this suppression mechanism.

As discussed above, there are situations in which spontaneously evoked emotions and automatic intuitive mechanisms are insufficient to deal with contextual demands so as to guide appropriate behavioral choices. In the moral domain, these demands are typical of situations involving moral dilemmas. A moral dilemma is a problem that entails dissonant choices of roughly comparable motivational strength, giving rise to a slow and effortful process often referred to as moral calculus (Gottfried, 1999; Moll et al., 2003). These processes presuppose the expression of the inner conflict between predicted outcomes of one's choices, and how the latter relate to personal preferences and values. Higher-order cognitive abilities, such as planning, executive flexibility, and strategy application, become decisive in these contexts. However, the neural representations underlying these cognitive processes must work in the service of actions that are essentially motivationally salient (i.e., linked with behaviorally important goals).

The cortico-limbic integration model of moral cognition (Moll, Zahn et al., 2005), in contrast to the cognitive control approach, proposes that competing representations of behavioral choices cannot be split into cognitive and emotional ones. Instead, the competition will occur among cognitive-emotional alternatives – e.g., should I opt for killing one innocent to save five other lives and suffer the angst of being a murderer forever, or opt for abstaining to do so and be responsible for causing the death of five people, thus committing a terrible act of omission? Should I indulge in tax evasion and thus be able to send my kid to a good school? In our view, rational or purely cognitive choices cannot be considered as real choices because they lack motivational power.

According to this view, all morally relevant experiences are considered to be essentially cognitive-emotional association complexes. Instead of competing with each other, cognition and emotion continuously interact in moral decision making. This view is in agreement with the finding that the PFC-mediated mechanisms are spontaneously engaged, whether or not decisions or behavioral outputs are required in moral scenarios, suggesting that the PFC does not only process information stored elsewhere in the brain, but is involved in representing aspects of morally salient contexts. Accordingly, certain PFC functions – for example, planning and representation of future outcomes – are believed to be central for enabling the experience of certain moral sentiments, such as anticipatory guilt, for example. These sentiments require anticipation and evaluation of possible future consequences of one's choices and social acts. Following this model, emotional states would not compete with cognitive or rational information: cognitive representations are part of the subjective experience of complex feelings, and provide essential ingredients for their emergence. Physiologically, interactions among cortical and subcortical limbic brain regions in moral cognition are still not well understood, but may result from temporal binding of neural activity across PFC-temporo-limbic networks (Moll, Zahn et al., 2005; W. Singer, 2001).

More specific to the topic of this review, recently published lesion studies bear direct relevance to roles of reason and emotion in moral cognition. These studies, carried out by Koenigs, Young, and colleagues (Koenigs et al., 2007) and by Ciaramelli and colleagues (Ciaramelli, Muccioli, Ladavas, & di Pellegrino, 2007), employed classical "trolley-type" dilemmas (Thomson, 1985) to investigate patterns of moral judgments in patients with bilateral damage to the VMPFC. They demonstrated that these patients endorsed "utilitarian" decisions in high-conflict scenarios – highly emotionally aversive choices that would nonetheless lead to greater aggregate welfare (e.g., more lives saved) – much more often than control subjects did. The increased preference of VMPFC patients for utilitarian choices could be interpreted according to different functional-anatomic hypotheses. One possibility would be that making more "rational," utilitarian choices in difficult dilemmas might have resulted from a general emotional blunting and reduced autonomic signaling arising from VMPFC damage – an interpretation that would fit with the somatic-marker hypothesis (Damasio, Tranel, & Damasio, 1990). This possibility, however, is not supported by the results of another study by Koenigs and Tranel (Koenigs & Tranel, 2007). In this study, the performance of VMPFC patients in the two-person Ultimatum game was investigated. In this "single-shot" game (participants interact only one time, anonymously), participants sometimes must choose between accepting an unfair but financially rewarding proposal (the economically "rational" choice), or rejecting it to punish the unfair player (the "emotional" choice). VMPFC patients opted more often than controls for rejecting unfair offers (i.e., they were more "emotional"). Therefore, while VMPFC patients made more utilitarian choices in trolley-type dilemmas (interpreted as "rational" responses), they opted more often for costly punishing, i.e., "emotional" responses associated with anger. Thus, the choice patterns observed in these morally salient experimental settings can neither be explained by a single mechanism of overall emotional blunting (Damasio et al., 1990), nor by the dual-process proposal, in which cognition and emotion processes compete for behavioral output in conflicting situations (Greene, 2007; Greene et al., 2004).

An alternative explanation would be the occurrence of a dissociation within the moral sentiment domain, with a selective impairment of prosocial sentiments – such as guilt and compassion (Moll & De Oliveira-Souza, 2007a, 2007b) – but spared other-critical sentiments, such as anger. It is likely that distinct brain regions have differential roles in enabling different aspects of emotional experience. The VMPFC, in particular, may be more critical for experience of prosocial sentiments associated with affiliative components (i.e., guilt, compassion, interpersonal attachment), whereas the DLPFC and lateral OFC/ insular cortex are more relevant for socially aversive sentiments (such as indignation and contempt) (Moll, Oliveira-Souza et al., 2005). A recent fMRI study corroborated this prediction in showing value-related guilt to be associated with subgenual cingulate cortex, and indignation/anger to be associated with lateral orbitofrontal-insular activations in healthy subjects (Zahn et al., 2009).

The "cold-blooded" utilitarian choices (Ciaramelli et al., 2007; Koenigs et al., 2007), and increased punishment of others in the Ultimatum game (Koenigs & Tranel, 2007) observed in VMPFC patients, may reflect an impairment in prosocial sentiments. Furthermore, the finding of decreased punishment of noncooperators following transient disruption of right DLPFC function by low-frequency repetitive transcranial magnetic stimulation, demonstrated in a recent study by Knoch, Pascual-Leone, Meyer, Treyer, and Fehr (2006), could arise from a decrease in aggressive inclinations – although the hypothesis of reduced cognitive control over anger cannot be ruled out. Finally, Sanfey, Rilling, Aronson, Nystrom, and Cohen (2003), using fMRI, reported increased DLPFC and insular activity when participants received unfair offers in the Ultimatum game. Activity in the insula, but not in the DLPFC, was correlated with rejection rates. The relative increase of DLPFC over insular activation associated with rational choices (accepted unfair offers), and the reverse pattern for emotional choices (rejections), has been used in favor of the hypothesis that the DLPFC mediates cognitive control over emotions (McClure et al., in press). It should be noted, however, that the level of DLPFC activity did not differ between accepted or rejected unfair offers. Therefore, changes in emotional engagement alone would be sufficient to explain behavioral effects.

In summary, these data do not support the notion either that moral reasoning is merely cortical and conscious, nor that emotions are merely limbic and implicit (Moll, Zahn et al., 2005; Nichols, 2002; Prinz, 2006). Though some brain regions are intrinsically tied to motivational/regulatory mechanisms and others are less so, this does not imply clear boundaries or competition between cognition and emotion. Instead, competition between behavioral options will only occur when choices are endowed with emotional salience.

MORAL MOTIVATIONS: PRIMITIVE OR UNIQUELY HUMAN?

The human moral instincts have been tackled by philosophers and scientists for a long time (Darwin, 1871/1982; Smith, 1759/1966). There is a growing awareness that the primitive affective-motivational building blocks of morality can be found in other social species as well (de Waal, 2001). Operationally, social motivations can be organized into two broad classes: one linked to approach and affiliation, and the other linked to aversion and rejection. While attachment promotes care, cooperation, and reciprocity toward in-group members, aversion fosters blame, prejudice, and group dissolution (de Waal, 1998; Moll et al., 2003; Schulkin, 2000). Such primitive social-motivational dispositions find a close correspondence to the prosocial and social-aversive counterparts at work in sophisticated psychological spheres of human moral cognition. These are manifested as moral sentiments and values that embody motivational elements of social attachment/aversion and culturally shaped social knowledge (Moll, Zahn et al., 2005; Schulkin, 2004).

Here we will briefly review the evidence on phylogenetically old mechanisms underlying prosocial motivations and social aversion, and how they relate to uniquely human expressions of morality. We will argue that sophisticated forms of human prosocial (e.g., cooperation, altruism, and empathy) and socially aversive inclinations (e.g., moral outrage and prejudice) are deeply entrenched with motivational-emotional neuro-endocrine mechanisms underlying primitive social instincts. It follows that the experience of moral sentiments and values essentially emerges from interlocking cognitive-motivational systems integrating and reshaping social instincts into uniquely human neural and psychological dimensions.

ATTACHMENT, MATERNAL INSTINCTS, AND COOPERATION WITH STRANGERS AND SOCIETAL CAUSES

The neurobiological systems enabling high degrees of maternal care and social bonding observed in placental mammals rely on key neuro-humoral systems regulating social attachment. These crucially depend on several subcortical and limbic structures, including the ventral striatum, septal nuclei, amygdala, and hypothalamus (Insel & Fernald, 2004; Keverne & Curley, 2004), as well as on a broad array of monoaminergic neurotransmitters (serotonin, dopamine), endogenous opioids and hormones (e.g., vasopressin, oxytocin) (Depue & Morrone-Strupinsky, 2005). Neuropeptides that promote affiliative states in animals include vasopressin, oxytocin, cocaine- and amphetamine-regulated transcript peptide, peptide Y. Distinct mediators may promote prosocial behaviors in different ways: for example, neuropeptide Y acts on the ventral striatum and perifornical region and has both anxiety-relieving properties and rewarding effects, while oxytocin facilitates social bonds and mediates animal contact and comfort (Insel & Young, 2001). Serotonin has also been shown to promote constructive social interactions by decreasing aggression (Young & Leyton, 2002), and might also be involved in regulating oxytocin expression.

Recent evidence has started to demonstrate the role of attachment-related neural mechanisms in humans. Structures of the brain reward system – i.e., the midbrain ventral tegmental area and ventral striatum, along with basal forebrain structures – were engaged when humans looked at their own babies or at their romantic partners (Aron et al., 2005; Bartels & Zeki, 2004). Other studies have provided causal evidence for the effects of oxytocin on human social behavior. In a sequential economic game involving trust, oxytocin levels were found to be higher in subjects who received a monetary transfer signaling an intention to trust, in comparison with an unintentional monetary transfer of the same amount from another player (Zak, Kurzban, & Matzner, 2004). Higher oxytocin levels were associated with increased likelihood of reciprocation. Decreasing social anxiety or fear might also be an important effect of oxytocin, a hypothesis that was strengthened by a recent pharmacological fMRI study. In this study, oxytocin was shown to decrease amygdala activation to fearful stimuli (Kirsch et al., 2005). In another study, intranasal administration of oxytocin induced more cooperation in an anonymous economic game by boosting interpersonal trust (Kosfeld, Heinrichs, Zak, Fischbacher, & Fehr, 2005). In this game, the first player chooses to transfer an amount of money (if any) to another player. The amount is multiplied, and the second player may choose how much she/he will transfer back to the first player (i.e., reciprocation). Exogenous oxytocin administration was associated with increased amounts transfers in the trust game by first movers.

These primitive neuro-humoral attachment mechanisms, highly preserved across several placental mammals, seem to provide key ingredients to the more sophisticated sphere of human morality. Because similar mechanisms can be adapted by evolution to serve novel functions across phylogenesis, we speculate that our proclivity to develop complex cultural constructs such as moral values may partially spring from integration of more "primitive" motivational systems with sophisticated cortical representations. In line with this hypothesis, a recent fMRI experiment provided evidence for a direct link between altruistic decision making in cultural settings to the functions of the brain reward and social attachment systems. In this study, subjects were scanned using functional MRI while they made real-life anonymous decisions about whether to donate to, or to oppose, a number of charities (Moll et al., 2006). Decisions, depending on trial type, could be either financially costly or noncostly to the participant. In other trials, participants were able to receive "pure" monetary rewards (without consequences for the charities). The charities were associated with causes with important societal implications, such as abortion, children's rights, nuclear energy, war, and euthanasia.

Both pure monetary rewards and decisions to donate activated the mesolimbic reward system, in agreement with the warm glow hypothesis – it feels good to be good (Andreoni, 1990). Interestingly, in comparison with the pure monetary reward condition, decisions to donate selectively activated the subgenual-septal area, which is intimately related to social attachment in other species (Freedman, Insel, & Smith, 2000; Young & Wang, 2004). When participants disliked the charities (e.g., many of them refused to make decisions that would benefit the National Rifle Association), the lateral OFC, an area more readily activated by experience of anger and disgust, was engaged. Furthermore, when decisions were costly to the participant – both costly donation and costly opposition – more anterior areas of the PFC were activated: the FPC and anterior OFC. This can be interpreted as a result of weighing the costs and benefits of decisions, and anticipating the consequences of one's decisions for oneself and for the charities. Noteworthy, during costly donations, these PFC areas showed increased functional connectivity with the subgenual-septal area (unpublished results). This indicates that moral motivations depend on the coactivation of limbic systems involved in affiliative rewards, and of the more recently evolved anterior PFC, which work cooperatively (instead of competitively) during decision making. Finally, these findings extended the role of fronto-limbic networks in social cooperation, from interpersonal economic interactions, as addressed by a number of previous studies (de Quervain et al., 2004; Delgado, Frank, & Phelps, 2005; King-Casas et al., 2005; Sanfey, Rilling, Aronson, Nystrom, & Cohen, 2003; T. Singer, Kiebel, Winston, Dolan, & Frith, 2004), to the realm of decisions based on internalized values and preferences shaped by culture.

Based on these findings, we have recently developed an "extended attachment" perspective on moral cognition, which aims to bridge between the neurobiology of primitive forms of attachment and complex moral cognition (Moll & De Oliveira-Souza, 2008). We have postulated that extended attachment is rooted on a unique proclivity of humans to develop affiliative links to culturally shaped elements. More specifically, we postulate that ancient mechanisms supporting basic forms of attachment in other species, such as pair-bonding (Insel & Young, 2001), evolved to enable the unique human ability to attach to culturally shaped associations of symbols with abstract meaning. This form of attachment might have played a major role in cooperation and indirect reciprocity during evolution, promoting altruistic behaviors within sociocultural groups and facilitating out-group moralistic aggression. The fundamental aspect underlying extended attachment is based on a functional reorganization of basic mechanisms of social attachment, present in many social species, into their human counterparts. The underlying neural architecture underpinning this ability putatively involves the connection of limbic/brainstem regions involved in basic mechanisms of interindividual bonding and attachment with phylogenetically recent association cortical systems. The specific mechanisms of cortico-limbic integration are in keeping with our earlier model of moral cognition (Moll, Zahn et al., 2005). We speculate that this kind of integration may play a central role in the uniquely human ability to attach motivational significance to abstract ideas, cultural symbols, and beliefs, supporting the high level of cooperation among non-kin typically observed in human societies. Recent studies provide preliminary support for this hypothesis (Krueger et al., 2007; Moll et al., 2006). As discussed before, extended attachment could not only drive intragroup altruism and cooperation, but also help demarcate outgroup boundaries, enhancing group distinctiveness and promoting aggression toward outgroups – a haunting feature that has permeated human evolution (Bowles, 2006; Bowles & Gintis, 2004). Although preliminary, recent imaging studies in humans have revealed that brain structures deeply involved in attachment – such as the subgenual cortex, septal area, and neighboring basal forebrain structures – are engaged not only when humans are presented to beloved ones (such as mothers to their babies or romantic partners to each other) in experimental settings (Aron et al., 2005; Bartels & Zeki, 2004), but also by donation to abstract societal causes while subjects feel compassion (Moll et al., 2006), and when individuals engage in "unconditional cooperation"; but not during "strategic cooperation" in economic games (Krueger et al., 2007). The extended attachment hypothesis is currently being tested in our laboratory using both behavioral and fMRI methods.

DISGUST, DOMINANCE, AND MORALISTIC AGGRESSION

In several animal species, aggression typically occurs in disputes concerning sex, territory, power, and food resources. Primates possess highly structured dominance hierarchies regulating access to food resources, mating, and other social privileges (Byrne & Whiten, 1988; de Waal, 1998). Social status marks one as a "good" or "poor" partner for future interactions. In humans, aggressiveness is underlined by feelings of anger, frustration, and, arguably, disgust, and contempt.

Neural and humoral systems underlying such behaviors have been studied in several species. There is extensive evidence pointing to the role of dopaminergic and serotonergic pathways. In primates, both dopamine and serotonin have modulatory effects on social interactions, depending on social status (Edwards & Kravitz, 1997; Morgan et al., 2002; Muehlenbein, Watts, & Whitten, 2004). Although enhanced dopaminergic and serotonergic action have been related to increased dominance, these neurochemical systems probably exert partially separable effects. Increased serotonergic activity leads to a decrease of harm avoidance and hostility, and an increase in dominance in social encounters in humans (Brody et al., 2000). It has been suggested that part of this effect may be mediated by regulation of oxytocin release, linked to social contact, or through the corticotropin-releasing hormone, linked to social withdrawal (Brody et al., 2000). In humans, D2-class receptor dopaminergic antagonism leads to a selective disruption in anger recognition, in line with the importance of dopamine mediating aggression in social-agonistic encounters (Lawrence, Calder, McGowan, & Grasby, 2002).

In addition to anger, disgust also plays a central role in social aversion. Interestingly, proto-forms of disgust found in nonhumans are linked to essentially nonsocial functions: distaste and nausea from exposure to potentially toxic or contaminated foods and odors have a clear adaptive function (Darwin, 1872/1965; Rozin, 1999; Rozin & Haidt, 1993). In humans, in contrast, disgust and its close relative, contempt, have clearly extended to the interpersonal realm. Differently from anger, disgust and contempt are slower to fade away, tend to "stick" or become a property of the object, and intensely devalue it (Haidt, 2003; Rozin, Lowery, Imada, & Haidt, 1999). Thus, in the same way that neural systems underlying primitive forms of pleasure and social bonding operate in complex social situations associated with human cooperation, neural systems underlying aversive responses related to physical properties of odors and foods seem to have been adapted to sustain social disapproval and "moralistic" aggression (Arsenio & Lemerise, 2004). Thus, while morality often promotes cooperation and helping, it can also motivate people to punish other individuals and social groups (Jones, 2007; Moll et al., 2003).

Moral values powerfully incite people to challenge others' beliefs and ideologies (Allport, 1954; Vogel, 2004). Previous research has consistently implicated a number of brain regions and circuits in social aversion, including brainstem regions, the amygdala, basal forebrain and hypothalamic nuclei, pirifom and cingulate cortex, and temporal and frontal connections (Calder, Lawrence, & Young, 2001; Mega, Cummings, Salloway, & Malloy, 1997; Moll, Oliveira-Souza et al., 2005; Volavka, 1999). In particular, the lateral OFC and neighboring agranular insula have been implicated in interpersonal aversive mechanisms (Bechara, Tranel, & Damasio, 2000; Kringelbach, 2005), including punishment of noncooperators in economic interactions (de Quervain et al., 2004; Sanfey et al., 2003), anger responses (Bechara et al., 2000; Blair, Morris, Frith, Perrett, & Dolan, 1999), and racial bias (Cunningham, Johnson et al., 2004). Another fMRI study directly showed that brain regions involved in basic forms of disgust and moral disgust are largely shared (Moll, de Oliveira-Souza et al., 2005). Accordingly, in the donation study described above, decisions to oppose charities, whether personally costly or not, were associated with activity in the lateral OFC and anterior insula, confirming the role of these regions in mediating aversive experiences in sophisticated cultural settings (Moll et al., 2006). In a recent study we found corroborating activation of lateral OFC and anterior insula, when subjects reported indignation/anger after imagining their best friend, to act counter to shared social values (e.g., "generosity") toward them during fMRI (Zahn et al., 2008).

THE NEURAL BASIS OF SOCIAL CONCEPTS AND MORAL VALUES

As outlined in the Introduction, moral cognition can be distinguished from general social cognition by identifying whether moral motivations are playing a role in guiding social behavior. In the previous section, we have described a theoretical view according to which two broad classes of moral motivations play important roles in moral cognition, embodied by the attachment and aversion components of moral sentiments and moral values. Although there is now cumulating evidence on the neural basis of moral sentiments, until recently no direct evidence was available on the representation of moral values. Moral or social values consist of abstract conceptual knowledge linked to emotional states and social actions (Schwartz, 1992). Therefore, the basis of moral values can only be established after identifying the basis of moral knowledge. Following our previous argument, moral knowledge when stripped from its motivations will be part of general social knowledge. The neural representation of general social knowledge, however, is also poorly understood. Wood and Grafman (2003) had proposed that social knowledge arises from knowledge of the sequences of social events and actions represented in the VMPFC. Other researchers, however, have stressed that when abstracted from the sequential context of action, social knowledge remains largely intact in patients with VMPFC damage (Eslinger & Damasio, 1985).

Recently, we have demonstrated that abstract conceptual social knowledge, which is independent of the sequential context of actions and emotions, is represented in the superior aTL (Zahn et al., 2007). Abstract conceptual social knowledge allows us to define the meaning of overarching social and/or moral values (e.g., intelligence, ambition, honor, politeness). Preserved aTL representations of this kind of knowledge may help explain the observation of intact abstract conceptual social knowledge and normal performance on certain social cognition tasks in patients with VMPFC damage (Eslinger & Damasio, 1985; Saver & Damasio, 1991).

This separation of stable abstract conceptual representations in the aTL that can be flexibly embedded within different contexts of action implementation and emotional qualities, as encoded in fronto-limbic circuits, could account for our ability to imbue social and moral values to a wide range of interpersonal and cultural settings. This independence of stable abstract conceptual and flexible context-dependent action-emotion representations could account for our ability to communicate about the sense of concepts, e.g., "politeness," in diverse cultural settings, despite a great variability of the exact actions and emotional flavors tied to these concepts in specific contexts. A polite greeting in Japan, for example, might be to bow one's head, in Germany to shake hands, and in the United States to say: "How are you?" Nevertheless, we are able to interpret these different kinds of behaviors as "polite." Conversely, the same social action (e.g., "a woman proposing to her boyfriend on a vacation") can be associated with different conceptual interpretations (e.g., "individualism," "boldness," or "desperation") depending on the sequential and cultural and personal context. This flexibility of associative links between social concepts and actions also enables us to flexibly interpret social behavior, because different associative links between social concepts and action contexts influence the emotional quality associated with the concept or action. A marriage proposal associated with boldness and individualism is more likely to lead to pride on the side of the agent, given that the person strives to act according to these values. This relinking of social actions and conceptual interpretations is successfully used to change emotional and moral evaluations of one's social behavior during the cognitive therapy of affective disorders (Beck, Rush, Shaw, & Emery, 1979).

In a subsequent study, we were able to corroborate the hypothesized neural basis of social values as consisting of the integration of representation of abstract conceptual social information with fronto-mesolimbic representations of the sequential context of action and emotional quality (Zahn et al., 2008). In this study, subjects had to imagine themselves acting in accordance with, or counter to, an important personal value (described by a single abstract social concept) toward their best friends (e.g., "Sam acts stingily toward Tom"). In a different condition, the agency-role was reversed, and subjects imagined their best friend acting toward them (e.g., "Tom acts stingily toward Sam"). Although valence, familiarity, and self-reference in self-agency and other-agency conditions were carefully matched, a distinctive signature for the different moral sentiments experienced during these conditions emerged: when acting against a social value, subjects most often reported guilt after the scan. Individual differences on the frequency with which each person reported guilt for not acting according to a value strongly increased subgenual cingulate and anterior VMPFC activation. This pattern of activation was different from the condition in which subjects imagined their best friend to act counter to the same social values. In this condition, indignation/anger was the most frequently reported moral sentiment, and this feeling was associated with increased activation in lateral orbitofrontal/anterior insular cortices. Despite these fronto-limbic differences in activation, specific for different contexts of agency and valence, there was no difference in the activation within the superior aTL between the different conditions. As in our study on abstract social concepts (Zahn et al., 2007), the same superior sector of the right aTL was activated for all types of moral sentiments (pride, gratitude, guilt, and indignation/anger), and activity increased with increasing richness of conceptual detail descriptive of social behavior.

These findings on separable neural representations for context-dependent and context–independent components of social and moral values provide a neurobiological mechanism that may explain the remarkable human ability to dynamically rearrange social concepts, actions, and emotional flavors to produce the rich variety of personal, moral, and social values that subtly steer our social lives.

CONCLUSIONS AND FUTURE DIRECTIONS

We have argued that moral cognition differs from other socially relevant abilities by its reliance on specific motivational mechanisms. We have further elaborated that an understanding of the neural basis of moral sentiments and values is central in order to make neurobiological predictions about the scope and limits of motivational forces that allow humans to behave altruistically or according to societal norms and needs.

Clinical and experimental studies now provide preliminary but solid evidence on the influence of cultural and biological factors on human morality. We have mentioned studies showing individual variability in the neural basis of moral cognition in healthy subjects and discussed findings pointing to impaired moral abilities in patients with acquired brain lesions and developmental macro-anatomical abnormalities. The identification of neural components and their relationships to psychological processes underlying moral cognition is providing critical knowledge for our understanding of human moral abilities. We have argued that deeply entrenched neurohumoral mechanisms, which are largely shared with other social species, are uniquely combined with cognitive abilities more recently developed in our species, such as conceptual abstraction and elaborate representation of future consequences of actions, to provide the motivational force associated with human moral sentiments.

In this vein, we have argued that these motivational mechanisms are not merely primitive evolutionary remnants that must be tempered and modulated by "rational" cortical systems. Instead, social attachment and aversion are crucial motivators of moral actions and are inextricably linked with moral evaluations and judgments. These motivations are deeply influenced by social learning and by individual biological differences.

This neural framework highlights the roles of social and moral knowledge in moral cognition, and how they interact with social-cultural factors that are unique to humans. This interaction of psychological, cultural and neurobiological factors in limiting or broadening moral abilities in humans can be explained within a neurocognitive model of integration across a fronto-temporo-mesolimbic brain network. Distinct functional roles of components of this network, such as the specific role of the superior aTL in representations of abstract social conceptual knowledge and the role of the subgenual-septal and anterior PFC regions in altruistic decisions, have been articulated. We have also presented evidence on categorical differences in patterns of activations for different moral sentiments, such as prosocial and other-critical feelings. These results raise hopes that the endeavor of elucidating functional subdivisions within the complex human neural system mediating moral cognition and behavior is worth pursuing. For instance, understanding individual differences in experiencing different kinds of moral sentiments and how they relate to culturally shaped beliefs and moral values, enabling moral commitments, may provide essential ingredients for novel theoretical constructs on how moral personality and identity develops and stabilizes over time, and how social contingencies affect personal choices.

REFERENCES

Allison, T., Puce, A., & McCarthy, G. (2000). Social perception from visual cues: role of the STS region. *Trends in Cognitive Sciences*, 4(7), 267–278.

Allman, J., Hakeem, A., & Watson, K. (2002). Two phylogenetic specializations in the human brain. *Neuroscientist*, 8(4), 335–346.

Allport, G. W. (1954). *The nature of prejudice*. Boston, MA: Beacon Press.

Anderson, S. W., Bechara, A., Damasio, H., Tranel, D., & Damasio, A. R. (1999). Impairment of social and moral behavior related to early damage in human prefrontal cortex. *Nature Neuroscience*, 2(11), 1032–1037.

Andreoni, J. (1990). Impure altruism and donations to public good: A theory of warm glow giving. *The Economic Journal*, 100(401), 464–477.

Aristotle. (1926). *The Nicomachean ethics* (E. t. b. H. Rackham, Trans.). London, New York: William Heinemann, G. P. Putnam's Sons.

Aron, A., Fisher, H., Mashek, D. J., Strong, G., Li, H., & Brown, L. L. (2005). Reward, motivation, and emotion systems associated with early-stage intense romantic love. *Journal of Neurophysiology*, 94(1), 327–337.

Arsenio, W. F., & Lemerise, E. A. (2004). Aggression and moral development: Integrating social information processing and moral domain models. *Child Development*, 75(4), 987–1002.

Bartels, A., & Zeki, S. (2004). The neural correlates of maternal and romantic love. *Neuroimage*, 21(3), 1155–1166.

Baumeister, R. F. (2005). *The cultural animal*. New York: Oxford University Press.

Bechara, A., Tranel, D., & Damasio, H. (2000). Characterization of the decision-making deficit of patients with ventromedial prefrontal cortex lesions. *Brain*, 123 (Pt. 11), 2189–2202.

Beck, A. T., Rush, A. J., Shaw, B. F., & Emery, G. (1979). *Cognitive therapy of depression*. New York: Guilford Press.

Berthoz, S., Armony, J. L., Blair, R. J. R., & Dolan, R. J. (2002). An fMRI study of intentional and unintentional (embarrassing) violations of social norms. *Brain*, 125(8), 1696–1708.

Blair, R. J., Morris, J. S., Frith, C. D., Perrett, D. I., & Dolan, R. J. (1999). Dissociable neural responses to facial expressions of sadness and anger. *Brain*, 122 (Pt. 5), 883–893.

Bowles, S. (2006). Group competition, reproductive leveling, and the evolution of human altruism. *Science*, 314(5805), 1569–1572.

Bowles, S., & Gintis, H. (2004). The evolution of strong reciprocity: cooperation in heterogeneous populations. *Theoretical Population Biology*, 65(1), 17–28.

Bozeat, S., Gregory, C. A., Ralph, M. A., & Hodges, J. R. (2000). Which neuropsychiatric and behavioural features distinguish frontal and temporal variants of frontotemporal dementia from Alzheimer's disease? *Journal of Neurology, Neurosurgery and Psychiatry*, 69(2), 178–186.

Brody, A. L., Saxena, S., Fairbanks, L. A., Alborzian, S., Demaree, H. A., Maidment, K. M. et al. (2000). Personality changes in adult subjects with major depressive disorder or obsessive-compulsive disorder treated with paroxetine. *Journal of Clinical Psychiatry*, 61(5), 349–355.

Burns, J. M., & Swerdlow, R. H. (2003). Right orbitofrontal tumor with pedophilia symptom and constructional apraxia sign. *Archives of Neurology*, 60(3), 437–440.

Byrne, R. W., & Whiten, A. (1988). *Machiavellian intelligence: Social expertise and the evolution of intellect in monkeys, apes and humans*. Oxford: Oxford University Press.

Calder, A. J., Lawrence, A. D., & Young, A. W. (2001). Neuropsychology of fear and loathing. *Nature Reviews Neuroscience*, 2(5), 352–363.

Casebeer, W. D. (2003). Moral cognition and its neural constituents. *Nature Reviews Neuroscience*, 4(10), 840–846.

Ciaramelli, E., Muccioli, M., Ladavas, E., & di Pellegrino, G. (2007). Selective deficit in personal moral judgment following damage to ventromedial prefrontal cortex. *Social Cognitive and Affective Neuroscience*, 2(2), 84–92.

Cleckley, H. M. (1976). *The mask of sanity* (5th ed.). St. Louis, MO: Mosby.

Cunningham, W. A., Raye, C. L., & Johnson, M. K. (2004). Implicit and explicit evaluation: fMRI correlates of valence, emotional intensity, and control in the processing of attitudes. *Journal of Cognitive Neuroscience*, 16(10), 1717–1729.

Daigneault, S., Braun, C. M., & Montes, J. L. (1999). [Hypothalamic hamartoma: Detailed presentation of a case]. *Encephale, 25*(4), 338–344.
Damasio, A. R., Tranel, D., & Damasio, H. (1990). Individuals with sociopathic behavior caused by frontal damage fail to respond autonomically to social stimuli. *Behavioral Brain Research, 41*(2), 81–94.
(1871/1982). *The descent of man and selection in relation to sex.* Princeton, NJ: Princeton University Press.
Darwin, C. (1872/1965). *The expression of emotions in man and animals.* Chicago: University of Chicago Press.
de Oliveira-Souza, R., Hare, R. D., Bramati, I. E., Garrido, G. J., Azevedo Ignacio, F., Tovar-Moll, F. et al. (2008). Psychopathy as a disorder of the moral brain: Fronto-temporo-limbic grey matter reductions demonstrated by voxel-based morphometry. *Neuroimage.*
de Oliveira-Souza, R., & Moll, J. (2000). The moral brain: A functional MRI study of moral judgment, *Neurology, 54*, A104.
de Quervain, D. J., Fischbacher, U., Treyer, V., Schellhammer, M., Schnyder, U., Buck, A., et al. (2004). The neural basis of altruistic punishment. *Science, 305*(5688), 1254–1258.
de Waal, F. (1998). *Chimpanzee politics power and sex among apes.* Baltimore: Johns Hopkins University Press.
Decety, J., & Jackson, P. L. (2004). The functional architecture of human empathy. *Behavioral and Cognitive Neuroscience Review, 3*, 71–100.
Delgado, M. R., Frank, R. H., & Phelps, E. A. (2005). Perceptions of moral character modulate the neural systems of reward during the trust game. *Nature Neuroscience, 8*(11), 1611–1618.
Depue, R. A., & Morrone-Strupinsky, J. V. (2005). A neurobehavioral model of affiliative bonding: Implications for conceptualizing a human trait of affiliation. *Behavioral and Brain Sciences, 28*(3), 313–350.
Edwards, D. H., & Kravitz, E. A. (1997). Serotonin, social status and aggression. *Current Opinions in Neurobiology, 7*(6), 812–819.
Ehrlich, P. R. (2000). *Human natures: Genes, cultures, and the human prospect.* Washington, D.C.: Island Press.
Eisenberg, N. (2000). Emotion, regulation, and moral development. *Annual Review of Psychology, 51*, 665–697.
Eslinger, P. J., & Damasio, A. R. (1985). Severe disturbance of higher cognition after bilateral frontal lobe ablation: Patient EVR. *Neurology, 35*(12), 1731–1741.
Eslinger, P. J., Flaherty-Craig, C. V., & Benton, A. L. (2004). Developmental outcomes after early prefrontal cortex damage. *Brain and Cognition, 55*(1), 84–103.
Eslinger, P. J., Grattan, L. M., Damasio, H., & Damasio, A. R. (1992). Developmental consequences of childhood frontal lobe damage. *Archives of Neurology, 49*(7), 764–769.
Fehr, E., & Fischbacher, U. (2003). The nature of human altruism. *Nature, 425*(6960), 785–791.
Fehr, E., & Rockenbach, B. (2004). Human altruism: Economic, neural, and evolutionary perspectives. *Current Opinion in Neurobiology, 14*(6), 784–790.

Fessler, D. (1999). Toward an understanding of the universality of second order emotions. In A. Hinton (Ed.), *Beyond nature or nurture: Biocultural approaches to the emotions* (pp. 75–116). New York: Cambridge University Press.

Freedman, L. J., Insel, T. R., & Smith, Y. (2000). Subcortical projections of area 25 (subgenual cortex) of the macaque monkey. *Journal of Comparative Neurology, 421*(2), 172–188.

Goodenough, O. R., & Prehn, K. (2004). A neuroscientific approach to normative judgment in law and justice. *Philosophical Transactions of the Royal Society of London, Series B: Biological Sciences, 359*(1451), 1709–1726.

Gottfried, K. (1999). Moral calculus and the bomb. *Nature, 401*(6749), 117.

Grafman, J. (1995). Similarities and distinctions among current models of prefrontal cortical functions. *Annals of the New York Academy of Sciences, 769*, 337–368.

Greene, J. D. (2007). Why are VMPFC patients more utilitarian? A dual-process theory of moral judgment explains. *Trends in Cognitive Sciences, 11*(8), 322–323; author reply 323–324.

Greene, J. D., Nystrom, L. E., Engell, A. D., Darley, J. M., & Cohen, J. D. (2004). The neural bases of cognitive conflict and control in moral judgment. *Neuron, 44*(2), 389–400.

Greene, J. D., Sommerville, R. B., Nystrom, L. E., Darley, J. M., & Cohen, J. D. (2001). An fMRI investigation of emotional engagement in moral judgment. *Science, 293*(5537), 2105–2108.

Haidt, J. (2001). The emotional dog and its rational tail: A social intuitionist approach to moral judgment. *Psychological Review, 108*(4), 814–834.

Haidt, J. (2003). The moral emotions. In R. J. Davidson, K. R. Scherer, & H. H. Goldsmith (Eds.), *Handbook of affective sciences* (pp. 852–870). Oxford: Oxford University Press.

Hare, R. D. (2003). *The hare psychopathy checklist-revised* (2nd ed.). Toronto: Multi-Health Systems.

Harenski, C. L., & Hamann, S. (2006). Neural correlates of regulating negative emotions related to moral violations. *Neuroimage, 30*(1), 313–324.

Heekeren, H. R., Wartenburger, I., Schmidt, H., Prehn, K., Schwintowski, H. P., & Villringer, A. (2005). Influence of bodily harm on neural correlates of semantic and moral decision-making. *Neuroimage, 24*(3), 887–897.

Heekeren, H. R., Wartenburger, I., Schmidt, H., Schwintowski, H. P., & Villringer, A. (2003). An fMRI study of simple ethical decision-making. *Neuroreport, 14*(9), 1215–1219.

Hitlin, S. (2003). Values as the core of personal identity: Drawing links between two theories of self. *Social Psychology Quarterly, 66*(2), 118–137.

Hume, D. (1739/1984). *A treatise of human nature.* New York: Penguin Classics.
   (1777a). *An enquiry concerning human understanding* (Vol. 2). London: T. Cadell.
   (1777b). *An enquiry into the principles of morals* (Vol. 2). London: T. Cadell.

Insel, T. R., & Fernald, R. D. (2004). How the brain processes social information: searching for the social brain. *Annual Review of Neuroscience, 27*, 697–722.

Insel, T. R., & Young, L. J. (2001). The neurobiology of attachment. *Nature Reviews Neuroscience, 2*(2), 129–136.

Jones, D. (2007). Moral psychology: The depths of disgust. *Nature, 447*(7146), 768–771.
Keverne, E. B., & Curley, J. P. (2004). Vasopressin, oxytocin and social behaviour. *Current Opinion in Neurobiology, 14*(6), 777–783.
Kiehl, K. A., Smith, A. M., Mendrek, A., Forster, B. B., Hare, R. D., & Liddle, P. F. (2004). Temporal lobe abnormalities in semantic processing by criminal psychopaths as revealed by functional magnetic resonance imaging. *Psychiatry Research, 130*(3), 297–312.
King-Casas, B., Tomlin, D., Anen, C., Camerer, C. F., Quartz, S. R., & Montague, P. R. (2005). Getting to know you: Reputation and trust in a two-person economic exchange. *Science, 308*(5718), 78–83.
Kirsch, P., Esslinger, C., Chen, Q., Mier, D., Lis, S., Siddhanti, S. et al. (2005). Oxytocin modulates neural circuitry for social cognition and fear in humans. *Journal of Neuroscience, 25*(49), 11489–11493.
Knoch, D., Pascual-Leone, A., Meyer, K., Treyer, V., & Fehr, E. (2006). Diminishing reciprocal fairness by disrupting the right prefrontal cortex. *Science, 314*(5800), 829–832.
Koenigs, M., & Tranel, D. (2007). Irrational economic decision-making after ventromedial prefrontal damage: Evidence from the Ultimatum game. *Journal of Neuroscience, 27*(4), 951–956.
Koenigs, M., Young, L., Adolphs, R., Tranel, D., Cushman, F., Hauser, M. et al. (2007). Damage to the prefrontal cortex increases utilitarian moral judgements. *Nature, 446*(7138), 908–911.
Kosfeld, M., Heinrichs, M., Zak, P. J., Fischbacher, U., & Fehr, E. (2005). Oxytocin increases trust in humans. *Nature, 435*(7042), 673–676.
Kringelbach, M. L. (2005). The human orbitofrontal cortex: Linking reward to hedonic experience. *Nature Review Neuroscience, 6*(9), 691–702.
Lawrence, A. D., Calder, A. J., McGowan, S. W., & Grasby, P. M. (2002). Selective disruption of the recognition of facial expressions of anger. *Neuroreport, 13*(6), 881–884.
Liu, W., Miller, B. L., Kramer, J. H., Rankin, K., Wyss-Coray, C., Gearhart, R. et al. (2004). Behavioral disorders in the frontal and temporal variants of frontotemporal dementia. *Neurology, 62*(5), 742–748.
Luo, Q., Nakic, M., Wheatley, T., Richell, R., Martin, A., & Blair, R. J. (2006). The neural basis of implicit moral attitude – an IAT study using event-related fMRI. *Neuroimage, 30*(4), 1449–1457.
MacIntyre, A. (1985). *After virtue* (2nd ed.). London: Duckworth.
MacLean, P. (1973). *A triune concept of the brain and behaviour: Hincks memorial lecture*. Oxford: University of Toronto Press.
Macmillan, M. (2000). *An odd kind of fame: Stories of Phineas Gage*. Cambridge, MA: MIT Press.
Maynard-Smith, J., & Szathmary, E. (1997). *The major transitions in evolution*. New York: Oxford University Press.
McClure, S. M., Botvinick, M. M., Yeung, N., Greene, J. D., & Cohen, J. D. (in press). Conflict monitoring in cognition-emotion competition. In J. J. Gross (Ed.), *Handbook of emotion regulation*. New York: Guilford.

Mega, M., Cummings, J., Salloway, S., & Malloy, P. (1997). The limbic system: An anatomic, phylogenetic, and clinical perspective. *Journal of Neuropsychiatry and Clinical Neuroscience*, 9(3), 315–330.

Mendez, M. F., Chow, T., Ringman, J., Twitchell, G., & Hinkin, C. H. (2000). Pedophilia and temporal lobe disturbances. *Journal of Neuropsychiatry and Clinical Neuroscience*, 12(1), 71–76.

Milinski, M., Semmann, D., & Krambeck, H. J. (2002). Reputation helps solve the "tragedy of the commons." *Nature*, 415(6870), 424–426.

Miller, E. K., & Cohen, J. D. (2001). An integrative theory of prefrontal cortex function. *Annual Review of Neuroscience*, 24, 167–202.

Moll, J., & de Oliveira-Souza, R. (2007a). Moral judgments, emotions and the utilitarian brain. *Trends in Cognitive Science*, 11, 319–321.

Moll, J., & de Oliveira-Souza, R. (2007b). Response to Greene: Moral sentiments and reason: Friends or foes? *Trends in Cognitive Science*, 11(8), 323–324.

Moll, J., & de Oliveira-Souza, R. (2008). "Extended attachment" and the human brain: Internalized cultural values and evolutionary implications. In J. Braeckman, J. Verplaetse & J. De Schrijver (Eds.), *The moral brain: Essays on the evolutionary and neuroscientific aspects of morality*, Springer.

Moll, J., de Oliveira-Souza, R., Bramati, I. E., & Grafman, J. (2002). Functional networks in emotional moral and nonmoral social judgments. *Neuroimage*, 16(3, Pt. 1), 696–703.

Moll, J., de Oliveira-Souza, R., & Eslinger, P. J. (2003). Morals and the human brain: A working model. *Neuroreport*, 14(3), 299–305.

Moll, J., de Oliveira-Souza, R., Eslinger, P. J., Bramati, I. E., Mourao-Miranda, J., Andreiuolo, P. A. et al. (2002). The neural correlates of moral sensitivity: A functional magnetic resonance imaging investigation of basic and moral emotions. *Journal of Neuroscience*, 22(7), 2730–2736.

Moll, J., de Oliveira-Souza, R., Moll, F. T., Ignacio, F. A., Bramati, I. E., Caparelli-Daquer, E. M. et al. (2005). The moral affiliations of disgust: A functional MRI study. *Cognitive Behavioral Neurology*, 18(1), 68–78.

Moll, J., Eslinger, P. J., & Oliveira-Souza, R. (2001). Frontopolar and anterior temporal cortex activation in a moral judgment task: Preliminary functional MRI results in normal subjects. *Arquivos de Neuro-Psiquiatria*, 59(3-B), 657–664.

Moll, J., Krueger, F., Zahn, R., Pardini, M., de Oliveira-Souza, R., & Grafman, J. (2006). Human fronto-mesolimbic networks guide decisions about charitable donation. *Proceedings of the National Academy of Sciences USA*, 103(42), 15623–15628.

Moll, J., Oliveira-Souza, R., Zahn, R., & Grafman, J. (2007). The cognitive neuroscience of moral emotions. In W. Sinnott-Armstrong (Ed.), *Moral psychology, Volume 3: Morals and the brain*. Cambridge, MA: MIT Press.

Moll, J., Zahn, R., de Oliveira-Souza, R., Krueger, F., & Grafman, J. (2005). Opinion: The neural basis of human moral cognition. *Nature Reviews Neuroscience*, 6(10), 799–809.

Morgan, D., Grant, K. A., Gage, H. D., Mach, R. H., Kaplan, J. R., Prioleau, O. et al. (2002). Social dominance in monkeys: Dopamine D2 receptors and cocaine self-administration. *Nature Neuroscience*, 5(2), 169–174.

Muehlenbein, M. P., Watts, D. P., & Whitten, P. L. (2004). Dominance rank and fecal testosterone levels in adult male chimpanzees (Pan troglodytes schweinfurthii) at Ngogo, Kibale National Park, Uganda. *American Journal of Primatology*, 64(1), 71–82.

Narvaez, D. (2005). The neo-Kohlbergian tradition and beyond: Schemas, expertise, and character. *Nebraska Symposium on Motivation*, 51, 119–163.

Narvaez, D., & Gleason, T. (2007). The relation of moral judgment development and educational experience to recall of moral narratives and expository texts. *Journal of Genetic Psychology*, 168(3), 251–276.

Nichols, S. (2002). Norms with feeling: Towards a psychological account of moral judgment. *Cognition*, 84(2), 221–236.

Ochsner, K. N., Ray, R. D., Cooper, J. C., Robertson, E. R., Chopra, S., Gabrieli, J. D. E. et al. (2004). For better or for worse: Neural systems supporting the cognitive down- and up-regulation of negative emotion. *Neuroimage*, 23(2), 483–499.

Park, K. (2000). The organic soul. In C. B. Schmitt & Q. Skinner (Eds.), *The Cambridge history of renaissance philosophy* (pp. 464–484). Cambridge: Cambridge University Press.

Prinz, J. (2006). The emotional basis of moral judgments. *Philosophical Explorations*, 9, 29–43.

Raine, A., & Yang, Y. (2006). The neuroanatomical bases of psychopathy: A review of brain imaging findings. In C. J. Patrick (Ed.), *Handbook of psychopathy* (pp. 278–312). New York: Guilford Press.

Rozin, P. (1999). The process of moralization. *Psychological Science*, 10, 218–221.

Rozin, P., & Haidt, J. (1993). Disgust. In M. Lewis & J. M. Haviland (Eds.), *Handbook of emotions*. New York: Guilford.

Rozin, P., Lowery, L., Imada, S., & Haidt, J. (1999). The CAD triad hypothesis: A mapping between three moral emotions (contempt, anger, disgust) and three moral codes (community, autonomy, divinity). *Journal of Personality and Social Psychology*, 76(4), 574–586.

Sanfey, A. G., Rilling, J. K., Aronson, J. A., Nystrom, L. E., & Cohen, J. D. (2003). The neural basis of economic decision-making in the Ultimatum Game. *Science*, 300(5626), 1755–1758.

Saver, J. L., & Damasio, A. R. (1991). Preserved access and processing of social knowledge in a patient with acquired sociopathy due to ventromedial frontal damage. *Neuropsychologia*, 29(12), 1241–1249.

Schaich Borg, J., Hynes, C., Van Horn, J., Grafton, S., & Sinnott-Armstrong, W. (2006). Consequences, action, and intention as factors in moral judgments: An fMRI investigation. *Journal of Cognitive Neuroscience*, 18(5), 803–817.

Schulkin, J. (2000). *Roots of social sensitivity and neural function*. Cambridge: MIT Press.

(2004). *Bodily sensibility: Intelligent action*. New York: Oxford University Press.

Schwartz, S. H. (1992). Universals in the content and structure of values – Theoretical advances and empirical tests in 20 countries. *Advances in Experimental Social Psychology*, 25, 1–65.

Shallice, T., & Burgess, P. (1996). The domain of supervisory processes and temporal organization of behaviour. *Philosophical Transactions of the Royal*

Society of London, Series B: Biological Sciences, 351(1346), 1405–1411; discussion 1411–1402.

Shin, L. M., Dougherty, D. D., Orr, S. P., Pitman, R. K., Lasko, M., Macklin, M. L. et al. (2000). Activation of anterior paralimbic structures during guilt-related script-driven imagery. Biological Psychiatry, 48(1), 43–50.

Singer, T., Kiebel, S. J., Winston, J. S., Dolan, R. J., & Frith, C. D. (2004). Brain responses to the acquired moral status of faces. 41, 653–662.

Singer, W. (2001). Consciousness and the binding problem. Annals of the New York Academy of Sciences, 929, 123–146.

Smith, A. (1759/1966). The theory of moral sentiments (6th ed.). New York: Kelly.

Stone, V. E., Cosmides, L., Tooby, J., Kroll, N., & Knight, R. T. (2002). Selective impairment of reasoning about social exchange in a patient with bilateral limbic system damage. Proceedings of the National Academy of Science USA, 99(17), 11531–11536.

Takahashi, H., Yahata, N., Koeda, M., Matsuda, T., Asai, K., & Okubo, Y. (2004). Brain activation associated with evaluative processes of guilt and embarrassment: An fMRI study. Neuroimage, 23(3), 967–974.

Tangney, J. P., Stuewig, J., & Mashek, D. J. (2007). Moral emotions and moral behavior. Annual Review of Psychology, 58, 345–372.

Thomson, J. (1985). The trolley problem. Yale Law Journal, 94, 1395–1415.

Tranel, D., Bechara, A., & Denburg, N. L. (2002). Asymmetric functional roles of right and left ventromedial prefrontal cortices in social conduct, decision-making, and emotional processing. Cortex, 38(4), 589–612.

Trivers, R. L. (1971). The evolution of reciprocal altruism. The Quarterly Review of Biology, 46, 35–57.

Vogel, G. (2004). Behavioral evolution. The evolution of the golden rule. Science, 303(5661), 1128–1131.

Volavka, J. (1999). The neurobiology of violence: An update. Journal of Neuropsychiatry and Clinical Neuroscience, 11(3), 307–314.

Weissenberger, A. A., Dell, M. L., Liow, K., Theodore, W., Frattali, C. M., Hernandez, D. et al. (2001). Aggression and psychiatric comorbidity in children with hypothalamic hamartomas and their unaffected siblings. Journal of the American Academy of Child and Adolescent Psychiatry, 40(6), 696–703.

Welt, L. (1888). Über Charakterveränderungen des Menschen. Deutsch Arch Klin Med, 42, 339–390.

Wood, J. N., & Grafman, J. (2003). Human prefrontal cortex: Processing and representational perspectives. Nature Reviews Neuroscience, 4(2), 139–147.

Young, L. J., & Wang, Z. (2004). The neurobiology of pair bonding. Nature Neuroscience, 7(10), 1048–1054.

Young, S. N., & Leyton, M. (2002). The role of serotonin in human mood and social interaction. Insight from altered tryptophan levels. Pharmacology, Biochemistry and Behavior, 71(4), 857–865.

Zahn, R., Moll, J., Krueger, F., Huey, E. D., Garrido, G., & Grafman, J. (2007). Social concepts are represented in the superior anterior temporal cortex. Proceedings of the National Academy of Science USA, 104(15), 6430–6435.

Zahn, R., Moll, J., Paiva, M., Garrido, G., Krueger, F., Huey, E. D. et al. (2009). The neural basis of human social values: evidence from functional MRI. *Cerebral Cortex, 19*(2), 276–283.

Zak, P. J., Kurzban, R., & Matzner, W. T. (2004). The neurobiology of trust. *Annals of the New York Academy of Science 1032,* 224–227.

Zeki, S., & Goodenough, O. (2004). Law and the brain: Introduction. *Philosophical Transactions of the Royal Society of London, Series B: Biological Sciences, 359*(1451), 1661–1665.

6

Triune Ethics Theory and Moral Personality

DARCIA NARVAEZ

Triune Ethics Theory (TET; Narvaez, 2008) is a meta-theory that draws together the findings of multiple research programs to propose three foundational ethical motivations. The three ethics – Security, Engagement, and Imagination – formed from evolved strata of the brain, are manifest in the moral lives of individuals and groups. The higher levels of moral functioning, Engagement and Imagination, depend on early nurturing for their optimal development. In this chapter, I describe the theory and its relation to moral personality, including how dispositions can be formed around one of the ethics, and situations can influence which ethic is activated.

Grounding Three Ethics

Triune Ethics Theory (TET) identifies three types of orientations that underlie human morality and that emerged from biological propensities in human evolution. Deriving its name and inspiration from MacLean's (1990) Triune Brain theory, Triune Ethics Theory identifies moral orientations that reflect in some sense MacLean's three evolutionary strata that resulted from "relatively long periods of stability in vertebrate brain evolution" (Panksepp, 1998, p. 43). Each stratum retains an identifiable mark on the brain and human behavior. TET notes their engineering of moral behavior in terms of cognitive and emotional propensities.

Emotion underlies basic functions in the brain. Emotional systems guide the animal in forming adaptive solutions to environmental demands. These systems involve "psychobehavioral potentials that are genetically ingrained in brain development" as "evolutionary operants" (Panksepp, 1998, p. 55). Centrally situated to interact dynamically with higher-order

---

Preparation of this chapter was facilitated by a grant from the Spencer Foundation.

cognitive structures and lower-level physiological and motor outputs, "emotive circuits change sensory, perceptual, and cognitive processing, and initiate a host of physiological changes that are naturally synchronized with the aroused behavioral tendencies characteristic of emotional experience" (Panksepp, 1998, p. 49). Emotional states affect "what is perceived and how it is processed, and the interpretations made of ongoing events subsequently influence emotional reactions and perceptual biases" (Bugental & Goodnow, 1998, p. 416). Cognition and, affect are interwoven, guiding memory formation and retrieval and perceptual vigilance, constraining the amount of attention available for reflective appraisal and response choice.

Many of the emotional component systems in the brain become integrated in early life as a function of bottom-up learning – "states constructed during early social development from more elemental units of visceral-autonomic experiences that accompany certain behavior patterns" (Panksepp, 1998, pp. 44–45). The brain's emotional command systems allow animals to adapt to life's challenges. An individual's unique brain pattern of emotional circuitry results from interaction with caregivers and other environmental supports. Recent animal and human research documents the importance of early experience on gene expression for emotional circuitry (Weaver, Szyf, & Meaney, 2002), personality formation (Schore, 2003a; 2003b), and cognition (Greenspan & Shanker, 2004). Environmental supports, particularly caregiver interaction with the offspring, influences whether genes are turned on or not, whether emotion regulation begins on a healthy path, and whether or not cognitive development is shaped for maximal growth.

Triune Ethics theory postulates that the emotional circuitry established early in life underpins the brain's architecture for morality and ethical behavior, influencing moral personality and potential for moral functioning. The three ethics can be described as "central motives" in the event-feature-emotion complexes that drive moral cognitive phenomena. As motivated cognition, when a particular ethic is active, it is presumed to influence perception, information processing, goal setting, and affordances (Moll, de Oliveira-Souza, Eslinger, Bramati, Mourao-Miranda, Andreiulo et al., 2002; Moll, Zahn, de Oliveira-Souza, Drueger, & Grafman, 2005). An activated ethic influences goal making, thereby shaping interpretation of normative claims. When an individual treats a particular orientation as a normative imperative that trumps other values, the orientation carries ethical significance. For example, the Ethic of Security is focused on self-preservation through safety and such things as personal or ingroup dominance. When the Security Ethic is highly active, the individual will have a difficult time focusing on the needs of others, because this ethic resides in brain and body systems that are self-focused. Actions that prioritize self and ingroup safety over the welfare of other lives will be deemed moral. The Ethic of Engagement is oriented to face-to-face emotional affiliation with others, particularly through caring relationships and social bonds; when it is active, the individual will be focused on the needs of others; compassionate action will seem most moral. Physiologically, the Security Ethic and the Engagement Ethic are based in incompatible systems. The former is related to increased stress hormones (norepinephrine/adrenaline) that tie up organism energy for fight or flight, while the latter is related to calming hormones (e.g., oxytocin) that fuel trust of others. When energized by the emotional systems of the brain, the Imagination Ethic can be linked to either Security (reptilian cleverness) or Engagement (compassion with wisdom). The Ethic of Imagination uses humanity's fullest reasoning capacities to adapt to ongoing social relationships and to address concerns beyond the immediate; it allows the individual to step back from and review instincts and intuitions.

Some basic preliminary information follows regarding underlying assumptions about how moral personality may be influenced by the three motivational systems. See Table 6.1 for a comparative sampling of characteristics across ethics.

TET and Personality

Moral personality finds its beginning with gestation, birth, and early life. Fetuses and babies are known to change growth patterns in different organs and systems based on maternal and environmental stress signals during sensitive developmental periods (Gluckman & Hanson, 2004; Henry & Wang, 1999). Early patterns establish orientations leading to dispositional habits and situational sensitivities for the expression of personality throughout life (Hrdy, 1999). Triune Ethics Theory proposes that these factors also impinge on moral personality.

The Importance of the Environment of Evolutionary Adaptedness (EEA)
Biology matters for moral functioning as individuals and as evolved mammals (see Narvaez & Vaydich, 2008). Human brain and body systems adapted to particular conditions of the Pleistocene era based on environmental supports; those conditions have been termed the "environment of evolutionary adaptedness" (EEA; Bowlby, 1988). Hewlett and Lamb (2005) describe the EEA – the type of early-life supports our biological systems

TABLE 6.1. *Sample characteristics of the three ethics*

	SECURITY (Instinct)	ENGAGEMENT (Intuition)	IMAGINATION (Deliberation & Narrative)
Characteristics	Focus on routine and tradition, territoriality, following precedent, struggle for dominance and status	Seat of emotion, memory for ongoing experience, sense of reality/truth, emotional-self-in-present, more right brain	Logical and imaginative problem solving, foresight, planning, learning, self-in-past, self-in-future, more left brain
Malleability	Closed system; subject to conditioning; Imitation	Initial brain wiring, shapeable intuition	Learned, constructed understanding; can be limited by other ethics
Basic emotions	Fear, rage, seeking, sorrow/panic (dominance)	Care, lust, play, awe	Coordinator of subcortical emotional areas
Learning	Little flexibility	Some flexibility	Great flexibility
Response to stress	Fight or flight	Tend and befriend	Disassociation (emotions and memory disengage)
Basic human needs	Personal autonomy (goal driven), instrumental efficacy	Trust people, belonging, social efficacy	Understanding, purpose self-enhancement
Moral dispositions (typical)	Ingroup loyalty, hierarchy, purity, concrete reciprocity, tradition, rules, rituals, symbols	Love and fellow feeling, justice, reciprocity, shame, responsiveness	Cognitive empathy, abstract reciprocity, reasoning, creative response
Morality	Self-protective (afferent), self-assertive (efferent), self-concerned interpersonal relations	Inclusive of immediate other, ingroup membership tied to emotional meaning	Inclusive of nonimmediate other, human heartedness when linked with Engagement Ethic
Dispositions that can harm self and others	Deception, control of others, aggression, mob – superorganism, goal seeking can be ruthless	Addictive dependency	Bandura's detachment (no connection), delusions (imagination with no logic), hyperrationality (logic and no imagination)
Power	Can shut down other brain areas, follows precedent	Compassion, empathy	Subvert instinct, overcome poor intuitions, alter emotions with cognitive framing, free "won't"

expect – summarizing the type of childcare in hunter-gatherer communities noted across anthropological studies (foraging community life is presumed to closely resemble human living during the Pleistocene). Not only does breastfeeding take place for 3–5 years, but:

> young children in foraging cultures are nursed frequently; held, touched, or kept near others almost constantly; frequently cared for by individuals other than their mothers (fathers and grandmothers, in particular) though seldom by older siblings; experience prompt responses to their fusses and cries; and enjoy multiage play groups in early childhood. (p. 15)

Adapted to particular conditions of the past, human brain and body systems are not adapted to the recent social practices of hospital births, infant formula, solo sleeping, or physical isolation. Does it make any difference? Aren't humans adaptive and resilient? Yes, and yes, within limits. Evidence is accumulating about the negative effects of the missing EEA. To take one of these features, touch, we know from animal studies that a dearth of touch in the early years is related to an underdevelopment of serotonin receptors (Kalin, 1999). Caregiving in the United States typically isolates infants from close human contact for long periods of time, and offers limited responsiveness and breastfeeding (Centers for Disease Control, 2004; Narvaez, 2008; Narvaez & Panksepp, 2009). It is likely that these practices influence serotonin receptor development. In fact, infants with faulty serotonin receptors are more likely to die of sudden infant death syndrome (Audero, Coppi, Mlinar, Rossetti, Caprioli, Al Banchaabouchi, Corradetti, & Gross, 2008; Paterson, Trachtenberg, Thompson, Belliveau, Beggs, Darnall, Chadwick, Krous, & Kinney, 2006). We also know that adults with faulty serotonin receptors are more likely to become depressed (Caspi, Sugden, Moffitt, Taylor, Craig, Harrington, McClay, Mill, Martin, Braithwaite, & Poulton, 2003) or anxious (Lesch, Bengel, Heils, Sabol, Greenberg, Petri, Clemens, Müller, Hamer, & Murphy, 1996), states that influence general as well as moral functioning. The United States has epidemics of anxiety and depression in real numbers (USDHHS, 1999). Because of the dearth of touch, Prescott (1996) came to the conclusion that most children in the U.S. are susceptible to somatosensory affectional deprivation (SAD), a condition related to depression, violent behavior, and stimulus seeking. Effects of childrearing on moral functioning are discussed further below and elsewhere (Narvaez, 2008; Narvaez & Vaydich, 2008).

Anthropological studies demonstrate that moral functioning is influenced by childrearing practices. Societies that stay in physical contact with their infants and children in the manner of the EEA are more likely to be peaceful societies (Prescott, 1996). Such experiences led to a cohesive social group that lived mostly in peaceful cooperation (Fry, 2006). One could postulate that the range of personality differences are much greater in "civilized" nations (toward the pathological and antisocial), as a result of modern childrearing practices, than they would be under the EEA (which would give psychologists much less to do).

Dispositional Effects
TET generates two hypotheses regarding moral personality. First, taking a dispositional view, a personality may cohere around being more or less oriented to each of the three ethics. A similar idea was proposed by Tomkins (Demos, 1995) who suggested that early socialization sets up life orientations ("ideo-affective postures") that the individual subsequently applies to many domains throughout life. The ideo-affective posture developed from early experience represents a socialized "set of loosely organized feelings and ideas about feelings" (Tomkins, 1965, p. 74) that resonate with particular organized ideologies, drawing individuals to particular viewpoints: a warm, supportive childhood leads a person to orient to an open, accepting posture ("humanistic") whereas a harsh, restrictive childhood leads to a defended, rejecting posture ("normative") toward people and toward life experiences in general. Similarly, TET proposes that during critical periods of brain and personality development (e.g., neonatal), "attachment" (Bowlby) and "trust" (Erikson) aspects of personality development are deeply influenced, affecting the structure and wiring of brain systems. The development of these systems is reflected in capabilities for moral functioning and is related to personality functions. For example, stressed early experience can lead to an enhanced orientation to self, and a depressed empathic response to others (Henry & Wang, 1998). (See Table 6.2 for possible developmental trends.) Situations can also influence which ethic is activated.

Situational Effects
Second, according to a social-cognitive view of moral personality (Cervone, 1999; Mischel, 1973), moral personality has a dispositional signature within particular situations: person and situation interact with dispositional regularity. TET suggests that individuals are morally driven, desiring the good as it is perceived in the moment. Thus, one's moral perspective may shift from one ethic to another, depending on the press of the situation and what that situation evokes in the moment. The individual may also experience the activation of conflicting ethics – shifting between Security (self-concern)

TABLE 6.2. *Possible crystallized ethical personality types*[1,2,3]

Initial Propensities Enhanced or Diminished by Caregivers
Drives for ATTACHMENT, SEEKING, PLAY, WONDER

Developmental Trajectory in Stress Conditions	Developmental Trajectory in Care Conditions
Emotions/Drives emphasized: FEAR, ANGER, PANIC/SORROW, outward SEEKING *Emotions/Drives suppressed*: LOVE (LUST/CARE /ATTACHMENT), PLAY, inward SEEKING	*Emotions/Drives emphasized*: LOVE (LUST/CARE /ATTACHMENT), PLAY, inward SEEKING *Emotions/Drives minimized*: FEAR, ANGER, PANIC/SORROW, outward SEEKING
Solo Security Orientation to feeling safe either with a constant defensive manner and through seeking high status or by following a set of rules or traditions. Sensitized to threat cues, the character will fight or flee (physically or psychologically) when threatened.	**Interpersonal Engagement** Embeddededness in intersubjectively safe and close nurturing relationships that provide engaged enactive participation in social life, rooted in sensorimotor sensibilities for justice from extensive experiences of non-verbal, then verbal, reciprocity and social exchange.
Ingroup Security Orientation to feeling safe either with a constant defensive manner or through following a set of prescriptions or rules or traditions. Sensitized to threat cues, the character will fight or flee (physically or psychologically) when threatened. The character is also oriented to feeling safe through having *others* following a set of prescriptions or rules or traditions. High status/power is sought. When threatened, the mind can be infected with mob mentality for aggression. Aggression is justified through perceived moral tit-for-tat.	**Ingroup Engagement** Orientation to maintaining harmony with familiar others through empathy and concern. The reaction to threat is to tend and befriend. The character may forget self in the moment and respond with compassion, playfulness, or wisdom, transcending immediate needs.

Imagination

Imagination for Self Building on previous levels, the person is oriented to developing multiple ways to maintain group power and security (narcissism; disorganized attachment). Aberrant imagination, detached from reality.	**Imagination for Engagement** Building on previous engagement capacities, the person is also oriented to helping familiar and unfamiliar others (including other societies and future generations) meet their needs to flourish in just and merciful ways.

[1] Documented emotional drives are in CAPS (see Panksepp, 1998).
[2] With maximal secure attachment, the child moves through the Security Ethics without crystallizing there. With therapy, adults can move beyond early crystallized security stances.
[3] Ethics may be shallow or deep.

and Engagement (concern for the other), for example, much like a Necker cube. Reflective capacities can override initial high emotion and guide selection among alternatives, but individuals may also select environments that match their dispositional moral orientations. Within the discussion of each ethic below, the two alternative theoretical stances toward personality are also discussed.

THREE ETHICAL ORIENTATIONS

The Ethic of Security

The Security Ethic represents the most primitive moral sense that humans display. It is rooted in the oldest parts of the brain, involving the R-complex (MacLean, 1990) or the extrapyramidal action nervous system (Panksepp, 1998). The R-complex in mammals drives territoriality, struggles for power, imitation, deception, and maintenance of routine and following precedent (MacLean, 1990). Emotion systems related to fear, rage, and seeking (exploring) reside here. For example, when safety is threatened, the parasympathetic system can trigger a fight-or-flight response (rage system); or the sympathetic system can induce freezing (fear system) to reduce pain and decrease the likelihood of bodily destruction.

The Ethic of Security is based primarily in these instincts, which revolve around safety, survival, and thriving in context, instincts shared with all animals and present from birth. Self-protective behaviors and values guard the life of the individual and the ingroup. Protecting the ingroup from outsiders is instinctual, based on the natural fear of strangers common to all animals. In safe environments, the R-complex remains calm, but when the R-complex feels threatened in humans, it can trigger tribalism, rivalry, and mob behavior – instinctive behaviors that subvert cortical activity and that are difficult to shut down (MacLean, 1990).

When humans use the R-complex to determine moral behavior (taking an action consciously or unconsciously to secure self or ingroup), it becomes a Security *Ethic*. When dominant, the Security Ethic focuses on securing survival through such things as ingroup purity (Altemeyer, 2006) or ingroup maintenance of hierarchy (Nisbett & Cohen, 1996), shown in terror management theory research (Rosenblatt, Greenberg, Solomon, Pyszczynski, & Lyon, 1989). When not tempered by other ethics, the Security Ethic is prone to ruthlessness and attaining a security goal at any cost, decreasing sensitivity to other, even moral, goals. When people are fearful for their own safety, they are less responsive to helping others (Mikulincer, Shaver, Gillath, & Nitzberg, 2005) and less able to reason carefully, because body energy (hormones, blood flow) is mobilized for safety (fight or flight). When threat is salient, individuals are more attracted to strongmen and tough policies on outsiders (Jost, Glaser, Kruglanski, & Sulloway, 2003), as happened in the United States after 9/11/2001 (Pyszczynski, Solomon, Greenberg, Maxfield, & Cohen, 2004) – any questioning of a strong military response or delving into alternative causes for the 9/11 attack was condemned as unpatriotic (traitorous). Such single-mindedness can lead not only to decreased sensitivity toward those who get in the way of efforts to stay safe or dominant, but also to an inability to change course, reflecting Simone Weil's view, "Evil when we are in its power is not felt as evil but as a necessity, or even a duty" (1947/1952). At the same time, what is considered evil by outsiders may be considered virtues or highly-prized principles by insiders (Skitka's "moral mandates"; Skitka & Morgan, this volume) – such as allegiant ingroup loyalty (me vs. not-me, not the loyalty of love), obedience, and self-control of soft emotion. There is nobleness in submitting to an authority figure and "completing the mission," or accomplishing a goal considered valuable by the tradition (e.g., military service). The Security Ethic responds to the safety or dominance wishes of self and ingroup members (real or imaginary), while shutting out the needs of anyone or anything else.

Extensive early childhood distress is likely to build a foundational sense of insecurity in face of uncertainty (what is different or unfamiliar) and promote a distrustful, less empathic view of the world, outcomes documented in attachment disorders (Eisler & Levine, 2002; Mikulincer & Shaver, 2005). A "stressed brain" formation due to neglect or trauma (Newman, Holden, & Delville, 2005), or to a shut down of the right brain from inadequate emotional nurturance (Schore, 2003b), are postulated to lead to a personality dominated by the default systems underlying the Ethic of Security. The dominance of the default systems is most easily seen in neglected and damaged children who react to others (and to change) with mistrust, aggression, and violence (Karr-Morse & Wiley, 1997); to behave prosocially may require extra effortful control, which quickly uses up energy resources and becomes overly difficult (Galliot, 2008).

The Security Ethic is part of lower evolution, driven by goodness of fit and self-interest (Loye, 2002), and has been important for individual and group survival. It can be described as a more primitive moral expression emphasizing actions that appear to promote a key goal of organisms – survival. Its motives are perceived as moral imperatives. Because the systems in which the Security Ethic is based are largely hardwired, they are not easily damaged, making this ethic the default when the development of the other ethics goes awry.

The Ethic of Engagement

The Ethic of Engagement represents the heart of morality. The second wave of brain evolution brought about a central component of mammalian brains, the limbic system and related structures (MacLean, 1990), also known as the visceral-emotional nervous system on the hypothalamic-limbic axis (Panksepp, 1998). These formations make mammals "smarter," allowing for emotional signaling both externally (sociality) and internally (learning; Konner, 2002); they are critical to emotion, identity, memory for ongoing experience, and an individual's sense of reality and truth (Burton, 2008; MacLean, 1990). Darwin identified these as the source for human's "moral sense" (see *Descent of Man*, 1871/1981; or his private notebooks, Gruber, 1974).

The functionality of mammalian emotional systems is dependent on caregiving. Coconstructed during an extended childhood (Eisenberg, 1995), the infant's nervous system is dependent on caregivers as "external psychobiological" regulators (Schore, 2001, p. 202). Gradually, external regulation is transformed into internal regulation as the brain matures in response to the interaction with the environment (ibid). Mammalian brains achieve stability by means of attachment relationships throughout life with social processes such as "*limbic resonance* – a symphony of mutual exchange and internal adaptation whereby two mammals become attuned to each other's inner states" (Lewis, Amini, & Lannon, 2000, p. 63). Human brains are reward-seeking structures that have evolved to obtain rewards primarily from social relationships (Nelson & Panksepp, 1998). Without this ongoing *limbic regulation*, mammals, especially young ones, slip toward "physiologic chaos" (Hofer, 1987; Lewis et al., p. 86).

The Engagement Ethic is rooted in the neurobiological systems underlying mammalian parental care and social bonding. These systems depend on multiple limbic and subcortical structures and multiple types of neurotransmitters that underlie values of compassion, social harmony, and togetherness ("moral sentiments"; Moll et al, this volume. The Engagement Ethic is similar to the "extended attachment" that Moll et al. describe). Fundamental to the Engagement Ethic are early and continuous experiences of attachment. As mentioned previously, the *environment of evolutionary adaptedness* (Bowlby, 1988) offers mammalian brains in the first few years of life nearly constant touch, frequent breastfeeding, immediate responsiveness to cries, and multiple (familiar) alloparents (Hewlett & Lamb, 2005). Proper care during development is required for normal formation of brain circuitries necessary for optimal cultural membership and moral functioning (Greenspan & Shanker 1999; Panksepp 1998; Schore, 2003a). With adequate care, the Engagement Ethic develops fully and leads to values of compassion, tolerance, and openness to others (Eisler & Levine, 2002). Indeed, caring moral exemplars are higher on agreeableness (Matsuba & Walker, 2004) the personal trait that captures these elements.

Inadequate care leads to deficiencies in brain structures, hormonal regulation, and system integration resulting in brain-behavioral disorders that are related to greater hostility and aggression toward others (Kruesi, Hibbs, Zahn, Keysor, Hamburger, Bartko, & Rapoport, 1992; Pollak & Perry, 2005), and greater depression and anxiety (Schore, 2003a; 2003b). When a brain is wired for self-concern, it is difficult to be prosocial, perhaps due in part to the effortful control required, which quickly uses up glycogen resources (Galliot, 2008).

Warm responsive parenting in early life is related to greater conscience and empathy (Thompson, this volume; Eisenberg, Fabes, & Spinrad, 2006). Indeed, World War II rescuers of Jews typically report positive home environments (Oliner, 2002; Oliner & Oliner, 1988). Walker and Frimer (this volume) found that, in comparison to brave exemplars, caring exemplars reported more positive childhood experiences that included secure attachment and involved mentors (indicating early life advantage, according to McAdams, this volume).

The Ethic of Imagination

The Ethic of Imagination represents the mind of morality, with its fullest expression in the human species. Although for moral exemplarity an Engagement Ethic orientation is fundamental (Colby & Damon, 1992), the fullest capacities for moral functioning unite the Ethic of Engagement with the Ethic of Imagination.

The third brain strata to evolve involves the neocortex and related thamalic structures (MacLean, 1990), a somatic-cognitive nervous system on the thalamic-neocortical axis (Panksepp, 1998). Focused primarily on the external world, it provides the capacity for problem solving and deliberative learning. Although incapable of generating emotions themselves, "the frontal lobes have emerged as the highest center for the emotions" (Konner, 2002, p. 135). These structures operate in coordination with the more primitive emotional systems in the older parts of the brain. That is, the mind "thinks *with* feelings" (Konner, 2002, p. 139), and when it does not, poor judgment and decision-making result (Damasio, 1999).

The Ethic of Imagination is represented primarily in these most recently evolved parts of the brain, particularly the prefrontal cortex (PFC). Connected with every distinct unit in the brain, the prefrontal cortex integrates information from the outside world with information internal to the organism itself (Goldberg, 2002). The PFC allows an adult to impede the perhaps impetuous emotional responses of the older parts of the brain and consider alternatives based on wider perspective taking. Triune Ethics Theory suggests that the real work of moral judgment and decision making has to do with the coordination of instincts, intuitions, reasoning and goals by the deliberative mind – the work of the Imagination Ethic.

Deliberative reasoning, one capacity of the Imagination Ethic, relies on explicit memory and develops slowly through experience and training, as Piaget and Kohlberg noted (Inhelder & Piaget, 1958; Kohlberg, 1984), and as empirically verified by recent neuroscience (Luna, Thulborn, Munoz, Merriam, Garver, Minshew et al., 2001). Because most learning takes place implicitly and without awareness, most knowledge is tacit and unavailable to consciousness (Keil & Wilson, 1999; Reber, 1985). A distinction has been made between the deliberative, conscious mind and the implicit mind or "adaptive unconscious" (Hassin, Uleman, & Bargh, 2005; Wilson, 2004). Deliberation complements the intuitive and instinctive aspects of the mind, which are now presumed to dominate human functioning (Bargh & Chartrand, 1999).The deliberative tools of the Imagination Ethic respond to, and coordinate, the intuitions and instincts of the Engagement Ethic and the Security Ethic, which operate according to conditioned and implicitly extracted moral "principles."

The Imagination Ethic uses at least two powerful tools. One is "free won't," the ability to countermand instincts and intuitions (Cotterill, 1999), an ability that allows humans to choose which stimuli are allowed to trigger emotional arousal or action sequences (Panksepp, 1998). The Imagination Ethic is rooted in typically left-brain activities of linear thinking, past and future orientation, and other aspects critical to an individual sense of self (Taylor, 2008). The conscious, deliberative mind allows the individual to consider choices and select activities and environments that foster particular intuitions in the subconscious part of the brain (Hogarth, 2001). When this is done for value purposes, it reflects the Imagination Ethic in action.

A second tool of the Imagination Ethic is the ability to frame behavior, to explain the past and imagine the future (Gazzaniga, 1985; Taylor, 2008), which contribute to building a life narrative and motivating the self (a focus of several chapters in this volume). Cultural narratives are often adopted and translated into personal narratives, propelling behavior. Narratives may promote peace or conflict, prosocial or antisocial views and enlist the resources of an individual to take up particular goals and actions. For example, Eidelson and Eidelson (2003) extracted five beliefs that promote group conflict, operating at the individual or group level: vulnerability, distrust, helplessness, injustice, and superiority – all of which provoke the Security Ethic. In contrast, redemptive narratives (McAdams, this volume) and gratitude framing (Emmons, this volume) are instances of ethical framing that promote the Engagement Ethic. Religious communities constantly discuss, model, and imitate moral exemplarity, bringing about a greater likelihood for chronic accessibility of particular constructs in their members, especially if alternatives are not presented. But the moral constructs emphasized by religious communities vary. For example, the Amish chronically activate compassion (Engagement) whereas Israeli and Palestinian extremists chronically activate a sense of injustice and threat (Security).

Like the brain areas related to the Engagement Ethic, brain areas related to the Ethic of Imagination require a nurturing environment to develop properly. Schore (2003a; 2003b) marshals a great deal of evidence to show how the development of the orbitofrontal cortex (OFC), critical for lifelong emotion regulation, is dependent on early coregulation by the caregiver in the first months of life. Poor care may permanently damage the OFC, predisposing the individual to psychiatric disorders, such as anxiety or depression, and suboptimal functioning throughout life. Taking decades to fully develop (Giedd, Blumenthal, & Jeffries 1999; Luna, Thulborn, Munoz, Merriam, Garver, Minshew et al., 2001), the prefrontal cortex and its specialized units can be damaged from environmental neglect or abuse, both early (Anderson, Bechara, Damasio, Tranel, & Damasio, 1999; Kodituwakku, Kalberg, & May, 2001) and late in development (Newman, Holden, & Delville, 2005). The prefrontal cortex is susceptible to damage in adolescence and early adulthood through physiologically addictive activities, such as binge drinking (Bechara, 2005) and violent video game play (Mathews, Kronenberger, Wang, Lurito, Lowe, & Dunn, 2005).

The work of the Imagination Ethic, which must be cultivated through deliberative study, offers the means for greater awareness outside the self. The Imagination Ethic enables a sense of community that extends beyond immediate relations, valuing universality and outsiders, and conceptualizing alternative sophisticated resolutions of moral problems. Although more detached from the basic emotional drives of the other ethics, the Imagination Ethic can be implicitly motivated by one of the other ethics. The open-heartedness of the Engagement Ethic fuels an imagination of helpfulness and altruism, while the closed rigidity of the Security Ethic fosters an imagination toward defense and perhaps offense. When the Engagement Ethic and the Imagination Ethic have been poorly nurtured by the caregiver and community, or there is significant trauma, the Security Ethic becomes the default system. To reiterate, humans are at their most moral, following Darwin's moral evolution, when the Ethic of Engagement (compassionate regard) is linked with the Ethic of Imagination (extended engagement).

IMPLICATIONS FOR MORAL PERSONALITY THEORY

Triune Ethics Theory emphasizes the importance of attending to the fundamental nature of organisms, mammals, and humans when considering moral functioning. Two aspects addressed here are that organisms are by nature goal driven, whether it be in seeking sustenance or stimulation, and the goals of the moment are considered good by the organism. Mammals are more keenly guided by emotions, and humans have the additional capacity for reasoned reflection. Because of the way human brains have evolved encompassing diverse systems, a person can have multiple, sometimes competing, goals.

Morality of the Moment

The view presented here is that all humans believe themselves to be moral agents in the moment, as they aim for what appears good in the moment – even the criminal attempts to "right wrongs" or restore justice to his or her world, even if it is through the processes of moral disengagement (Bandura, 1999). It is against commonsense and nature for creatures to aim for what they think is bad in the moment. "Good" is what the organism believes will meet the current drive or aim. Goals are not always conscious motives. Humans are made up of multiple competing biological systems with their own goals, or good ends (e.g., goals for energy, rest, being safe, affiliation, transcendence, etc.). At any given moment, it is likely that a person has more than one goal of interest, whose priority may shift with changing appraisals of the situation. Bandura (1999) has shown how one's goals and interests can lead to moral disengagement, a process that involves typically, in TET terminology, shutting down the Engagement Ethic and focusing on Security Ethic goals, all for what seems "right" in the moment.

The individual's internal aims and drives interact with the situation in various ways. Organisms respond to environmental press (social and nonsocial) by shifting goals or subgoals. Affective expectancies (e.g., fear, love) influence perceptual sensitivities (Wilson, Lisle, Kraft, & Wetzel, 1989). Perceived affordances (social, physical, and action possibilities) are influenced by prior experience and expertise (Neisser, 1976), as well by current goals (Gibson, 1979). Based on experiences and goals, one is attracted to rhetoric that supports those goals, regardless of accuracy (Burton, 2008). The situation also affects behavioral outcome expectancies and preferred subgoals (Mischel's "subjectively valuable outcomes," 1973, p. 270). For example, when a person is threatened, he is more attuned to threat cues. The affordances noticed centralize around self-advantageous and ingroup-advantageous actions; "shoot to kill" sounds like a more reasonable command, and goals of control may be more attractive – all of which contribute to using a Security Ethic. Situations provide a "press" toward one ethic or another – the "power of the situation," as reflected in behavior of most inmates in Nazi concentration camps (Levi, 1958) or the guards at Abu Ghraib Prison (Zimbardo, 2007). Laboratory studies show that Security goals or Engagement goals can be primed, influencing both subsequent helping behavior and attitudes toward, and treatment of, outgroup members (terror management studies; Hart, Shaver, Goldenberg, 2005; Mikulincer & Shaver, 2001).

Goal focus is a shifting, situational aspect of moral functioning. But as seen in moral exemplar research, some people have chronic moral goals as well.

Dispositional Multiplicity of Moral Personality

Several theorists are questioning the psychological feasibility of a singular notion of identity (Cervone & Tripathi, this volume; Markus & Nurius, 1986; Wong, this volume). TET agrees that the individual potentially has multiple identities and multiple moral identities. The three ethical motivations may conflict: for example, a person may struggle against feeling threatened while trying to maintain a sense of compassion. The individual may feel a sense of "moral ambivalence" because of underlying "moral value pluralism" (Wong, 2006). For instance, as a person is victimized, does one stand by like everyone else in order to avoid looking foolish, or does one put self-concern aside and operate from compassion and intervene? Small and large choices like these are daily affairs; the different ethics offer strikingly different courses of action. An individual's moral identity can shift with how the individual apprehends the demands of the context and their capacity to meet them.

Because each ethic is available to some degree in each person (although damaged or deficient brains may offer fewer resources for engagement or imagination), the self is not necessarily consistent in its moral orientation. There are several examples of shifting moral identities in this volume. For example, Aquino points out how a person's competing identities or working self-concepts (Markus & Kunda, 1986) are evoked by situational affordances. Aquino and colleagues find that different moral identities are activated through financial rewards, role models, and situational norms. Monin and Jordan (this volume) reveal how individuals keep moral balance sheets, which allow for self-sanctioned indiscretion after paying one's moral dues with effortful moral behavior. A person may flip between ethical stances, as did the Nazi, Joseph *Goebbeis,* who showed moments of compassion toward Jews, which he later offset with greater cruelty (Arpaly, 2003). Aquino and Freeman points out the flexibility in defining morality, which leads to an easy moral disengagement so that a person can take a desired immoral action (Bandura et al., 1996).

More mature personalities may be more consistent (i.e., Loevinger, 1972). Some individuals may not be overpowered by a situation (Frankl, 1963), displaying an idiosyncratic person-by-context personality signature. Chronic personality orientations probably shift less between ethics, or have primary controls to keep from shifting into an unfamiliar direction. For example, although aggression cues promote hostile thoughts and actions in most people, individuals high in agreeableness may activate prosocial responses instead (Meier, Robinson, & Wilkowski, 2006). Expertise in self-forgetting and compassionate response may prevent Security Ethic activation (e.g., among Buddhist monks).

Dispositional moral orientations rely on sensitive periods of development. In the first few years of life, the ground is laid for engagement and imagination. But there appear to be other sensitive periods, such as early adolescence (for engagement) and emerging adulthood (especially for imagination; Narvaez, Getz, Rest, & Thoma, 1999).

CONCLUSION

The primary contribution of Triune Ethics Theory is to point out the importance of initial conditions for human development and how these may influence brain structures and circuitry, affecting moral functioning in sometimes subtle ways. In order to act with situation-appropriate compassion and imagination – the heart and mind of morality – individuals must have capabilities for self-regulation (e.g., self-soothing) and connecting to others (e.g., social limbic resonance), based on well-developed limbic and cortical structures established in early life, or in subsequent sensitive periods of development (which could include psychotherapy).

Ethical capacities rely on longstanding childrearing and social practices that are often missing in modern societies. Even if neglect is less than profound, its effects on the formation of systems that promote the Engagement Ethic can be long lasting. A child who spends a great deal of time alone in his or her room develops a different social orientation and embodied understanding of the social world than a child who co-sleeps with parents and siblings and is never isolated. As Lewis et al. (2000) point out:

> A child enveloped in a particular style of relatedness learns its special intricacies and particular rhythms, as he distills a string of instances into the simpler tenets they exemplify. As he does so, he arrives at *an intuitive knowledge of love that forever evades consciousness.* (p. 116, emphasis added)

TET also leads one to conclude that the approaches typically taken toward moral education – advocacy by adults for particular behaviors, or reasoned reflection about one's ideals, and shaping one's behavior accordingly from the top down – are upside down. Instead, moral selves emerge from lived experience that is largely stored in nonconscious neurological and endocrine systems (Damasio, 1999). Immersion in good relationships and communities fosters the intuitions upon which rationality is built (Greenspan & Shanker, 2004). Then, after immersion in a complex social world, explicit discussion and guidance about good behavior makes sense as skills are honed toward expertise (Narvaez, 2006).

In the EEA of the Pleistocene era, humans lived in small, tight-knit groups. There, a *good* life and a life that survived/reproduced/thrived were the same thing. Contrarily, in the "civilized" world, individuals are able to survive physically even though they are socially or morally deformed and live "bad" lives (lives of disorganized emotion, cognition, and behavior that cause harm to themselves and others). Starting life without the rich soil provided by mutually responsive caregivers leaves a child with shallow roots in sociomoral functioning, tenuous self-regulation, and a self-oriented neurobiology. Children with these characteristics are less compliant with adults and rules (Kochanksa, Aksan, Prisco, & Adams, 2008), more dangerous to themselves and their communities (Karr-Morse & Wiley, 1997), and must spend a greater amount of more limited energy to self-regulate for life success. It is time to pay attention to the types of biologically supportive environments that promote optimal moral formation and alleviate the maternal and familial stressors that promote stunted moral growth.

REFERENCES

Altemeyer, R. (2006). *The authoritarians*. Lulu.com: Robert Altemeyer.
Anderson, S. W., Bechara, A., Damasio, H., Tranel, D., & Damasio, A. R. (1999). Impairment of social and moral behavior related to early damage in human prefrontal cortex, *Nature Neuroscience*, 2, 1032–1037.
Aquino, K., & Freeman, D. (this volume). Moral identity in business situations: A social-cognitive framework for understanding moral functioning. In D. Narvaez & D. K. Lapsley (Eds.), *Personality, identity, and character explorations in moral psychology* (pp. 375–395). New York: Cambridge University Press.
Arpaly, N. (2003). *Unprincipled virtue: An inquiry into moral agency*. New York: Oxford University Press.
Audero, E., Coppi, E., Mlinar, B., Rossetti, T., Caprioli, A., Al Banchaabouchi, M., Corradetti, R., & Gross, C. (2008). Sporadic autonomic dysregulation and death associated with excessive serotonin autoinhibition. *Science*, 321, 130–133.
Bandura, A. (1999). Moral disengagement in the perpetration of inhumanities. *Personality and Social Psychology Review*, 3(3), 269–275.
Bargh, J. A. (1989). Conditional automaticity: Varieties of automatic influence in social perception and cognition. In J. S. Uleman & J. A. Bargh (Eds.), *Unintended thought* (pp. 3–51). New York: Guilford.
Bauerlein, M. (2008). *The dumbest generation: How the digital age stupefies young Americans and jeopardizes our future*. New York: Tarcher/Penguin.
Bechara, A. (2005). Decision making, impulse control and loss of willpower to resist drugs: A neurocognitive perspective. *Nature Neuroscience* 8, 1458–1463.
Bowlby, J. (1973). *Attachment and loss*. New York: Basic Books.
  (1988) *A secure base: Parent-child attachment and healthy human development*. New York: Basic Books.
Bugental, D. B., & Goodnow, J. J. (1998). *Socialization processes*. In W. Damon (Series Ed.) &. N. Eisenberg (Vol. Ed.), *Handbook of child psychology, 5th. ed.* (pp. 389–462). New York: John Wiley & Sons.
Burton, R. A. (2008). *On being certain: Believing you are right even when you are not*. New York: St. Martin's Press.
Caspi, A., Sugden, K., Moffitt, T. E., Taylor, A., Craig, I. W., Harrington, W., McClay, J., Mill, J., Martin, J., Braithwaite, A., & Poulton, R. (2003). Influence of life stress on depression: Moderation by a polymorphism in the 5-HTT gene. *Science*, 301, 386–89.
Centers for Disease Control. (2004). *National Immunization Survey*. Atlanta, GA: CDC.
Cervone, D. (1999). Bottom-up explanation in personality psychology: The case of cross-situational coherence. In D. Cervone & Y. Shoda (Eds.), *The coherence of personality: Social-cognitive bases of personality consistency, variability, and organization* (pp. 303–341). New York: Guilford Press.

Cervone, D., & Tripathi, R. (this volume). The moral functioning of the person as a whole: On moral psychology and personality science. In D. Narvaez & D. K. Lapsley (Eds.), *Personality, identity, and character explorations in moral psychology* (pp. 30–51). New York: Cambridge University Press.

Champagne, F. A., & Meaney, M. J. (2006). Stress during gestation alters maternal care and the development of offspring in a rodent model. *Biological Psychology*, 59, 1227–1235.

Cotterill, R. (1998). *Enchanted looms*. Cambridge: Cambridge University Press.

Damasio, A. (1994). *Descartes' error*. New York: Avon Books.

   (1999). *The feeling of what happens*. London: Heineman.

Darley, J., & Batson, C. D. (1973). From Jerusalem to Jericho: A study of situational and dispositional variables in helping behavior. *Journal of Personality and Social Psychology*, 27, 100–108.

Dentan, R. K. (1968). *The Semai: A nonviolent people of Malaya*. New York: Harcourt Brace College Publishers.

Demos, E. V. (1995). *Exploring affect: The selected writings of Silvan S. Tomkins*. Cambridge: Cambridge University Press.

Eidelson, R. J., & Eidelson, J. I. (2003). Dangerous ideas: Five beliefs that propel groups toward conflict. *American Psychologist*, 58, 182–192

Eisenberg L. (1995). The social construction of the human brain. *American Journal of Psychiatry*, 152, 1563–1575.

Eisenberg, N., Fabes, R. A., & Spinrad, T. L. (2006). Prosocial development. In W. Damon (Series Ed.) &. N. Eisenberg (Vol. Ed.), *Handbook of child psychology*, 6th. ed. (pp. 646–718). New York: John Wiley & Sons.

Eisler, R. & Levine, D. S. (2002). Nurture, nature, and caring: We are not prisoners of our genes. *Brain and Mind*, 3, 9–52.

Frankl, Viktor E. (1963). *Man's search for meaning*. New York: Simon & Schuster.

Franklin, K. M., Janoff-Bulman, R., & Roberts, J. E. (1990). Long-term impact of parental divorce on optimism and trust: Changes in general assumptions or narrow beliefs. *Journal of Personality and Social Psychology*, 59, 743–755.

Fry, D. P. (2006). *The human potential for peace: An anthropological challenge to assumptions about war and violence*. New York: Oxford University Press.

Galliot, M. T. (2008). Unlocking the energy dynamics of executive functioning: Linking executive functioning to brain glycogen. *Perspectives on Psychological Science*, 3(4), 245–263.

Gazzaniga, M. S. (1995). Consciousness and the cerebral hemispheres. In M. S. Gazzaniga (Ed.), *The cognitive neurosciences* (pp. 1391–1399). Cambridge, MA: MIT Press.

Gibson, J. (1979). *The ecological approach to perception*. Hillsdale, NJ: Lawrence Erlbaum Associates.

Giedd, J. N., Blumenthal, J., Jeffries, N. O. et al. (1999). Brain development during childhood and adolescence: A longitudinal MRI study. *Nature Neuroscience*, 2(10), 861–3.

Gluckman, P., & Hanson, M. (2004). *The fetal matrix: Evolution, development and disease*. New York: Cambridge University Press.

Goldberg, E. (2002). *The Executive brain: Frontal lobes and the civilized brain*. New York: Oxford University Press.

Greenspan, S. I., & Shanker, S. I. (2004). *The first idea.* Cambridge, MA: Da Capo Press.

Gruber, H. (1974). *Darwin on man: A psychological study of scientific creativity.* Chicago: University of Chicago Press.

Hart, J., Shaver, P. R., & Goldenberg, J. L. (2005). Attachment, self-esteem, worldviews, and terror management: Evidence for a tripartite security system. *Journal of Personality and Social Psychology, 88* (6), 999–1013.

Hassin, R. R., Uleman, J. S., & Bargh, J. A. (Eds.) (2005). *The new unconscious.* New York: Oxford University Press.

Henry, J. P., & Wang, S. (1998). Effects of early stress on adult affiliative behavior, *Psychoneuroendocrinology 23*(8), 863–875.

Hewlett, B. S., & Lamb, M. E. (2005). *Hunter-gatherer childhoods: Evolutionary, developmental and cultural perspectives.* New Brunswick, NJ: Aldine.

Hofer, M. A. (1994). Hidden regulators in attachment, separation, and loss. In N. A. Fox (Ed.), Emotion regulation: Behavioral and biological considerations. *Monographs of the Society for Research in Child Development, 59,* 192–207.

—— (1987). Early social relationships as regulators of infant physiology and behavior. *Child Development, 58*(3), 633–647.

Hogarth, R. M. (2001). *Educating intuition.* Chicago, IL: University of Chicago Press.

Hrdy, S. B. (1999). *Mother Nature: Maternal instincts and how they shape the human species.* New York: Ballantine.

Inhelder, B., & Piaget, J. (1958). *The growth of logical thinking from childhood to adolescence.* New York: Basic Books.

Jacoby, S. (2008). *The American age of unreason.* New York: Pantheon.

Jackson, M. (2008). *Distracted: The erosion of attention and the coming dark age.* Amherst, NY: Prometheus.

Jost, J. T., Glaser, J., Kruglanski, A. W., & Sulloway, F. J. (2003). Political conservatism as motivated social cognition. *Psychological Bulletin, 129*(3), 339–375.

Kalin, N. H. (1999). Primate models to understand human aggression. *Journal of Clinical Psychiatry, 60* (15), 29–32.

Karr-Morse, R., & Wiley, M. S. (1997). *Ghosts from the nursery: Tracing the roots of violence.* New York: Atlantic Monthly Press.

Keil, F. C., & Wilson, R. A. (1999). *Explanation and cognition.* Cambridge, MA: MIT Press.

Kochanska, G. (2002b). Mutually responsive orientation between mothers and their young children: A context for the early development of conscience. *Current Directions in Psychological Science, 11,* 191–195.

Kodituwakku, P. W., Kalberg, W., & May, P. A. (2001). The effects of prenatal alcohol exposure on executive functioning. *Alcohol Research and Health, 25*(3), 192–198.

Kohlberg, L. (1984). *Essays on moral development, Volume 2: The psychology of moral development.* San Francisco: Harper & Row.

Konner, M. (2002). *The tangled wing.* New York: Owl Books.

Kruesi, M. J., Hibbs, E. D., Zahn, T. P., Keysor, C. S., Hamburger, S. D., Bartko, J. J., & Rapoport, J. L. (1992). A 2-year prospective follow-up study of children and adolescents with disruptive behavior disorders. Prediction by cerebrospinal fluid 5-hydroxyindoleacetic acid, homovanillic acid, and autonomic measures? *Archives of General Psychiatry, 49*(6):429–435.

Lapsley, D. & Narvaez, D. (2004). A social-cognitive view of moral character. In D. Lapsley & D. Narvaez (Eds.), *Moral development: Self and identity* (pp. 189–212). Mahwah, NJ: Lawrence Erlbaum Associates.

Lesch, K., Bengel, D., Heils, A., Sabol, S. Z., Greenberg, B. D., Petri, S., Clemens, R., Müller, J. B., Hamer, D. H., & Murphy, D. L. (1996). Association of anxiety-related traits with a polymorphism in the serotonin transporter gene regulatory region. *Science, 274*, 1527–31.

Levi, P.(1959) *Survival in Auschwitz*. New York: Touchstone.

Lewis, T., Amini, F., & Lannon, R. (2000). *A general theory of love*. New York: Vintage.

Loevinger, J. (1976) *Ego development*. San Francisco: Jossey-Bass.

Loye, D. (2002). The moral brain. *Brain and Mind, 3*, 133–150.

(2000). *Darwin's lost theory of love*. New York: Writer's Press.

Luna, B., Thulborn, K. R., Munoz, D. P., Merriam, E. P., Garver, K. E., Minshew, N. J. et al. (2001). Maturation of widely distributed brain function subserves cognitive development. *NeuroImage, 13*(5), 786–793.

MacLean, P. D. (1973). *A triune concept of the brain and behavior*. Toronto: University of Toronto Press.

(1990). *The triune brain in evolution: Role in paleocerebral functions*. New York: Plenum.

Markus, H., & Kunda, Z. (1986). Stability and malleability of the self-concept. *Journal of Personality and Social Psychology, 51*(4), 858–866.

Markus, H., & Nurius, P. (1986). Possible selves. *American Psychologist, 41*, 954–969.

Mathews, V. P., Kronenberger, W. G., Wang, Y., Lurito, J. T., Lowe, M. J., & Dunn, D. W. (2005). Media violence exposure and frontal lobe activation measured by functional magnetic resonance imaging in aggressive and nonaggressive adolescents. *Journal of Computer Assisted Tomography, 29* (3), 287–292.

Matsuba, M. K., & Walker, L. J. (2004). Extraordinary moral commitment: Young adults involved in social organizations. *Journal of Personality, 72* (2), 413–436.

McAdams, D. (this volume). The moral personality. In D. Narvaez & D. K. Lapsley (Eds.), *Personality, identity, and character: Explorations in moral psychology* (pp. 11–29). New York: Cambridge University Press.

Meier, B. P., Robinson, M. D., & Wilkowski, B. M. (2006). Turning the other cheek: Agreeableness and the regulation of aggression-related primes. *Psychological Science, 17*(5), 136–142.

Mikulincer, M., & Shaver, P. R. (2005). Attachment security, compassion, and altruism. *Current Directions in Psychological Science, 14*, 34–38.

Mikulincer, M., Shaver, P. R., Gillath, O., & Nitzberg, R. A. (2005). Attachment, caregiving, and altruism: Boosting attachment security increases compassion and helping. *Journal of Personality and Social Psychology, 89* (5), 817–839.

Mischel, W. (1973). Towards a cognitive social learning theory reconceptualization of personality. *Psychological Review, 80*, 252–283.

Moll, J., de Oliveira-Souza, R., Eslinger, P. J., Bramati, I. E., Mourao-Miranda, J., Andreiulo, P. A. et al. (2002). The neural correlates of moral sensitivity: A functional magnetic resonance imaging investigation of basic and moral emotions. *Journal of Neuroscience, 22*, 2730–2736.

Moll, J., Zahn, R., de Olivera-Souza, R., Krueger, F., & Grafman, J. (2005). The neural basis of human moral cognition. *Nature Reviews: Neuroscience, 6*, 799–809.

Moll, J., de Oliveira-Souza, R., & Zahn, R. (this volume). Neuroscience and morality: Moral judgments, sentiments and values. In D. Narvaez & D. K. Lapsley (Eds.), *Personality, identity, and character: Explorations in moral psychology* (pp. 106–135). New York: Cambridge University Press.

Monin. B., & Jordan, A. (this volume). The dynamic moral self: A social psychological perspective. In D. Narvaez & D. K. Lapsley (Eds.), *Personality, identity, and character: Explorations in moral psychology* (pp. 341–354). New York: Cambridge University Press.

Narvaez, D. (2008). Triune ethics: The neurobiological roots of our multiple moralities. *New Ideas in Psychology, 26*, 95–119.

Narvaez, D., & Vaydich, J. (2008). Moral development and behaviour under the spotlight of the neurobiological sciences. *Journal of Moral Education, 37*(3), 289–313.

Neisser, U. (1976). *Cognition and reality*. New York: W.H. Freeman and Company.

Nelson, E. E., & Panksepp, J. (1998). Brain substrates of infant–mother attachment: Contributions of opioids, oxytocin, and norepinephrine. *Neuroscience and Biobehavioral Reviews, 22*, 437–452.

Newman, M. L., Holden, G. W., & Delville, Y. (2005). Isolation and the stress of being bullied. *Journal of Adolescence, 28*, 343–357.

Nisbett, R., & Cohen, D. (1996). *Culture of honor*. New York: Westview Press.

Oliner, S. P. (2002). Extraordinary acts of ordinary people: Faces of heroism and altruism. In S. G. Post, L. G. Underwood, J. P. Schloss, & W. B. Hurlbut (Eds.), *Altruistic love: Science, philosophy, and religion in dialogue* (pp. 123–139). New York: Oxford University Press.

Oliner, S. P., & Oliner, P. M. (1988). *The altruistic personality: Rescuers of Jews in Nazi Europe*. New York: Free Press.

Panksepp, J. (1998). *Affective neuroscience: The foundations of human and animal emotions*. New York: Oxford University Press.

Paterson, D., Trachtenberg, F. L., Thompson, E. G., Belliveau, R. A., Beggs, A. H., Darnall, R., Chadwick, A. E., Krous, H. F., Kinney, H. C. (2006). Multiple serotonergic brainstem abnormalities in sudden infant death syndrome. *Journal of the American Medical Association, 296*, 2124–2132.

Pollak, S. D., & Perry, B. (2005). Early neglect can hinder child's relationships. *Proceedings of the National Academy of Sciences*, Nov. 21–25.

Prescott, J. W. (1996). The origins of human love and violence. *Pre- and Perinatal Psychology Journal, 10* (3), 143–188.

Putnam, R. D. (2001). *Bowling alone: The collapse and revival of American community*. New York: Simon & Schuster.

Pyszczynski, T., Solomon, S., Greenberg, J., Maxfield, M., & Cohen, F. (2004). Fatal attraction. The effects of mortality salience on evaluations of charismatic, task-oriented, and relationship oriented leadership. *Personality and Social Psychology Bulletin, 32* (4), 525–537.

Reber, A. S. (1993). *Implicit learning and tacit knowledge: An essay on the cognitive unconscious*. New York: Oxford University Press.

Rosenblatt, A., Greenberg J., Solomon S., Pyszczynski, T., & Lyon D. (1989). Evidence for terror management theory: I. The effects of mortality salience on reactions to those who violate or uphold cultural values. *Journal of Personality and Social Psychology*, 57(4), 681–90.

Shenkman, R. (2008). *Just how stupid are we: Facing the truth about the American voter*. New York: Basic Books.

Schore, A. N. (2001). The effects of early relational trauma on right brain development, affect regulation, and infant mental health. *Infant Mental Health Journal*, 22, 201–269.

(2003a). *Affect regulation and the repair of the self*. New York: Norton.

(2003b). *Affect dysregulation and disorders of the self*. New York: Norton.

Skitka, L. J., & Morgan, G. S. (this volume). The double-edged sword of a moral state of mind. In D. Narvaez & D. K. Lapsley (Eds.), *Personality, identity, and character explorations in moral psychology* (pp. 355–374). New York: Cambridge University Press.

Taylor, J. B. (2008). *My Stroke of insight: A brain scientist's personal journey*. New York: Viking Press.

Thomas, E. M. (1959). *The armless people*. New York: Vintage.

Thompson, R. (this volume). Early foundations: Conscience and the development of moral character. In D. Narvaez & D. K. Lapsley (Eds.), *Personality, identity, and character explorations in moral psychology* (pp. 159–184). New York: Cambridge University Press.

Tomkins, S. (1965). Affect and the psychology of knowledge. In S. S. Tomkins & C. E. Izard (Eds.), *Affect, cognition, and personality*. New York: Springer.

Twenge, J. M. (2000). The age of anxiety? Birth cohort change in anxiety and neuroticism, 1952–1993. *Journal of Personality and Social Psychology*, 79(6) 1007–1021.

U. S. Department of Health and Human Services, Substance Abuse and Mental Health Services Administration. (1999). *Mental health: A report of the surgeon general*. Rockville, MD: Center for Mental Health Services, National Institutes of Health, National Institute of Mental Health.

Walker, L. J., & Frimer, J. (this volume). Moral personality exemplified. In D. Narvaez & D. K. Lapsley (Eds.), *Personality, identity, and character explorations in moral psychology* (pp. 232–255). New York: Cambridge University Press.

Weaver, I. C., Szyf, M., & Meaney, M. J. (2002). From maternal care to gene expression: DNA methylation and the maternal programming of stress responses. *Endocrine Research*, 28, 699.

Weil, S. (1947/1952). *Gravity and grace*. New York: Routledge Kegan Paul.

Wilson, T. D. (2004). *Strangers to ourselves*. New York: Belknap.

Wong, D. B. (2006). *Natural moralities*. New York: Oxford University Press.

Wong, D. B. (this volume). Pluralism and moral identity. In D. Narvaez & D. K. Lapsley (Eds.), *Personality, identity, and character explorations in moral psychology* (pp. 79–105). New York: Cambridge University Press.

Zimbardo, P. (2007). *The Lucifer effect: Understanding how good people turn bad*. New York: Random House.

7

Early Foundations: Conscience and the Development of Moral Character

ROSS A. THOMPSON

The themes of moral self, identity, and character underscore the complex foundations of mature moral conduct. Adults act from a sense of self in which moral integrity may be an important component. They respond to everyday ethical challenges by enlisting identities – professional, familial, religious – that provide guidance. Adults are also integrated into networks of social relationships that motivate moral conduct, in communities that may either support or undermine acting on the basis of moral character. It is not surprising that the influences on moral self, identity, and character have inspired centuries of philosophical reflection on the nature of human conduct and, more recently, nearly a century of intensive psychological study. The themes of this volume are genuinely a lifespan developmental concern.

Well ... *almost* lifespan. This is because despite concerted interest in the origins of moral character in childhood, adolescence, and adulthood, developmental influences in infancy and early childhood have been long neglected. Moral development in classic theories describes how the child abandons the egocentric, authoritarian orientation of the early years in favor of a more mature, humanistic orientation. As a consequence, researchers have naturally been more interested in the developmental influences and transitions of middle childhood and beyond. The purpose of this chapter is to argue, however, that the time is long overdue for a reconsideration of the foundations of moral character in early childhood. Although classic theories capture much that is true about the early origins of moral character, research on young children during the past 25 years has contributed to a new understanding of the basis of early morality that shares much in common with later years in the emphasis on cooperation in close relationships, emotion understanding, sensitivity to others' needs, and an emerging moral self. Taken together, these studies suggest that to a greater extent than traditionally realized, children and adolescents build on an early foundation in the development of moral character and self.

The chapter begins with a survey of classic moral development theories that continue to shape contemporary thinking about early childhood morality. Next is an overview of current research findings concerning infants and young children that relate to these formulations. Although little of this research is directly concerned with early morality, it addresses the psychological foundations that are believed to be at the heart of a young child's capacities to act morally, such as the ability to understand others' needs and feelings in a nonegocentric manner, awareness of intentionality in prohibitive violations, the constructive understanding of behavioral standards, moral affect (including empathy), and whether the self is conceptualized in morally relevant terms. Following this, the research literature on early conscience is summarized, with particular attention to the relational foundations of conscience development. The chapter closes with some conclusions about future directions for moral development theory and research.

EARLY CHILDHOOD IN CLASSIC MORAL DEVELOPMENT THEORIES

Prevailing theories of moral development describe infants and young children as obedience-oriented and self-interested – or in Piaget's word, "premoral." Although their explanations for this early orientation differ, psychoanalytic, behavioral, and cognitive-developmental theorists are surprisingly consistent in describing early childhood morality as fundamentally different from the moral perspective of later years, and this view strongly influences contemporary thinking.

To psychoanalytic thinkers, morality emerges from the reining in of instinctual drives by social controls that become progressively internalized. In this theory, the young child's dependency on parental love creates the incentives for compliance and the sanctions for noncompliance: anxiety over the loss of parental love, fear of punishment, and emotional reliance on the parent each motivate moral growth (Freud, 1940). In particular, the child's identification with the parent late in the preschool years promotes internalization of the adult's values and the emergence of internalized guilt when those values are violated. These formulations are consistent with some contemporary views of the relational incentives for moral internalization (Hoffman, 1988) and early conscience development (Kochanska, 1993).

Young children are portrayed in psychoanalytic theory as externalized in their moral orientation and motivated to avoid the consequences of noncompliance (loss of love, punishment) until parental values are eventually adopted.

Although learning theorists have a much different network of explanatory processes for describing moral development, they are consistent with the psychoanalytic view in their description of the young child as morally externalized and responding to the sanctions of caregivers as well as their example (Bandura, 1991; Skinner, 1971). Preschoolers are especially reliant on immediate rewards and sanctions because they have not yet acquired the self-regulatory capacities emphasized in some cognitive social learning formulations (Bandura, 1991). Learning views have also influenced contemporary thinking about early morality, particularly the importance of the young child's responsive imitation of the parent as a contributor to cooperation and compliance (Forman, Aksan, & Kochanska, 2004; Forman & Kochanska, 2001).

The ideas of cognitive-developmental theorists Piaget (1932) and Kohlberg (1969) have had the strongest influence on contemporary thinking about moral development. Piaget (1932) described young children as initially premoral and, late in the preschool years, as moving into a stage of heteronomous morality characterized by unilateral respect for authority, an absolutist understanding of rules, a consequentialist (rather than intentions-based) approach to wrongdoing, and belief in immanent justice. The decline in egocentrism and increased experience in cooperative, egalitarian peer relationships leads, he believed, to the more autonomous moral orientation of middle childhood that focuses on the human origins and purposes of rules and compliance. Kohlberg (1969) extended the Piagetian formulation in his characterization of young children as preconventional thinkers, characterized by a self-serving morality that respects punishments and rewards but seeks the best possible personal outcomes, while also recognizing that others are similarly motivated. The preconventional moralist is, like Piaget's heteronomist moralist, consequentialist, obedience oriented, and externalized. Kohlberg emphasized the cognitive developmental origins of changes in moral judgment, particularly the decline in egocentrism, that enables children gradually to better understand the perspectives of other people and the social interactions that can contribute to cognitive-moral conflict.

All three of these theoretical views offer useful portrayals of many aspects of early childhood morality. The infant's and young child's reliance on close relationships with caregivers provides the impetus, they each recognize, for cooperation and compliance, although the internal processes mediating this differ (e.g., anxiety over love withdrawal, fear of punishment, preoperational thought leading to unilateral respect). Furthermore, each theory emphasizes that young children respond to parental rewards and punishments that convey standards of approved and disapproved conduct. Each theory also emphasizes how moral motivation is influenced by the developmental limitations of early childhood, whether conceived in terms of pre-Oedipal psychological structures, deficiencies in self-regulatory processes, or cognitive immaturity.

Perhaps for this reason, one of the most striking consistencies across these classic theories is the discontinuity between the moral (or premoral) orientation of early childhood and that of later years. Whether portrayed in terms of preconventional vs. conventional morality, heteronomous vs. autonomous moral orientation, pre-Oedipal vs. post-Oedipal introjections, externalized vs. internalized morality, or reliance on external controls vs. self-regulation, each theory describes greater discontinuity in the transition from early childhood to later childhood than for any other developmental transition in moral orientation. In a sense, mature morality develops as the child progressively overcomes the deficiencies and limitations of early childhood, whether considered in terms of cognitive egocentrism, dependency on parent-child relationships, or the reliance on external rather than internalized controls over behavior.

Decades of research on these alternative theoretical formulations have confirmed, questioned, and refined these ideas, of course (see Turiel, 2006, for a helpful review). What has remained consistent over time has been the naturally greater interest of moral development researchers in the more reasoned, relational, and humanistic morality of later years over the self-interested, authoritarian moral orientation expected of young children (see Carlo & Edwards, 2005; Lapsley & Narvaez, 2004; Turiel, 2006). This is important because the past three decades have also witnessed astonishing advances in other fields of developmental science concerned with infants' and young children's cognitive, emotional, and sociomoral development, to be reviewed below (see also Thompson, 2006a). Together, these studies have contributed to a new understanding of early childhood development that is fundamentally post-Piagetian and also poses new questions for classic moral development theories. If infants and preschoolers are not egocentric but are instead deeply interested in understanding others' feelings and goals, for example, what does this mean for the self-concerned morality believed to derive from cognitive egocentrism? If toddlers exhibit an early sensitivity to violations of their own standards and expectancies, what are the implications of this for the view that moral values arise primarily from the internalization of parental standards? If conscience development in preschoolers is motivated not by parental talk about rules and the consequences of violating them, but instead by discussion of people's feelings, what does this mean for the humanistic bases for early morality?

As these questions imply, much of the research on young children that is relevant to early childhood morality is focused on broader features of early social understanding, self-awareness, and social relationships. New research also has explored specific features of early conscience and moral understanding. In the next sections, this research literature is reviewed and discussed with respect to its relevance to the construction of a new view of moral character and conduct in early childhood.

CONCEPTUAL AND SOCIAL FOUNDATIONS OF EARLY MORALITY

Moral development is based at any age on the conceptual capabilities of the child, self-understanding, and the networks of social relationships that guide moral conduct. No one would expect a young child, for example, to exercise postconventional moral judgment or exhibit a psychologically differentiated moral self. Developmental research in a variety of areas is yielding, however, a new portrayal of the conceptual, self-aware, and relational foundations of early morality.

Early Social and Emotional Understanding

One of the most important changes in contemporary thinking about early childhood derives from carefully designed experimental studies of infants' social understanding. They show that before the end of the first year, infants demonstrate an awareness of the subjectivity underlying people's attention, behaving, and feeling. For example, infants use pointing to redirect an adult's attention to something of interest, often to change their behavior (such as retrieving an object the infant wants; Tomasello, Carpenter, & Lizkowski, 2007), and they infer the goals underlying simple actions they observe in others, like reaching (Woodward, 1998). By 12 months, infants look to a parent when faced with an ambiguous event and, based on the adult's positive or negative emotional expressions, respond with approach or avoidance (Moses, Baldwin, Rosicky, & Tidball, 2001). By 18 months, toddlers will hand a friendly experimenter the broccoli that the adult clearly prefers as a snack rather than the crackers the child prefers (Repacholi & Gopnik,

1997), and will imitate an adult's intended action, even if the action was not completed (Meltzoff, 1995). Studies like these provide convincing evidence that rather than confusing their own perceptions, feelings, and desires with those of another person because of egocentrism, infants and toddlers are aware of these differences early and, equally important, strive to understand the mental states in others that account for these differences.

With increasing age, there are further advances in what is now called "theory of mind" – that is, young children's beliefs about mental states and behavior (Wellman, 2002). From their early understanding of the influence of intentions, desires, and emotions on behavior, young children begin to comprehend the importance of beliefs after age three and, in particular, how thoughts and ideas can be inconsistent with the reality to which they refer. Moreover, by ages five or six children begin to perceive people in terms of their individual traits and motives, and can offer accurate predictions of behavior based on the psychological characteristics they infer in others (Heyman, Gee, & Giles, 2003; Heyman & Gelman, 2000).

Taken together, this expanding research literature underscores that infants and young children are aware early on of the differences between their own subjective states and those of others; are developing considerable knowledge of how differences in intention, desire, feeling, and beliefs are associated with behavior; and are sensitive to individual differences in the psychological characteristics that cause people to act differently. Although they have far to go before they attain a mature understanding of the internal motivators of behavior, these findings explain why few contemporary researchers of early childhood describe young children as egocentric in any comprehensive sense. Young children may still act in a self-interested manner, but, like adults, they do not do so because they are unaware of others' feelings and goals.

Social Referencing

As described earlier, one reflection of infants' social and emotional sensitivity is when they encounter novel situations, people, or objects and turn to trusted adults. Experimental studies show that the adults' facial expressions, coupled with their attention toward the ambiguous event, significantly affect the infant's subsequent behavioral response (see Baldwin & Moses, 1996; Moses et al., 2001; see Thompson, 2006a for a review). Infants more readily approach a novel object or person when adults look positive or reassuring, but are more likely to withdraw or avoid the event when adults look concerned or upset. Social referencing is important because it is an early means by which infants vicariously appropriate an understanding of events through the signals provided by another, and thus, in a broader sense, it is an early step to socially constructed meaning systems.

Viewed in this light, it is apparent how social referencing can contribute to the early acquisition of behavioral standards. Parents commonly display cautionary facial or vocal expressions when infants approach potentially dangerous situations, and they exhibit anticipatory cues of disapproval when toddlers are about to engage in forbidden activity. In doing so, they endow these activities with negative affective valence for the child. Indeed, during the second year, toddlers can be observed looking back to the parent when approaching a previously forbidden object or activity, as if to enlist the adult's emotional expressions to clarify or confirm the child's expectations about sanctioned conduct (Emde, Biringen, Clyman, & Oppenheim, 1991; Emde & Buchsbaum, 1990). In other circumstances, caregivers also use their emotional signals to induce sympathy for someone who has been harmed by the young child's actions.

In these and other ways, social referencing connects behavioral standards to the emotional signals of people to whom the infant is emotionally attached. Much less is known about how social referencing may also guide young children's evaluations of themselves when adults convey emotionally salient signals either to the child or to the outcomes of the child's activity. As described later, such evaluations are important contributors to the earliest appearance of self-evaluative emotions like pride, guilt, and shame in young children, but their efficacy is contingent on when infants and toddlers can view *themselves* as the referential targets of an adult's evaluative emotional expressions.

Sensitivity to Standards

Classic moral development theories portray young children as acquiring norms and standards from adult authorities (such as through social referencing). Although this is certainly true, it neglects the young child's active role in the construction of behavioral expectations. There is reason to believe that young children begin developing early normative expectations for everyday experience. Toward the end of the second year, for example, toddlers become increasingly concerned with how things ought to be, whether it concerns the conventional nominal references for the words they are rapidly learning (Tomasello & Rakoczy, 2003); or their expectations for daily routines (leading them to be inflexible about bedtime or morning rituals; Hudson, 1990); or even their appearance (by 19 months, toddlers

Normal teddy bear

Morally violated teddy bear

FIGURE 7.1. Variations in the toys shown to children.

Early Foundations 167

Abnormal teddy bear

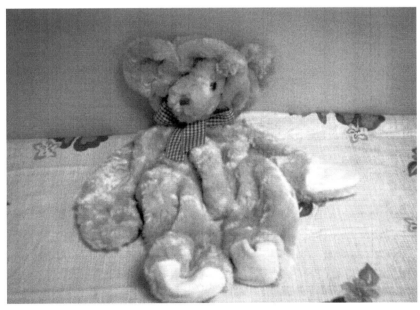
Functionally different teddy bear

FIGURE 7.1. (cont.)

show evident embarrassment when detecting a spot of rouge on their noses in the mirror; Lewis, 2000). In these and other behavioral domains, they are constructing representations of how things are done, and are sensitive to – sometimes responding aversively to – violations of these conventional normative expectations.

In the moral domain, Kagan (2005) has likewise noted that 19-month-olds respond negatively and with concern when faced with objects that have been marred, damaged, or disfigured. When they notice missing buttons from garments, torn pages in a book, or broken toys, he notes, they react with heightened interest and attention, negative evaluations (e.g., "It's yukky!"), touching the flaw, and concern about who was responsible (see also Kochanska, Casey, & Fukumoto, 1995; Lamb, 1993). Kagan interprets these responses as an emerging moral sense, because these damaged objects violate implicit norms of wholeness and intactness that parents typically enforce through sanctions on breaking or damaging objects.

In my lab, I explored this further in a study (with Meredith McGinley) on toddlers' responses to objects that were different from the norm in various ways. We were interested in understanding whether the sensitivity that Kagan and others have observed is specific to objects that are different in ways implying wrongdoing (i.e., broken or damaged), or whether children respond comparably to objects that are different in other ways, such as being the wrong color. Thus we compared toddlers' responses to toys that were different from the norm in several specific ways. Some were obviously broken or damaged – such as a broken cup, or a teddy bear with one eye missing. Others were functionally impaired without being broken – such as a cup with a finished hole at the bottom (so it could not hold liquid), or a teddy bear without stuffing. Some were functional and intact but simply looked abnormal (for example, a cup with a handle at an unusual angle, or a teddy bear in psychedelic colors and with wings). An example of these variations for the teddy bear can be found in Figure 7.1. In addition to the teddy bear and the cup, similar variations were created for a doll's blanket and a small, child-size table.

Thirty toddlers ranging in age from 14 to 23 months were individually shown a normal toy and each of the three variations of the toy in counterbalanced order, and then, when each had been presented individually, all four toys were presented together and the child was invited to indicate which was preferred. From videotaped records, the duration of the child's looking at each toy, emotional expressions toward each toy, and touching the unusual features of the toy were coded reliably. The results showed that regardless of age, young children showed no differential responding to the objects implying wrongdoing. Instead, they responded with interest, affect, and attention to all forms of atypicality, whether objects were damaged, functionally impaired, or simply looked abnormal.

These findings suggest that rather than reflecting an emerging moral sense, toddlers' responses to broken toys and disfigured objects is part of a more general sensitivity to objects and events that are different from the conventional norms that young children are constructing. Just as young preschoolers play games involving misnaming familiar animals or misusing familiar household objects (e.g., stirring in a bowl with a banana), they are interested in cups with strange handles, teddy bears with an eye missing, and other variations on the norm. Even though responses to broken or disfigured objects are not unique in young children's sensitivity to atypicality, however, this sensitivity probably becomes enlisted into an early moral sensibility as children become aware that broken and marred objects are also disapproved. In these instances, what is atypical is interesting not only because it violates the norm, but also because it is forbidden.

Obligation and Intention

The research on children's sensitivity to violations of conventional standards seems consistent with Piaget's (1932) portrayal of preschoolers as consequentialist in their moral orientation. In other words, young children seem focused on whether normative expectations are fulfilled, regardless of the reason why, and experimental studies highlight young children's sensitivity to violations of prohibitory rules (Harris & Nunez, 1996). On the other hand, research earlier reviewed also indicates that infants and young children are attuned to the intentions underlying human behavior. Does this influence their judgments of rule violation? Nunez and Harris (1998) found that children as young as three distinguished prohibitive situations (e.g., "Sally's mum says that if she plays outside she must keep her hat on") in which a story character violated the prohibition intentionally (Sally goes outside and takes off her hat) or accidentally (the wind blows off Sally's hat). Young children judged the story character as much more naughty when violations were intentional. Thus young children's deontic judgments are more nuanced than classic moral development theories portray. Preschoolers are concerned with normative obligations, but they also attend to the intentionality of human violations.

Young children's psychological awareness nuances their moral judgments in other ways also. Lagattuta (2005) examined young children's understandings of the emotional consequences of compliance with a prohibition (that frustrates what one desires to do) versus transgression (that fulfills the desire). When children were interviewed about how a story character would feel after complying with or violating a prohibitive rule (e.g., running into the street to retrieve a ball after being told not to run into the street), four- and five-year-olds attributed more negative emotion to the compliant story character and more positive emotions to the violator, explaining their judgments with reference to the story character's goals being satisfied or not. By contrast, seven-year-olds and adults more often attributed positive or mixed emotions to compliance, and negative or mixed emotions to story characters who transgressed. Thus a conceptual and emotional challenge for young children faced with everyday moral dilemmas is the conflict between the satisfaction of present desires and the longer-term consequences of violating a prohibition. In a sense, they are aware that violating prohibitions is bad, but that compliance can make you sad.

Young children's deontic judgments are also nuanced by their awareness of different domains of rules. Although children as young as two regard rule-breaking as "bad," during their third year they begin to distinguish between moral rules (which are universally applicable) and social-conventional rules (which are relative to location and time), viewing violations of moral rules as more serious and less revocable (Smetana, 1985; Smetana & Braeges, 1990). These domain distinctions are incorporated into parents' socialization strategies, which emphasize the human consequences of moral violations and the threats to social order posed by social-conventional violations, even when children are young (Smetana, 1989; Smetana, Kochanska, & Chuang, 2000).

Another way that young children are sensitive to human concerns is with respect to fairness. Research by Killen and her colleagues has shown that preschoolers regard straightforward social exclusion, such as by gender or race, as being wrong, even though they recognize the utility of exclusion for social-conventional purposes, such as to enhance group achievement (Killen, Piscane, Lee-Kim, & Ardile-Rey, 2001; Theimer, Killen, & Stangor, 2001). Thus an early sense of fairness and equity is apparent but fragile – most evident when young children's self-interest is not involved, and awaiting the more sophisticated conceptions of equity, need, and other distributive justice principles that emerge in middle childhood (Damon, 1977).

Taken together, it is certainly true that young children comply with the behavioral standards enforced by parents, but a more complete story is that young children are co-constructing behavioral expectations, as parental messages are integrated with their own developing, intuitive moral sensibility. In their efforts to comprehend how things are typically – and therefore *should be* – done, preschoolers are sensitive to violations of prohibitive rules, but also to differences in the violator's intentions, the emotional dimensions of compliance and defiance, and the imperative strength of different rule domains. Their early awareness of the human consequences associated with violating moral rules is reflected also in the emergence of a beginning sense of fairness that is also based in human considerations. Together this suggests that young children are not just oriented toward obedience to rules, but also to the humanistic dimensions of rules and one's obligation to obey.

Moral Affect

A focus on moral judgment can make moral development appear to be a coldly cognitive phenomenon. But even casual acquaintance with infants and young children confirms the hot emotions involved in compliance, rule violation, negotiation over conflicting desires, misunderstanding of intent, and other issues in parent-child moral socialization.

Emotions are particularly influential in the growth of the moral self during the second year, especially the emergence of self-referential emotions like pride, guilt, shame, and embarrassment (Barrett, 2005; Lagattuta & Thompson, 2007; Lewis, 2000). Although identifying complex self-referential emotions like these is empirically challenging (especially when young children's self-awareness is so rudimentary), researchers have succeeded in reliably distinguishing a constellation of guiltlike behaviors (e.g., spontaneous confession, efforts at reparation); shamelike behaviors (e.g., avoidance of the adult, anxious mannerisms); and embarrassment (e.g., gaze aversion and self-touching) with predictable associations emerging between guilt- and shamelike responses and morally relevant behavior. Kochanska, Gross, Lin, and Nichols (2002), for example, observed young children's emotional and behavioral responses at 22, 33, and 45 months to experimental situations involving rigged mishaps in which children believed they had damaged the experimenter's special toy. Individual differences in these behaviors were stable over time and were modestly predictive of a battery of assessments of conscience at 56 months, which included compliance with rules, moral themes in story-completion responses, and the child's self-reported moral behavior.

Parental responses to young children's successes and failures, compliance and disobedience are significant influences on early manifestations of pride, guilt, and shame (Stipek, 1995; Stipek, Recchia, & McClintic, 1992). Young children's anticipation of parental reactions is one reason for their emotional responses to success or failure. Kelly, Brownell, and Campbell (2000) found, for example, that mothers' negative evaluations of their toddler's behavior during a challenging task at 24 months predicted children's shame responses during subsequent achievement tasks at age three. Although it is likely that the responses that developmental scientists describe as early guilt or shame are based on anticipated parental reactions to failure or misbehavior, young children's sensitivity to violations of normative standards (some of which are not sanctioned by parents), and their investment in a positive sense of self at this age (Thompson, 2006a), together suggest that early expressions of guilt and shame are more than generalized conditioned anxiety responses. In a sense, the "good boy – good girl" morality described by Kohlberg as characteristic of conventional morality, entailing a commitment to moral conduct to maintain esteem in the eyes of others and support self-esteem, shares many characteristics with early childhood morality.

Empathy is another emotional resource for moral conduct that also emerges in early childhood (Bischof-Kohler, 1991; Thompson, 1998; Zahn-Waxler, 2000). Consistent with the advances in social and emotional understanding earlier described, young children respond with concerned attention to the sight and sound of another person's distress. But because empathy is an emotionally and motivationally complex experience for young children, who are often unsure what to do or incapable of assisting the distressed person, their emotional arousal may or may not be accompanied by comforting or prosocial initiatives. This makes indexing empathy in terms of helping behavior inappropriate, especially for younger children. Empathy may appear developmentally earlier than reliable prosocial initiatives, and may appear independently of prosocial behavior, which, in turn, is also not contingent on an empathic response.

Moral Self

When preschoolers are asked to provide open-ended verbal descriptions of themselves, they typically describe their physical characteristics, behavior, and activities (Keller, Ford, & Meacham, 1978). However, when they can respond to more structured prompts that are less reliant on verbalization skills, young children identify not only external features of themselves but also their internal characteristics and traits (Marsh, Ellis, & Craven, 2002; Measelle, Ablow, Cowan, & Cowan, 1998). Five-year-olds can reliably describe themselves in terms of their dominant affect, tendency toward anxiety or depression, social acceptance, feelings about themselves, and academic competencies, and these self-descriptions are validated by their external correlates in parental and teacher perceptions of the child.

Using these new methods, Kochanska (2002a) has identified individual differences in a nascent "moral self" that emerges by age five. Preschoolers with a strong moral component to their self-awareness are more likely to endorse statements describing themselves as someone who feels badly about doing the wrong thing, apologizes for wrongdoing, tries to make amends or reparation, and related behavior. In her research, Kochanska has found that individual differences in this feature of self-awareness are predicted by earlier differences in children's observed responses to wrongdoing in the lab, and related morally relevant behaviors (Kochanska et al., 2002). This research is clearly at an early stage, but merits follow-up study to elucidate how the emergence of psychological self-conceptions might provide early foundations for the development of a more mature moral self and moral character.

Interim Conclusion

As students of infancy and early childhood have explored these and related topics, their studies have yielded an increasing variety of findings that are not easily understood within the context of traditional portrayals of early childhood. In several studies, for example, Warneken and Tomasello (2006, 2007) have shown that infants as young as 14 months old behave prosocially toward unfamiliar adults in the absence of reward or praise for doing so. In a series of laboratory experiments, an adult was engaged in simple tasks that he or she could not complete without simple assistance from the child (e.g., retrieving a marker the adult was using for drawing that accidentally fell on the floor; opening a cabinet for an adult with his arms full of books). All but two of the 18-month-olds (and two-thirds of the 14-month-olds) helped readily, most within a few seconds of the adult's apparent need; by contrast, toddlers did not assist when the same situations arose from the adult's deliberate action (e.g., tossing the marker on the floor rather than dropping it accidentally), and thus when no help was needed. We have replicated these findings in our lab.

Although we might disagree with the authors' description of this activity as "altruistic helping," it is apparent that the social-cognitive capabilities of the toddlers in these studies are more sophisticated than conventionally expected. Interpreting others' goals and needs, enacting behavior with a stranger that advances those goals, awareness of others' feelings, and – beyond this experimental context – sensitivity to intentionality in prohibitive violations, identifying normative expectations for behavior, and the early emergence of a "moral self" are each developmental phenomena in the early years that suggest the need for a new portrayal of early moral sensibility.

The studies reviewed in this section, however, were not primarily focused on early conscience or moral development. The research on conscience, to which we now turn, offers a similar portrayal of young children who are sensitive and intuitive moralists, and whose orientation shares much in common with the more sophisticated forms of moral judgment, character, and identity of later years.

CONSCIENCE DEVELOPMENT IN EARLY CHILDHOOD

What is "conscience"? Consistent with the rich history of this concept within psychological theory, current researchers define conscience as the cognitive, affective, relational, and other processes that influence how young children construct and act consistently with generalizable, internal standards of conduct (Kochanska & Aksan, 2004; Thompson, Meyer, & McGinley, 2006). Researchers have used a wealth of measures to study early conscience development, including young children's cooperation with their caregivers at required tasks (such as cleaning up), unsupervised compliance with a behavioral standard, moral affect (including guilt and shame), moral reasoning (involving simplified semiprojective moral dilemmas), prosocial affect (such as empathy), prosocial behavior, and indicators of an emergent "moral self" in preschoolers (see Thompson et al., 2006, for a review). Many of these approaches are comparable to those that have been used for years with older children. Contemporary research on conscience development is distinctive, however, not only for the younger ages of the children that are studied, but also for a view of early morality that builds on contemporary thinking about close relationships, early social and emotional understanding, and the developing self.

Parent-Child Relationships and Early Conscience

Classic moral development theories describe parent-child relationships as central to early moral development, but portray relational incentives in bivalent ways: rewards and punishments, love and anxiety over loss of love, respect and fear. Informed by attachment theory, contemporary students of early conscience development acknowledge these incentives and add to them the emotional attachment shared by parent and child as an important gateway for values transmission and internalization. To Kochanska (2002b), for example, the parent-child relationship enlists young children into a mutually responsive system of reciprocal cooperation that sensitizes them to the mutual obligations of close relationships. Although preschoolers obviously cannot be equal contributors to such a relationship, they are nevertheless motivated by the adult's warm responsiveness to react cooperatively and positively to the adult's initiatives. Such a relationship also orients young children to the human dimensions of moral conduct (e.g., consequences for another), and make children more receptive to the parent's socialization initiatives (see also Maccoby, 1984, and Waters, Kondo-Ikemura, Posada, & Richters, 1991, for similar approaches).

The view that a positive parent-child relationship orients young children to respond cooperatively to the parent's socialization initiatives has been supported in several longitudinal studies in which the mutual responsiveness and shared positivity of parent-child interaction have been found to predict later measures of conscience, such as the child's cooperative conduct and rule-compliance without supervision (Kochanska, Forman, & Coy, 1999; Kochanska & Murray, 2000; Laible & Thompson, 2000; see review by Kochanska, 2002b). One reason is that mothers in these relationships use less power assertion and less coercive influence techniques, and thus elicit less emotional reactivity from offspring during discipline encounters (Kochanska, Aksan, Prisco, & Adams, 2008). Consistent with this view, researchers have found that a secure parent-child relationship is associated with conscience development in early childhood, with securely attached children responding more cooperatively and with greater internalization of values than insecurely attached children (Kochanska, 1995; Laible & Thompson, 2000; see Thompson, in press, for a review). Kochanska's (1991, 1995) research has shown that a secure attachment is especially influential for children who are temperamentally relatively fearless, for whom the emotional incentives of the mother-child relationship (rather than the anxiety provoked by discipline practices) are motivational.

As these findings suggest, the influence of specific parental socialization practices may be mediated by the broader quality of the parent-child relationship in shaping early conscience. In a longitudinal study, Kochanska, Aksan, Knaack, and Rhines (2004) found that for securely attached children (assessed at 14 months), the parent's responsiveness and use of gentle discipline (from 14 to 45 months) predicted conscience (assessed at 56 months), but for insecurely attached children there was no such association. As with temperamental variability, therefore, parental discipline practices cannot be expected to have the same influence on children who differ in the security of attachment, suggesting that the early socialization of conscience is a process of parent-child interactive effects, rather than main effects of socialization strategy.

Parental Practices: Discipline and Conversation

As with older children, researchers have found that discipline practices that emphasize reasoning and provide young children with justifications are more likely to foster the internalization of values, even though preschoolers may also assert their autonomy through negotiation (Crockenberg & Litman, 1990; Kuczynski & Kochanska, 1990). Parental explanations may be especially important in early childhood for clarifying issues of causality, responsibility, and obligation that may be unclear in the minds of young children as they are caught up in conflicts involving salient emotions and desires. An adult's explanations may also be important for helping young children comprehend the human consequences of the child's behavior.

Parent-child talk during the disciplinary encounter – the traditional focus of research on moral socialization – has advantages and disadvantages for fostering moral internalization. Parents' explanations are directly tied to the prohibitive violation, but the child's emotional arousal may undermine thoughtful processing of the adult's message, especially if the child is young (Thompson, 2006a). There is increasing evidence, however, that parent-child conversation outside of the immediate discipline context is influential in conscience development. Laible and Thompson (2000) recorded conversations between four-year-olds and their mothers about past events in which the child either misbehaved or behaved appropriately. Mothers who more frequently discussed people's feelings in these conversations had children who, in independent assessments, were more advanced in conscience development. Even though maternal references to rules and the consequences of violating them were also identified in these mother-child conversations, it was only maternal references to emotions that predicted conscience in young children. These findings were subsequently replicated in a prospective longitudinal study in which maternal references to feelings (but not references to rules and moral evaluations) during conflict with the child at 30 months predicted the child's conscience development six months later (Laible & Thompson, 2002). Similarly, in another study, two- to three-year-old children whose mothers used reasoning and discussed humanistic concerns in resolving conflict with them were more advanced in moral understanding in kindergarten and first grade (Dunn, Brown, & Maguire, 1995). Together, these findings suggest that what is important about parent-child conversations is not the clear and consistent articulation of rules and the consequences of rule violation, but how they sensitize young children to the human dimensions of misbehavior and good behavior, and help young children to comprehend the effects of their actions on others' feelings.

These conversational effects are consistent with a broader research literature documenting the influence of parental discourse for young children's representations of their experiences, themselves, and other people (see Thompson, 2006b, and Thompson, Laible, & Ontai, 2003, for reviews). Studies of early parent-child conversation show that when parents talk in a rich and elaborative manner with their young offspring, preschoolers are likely to acquire deeper memory of shared events and achieve greater understanding compared to children who participate in more directive or unelaborated conversations (Nelson & Fivush, 2004). With respect to early conscience, research also shows that mothers who take the initiative to resolve conflict with offspring, using justifications to explain and clarify their requests, and who manage to avoid aggravating tension (such as through threats or teasing), have children who are longitudinally found to be more advanced in assessments of conscience (Laible, 2004; Laible & Thompson, 2002). By contrast, mothers who are more conversationally "power assertive" when recounting the child's misbehavior in the recent past – conveying a critical or negative attitude, feelings of disappointment or anger, or providing reproach or punishment – have preschoolers with lower scores on measures of moral cognition (Kochanska, Aksan, & Nichols, 2003). The positive conversational qualities that are associated with enhanced early conscience development are observed especially in securely-attached mothers and children, which may help to explain why secure children are likely to score higher on measures of early conscience (Laible, Panfile, & Makariev, 2008).

These conclusions are consistent, of course, with the well-documented effects of inductive discipline practices on moral internalization with older children. But these findings suggest that the benefits of a parent's rational justifications and humanistic appeals are also apparent in early childhood, and in conversational contexts that are both within and outside of the specific discipline encounter. Furthermore, these studies suggest that conversational quality and the broader quality of the parent-child relationship are each important to early conscience development. In secure relationships – as a marker of relationships characterized by an orientation of mutual cooperation and responsiveness – mothers and children are also more likely to discuss moral conflicts in a manner facilitating the child's moral growth.

CONCLUSION

The story of the development of moral character and moral self that emerges from these research literatures is far richer and more interesting than the classic view of early morality from psychoanalytic, learning, and cognitive-developmental traditions. It is also very consistent with the portrayal of moral development in middle childhood from the same classic theories. Young children incorporate into an early developing moral sensibility their sensitivity to others' feelings, desires, goals, and needs, and respond in ways that balance recognition of others' interests with their own. They are also aware of the nuances of moral compliance, such as the importance of intention in prohibitive violation, the different domains of social rules, and the emotional consequences of compliance and violation. Their early developing awareness of normative standards becomes enlisted into moral sensibility as they recognize that some things (damage, harm, certain conduct) is not only nonnormative but also disapproved. In all of these conceptual discoveries, they are guided by their relationships with caregivers. These relationships are not only avenues for the transmission of rules but also of humanistic values, an orientation toward cooperation and prosociality that is shaped by the general quality of the parent-child relationship, and by conversation that occurs within and outside the discipline encounter. As a consequence of these relational influences, young children experience salient moral emotions – such as pride, guilt, and shame – that are closely tied to caregivers' evaluations of their conduct, and they are developing a sense of themselves as moral actors that is forged by close relational experience.

These characteristics of early childhood morality are nicely captured in a recent longitudinal study of the morally relevant conversations of two young children documented from the CHILDES database (MacWhinney, 2000). In their analyses of the spontaneous verbal utterances of these children between the ages of two and a half and five, Wright and Bartsch (2008) document how each child was an active interpreter of his or her moral behavior and that of others, applying rapidly developing conceptual skills to the analysis of everyday moral conflicts. The children, Abe and Sarah, rarely talked about moral rules or standards, but frequently evaluated the goodness and badness of people's dispositions and actions by appealing to others' feelings and welfare (e.g., at two years Abe said "I think they are mean to that man because they put him in that glue"). Each child also interlaced emotion concepts into their moral appraisals, commenting about the negative feelings associated with wrongdoing, but also about loving certain people and other positive affects (e.g., at three and a half years, Abe said "I'm picking up mine because I want you to be happy"). Each child remarked more commonly on the internal than the external motivators of moral conduct, such as the feelings underlying or resulting from specific conduct.

Developmental science needs a new theory of moral development to accommodate these and other findings discussed in this chapter. Such a theory would provide a fresh portrayal of the early foundations of moral character in the experiences and thinking of early childhood, as well as describing how the conceptual and self-reflective advances of later years build on this foundation to foster more sophisticated moral judgments, conduct, and identity to come. Equally important, such a theory would offer insight into how early relationships and experiences create a legacy of moral sensitivity, self-awareness, and dispositions to others that are likely to influence moral conduct in later years. It is long past time for such a theory to guide a new research literature on moral development that is *truly* lifespan in orientation.

REFERENCES

Baldwin, D., & Moses, L. (1996). The ontogeny of social information-processing. *Child Development*, 67, 1915–1939.

Bandura, A. (1991). Social cognitive theory of moral thought and action. In W. M. Kurtines & J. H. Gewirtz (Eds.), *Handbook of moral behavior and development*, Vol. 1 (pp. 45–103). Hillsdale, NJ: Lawrence Erlbaum Associates.

Barrett, K. C. (2005). The origins of social emotions and self-regulation in toddlerhood: New evidence. *Cognition and Emotion*, 19, 953–979.

Bischof-Kohler, D. (1991). The development of empathy in infants. In M. E. Lamb & H. Keller (Eds.), *Infant development: Perspectives from German-speaking countries* (pp. 245–273). Hillsdale, NJ: Lawrence Erlbaum Associates.

Carlo, G., & Edwards, C. P. (Eds.) (2005). *Moral motivation through the life span. Nebraska Symposium on Motivation*, Vol. 51. Lincoln, NE: University of Nebraska Press.

Crockenberg, S., & Litman, C. (1990). Autonomy as competence in 2-year-olds: Maternal correlates of child defiance, compliance, and self-assertion. *Developmental Psychology*, 26, 961–971.

Damon, W. (1977). *The social world of the child*. San Francisco: Jossey-Bass.

Dunn, J., Brown, J., & Maguire, M. (1995). The development of children's moral sensibility: Individual differences and emotion understanding. *Developmental Psychology*, 31, 649–659.

Emde, R., Biringen, Z., Clyman, R., & Oppenheim, D. (1991). The moral self of infancy: Affective core and procedural knowledge. *Developmental Review*, 11, 251–270.

Emde, R., & Buchsbaum, H. (1990). "Didn't you hear my Mommy?" Autonomy with connectedness in moral self-emergence. In D. Cicchetti & M. Beeghly (Eds.),

The self in transition: Infancy to childhood (pp. 35–60). Chicago: University of Chicago Press.

Forman, D., & Kochanska, G. (2001). Viewing imitation as child responsiveness: A link between teaching and discipline domains of socialization. *Developmental Psychology, 37*, 198–206.

Forman, D., Aksan, N., & Kochanska, G. (2004). Toddlers' responsive imitation predicts preschool-age conscience. *Psychological Science, 15*, 699–704.

Freud, S. (1940). *An outline of psycho-analysis* (J. Strachey, Trans.). New York: Norton.

Harris, P., & Nunez, M. (1996). Understanding of permission rules by preschool children. *Child Development, 67*, 1572–1591.

Heyman, G., Gee, C., & Giles, J. (2003). Preschool children's reasoning about ability. *Child Development, 74*, 516–534.

Heyman, G., & Gelman, S. (2000). Preschool children's use of trait labels to make inductive inferences. *Journal of Experimental Child Psychology, 77*, 1–19.

Hoffman, M. L. (1988). Moral development. In M. H. Bornstein & M. E. Lamb (Eds.), *Developmental psychology: An advanced textbook* (2nd Ed., pp. 497–548). Hillsdale, NJ: Lawrence Erlbaum Associates.

Hudson, J. (1993). Understanding events: The development of script knowledge. In M. Bennett (Ed.), *The child as psychologist: An introduction to the development of social cognition* (pp. 142–167). New York: Harvester Wheatsheaf.

Kagan, J. (2005). Human morality and temperament. In G. Carlo & C. Pope-Edwards (Eds.), *Moral motivation through the lifespan. Nebraska Symposium on Motivation*, Vol. 51 (pp. 1–32). Lincoln, NE: University of Nebraska Press.

Keller, A., Ford, L., & Meacham, J. (1978). Dimensions of self-concept in preschool children. *Developmental Psychology, 14*, 483–489.

Kelly, S. A., Brownell, C. A., & Campbell, S. B. (2000). Mastery motivation and self-evaluative affect in toddlers: Longitudinal relations with maternal behavior. *Child Development, 71*, 1061–1071.

Killen, M., Pisacane, K., Lee-Kim, J., & Ardila-Rey, A. (2001). Fairness or stereotypes? Young children's priorities when evaluating group exclusion or inclusion. *Developmental Psychology, 37*, 587–596.

Kochanska, G. (1991). Socialization and temperament in the development of guilt and conscience. *Child Development, 62*, 1379–1392.

(1993). Toward a synthesis of parental socialization and child temperament in early development of conscience. *Child Development, 64*, 325–347.

(1995). Children's temperament, mother's discipline, and security of attachment: Multiple pathways to emerging internalization. *Child Development, 66*, 597–615.

(2002a). Committee compliance, moral self, and internalization: A mediated model. *Developmental Psychology, 38*, 339–351.

(2002b). Mutually responsive orientation between mothers and their young children: A context for the early development of conscience. *Current Directions in Psychological Science, 11*, 191–195.

Kochanska, G., & Aksan, N. (2004). Conscience in childhood: Past, present, and future. *Merrill-Palmer Quarterly, 50*, 299–310.

Kochanska, G., Aksan, N., Knaack, A., & Rhines, H. (2004). Maternal parenting and children's conscience: Early security as a moderator. *Child Development, 75,* 1229–1242.

Kochanska, G., Aksan, N., & Nichols, K. E. (2003). Maternal power assertion in discipline and moral discourse contexts: Commonalities, differences, and implications for children's moral conduct and cognition. *Developmental Psychology, 39,* 949–963.

Kochanska, G., Aksan, N., Prisco, T. R., & Adams, E. E. (2008). Mother-child and father-child mutually responsive orientation in the first 2 years and children's outcomes at preschool age: Mechanisms of influence. *Child Development, 79,* 30–44.

Kochanska, G., Casey, R., & Fukumoto, A. (1995). Toddlers' sensitivity to standard violations. *Child Development, 66,* 643–656.

Kochanska, G., Forman, D., & Coy, K. (1999). Implications of the mother-child relationship in infancy for socialization in the second year of life. *Infant Behavior & Development, 22,* 249–265.

Kochanska, G., Gross, J., Lin, M.-H., & Nichols, K. (2002). Guilt in young children: Development, determinants, and relations with a broader system of standards. *Child Development, 73,* 461–482.

Kochanska, G., & Murray, K. (2000). Mother-child mutually responsive orientation and conscience development: From toddler to early school age. *Child Development, 71,* 417–431.

Kohlberg, L. (1969). Stage and sequence: The cognitive-developmental approach to socialization. In D. A. Goslin (Ed.), *Handbook of socialization theory and research* (pp. 347–480). Chicago: Rand McNally.

Kuczynski, L., & Kochanska, G. (1990). Development of children's noncompliance strategies from toddlerhood to age 5. *Developmental Psychology, 26,* 398–408.

Lagattuta, K. H. (2005). When you shouldn't do what you want to do: Young children's understanding of desires, rules, and emotions. *Child Development, 76,* 713–733.

Lagattuta, K., & Thompson, R. A. (2007). The development of self-conscious emotions: Cognitive processes and social influences. In R. W. Robins & J. Tracy (Eds.), *Self-conscious emotions* (2nd Ed.) (pp. 91–113). New York: Guilford.

Laible, D. (2004). Mother-child discourse about a child's past behavior at 30-months and early socioemotional development at age 3. *Merrill-Palmer Quarterly, 50,* 159–180.

Laible, D., Panfile, T., & Makariev, D. (2008). The quality and frequency of mother-toddler conflict: Links with attachment and temperament. *Child Development, 79,* 426–443.

Laible, D., & Thompson, R. A. (2000). Mother-child discourse, attachment security, shared positive affect, and early conscience development. *Child Development, 71,* 1424–1440.

(2002). Mother-child conflict in the toddler years: Lessons in emotion, morality, and relationships. *Child Development, 73,* 1187–1203.

Lamb, S. (1993). First moral sense: An examination of the appearance of morally related behaviours in the second year of life. *Journal of Moral Education, 22,* 97–109.

Lapsley, D. K., & Narvaez, D. (Eds.) (2004). *Moral development, self, and identity.* Mahwah, NJ: Lawrence Erlbaum Associates.

Lewis, M. (2000). Self-conscious emotions: Embarrassment, pride, shame, and guilt. In M. Lewis & J. Haviland-Jones (Eds.), *Handbook of emotions* (pp. 563–573). New York: Guilford.

Maccoby, E. E. (1984). Socialization and developmental change. *Child Development, 55,* 317–328.

MacWhinney, B. (2000). *The CHILDES project: Tools for analyzing talk.* Vol. 2. *The database* (3rd Ed.). Mahwah, NJ: Lawrence Erlbaum Associates.

Marsh, H. W., Ellis, L. A., & Craven, R. G. (2002). How do preschool children feel about themselves? Unraveling measurement and multidimensional self-concept structure. *Developmental Psychology, 38,* 376–393.

Measelle, J. R., Ablow, J. C., Cowan, P. A., & Cowan, C. P. (1998). Assessing young children's views of their academic, social, and emotional lives: An evaluation of the self-perception scales of the Berkeley Puppet Interview. *Child Development, 69,* 1556–1576.

Meltzoff, A. N. (1995). Understanding the intentions of others: Re-enactment of intended acts by 18-month-old children. *Developmental Psychology, 31,* 838–850.

Moses, L., Baldwin, D., Rosicky, J., & Tidball, G. (2001). Evidence for referential understanding in the emotions domain at twelve and eighteen months. *Child Development, 72,* 718–735.

Nelson, K., & Fivush, R. (2004). The emergence of autobiographical memory: A social-cultural developmental theory. *Psychological Review, 111,* 486–511.

Nunez, M., & Harris, P. L. (1998). Psychological and deontic concepts: Separate domains or intimate connection? *Mind & Language, 13,* 153–170.

Piaget, J. (1932). *The moral judgment of the child* (M. Gabain, Trans.). London: Routledge, and Kegan Paul.

Repacholi, B., & Gopnik, A. (1997). Early reasoning about desires: Evidence from 14- and 18-month-olds. *Developmental Psychology, 33,* 12–21.

Skinner, B. F. (1971). *Beyond freedom and dignity.* New York: Knopf.

Smetana, J. G. (1985). Preschool children's conceptions of transgressions: The effects of varying moral and conventional domain-related attributes. *Developmental Psychology, 21,* 18–29.

(1989). Toddlers' social interactions in the context of moral and conventional transgressions in the home. *Developmental Psychology, 25,* 499–508.

Smetana, J., & Braeges, J. (1990). The development of toddler's moral and conventional judgments. *Merrill-Palmer Quarterly, 36,* 329–346.

Smetana, J., Kochanska, G., & Chuang, S. (2000). Mothers' conceptions of everyday rules for young toddlers: A longitudinal investigation. *Merrill-Palmer Quarterly, 46,* 391–416.

Stipek, D. (1995). The development of pride and shame in toddlers. In J. Tangney & K. Fischer (Eds.), *Self-conscious emotions* (pp. 237–252). New York: Guilford.

Stipek, D., Recchia, S., & McClintic, S. (1992). Self-evaluation in young children. *Monographs of the Society for Research in Child Development*, 57 (Serial No. 226).

Theimer, C., Killen, M., & Stangor, C. (2001). Preschool children's evaluations of exclusion in gender-stereotypic contexts. *Developmental Psychology*, 37, 18–27.

Thompson, R. A. (1998). Empathy and its origins in early development. In S. Braten (Ed.), *Intersubjective communication and emotion in early ontogeny* (pp. 144–157). Cambridge: Cambridge University Press.

(2006a). The development of the person: Social understanding, relationships, self, conscience. In W. Damon & R. M. Lerner (Eds.), *Handbook of child psychology* (6th Ed.), Vol. 3. *Social, emotional, and personality development* (N. Eisenberg, Vol. Ed.) (pp. 24–98). New York: Wiley.

(2006b). Conversation and developing understanding: Introduction to the special issue. *Merrill-Palmer Quarterly*, 52, 1–16.

(in press). Early attachment and later development: Familiar questions, new answers. In J. Cassidy & P. R. Shaver (Eds.), *Handbook of attachment* (2nd Ed.). New York: Guilford.

Thompson, R. A., Laible, D., & Ontai, L. (2003). Early understanding of emotion, morality, and the self: Developing a working model. In R. Kail (Ed.), *Advances in Child Development and Behavior*, Vol. 31 (pp. 137–171). San Diego: Academic.

Thompson, R. A., Meyer, S., & McGinley, M. (2006). Understanding values in relationship: The development of conscience. In M. Killen & J. Smetana (Eds.), *Handbook of moral development* (pp. 267–297). Mahwah, NJ: Lawrence Erlbaum Associates.

Tomasello, M., Carpenter, M., & Lizkowski, U. (2007). A new look at infant pointing. *Child Development*, 78, 705–722.

Tomasello, M., & Rakoczy, H. (2003). What makes human cognition unique? From individual to shared to collective intentionality. *Mind & Language*, 18, 121–147.

Turiel, E. (2006). The development of morality. In W. Damon & R. M. Lerner (Eds.), *Handbook of child psychology* (6th Ed.), Vol. 3. *Social, emotional, and personality development* (N. Eisenberg, Vol. Ed.) (pp. 789–857). New York: Wiley.

Warneken, F., & Tomasello, M. (2006). Altruistic helping in human infants and young chimpanzees. *Science*, 311, 1301–1303.

(2007). Helping and cooperation at 14 months of age. *Infancy*, 11, 271–294.

Waters, E., Kondo-Ikemura, K., Posada, G., & Richters, J. (1991). Learning to love: Mechanisms and milestones. In M. Gunnar & L. Sroufe (Eds.), *Self processes and development. Minnesota Symposia on Child Psychology*, Vol. 23 (pp. 217–255). Hillsdale, NJ: Lawrence Erlbaum Associates.

Wellman, H. (2002). Understanding the psychological world: Developing a theory of mind. In U. Goswami (Ed.), *Handbook of childhood cognitive development* (pp. 167–187). Oxford: Blackwell.

Woodward, A. (1998). Infants selectively encode the goal object of an actor's reach. *Cognition*, 69, 1–34.

Wright, J.C., & Bartsch, K. (2008). Portraits of early moral sensibility in two children's everyday conversations. *Merrill-Palmer Quarterly, 54*, 56–85.

Zahn-Waxler, C. (2000). The development of empathy, guilt, and internalization of distress: Implications for gender differences in internalizing and externalizing problems. In R.J. Davidson (Ed.), *Anxiety, depression, and emotion* (pp. 222–265). New York: Oxford University Press.

8

The Development of the Moral Personality

DANIEL K. LAPSLEY AND PATRICK L. HILL

That moral rationality attaches to selves who have personalities is a notion so commonplace that it is likely to be contested only in certain quarters of academic psychology. Yet ever since Kohlberg's landmark articulation of the "cognitive developmental approach to socialization" (Kohlberg, 1969), there was a way of talking about moral development that scarcely required reference to personality. One could describe the ontogenesis of moral reasoning without invoking the usual indicators of personality, such as traits, dispositions, or character. If anything, personological considerations were regarded as sources of bias, backsliding, and special pleading that had to be surmounted in order to render judgments from the "moral point of view." Moreover, for Kohlberg, the moral stage sequence could not be used to describe persons or to chart individual differences, and he was opposed to the use of the stage theory as a way to make "aretaic judgments" about the moral worthiness of individuals. Moral stages were not, after all, "boxes for classifying and evaluating persons" (Colby, Kohlberg, Gibbs, & Lieberman, 1983, p. 11). Instead moral stages serve as a taxonomic classification of different kinds of sociomoral operations. They describe forms of thought organization of an ideal rational moral agent – an epistemic subject – and hence cannot be "reflections upon the self" (Kohlberg, Levine, & Hewer, 1983, p. 36).

But there has been a discernible movement, in both ethical theory (Flanagan & Rorty, 1990; Taylor, 1989) and moral development (Blasi, 2005; Hart, 2005; Lapsley & Narvaez, 2004; Narvaez & Lapsley, 2009; Walker & Frimer, this volume) to draw a tighter connection between moral agency and personality. At least among psychologists, the desire for thicker conceptions of the moral self was motivated partly by a desire to offer a compelling account of the relationship between moral judgment and moral action (Blasi, 1983). Moreover, it has proven difficult to tell a coherent developmental story about the origins of moral rationality without reference to the developmental processes that frame the emergence of selfhood in early childhood (Narvaez & Lapsley, 2009; Thompson, this volume).

There are at least two impediments to research on the development of the moral personality. First, although a number of conceptions of moral self-identity and personality have emerged recently (Aquino & Freeman, this volume; Blasi, 2005, this volume; Walker & Hennig, 1998), these models start from the perspective of mature adult functioning. Consequently, we lack precise specification of the developmental processes, influences, or pathways that yield these models as an outcome (Narvaez & Lapsley, 2009). Second, personality itself is understood in different ways, and it is not clear which of the various options for conceptualizing personality is the best candidate for developmental analysis in the moral domain. If moral self-identity, or "character," is the moral dimension of personality, then our accounts of these constructs must be compatible with well-attested models of personality. But *which* models?

Personality science provides a number of options, all of which have implications for understanding the personological dimensions of moral functioning. Indeed, a commitment to theoretical and methodological pluralism is a prudent and useful strategy at this early stage of inquiry. Still, one has to start somewhere. Our own preference is for a social cognitive-developmental account of the moral personality, not the least because of its meta-theoretical compatibility with ecological-contextualist models of development (Lapsley & Narvaez, 2004), and its strong integrative potential with theoretical accounts of mature social cognitive functioning (Olson & Dweck, 2008). That said, other approaches hold promise for understanding patterns of continuity and change in moral dispositions (Caspi, Roberts, & Shiner, 2005; Robins & Tracey, 2003), and broad integrative perspectives among the various models of personality are within reach (Caspi & Shiner, 2006; McAdams, this volume).

Our goal in this chapter is to explore some features of personality science that seem to offer promising directions for integrative study of moral development. We begin by considering some broad issues concerning the basic units of personality and recent advances in understanding the structure and types of personality. We then extract five themes from the extant empirical literature on personality development and explore their implications for theory and research in the moral character development literature. We then take up the social cognitive option. After noting the two traditions of social cognitive development, we attempt to explicate a possible developmental course for the social cognitive mechanisms that seem to underlie moral self-identity, as well as prospects for future integrative research.

MODELS OF PERSONALITY

The Two Disciplines

Cervone (2001, 2005, this volume) argues that personality psychology divides into two disciplines on the question of how best to represent the basic structural units of personality. One discipline focuses on *traits* as the basic unit of analysis. The second discipline focuses on *social cognitive* constructs – such as scripts, schemas, and prototypes – as the unit of analysis (Mischel, 1990). According to Cervone, the traits approach accounts for personality structure by classifying between-person variability using latent variable taxonomies identified by factor analysis, of which the Big Five (extraversion, neuroticism, conscientiousness, agreeableness, openness-to-experience) is a prominent example (McCrae & Costa, 1999).

Moreover, the five-factor trait approach is said to adopt an explanatory strategy that is "Aristotelian" (Cervone, Shadel, & Jencius, 2001). For Kurt Lewin (1931) an explanatory strategy is Aristotelian if it considers abstractly defined classes as the essential nature of an object, and appeals to such classifications to explain behavior. To understand the essence of an object, one looks to the class of things under which it is subsumed. These essential qualities refer typically to statistical averages, with the added assumption that essential qualities do not vary by context and do not change over time. This follows from an Aristotelian conception of lawfulness, for which objects or events occur with regularity in the same way and without exception. Lewin (1931), writing almost eight decades ago, thought that contemporary psychology was rife with Aristotelian explanations. "Present day child psychology," he writes, "exemplify clearly the Aristotelian habit of considering abstractly defined classes as the essential nature of the particular object and hence as the 'explanation' of its behavior" (p. 153). One example is the case of taking the negative behavior of three-year-olds as evidence of the "negativism" characteristic of that age, as indicating something of its essential reality, and then using negativism as the explanation of their behavior. Other examples included explanations of character and of temperament. "Here, as in a great many other fundamental concepts, such as that of ability, talent and similar concepts ... present day psychology is really reduced to explanations in terms of Aristotelian 'essences'" (p. 153).

Cervone et al. (2001) want to show that old explanatory habits die hard, and so press Lewin's (1931) case against the five-factor model. On their view the Big Five factors refer to "statistical properties of populations, not individual persons" (Cervone & Shoda, 1999, p. 28); and proffer an explanation of personality that is "prototypically Aristotelian" (Cervone et al., p. 37) in that it refers simply to the abstract properties of the object ("conscientiousness") whose action is being explained. As Cervone et al. (2001, p. 37) put it, "Explanation is in terms of hypothetical constructs that are essential qualities of an individual that correspond to his or her overall average tendency to perform given types of action," and quite irrespective of situational context. Indeed, the immutable cross-situational consistency and temporal stability of dispositional tendencies is a deeply held assumption of essentialist trait psychology (or else is a deeply held caricature of traits, see Caspi & Shiner, 2006).

In contrast, the social cognitive approach understands personality structure in terms of within-individual, cognitive-affective mechanisms that are "in the head," as it were (Mischel, 1990). These cognitive mechanisms include *knowledge structures* that are used to encode features of situations – *self-reflective* processes through which individuals construct self-beliefs and attributions that contribute to affective and behavioral tendencies, and *self-regulatory* processes through which individuals set goals, evaluate progress, and maintain a motivational focus (Bandura, 1986, 1999) Moreover, in contrast to trait taxonomic approaches, social cognitive theory assumes that personal and situational variables interpenetrate and are mutually implicative. Psychological systems are in dynamic interaction with changing situational contexts (Cervone, 2005). This reciprocal determinism highlights the role of sociocultural contexts for shaping the contours of personality development, but also the active role of the agent who selects and moves into environments and shapes them to his or her own interests.

The dynamic interactions of persons and contexts also points to the explanatory strategy of the social cognitive approach. If the explanatory strategy of the five-factor model is Aristotelian, the explanatory strategy of social cognitive theory is "Galilean" (Cervone et al., 2001). The Galilean strategy looks for functional and causal explanations (Lewin, 1931). In doing so, it does not reference class membership or the essential qualities of the object or average dispositional tendencies, but rather underlying mechanisms that are reciprocally interactive with the environment (Bandura, 1986). In social cognitive theory, dispositional coherence is to be found at the intersection of Person × Context interactions (or else as a precipitate of transactions with environments, if not quite interactions in the statistical sense). Actions are explained "by reference to the interacting character of the object and the environmental context in which the action occurs" (Cervone et al., 2001, p. 37). This approach accounts for both stability and idiosyncratic behavior. There is both a stable behavioral signature but also situational variability. And social cognitive theory assumes that psychological qualities develop dynamically over time (Cervone et al, 2001; Cervone & Shoda, 1999).

The Trait Dispositional Approach

Although there is an "essentialist" reading of the five-factor theory (McCrae et al., 1999, 2000), many other researchers working on trait dispositions would not recognize the terrain surveyed by Cervone et al. (2001). Caspi, Roberts, and Shiner (2005) assert, for example, that the antimony between traits and social cognitive theory is exaggerated; and that the two approaches are not only complementary and mutually informative, but also capable of useful integration. They write: "By integrating social cognitive constructs (e.g., mental representations, encoding processes) into research on traits, developmentalists can advance understanding of how traits are directly manifested at different ages" (Caspi et al., 2005, p. 461).

There is also convergence on how to understand the person-situation debate and, in turn, the nature of traits. The person-situation debate consumed researchers for many years, and pitted social psychologists against personologists on the question of whether dispositional traits were consistently displayed across situations (the personologist position) or were trumped by the demand characteristics of situations (the social psychologist position). Some moral development researchers (Kohlberg, 1987) and philosophers (Doris, 2002; Harman, 2000; cf. Flanagan, this volume) took sides, joining the situationist attack on the reality of traits (and cognate concepts, such as virtues and character); or else, in the case of Kohlberg, accepting the situationist evidence against traits, but looking elsewhere (moral reasoning) for behavioral consistency. Personologists, for their part, mounted an impressive counterattack that demonstrated at least heterotypic dispositional consistency across situations (and continuity over time), or else consistency at the broader level of psychological meaning of situations (or broader trait descriptions), as opposed to consistency of specific, discrete behavior (Epstein, 1979; Epstein & O'Brien, 1985; Funder & Colvin, 1991; Funder & Ozer, 1983; Shoda, Mischel & Wright, 1994).

The person-situation debate turns on what to think about the ontological reality of traits (Caspi & Shiner, 2006), and on at least two conceptions of traits, there is little daylight between trait and social cognitive theory. For example, the *dispositional* conception holds that traits are tendencies to behave in certain ways given certain activating conditions. Personality traits are "if-then" conditional propositions, such as, "*if* Jones is put in a situation where demands are placed upon his sense of competency, *then* he is aggressive." This view is consonant with the social-cognitive conception of dispositions and of person-situation interactions (Mischel, 1990; Shoda, Mischel, & Wright, 1993, 1994; Wright & Mischel, 1987, 1988) and is not disputed by trait theorists, either (Caspi & Shiner, 2006). Indeed, as noted above, personologists have insisted on incorporating the psychological meaning of situations into the investigation of behavioral consistency across situations (Funder & Colvin, 1991). It is now a widely shared view that persons and situations interact in complex ways (Higgins, 1990; Kendrick & Funder, 1988); that the person-situation distinction is a false one (Funder, 1996); that situational specificity and behavioral consistency are not antagonistic positions (Ozer, 1986); and that traits are not static, nondevelopmental and immutable essences, but are instead organizational constructs that operate dynamically in transaction with environments (Caspi, 1987; Caspi & Shiner, 2006).

With respect to the dispositional notion of personality structure, then, there is much common ground between many trait and social cognitive theorists. Moreover modern trait theory embraces a *realist* conception of traits that is decidedly "Galilean" in its desire to postulate underlying causal mechanisms. As Caspi and Shiner (2006, p. 301) put it, "Whereas the dispositional, if-then conception of traits is agnostic with regard to explanation, a realist conception attempts to postulate underlying processes that lead traits to cause certain intentional states." On this view, personality traits are real characteristics of individuals (Funder, 1991, 1995). Although personality structure, for the trait theorist, could mean the pattern of covariation of traits across individuals, it can also refer to the organization of traits within individuals (Caspi & Shiner, 2006). Even here, though, dispositional and realist conceptions of traits are not antithetical, and theorists from either side of the "two disciplines" can properly claim a Galilean commitment to investigate real properties of individuals that interact dynamically with settings and contexts.

So if there are two disciplines, there is perhaps more that is shared than is contested between them. Of course, the two disciplines differ on just what are the real properties of individuals that account for dispositional coherence. Traits and social cognitive constructs are very different things, although not necessarily incommensurable things. Yet the two disciplines are not far apart in their understanding of person-context interactions, of dispositional and realist conceptions of the units of personality, or in their Galilean commitment to identify underlying causal mechanisms. The integrative spirit abides here.

Personality Types

Research on the structure of personality focuses on attempts to understand the variables or dimensions along which individuals differ. Another strategy is to emphasize not the variable but the person as the unit of study. A person-centered strategy attempts to identify how personality dimensions cohere within individuals (typically by means of Q-sort descriptions), and then to determine the resemblance of these descriptions across samples of individuals (typically by means of inverse factor analysis). Where the trait approach attempts to show the relative standing of individuals on single variables, the person-centered approach wants to show how variables are organized within the person. The goal is to identify clusters of individuals, or personality *types,* who share certain personality attributes. In a classic study, J. Block (1971) identified three important personality types (among others): *resilient, overcontrolled,* and *undercontrolled.* These types vary on two dimensions, *ego resiliency* (resilient) and *ego control* (overcontrolled, undercontrolled). Ego resiliency refers to an "ability to modify one's behavior in accordance with contextual demands" (Block & Block, 1980, p. 48). Resilient individuals are able to flexibly adapt to changing situations, particularly those that are stressful, frustrating, or demanding. Ego control refers to the "degree of impulse control and modulation" (Block & Block, 1980, p. 41), with overcontrolled individuals clamping down hard on impulses and permitting little modulation; and undercontrolled individuals giving freer reign to impulses and permitting wider modulation of them.

The three personality types have been observed in studies of children and adolescents in North America, Europe, and New Zealand (Asendorpf, Borkenau, Ostendorf, & Van Aken, 2001; Hart, Hofmann, Edelstein, & Keller, 1997; Robins, John, Caspi, Moffitt, & Stouthamer-Loeber, 1996). In addition to replicability, three additional findings are of interest. First, this typology predicts patterns of adaptation. Typically resilient children and adolescents show a good profile of adjustment. Overcontrolled children tend toward internalizing symptoms, social withdrawal, and self-esteem problems, and undercontrolled children show a more pervasive pattern of behavioral and emotional problems, including aggressive behavior (Hart et al., 1997; Huey & Weisz, 1997; Robins et al., 1996).

Second, the three personality types identified in early childhood predict outcomes later in development. Hart et al. (1997) showed, for example, using growth curve analyses, that resilient children at age 7 had higher levels of academic achievement and lower levels of concentration difficulties throughout adolescence. In a related study, Hart, Keller, Edelstein, and Hoffman (1998) showed that ego resiliency in early childhood predicted faster acquisition of friendship understanding between ages 7 and 15, and of moral judgment between 12 and 19, than did the ego control dimensions. Ego resiliency appears, then, to be a robust predictor of important acquisitions of social cognitive development, including moral reasoning, and calls attention to the role of personality in the moral formation of children.

Third, the personality types appear to converge with the Big Five (Asendorpf & Van Aken, 1999; Robins et al., 1996). In one study (van Leeuwen, De Fruyt, & Mervielde, 2004), resilient individuals were associated with socially adjusted factors, such as agreeableness, extraversion, openness to experience, but not neuroticism. Overcontrolled individuals, on the other hand, were high in neuroticism, low in extraversion; while undercontrolled individuals scored lower on agreeableness and conscientiousness. The apparent convergence of types and traits, along with evidence that traits are comparatively stronger predictors of various outcomes (van Leeuwen et al., 2004; Caspi & Shiner, 2006), have led some researchers to conclude that type membership is of interest only to the extent that it points to trait characteristics (Costa, Herbst, McCrae, Samuels, & Ozer, 2002). The integrative spirit appears to abide here as well.

Our interest in wading into these issues is not, of course, to resolve them, but rather to establish the terms of reference for considering how contemporary models of personality and allied empirical literatures can help frame our understanding of the moral personality. In the next section we review some key themes that emerge from recent reviews of the personality development literature that moral psychology will need to consider, and then we review what is known about the relationship between personality traits, types, and moral development.

DISPOSITIONS AND MORAL DEVELOPMENT

Five Themes from Personality Development for Moral Development

The personality development literature has profited from recent analytical (Caspi & Shiner, 2006; Caspi, Roberts, & Shiner, 2005; Shiner, 1998) and meta-analytical (Roberts & DelVecchio, 2000) reviews of its sprawling literature. Our aim here is to identify themes that emerge from these and other reviews that strike us as particularly important for framing research on the development of the moral personality.

Temperament and Personality. First, the distinction between temperament and personality may not be a rigid one, at least with regard to their respective structural properties. Temperament refers to "individual differences in reactivity and self-regulation in nonhuman animals and young infants" (Rothbart & Bates, 2006, p. 100). Often temperament traits are considered on a lower-order of generality than are personality traits, and more closely tied to genetic-biological foundations. Moreover, temperament is thought to provide the building blocks of later personality, or else point to qualities that have to be assembled into broader dispositional patterns.

Indeed, several narrow, lower-order temperament dimensions have been identified – such as fear/inhibition, irritability, activity level, attentional focusing, and inhibitory control, among others (Rothbart & Bates, 2006). But factor analytic research has shown that narrow bands of temperament tend to coalesce into three broader, higher-order dimensions, identified as *surgency, negative affectivity,* and *effortful control* (Rothbart, Ahadi, Hershey, & Fisher, 2001), which are related conceptually to three of the Big Five factors – *extraversion, neuroticism,* and *conscientiousness,* respectively (Rothbart & Bates, 2006). Moreover, temperament dimensions show up in samples of older children and adolescents (Capaldi & Rothbart, 1992; Putnam et al., 2001), and are empirically related to Big Five factor scores in adults (Rothbart, Ahadi, & Evens, 2000). Shiner and Caspi (2003; also, Caspi et al., 2005; Caspi & Shiner, 2006; Shiner, 1998) have proposed a taxonomy of childhood personality that underscores the hierarchical nature of lower-order temperament and higher-order (Big Five) personality traits. For example, in their taxonomy, extraversion as a personality dimension is composed of lower-order traits of sociability and energy/activity level. Agreeableness includes prosocial tendencies and a lack of willfulness or antagonism. Neuroticism subsumes fear, anxiety, sadness, and so on.

This first theme highlights the fact that stable dimensions of temperament emerge early, persist into later developmental periods, and are elaborated into broader dimensions of individual differences. This underscores the importance of examining both lower- and higher-order temperament dimensions as the first place to look for emergent signs of a moral orientation (Eisenberg, 2000). There is some evidence, for example, that individual differences in dispositional regulation are related to the experience of moral emotions, such as guilt and shame (Rothbart, Ahadi, & Hershey, 1994). The display of prosocial behaviors may tap into a complex of dispositional factors that add up to broader traits, such as agreeableness or conscientiousness.

Moreover, there is mounting evidence, particularly from Nancy Eisenberg's lab, that dimensions such as negative emotionality, impulsivity, and effortful control are related to an array of childhood outcomes, including problem-behavior (Eisenberg et al., 1996, 2000, 2005), quality of social functioning (Eisenberg, Fabes, Guthrie, & Reisser, 2000), and resilient adjustment (Eisenberg, Spinrad, Fabes, Reisser, Cumberland, & Shepard et al., 2004). Studies that chart similar relationships with prosocial moral behavioral outcomes are comparatively slight. There is some evidence that children with sociable or agreeable temperaments are more likely to demonstrate concern for others (Hastings, Zahn-Waxler, & McShane, 2006). In addition, negative emotionality (Eisenberg, Fabes, Murphy, Karbon, Smith, & Maszk, 1996) and anger (Denham, 1986) counterindicates prosocial behavior, sympathy, and concern for others.

Finally, the first theme underscores two important claims of the "new Big Five" model of moral personality outlined by McAdams (this volume; McAdams & Pals, 2006). In his layered account of the moral personality, McAdams argues that genetically based temperament dimensions are transformed into Level 2 dispositional traits, and that dispositional traits underwrite the Level 3 characteristic adaptations of childhood. As we have seen, both claims are well grounded by the extent literature, although more research anchored clearly in the moral domain is needed.

Elaboration of Temperament. But how is temperament elaborated into dispositional personality traits? Caspi and Shiner (2006) propose seven mechanisms. The first mechanism (*"learning"*) suggests that temperament might shape the child's experience of what is reinforcing (e.g., agreeable and neurotic children might find novel, complex stimuli differentially rewarding). Temperament might evoke or shape the response of others to the child (*"environmental elicitation"*). Highly extraverted children, for example, might enlist the support of peers more reliably than introverted children. Temperament might influence the way children interpret their experiences (*"environmental construal"*). For example, children low on agreeableness might misconstrue the ambiguous social cues of others as hostile intent or as an unwelcome imposition. Temperament might influence how children make *"social and temporal comparisons."* A neurotic child might disbelieve that he or she is as good as anybody else in a certain domain, or has shown growth or improvement over time. Temperament could shape the choices children make (*"environmental selection"*). By choosing certain environments, individuals place themselves into contexts that canalize their dispositional tendencies. Finally, by means of "*environmental manipulation*," temperament might influence the way children move into environments and shape, manipulate, and alter them. A child high on extraversion might exert more leadership over peers, and thereby shape peer activities around one's own interests.

These mechanisms illustrate how personality unfolds in the dynamic transaction between dispositional tendencies and context, a theme that is quite at home in developmental science, a theme we take up next. We note, too, that the appeal to temperament in several of these mechanisms masks significant contributions of social cognitive development, which might, in fact, provide the more powerful explanatory framework. Environmental construal, for example, requires mechanisms of interpretation that invoke the literatures of social information processing. Social and temporal comparisons hinge on patterns of self-beliefs. Environmental selection invites consideration of the motivational properties of self-goals. Perhaps the safe lesson is that both dispositional and social cognitive perspectives are required to account adequately for the elaboration of moral personality.

Persons and Contexts. Dispositional tendencies, although stable and enduring, are amenable to moderation by contextual influence. There is ample confirmation of this in the personality development literature (Caspi & Shiner, 2006; Rothbart & Bates, 2006). For example, dysregulation traits in young children – such as impulsivity and resistance to control – are related to problem behavior, but the effects are especially pronounced when impulsive and resistant children have parents who are harshly punitive. Similarly, negative emotionality foreshadows externalizing behaviors, but especially in children exposed to adverse rearing conditions. Angry parenting is associated with externalizing behavior in children, but the relationship is stronger in children low in agreeableness. Parental control is associated with lower levels of antisocial behavior in adolescence, but such parenting may be particularly important for adolescents who are impulsive. Similar moderating effects are reported in the development of conscience, as we will see. Clearly, dispositional tendencies are not destiny. Children's transactions with parents, peers, schools, and neighborhoods moderate the influence of personality traits; and the search for moderators and mediators should pay dividends in the study of the moral personality. Indeed, Hart and Matsuba (this volume) show how neighborhood effects influence prosocial behavior and moral identity.

Continuity and Consequences. Personalities are not easy to change, however, and dispositions can influence a wide variety of outcomes across the lifecourse, which is why moral psychology cannot afford to neglect them.

The rank-order stability of personality is remarkably high from early childhood to adulthood (Roberts & DelVecchio, 2000), and its influence on adaptation, competence, and adjustment is pervasive (Rothbart & Bates, 1998). Research shows, for example, that childhood personality characteristics predict indices of adaptation ten (Shiner, 2000) and twenty (Shiner, Masten, & Roberts, 2003) years later, and that the young child is, indeed, "father of the man" (Caspi, 2000). Two examples will make the point.

Caspi (2000; also Caspi & Silva, 1995) identified undercontrolled, inhibited, and well-adjusted temperament types in the Dunedin sample (Silva & Stanton, 1996) of three-year-olds, and then tracked them at various times up through young adulthood. Remarkably, temperament measured at age three predicted behavioral problems in childhood and adolescence and the structure of personality at age 18. But three-year-old temperament also predicted the quality of interpersonal relationships, the extent of social support, employment status, psychiatric risk, and criminality in young adulthood.

Shiner (2000) identified four higher-order dispositions (Mastery Motivation, Academic Conscientiousness, Surgent Engagement, Agreeableness) in a community of sample of 8- to 12-year-old children, and then attempted to predict both concurrent and longitudinal adaptation ten years later (and twenty years later, Shiner et al., 2003). Her results showed that "childhood personality traits evidence robust, conceptually coherent relationships with adaptation both concurrently and across time" (p. 310). For example, the average correlation of childhood Mastery Motivation with indices of academic achievement, conduct (rule-abidingness vs. antisocial behavior) and peer social competence ten years later was $r = .34$ (the average of the concurrent relationship was $r = .30$). The average correlation of Agreeableness across the three indices of adaptation was $r = .31$ (concurrent $r = .24$). To put this in perspective: the magnitude of these correlations fall within the top third of correlations reported in psychological research (Hemphill, 2003).

Of course, the continuity of personality also reflects the influence of transactions with environments (Caspi, 2000). We are producers of our own development (Lerner & Busch-Rossnagel, 1981) to the extent that our personality evokes consistent patterns of response from others; or else we actively select environments, friends, groups, and settings that support our dispositional tendencies. But our main point here is that the ubiquity of personality, and its pervasive and long-term influence on the way one's life goes, should figure more prominently in accounts of the moral life. There is no reason to suppose that dispositional tendencies influence every other facet of human experience, but leaves the moral domain untouched.

Take, for example, Blasi's (2005) influential account of moral character. Found lurking here are notions that bear striking resemblance to dispositional constructs. Much like a good trait theorist, Blasi distinguishes lower- and higher-order virtues. Of particular interest are two clusters of higher-order traits. One cluster is called "willpower" (or, alternatively, self-control). Willpower as self-control is a toolbox of skills that permit self-regulation in problem-solving. Breaking down problems, goal-setting, focusing attention, avoiding distractions, resisting temptation, staying on task, persevering with determination and self-discipline – these are the skills of willpower. The second cluster of higher-order traits are organized around the notion of "integrity," which refers to internal self-consistency. Being a person of one's word, being transparent to oneself, being responsible, self-accountable, sincere, resistant to self-deception – these are the dispositions of integrity. Integrity is felt as *responsibility* when one constrains the self with intentional acts of self-control in the pursuit of moral aims. Integrity is felt as *identity* when one imbues the construction of self-meaning with moral desires.

Clearly there are a host of empirical questions embedded in this account, not the least of which is how to account empirically for the two higher-order clusters, their relationship to each other, and to important prosocial and moral behavioral outcomes. But it is not difficult to see that at least one of the clusters – willpower as self-control – is a full toolbox of temperament and personality trait dispositions.

Special Status of Early Adulthood. Although much research is directed properly to the early organization of personality and its forward-leaning influence on developmental outcomes, there is now increasing evidence that early adulthood might also be a fertile period for investigation. In a meta-analysis of 92 longitudinal samples, Roberts, Walton, and Viechtbauer (2006) found that mean-level change in personality is found predominantly in young adulthood, particularly for traits such as conscientiousness, emotional stability, and social dominance-extraversion. They note that adolescence may be a period of "personality trait moratorium," just as it is an identity moratorium, a time of exploration not just in terms of identity commitments but in dispositional qualities as well. But these qualities become consolidated when individuals make the transition to adulthood. "It is during young adulthood," they write, "when people begin to confront the realities of becoming an adult and when we find significant gains in personality traits" (p. 20). As a result the authors suggest that the window for investigating personality development be opened a bit wider to include this part of the lifecourse. The implication is straightforward for researchers interested in moral self-identity and moral personality.

Traits, Types, and Moral Functioning

Traits. A number of research programs have worked dispositional variables into their investigation of topics in the moral domain. For example, Walker and his colleagues examined the personality of moral exemplars in terms of the Big Five taxonomy. One studied showed that the personality of moral exemplars was oriented toward conscientiousness and agreeableness (Walker, 1999). Agreeableness also characterized young adult moral exemplars (Matsuba & Walker, 2005). In a study of brave, caring, and just Canadians, Walker and Pitts (1998) found that brave exemplars aligned with a complex of traits associated with extraversion; caring exemplars aligned with agreeableness; and just exemplars with a mixture of conscientiousness, emotional stability, and openness to experience. This pattern was largely replicated by Walker and Hennig (2004). More recently Walker and Frimer (this volume) have utilized several layers of the "new Big Five" (McAdams, this volume) to good advantage in their analysis of the dispositional traits, characteristic adaptations, and life narratives of brave and caring exemplars.

Types. Hart (2005; Hart & Matsuba, this volume) proposed a model of moral identity that also carves out a significant role for both disposition and characteristic adaptations. In this model, moral identity is influenced by (1) enduring dispositional and (2) social (family, culture, social class) characteristics that change slowly and are beyond the volitional control of the child. Children, after all, do not choose their personality traits or their family, their neighborhood or other social conditions of their rearing. Yet these early childhood factors exert a long influence on adolescent moral identity. In one study Hart, Atkins, and Fegley (2003) showed that adolescents whose personality profile was judged "resilient" when they were children were more likely to be engaged in voluntary community service in adolescence than were teens who had undercontrolled or overcontrolled personality profiles as children.

Prosocial Behavior. There have been attempts to understand the dispositional basis of prosocial behavior. For example, there is considerable evidence of a relationship between empathy-related responding and children's prosocial behavior (Eisenberg, Spinrad, & Sadovsky, 2006). Moreover, sociability appears to influence children's helping behavior, particularly helping behavior that is emitted spontaneously, toward strangers and in unfamiliar settings (Eisenberg, Fabes, & Spinrad, 2006). Eisenberg and her colleagues also investigated whether there is a dispositional or personological basis for prosocial behavior. In one study, spontaneous, other-oriented prosocial sharing behavior (but not low-cost helping or compliant prosocial behavior) observed at ages four to five predicted actual and self-reported prosocial behavior up to 17 years later, a relationship that was partially mediated by sympathy (Eisenberg, Guthrie, Murphy, Shepard, Cumberland, & Carlo, 1999). Similarly, self-reports of prosocial dispositions in early adulthood often related to self-reports of sympathy, empathy, and prosocial behavior 10 to 16 years earlier (Eisenberg, Guthrie, Cumberland, Murphy, Shepard, Zhou, & Carlo, 2002). These studies support the claim that there is a prosocial personality disposition that emerges in early childhood and is consistent over time, although the manifestation of the "altruistic personality" may vary with the demand characteristics of social contexts (Carlo, Eisenberg, Troyer, Switzer, & Speer, 1991, Carlo et al., this volume).

Conscience. Kochanska's research program documents the interplay of temperament, parenting, and the emergence of the moral self (Kochanska, 2002a; Kochanska & Aksan, 2004; Kochanska, Aksan, & Koenig, 1995; Kochanska et al., 2004; Thompson, this volume). Her model of emerging morality begins with the quality of parent-child attachment. A strong, mutually responsive relationship with caregivers orients the child to be receptive to parental influence (Kochanska, 1997a, 2002b).

This "mutually responsive orientation" (MRO) is characterized by shared positive affect, mutually coordinated enjoyable routines ("good times") and a "cooperative interpersonal set" that describes the joint willingness of parent and child to initiate and reciprocate relational overtures. It is from within the context of the MRO, and the secure attachment that it denotes, that the child is eager to comply with parental expectations and standards. There is "committed compliance" on the part of the child to the norms and values of caregivers that, in turn, motivates moral internalization and the work of "conscience." This was documented in a recent longitudinal study. Children who had experienced a highly responsive relationship with mothers over the first 24 months of life strongly embraced maternal prohibitions and gave evidence of strong self-regulation skills at preschool age (Kochanksa, Aksan, Prisco, & Adams, 2008).

Kochanska's model moves, then, from security of attachment to committed compliance to moral internalization. This movement is also expected to influence the child's emerging internal representation of the self. As Kochanska et al. (2002a) put it:

> "Children with a strong history of committed compliance with the parent are likely gradually to come to view themselves as embracing the parent's values and rules. Such a moral self, in turn, comes to serve as the regulator of future moral conduct and, more generally, of early morality." (p. 340)

But children bring something to the interaction, too – namely, their temperament. Indeed, Kochanska (1991, 1993) argues that there are multiple pathways to conscience, and that one parenting style is not uniformly more effective irrespective of the temperamental dispositions of the child. She suggests, for example, that children who are highly prone to fearful reactions would profit from gentle, low power-assertive discipline. This "silken glove" approach capitalizes on the child's own discomfort to produce the optimal level of anxiety that facilitates the processing and retention of parents' socialization messages. But for "fearless" children another approach is called for, not the "iron hand," which would only make the fearless child angry, highly reactive, and resistant to socialization messages (Kochanska, Aksan, & Joy, 2007), but rather one that capitalizes on positive emotions (rather than on anxiety).

Here, then, are two pathways to the internalization of conscience. For fearful children, it leads through the soft touch of gentle discipline; for fearless children, it leads through the reciprocal positive parent-child relationship. This has now been documented in a number of studies (Kochanska, 1997b; Kochanska, Forman, Aksan, & Dunbar, 2005). Moreover, this model is drawing increasing interest as a possible developmental grounding for the emergence of mature forms of moral self-identity (Lapsley, 2007; Narvaez & Lapsley, in press).

THE SOCIAL COGNITIVE DEVELOPMENT OF THE MORAL PERSONALITY

To this point we have explored the contribution of the trait dispositional discipline of personality science to understanding moral personality. We now turn our attention to the social-cognitive, the second discipline of personality. The expression "social cognitive development" signifies two rather different research traditions. The older tradition investigated (often stage-) developmental variation in domains – such as person perception, interpersonal- and self-understanding, and, of course, moral development (Damon, 1977; Damon & Hart, 1982; Livesly & Bromley, 1973; Shantz, 1975; Selman, 1980).

More recently, Olson and Dweck (2008) have proposed a "blueprint" for social cognitive development (SCD) that attempts to bridge the divide between cognitive and social development. In the manner of cognitive development, mental representations and cognitive processes are the core of SCD. These are, after all, the "means by which children package their experiences and carry them forward" (Dweck & London, 2007, p. 121). But cognitive processes also are deeply embedded in social relationships both as antecedents and outcomes. Four goals are outlined to facilitate SCD research (Olson & Dweck, 2008): *Identify* and then assess a social cognitive mental representation or process, *manipulate* it to see how it changes some aspect of the child's functioning, investigate its *antecedents*, and *compare* how the representations or processes work in natural settings and in the lab.

Lapsley and Narvaez (2004; also Aquino & Freeman, this volume) have proposed a social cognitive account of the moral personality. Although social cognitive theory draws attention to cognitive-affective mechanisms that influence social perception, these mechanisms also serve to create and sustain patterns of individual differences. If schemas are easily primed and readily activated ("chronically accessible"), then they direct our attention selectively to certain features of our experience. This selective framing disposes one to select schema-compatible tasks, goals, and settings that canalize and maintain our dispositional tendencies (Cantor, 1990). We choose environments, in other words, that support or reinforce our schema-relevant interests, which illustrates the reciprocal nature of person-context transaction. Moreover, we tend to develop highly practiced behavioral routines in those areas of our experience that are regulated by chronically accessible schemes. In these areas of our social experience, we become "virtual experts," and in these life contexts, social cognitive schemas function as "a ready, sometimes automatically available plan of action" (Cantor, 1990, p. 738). In this way, chronically accessible schemas function as the cognitive carriers of dispositions.

Social cognitive theory asserts, then, that schema accessibility and conditions of activation are critical for understanding how patterns of individual differences are channeled and maintained. From this perspective, Lapsley and Narvaez (2004) claim that a moral person, or a person who has a moral identity or character, is one for whom moral categories are chronically accessible. If having a moral identity is just when moral notions are central, important, and essential to one's self-understanding, then notions that are central, important, and essential are also those that are chronically accessible for appraising the social landscape. Chronically accessible moral schemas provide a dispositional readiness to discern the moral dimensions of experience, as well as to underwrite the discriminative facility in selecting situationally appropriate behavior.

Five Advantages. A social cognitive model of moral personality has at least five attractive features (Narvaez & Lapsley, 2009). First, social cognitive theory accords with the paradigmatic assumptions of ecological "systems" models of development (Lerner, 2006). Both developmental systems and social cognitive theory affirm that a dispositional behavioral signature is to be found at the intersection of Person × Context interactions. This alignment increases the probability of articulating robust, integrative social cognitive developmental models of moral personality.

Second, it provides an explanation for the model of moral identity favored by Blasi (1984), who argues that one has a moral identity just when moral categories are essential, central, and important to one's self-understanding. A social cognitive interpretation would add that moral categories that are essential, central, and important for one's self-identity would also be ones that are chronically accessible for interpreting the social landscape. These categories would be on-line, vigilant, easily primed, easily activated, for discerning the meaning of events, for noticing the moral dimensions of experience, and, once activated, to dispose one to interpret events in light of one's moral commitments.

Third, this model accounts for the felt necessity of moral commitments experienced by moral exemplars, their experience of moral clarity or felt conviction that their decisions are evidently appropriate, justified, and true. Typically moral exemplars report that they "just knew" what was required of them, automatically as it were, without the experience of working through an elaborate decision-making calculus (Colby & Damon, 1992). Yet this is precisely the outcome of preconscious activation of chronically accessible constructs that it should induce strong feelings of certainty or conviction with respect to social judgments (Bargh, 1989; Narvaez & Lapsley, 2009).

Fourth, the social cognitive framework is better able to account for the implicit, tacit, and automatic features of moral functioning (Narvaez & Lapsley, 2005). There is growing recognition that much of human decision making is under nonconscious control (Bargh, 2005) and occurs with an automaticity that belies the standard notions of rational, deliberative calculation (Bargh & Chartrand, 1999). Though this possibility offends traditional accounts of moral development, there is no reason to think that automaticity is evident in every domain of decision making except the moral domain (Narvaez & Lapsley, 2009). However, unlike the social intuitionist model (Haidt, 2001), which frontloads automaticity prior to judgment and reasoning as a result of intuitions that are constitutive of human nature (and hence prior to learning and enculturation), the social cognitive approach to moral personality locates automaticity on the backend of development as the result of repeated experience, of instruction, intentional coaching, and socialization (Lapsley & Hill, in press). It is the automaticity that comes from expertise in life domains, where we have vast experience and well-practiced behavioral routines (Cantor, 1990).

Finally, a social cognitive model of the moral personality can account for situational variability in the display of a virtue (Cervone, this volume). The accessibility of social cognitive schemas underwrites not only the discriminative facility in the selection of situationally appropriate behavior, but also the automaticity of schema activation that contributes to the tacit, implicit qualities often associated with the "habits" of moral character (Lapsley & Narvaez, 2006).

Recent research has attempted to document the social cognitive dimensions of moral cognition. For example, research shows that conceptions of good character (Lapsley & Lasky, 1999) and of moral, spiritual, and religious persons (Walker & Pitts, 1998) are organized as cognitive prototypes. Moreover, moral chronicity appears to be a dimension of individual differences that influences spontaneous trait inference and text comprehension (Narvaez, Lapsley, Hagele, & Lasky, 2006). In two studies, Narvaez et al. (2006) showed that moral chronics and nonchronics respond differently to the dispositional and moral implications of social cues.

Social Cognitive Development. Of course, all social cognitive theories share a common defect, which is the absence of a developmental account of the pathways that bring individuals to adult forms of functioning specified by the theory. Lapsley and Narvaez (2004) speculate on the developmental grounding of their social cognitive account of the moral personality. They argue that moral chronicity is built on the foundation of generalized event representations that characterize early sociopersonality development (Thompson, 1998). Event representations have been called the "basic building blocks of cognitive development" (Nelson & Gruendel, 1981, p. 131). They are working models of how social routines unfold and of what one can expect of social experience. These prototypic knowledge structures are progressively elaborated in the early dialogues with caregivers, who help children review, structure, and consolidate memories in scriptlike fashion (Fivush, Kuebli, & Chubb, 1992).

But the key characterological turn of significance for moral personality is how these early social-cognitive units are transformed from episodic into autobiographical memory. At some point, specific episodic memories must be integrated into a narrative form that references a self whose story it is. The mechanisms that drive this integration are both cognitive and social. On the cognitive front, autobiographical memory development shows two important achievements during the preschool years. First, children begin to include subjective interpretations of the events (Fivush, 2001), which include markers of the personal significance of the event for the self. Second, children's event memories show greater grammatical and emotional detail (Fivush & Haden, 1997), which signals increasing maturity as a "storyteller."

But socialization experiences are also crucial. Parents help children organize events into personally relevant biographical memories by the frequency and kinds of questions they ask about daily routines or recent experiences. Parental interrogatives ("What happened when you pushed your sister? What should you do next?") are a scaffold that helps children structure events in narrative fashion, which provide, in turn, as part of the self-narrative, action-guiding scripts ("apologize when you harm") that become frequently practiced, overlearned, routine, habitual, and automatic (a type of moral expertise development; Narvaez & Lapsley, 2005). Parental interrogatives might also include reference to norms, standards, and values, so that the moral ideal-self becomes part of the child's autobiographical narrative. In this way parents help children identify morally relevant features of their experience and encourage the formation of social cognitive schemas that are chronically accessible (Lapsley & Narvaez, 2004).

If the Lapsley-Narvaez model is plausible, it would then suggest that the most important forms of moral character formation are not the result of an intervention, nor are they the product of a formal curriculum, and they do not take place primarily in schools. Rather they are grounded by the prosaic transactions in the daily family and social life of the young child. The banality and ubiquity of moral character formation, its ordinariness, the way it ramifies into developmental and personality constructs and processes of all kinds, points to a pressing need for comprehensive, intentional, integrative, and interdisciplinary approaches to studying this model.

Indeed, we are now beginning to see with more clarity how topics of long interest to developmental science – topics such as social referencing, internal working models, event representation, theory of mind, self-regulation – have implications for the developing moral self (Thompson, this volume), even though these are not typically considered contributions to a moral development literature. How these acquisitions are carried forward, how they take on dispositions and are moderated by transactions with the world, and how they come to influence behavior and under what conditions – these are the pressing questions before the new field of moral personality development.

CONCLUSION

We should like to conclude, then, with some ideas about the future development of the nascent field of moral personality development that are suggested by the present review. Clearly there is a case, first of all, for future research to examine both lower- and higher-order temperament dispositions for emergent signs of the moral self. On one level, this is a call for more research on the dispositional antecedents of behavior that is demonstrably prosocial. But on another level it calls for investigations into the dispositional sources of variation in social and cognitive achievements that are crucial for the early organization of the moral personality, such as self-regulation, self-conscious emotions, theory of mind, event representation, among others. These acquisitions seem to underlie, for example, the emerging sense of what is normative and what one ought to do (Narvaez & Lapsley, 2009; Thompson, this volume), an understanding that goes to the heart of what it means to be a moral person. Is there a dispositional element to these social cognitive acquisitions? This question might well guide integrative research in the development of the moral personality.

A second possible future concerns research on the manner in which dispositions are elaborated in the service of prosocial behavior. We noted earlier how some of the mechanisms of elaboration proposed by Caspi and Shiner (2006) require significant social cognitive competencies. For example, *environmental construal* might well govern the transformation of temperament into personality, but its social cognitive elements are well known to developmental researchers (Dodge, 1980; Dodge & Frame, 1982). Similarly, the study of *social and temporal comparisons* and *environmental selection* as mechanisms for elaborating temperament might profit from social cognitive literatures on self-beliefs (Caprara, Barbaranelli, Pastorelli & Cervone, 2004) and self-guides (Higgins, 1987), respectively.

A third line of research would test directly a key empirical claim of Lapsley-Narvaez that individuals with a strong moral identity – which is to say, individuals for whom moral notions are central, important, and essential to self-understanding – would also have moral notions chronically accessible for guiding social information processing.

A fourth line of research should examine the empirical implications of Blasi's (2005) model of moral character. The notions of willpower and integrity are key higher-order virtues that underwrite the second-order volitions and moral desires of the subjective self-as-agent (Lapsley, 2007). Yet, as we have seen, these components of moral self-identity are built on a foundation of dispositional constructs, the implication of which has not been examined directly.

Perhaps one strategy is to approach this problem with the organizing framework of the "new Big Five" (McAdams & Pals, 2006). This framework for integrating personality science has already shown its conceptual (McAdams, this volume) and empirical (Walker & Frimer, this volume) utility for moral psychology; and it invites new investigations into how dispositional traits map into characteristic moral adaptations, and how these contribute to individual differences in the thematic narratives that individuals construct to make sense of their lives. Moral identity may turn out to be not so much a matter of chronically accessible schemas (at the level of "characteristic" adaptations), but rather a kind of self-narrative that makes sense of one's being-in-the-world.

Moreover, for all the importance of early childhood, the study of moral personality development cannot neglect the adult lifespan, and particularly early adulthood, which seems to be a period of particular ferment for the construction of moral self-identity (and its presumptive narrative structure). The question of what it means to be a moral person is a lifelong concern, and our developmental work must follow accordingly. But the division of labor whereby personologists and social psychologists focus on adults, while developmentalists focus on children, is not helpful. Fortunately, the pace of integrative research across fields is increasing, and the blueprint for social cognitive development (Olson & Dweck, 2008) is also a welcome step in this direction.

Finally, on a methodological note, the field of moral personality research would profit from new ways to measure the constructs of interest. Particularly glaring is the relative lack of assessment strategies for measuring such foundational constructs as "moral identity." We have taken some steps in this direction by constructing a Q-sort assessment of moral identity that is showing promising results (Jimenez, Nawrocki, Hill, & Lapsley, 2008), although much more research is required.

Moreover, though we talk about dispositional traits, adopt variable-centered measurement strategies, and understand the personality as something that is layered, the truth is that the object of study is a whole person. We are sympathetic to the point raised by Robins and Tracey (2003) that person-centered strategies might prove more attractive to developmental researchers who want to study the child holistically. With such strategies we can ask: How do moral qualities cohere within individuals? Are there different moral types?

These questions are central to some basic claims about moral personality. It is believed widely that moral identity is a dimension of individual differences, and in a double sense. First, people differ on how central moral notions are to their sense of self-understanding. Some individuals construct their self-understanding on moral grounds; others have only a glancing acquaintance with morality but construct the self around other priorities. Second, even among those who value morality as a source of self-definition, there are different ways of living a moral life well – some might orient to justice, some to care, and still others to utility or virtues (and so on). These dual claims about individual differences in moral identity have never been tested adequately, yet doing so would seem to be a high priority for a field of moral personality development. A person-centered assessment strategy that identifies a typology of moral personality in this way would open up a fascinating and productive line of research.

REFERENCES

Asendorpf, J. B., & Van Aken, A. G. (1999). Resilient, overcontrolled and undercontrolled personality prototypes in childhood: Replicability, predictive power and the trait-type issue. *Journal of Personality and Social Psychology*, 77, 815–832.

Bandura, A. (1986). *Social foundations of thought and action: A social cognitive theory*. Englewood Cliffs, NJ: Prentice-Hall.

(1999). Social cognitive theory of personality. In D. Cervone & .Y. Shoda (Eds.), *The coherence of personality: Social cognitive bases of consistency, variability and organization* (pp. 185–241). New York: Guilford.

Blasi, A. (1983). Moral cognition and moral action: A theoretical perspective. *Developmental Review*, 3, 178–21.

(2005). Moral character: A psychological approach. In D. K. Lapsley & F. C. Power (Eds.), *Character psychology and character education* (pp. 18–35). Notre Dame, IN: University of Notre Dame Press.

Block, J. (1971). *Lives through time*. Berkeley, CA: Bancroft.

Block, J. H., & Block, J. (1980). The role of ego control and ego resiliency in the organization of behavior. In W. A. Collins (Eds.), *Minnesota Symposium on Child Psychology, Vol. 13* (pp. 39–101). Hillsdale, NJ: Lawrence Erlbaum Associates.

Caprara, G. V., Barbaranelli, C., Pastorelli, C., & Cervone, D. (2004). The contributions of self-efficacy beliefs to psychosocial outcomes in adolescence: Predicting beyond global dispositional tendencies. *Personality and Individual Differences*, 37, 751–763.

Carlo, G., Eisenberg, N., Troyer, D., Switzer, G., & Speer, A. L. (1991). The altruistic personality: In what contexts is it apparent? *Journal of Personality and Social Psychology*, 61, 450–458.

Caspi, A. (2000). The child is father of the man: Personality continuities from childhood to adulthood. *Journal of Personality and Social Psychology*, 78, 158–172.

(1987). Personality in the life course. *Journal of Personality and Social Psychology,* 53, 1203–1213.

Caspi, A., Roberts, B. W., & Shiner, R. (2005). Personality development: Stability and change. *Annual Review of Psychology,* 56, 453–484.

Caspi, A., & Shiner, R. L. (2006). Personality development. In W. Damon & R. M. Lerner (Eds.), *Handbook of child psychology* (6th Ed., Vol. 3, Nancy Eisenberg, Vol. Ed., *Social, emotional and personality development,* pp. 300–365). New York: Wiley.

Caspi, A. & Silva, P. A. (1995). Temperamental qualities at age 3 predict personality traits in young adulthood: Longitudinal evidence from a birth cohort. *Child Development,* 66, 486–491.

Cervone, D. (2005). Personality architecture: Within person structures and processes. *Annual Review of Psychology,* 56, 423–452.

(1991). The two disciplines of personality psychology. *Psychological Science,* 2, 371–377.

Cervone, D., Shadel, W. G., & Jencius, S. (2001). Social cognitive theory of personality assessment. *Personality and Social Psychology Review,* 5, 33–51.

Cervone, D., &. Shoda, Y. (Eds.) (1999). *The coherence of personality: Social cognitive bases of consistency, variability and organization* (pp. 185–241). New York: Guilford

Colby, A., Kohlberg, L., Gibbs, J., & Lieberman, M. (1983). A longitudinal study of moral judgment. *Monographs of the Society for Research in Child Development,* 48 (1–2, Serial No. 200). Chicago: University of Chicago Press.

Damon, W. (1977). *The social world of the child.* San Francisco: Jossey-Bass.

Dodge, K. A. (1980). Social cognition and children's aggressive behavior. *Child Development,* 51, 620–635.

Dodge, K. A., & Frame, J. M. (1982). Social cognitive biases and deficits in aggressive boys. *Child Development,* 53, 620–635.

Doris, J. M. (2002). *Lack of character: Personality and moral behavior.* New York: Cambridge University Press.

Dweck, C., & London, B. E. (2007). The role of mental representations in social development. In G. W. Ladd (Ed.), *Appraising the human development science: Essays in honor of Merrill Palmer Quarterly* (pp. 121–137). Detroit, MI: Wayne State University Press.

Eisenberg, N. (2000). Emotion, regulation and moral development. *Annual Review of Psychology,* 51, 665–697.

(2006). Prosocial development. In W. Damon & R. M. Lerner (Eds.), *Handbook of child psychology* (6th. Ed, Vol. 3, N. Eisenberg, Vol. Ed., *Social, emotional and personality development,* pp. 646–718). New York: Wiley.

Eisenberg, N., Guthrie, D. K., Cumberland, A., Murphy, B. C., Shepard, S. A., Zhou, Q., & Carlo, G. (2002). Prosocial development in early adulthood: A longitudinal study. *Journal of Personality and Social Psychology,* 82, 993–1006.

Eisenberg, N., Guthrie, D. K., Murphy, B. C., Shepard, S. A., Cumberland, A., & Carlo, G. (1999). Consistency and development of prosocial dispositions: A longitudinal study. *Child Development,* 70, 1360–1372.

Eisenberg, N., Spinrad, T. L., & Sadovsky, A. (2006). Empathy-related responding in children. In M. Killen & J. G. Smetana (Eds.), *Handbook of moral development* (pp. 517–549). Mahwah, NJ: Lawrence Erlbaum Associates.

Flanagan, O. & Rorty, A. O. (Eds). (1990). *Identity, character and morality: Essays in moral psychology*. Cambridge, MA: The MIT Press.

Funder, D. C. (1991). Global traits: A neo-Allportian approach. *Psychological Science, 2*, 31–39.

(1995) On the accuracy of personality judgments: A realist approach. *Psychological Review, 102*(4), 652–670.

(1996). Towards a resolution of the personality triad: Persons, situations and behaviors. *Journal of Research in Personality, 40*, 21–34.

Funder, D. C., & Colvin, C. R. (1991). Explorations in behavioral consistency: Properties of persons, situations and behaviors. *Journal of Personality and Social Psychology, 60* (5), 773–794.

Funder, D. C., & Ozer, D. J. (1991). Behavior as a function of the situation. *Journal of Personality and Social Psychology, 44*, 107–112.

Harman, G. (2000). The nonexistence of character traits. *Proceedings of the Aristotelian Society, 100*, 223–226.

Hart, D. (2005). The development of moral identity. *Nebraska Symposium on Motivation, 51*, 165–196.

Hart, D., Atkins, R., & Fegley, S. (2003). Personality and development in childhood: A person-centered approach. *Monographs for the Society for Research in Child Development*. Hillsdale, NJ: Lawrence Erlbaum Associates.

Hart, D., Hofmann, V., Edelstein, W., & Keller, M. (1997). The relation of childhood personality types to adolescent behavior and development: A longitudinal study of Icelandic children. *Developmental Psychology, 33*, 195–205.

Hart, D., Keller, M., Edelstein, W. & Hofmann, V. (1998). Childhood personality influences on social cognitive development: A longitudinal study. *Journal of Personality and Social Psychology, 74*(5), 1278–1289.

Hastings, P. D., Zahn-Waxler, C., & McShane, K. (2006). We are, by nature, moral creatures: Biological bases of concern for others. In M. Killen & J. G. Smetana (Eds.), *Handbook of moral development* (pp. 483–516). Mahwah, NJ: Lawrence Erlbaum Associates.

Hemphill, J. F. (2003). Interpreting the magnitudes of correlation coefficients. *American Psychologist, 58*, 78–80.

Higgins, E. T. (1987). Self-discrepancy. A theory relating self and affect. *Psychological Review, 94*, 319–340.

(1990). Personality, social psychology, and person-situation relations: Standards and knowledge activation as a common language. In L. A. Pervin (Ed.), *Handbook of personality: Theory and research* (pp. 303–338). New York: Guilford Press.

Huey, S. J., & Weisz, J. R. (1997). Ego control and ego resiliency and the five-factor model as predictors of behavioral problems in clinic-referred children and adolescents. *Journal of Abnormal Psychology, 106*, 404–415.

Jimenez, J. A., Nawrocki, L., Hill, P. L., & Lapsley, D. K. (2008). *Assessing moral identity development: Validation of a moral identity Q-sort*. Paper presented at the Annual Meeting of the Midwestern Psychological Association, Chicago.

Kendrick, D. T., & Funder, D. C. (1988). Profiting from controversy: Lessons from the person-situation debate. *American Psychologist, 43*(1), 23–34.

Kochanska, G. (1991). Socialization and temperament in the development of guilt and conscience. *Child Development, 62*, 1379–1392.

(1993). Toward a synthesis of parental socialization and child temperament in early development of conscience. *Child Development, 64,* 325–347.

(1997a). Mutually-responsive orientation between mothers and their children: Implications for socialization. *Child Development, 68,* 94–112.

(1997b). Multiple pathways to conscience for children who have different temperaments: From toddlerhood to age 5. *Developmental Psychology, 33,* 228–240.

(2002a). Committed compliance, moral self and internalization: A mediated model. *Developmental Psychology, 38,* 339–351.

(2002b). Mutually-responsive orientation between mothers and their children: A context for the early development of conscience. *Current Directions in Psychological Science, 11,* 191–195.

Kochanska, G., & Aksan, N. (2004). Conscience in childhood: Past, present and future. *Merrill-Palmer Quarterly, 50,* 299–310.

Kochanska, G., Aksan, N., & Joy, M. E. (2007). Children's fearfulness as a moderator of parenting in early socialization: Two longitudinal studies. *Developmental Psychology, 43,* 222–237.

Kochanska, G., Aksan, N., Prisco, T. R., & Adams, E. E. (2008). Mother-child and father-child mutually responsive orientation in the first two years and children's outcomes at preschool age: Mechanisms of influence. *Child Development, 79,* 30–44.

Kochanska, G., Forman, D. R., Aksan, N., & Dunbar, S. B. (2005). Pathways to conscience: Early mother-child mutually-responsive orientation and children's moral emotion, conduct and conduct. *Journal of Child Psychology and Psychiatry, 46,* 19–34.

Kohlberg, L. (1969). Stage and sequence: The cognitive-developmental approach to socialization. In D. Goslin (Ed.), *Handbook of socialization theory and research* (pp. 347–480). Chicago, IL: Rand McNally.

(1987). The young child as a philosopher. In L. Kohlberg (Ed., with colleagues), *Child psychology and childhood education: A cognitive-developmental view* (pp. 13–44). New York: Longman.

Kohlberg, L., Levine, C., & Hewer, A. (1983). *Moral stages: A current formulation and a response to critics.* In J. A. Meacham (Ed.), *Contributions to human development (Vol. 10).* Basel: Karger.

Lapsley, D. K. (2007) Moral self-identity as the aim of education. In L. Nucci & D. Narvaez (Eds). *Handbook of moral and character education.* Mahwah, NJ: Lawrence Erlbaum Associates.

Lapsley, D. K., & Hill, P. L. (2008). On dual processing and heuristic approaches to moral cognition. *Journal of Moral Education, 37,* 313–332.

Lapsley, D. K., & Narvaez, D. (Eds., 2004a). *Moral development, self and identity.* Mahwah, NJ: Lawrence Erlbaum Associates.

Lapsley, D. K., & Narvaez, D. (2004b). A social-cognitive approach to the moral personality. In D. K. Lapsley & D. Narvaez (Eds.), *Moral development, self and identity* (pp. 189–212). Mahwah, NJ: Lawrence Erlbaum Associates.

Lerner, R. M. (2006). Developmental science, developmental systems and contemporary theories of human development. In W. Damon & R. M. Lerner (Eds.), *Handbook of child psychology.* (6th Ed., Vol. 1, R. M. Lerner, Vol. Ed., *Theoretical models of human development,* pp. 1–17). New York: Wiley.

Lerner, R. M., & Busch-Rossnagel, N. (Eds.) (1981). *Individuals as producers of their own development: A lifespan perspective*. New York: Academic Press.

Lewin, K. (1931). The conflict between Aristotelian and Galilean modes of thought in contemporary psychology. *Journal of General Psychology, 5*, 141–177.

Livesly W. J., & Bromley, D. B. (1973). *Person perception in childhood and adolescence*. London: Wiley.

Matsuba, K., & Walker, L. J. (2005). Young adult moral exemplars: The making of self through stories. *Journal of Research on Adolescence, 15*, 275–297.

McAdams, D., & Pals, J. L. (2006). The new big 5: Fundamental principles for an integrative science of personality. *American Psychologist, 61*, 204–217.

McCrae, R. R., & Costa, P. T. (1999). A five-factor theory of personality. In L. A. Pervin & O. P. John (Eds.), *Handbook of personality: Theory and research* (2nd ed., pp. 139–154). New York: Guilford.

McCrae, R. R., Costa, P. T., Ostendorf, F., Angleitner, A., Hrebickova, H., Avia, M. D., Sanz, J., Sanchez-Bernardos, M. L., Kusdil, M. E., Woodfield, R., Saunders, P. R., & Smith, P. B. (2000). Nature over nurture: Temperament, personality, and life span development. *Journal of Personality and Social Psychology, 78*, 173–186.

McCrae, R. R., Costa, P. T., Pedroso de Lima, M., Simoes, A., Ostendorf, F., Angleitner, A., Marusig, I., Bratko, D., Caprara, G. V., Barbaranelli, C., & Chae, J-H. (1999). Age differences in personality across the adult lifespan: Parallels in five cultures. *Developmental Psychology, 35*, 466–477.

Mischel, W. (1990). Personality dispositions revisited and revised: A view after three decades. In L. A. Pervin (Ed.), *Handbook of personality: Theory and research* (pp. 111–134). New York: Guilford Press.

Narvaez, D., & Lapsley, D. (2005). The psychological foundations of everyday morality and moral expertise. In D. Lapsley & C. Power (Eds.), *Character psychology and character education* (pp. 140–165). Notre Dame: IN: University of Notre Dame Press.

Narvaez, D., & Lapsley, D. K. (2009). Moral identity and the development of moral character. In D. Medin, L. Skitka, D. Bartels, & C. Bauman (Eds.), *Moral cognition and decision-making, Vol. 50 of Psychology of Learning and Motivation series (pp. 237–274)*. Elsevier.

Olson, K. B., & Dweck, C. (2008). A blueprint for social cognitive development. *Perspectives on Psychological Science, 3*, 193–202.

Ozer, D. J. (1986). *Consistency in personality: A methodological framework*. Berlin: Springer-Verlag.

Robins, R. W., & Tracy, J. L. (2003). Setting an agenda for a person-centered approach to personality development. *Monographs of the Society for Research in Child Development, 68* (Serial No. 272), 110–122.

Roberts, B. W., & DelVecchio, W. F. (2000). The rank-order consistency of personality traits from childhood to old age: A quantitative review of longitudinal studies. *Psychological Bulletin, 126*, 3–25.

Roberts, B. W., Walton, K. E., & Viechtbauer, W. (2006). Patterns of mean-level change in personality traits across the lifecourse: A meta-analysis of longitudinal studies. *Psychological Bulletin, 13*(2), 1–25.

Rothbart, M. K., Ahadi, S. A., Hershey, K. L., & Fisher, P. (2001). Investigations of temperament at 3 to 7 years: The children's behavior questionnaire. *Child Development, 72,* 1394–1408.

Rothbart, M. K., Ahadi, S. A., & Evans, D. E. (2000). Temperament and personality: Origins and outcomes. *Journal of Personality and Social Psychology, 78,* 122–135.

Rothbart, M. K., Ahadi, S. A., & Hershey, K. L. (1994). Temperament and social behavior in children. *Merrill-Palmer Quarterly, 40,* 21–39.

Rothbart, M. K., & Bates, J. E. (1998). Temperament. In W. Damon (Editor-in-Chief), & N. Eisenberg (Vol. Ed.), *Handbook of child psychology: Vol. 3. Social, emotional and personality development* (5th Ed., pp. 105–176). New York: Wiley.

—— (2006). Temperament. In W. Damon & R. M. Lerner (Eds.), *Handbook of child psychology* (6th Ed., Vol. 3, Nancy Eisenberg, Vol. Ed., *Social, emotional and personality development,* pp. 99–166). New York: Wiley.

Shantz, C. (1975). The development of social cognition. In E. M. Hetherington (Ed.), *Review of child development theory and research. Vol. 5.* Chicago: University of Chicago Press.

Shiner, R. L. (1998). How shall we speak of children's personalities in middle childhood? A preliminary taxonomy. *Psychological Bulletin, 124,* 308–332.

—— (2000). Linking childhood personality with adaptations: Evidence for continuity and change across time into late adolescence. *Journal of Personality and Social Psychology, 78,* 310–325.

Shiner, R. L., & Caspi, A. (2003). Personality differences in childhood and adolescence: Measurement, development and consequences. *Journal of Child Psychology and Psychiatry, 44*(1), 2–32.

Shiner, R. L., Masten, A. S., & Roberts, J. M. (2003). Childhood personality foreshadows adult personality and life outcomes two decades later. *Journal of Personality, 7,* 1145–1170.

Shoda, Y., Mischel, W., & Wright, J. C. (1993). The role of situational demands and cognitive competencies in behavior organization and personality coherence. *Journal of Personality and Social Psychology, 65,* 1023–1035.

Shoda, Y., Mischel, W., & Wright, J. C. (1994). Intraindividual stability in the organization and patterning of behavior: Incorporating psychological situations into the ideographic analysis of personality. *Journal of Personality and Social Psychology, 67,* 674–687.

Silva, P. A., & Stanton, W. (Eds.), (1996). *From child to adult: The Dunedin study.* Oxford: Oxford University Press.

Van Leeuwen, K., De Fruyt, F., & Mervielde, I. (2004). A longitudinal study of the utility of the resilient, overcontrolled, and undercontrolled personality types as predictors of children's and adolescents' problem behavior. *International Journal of Behavioral Development, 28,* 210–220.

Walker, L. J. (1999). The perceived personality of moral exemplars. *Journal of Moral Education, 28,* 145–162.

Walker, L. J., & Hennig, K. H. (1998). Moral functioning in the broader context of personality. In S. Hala (Ed.), *The development of social cognition* (pp. 297–327). East Sussex, UK: Psychology Press.

Walker, L. J., & Hennig, K. H. (2004). Differing conceptions of moral exemplarity: Just, brave and caring. *Journal of Personality and Social Psychology*, 86, 629–647.
Walker, L. J., & Pitts, R. C. (1998). Naturalistic conceptions of moral maturity. *Developmental Psychology*, 34, 403–419.
Wright, J. C., & Mischel, W. (1987). A conditional approach to dispositional constructs: The local predictability of social behavior. *Journal of Personality and Social Psychology*, 55, 454–469.
  (1988). Conditional hedges and the intuitive psychology of traits. *Journal of Personality and Social Psychology*, 55, 456–469.
Young, S. K., Fox, N., & Zahn-Waxler, C. (1999). The relations between temperament and empathy in 2-year olds. *Developmental Psychology*, 35, 1189–1197.

9

Urban Neighborhoods as Contexts for Moral Identity Development

DANIEL HART AND M. KYLE MATSUBA

Traditionally, research on moral identity has been preoccupied with identifying individual-level factors, such as traits or motives, associated with moral outcomes. In our current work we expand the field by examining how the construction of a *moral identity* is affected by broad social factors, particularly as they relate to urban poverty. We were interested in asking: What characteristics of adolescents and the worlds in which they live allow for the pursuit of moral projects? And, how can we – as parents, members of institutions, and citizens – foster the development of these characteristics in our youth and their social contexts? In addressing these questions, we first suggest that moral identity is formed in poor neighborhoods just as in any other neighborhoods, but that the conditions characteristic of urban poverty make such constructions more difficult to achieve. Nevertheless, it is possible for youth to develop a moral identity, and we provide tentative suggestions to help foster such development for adolescents living in poor urban neighborhoods.

A MODEL OF MORAL IDENTITY

Moral identity can be described as a commitment consistent with one's sense of self to lines of action that promote or protect the welfare of others. Our use of moral identity brings to the fore three qualities of moral life. First, moral life involves some awareness of, and reflection upon, obligations, virtues, and lines of action. This kind of consideration is captured well in Erikson's (1968) notion of identity. While there is much evidence to support the conclusion that many moral decisions are made quickly and automatically without much reflection (Bargh & Morsella, 2008), in our view moral identity is at least occasionally salient in awareness, and the object of conscious consideration. In a modern world in which values vary across contexts, it seems inevitable that one's commitments to others' welfare will conflict with those of still others, or with the prevailing norms for situations, and that reflection upon one's own moral choices will arise.

Second, moral life often coheres around specific obligations and domains, and this specificity of moral life can be captured by the notion of moral identity. Moral exemplars typically exhibit distinction in just a few areas of life, and only in some pursuits. For example, in studies by Colby and Damon (1992) and Walker and Frimer (2007), morally remarkable achievements in adulthood are most often realized through consistent efforts to a cause extended through long periods of time. Piliavin's (Piliavin & Callero, 1991; Lee, Piliavin, & Call, 1999) fascinating research on blood donation suggests how individuals become attached to a specific line of action – blood donation, which in turn contributes to the elaboration of thoughts and emotions tied to this action. The specificity of moral life is not well-captured by notions such as moral personality, or by stage notions of moral judgment, because both refer to tendencies (action or reasoning) that are evident in individuals across situations.

Thirdly, moral life is often social in nature, influenced by social factors. While there are clearly internal dispositions that contribute to moral behavior – and these shall be discussed in later sections – the social construction and maintenance of morality should not be ignored (Doris, 1998). Remarkable moral achievement is rarely done in social isolation (Colby & Damon, 1992; Hart & Fegley, 1995). Alternatively, one of the lessons that psychology and philosophy can glean from the study of genocide is that social factors can also produce moral collapse (Glover, 1999; Gourevitch, 1998).

The Sources of Moral Identity

Figure 9.1 depicts our model of moral identity. The model suggests that there are six constituents to moral identity arranged in two vertical layers. We discuss each layer in turn.

Enduring qualities. The first layer, at the left edge of the figure, is constituted of enduring personality and social characteristics that form the foundation for much of child and adolescent development. The kinds of personality and social characteristics in this layer change slowly and may be outside of children's and adolescents' volitional control.

Personality is constituted of the enduring behavioral and emotional tendencies of the individual, and these typically vary from person to person. For example, a person with pronounced extraversion tendencies typically is

216   Daniel Hart and M. Kyle Matsuba

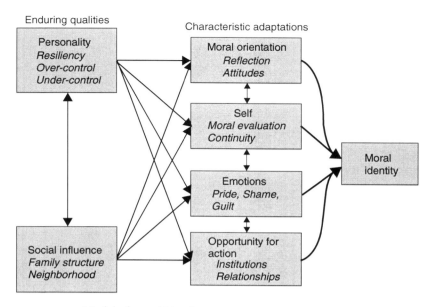

FIGURE 9.1. Model of moral identity.

gregarious and outgoing in social situations, in contrast to someone low in extraversion. There is considerable research indicating that personality traits are fairly stable over time (Roberts & DelVecchio, 2000) and have biological roots (Caspi, Roberts, & Shiner, 2005).

Three aspects of personality research are relevant to our discussion here. First, there is considerable evidence to indicate that dispositional personality is linked to prosocial and moral behavior (for a review, see Matsuba, Hart, & Atkins, 2007). Second, the relation of personality to prosocial behavior is broad rather than specific. This means that no single personality trait seems to be responsible for prosocial and moral behavior; instead, broadly resilient profiles of personality seem predictive of volunteering (Atkins, Hart, & Donnelly, 2005; Matsuba, Hart, & Atkins, 2007). Third, there is little research to indicate that childhood personality traits can be affected in targeted interventions. Similarly, broad patterns of family functioning have proven difficult to alter (St. Pierre, Layzer, Goodson, & Bernstein, 1997). We shall return to the discussion of neighborhood characteristics and social class; for now it suffices to point out that these two are stable characteristics of children's life-worlds.

The middle layer in Figure 9.1 corresponds to the set of qualities that McAdams and Pals (2006; McAdams, this volume) has called "characteristic adaptations." Our working hypotheses are that: (a) this middle layer in the figure mediates the relations of enduring characteristics – the qualities on the left side of the figure – to moral identity; (b) this middle layer is more malleable than the enduring qualities; and (c) this middle layer is linked to particular sets of activities.

Moral orientation refers to moral cognition, values, attitudes, and reflection. Not surprisingly, there is substantial evidence to explain how moral orientation develops in childhood (see Thompson, this volume). There is also substantial evidence to suggest that individuals pursuing lines of moral action often judge that they have obligations to do so (Colby & Damon, 1992). The extended involvement in an activity or practice is infused with beliefs and judgments that the pursuit is morally worthy. In our previous research, we have found that adults who believe they are obligated to participate in their communities are more likely to volunteer than those without such beliefs (Matsuba, Hart, & Atkins, 2007). Moreover, Schlenker, Miller, and Johnson (this volume) found the value of integrity to be an important characteristic associated with ethical behavior.

Images of self also contribute to moral identity. In our studies of urban adolescents who have demonstrated remarkable commitments to care for others (Hart & Fegley, 1995), we found that these adolescents' conceptions of self are more connected to the past and future, integrate more moral terms, and are more adult-oriented compared to adolescents without such commitments. As well, adults who volunteer many hours a month are more likely than adults who rarely volunteer to provide life narratives in which themes of agency are common (Loughman, 2008). Similarly, regular volunteers are more likely than infrequent volunteers to believe that they control their contributions to the welfare of others. In summary, then, moral identity seems supported by images of the self as agentic, moral, and continuous over time.

The *moral emotions* – shame, guilt, pride – also contribute to the development of moral identity (see Thompson, this volume). Hart and Matsuba (2007) have argued that while shame and guilt inhibit immoral behavior and may motivate compensatory action when moral norms are transgressed, pride is especially important in maintaining commitment to moral lines of action. Those who feel pride in their volunteer activities donate more hours than those who do not feel such pride.

Finally, *social relationships* and *opportunities* are critical for the formation and maintenance of moral identities. Most moral identities are formed in the contexts of social relationships and institutions. For example, volunteers report that their volunteer participation is usually the result of an invitation from a friend or colleague, rather than the product of solitary deliberation resulting in the choice of a particular altruistic activity (Independent Sector, 2001). Our research with urban adolescents suggested that those involved in remarkable caring activities most often were receiving support in one form or another from institutions – churches, civic organizations, and so on (Hart & Fegley, 1995). Moral action often has an institutional base. Moreover, not only is moral activity often based in institutions, but the meaning of the activity is shaped profoundly by the ideology of the institution within which it takes place. Social relationships and social institutions are tremendously important in the formation of moral identities.

To summarize, in our view, the ideal constellation of psychological and social qualities for commitment to moral projects includes: a resilient personality; sophisticated moral reflection, and prosocial values and attitudes; the ability to feel pride that is linked to one's moral activities; and, finally, a set of social relationships that both draw one into moral projects and protect one against moral collapse.

However, we posit that the relations among the components are relatively weak. This means that no single personality profile or background factor is prerequisite to moral accomplishment: The world has seen remarkable moral achievements from deeply neurotic people. And yet the failure of any element has the potential to have corrosive effects on the others. In our discussion of neighborhoods, we shall focus on the negative consequences that factors associated with neighborhood poverty might have on the various components of identity.

THE QUALITIES OF POOR URBAN NEIGHBORHOODS

What are poor urban neighborhoods like? We emphasize three qualities: stress, institutional density, and youthfulness, each of which has distinct effects on the components of the model.

Stress

High-poverty neighborhoods are often quite stressful. Evans (2004) found that children of low-income families were much more likely than children living in affluent families to be chronically exposed to neighborhood violence, pollution, and loud noise, as well as to live in decrepit housing. There are no data suggesting that chronic exposure to high levels of stress is beneficial, and much evidence to indicate that it can be deleterious for physical health (Shishehbor, Litaker, Pothier, & Lauer, 2006) and successful adjustment.

Personality. Our work suggests that chronic stress is associated with undesirable change in childhood personality. In much of this work, childhood personality is characterized in terms of a threefold typology: resilient, over-controlled, and under-controlled (see Hart, Atkins, & Fegley, 2003 for a review). These personality types measured in childhood are associated in predictable ways with adolescent academic progress (resilients do best; Hart, Atkins, & Fegley, 2003), aggression (under-controlled are highest; Atkins, 2007), sexual behavior (under-controlled are first to debut; Atkins & Hart, 2008), and volunteering (resilients are highest; Atkins, Hart, & Donnelly, 2005). Previous research has shown that children living in families with high levels of risk for stress (i.e., poverty, father absence, low-quality home environments) are more likely to change from resembling the resilient personality type in early childhood (three- & four-year-olds) to greater similarity with the under-controlled type in middle childhood (five- & six-year-olds) (Hart, Atkins, & Fegley, 2003).

In a recent study (Hart, Atkins, & Matsuba, 2008), we examined the relation between neighborhood poverty level, a proxy for exposure to the kinds of chronic stresses described earlier, and undesirable personality change. Participants in the study were drawn from the child sample of the 1977 National Longitudinal Survey of Youth (NLSY). The participants were born to a representative sample of women between the ages of 14 and 21 in 1977. Since 1985, the children born to these women have been tested and interviewed, and their mothers questioned about their children, every two years. When the children were three, four, five, and six years-of-age, mothers rated them on thirty temperament items, as well as on behavior problems. The thirty temperament items were used to estimate the similarity of the children to the three personality types previously described (resilient, over-controlled, under-controlled; details can be found in Hart, Atkins, & Matsuba, 2008). The neighborhood poverty rate for each child's neighborhood was estimated using U.S. Census data for the census tract of the family's residence. Family income, family characteristics (i.e., single head of household versus two-parent household, number of siblings), maternal educational attainment, and the quality of the home environment (assessed with the HOME scale) were also indexed. To assess the relation of personality to neighborhood poverty, the Time 2 (when the children were either five or six years of age) personality scores (i.e., scores for resilience, over-control, under-control, total behavior problems) were regressed on Time 1 (when the children were either three or four years of age) neighborhood poverty, and measures of other variables (i.e., family characteristics, home environment, maternal education). Our results indicated that living in high-poverty neighborhoods was associated with undesirable personality change. For example, regression-based estimates of personality change suggested that children living in very poor neighborhoods could expect to increase about 0.3 of a standard deviation in behavior problems over the course of a two-year period; similar estimates were derived for the personality type variables of resilience and over-control. In other words, the changes in personality associated with life in high-poverty neighborhoods lead children away, rather than toward, the personality we posit (Figure 9.1) to be optimally supportive of moral identity.

Moral orientation. High poverty neighborhoods can also be corrosive to moral attitudes and values. For example, Hart, Atkins, Markey, and Youniss (2004) examined the association of neighborhood poverty levels with adolescents' *tolerance for divergent perspectives.* Tolerance is fundamental for democracy, especially in increasingly multicultural societies like the United States (see Sullivan & Transue, 1999). Hart et al. found that, controlling for a variety of background and demographic factors, adolescents living in poor neighborhoods were less likely to be tolerant of divergent perspectives than were adolescents residing in affluent neighborhoods (see also Persell, Green, & Gurevich, 2001). Tolerance is likely to be an effortful extension of goodwill toward others who disagree with the self. The energy to extend goodwill may be diminished by the chronic stresses associated with life in poor urban neighborhoods.

Institutional Density

Opportunities. Poor neighborhoods are less able to provide the opportunities for productive engagement that we propose to be essential for the development of moral identity. According to our model (Figure 9.1), institutions and relationships provide opportunities for the enactment of moral identities. Blood donors acquire this identity through affiliation with blood banks; poverty activists usually are associated with organizations aimed at redressing problems arising from poverty; environmental activists band together in organizations like Greenpeace, Sierra Club, and so on. Neighborhoods with rich networks of organizations that have moral goals provide more opportunities for the elaboration of moral identities than neighborhoods thin in associational opportunities.

Adolescents in poor communities form fewer of these associations than adolescents in affluent communities. Hart, Marmorstein, Atkins, and Youniss (2008) used data from the National Longitudinal Study of Adolescent Health (ADD Health), with a large, nationally representative

Urban Neighborhoods as Contexts for Moral Identity Development 221

sample of American adolescents, to estimate the association between neighborhood poverty and the number of school clubs and teams of which an adolescent was a member. Neighborhood poverty level was estimated using U.S. Census data for the census tract of adolescents' residences. Participants reported membership status (member, nonmember) in 33 different organizations, with the number of memberships summed. We regressed the number of memberships on neighborhood poverty level. Figure 9.2 depicts the association between number of clubs and teams to which an adolescent belongs as a function of neighborhood poverty. Clearly, adolescents who live in affluent neighborhoods are more likely than those living in poor neighborhoods to report club and team affiliations. One possible explanation for this association is that adolescents in poor neighborhoods attend poor schools that lack the funds to provide the full range of extracurricular activities found in affluent neighborhoods. Whatever the explanation, the dearth of opportunities is likely to deprive adolescents of the opportunities to form moral identities.

Further, other sorts of institutional opportunities are probably absent in poor areas. Rupasingha, Goetz, and Freshwater (2006) analyzed the relationship of social capital measured at the level of counties to demographic characteristics of those counties. We have used their data to show the relation of the number of nonprofit civic associations per 10,000 inhabitants to the poverty rate. This relationship is depicted in Figure 9.3. The results indicate that the number of nonprofit civic organizations declines as the poverty rate increases. Similar trends are observed for other types

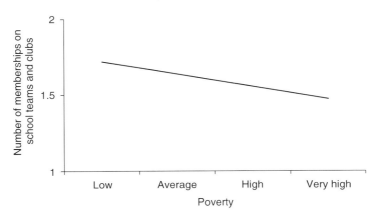

FIGURE 9.2. Association between the percent of the population under the age of 17 and neighborhood poverty.

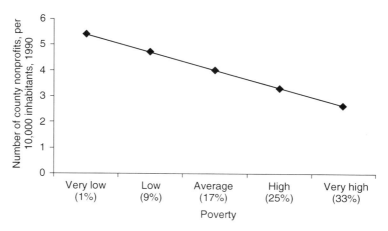

FIGURE 9.3. Association between the number of nonprofit civic groups and poverty rates.

of nonprofit organizations, such as churches. To the extent that these organizations provide important opportunities for adolescents to form moral identities, their relative absence in poor communities makes it more difficult for adolescents to form moral identities.

Youthfulness

Finally, poor urban neighborhoods are also youthful, or *high in child saturation*. Child saturation refers to the proportion of a population that is young. Consider Camden, New Jersey, where we do much of our work (for examples, see Hart & Fegley, 1995; Hart, Atkins, & Ford, 1998). According to 2000 U.S. Census data, there is one person under the age of 16 for every two over that age in Camden. In one census tract in Camden, there was one person under the age of 16 for every person over that age. A typical city in New Jersey has a much different ratio. Bayonne, New Jersey, for example has one person under the age of 16 to four persons over the age of 16.

Poor communities are higher in child saturation than are affluent communities. The correlation between a city or town's poverty rate in 2000 and the percentage of its population below the age of 18 is .23.[1] Neighborhoods are represented in U.S. Census data by census tracts; the correlation between a tract's poverty rate and its child saturation is .24. This means that the

---

[1] This number is generated using U.S. Census 2000 data from Geolytics.

nation's population of children is disproportionately likely to be living in high-poverty neighborhoods. It is worth noting that this is a new phenomenon; the correlation between poverty rate and child saturation for census tracts was essentially zero in 1970.[2]

Children and adolescents in communities in which a large fraction of the population is constituted of children and adolescents (child-saturated environments) will interact more often with peers, and consequently will be more influenced by them, than will an adolescent in a community with relatively few children and many adults (adult-saturated environment). This assumption rests on the notion that social influence is a product of the persons with whom an individual interacts on a daily basis. What do children and adolescents learn from each other? What might children and adolescents learn from adults? What kinds of values might be transmitted by adults versus those acquired from adults? These were questions we were interested in exploring in this paper.

To begin with, we investigated child saturation and volunteering behavior. If social influence operates as we suggest, then child-saturated environments are better than adult-saturated ones for the acquisition by adolescents of any activity requiring collaboration and mobilization. Volunteering is one such activity; consequently we hypothesized that adolescents in child-saturated environments would be more likely to volunteer than adolescents in adult-saturated environments.

To test this hypothesis, we made use of data from the National Household Educational Survey of 1999 (NHES-99). The NHES-99 was a telephone-interview study of nationally representative households from across the United States. Approximately 6000 children and adolescents in grades 6–12 were asked if they had been voluntarily involved (i.e., not to meet a school-mandated requirement) in community service in the current school year. We also calculated the poverty rate and child saturation quotient for their neighborhoods (zip codes). Figure 9.4 provides estimates from a logistic regression equation (see Hart, Atkins, Markey, & Youniss, 2004) predicting volunteering from the interaction of poverty rate and child saturation (controlling for family demographics and child characteristics). This effect has been replicated in two additional national samples.

In low poverty neighborhoods, with approximately a 3% poverty rate, the rate of volunteering was nearly twice as high in neighborhoods with 40% children than it was in neighborhoods with 20% children. In moderate poverty neighborhoods, approximately 21%, child saturation had no effect

---

[2] Calculated using the Neighborhood Change Database from Geolytics.

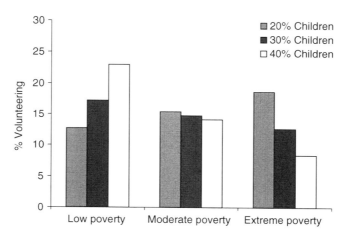

FIGURE 9.4. Youth volunteering as a function of the interaction between poverty level and child saturation.

on volunteering. Finally, in extremely poor neighborhoods, 40% poverty, neighborhoods with 40% children had extremely low rates of volunteering. The conjunction of extreme poverty and an extremely youthful populace appears to overwhelm a community's capacity to provide opportunities for children and adolescents to contribute through volunteering to the public good.

Value acquisition might also be influenced by neighborhood child saturation. To investigate this possibility, we have begun using the 1988 National Educational Longitudinal Study (NELS:88). The participants of the NELS:88 formed a representative sample of eighth graders in 1988, the time of the first survey, and were assessed again in 1990 and 1992 (Time 2 and Time 3 respectively). The sampling design of the NELS:88 provided for clusters of adolescents at each school. At Time 2 and Time 3, participants were asked to judge statements representing different values. A principal components analysis suggested four sets of values: achievement (e.g., "it's important to be successful in one's line of work"), social (e.g., "it's important to find the right person to marry"), independence (e.g., "it's important to get away from my parents"), and civic/moral (e.g., "it's important to work to correct economic inequalities"). Factor scores were used to represent these sets of values at Time 2 and Time 3.

Neighborhood poverty and child saturation were estimated using U.S. Census data for the zip codes of participants' home residences. We included in our analyses only participants who remained in the same residence at all three testing times, reasoning that neighborhood effects are unlikely to be evident among those who live in a neighborhood for a very short period of time. Value scores were regressed on neighborhood poverty and child saturation indices, with child and family demographics entered as covariates. Because of the sampling design, which resulted in clusters of participants living in the same neighborhoods, we used a multilevel modeling approach (Singer, 1998).

First, our analyses indicated neighborhood effects for achievement, independence, and civic/moral values (but not for social values); in other words, participants living in the same neighborhood were more similar to each other in their values than they were, on average, to participants living in other neighborhoods. Second, neighborhood poverty was a significant predictor of adolescents' endorsement of achievement values; adolescents living in poor communities were more likely than adolescents living in affluent ones to judge that getting a well-paying job and doing well in school were important. Both neighborhood poverty and neighborhood child saturation were positively associated with the valuing of independence. Finally, neighborhood child saturation was inversely associated with the endorsement of moral/civic values: adolescents living in communities in which a large fraction of the community was composed of children seemed less inclined to value broad social concerns than adolescents in neighborhoods lower in child saturation.

These findings suggest that adolescents living in communities high in child-saturation, in comparison to adolescents living in neighborhoods rich with adults, are more likely to value independence achieved by "breaking loose" of families and communities. While more research is clearly needed to explicate these findings, our tentative interpretation is that adults help connect adolescents to communities and social institutions. With a paucity of adults in the neighborhood, adolescents may have a difficult time discerning paths connecting them to the larger community and its concerns. Instead the presence of many children in a neighborhood may encourage adolescents' participation in activities that promote their own self-interests.

To summarize, child-saturated neighborhoods can increase the frequency of volunteering, a behavior that is typically considered prosocial. This effect probably occurs through the influence of peers on personality, and by increasing the opportunities adolescents have for participation in volunteering. However, there is little to recommend high levels of child-saturation in combination with high levels of poverty. In such locations, volunteering is depressed. It appears as if the large population of youth, combined with a lack of resources, may overwhelm a community's ability to provide opportunity for development. Moreover, high child saturation may be associated with youth valuing independence over community.

Poverty and Moral Identity Development

Poverty in the United States is associated with stress and child saturation, and inversely correlated with institutional density, which impact the development of a moral identity. First, stress undermines personality development: children living in high poverty neighborhoods become less resilient with time. These changes weaken the foundation (i.e., the enduring qualities of the model depicted on the left edge of Figure 9.1) upon which moral identity is built. Second, high levels of neighborhood poverty are also associated with low levels of tolerance for divergent views, part of a cardinal virtue for a democratic society, and one of the moral attitudes constituting the moral orientation component at the top, middle of Figure 9.1. Third, the exploration of moral identities, we argued, often takes place in the context of social institutions. Institutions are one source of opportunities – a key component depicted at the bottom, middle of Figure 9.1 for the formation of immoral identities. Finally, child saturation can mobilize and energize prosocial behavior such as volunteering. However, high child saturation joined with poor neighborhoods appears to depress prosocial activity. Moreover, child saturation appears to be inversely correlated with moral/civic attitudes concerning the community.

In sum, our review suggests that there is little to recommend high-poverty neighborhoods as a context for the development of a moral identity in these current times within the United States. There are no findings to suggest that high-poverty neighborhoods have hidden benefits, or that some children fare better in them compared to low-poverty neighborhoods.

INTERVENTIONS

While conditions are not optimum for moral growth in America's poorest neighborhoods, there are reasons for optimism. First of all, there is abundant evidence to indicate that moral flourishing regularly occurs in poor urban areas. Despite the stressors associated with economic inequality, children, adolescents, and adults in poor neighborhoods regularly contribute to the welfare of others. For example, Hart and Fegley (1995) studied adolescents in one of America's poorest cities, Camden, New Jersey, and found many adolescents involved in genuinely altruistic activities. These activities included dedicated work with the Salvation Army and NAACP, founding a scout troop for homeless youth, work in soup kitchens, and so on. Despite obstacles, adolescents in poor neighborhoods usually develop in very positive directions. News reports about violence, unemployment, and academic failure in urban areas promote an image of entire populations of adolescents failing to stay on the path to healthy development; in fact, the reality is that most urban adolescents successfully negotiate their teenage years to become productive members of society.

The high level of success among urban adolescents in high-poverty neighborhoods does not, of course, extend to all. There are many ways for adolescents to fail in high-poverty neighborhoods. To reduce the number of adolescents who fall off the track to healthy development, the risks and obstacles posed by their neighborhoods must be reduced. There are no easy answers to the problems posed by urban poverty, but it seems likely that current policies resulting in the confluence of poverty, child saturation, and a lack of social institutions are probably not the solution.

Second, while the conditions for the formation of moral identity in poor neighborhoods are not ideal, the model depicted in Figure 9.1 suggests that no single element is key, which in turn suggests that interventions may be effective by targeting multiple elements in the model. As noted earlier, effecting change through intervention on the enduring characteristics that serve as the foundation for moral identity – social class, family conditions, personality, all depicted on the left edge of the model – is likely to be difficult, long-term work, but worthwhile nonetheless. In our view, interventions are likely to produce results by targeting the mediating elements in the center of the model – moral orientation, self and identity, moral emotions, and opportunities.

Our experience with the Camden STARR (Sports Teaching Adolescents Responsibility and Resiliency) Program, a youth development program in one of America's poorest cities, suggests that adolescents who are members of an ongoing social group are easily recruited for community service (Hart, Atkins, & Watson, 2005), and they readily appreciate the value of participation. The problem is that there are too few opportunities for adolescents to engage in community service activities. In poor urban neighborhoods, because community service opportunities are associated with institutions, and because institutions and their associated social capital are less likely to be found in poor and highly child-saturated and racially diverse areas (Rupasingha, Goetz, & Freshwater, 2006), social structures that do exist in these areas need to be supported to provide opportunities for adolescents to become involved.

Recruiting adolescents to community service – work in their neighborhoods that benefits others, such as working in soup kitchens, cleaning parks, tutoring children, and so on – is one effective strategy to promote moral and civic development (for reviews, see Donnelly, Atkins, & Hart, 2006; Hart, Matsuba, & Atkins, 2008). In a recent analysis of national longitudinal data, Hart, Donnelly, Youniss and Atkins (2007) found that adolescents involved in community service in high school were substantially more likely as young adults to volunteer. Moreover, Hart et al. discovered that both adolescents who were required to perform, as well as those who voluntarily performed, community service benefited nearly equally from their participation.

SUMMARY

Moral identity, a commitment to advance the welfare of others that is consistent with one's self-image and moral goals, emerges from the interplay of family background, personality, moral cognitions and attitudes, self-perceptions and moral emotions, and social relationships and interactions with social institutions. No single element is the keystone; there are multiple routes to moral identity formation.

For adolescents, the resources available to construct a moral identity vary systematically with neighborhood environment. Adolescents living in America's poorest neighborhoods experience stress, child saturation, and institutional scarcity at levels that make the formation of moral identity more difficult. For this reason and many others, high levels of urban poverty are to be decried: there is nothing to recommend social policies that promote or allow these conditions to persist.

While most adolescents in even the most challenging neighborhoods persist, and eventually succeed, in forming moral identities, intervention is clearly warranted for the many who struggle. Research suggests that providing opportunities for adolescents to explore lines of moral action through participation in community service can be effective. Our experience with adolescents living in high-poverty neighborhoods is that they understand the issues around service work, and enjoy and benefit from their work, when given the opportunity to serve.

REFERENCES

Atkins, R. (2007). The association of personality type in childhood with violence in adolescence. *Research in Nursing and Health, 30*, 308–319.

Atkins, R., & Hart, D. (2008). The under-controlled do it first: The association of childhood personality and early sexual debut. *Research in Nursing and Health*, 31, 626–639.

Atkins, R., Hart, D., & Donnelly, T. (2005). The association of childhood personality type with volunteering during adolescence. *Merrill-Palmer Quarterly*, 51, 145–162.

Bargh, J. A., & Morsella, E. (2008). The unconscious mind. *Perspectives on Psychological Science*, 3(1), 73–79.

Caspi, A., Roberts, B. W., & Shiner, R. (2005). Personality development: Stability and change. *Annual Review of Psychology*, 56, 453–484.

Colby, A., & Damon, W. (1992). *Some do care: Contemporary lives of moral commitment.* New York: Free Press.

Donnelly, T. M., Atkins, R., & Hart, D. (2006). Parental influences on youth activism. In L. R. Sherrod, R. Kassimir, & C. Flanagan (Eds.), *Youth activism: An international encyclopedia, Volume II* (pp. 454–456). Westport, CT: Greenwood Publishing Company.

Doris, J. M. (1998). Persons, situations, and virtue ethics. *Noûs*, 32, 504–530.

Erikson, E. H. (1968). *Identity, youth, and crisis.* New York: Norton.

Evan, G. W., (2004). The environment of childhood poverty. *American Psychologist*, 59, 77–92.

Glover, J. (1999). *Humanity: A moral history of the twentieth century.* New Haven, CT: Yale University Press.

Gourevitch. P. (1998). *We wish to inform you that tomorrow we will be killed with our families: Stories from Rwanda.* New York: Farrar, Straus and Giroux.

Hart, D., Atkins, R., & Donnelly, T. M. (2006). Community service and moral development. In M. Killen & J. Smetana (Eds.), *Handbook of Moral Development* (pp. 633–656). Hillsdale, NJ: Lawrence Erlbaum Associates.

Hart, D., Atkins, R., & Fegley, S. (2003). Personality and development in childhood: A person-centered approach. *Monographs of the Society for Research in Child Development*, 68(1, Serial No. 272).

Hart, D., Atkins, R., & Ford, D. (1998). Urban America as a context for the development of moral identity in adolescence. *Journal of Social Issues*, 54, 513–530.

Hart, D., Atkins, R., Markey, P., & Youniss, J. (2004). Youth bulges in communities: The effects of age structure on adolescent civic knowledge and civic participation. *Psychological Science*, 15, 591–597.

Hart, D., Atkins, R., & Watson, N. C. (2005). How to start your own youth development micro-program. *SRA Newsletter*, Spring 1.

Hart, D., Donnelly, T. M., Youniss, J., & Atkins, R. (2007). High school predictors of adult civic engagement: The roles of volunteering, civic knowledge, extracurricular activities, and attitudes. *American Educational Research Journal*, 44, 197–219.

Hart, D., & Fegley, S. (1995). Altruism and caring in adolescence: Relations to moral judgment and self-understanding. *Child Development*, 66, 1346–1359.

Hart, D., Marmorstein, N., Atkins, R., & Youniss, J. (2008). *Neighborhood and National Child Saturation Predicts IQ and Achievement.* Unpublished paper.

Hart, D., & Matsuba, M. K. (2007). Pride and moral life. In J. Tracy, R. Robins, & J. Tangney (Eds.), *The self-conscious emotions: Theory and research* (pp. 114–133). New York: Guilford.

Hart, D., Matsuba, M. K., & Atkins, R. (2008). The moral and civic effects of learning to serve. In L. Nucci & D. Narvaez (Eds.), *Handbook on Moral and Character Education* (pp. 484–499). New York: Lawrence Erlbaum Associates.

Independent Sector. (2001, November). Giving and volunteering in the United States. Retrieved May 24, 2008, from http://www.independentsector.org/PDFs/GV01keyfind.pdf.

Lee, L., Piliavin, J., & Call, V. (1999). Giving time, blood and money: Similarities and differences. *Social Psychological Quarterly*, 62(3), 276–290.

Loughman, J. (2008). *Life story Lanauage and themes Associated with Volunteerism*. Unpublished honors thesis, Rutgers University, camden, NJ.

Matsuba, M. K., Hart, D., Atkins, R. (2007). Psychological and social-structural influences on involvement in volunteering. *Journal of Research on Personality*, 41, 889–907.

McAdams, D. P. (2008). The moral personality. In D. Narvaez & D. Lapsley (Eds.), *Moral self, identity and character: Prospects for a new field of study*. New York: Cambridge University Press.

McAdams, D. P., & Pals, J. L. (2006). A new Big Five: Fundamental principles for an integrative science of personality. *American Psychologists*, 61, 204–217.

Persell, C. H., Green, A., & Gurevich, L. (2001). Civic society, economic distress, and social tolerance. *Sociological Forum*, 16, 203–230.

Piliavin, J. A., & Callero, P. L. (1991). *Giving blood: The development of an altruistic identity*. Johns Hopkins University Press.

Roberts, B. W., & DelVecchio, W. F. (2000). The rank-order consistency of personality traits from childhood to old age: A quantitative review of longitudinal studies. *Psychological Bulletin*, 126(1), 3–25.

Rupasingha, A., Goetz, S. J., & Freshwater, D. (2006). The production of social capital in US counties. *Journal of Socio-Economics*, 35, 83–101.

Schlenker, B. R., Miller, M. L., & Johnson, R. M. (2008). Moral identity, integrity, and personal responsibility. In D. Narvaez & D. Lapsley (Eds.), *Moral self, identity and character: Prospects for a new field of study*. New York: Cambridge University Press.

Shishehbor, M. H., Litaker, D., Pothier, C. E., & Lauer, M. S. (2006). Association of socioeconomic status with functional capacity, heart rate recovery, and all-cause mortality. *Journal of the American Medical Association*, 295, 784–792.

Singer, J. D. (1998). Using SAS PROC MIXED to fit multilevel models, hierarchical models, and individual growth models. *Journal of Educational and Behavioral Statistics*, 24(4), 323–355.

St. Pierre, R. G., Layzer, J. I., Goodson, B. D., & Bernstein, L. S. (1997). *National impact evaluation of the comprehensive child development program: Final report*. Cambridge, MA: Abt Associates. Retrieved June 21, 2008, from http://www.mathematica-mpr.com/publications/redirect_pubsdb.asp?strSite=pdfs/ehsfinalvol1.pdf.

Sullivan, J. L., & Transue, J. E. (1999). The psychological underpinnings of democracy: A selective review of research on political tolerance, interpersonal trust, and social capital. *Annual Review of Psychology, 50,* 625–650.

Thompson, R. A. (2008). Early foundations: Conscience and the development of moral character. In D. Narvaez & D. Lapsley (Eds.), *Moral self, identity and character: Prospects for a new field of study.* New York: Cambridge University Press.

Walker, L. J., & Frimer, J. A. (2007). Moral personality of brave and caring exemplars. *Journal of Personality and Social Psychology, 93*(5), 845–860.

10

Moral Personality Exemplified

LAWRENCE J. WALKER AND JEREMY A. FRIMER

In the absence of a compelling model of moral functioning, the field of moral development has been languishing and is in critical need of resuscitation. Although in recent years some important conceptual insights have been advanced, corresponding empirical paradigms have been in short supply; and so the most promising theories remain largely unsubstantiated and without practical "legs." As a further consequence, moral educators have had few viable frameworks on which to base intervention efforts. This vacuity is primarily attributable to the once inordinate interest in moral rationality, an interest that initially gave spark to the field and fanned its flames for a time, but is an enterprise now reduced to a few smoldering embers.

This focus on moral cognition arose through the magisterial contributions of Piaget (1932/1977) and Kohlberg (1969) who heralded the cognitive revolution within psychology. These structural-developmental theorists forcefully advocated the notion that the fundamental core of moral functioning entailed processes of deliberative moral judgment. Their models embraced the formalist assumptions of the philosophical mindset of the Enlightenment Era, which conceptualized human nature dualistically, pitting rationality against personality. Moral rationality was hoisted onto a pedestal, regarded as not only necessary to define the moral quality of situations, but also as imbued with sufficient oomph to motivate moral action. In striking contrast, however, emotions, personal desires, and other aspects of personality were tossed into the garbage "bag of virtues" (Kohlberg, 1981, p. 78), regarded as potentially contaminating influences that the moral agent must eschew in order to adhere to the purer dictates of reason.

The structural-developmental paradigm had an exceedingly good run, compared to the typical fate of most flash-in-the-pan psychological theories. Part of its success can be attributed to the well-choreographed interplay between bold theory and compelling evidence, made possible by the development and refinement of a measure of moral reasoning (Colby & Kohlberg, 1987). Kohlberg's conceptual and empirical package established and legitimized the field of moral development, and then dominated its research agenda for over a generation, making significant and enduring contributions to our understanding of important aspects of the domain. But its limitations have become glaringly apparent, even to its most ardent acolytes. At a theoretical level, the conceptual skewing (with its singular focus on moral rationality and resulting neglect of moral personality) represents an untenable and unnecessarily narrow demarcation of what is undoubtedly a broader and more complex domain. At an empirical level, the now abundant evidence cumulatively indicates that moral cognition lacks passable predictive validity – what is more commonly known as the "judgment/action gap" (Straughan, 1986) – with moral reasoning typically explaining a mere 10% of the variability in moral action (Blasi, 1980; Walker, 2004). The moral reasoning construct seemingly does not provide the motivational compulsion for moral action and does not fully account for the breadth of moral functioning. So the field, once flourishing in the house of this construct, now ventures timidly and with speculation over what lies beyond, in the great outdoors.

Perhaps it is time to take a look at the potential relevance to moral functioning of the oft-disparaged aspects of personality, an appeal now being voiced with increased conviction (Blasi, 2004; Campbell & Christopher, 1996; Walker & Hennig, 1997. Also see McAdams, this volume, for arguments regarding the viability of the construct of moral personality). To be explicit about our intent here: it is not to *supplant* an emphasis on moral cognition with a similarly skewed emphasis on moral personality; rather our objective is to *augment* our understanding of moral cognition with an appreciation of the personological factors associated with moral action in order to provide a more balanced and comprehensive explanation of moral motivation and functioning. Processes of moral cognition, both intuitive and deliberative, are essential to an appropriate understanding of moral functioning; however, they are simply not sufficient. To be clear, we are advocates for an era of construct plurality for the moral domain (Frimer & Walker, 2008).

The primary purpose of the research presented in this chapter is to explore the personality variables associated with moral action in an attempt to identify those which are morally relevant and which hold some promise for bridging the judgment/action gap. One potential strategy here would involve using existing empirical templates to address the new questions surrounding moral personality; an alternate strategy would be to develop new measures, directly derivative from theory. The benefit of the latter strategy is its targeted precision at the constructs of interest, whereas the former strategy skips some of the methodological labor of measure development for what may be the same predictive reward. A conceptual and empirical discussion of the relative merits of each approach remains important work for the near future. Notwithstanding, the two approaches should provide vastly congruent and complementary data.

The empirical strategy adopted here is that of the former. Implementing existing empirical paradigms, we undertook a systematic and comprehensive assessment of the personality of a sample of moral exemplars, people who had been identified as engaging in noteworthy moral action. Research on moral exemplars can be especially informative (Walker, 2002) because processes of moral functioning are cast in more striking relief, and because the holistic study of exemplars' lives is particularly revelatory of the complexity and balancing of various virtues. However, exemplars are, by definition, relatively scarce, and so research with them is similarly infrequent and often methodologically constrained.

Typically, research with moral exemplars has entailed qualitative case-study analyses. Although such studies can yield suggestive and heuristic findings (Colby & Damon, 1992; Midlarsky, Jones, & Corley, 2005; Monroe, 2002; Oliner, 2003; Oliner & Oliner, 1988), the lack of objective measures makes it difficult to discern the meaning of posited constructs and the lack of appropriate comparison groups makes it impossible to determine to what extent the moral exemplars are, indeed, atypical (and exemplary). There is some exemplar research that has employed systematic methodology and comparison groups (Hart & Fegley, 1995; Matsuba & Walker, 2004, 2005; Reimer & Wade-Stein, 2004), but those studies often entailed a rather circumscribed assessment of psychological functioning, were conducted with adolescent and young adult samples (a portion of the lifespan when aspects of the moral personality are relatively nascent and unconsolidated), and/or focused on a single type of moral exemplarity (volunteering).

This facet of much previous research – the focus on one type of moral exemplarity – prompts the observation that most theoretical conceptions of moral functioning similarly posit a singular ideal of moral maturity or moral excellence. Kohlberg's (1981) principles of justice and Gilligan's (1982) ethic of care illustrate the point. But the move beyond stage sequences and the newfound interest in the moral personality raise the questions of whether it is defensible to posit multiple ideals of moral excellence, and whether different varieties of moral personality might indeed be discernable (Flanagan, 1991; Walker & Hennig, 2004).

This preamble allows us to sketch out the design of our research project: it entailed the broad-band assessment of the personality of two quite different types of moral exemplars (namely, brave vs. caring), who not only were contrasted with each other, but also with matched comparison groups comprised of "ordinary" individuals.

Herein lay the two research questions that frame our project: First, can mature moral functioning be exemplified in different ways, challenging the univocal models that have dominated the field? The extent to which brave and caring exemplars evidence psychological profiles that are both unique *and* adaptive would be indicative of different manifestations of moral excellence. For example, we expect that caring exemplars will evidence a more communal and nurturing profile, and the brave exemplars a more agentic and dominant one (as suggested by naturalistic conceptions, Walker & Hennig, 2004). Second, is there a foundational core to moral functioning? The extent to which these quite different types of moral exemplars share personality characteristics, characteristics that also distinguish them from comparison groups, would reference the basic aspects of the moral personality. Thus, our intent is to examine both what differentiates contrasting types of moral exemplars and what commonalities they share.

A critical methodological issue for our enterprise concerns the veridical identification of moral exemplars (Wolf, 1982). Of course, the identification of exemplars requires that their moral actions be known to others and recognized; inevitably, those whose good deeds are inconspicuous, for whatever reason, will be omitted from study. Also, moral exemplars are frequently controversial figures (those involved in social activism, for example), garnering mixed evaluations: one person's hero can be another's villain, and, furthermore, none of these is completely unblemished. The approach to this issue taken by some researchers (Colby & Damon, 1992) has been to rely on the evaluations of experts to identify exemplars; however, experts tend to define a domain more narrowly than do laypeople and to favor particular ideological frameworks (Sternberg, Conway, Ketron, & Bernstein, 1981). Other researchers (Matsuba & Walker, 2004), in contrast, have tapped folk conceptions of moral excellence by asking laypeople to identify moral exemplars, but that approach leaves the nominating criteria somewhat unclear and unsubstantiated. Some researchers (Oliner & Oliner, 1988) have simply chosen to study moral exemplars of specific interest (e.g., Holocaust rescuers) or to access samples of convenience. These various approaches illustrate the fact that people do identify different types of moral exemplars (Walker, Pitts, Hennig, & Matsuba, 1995).

BRAVE AND CARING EXEMPLARS

In the present research, our approach was to compare two contrasting types of exemplars (brave vs. caring) whose moral actions were fairly unambiguous and noncontroversial. Both bravery and care are well represented in philosophical writings as emblematic of moral excellence (Miller, 2000; Noddings, 1984). Our brave and caring exemplars were identified in the same way through the Canadian honors system: initial nominations came from members of the general community; these nominations were vetted by an independent advisory committee; if approved, people were recognized by a national award conferred by the governor-general of Canada (the de facto head of state).

The brave exemplars in our study were recent recipients of the Medal of Bravery, a civilian award that recognizes individuals who have risked their lives to save others and who have persisted in their rescue attempts despite considerable danger. The caring exemplars were recent recipients of the Caring Canadian Award, a parallel award that recognizes volunteers who have demonstrated extraordinary and long-term commitment in providing care to others or in supporting community service or humanitarian causes. The sample involved 25 brave and 25 caring exemplars, drawn from all ten Canadian provinces. Interestingly, these two groups of exemplars did not differ in the distribution of gender or ethnicity, nor in level of education; however, the caring exemplars were considerably older than the brave exemplars, a finding that potentially complicates any interpretation of personality differences between them. This age disparity might be expected, given that the brave exemplars were recognized for heroism in dangerous contexts where younger adults are more often involved, whereas the caring exemplars were recognized for long-term volunteer service and were, consequently, somewhat older.

One of the notable design strengths of our study was the inclusion of carefully matched comparison groups. This feature allowed for much stronger conclusions about the association between personality and moral action than would have been appropriate in previous research. Comparison participants were drawn from the general community and were closely matched, on a case-by-case basis, to exemplar participants on four demographic variables (gender, ethnicity, level of education, and age). Thus, there were 25 comparison participants individually matched to brave exemplars, and 25 comparison participants individually matched to caring exemplars, for a total sample of 100. More detailed information regarding the sample for this project, its methodology and results, is reported by Walker and Frimer (2007).

THE EMPIRICAL PARADIGM OF MORAL PERSONALITY

Our intent was to provide an extensive examination of the personality of moral exemplars by using multiple measures and a broadband assessment. McAdams's (1995b; this volume) three-level typology of personality description provided the empirical paradigm that guided our assessment. Each level of the typology has its particular advantages (and limitations) but, in concert, the three levels provide a comprehensive profile.

The first level of personality description reflects *dispositional traits* – the dimensions of personality that are broad, stable, decontextualized, and implicitly comparative. The second level is that of *characteristic adaptations* – the motivational, developmental, and strategic aspects of personality functioning that are more particular to contexts. The third level is that of integrative *life narratives* – the aspects of personality involving the psychosocial construction of a personal identity and a framework for deriving a sense of unity, purpose, and meaning in life.

To assess personality at all three levels, we used several measures. At the level of dispositional traits, we had participants complete Wiggins's (1995) Revised Interpersonal Adjective Scales in which they rate the accuracy of 124 trait terms in describing themselves. This personality inventory taps the circumplex dimensions of *dominance* and *nurturance*. These two modalities involve the granting or withholding of power/status and of affection/affiliation, respectively, and are widely held to be fundamental in human functioning.

At the level of characteristic adaptations, we were particularly interested in the goal motivational aspects of personality and so had participants complete Emmons's (1999) Personal Strivings List. On this measure, participants are asked to reflect on and then to write down a list of at least ten to fifteen of their personal strivings or goals, that is, the things they are "typically trying to do." The notion that moral desires – rather than cognitive competencies – are what fundamentally motivate moral action suggests the probable relevance of personal strivings to the moral domain. We coded participants' personal strivings for five major categories of motivation that were thought to be particularly germane: (a) *power* (concern with influencing others); (b) *affiliation/intimacy* (concern for maintaining relationships and commitment to another); (c) *generativity* (concern for the next generation and of giving of oneself for others); (d) *spiritual self-transcendence* (a divine awareness and other concerns that transcend the self); and (e) *identity/personal growth* (concern for greater self-understanding and self-development).

At the third level of personality description, we assessed integrative narratives of the self in the context of a lengthy life-review interview (McAdams, 1995a), in which participants were essentially asked to construct the story of their life. The initial part of the interview was rather open-ended: here, participants were prompted to describe in some detail the main chapters of their life story. Then they were asked to focus, in turn, on several specific events that were critical in their life story (a high point, low point, turning point, earliest memory, important childhood memory, important adolescent memory, and important adult memory): they were asked to share not only concrete details but also, more important, the significance of the event and what it conveyed about who they are as persons. Appropriate parts of the life-review interview were coded (relying on various coding schemes provided by McAdams) for seven relevant personality variables: (a) themes of *agency* (self-mastery, status/victory, achievement/responsibility, and empowerment); (b) themes of *communion* (love/friendship, dialogue, caring/help, and unity/togetherness); (c) overall *affective tone* (degree of pessimism vs. optimism); (d) *redemption/contamination* sequences (the construal of life events either such that an initially negative state is salvaged in some way, or such that an initially positive state is irreconcilably tainted by a negative outcome – redemption vs. contamination, respectively); (e) *sensitization to the needs of others* (the extent to which the participant indicates being exposed to the needs of others in early life); (f) *helpers/enemies* (the presence of people who, in early life, influenced the participant in an explicitly positive way and the relative absence of "enemies" who were detrimental); and (g) the security of childhood *attachments* in various relationships. The latter three variables (sensitization to the needs of others, helpers/enemies, and attachments), as a cluster of themes, comprise what McAdams, Diamond, de St. Aubin, and Mansfield (1997) conceptualize as early-life advantage, the recollection of a highly positive childhood that was formative of prosocial goals and commitments.

The measures and personality variables assessed in this study are outlined in the left-hand columns of Table 10.1. It was anticipated that the multiple personality measures and the broad range of personality variables assessed would facilitate a comprehensive examination of the moral personality.

DIFFERENT PERSONALITY PROFILES

One of the main questions framing our research was whether mature moral functioning can be manifest in different moral personalities, challenging the contrary notion implicit in theories that posit singular visions of moral

TABLE 10.1. *Summary of findings*

Measures	Level of personality description	Personality variable	Different personality profiles?[a]	Foundational core?[b]
Revised Interpersonal Adjective Scales	Dispositional traits	Dominance		
		Nurturance	✓	
Personal Strivings List	Characteristic adaptations	Power		
		Affiliation/intimacy	†	
		Generativity	✓	
		Spiritual self-transcendence		
		Identity/personal growth		
Life-Review Interview	Integrative life narratives	Agency		✓
		Communion	†	✓
		Affective tone	✓	
		Redemption/contamination		✓
		Sensitization to the needs of others	†	
		Helpers/enemies		✓
		Attachments	†	✓

[a] For the findings regarding different personality profiles, a ✓ indicates that caring exemplars scored higher than brave exemplars at $p \leq .001$, whereas a † indicates a marginally significant difference with $.007 \leq p \leq .04$.
[b] For the findings regarding the foundational core of the moral domain, a ✓ indicates that both groups of exemplars scored higher than their comparison groups at $p < .001$.

excellence. The brave and caring exemplars in our project, although identified and recognized in similar ways, had engaged in quite different forms of moral action. So we now turn to an overview of their personality profiles and then flesh out these differences with illustrative material.

The interpretive challenge in making such a comparison is the confound, noted earlier, between the type-of-award variable and age – the brave exemplars were almost a generation younger than the caring exemplars. Thus, any personality differences revealed between brave and caring exemplars might be attributable instead to a developmental or cohort effect. To address the possibility of this confound, two preliminary analyses were undertaken with the comparison-group participants (who are demographically identical to the exemplars): one examined the correlations between age and each of the personality variables for the comparison-group participants; the other examined personality differences between the brave and caring comparison groups. Both sets of analyses consistently revealed nonsignificant effects, indicating that the age difference between the exemplar groups does not present an interpretive obstacle.

Having dealt with the potential confound between the award variable and age, we now turn to a direct comparison of the personality profiles of brave and caring exemplars. Analyses revealed pronounced differences (with $ps \leq .001$ and with large effect sizes of $\eta^2 \geq .20$) between the two types of exemplars on three personality variables – nurturance, generativity, and affective tone – variables, incidentally, representing all three levels of personality description. Weaker differences on four other variables – affiliation/intimacy, communion, sensitization to the needs of others, and quality of attachments – were also suggested by analyses (the differences on these four variables were marginally significant when using an alpha level adjusted for the experiment-wise error rate, but all $ps < .05$ and with medium effect sizes of $\eta^2 \geq .09$). These findings are summarized in Table 10.1.

Strikingly, each one of these personality differences favored caring over brave exemplars. Contrary to our hypothesis, the brave exemplars did not "outscore" the caring exemplars on even one personality variable. But before drawing conclusions about the "banality of heroism" (Franco & Zimbardo, 2006), we will later reveal that the brave exemplars were by no means common. The present findings suggest, however, that brave personalities are somewhat less exemplary than caring ones. In retrospect, this is not unsurprising in that the caring exemplars were recognized for long-term commitment to caring action, whereas the brave exemplars were recognized for a single heroic act. Situational pressures could have had a stronger causal role in bringing out exemplary moral action from only somewhat exemplary individuals.

We now illustrate some of the empirical differences between brave and caring exemplars. One consistent theme running through this pattern of personality differences was the strong communal orientation to others demonstrated by caring exemplars, as shown by their elevated scores on personality traits reflecting the nurturance dimension, on both generativity and affiliation/intimacy strivings, and on themes of communion in their life narratives. For example, on the warm–agreeable trait terms most closely associated with the nurturance dimension of the interpersonal circumplex (e.g., kind, accommodating, charitable, sympathetic), caring exemplars scored over one standard deviation higher than the brave exemplars.

In terms of goal motivation as expressed in personal strivings, caring exemplars had over twice as many generativity strivings as did brave exemplars and over 50% more affiliation/intimacy strivings. In previous research, McAdams et al. (1997) found that outstanding teachers and community volunteers evidenced higher levels of generative concern than comparison participants, implicating the relevance of generativity for moral action. In Emmons's (1999) conceptualization, generativity entails not only a desire to create something, leave a legacy, and have an enduring influence, but also a desire to give of oneself to others and, more particularly, for purposeful interaction with the younger generation. Such generative concern is illustrated by a few examples of the personal strivings of caring exemplars in this study who were responding to the prompt, "I typically try to …":

- make my community a better place to be.
- do at least one good deed daily – often anonymously.
- create a role model for my kids and other youth.
- enrich everyone around me with unerring faith, hope, and positive thinking.
- make time to advocate for women who are from a "low-income" bracket.

The moral motivation in such personal concerns is transparent and seems to be an important component of the caring exemplars' framing of their lives.

A strong orientation toward affiliation and intimacy also was found to characterize the goal motivation of caring exemplars. This relational theme encompasses a range of strivings including the seeking of acceptance and security in relationships, establishing and maintaining friendships, commitment to and concern for another, positive interpersonal affect, and reciprocal communication and sharing. Midlarsky et al.'s (2005) finding of exceptional empathic concern among Holocaust rescuers, and Matsuba and Walker's (2004) finding that their young-adult moral exemplars scored highly on the other-model dimension of adult attachment, are consistent with our finding of a higher level of affiliation/intimacy strivings among caring exemplars. A few examples of such relational strivings in the present data are:

- call lonely friends as often as possible.
- be sensitive to the physical and emotional needs of my wife.

- entertain others and create a happy environment.
- be liked and be needed.
- live in harmony in human relationships particularly in the home.

Such goals, seemingly fundamental in the lives of caring exemplars, frequently focus on altruistic concerns and the nurturing of relationships.

This notion of an enhanced orientation to others was also evidenced by considerably more frequent themes of communion in the life stories of caring exemplars than in those of brave exemplars (by a ratio of 3:2). McAdams's (1993) conception of communion encompasses several ideas, including ones referencing love and friendship, meaningful and mutual dialogue among people, the provision of care and help for another, and experiences of being a part of a larger community. In outlining the major chapters in their life story, and in identifying and making sense of significant life events, caring exemplars were more likely to incorporate communal themes in their self-understanding. Note that this orientation to others was pervasive across the levels of personality analysis, seen not only in terms of dispositional traits and characteristic adaptations, but also at the deeper level of integrative life narratives.

In addition to these four personality variables tapping an orientation to others, caring exemplars also had a generally more optimistic affective tone to their life narratives than did brave exemplars (whose interviews tended to more mixed or neutral in affective tone). Dispositional optimism has frequently been implicated in adaptive coping and better adjustment (Peterson, 2000). The case studies analyzed by Colby and Damon (1992) suggested that hopefulness and positivity were important factors underlying extraordinary moral commitment. Although it is difficult to convey the overall affective tone of someone's life story with a few excerpts from an interview, the following ones illustrate the pervasive optimism of one caring exemplar in our study (who was recognized for her extraordinary community service):

> I grew up ... with a lot of love and maybe some hardships; you know, holes in the socks and things like that. And we laugh about it now, but that was how it was. And not a lot of extras – no extras, really, at all. But always feeling ... that I was sort of a child of God, that I was looked after, that I didn't have anything to worry about; and that feeling has stayed with me all my life. So, you know, I grew up, as we say, without a whole lot, but it was a great childhood.
>
> My [nursing] career has spanned 15 years in maternity and 25 in emergency room. And to me, it was such a privilege to be able to be there ... to

be able to work in that kind of a situation I think allowed me to grow ... to really start to feel that I could give back to people. And it was easy for me; it was never a hardship; it still isn't. So those were really good years.... When I went to work, I didn't even think about home or anything else. I went and I absolutely loved it, and I could laugh and cry and do whatever I had to do, but I loved every minute of being there. And some people don't understand that, but I did. And I don't think there was ever one shift where I didn't really enjoy it to the utmost. So again, that was something that was given to me and I recognize that.

Pervasive optimism in the context of long-term commitment to caring service should come as some surprise. After all, these volunteers often worked in situations that entailed destitution, desperation, and disenfranchisement. In spite of their elevated exposure to challenging environments, the caring exemplars in some sense defy their environments in exuding positivity. A purely contextual (as opposed to dispositional) explanation of moral exemplarity would have to posit the opposite finding of attitudes of discouragement and cynicism. The present data imply the working of an agentic personality that somehow transduces the negativity of difficult contexts into expressions of hope and affirmation.

One of the unanticipated findings of the study was that a disproportionate number of caring exemplars had suffered the death of one or more children. The death of a child is prototypic of the out-of-sequence, ofttimes traumatic events with which most people typically have great difficulty coping, even over the long term, often falling into anger or despair. But here, despite the fact that a sizable number of caring exemplars had had to contend with their own child's death, they were found to evidence optimism and positivity. It appears that these extraordinary people cope by discerning some meaning and benefit from a tragedy and by deliberately fostering a positive attitude toward life. The following interview excerpt with a caring exemplar illustrates this phenomenon. The daughter of this participant had been involved in aid work in a developing nation when she was stricken with a terminal illness.

> By this time, she'd gotten ... me into a lot of things, into Amnesty [International] letter writing.... And so, of course, when she told me that the cancer had metastasized, I guess I had tears, and she said, "Mom, there are lots of things worse than me having breast cancer ... like being in prison and being tortured." ... So doing voluntary work has been a godsend for me. You know, that I was motivated and able.
>
> People used to say to me, "It's not fair that [your daughter] should die so young. Look at all the good she could have done in this world. Look

at how she was helping people; and then she goes and, you know, gets cancer. Well, it's not fair." And I'd always say, "No, [she] has accomplished more by her death than had she lived," and I still see it that way.

One of the unanswered questions here is whether these participants were predisposed to such positivity throughout their life, or rather that it is a reflection of some element of posttraumatic growth.

The remaining variables that were found to distinguish the personality functioning of caring and brave exemplars involved two aspects of early-life advantage: the quality of childhood attachments and sensitization to the needs of others. Participants were never explicitly questioned regarding such relationships and experiences in the context of the life-review interview, so the coding very much reflects the spontaneous mention of significant people and events in childhood and adolescence. Quality of attachments was rated for six different relationships: mother, father, grandparents, siblings, friendship/school, and church/religion. Overall, in the life stories of caring exemplars, there was greater evidence for secure childhood attachments than in those of brave exemplars, suggestive of contexts of nurture, trust, and interpersonal connection.

The other early-advantage variable – sensitization to the needs of others – reflects the experience of exposure to people who require special care, an experience that prompts an expansion of one's scope of concern. Such awareness of the needs and suffering of others was more pronounced in the recollections of caring than brave exemplars. Examples from these interviews include experiences of helping refugee families adapt, befriending a child afflicted with polio, dealing with the suicide attempt of a teenage friend, and visiting a lonely neighbor who was an invalid. Whether such early-life experiences were indeed formative of a caring personality, or rather that such memories are merely reconstructions as one attempts to impose meaning on one's life, is indeterminate; nevertheless, this process is informative of the forging of a moral identity.

In summary, these analyses provide ample evidence for different moral personalities – brave and caring exemplars were found to have rather divergent personality profiles. Notably, however, when differences were found, they favored caring over brave exemplars: the personality of caring exemplars was considerably more "exemplary," as embodied by the pervasive communal orientation of their character, the fundamental optimism, and the recollections of early-life advantage.

These findings resurrect the intractable issue of the agentic versus situational causes of behavior. In our study, the brave exemplars reacted heroically in a life-and-death rescue, and the operation of powerful situational factors was probably implicated in their action. The caring exemplars, on the other hand, had engaged in long-term volunteer service, and the instigation and maintenance of such activity were probably more dependent on deeply instilled aspects of character and motivation. However, we should be careful not to portray too strong a contrast between these two types of exemplars. Brave exemplars obviously also have a caring and strongly altruistic orientation: they did risk their lives to rescue another. Caring exemplars frequently have to be heroic and brave in confronting injustice, advocating for the disadvantaged, and overcoming challenges. Given the methodological difficulties in directly assessing motivation for moral action, most notably socially desirable responding, it will be difficult to generate data that can empirically inform the interaction between personological and situational factors.

One may be drawn to the apparent conclusion that the behaviors of the brave exemplars were merely situationally induced, whereas the personalities of the caring exemplars caused their behaviors. At this juncture, the suggestion that the brave exemplars were quite commonplace in their personality has some currency – but that would be a distinctly premature and, as it turns out, incorrect conclusion. The next section of this chapter will explore differences between exemplar and comparison participants and, not to give away the whole story, brave exemplars were found to score higher on several personality variables than comparison participants (confirming their exemplarity). However, it just so happens that caring exemplars also scored higher on the same variables.

FOUNDATIONAL CORE

The second major question framing our research asked whether we could identify aspects of the psychological core to moral functioning. Our analytic strategy was to determine the personality characteristics that these two contrasting types of moral exemplars clearly share, but which, at the same time, distinguish them from comparison-group participants. Such commonalities in personality functioning implicate some basic aspects of the moral personality.

We only counted a personality variable as core to the domain if analyses indicated, for that particular variable, that the brave exemplars differed from their comparison group, and similarly, that the caring exemplars differed from their comparison group. That is, both of these quite different exemplar types needed to evidence the same personality exemplarity. Our analyses identified five personality variables as foundational – themes of agency and of communion, redemption/contamination sequences, helpers/ enemies in early life, and quality of childhood attachments – with the differences between exemplar and comparison groups being quite pronounced (with all $ps < .001$ and with large effect sizes of $\eta^2 \geq .16$). These findings are summarized in Table 10.1.

In the life narratives of exemplars, the central themes of both agency and communion were frequently voiced (with 68% more agency than the comparison groups and 82% more communion). Agency and communion represent a motivational duality that entails orthogonal psychological tendencies, ones that are relatively broad and multidimensional. The convergence of both agency and communion in psychological functioning is held to represent a particularly adaptive and well-adjusted motivational style (McAdams, 1993; McAdams, Hoffman, Mansfield, & Day, 1996): mitigating agency with communal concerns is a major life challenge (Bakan, 1966). The agentic aspects of (both brave and caring) exemplars' personality reflect their significant engagement in action in often difficult and challenging circumstances. Such action demands self-control and self-awareness, independence, assumption of responsibility, relentless pursuit of goals, and a sense of empowerment. The communal aspects of exemplars' personality reflect their application of agency to projects of helping, serving, and connecting with others. Such action demands a sustained orientation to others, concern for their welfare and well-being, interpersonal sensitivity and connection, openness, and positive emotionality.

The following excerpts from the interview with a caring award recipient (who was recognized for his extraordinary volunteer service with poor children in isolated communities) illustrate this conjoining of agency and communion:

> [When I was] a young student, a police officer came into our school – still remember his name; he was a youth liaison officer – and his whole persona, his whole reflection on life was helping people as opposed to hindering people (or that adage, "getting the bad guy"), which is a philosophy that I adopted as a police officer in much later years.
>
> It was a big decision, of course, to embark on something [police training] that you've wanted, but you're not really sure of the unknowns. But we made the decision and I did successfully complete training. Very difficult ... it was a real challenge, not just physically. I worked out very, very hard for months.

[My wife and I] sat back Christmas Eve one year [and] looked at all the gifts under our tree. We'd got the kids to sleep and all the other gifts had come out that had been hidden away. It was a true mass of gifts to be opened.... We then realized how fortunate our kids were and how fortunate we were [and decided], that regardless of how the impact was going to be, or how minimal or how large it was going to be, we were going to start a program the following year [to collect and deliver gifts for disadvantaged children].

It was so refreshing to go back into a community as a police officer, especially when we went in in uniform.... But, as opposed to going in and delivering bad news, ... here you are going in bestowing gifts, unsolicited gifts, and caring. It's not what the gift represents itself; it's not the doll or the truck. It's the fact that somebody's taken the time to organize something like this, actually physically wrap the gifts.... We try and go back year after year after year. It's a true demonstration that you've made a commitment.

The agentic themes apparent here include a strong sense of achievement and responsibility, the empowerment induced by an influential authority figure, and the self-mastery that came through the transformation in self-awareness and the realization of new goals. The communal themes referenced here focus on empathic care and concern for the emotional well-being of others.

Another foundational personality variable that was common to both types of exemplars and distinguished them quite dramatically from comparison groups was the prevalence of redemption sequences (and the relative absence of contamination sequences). The life stories of exemplars were coded as having 66% more redemption sequences and 51% fewer contamination sequences than the accounts of comparison participants. McAdams (2006) argues that it is not the recalled events themselves that are important in assessing personality functioning, rather it is how such events are construed and what meaning is derived from them. In his conceptualization, a redemption sequence is one in which a demonstrably negative state leads to a positive one; the initial negative state is redeemed or salvaged in some way. In a complementary manner, a contamination sequence is one in which a positive state leads to a noticeably negative one; the initial positive state is irreconcilably contaminated or tainted by a negative outcome – the negativity overwhelms the previous positivity. The extant evidence (McAdams, 2006) indicates that redemptive construals are associated with psychological well-being and represent the most important and pervasive theme among generative adults, whereas contamination is more consistently associated with measures of psychological distress.

Among the exemplars in our project, there was a strong tendency to reframe critical life events redemptively, as the following four descriptions reveal (the first two examples are from brave exemplars, the last two from caring ones):

> The painful experience of his parents' divorce is construed as an opportunity for personal development. ("I came to discover who I was, and what I wanted in my life, and what I didn't want in my life. But in that family structure, that was what I would say was really oppressive, it wasn't possible for me.")
>
> In the aftermath of the murder of her best friend, a young woman describes being able to deliver the eulogy at the funeral as a high point, her most significant achievement. ("This was how I really felt about her, and I got the opportunity to say it, and people got to hear it, and a lot of people said … 'That was incredible, it was beautiful,' and the boys hated me because I made them all cry.")
>
> A positive benefit of a diagnosis of breast cancer is understood as reenergizing her creative side. ("Out of that, you know, has come this wonderful, well, it's almost like a happy reunion with my art and realizing the gift that came from the tragedy.")
>
> The sudden death of his son induces a positive change in values. ("Things that may have seemed important don't seem so important anymore. It certainly gets your priorities a little straighter and it gives you a different sense of what you value.")

These accounts illustrate the capability, and often the conscious choice, to discern or to construct some benefit or positive outcome from adversity. Redemptive construals of transformative life experiences – this process of benefit-finding – represent a particularly adaptive form of personality functioning that can often foster and sustain moral action in challenging and difficult contexts.

Finally, two related features of early-life advantage (quality of attachments and helpers/enemies) also figured prominently in the foundational core of the moral personality, reflective of people's retrospective construal of formative relationships through their childhood and adolescence (McAdams et al., 1997). These intimations of a childhood that was positively valenced in terms of secure and scaffolding relationships were inferred from incidental references to significant people in participants' life stories since there was no explicit probing in this regard. Exemplars' relationships overall were rated as being significantly more secure than those of comparison participants, suggestive of nurturing and steadfast contexts for development.

In terms of the explicit identification of helpers and enemies in the narratives, the frequency of enemies (those who are described as detrimental and oppositional) was relatively low and did not differ significantly between groups. However, the frequency of helpers in the recollections of exemplars was almost three times that of comparison participants. A helper is someone whose actions are construed as scaffolding or benefiting the respondent in an explicitly positive way. A sampling of the helpers mentioned by our exemplars included: a mother who taught responsibility and self-sufficiency, a principled father who instilled a moral standard, a loving grandmother who showed the meaning of "grace," a caring aunt who paid for surgery to repair a congenital deformity, a neighbor who provided daily encouragement, a stimulating teacher who encouraged intrinsic learning, and a coach who fostered excellence in every aspect of life.

These positive childhood experiences, involving secure attachments and influential mentors, suggest an early realization of being particularly advantaged in some way, and may be pivotal in the fashioning of an identity that entails a sense of efficacy, prosocial motivation, and a strong commitment to moral concerns.

In summary, then, we were able to discern some conspicuous commonalities in the personality functioning of brave and caring exemplars, indicative of the psychological core of the moral domain. These commonalities were found despite their considerably different types of moral action and their typically different stages in the adult lifespan. Our evidence regarding the foundational core is that it frequently entails the convergence of agency and communion, adaptive aspects of personality that seem instrumental for moral action. Further, the redemptive reframing of significant life events in order to construct some positive benefit seems to be a coping strategy that sustains prosocial commitment in the face of difficulties. And, finally, a life narrative that references a highly positive childhood, conferring some early-life advantage, seems integral to an identity that is pervaded by moral concerns. We cannot determine from our data, of course, whether such recollections of an advantaged early life are indeed reflective of actual experiences or instead represent construals of one's life in terms of present understandings. Regardless, such intimations do reflect important components of the moral personality.

The differences between exemplar and comparison participants were most obvious in the life-narrative data, in the forging of a personal identity.

Blasi (1993, 2004) and Frimer and Walker (2008) have argued that a moral identity is a fundamental explanatory construct in moral functioning. The aspects of personality captured at lower levels of personality description (viz., dispositional traits and characteristic adaptations) may not as readily tap the complex processes of self-continuity, self-coherence, and identity formulation as individuals develop and confront changing contexts and new challenges. Such personological processes, operative in and constitutive of a moral identity, are seemingly best assessed in terms of individuals' self-narratives.

TOWARD BRIDGING THE JUDGMENT/ACTION GAP

This project was premised on the well-established observation that moral judgment fails to be a viable contender in adequately explaining moral action, with the proposition that personality variables might serve to help bridge the judgment/action gap. Our design allowed a test of both the premise and the proposition. In addition to the personality variables described earlier, participants were prompted to discuss a real-life moral conflict in the context of their life review, and their reasoning in handling this dilemma was coded for moral stage (Colby & Kohlberg, 1987; Walker et al., 1995), yielding a standard index of moral judgment.

To test the premise about the explanatory power of moral cognition, we conducted logistic regression analyses, using moral reasoning as a predictor of moral-action status (as exemplar or comparison). For the brave groups, moral reasoning did not predict moral action whatsoever (with Nagelkerke $R^2 = .00$); that is, brave exemplars and their comparison group were indistinguishable in terms of level of moral reasoning. For the caring groups, moral reasoning was a significant but weak predictor of moral action ($R^2 = .20$); with caring exemplars somewhat more advanced in moral reasoning than their comparison group. Thus, our data are consistent with the claim that moral cognition, at best, only weakly predicts behavior.

To test the proposition about the potential relevance of personological factors to moral functioning, we again conducted logistic regression analyses, entering moral reasoning in the first block as a control variable, and then entering the 14 personality variables in the second block to determine whether they added to the explanatory equation. For the brave groups, the addition of personality variables significantly improved the prediction of moral action from $R^2 = .00$ (with moral reasoning alone) to $R^2 = .68$ (with the addition of personality variables). For the caring groups, the addition of personality variables similarly improved the prediction of moral action from $R^2 = .20$ to .87 – almost completely accounting for the variability in the data. Thus, these analyses yield unequivocal support for the hypothesis that aspects of the moral personality do augment moral cognition and substantially close the judgment/action gap.

CODA: BRINGING THINGS TOGETHER AND MOVING THEM FORWARD

Our research project was framed as an attempt to encourage a more inclusive and comprehensive understanding of moral functioning: trying to break out of the rationalistic fetters that have bound the field and to consider empirically the moral relevance of aspects of personality. Indeed, our evidence is that moral cognition does not well explain morally exemplary action, a conclusion previously suggested by Colby and Damon's (1992) case studies. In contrast, however, several personality variables clearly distinguished moral exemplars from comparison participants and were found to substantially close the explanatory gap between judgment and action.

Our focus on two types of moral action – heroic rescues and caring service – finessed complementary aims: to identify contrasting ideals of moral maturity, on the one hand, and to identify the personological core to moral functioning, on the other. We anticipated finding divergence in their personality profiles, with each exemplar group evidencing adaptive advantages relative to the other. Instead, the caring exemplars scored a shutout victory over the brave exemplars. This must be interpreted in the context of the finding that both the brave and caring groups outscored comparison participants. A tentative proposition thus seems warranted: that the brave and caring exemplars, as well as their comparison groups comprised of "ordinary" individuals, lie on a single axis of "personological exemplarity." In other words, the brave exemplars were more adaptive than their comparisons, and the caring exemplars were more adaptive still. This model of exemplarity stands in contrast to the notion of a branch point, where high moral functioning can equally be manifested in different ways. But before such a proposition is accepted, an even-handed replication is necessary, one in which contrasting types of exemplars have engaged in comparable amounts of morally exemplary action.

Of course, bravery and care do not begin to exhaust the realm of moral exemplarity – the just exemplar being a notable omission from our design, given its prominence in ethical theory and in everyday conceptions (Rawls, 1971; Walker & Hennig, 2004), while other examples abound. The empirical study of other types of moral action may implicate psychological processes left unexplored at present.

Despite the wide-ranging differences in the personality profiles of our brave and caring exemplars, they also shared several commonalities that also distinguished them from ordinary individuals. These commonalities evince the psychological essentia of the moral personality. Most notably, this foundational core includes the converging motivational duality of agency and communion, the redemptive reframing of life events, and an identity that references a beneficially formative childhood.

A frequent observation is that achieving excellence in one aspect of character may come at some cost, that a shadow-side or psychological handicap may somehow be implicated (Lapsley & Narvaez, 2006). We found no evidence of psychological impairment associated with moral exemplarity in our study, but our measures were not particularly designed to assess maladaptive aspects of personality. A profitable direction for future research will be to flesh out the complexity in the balancing of various virtues, to explore how a personal strength can also entail a vulnerability, and how weakness can promote growth. Another research question prompted by the present findings is the extent to which moral exemplarity differs from "generic exemplarity" in other domains: think of academic or entrepreneurial achievement as contrasts, for example. Likewise, the dissimilarities in psychological functioning between moral exemplars and immoral ones (such as psychopaths) may be particularly informative of the processes underlying moral behavior.

A final consideration in our concluding thoughts concerns the critical issue of psychological causality. Here the question, posed starkly, is: Does moral personality function analogously to an operator's manual, causing exemplary moral action; or does involvement in significant action prompt a reworking of one's personality, with personality being more analogous to a documentary? This is certainly not an easily resolved question (Midlarsky et al., 2005). There is abundant evidence in social psychological research to indicate both that attitudes affect behavior and that engaging in behavior induces attitude change (e.g., see Bem's, 1972, self-perception theory). In our study, no determination of the causal connection between personality and action was attempted and, hopefully, none was implied in our discussion. At this point, it sufficed for us to demonstrate that some personality variables were associated with exemplary action. Our assessment of exemplars' personality was, of course, done subsequently to their heroic rescues or long-term volunteer service (and the recognition that such action garnered); and neither such actions nor the award were likely to have been inconsequential events in most people's lives and self-understandings. An alternate methodological approach would be to conduct prospective longitudinal studies in an attempt to identify the personological precursors of moral action, but this approach would require large samples, and it is not apparent what outcome index of moral action would be most appropriate.

The impetus for our research project was to salvage the foundering ship that has become the moral development enterprise. In describing and empirically validating the signature moral personality variables, we hope to have provided abundant ammunition to empirical researchers. The far-reaching theorizing on the topic of moral personality and character of recent years may now duly come to fruition. With more clearly delineated means of testing theory, we anticipate widespread flag-raising, and new and exciting armada of moral psychological research. The empirical cannons lie trembling in anticipation; the time approaches for determining the weak-hulled from the seaworthy, the old-fashioned way.

REFERENCES

Bakan, D. (1966). *The duality of human existence: An essay on psychology and religion*. Chicago, IL: Rand McNally.

Bem, D. J. (1972). Self-perception theory. In L. Berkowitz (Ed.), *Advances in experimental social psychology* (Vol. 6, pp. 1–62). New York: Academic Press.

Blasi, A. (1980). Bridging moral cognition and moral action: A critical review of the literature. *Psychological Bulletin, 88*, 1–45.

(1993). The development of identity: Some implications for moral functioning. In G. G. Noam & T. E. Wren (Eds.), *The moral self* (pp. 99–122). Cambridge, MA: MIT Press.

(2004). Moral functioning: Moral understanding and personality. In D. K. Lapsley & D. Narvaez (Eds.), *Moral development, self, and identity* (pp. 335–347). Mahwah, NJ: Lawrence Erlbaum Associates.

Campbell, R. L., & Christopher, J. C. (1996). Beyond formalism and altruism: The prospects for moral personality. *Developmental Review, 16*, 108–123.

Colby, A., & Damon, W. (1992). *Some do care: Contemporary lives of moral commitment*. New York: Free Press.

Colby, A., & Kohlberg, L. (1987). *The measurement of moral judgment* (Vols. 1–2). New York: Cambridge University Press.

Emmons, R. A. (1999). *The psychology of ultimate concerns: Motivation and spirituality in personality*. New York: Guilford.

Flanagan, O. (1991). *Varieties of moral personality: Ethics and psychological realism*. Cambridge, MA: Harvard University Press.

Franco, Z., & Zimbardo, P. (2006, Fall/Winter). The banality of heroism. *Greater Good, 3*(2), 30–35.

Frimer, J. A., & Walker, L. J. (2008). Towards a new paradigm of moral personhood. *Journal of Moral Education, 37*, 333–356.

Gilligan, C. (1982). *In a different voice: Psychological theory and women's development.* Cambridge, MA: Harvard University Press.

Hart, D., & Fegley, S. (1995). Prosocial behavior and caring in adolescence: Relations to self-understanding and social judgment. *Child Development, 66,* 1346–1359.

Kohlberg, L. (1969). Stage and sequence: The cognitive-developmental approach to socialization. In D. A. Goslin (Ed.), *Handbook of socialization theory and research* (pp. 347–480). Chicago, IL: Rand McNally.

(1981). *Essays on moral development: Vol. 1. The philosophy of moral development.* San Francisco: Harper & Row.

Lapsley, D. K., & Narvaez, D. (2006). Character education. In W. Damon & R. M. Lerner (Series Eds.) & K. A. Renninger & I. E. Sigel (Vol. Eds.), *Handbook of child psychology: Vol. 4. Child psychology in practice* (6th ed., pp. 248–296). New York: Wiley.

Matsuba, M. K., & Walker, L. J. (2004). Extraordinary moral commitment: Young adults working for social organizations. *Journal of Personality, 72,* 413–436.

(2005). Young adult moral exemplars: The making of self through stories. *Journal of Research on Adolescence, 15,* 275–297.

McAdams, D. P. (1993). *The stories we live by: Personal myths and the making of the self.* New York: Guilford.

(1995a). *The life story interview* (Rev.). Unpublished manuscript, Northwestern University, Evanston, IL.

(1995b). What do we know when we know a person? *Journal of Personality, 63,* 365–396.

(2006). *The redemptive self: Stories Americans live by.* New York: Oxford University Press.

(2009). The moral personality. In D. Narvaez & D. K. Lapsley (Eds.), *personality, identity, and character: Explorations in moral psychology.* New York: Cambridge University Press.

McAdams, D. P., Diamond, A., de St. Aubin, E., & Mansfield, E. (1997). Stories of commitment: The psychosocial construction of generative lives. *Journal of Personality and Social Psychology, 72,* 678–694.

McAdams, D. P., Hoffman, B. J., Mansfield, E. D., & Day, R. (1996). Themes of agency and communion in significant autobiographical scenes. *Journal of Personality, 64,* 339–377.

Midlarsky, E., Jones, S. F., & Corley, R. P. (2005). Personality correlates of heroic rescue during the Holocaust. *Journal of Personality, 73,* 907–934.

Miller, W. I. (2000). *The mystery of courage.* Cambridge, MA: Harvard University Press.

Monroe, K. R. (2002). Explicating altruism. In S. G. Post, L. G. Underwood, J. P. Schloss, & W. B. Hurlbut (Eds.), *Altruism and altruistic love: Science, philosophy, and religion in dialogue* (pp. 106–122). New York: Oxford University Press.

Noddings, N. (1984). *Caring: A feminine approach to ethics and moral education.* Berkeley, CA: University of California Press.

Oliner, S. P. (2003). *Do unto others: Extraordinary acts of ordinary people.* Boulder, CO: Westview.

Oliner, S. P., & Oliner, P. M. (1988). *The altruistic personality: Rescuers of Jews in Nazi Europe*. New York: Free Press.

Peterson, C. (2000). The future of optimism. *American Psychologist, 55,* 44–55.

Piaget, J. (1977). *The moral judgment of the child* (M. Gabain, Trans.). Harmondsworth, England: Penguin. (Original work published 1932.)

Rawls, J. (1971). *A theory of justice*. Cambridge, MA: Harvard University Press.

Reimer, K., & Wade-Stein, D. (2004). Moral identity in adolescence: Self and other in semantic space. *Identity, 4,* 229–249.

Sternberg, R. J., Conway, B. E., Ketron, J. L., & Bernstein, M. (1981). People's conceptions of intelligence. *Journal of Personality and Social Psychology, 41,* 37–55.

Straughan, R. (1986). Why act on Kohlberg's moral judgments? (Or how to reach Stage 6 and remain a bastard). In S. Modgil & C. Modgil (Eds.), *Lawrence Kohlberg: Consensus and controversy* (pp. 149–157). Philadelphia, PA: Falmer.

Walker, L. J. (2002). Moral exemplarity. In W. Damon (Ed.), *Bringing in a new era in character education* (pp. 65–83). Stanford, CA: Hoover Institution Press.

(2004). Gus in the gap: Bridging the judgment–action gap in moral functioning. In D. K. Lapsley & D. Narvaez (Eds.), *Moral development, self, and identity* (pp. 1–20). Mahwah, NJ: Lawrence Erlbaum Associates.

Walker, L. J., & Frimer, J. A. (2007). Moral personality of brave and caring exemplars. *Journal of Personality and Social Psychology, 93,* 845–860.

Walker, L. J., & Hennig, K. H. (1997). Moral development in the broader context of personality. In S. Hala (Ed.), *The development of social cognition* (pp. 297–327). East Sussex, England: Psychology Press.

(2004). Differing conceptions of moral exemplarity: Just, brave, and caring. *Journal of Personality and Social Psychology, 86,* 629–647.

Walker, L. J., Pitts, R. C., Hennig, K. H., & Matsuba, M. K. (1995). Reasoning about morality and real-life moral problems. In M. Killen & D. Hart (Eds.), *Morality in everyday life: Developmental perspectives* (pp. 371–407). Cambridge: Cambridge University Press.

Wiggins, J. S. (1995). *Interpersonal Adjective Scales: Professional manual*. Odessa, FL: Psychological Assessment Resources.

Wolf, S. (1982). Moral saints. *Journal of Philosophy, 79,* 419–439.

11

Greatest of the Virtues? Gratitude and the Grateful Personality

ROBERT A. EMMONS

> In gratitude for your good fortune, you must render in return some sacrifice of your own life for other life. – Albert Schweitzer

Elizabeth Bartlett, professor of political science at a Midwestern university, received a heart transplant at the age of 42. All other options for treating her life-threatening chronic tachycardia (irregular heartbeat) had been exhausted. Four years earlier, she had suffered a cardiac arrest, and medication failed to improve her condition. In a book chronicling her journey, she describes the insufficiency of the gratitude she felt in the wake of her new lease on life:

> Yet I have found that it is not enough for me to be thankful. I have a desire to do something in return. To do thanks. To give thanks. Give things. Give thoughts. Give love. So gratitude becomes the gift, creating a cycle of giving and receiving, the endless waterfall. Filling up and spilling over. To give from the fullness of my being. This comes not from a feeling of obligation, like a child's obligatory thank-you notes to grandmas and aunts and uncles after receiving presents. Rather, it is a spontaneous charitableness, perhaps not even to the giver but to someone else, to whoever crosses one's path. It is the simple passing on of the gift. (Bartlett, 1997, p. 124)

Gratitude in response to received goodness. It is a natural emotional reaction and quite likely a universal tendency to respond positively to another's benevolence. The word gratitude is derived from the Latin *gratia*, meaning favor, and *gratus*, meaning pleasing. All derivatives from this Latin root have to do with kindness, generousness, gifts, the beauty of giving and receiving, or getting something for nothing. Gratitude is pleasing. It feels good. Yet as this brief passage from Bartlett illustrates, gratitude is more than a pleasant feeling. Gratitude is also motivating. There is an energizing and motivating quality to gratitude. It is a positive state of mind that gives rise to the "passing on of the gift" through positive action. As such, gratitude serves as a key link in the dynamic between receiving and giving. It is not only a response to kindnesses received, but it is also a motivator of future benevolent actions on the part of the recipient. In the language of evolutionary dynamics, gratitude leads to "upstream reciprocity" (Nowak & Roch, 2007) or the passing on of benefits to third parties instead of returning benefits to one's benefactors. As much of human life is about giving, receiving, and repaying, gratitude is a pivotal concept for human social interactions. Moreover, there is increasing evidence, reviewed later, that gratitude may spur spontaneous acts of altruism.

For centuries, theologians, moral philosophers, and writers have identified gratitude as an indispensable manifestation of virtue and excellence of character. Gratitude is a virtue as well as an emotion, the possession of which enables a person to live life well. The Roman philosopher Cicero held that "Gratitude is not only the greatest of virtues, but the parent of all the others." Cicero's contemporary, Seneca, maintained that "He who receives a benefit with gratitude repays the first installment on his debt." Adam Smith (1790/1976) defined gratitude as "The sentiment which most immediately and directly prompts us to reward" (p. 68). Similarly, across time, ingratitude has been treated as a serious vice. Ingratitude is the "essence of vileness," wrote the great German philosopher Immanuel Kant. Despite these powerful assertions, opinion concerning gratitude's status as a virtue is far from unanimous. La Rochefoucauld opined that "Gratitude in the generality of men is only a strong and secret desire of receiving greater favours" (cited in Emmons, 2007, p. 16). Aristotle found gratitude incompatible with magnanimity and therefore did not include it in his list of virtues. Magnanimous people, according to Aristotle, insist on their self-sufficiency and therefore find it demeaning to be indebted to others.

Despite such acclaim from most virtue theorists, gratitude has never, until recently, been systematically examined or studied by scientific psychologists. It is possible that psychology has ignored gratitude because it appears, on the surface, to be a very obvious emotion, lacking in interesting complications – we receive a gift (from friends, from family, from God), and then we feel pleasurably grateful. But gratitude is a deeper, more complex phenomenon that plays a critical role in human happiness and in human social relationships. Beneath the warm feelings of gratitude resides an imperative force, a force that compels us to return the benefit we have received. Gratitude has a clearly specified action tendency connected to it, as is also stipulated by emotion theorists (Lazarus & Lazarus, 1994). This duty to return led the social psychologist Barry Schwartz (1967) to speak of the "gratitude imperative." Part of gratitude's magnetic appeal lies in its power to evoke a focus by the recipient on the benevolence of others, thereby ensuring a perception that kindness has been offered; and its beneficial consequences frequently are the motive to respond favorably toward another. Whether viewed as a personality disposition or an emotional state, there is a connection between gratitude and generosity. Thus the idea that the capacity to receive and be grateful fosters the desire to return goodness is theoretically plausible and empirically viable. Recent research and theory to be reviewed in this chapter has begun to explore gratitude's distinct social causes and effects.

WHAT IS GRATITUDE?

Before presenting the research evidence on gratitude and social behavior, a brief conceptual analysis of gratitude is warranted. Gratitude stems from the perception that one has benefited due to the actions of another person. There is an acknowledgement that one has received a gift, and an appreciation of and recognition of the value of that gift. The gift is something of value given to one unearned and undeserved by one moral agent at some cost to that agent and for the benefit of the recipient. Thus, a grateful state usually requires a relationship, and insomuch as actions between human beings are legitimate moral concerns, gratitude is relevant to the moral life (Shelton, 2004).

Since gratitude is more than a feeling, it requires a willingness to recognize (a) that one has been the beneficiary of someone's kindness; (b) that the benefactor has intentionally provided a benefit, often incurring some personal cost; and (c) that the benefit has value in the eyes of the beneficiary. In gratitude we recognize the other's moral agency – that he or she could have done otherwise but chose to intentionally provide a benefit – hence the concern with our well-being – and that the giver had correctly grasped the character of our moral situation (that we were in need of the benefit).

Gratitude also implies humility – a recognition that we could not be who we are or where we are in life without the contributions of others. Gratitude also requires a recognition that it is possible for other moral agents to act toward us with benevolent selfless motives. In gratitude we remember the contributions that others have made for the sake of our well-being. On the recipient side, we acknowledge having received a benefit, and we realize that the giver acted intentionally in order to benefit us. Gratitude has a critically important broader sense (of gratitude to God) that has been discussed extensively by religious thinkers (Carman & Streng, 1989). This form of gratitude is an affirmation of the goodness in one's life, and the recognition that the sources of this goodness lie at least partially outside the self; it is a way of saying "yes" to life. Equally important is the recognition that one is not 100% responsible for these good things by oneself – that responsibility lies with other people, specific circumstances, fate, or God. Without this recognition, we would most likely have pride (taking sole credit for success) without gratitude.

THE "MORAL MEMORY OF MANKIND"

Gratitude is a positive emotion, but it is different from generic pleasantness because gratitude is typically preceded by the perception that one has benefited from another person's generosity. A social psychological view on gratitude emphasizes the interpersonal relationships and social interactions in which gratitude is shaped. Gratitude is always embedded in a relationship between two parties. The capacity to be grateful and generous develops within the context of a social relationship. The primary function of gift giving – creating social ties – is clearly demonstrated in the interaction between mother and child: the bond is only kept alive and intact if there is some degree of positive reciprocity. Gratitude plays a crucial role in establishing and maintaining social relations. In his essay *Faithfulness and Gratitude,* sociologist Georg Simmel called gratitude "the moral memory of mankind" (1950, p. 388). By mutual giving, people become tied to each other by a web of feelings of gratitude. Although it has psychological feelings at its base, its main function is social, according to Simmel. Gratitude functions within the chain of reciprocity. Gift exchange and the concomitant feelings of gratitude are at the basis of a system of mutual obligations among people, and as such, function as the moral cement of human society and culture. Simmel refers to the role of gratitude in fostering the continuity of social life. Gratitude connects people with what has gone on before, and gives them the continuity of interactional life. He conducts a mental experiment by imagining what would happen if every grateful action based on benefits received in the past were suddenly eliminated: society would definitely break apart. Gratitude not only creates and smooths interpersonal relationships, it also fulfills important cohesive functions for society and culture as such.

The social nature of the principle of reciprocity is illustrated in the primate research data collected by Frans de Waal and his coworkers

(Bonnie & de Waal, 2004). After having offered ample illustrations of chimpanzees and capuchins sharing and exchanging food, de Waal asks the crucial question about *why* they do so. In his experiments, he has observed chimpanzees when they see a caretaker arrive with bundles of blackberry, sweet gum, beech, and tulip branches. Characteristically, a general pandemonium ensues: wild excitement, hooting, embracing, kissing, and friendly body contact, which he calls a "celebration." De Waal considers it a sign indicating the transition to a mode of interaction characterized by friendliness and reciprocity. Celebration is followed by a pattern of reciprocal giving and receiving: those who share with others will also receive from others, and those who are poor givers will be poor recipients as well. Capuchins and chimpanzees have at least a rudimentary mental capacity to keep track of what they have given and received and apply this capacity whenever it is appropriate (see Bonnie & de Waal, 2004). Therefore, reciprocal exchanges of social services among chimps and capuchins may rest on psychological mechanisms as complex as gratitude.

DOES GRATITUDE MOTIVATE MORAL ACTION?

By experiencing gratitude, a person is motivated to carry out prosocial behavior, energized to sustain moral behaviors, and is inhibited from committing destructive interpersonal behaviors. Because of its specialized functions in the moral domain, gratitude is similar in some respects to empathy, sympathy, guilt, and shame. Whereas empathy and sympathy operate when people have the opportunity to respond to the plight of another person, and guilt and shame operate when people have failed to meet moral standards or obligations, gratitude operates typically when people acknowledge that they are the recipients of prosocial behavior. In a review of the literature on gratitude (McCullough, Kirkpatrick, Emmons, & Larsen, 2001), my colleagues and I contended that gratitude serves as a *moral barometer* or benefit detector, providing individuals with an affective readout that accompanies the perception that another person has treated them prosocially. Gratitude also serves as a *moral motive*, stimulating people to behave prosocially after they have been the beneficiaries of other people's prosocial behavior. Accruing research evidence has ratified the hypothesis that one function of gratitude is to stimulate moral, especially prosocial, action, and in so doing, makes a strong case for the role of gratitude in living a moral, constructive life.

But gratitude is not the only emotional reaction to receiving a benefit. Individuals may react with feelings of indebtedness, an unpleasant emotional state that motivates people to repay not out of generosity, but out of a desire to reduce inequity. Similarly, receiving a benefit might trigger the norm of reciprocity, which states that people should help those who have helped them, and should not injure those who have helped them. Despite its status as a virtue, research has only begun to differentiate the effect of these three reactions to benevolence on subsequent prosocial behavior.

An increasing number of studies have begun to test the *moral motive* hypothesis. Research on reactions to aid and reciprocity – which seem relevant to the motivational value of gratitude – has been dominated by the assumption that the key motive for moral behavior in reciprocity situations is inequity or indebtedness. Yet three new studies provide strong initial evidence that gratitude shapes prosocial responding by increasing the likelihood that one will engage in effortful helping behavior. Moreover, these studies have been able to differentiate the unique effects of gratitude as a moral motive from the general effects of positive mood on helping behavior. Gratitude and indebtedness have distinct patterns of thought-action tendencies. Grateful responses are more strongly associated with inclination for future altruism than indebtedness and feelings of obligation.

One particularly informative set of studies examined gratitude experimentally by employing interpersonal emotion inductions and requests for assistance. Research by David DeSteno and Monica Bartlett at Northeastern University showed that gratitude increased efforts to assist a benefactor even when such efforts were costly, as opposed to simple awareness of reciprocity norms, or general positive affect; and it is gratitude that drove helping behavior (Bartlett and DeSteno, 2006). In their creative studies, participants worked on a computer-generated task where the screen suddenly went blank as they were about to receive their score. A confederate "discovered" that the monitor's plug had been pulled partially out of the power strip. With the confederate's assistance in restoring power, the participant's scores were subsequently displayed. Upon leaving the laboratory, the participant was asked to assist in another, ostensibly unrelated experiment that involved completing a tedious and taxing survey. Increased helping was found to be related to gratefulness toward the confederate in receiving the favor during the computer task, not from an awareness of reciprocity norms (manipulated by not having a benefactor provide a favor) or positive emotions (elicited through viewing a funny movie clip).

In another important series of studies conducted by Jo-Ann Tsang at Baylor University, gratitude was differentiated from positive affect by pairing a condition in which participants received a favor from another participant with a control condition in which participants received an identical positive outcome caused "by chance" (Tsang, 2006, 2007). Participants received a positive outcome either as a favor or by chance, and were then given an opportunity to distribute raffle tickets to their partner in a subsequent task. The value of the favor was also manipulated. Participants receiving a favor subsequently distributed more tickets to the other student; participants receiving more valuable favors also distributed more. Self-reported grateful motivation predicted distribution better than did indebtedness, and grateful motivation mediated the relationship between favor and distribution. This study was important because it utilized behavioral measures of gratitude, involved costly reciprocating behavior, and distinguished between gratitude and indebtedness as a motivator of prosocial behavior.

Watkins, Scheer, Ovnicek, and Kolts (2006) used vignette studies to investigate the relationship between indebtedness and gratitude. They found that as reciprocity expectations on the part of the benefactor increased, feelings of gratitude decreased and feelings of indebtedness increased. Distinct thought-action tendencies were found to be associated with gratitude, and indebtedness, respectively. Gratitude covaried with positive emotions and approach tendencies, whereas indebtedness covaried with negative emotions and was not linked to any prosocial tendencies. Furthermore, gratitude inhibited antisocial tendencies (showing irritation, resentment, ignoring or insulting the benefactor), whereas indebtedness did not.

The overall pattern from these three separate, but related, lines of research on gratitude and prosocial behavior suggests that, in the prosocial realm, there is something unique about gratitude. Its motivational function is distinct from indebtedness, the reciprocity norm, and general positive affect. These experimental studies support the *moral motive* hypothesis (McCullough et al, 2001) in which grateful recipients of prosocial actions are motivated *by gratitude* to behave prosocially themselves. Whether this motivation stems from altruistic versus egoistic concerns (Tsang, 2007), however, is a different and valuable question in its own right, and is in need of further empirical study. Gratitude may also motivate prosocial behavior by influencing psychological states that support generosity and cooperation. For example, Dunn and Schweitzer (2005, Study 3) found that participants who described a time in the past when they felt grateful toward someone (thereby creating grateful emotion in the present) subsequently reported higher levels of trust toward a third party than did participants who were asked to describe a time they felt angry, guilty, or proud.

After appraising the evidence that gratitude fosters moral behavior, McCullough, Kimmeldorf, and Cohen (2008) raised the possibility that gratitude evolved to facilitate social exchange. Compelling evidence suggests that gratitude evolved to stimulate not only direct reciprocal altruism but also "upstream reciprocity" (Nowak & Roch, 2007): the passing on of benefits to third parties instead of returning benefits to one's benefactors.

THE PERSONALITY BASIS OF GRATITUDE

Feeling grateful is not the same as being a grateful person. To describe a man – Garrett, for example – by saying that he always seems to have a deeply grateful heart, no matter what the circumstance, is far more compelling than to comment merely that Garrett is appreciative or grateful for some favor that he has received. To have the virtue of gratitude, it is insufficient to feel grateful occasionally. A grateful person is one who is prone to feeling gratitude frequently across a range of situations. He or she is one who *regularly* affirms the goodness in his or her life and recognizes that the sources of this goodness lie at least partially outside of themselves. The grateful disposition is a generalized tendency to recognize and respond with positive emotions to the role of other moral agents' benevolence in the positive experiences and outcomes that one obtains. Conversely, the regular failure to feel gratitude in situations that call for it suggests a lack of the virtue. But the grateful disposition is not monolithic. It consists of several dimensions or facets.

The first facet of the grateful disposition might be called gratitude *intensity*. A person with a strong grateful disposition who experienced a positive event would be expected to feel more intensely grateful than would someone less disposed toward gratitude, who experienced the same positive event. A second facet of the grateful disposition might be called gratitude *frequency*. Someone with a strong grateful disposition might report feeling grateful several times per day, and gratitude might be elicited by even the simplest favor or act of politeness. Conversely, for someone less disposed toward gratitude, such a favor or act of politeness might be insufficient to elicit gratitude. As a result, the person with a weaker grateful disposition might experience less gratitude within a specified time period (e.g., hours, days, or weeks). A third facet of the grateful disposition might be called gratitude *span*. Gratitude span refers to the number of life circumstances for which a person feels grateful at a given time. Someone with a strong grateful disposition might be expected to feel grateful for their families, their jobs, their health, and life itself, along with a wide variety of other benefits. Someone less disposed toward gratitude might be aware of experiencing gratitude for fewer aspects of their lives. A fourth facet of the grateful disposition might be called gratitude *density*. Gratitude density refers to the number of persons to whom one feels grateful for a single positive outcome or life circumstance. When asked to whom one feels grateful for a certain outcome – say, obtaining a good job – someone with a strong grateful disposition density might list a large number of others, including parents, elementary school teachers, tutors, mentors, fellow students, and God. Someone less disposed toward gratitude might feel grateful to fewer people for such a benefit. These considerations have informed the development of individual difference measures of gratitude.

Three self-report measures of gratitude as a personality disposition have been constructed: the GRAT (the Gratitude, Resentment, and Appreciation Test; Watkins et. al., 2004), the Gratitude Questionnaire (GQ; McCullough, Emmons, & Tsang, 2002), and the Gratitude toward God scale (Krause, 2005). Items on the GQ reflect gratitude intensity (e.g., "I feel thankful for what I have received in life"), gratitude frequency (e.g., "Long amounts of time can go by before I feel grateful to something or someone"), gratitude span (e.g., "I sometimes feel grateful for the smallest things"), and gratitude density (e.g., "I am grateful to a wide variety of people"). Items on the GRAT tap appreciation of simple pleasures ("Often I think, 'What a privilege it is to be alive'"), a sense of deprivation ("I really don't think that I've gotten all the good things that I deserve in life"), and appreciation for others ("I couldn't have gotten where I am today without the help of many people"). Another measure assesses gratitude toward God, and includes items such as "I am grateful to God for all he has done for me," and "As I look back on my life, I feel I have been richly blessed by God." These individual difference measures emphasize the emotional component of gratitude more so than the moral component of reciprocity.

People who score highly on measures of gratitude as an affective trait tend to experience a high degree of life satisfaction and positive affects, such as happiness, vitality, and hope. They also experience relatively low levels of negative affects, such as resentment, depression, and envy. McCullough and colleagues (McCullough et al., 2002) found that they also scored higher on measures of prosocial behavior, empathy, forgiveness, religiousness, and spirituality. Among the Big Five, the grateful disposition seems related most strongly to agreeableness (positively) and neuroticism (negatively). For people who are dispositionally prone to feel grateful, the amount of gratitude in their daily moods is determined so thoroughly by personality processes that their moods are resistant to the effects of gratitude-relevant daily life events (e.g., experiencing many discrete gratitude-eliciting events; experiencing gratitude to a large number of people), and their discrete emotional responses to these daily events (i.e., feeling intense episodes of grateful emotion in response). Recent research has shown that individuals who report habitually experiencing gratitude engage more frequently in prosocial behaviors than do individuals who experience gratitude less often. Individual differences in gratitude are related to individual differences in personality factors that have typically been linked to prosocial emotions and behavior – namely, high agreeableness, empathy, and forgiveness – as well as low narcissism and envy.

Furthermore, data are not limited to what grateful people report about their own experience. Nonself-report data indicate positive correlates and consequences of gratitude. The informants of people with strong dispositions toward gratitude reported that these grateful friends engaged in more prosocial behaviors (e.g., loaning money, providing compassion, sympathy, and emotional support) in the previous month than did the informants of less grateful individuals. Grateful individuals were also rated by their informants as engaging in supportive behaviors more frequently than were less grateful individuals.

WHY IS GRATITUDE GOOD?

Be it as a state or trait emotion, gratitude has clearly been linked to positive social outcomes, including empathy, generosity, forgivingness, and the provision of social support. Indeed, grateful people tend to be helpful people. Moreover, expressing gratitude seems to intensify our already felt positive affect in response to being the recipient of a benefactor's kind behavior (e.g., giving a gift). "It is as if our enjoyment is incomplete unless some praise or gratitude is expressed to the source of our enjoyment" (Watkins, 2004, p. 167). Subsequently, capitalizing on positive experiences by processing them post hoc seems to be psychologically beneficial. Indeed, the ability to notice positive occurrences in one's life, and to enjoy them, allows us to have more fulfilling experiences. In addition, gratitude is associated positively with a wide variety of measures of subjective well-being (McCullough et al, 2002). Other work shows that gratitude is easily cultivated and is efficacious in kindling positive emotions and beneficial relational outcomes in adults and in children (Emmons & McCullough, 2003; Froh, Sefick, & Emmons, 2008). These findings suggest that further work on gratitude may foster important insights into the links between personality, emotion, social life, and psychological well-being.

What accounts for the link between gratitude and positive outcomes, whether these outcomes be psychological, social, or physical? There are three primary explanations. First, *gratitude strengthens social ties*. It is the relationship strengthening emotion. It cultivates an individual's sense of interconnectedness. Gratitude is indeed the "moral memory of mankind." Roger, a man we interviewed in our research on gratitude and quality of life in patients with chronic neuromuscular disease, who was on the verge of losing his home due to escalating medical bills and an extended period of unemployment, wrote in his gratitude journal:

> I was scheduled back to work August 7, 2000, and my co-workers and friends threw a benefit for me at a rock-n-roll club called "the Double Door." Located in a[n] "upcoming" neighborhood the place was known as an opening stage for the Rolling Stones tour. My building manager spearheaded the effort organizing a raffle of restaurants' dinners, sports items and free buffet and music. My wife Sue felt guilty not having been part of the planning or promotion, we felt like this was asking too much of our friends and families but we weren't in charge so we sat back and just appreciated the effort and hard work being done on our behalf. Was it gonna be a bust? Or success? We didn't know but Sue, Brian and the three boys were gonna show up to thank anyone who showed up. Well the big day came after much anticipation. About two hundred people showed up, bought raffle tickets, drank, danced, partied and ate till 1 a.m. closing! We saw so many friends and coworkers and it was a trult great night. We went up on stage to thank everyone amid joy, tears, and hugs. My manager cut me a check for over $35,000 the next week! Without that check my house/car would have been on the market. Insurance picked up the majority of bills, but weekly tests and medication and follow-up ran into the thousands. My doctor and nurse also attended and our priest stopped by for a few beers – I keep thinking of more highlights as I write. I truly felt like George Bailey in "It's a Wonderful Life!" I feel myself almost tearing up as I write. My heart warms as I see the people that attended. I also feel a need to help or reach out to others whenever I can help by speaking or just listening. (Emmons, 2007, pp. 9–10)

One just needs to try to imagine human relationships existing without gratitude. As a social emotion, expressions of gratitude and appreciation are essential to successful, vital, and thriving long-term relationships. By way of contrast, ingratitude leads inevitably to a confining, restricting, and "shrinking" sense of self. Emotions like anger, resentment, envy, and bitterness tend to undermine happy social relations. But the virtue of gratitude is not only a firewall of protection against such corruption of relationships; it contributes positively to friendship and civility, because it is both benevolent (wishing the benefactor well) and just (giving the benefactor his due, in a certain special way). A grateful outlook can even dominate the life of an entire culture, as can be seen in certain Eastern cultures, in which individuals view themselves as recipients of endless ancestrally bestowed blessings (Carman & Streng, 1989).

A second reason for the power of gratitude is *that gratitude increases one's sense of personal worth*. Implicit in the experience of gratitude is the recipient's "theory of mind" from which he or she infers another's well-meaning intention and in turn feels loved and esteemed. That is to say, we can logically infer that a person feeling grateful might be more inclined to feel loved and cared for by others. If someone has incurred a personal cost by helping me out, then how can I not infer that I have value in that person's eye? It might be this link that explains why gratitude can be a powerful antidote to a depressed view of life. A critical element in gratitude is the recipient's acknowledgment that the gift was given out of compassion, generosity, kindness, and/or love (and often, but not always, selflessness – always at least, though, some effort or loss or energy spent by the giver). One of the reasons gratitude makes us happier is that it forces us to abandon a belief that may accompany severe depression: that the world is devoid of goodness, love, and kindness and is nothing but randomness and cruelty. Repeated patterns of perceived benevolence may lead the depressed person to reorganize his or her self-schema ("I guess I'm not such a loser after all"). By feeling grateful, we are acknowledging that someone, somewhere, is being kind to us. And therefore not just that we are worthy of kindness (vs. everyone else), but that kindness indeed exists in the world and, therefore, that life may be worth living.

A third reason that accounts for the power of gratitude, already expounded upon in this chapter, is that gratitude not only creates a strong desire to reciprocate, but also stimulates prosocial behavior, including acts of volunteerism, generosity, forgiveness, and compassion. Grateful people look forward to helping those who have helped them. Grateful people are more likely to creatively engage their capacities – their time, talents, and treasures – in the service of others. In the words of Charles Shelton (2004):

> Gratitude is viewed as a way of life which is best defined as an interior depth we experience which orients us to an acknowledged dependence out of which flows a profound sense of being gifted. This way of being, in turn, elicits a humility just as it nourishes our goodness. As a consequence, when truly grateful, we are led to experience and interpret life situations in ways that call forth from us an openness to and engagement with the world through purposeful actions in order to share and increase the very good we have received. (p. 273)

As an integral element of moral character, gratitude is an open and receptive stance toward the world that energizes people to return the goodness they have received. Gratitude's intrinsic function is to affirm the good in life, embrace that good, and then transform the good in purposeful actions to accomplish something that is at once meaningful to the self and of consequence to the world beyond the self.

Consider Shauna Marsh. As a high school freshman in Southern California in 2003, Shauna started a national campaign to collect and distribute one million letters, e-mails, and cards of thanks and appreciation to our current and past military service members. Within a year and a half of launching her vision, more than 1.5 million people had written letters to service people stationed abroad; three years later the total surpassed 4 million. Naming her service project "A Million Thanks," Shauna recalled "I just decided to go for it. It never occurred to me that I wouldn't succeed. I had an invincible mental image and knew no one would stop me. My friends loved the idea and wanted to help" (Metzler, 2006).

CONCLUSIONS

Gratitude is a personal asset as well as a moral virtue: a capacity one has to learn. Moreover, gratitude has been analyzed as the moral basis of reciprocity. By acting as a moral obligation to give in return, gratitude not only serves to reinforce bonds at the level of social relationships, it is also a means for establishing social cohesion and creating a shared culture. It is important, at this point, to emphasize that a sense of indebtedness is not in any way contrary to gratitude, but rather its moral core.

In the history of ideas, gratitude has had surprisingly few detractors. Aside from a few harsh words from a small handful of cynics, nearly every thinker has viewed gratitude as a sentiment with virtually no downside. As Comte-Sponville (2001) pointed out, gratitude is "the most pleasant of the virtues, and the most virtuous of the pleasures" (p. 132). It is virtuously pleasant because experiencing it not only uplifts the person who experiences it, but it edifies the person to whom it is directed as well. But the fact that people typically consider gratitude a virtue and not simply a pleasure also points to the fact that it does not always come naturally or easily. Gratitude must, and can, be cultivated. And by cultivating the virtue, it appears that people may get the pleasure of gratitude, and all of its other concomitant benefits, gratuitously included.

The science and discipline of gratitude is still in its infancy, and much is not known. A distinguished emotions researcher recently commented that, if a prize were given for the emotion most neglected by psychologists, gratitude would surely be among the contenders. Basic issues – such as the emotional structure of gratitude, its uniqueness from other positive emotions, the consequences of its experience and expression for emotional, physical, and relational well-being, and the cognitive mechanisms that sustain gratitude over time – require further study. Little is also known about cross-cultural experiences and expressions of gratitude, an area in which the comparative study of world religions might prove instructive (cf. Carman & Streng, 1989). Gratitude has attracted scholarly attention from the disciplines of moral philosophy, religious studies, evolutionary psychology, clinical psychology, sociology, anthropology, organizational studies, nursing and medicine, affective science, and personality and social psychology. Therefore it would be most surprising if further progress in exploring its contours were not anchored firmly within an interdisciplinary ethic, a prescription that is encouraged by the perspectives on moral behavior exemplified throughout this volume.

REFERENCES

Anderson, L. M., Giacalone, R. A., & Jurkiewicz, C. L. (2007). On the relationship between hope and gratitude to corporate social responsibility. *Journal of Business Ethics, 70,* 401–409.

Bartlett, E. A. (1997). *Journey of the heart: Spiritual insights on the road to a transplant.* Duluth, MN: Pfeifer-Hamilton.

Bartlett, M. Y., & DeSteno, D. (2006). Gratitude and prosocial behavior: Helping when it costs you. *Psychological Science, 17,* 319–325.

Bonnie, K. B., & deWaal, F. (2004). Primate social reciprocity and the origin of gratitude. In R. A. Emmons & M. E. McCullough, (Eds.), *The psychology of gratitude.* New York: Oxford University Press.

Carman, J. B., & Streng, F. J. (Eds.) (1989). *Spoken and unspoken thanks: Some comparative soundings.* Dallas, TX: Center for World Thanksgiving.

Comte-Sponville, A. (2001). *A small treatise on great virtues: The uses of philosophy in everyday life.* New York: Henry Holt.

Dunn, J. R., & Schweitzer, M. E. (2005). Feeling and believing: The influence of emotion on trust. *Journal of Personality and Social Psychology, 88,* 736–748.

Emmons, R. A. (2007). *Thanks! How the new science of gratitude can make you happier.* New York: Houghton-Mifflin.

Emmons, R. A., & McCullough, M. E. (2003). Counting blessings versus burdens: An experimental investigation of gratitude and subjective well-being in daily life. *Journal of Personality and Social Psychology, 84,* 377–389.

Emmons, R. A., & McCullough, M. E. (Eds.) (2004). *The psychology of gratitude.* New York: Oxford University Press.

Froh, J. J, Sefick, W. J., & Emmons, R. A. (2008). Counting blessings in early adolescents: An experimental study of gratitude and subjective well-being. *Journal of School Psychology, 46,* 213–233.

Gray-Greiner, S. (2004). *The "Gift of Life": The Role of Gratitude in Donating and Receiving Transplant Organs*. Unpublished doctoral dissertation, University of California, Davis.

Krause, N. (2006). Gratitude toward God, stress, and health in late life. *Research on Aging, 28*, 163–183.

Lazarus, R. S., & Lazarus, B. N. (1994). *Passion and reason: Making sense of our emotions*. New York: Oxford University Press.

McCullough, M. E., Emmons, R. A., & Tsang, J. (2002). The grateful disposition: A conceptual and empirical topography. *Journal of Personality and Social Psychology, 82*, 112–127.

McCullough, M. E., Kilpatrick, S., Emmons, R. A., & Larson, D. (2001). Gratitude as moral affect. *Psychological Bulletin, 127*, 249–266.

McCullough, M. E., Kimeldorf, M. B., & Cohen, A. D. (2008). An adaptation for altruism? The social causes, social effects, and social evolution of gratitude. *Current Directions in Psychological Science, 17*, 281–285.

Metzler, B. R. (2006). *Passionaries: Turning compassion into action*. West Conshohocken, PA: Templeton Foundation Press.

Nowak, M. A., & Roch, S. (2007). Upstream reciprocity and the evolution of gratitude. *Proceedings of the Royal Society B: Biological Sciences, 274*, 604–609.

Pruyser, P. W. (1976). *The minister as diagnostician: Personal problems in pastoral perspective*. Philadelphia, PA: Westminster Press.

Schwartz, B. (1967). The social psychology of the gift. *American Journal of Sociology, 73*, 1–11.

Shelton, C. C. S. (2004). Gratitude: Some moral considerations. In R. A. Emmons & M. E. McCullough (Eds.) *The psychology of gratitude* (pp. 259–281). New York: Oxford University Press.

Simmel, G. (1950). *The sociology of Georg Simmel*. Glencoe, IL: Free Press.

Smith, A. (1976). *The theory of moral sentiments* (6th Ed.). Oxford: Clarendon Press: (Original work published 1790.)

Tsang, J. (2006). Gratitude and prosocial behavior: An experimental test of gratitude. *Cognition and Emotion, 20*, 138–148.

    (2007). Gratitude for small and large favors: A behavioral test. *The Journal of Positive Psychology, 2*, 157–167.

Watkins, P. C. (2004). Gratitude and subjective well-being. In R. A. Emmons & M. E. McCullough (Eds.) *The psychology of gratitude* (pp. 167–192). New York: Oxford University Press.

    (2003). Gratitude and happiness: Development of a measure of gratitude and relationships with subjective well-being. *Social Behavior and Personality, 31*, 431–452.

Watkins, P. C., Scheer, J., Ovnicek, M., & Kolts, R. (2006). The debt of gratitude: Dissociating gratitude and indebtedness. *Cognition and Emotion, 20*, 217–241.

12

The Elusive Altruist: The Psychological Study of the Altruistic Personality

GUSTAVO CARLO, LISA M. PYTLIKZILLIG,
SCOTT C. ROESCH, AND RICHARD A. DIENSTBIER

Few topics through the ages have garnered as much scholarly attention as altruism. Across many different philosophical, theological, and scientific disciplines, scholars have critically debated and researched the topic of altruism posing such questions as: Are humans innately good or bad? Are there actions that are selflessly motivated? Or do all behaviors stem from selfish motives? Questions such as these spark heated debate and much controversy because the answers have tremendous theoretical and practical implications for human nature and functioning. Since psychology is a relatively young science, the study of altruism in psychology is also relatively new and continues to be a focal point for debate and controversy.

The tremendous interest in altruism stems in part from a desire to understand individuals who commit themselves to acts of heroism and sacrifice to assist others – sometimes at risk for their own life or well-being (Staub, 2005). Such individuals have sometimes been termed *moral* or *care exemplars* by scholars (Colby & Damon, 1992), and many such individuals have been identified in history (e.g., Mahatma Gandhi, Martin Luther King, Mother Teresa). However, there are many others not so recognized who commit such acts in relative obscurity in our local communities and across the world. It is not that such individuals always behave altruistically, but rather that some individuals exhibit such acts relatively frequently across time and situations. Furthermore, although those individuals might feel obligated, or feel it a duty, to help others, such duty or obligation is primarily intrinsically rather than extrinsically based.

The authors appreciated greatly the contributions and assistance of Shelley Freeman, Scott Hemenover, Roger C. Lott, and Sherri Lowrey. The Gallup Research Center and the Office of the Research Council provided funding support to the first author.

Some scholars have speculated that the behaviors of moral and care exemplars might reflect a set of personality characteristics or traits (sometimes linked to a moral identity) that motivate them to act altruistically. This has led social scientists to identify a cluster of personal traits associated with altruistic behaviors. Different terms have been used to label such traits, but the most common term is the *altruistic personality* (Oliner & Oliner, 1988; Staub, 1974). One can define the altruistic personality as a set of selflessly motivated personal tendencies aimed at benefiting others. The central focus of the present chapter is to examine the evidence for an altruistic personality. We review prior theoretical perspectives and conceptualizations of altruism and related empirical studies. We then present new data designed to examine the concept of altruism and the altruistic personality from a different perspective, that of a helper who helps indirectly through risking the lives of others. Finally, we provide theoretical and methodological suggestions for furthering and advancing the study of altruism.

ALTRUISM IN ALL ITS GLORY

One of the core aspects of debate and controversy is how to define altruism. There are many different conceptualizations of altruism across many different disciplines of study. However, for purposes of the present chapter, we will focus on key definitions that have been proposed by contemporary psychologists. To begin, it is important that we discuss altruism and other forms of prosocial behaviors. We define *prosocial behaviors* as a set of actions that benefit others, or that are regarded by society or culture as beneficial to others (Carlo, 2006; Dovidio, Piliavin, Schroeder, & Penner, 2006; Eisenberg & Fabes, 1998; Penner, Dovidio, Piliavin, & Schroeder, 2005; Staub, 1978). Prosocial behaviors include such actions as comforting or assisting someone in distress, sharing or donating resources with someone in need, and volunteering in charitable organizations. However, prosocial behaviors can result from a host of motives and for many different reasons. Individuals might donate money, for example, to gain approval from others. They might volunteer in a charitable organization because it is a requirement for service learning credit in school. In general, then, prosocial behaviors are deemed socially desirable behaviors that benefit our society, and such behaviors are central to understanding morality.

Altruism can be considered a special subset of prosocial behaviors. For the purposes of this chapter, altruism refers to the subset of actions that not only benefit others, but also are *primarily* motivated by the desire to benefit others, regardless of other conditions and simultaneous, but secondary, motivations (Carlo & Randall, 2001). Several theorists distinguish between prosocial behaviors that are egoistic – self-serving and primarily motivated by self-enhancement desires (e.g., to improve one's image or self-esteem, or to avoid guilt) – and prosocial behaviors that are altruistic – other-serving and primarily motivated by the desire to help others (Dovidio et al., 2006). Though not part of the central definition of altruism as discussed in this chapter, altruism is often engaged in the absence of obvious external rewards, is voluntary (not coerced), and usually incurs a cost to the self. Furthermore, persons who regularly engage in such behaviors may be described as having altruistic personalities. Using this definition of altruism is challenging, however, because it requires one to discern primary intention. Although altruism sometimes results in positive consequences to the self (as well as to others), the key is whether the primary intention was to benefit others, a factor that cannot always be accurately assessed and one of the focal points of controversy in the literature.

Critics and skeptics of the notion of altruism point out that we can never accurately assess the primary intention of prosocial behaviors. Of course, such criticisms are not uncommon in psychology, as it is challenging to accurately infer the underlying motive of any action. However, it is still useful to attempt such distinctions. Just as in the study of aggression, there are important qualitative and practical reasons to attempt to distinguish between aggressive actions that are intentionally produced (e.g., murder in the first degree) and those that are unintentional (e.g., manslaughter), it is also useful to acknowledge that actions that are primarily intended to benefit others are different from, and should be more valued than, prosocial behaviors that are intended to harm others (e.g., using prosocial behaviors to manipulate others) or that are primarily conducted for selfish reasons (e.g., to promote one's social status) (Hawley, Little, & Pasupathi, 2002).

By emphasizing the underlying intentions of prosocial behaviors, actions that could benefit both the helper and the recipient are not excluded. However, other scholars have proposed that purely altruistic behavior should be devoid of any self-benefits (Aronson, Wilson, & Akert, 2004; Macaulay & Berkowitz, 1970). In that case, one could argue that because most prosocial behaviors have positive consequences to one's self, *pure* altruism does not exist. Proponents of altruism instead note that even when there are nonmaterial rewards or costs to the actor, one can assess the relative material rewards and costs to the actor (Batson, 1991). Distinguishing between prosocial actions that are enacted under high material costs to one's self, and under low material costs to one's self, may be important. Although one can debate whether prosocial actions are devoid of *any* self-reward, there is still considerable value in understanding prosocial actions that are devoid of material rewards or conducted under high cost to one's self. Nevertheless, we define altruism in terms of primary motives instead of outcomes.

Other strengths of defining altruism in terms of primary intent are that it avoids the pitfalls of distinguishing between long-term and short-term consequences of prosocial behaviors. That is, if one focuses on the consequences of prosocial actions, there is always a question of whether one ought to consider beneficial short- or long-term consequences, which sometimes conflict. In addition, the definition circumvents the question of whether material consequences (e.g., goods, resources) or nonmaterial consequences (e.g., approval, self-esteem enhancement) are more important to consider. According to the definition presented in this chapter, all benefits to others or to one's self are considered relatively equal, because the focus is instead on the primary motive driving the action. It is important to note that intentions do not necessarily equate with explicit, effortful, or deliberate actions – one could conceive of altruistic actions driven by relatively automatic, nonconscious mechanisms whose primary end goal is to benefit others (akin to the notion of moral chronicity and expertise; see Narvaez, 2005).

Altruism, when defined in terms of primary motives, is also therefore defined in part as arising from intrinsic processes, emphasizing the importance of personality. As will be discussed in more detail later, some of the personality characteristics that have been found to be importantly and positively related to altruistic behavior include perspective taking, empathy, sympathy, social responsibility, internalized values or principles, moral reasoning, and a strong prosocial or moral identity (Staub, 2005). In contrast, other types of prosocial behaviors might be motivated by extrinsic concerns (e.g., social power, social approval, money) or by the avoidance of punishment. Thus, some of the personality traits that are related more broadly to prosocial behavior, but not to altruism per se, include distress sensitivity and the desire to avoid or reduce distress, impulsivity, and self-regulation (Batson, 1998; Cialdini, Brown, Lewis, Luce, & Neuberg, 1997; Staub, 1978).

BIOLOGICAL AND EVOLUTIONARY BASIS OF ALTRUISM

If altruism exists, then it would be reasonable to expect that it would have some biological and evolutionary foundation. Indeed, though evolutionary theorists are more likely to look at the consequences of behaviors instead of motives when identifying altruistic actions (Penner, Dovidio, et al., 2005), the study of altruism has deep roots in evolutionary theory (Sober & Wilson, 1998; Wilson, 1978). Ethologists have pointed out that altruism serves an adaptive function in the survival of the human species. Thus, although some acts of altruism might pose high risk to the survival of the organism, the survival of the genetic pool takes precedence over the organism's individual survival.

Three main theories have been proposed to account for high-risk altruistic behaviors: genetic similarity, kin selection, and reciprocal altruism. The *genetic similarity hypothesis* refers to altruistic acts that are likely to enhance the survival of organisms that are deemed physically similar to oneself because of common genetic information. *Kin selection* refers to the likelihood of enhancing the close genetic heritage of relatives for future generations. Finally, the *reciprocal altruism hypothesis* suggests that such acts might occur if organisms anticipate mutually beneficial behaviors (Penner, Brannick, Webb, & Connell, 2005; Sober & Wilson, 1998). In all cases, the key is the extent to which altruistic behaviors might increase the survival rate of the genetic pool rather than the survival of an individual organism (de Waal, 1996).

Much research has been devoted to systematically recording altruisticlike behaviors among several animal species. Although such behaviors have been observed in chimpanzees and among the great apes, evidence of altruism has also been observed in other species, such as elephants, dogs, and birds. Among those animal species, behaviors such as comforting and nurturance, grief and sorrow, cooperation, and self-sacrifice have been recorded (see de Waal, 1996, for examples). Indeed, even among lowerorder animals such as social insects (e.g., bees, wasps, ants), self-sacrificial behaviors are not uncommon (Wilson, 1978). Despite these observations, debate continues on whether those displays are relevant to explain "human altruistic actions," since altruisticlike actions in other animals and social insects can be explained through simple mechanisms (e.g., the pain and pleasure principle), rather than more sophisticated mechanisms that have been cited in human altruistic actions (e.g., internalized moral principles or even empathy and sympathy).

Research on humans yields additional evidence for the biological and evolutionary basis of altruism. A number of neurophysiological mechanisms have been linked to altruistic traits (e.g., empathy) and behaviors (e.g., cooperation, nurturance, sociability). For example, consistent with existing theory (Eisenberg & Fabes, 1992; Rothbart, Ahadi, & Hershey, 1994), the hypothalamic pituitary adrenal axis and frontal cortical region are associated with arousability and self-regulation, and these regions could be associated with prosocial responding. Moreover, central neuropeptides, such as oxytocin and vasopressin, have been linked to affiliative behaviors during mother-infant bonding and other positive social behaviors (Carter, 1998; Young, Lim, Gingrich, & Insel, 2001). Other research suggests that the ventromedial prefrontal cortex (VMPC) plays a role in producing social emotions, such as compassion and guilt. Recent research by Damasio and colleagues found that damage to the VMPC was associated with increased willingness to sacrifice one person for the sake of others (e.g., by pushing a person off of a bridge to stop a boxcar from hitting five other people), possibly indicating reductions in moral emotions that inhibit actions such as empathetic concern for the individual being sacrificed, or distress and guilt over being the agent responsible for the sacrifice (Koenigs et al., 2007).

The rapidly developing area of neurobiology has yielded provocative theories and research that hold much promise in advancing our understanding of altruism and morality (Narvaez, 2008). Recently, a number of investigators using brain-scanning techniques have suggested that specific brain regions are associated with moral emotions and moral decision making (Greene, Sommerville, Nystrom, Darley, & Cohen, 2001; Lamm, Batson, & Decety, 2007; Moll, Eslinger, & de Oliveira-Souza, 2001). Some such studies have identified *mirror neurons*, specialized neurons that fire both when a person performs an action (e.g., crying, laughing) and when a person watches someone else performing the same action. Mirror neurons then may play an important role in the experience of empathy (Quartz & Sejnowski, 2003).

There is also growing evidence for the biological and genetic basis of altruistic responding in humans. For example, behavioral genetic studies of twins have yielded evidence of a strong genetic heritability component in empathy (Emde et al., 1992; Matthews, Batson, Horn, & Rosenman, 1981; Zahn-Waxler, Robinson, & Emde, 1992). Furthermore, temperament is associated with empathy and prosocial behaviors (Eisenberg, 2005; Rothbart et al., 1994). Empathylike responding is present in infants, and prosocial behaviors are exhibited in children as young as 18 months of age (Hoffman, 1991; Preston & de Waal, 2002). And finally, there is accumulating evidence on the temporal stability of empathy and prosocial behaviors across the life span (Carlo, Crockett, Randall, & Roesch, 2007; Davis & Franzoi, 1991; Eisenberg et al., 1999; Romer, Gruder, & Lizzadro, 1986). Indeed, the magnitude of the stability coefficients across several age periods are relatively high and similar to those found in studies of aggression (see Carlo, 2006).

The recent advances in medical technology provide a promising glimpse into the future of research on the biological bases of altruism and related responses. Combined with comparative and translational research approaches, such techniques will no doubt lead to further discoveries in this area. For example, there is existing research with rodents showing the effects of early maternal care experiences (including nurturant behaviors) on distress sensitivity (Liu et al., 1997). Other animal models could provide useful information on impulsivity and self-regulation processes – mechanisms associated with prosocial responding (Eisenberg, 2005; Staub, 1978). Finally, information on the genetic basis of emotional sensitivity and nurturance in animals could provide valuable insights on the genetic-environment link.

PSYCHOLOGICAL RESEARCH ON ALTRUISM

While research on the evolutionary or biological bases of altruism suggests its likely existence, that research still needs to be linked to psychological research on altruism. In much of the early work on prosocial behaviors, scholars were mostly interested in understanding why many individuals do not help others in emergency situations, and much of the focus was on external situation factors, instead of on internal individual differences of the actors (Latané & Darley, 1970). Factors such as physical attractiveness of the victim, number of bystanders, and perceived similarity were significant predictors of prosocial behaviors (Aronson & Aronson, 2007). These studies yielded important evidence on the impact of the group, the social context, and the characteristics of the victim on prosocial behaviors. Although not the primary focus of these early studies, there were some individuals who were willing to help others, sometimes under risky circumstances. Nevertheless, these early scholars asserted that individual differences in helping were accounted for mostly by situational factors.

An obstacle challenging the relevance of the early work on prosocial behavior to the study of altruism is that it was difficult to ascertain whether the prosocial behaviors were motivated by selfless intentions. In an attempt to directly address this challenge, Batson (1998) posited that altruistic acts occur under specific circumstances. He also posited that empathy (i.e., a vicarious emotion that results in feeling the same as another), and sympathy (i.e., feelings of sorrow and concern for another), in particular, are the primary motives for altruistic behaviors, and he presented systematic evidence in support of this contention. In a series of studies, individuals are presented with an opportunity to assist a needy other under two different circumstances (Batson, 1991). In one condition, individuals could choose to volunteer to assist someone in an easy-to-escape scenario. In the other condition, individuals could choose to volunteer under a difficult-to-escape scenario. The key to ascertaining the underlying motive was whether individuals chose to help, even when they could avoid it under little threat to self (i.e., the easy-escape scenario). Across a series of different scenarios, these and other researchers have presented evidence that there are some individuals who choose to help in the easy-escape condition. Furthermore, those individuals score relatively high on measures of state empathy or empathic concern. In contrast, empathic concern did not predict helping in the difficult-escape condition. On the basis of their findings, Batson concluded that altruism exists under specific circumstances that trigger empathic reactions from individuals.

Despite the accumulating evidence in support of Batson's assertions, scholars such as Cialdini and his colleagues have questioned whether Batson induces empathic reactions in those studies (Cialdini et al., 1997). According to this group of scholars, sadness rather than empathic concern is induced. Thus, Cialdini proposed a "negative state relief (NSR) model," in which prosocial behaviors that appear altruistic actually result from attempts to improve mood and reduce sadness. Cialdini and his colleagues have conducted a series of studies aimed at showing that when sadness is induced, resulting prosocial actions help to improve mood.

Although it is beyond the scope of the present chapter to address each point and counterpoint in this ongoing debate, it is possible that both Batson and Cialdini are correct. Both sadness and empathy (or sympathy, feelings of sadness, sorrow, or concern for another) might be induced when individuals are exposed to someone in need. In fact, one might expect that sadness is an aspect of empathy and vice versa, suggesting an overlap between the constructs. Penner and his colleagues (Penner, Dovidio, et al., 2005, p. 368) reached a similar conclusion:

> Although most researchers agree that empathic arousal is fundamental to many kinds of helping (Davis 1994), there is much less agreement about the nature of this emotion and how it actually motivates people to help. *Empathic arousal* may produce different emotions. In severe emergency situations, bystanders may become upset and distressed (Piliavin et al. 1981); in less critical, less intense problem situations, observers may feel sad (Cialdini et al. 1987), tense (Hornstein 1982), or concerned and compassionate (Batson 1991). How arousal is interpreted can shape the nature of prosocial motivation. Feeling upset, personally distressed, guilty, or sad produces egoistically motivated helping with the goal of relieving one's own negative emotional state (Batson 1991, Cialdini et al. 1997, Piliavin et al. 1981). Feelings of empathic concern, such as sympathy and compassion, arouse altruistic motivation with the primary goal of improving the welfare of the person in need (Batson, 1991).

In a meta-analytic review of the literature, Carlson and Miller (1987) found overall supportive evidence for the empathy-altruism hypothesis, and little overall support for Cialdini's NSR model. It is also likely that there are prosocial behavioral situations where simultaneous, or conflicting, selfish and selfless motives exist (Batson, 1998; Carlo, Allen, & Buhman, 1999). Thus, even if sadness is induced when someone is in distress, the question remains whether empathy is a relatively strong independent predictor of prosocial behavior.

Although Batson's research suggests that altruism does exist, there is an interesting caveat to his conclusions. Given his emphasis on empathy as a predictor of prosocial behavior, one might expect individual differences in trait empathy to account for some of the individual differences in helping. (This line of thought would also apply to Cialdini's NSR model, as those who help under easy-to-escape conditions may be high on distress sensitivity.) However, in reviewing the existing literature on altruism, Batson noted that, although "it appears that the empathy-altruism hypotheses should tentatively be accepted as true" (p. 302), evidence to support the notion of an altruistic personality is not clear, and more research is needed (Batson, 1998). Thus, the notion of altruistic personality might be considered even more controversial than the notion of whether altruism exists. Nonetheless, there has been increasing attention to the correlates and development of traits associated with altruism. This body of research, which we turn to next, has broadened the scope of the work on altruism.

CONCEPTIONS OF THE ALTRUISTIC PERSONALITY

When one considers the various reasons why studying altruism is of interest to psychologists, one has to regard understanding individual differences in altruism as foremost on that list of reasons, raising the possibility of persons with an altruistic personality.

One integrative approach to examining the altruistic personality focuses on moral/care exemplars and moral identity. The research on moral and care exemplars implies that there are individuals whose sense of morality is central to their self-concept (Blasi, 2004). This follows from the notion that individuals develop a moral identity, and that moral identity impacts moral action. *Moral identity* refers to a broad set of characteristics that affects how individuals perceive themselves and others on moral issues. It involves both cognitive and affective processes, and it is presumed to guide and motivate moral action (Hardy & Carlo, 2005).

Although many of the examples discussed by scholars have been historically documented, most altruistic actions occur in relative obscurity. For example, in the United States alone, thousands of individuals generously volunteer time assisting others through food banks, homeless shelters, and other community organizations. Other instances of altruistic behaviors include when parents take risks to save a child, when firefighters risk their lives to save the life of another, or when soldiers throw themselves on a live grenade to save their comrades. It is important to note that altruistic acts might result partially from formal obligations or duties. However, the central question remains whether their primary motive is based on those formal obligations (extrinsic) or whether it is based on personal obligations (intrinsic). For example, firefighters might have an obligation to assist others as part of their job duties, or they might have pursued such jobs for monetary reasons. However, for some firefighters, their intrinsic desire to help others might have led to their pursuit of that specific career. The fact that they get paid to work their jobs does not necessarily tell us what their primary intent or motive is. Furthermore, for some of those workers, they could have chosen other, perhaps less risky, careers.

The research on moral exemplars and moral identity has been growing in recent years. In one of the early studies on moral exemplars, Oliner and Oliner (1988) interviewed hundreds of persons who rescued Jews during the Holocaust in World War II. These scholars found several common traits among the rescuers (versus nonrescuers) including a strong sense of social responsibility, internalized moral values of caring for others, and compassion for others less fortunate than themselves. Colby and Damon (1992) systematically interviewed 23 Americans nominated for their moral exemplarity, to identify their characteristics. These are individuals who were committed to prosocial actions, often over long periods of time, showing evidence of temporally stable altruistic personality traits. Other studies of moral exemplars have focused on relatively more obscure instances of altruism. For example, Hart and Fegley (1995) showed that care exemplars could be identified in a low SES, inner-city community. They asked African American and Latino adolescents to nominate peers who exhibit unusual committed acts of caring and kindness to others and in their community. Among several differences, the nominated peers (care exemplars) were more likely than a comparison group of adolescents to describe themselves in terms of a cluster of moral personality traits and goals, and they had more articulated beliefs and concepts about themselves. Such findings indicate that, even under adverse circumstances, individuals are capable of linking self-concepts to committed acts of caring (see also Matsuba & Walker, 2004, 2005).

The study of moral identity using information processing approaches provides evidence for the central role of traits in morality. Following a naïve psychological model, Walker and Pitts (1998) showed that lay individuals have multidimensional conceptions of the traits of everyday moral persons that include caring, justice, and spirituality. The investigators noted that, by asking individuals to list the traits of persons with strong character, trait conceptions of morality are broader and more complex than previously believed. Lapsley and Lasky (2001) introduced an information-processing approach to studying moral identity. Investigators proposed, and found evidence, that individuals with strong moral identity had information-processing biases that would elicit faster cognitive reaction times and better memory recall when exposed to moral terms (see also Narvaez, Lapsley, & Hagele, 2006). The findings suggest that individuals with strong moral identity exhibit moral expertise, probably resulting from frequent morally relevant experiences and rehearsal over time (see also Narvaez, 2005). Their findings suggest that individuals with an altruistic personality might have developed relatively automatic cognitive biases and processes that facilitate altruistic responding.

A second approach to the study of the altruistic personality is offered by social and personality psychologists. In one of the earliest studies of the altruistic personality, Staub (1974) asked individuals to complete a number of conceptually related personality measures. Then, the participants were presented with an opportunity to help three to six weeks later. Staub found that many of the prosocial personality traits appeared to interact with the situation to predict certain helping behaviors. For example, when participants were given permission to interrupt their task (e.g., to get a cup of coffee from an adjoining room), but not under conditions where they were given no instructions or told not to interrupt their task, participants who scored high (at least Stage 5) on Kohlberg's measure of moral reasoning offered more help to someone experiencing severe stomach distress than those who scored lower.

Beyond moral reasoning and the study of dispositional empathy and sympathy previously described (Batson, 1998), personality researchers have investigated other trait variables that have been linked to altruism, including sympathy, perspective taking, and social responsibility (Archer, Diaz-Loving, Gollwitzer, Davis, & Founshe, 1981; Batson, Bolen, Cross, & Neuringer-Benefiel, 1986; Berkowitz & Lutterman, 1968; Bierhoff, Klein, & Kramp, 1991; Carlo, Eisenberg, Troyer, Switzer, & Speer, 1991; Davis & Franzoi, 1991; Eisenberg et al., 1989; Penner, Fritzche, Craiger, & Freifeld, 1995; Schwartz & Howard, 1984; Staub, 1978). In one study (Carlo et al., 1991), college students were administered a number of personality measures deemed relevant to prosocial behavior, and subsequent factor analyses revealed two major factors: a prosocial factor comprised of empathic concern, perspective taking, social responsibility, and ascription of responsibility; and a distress factor comprised of personal distress and affective intensity. Carlo et al. (1991) reported that participants who scored high on the prosocial personality factor were more likely to help others when escape from a request to help was easy, particularly when the cues of distress were strong. In contrast, the arousability (distress) personality factor was related positively to helping, but only in the difficult escape, low emotional evocativeness situation.

In addition to the personality variables noted above, scholars have noted that the agreeableness dimension of the Big Five personality model – which includes warmth, sympathy, helping, and trust (Costa & McCrae, 1992; Graziano, 1994) – is conceptually related to an altruistic personality. Indeed, there is evidence that volunteers tend to exhibit high levels of agreeableness (Carlo, Okun, Knight, & de Guzman, 2005; see Batson, 1998). In contrast, by definition, trait neuroticism, affective intensity, and personal distress reflect highly arousing, egoistically motivated emotional tendencies (Costa & McCrae, 1992; Davis & Franzoi, 1991), and there is evidence that these traits are associated with no helping or helping only in difficult-to-escape situations (Batson, 1991; Carlo et al., 1991; Carlo et al., 1999).

A STUDY OF VOLUNTEERING OTHERS TO HELP

While theorists and researchers have examined volunteering one's self as an indicator of altruism, volunteering others has not been examined similarly. Individuals in leadership positions are often asked to decide whether to send individuals into potentially dangerous situations to assist others who are in need. For example, politicians and military leaders often have to decide whether to send troops into areas of turmoil to save the lives of others. Police and firefighter chiefs are often faced with similar circumstances. It is important to note that, even though such persons might be placed or choose to place themselves in such positions (even for pay), they can still choose whether to oblige or place themselves or others in positions of high risk.

We presumed that prosocial dispositions, such as sympathy, social responsibility, agreeableness, and perspective taking, would be important and relevant considerations in making such decisions, along with other factors such as salience, proximity, risk, and extent of need, humanization, similarity, and ingroup/outgroup factors, which have previously been found to affect helping decisions and behavior (Bandura, 2004; Latané & Darley, 1970; Penner, Dovidio et al., 2005). Based upon prior research on volunteering one's self (Penner & Finkelstein, 1998; Penner et al., 1995; Staub, 1978), it was expected that individuals with high levels of perspective taking, sympathy, social responsibility, and agreeableness would be more likely to volunteer *themselves* even under risky circumstances. However, in scenarios where one is the leader in charge of sending others into risky situations, there are often two sets of "others" that one can be concerned for: those volunteers who will be sent to help, and those who might be helped. On one hand, those who might benefit from help might have more serious and thus salient needs than the helping volunteers. On the other hand, the leaders might live and work more proximally to the volunteer helpers than to those needing help, making concerns for the safety of the volunteers more salient and powerful. In addition, to the extent that the volunteers are more likely to be similar to the leader, part of his/her ingroup, and have personal relationships with the leader, the leader may be more concerned about the safety of the volunteers relative to the others in need of help.

Prior to deciding to risk the lives of other volunteers, a leader probably will be gathering information and be especially attentive to the needs of those whose lives he/she might be risking for the cause, and whether or not the cause merits the risks. In such situations, prosocial traits would be associated with *reducing* other potential helpers' risks. For example, the sense of social responsibility that stimulates self-volunteering in a risky situation should dissuade one from placing other potential helpers at risk in that situation. Similarly, sympathy might induce concern for others who could be put into risky circumstances. Furthermore, when volunteering others in risky circumstances, traits that reflect self-focused motives to avoid helping might become central and related to being *more* willing to risk *others* lives. For example, high levels of personal distress and neuroticism could lead individuals to avoid risky circumstances for themselves. However, these individuals might be willing to volunteer others (particularly outgroup members). Thus, while those personality variables usually inhibit placing one's self in danger by volunteering, they could contribute to committing others to help.

In the present study, participants (77 male and 62 female undergraduates from a Midwestern state university) received a battery of questionnaires, including a demographic information sheet, measures of personality, and one of three measures of intention to volunteer. Measures of personality were selected to replicate and extend prior research (Batson et al., 1986;

Carlo et al., 1991; Eisenberg et al., 1989; Staub, 1978), and included the full agreeableness and neuroticism scales from a five-factor adjective checklist measure of personality (Trapnell & Wiggins, 1990); three of four of the empathy subscales from the Thoughts and Feelings Questionnaire (Davis, 1983); a measure of social responsibility (Berkowitz & Lutterman, 1968); and a shortened version of a social desirability scale (Crowne & Marlowe, 1964).

Intent to volunteer was assessed by participants' willingness to volunteer in six social-cause scenarios involving high risk. The disease scenario involved the need to prevent the spread of a devastating disease (reminiscent of the then-recently publicized Ebola virus) by removing and burning infected dead bodies, despite the risk that those undertaking this task could become infected themselves. Other scenarios included the need to stop illegal logging in a rainforest, the need for a watchdog group to fight residential gang and drug problems, the need to stop globally hazardous oil fires after the Gulf War, the need for healthy human subjects in drug testing, and the need for volunteers to go on a risky reconnaissance mission in Sarajevo.

There were three helping conditions for each scenario: (1) self-volunteerism – a willingness to voluntarily expose oneself to dangers and risks for the social cause; (2) ingroup-volunteerism – a willingness to risk the lives of one's ingroup for the social cause; and (3) outgroup-volunteerism – a willingness to risk the lives of persons in one's outgroup. In each scenario, the questions focused on weighing risks to the volunteer helper(s) in decisions about whether or not to offer help. For example, in the rainforest scenario reflecting the self-volunteerism condition, the reader was asked to take the role of a Green Peace volunteer and was asked to indicate whether he or she personally "would not help with this cause under any conditions," or if he or she would help if the chances that he or she would be harmed were of a certain proportion (e.g., 0 in 1000, 1 in 1000, 1 in 100, 1 in 25, 1 in 10, 1 in 5). In contrast, in the ingroup-volunteerism condition, participants were asked to take the role of a president of a chapter of Green Peace, and to make a decision to send or not to send other chapter members to assist with the rainforest cause ("I would send the volunteers if I believed that only [a number between 0 to 100 of them would get sick or attacked," OR, "I would not send any volunteers.") The outgroup-volunteerism condition was similar to those used for the ingroup-volunteerism condition, except that participants were asked to take the role of a Green Peace volunteer stationed in Brazil who was responsible for deciding whether to send Brazilian volunteers into the forest. To avoid participant suspicions regarding our hypotheses, each participant was presented two scenarios that reflected the self-volunteering, ingroup volunteering, and outgroup volunteering condition (a total of six scenarios, one for each social cause).

A Varimax-rotated, principal components factor analysis of the personality measures resulted in the extraction of two factors with eigenvalues greater than one, with the first factor reflecting a prosocial trait consisting of sympathy, perspective taking, agreeableness, and social responsibility (loadings were .86, .72, .85, and .56, respectively), and the second factor reflecting a distress trait consisting of personal distress and neuroticism (loadings were .87 and .86, respectively). The factor scores were used in subsequent analyses. The interrelations among measures of intent to volunteer under the three conditions ranged from .19 to .61. Preliminary analyses indicated no significant main effects of social desirability, and only one significant interaction. Thus, social desirability was not included in subsequent analyses. Only significant effects are summarized.

As can be seen in Table 12.1, for volunteering self, individuals who scored relatively high on the trait prosocial composite were more likely to volunteer themselves than those who scored relatively low. Furthermore, males were more likely to volunteer themselves than females. In the second step, there was a significant two-way interaction. Graphic plots showed that persons with low levels of prosocial dispositions and high levels of distress/neuroticism were least likely to volunteer themselves. For volunteering ingroup members, in the second step, there were significant two-way interactions. In the third step, there was a significant Gender × Trait Prosocial × Trait Distress interaction effect. Subsequent analyses showed that men, but not women, who reported high levels of prosocial dispositions and high levels of distress were most likely to volunteer ingroup members.

For volunteering outgroup members, in the second step, there were significant two-way interactions. Furthermore, in the third step, there was a significant Gender × Trait Prosocial × Trait Distress interaction effect. Among men low in prosocial traits, being high in distress related to a lesser likelihood of volunteering others (in this case outgroup others) for the cause; among men high in prosocial traits, distress related to greater likelihood of volunteering others for the cause. Among women, higher distress more generally related to less volunteering of others.

As expected, individuals who reported high levels of prosocial traits were more likely to volunteer themselves. However, this was true especially when trait distress was high rather than low, suggesting that distress might provide an energizing function. These findings are consistent with prior theory and research that suggests that personal distress/neuroticism

TABLE 12.1. *Hierarchical multiple regression analysis results (r^2 and unstandardized betas) predicting volunteerism in each condition*

Variable entered	Self	Ingroup	Outgroup
Step 1:			
F change:	F chg (3,126) = 5.76, R^2 = .12**	F chg (3,126) = .67, R^2 = .02	F chg (3,126) = 1.84, R^2 = .04
Gender (M = −1, F = 1)	−.31**	−.07	−.17
Prosocial	.21*	.04	.00
Distress	−.08	−.08	−.06
Step 2:			
F change:	F chg (3,123) = 2.07, R^2 = .04	F chg (3,123) = 6.88, R^2 = .14***	F chg (3,123) = 4.78, R^2 = .10**
Gender (M = −1, F = 1)	−.29**	−.04	−.14
Prosocial	.24**	.08	.03
Distress	−.10	−.11	−.09
Gender × Prosocial	−.12	−.23*	−.28**
Gender × Distress	−.16	−.35***	−.23*
Prosocial × Distress	.24*	.39***	.32**
Step 3:			
F change:	F chg (1,122) = .01, R^2 = .01	F chg (1,122) = 14.30, R^2 = .09***	F chg (1,122) = 4.05, R^2 = .03*
Gender (M = −1, F = 1)	−.29**	−.15	−.21*
Prosocial	.24*	.21*	.11
Distress	−.10	.07	.01
Gender × Prosocial	−.12	−.25**	−.29**
Gender × Distress	−.16	−.31**	−.20*
Prosocial × Distress	.24*	.36***	.30**
Gender × Prosocial × Distress	.01	−.36***	−.20*

*p < .05, **p < .01, ***p < .001

(the components of the distress factor) has arousal properties that might enhance action (Carlo et al., 1999; Hoffman, 1982; Tomkins, 1970). In most prior research on prosocial behaviors, individuals were faced with less physically dangerous situations. In those circumstances, low-to-moderate levels of arousal (stemming from sympathy reactions) combined with prosocial dispositions might be sufficient for prosocial behaviors. Because level of arousal is linked to personal distress and sympathy responding, and these responses are linked to different behavioral responses (Batson, 1998; Hoffman, 1982), it might be necessary to account for emotional arousability in volunteering situations.

The pattern of relations regarding volunteering ingroup others and outgroup others was more complex. The hypotheses that higher scores on the distress factor would relate to reduced self-volunteerism, while higher scores on the prosocial trait factor would relate to reduced volunteering of others, were primarily supported in the data from women, and not from men. Furthermore, the hypothesis that higher scores on the distress factor would predict greater willingness to volunteer outgroup members was only supported by men who scored high on the prosocial factor. High levels of both prosocial dispositions and distress were associated with higher levels of sending others to help in risky situations for men; while women scoring high on both the prosocial and distress factors showed the least willingness to volunteer others. It might be that volunteering others in risky situations is perceived by men as a form of instrumental helping that is consistent with the masculine gender stereotype (cf. Eagly & Crowley, 1986), and with how men and women are socialized (Huston, 1983). Although more research is needed to examine these gender-related patterns, the data show the relevance of altruistic personality traits on volunteering others.

CONCLUSIONS

Debate and controversy surrounding the existence of altruism and the notion of an altruistic personality will no doubt continue in the foreseeable future. The challenge of accurately inferring the underlying intention of prosocial behaviors is great. Nonetheless, we have observed similar challenges in other areas of study, such as aggression. Thus far, the empirical evidence for selfless traits and motives is as impressive as the evidence for selfish traits and motives. Clearly, research on both selfish and selfless traits, motives, and behaviors have furthered our understanding of human nature and functioning. However, the beneficial consequences of altruism are far-reaching and significant in the betterment of our society. For this reason alone, there is tremendous need for continued research on altruism.

What can we conclude from the evidence to date on the existence of an altruistic personality? The combination of social/personality approaches and moral identity/exemplar approaches yield an impressive set of findings using different methodologies in the study of altruism. As Dovidio and his colleagues (2006) surmised, "there is a convergence of findings across a fair number of different studies that lead us to conclude that: (a) there is such a thing as a 'prosocial personality,' and (b) differences in this personality attribute are associated with differences in prosocial actions that range from willingness to help a distressed individual, to heroic rescues of people whose lives were in danger, to willingness to serve as a volunteer" (p. 265). Based on the existing research across social and developmental psychology (as well as research in other disciplines, including economics, political science, sociology, anthropology, and ethology), we would concur with their conclusions regarding the accumulating evidence for the existence of an altruistic personality.

Of course, despite these promising methods and evidence, a number of gaps in the study of altruism remain. First, future studies are needed using longitudinal designs to examine expression of, and changes in, altruistic traits and behaviors across time. While prior personality studies have focused on the examination of altruistic or prosocial traits as defined by survey instruments and the effects of mean levels of altruistic traits on behaviors across situations, recent methods for investigating personality increasingly include the use of repeated measures gathered *in situ*. Short-term repeated measures studies, such as experience-sampling studies (Bolger, Davis, & Rafaeli, 2003; Csikszentmihalyi & Larson, 1992), or studies that examine profiles of behaviors in multiple types of situations (Mischel, 2004), could be used to better understand the combined effect of situations and personality factors predicting altruistic behaviors. Such studies, as they have been applied to other personality traits as well, could also be used to clarify the nature of altruistic personality. For example, little is known about the extent and stability of intraindividual variability in altruistic motivations and behaviors, as the study of stable patterns of variability in "states" paralleling personality traits is still in its infancy (Fleeson & Leicht, 2006).

Second, and related to the last aforementioned point, studies in early childhood and adolescence are needed to discover the origins and development of altruism. There are studies of moral conscience in early childhood and adolescence that could be linked to the existing social and personality studies conducted in late adolescence and young adulthood. In these studies, researchers have presented evidence for a moral personality cluster in the toddler years (Kochanska et al., 1996). Furthermore, these developmental scholars have linked early moral conscience to temperament and to parenting processes, and there is evidence of moral personality clusters in adolescence (Laible, Eye, & Carlo, in press). Developmental studies of moral and care exemplars would also be useful to determine the origins and predictors of such individuals (Hardy & Carlo, 2005). Eventually, such studies will need to be linked to other socialization agents, such as peers and media (see Carlo, 2006).

Third, more studies on the biological bases of altruism are needed. Studies utilizing animal models and advanced medical technologies may provide powerful tools for new discoveries. Such models will need to be integrated with socialization models to provide integrative frameworks on the dynamic interplay of biology and environment. And fourth, research beyond the influence of proximal socializing agents of altruism is needed. That is, studies that examine the cross-cultural and broader social contextual factors associated with altruism are needed, especially given the prior evidence on the importance of prosocial behaviors and cooperative behaviors in other (e.g., collectivist-oriented) societies. Thus far, the bulk of the research has been conducted in European American samples from North America.

One cannot underestimate the important implications of understanding altruism for improving our society. As we emerge into a more globalized society and face the common challenges of the twenty-first century across societies, the study of altruism may assist in addressing the many global challenges and issues that will undoubtedly arise. As it is important to understand the negative aspects of human functioning (e.g., aggression, violence) in order to raise awareness and to develop more effective solutions, it will be equally important to understand the positive aspects of human functioning. A focus on the positive aspects of human functioning will facilitate the development of more balanced, comprehensive solutions designed to enhance the personal and environmental factors that promote and foster a more caring, beneficent, and thriving society.

REFERENCES

Archer, R. L., Diaz-Loving, R., Gollwitzer, P. M., Davis, M. H., & Founshe, H. C. (1981). The role of dispositional empathy and social evaluation in the empathic mediation of helping. *Journal of Personality and Social Psychology, 40,* 786–796.

Aronson, E., & Aronson, J. (2007). *The social animal.* New York: Worth/Freeman.

Aronson, E., Wilson, T. D., & Akert, R. M. (2004). *Social Psychology*. Upper Saddle River, NJ: Pearson Prentice Hall.

Bandura, A. (2004). Selective exercise of moral agency. In T. A. Thorkildsen & H. J. Walberg (Eds.), *Nurturing morality* (pp. 37–57). Boston: Kluwer Academic.

Batson, C. D. (1991). *The altruism question: Toward a social-psychological answer*. Hillsdale, NJ: Lawrence Erlbaum Press.

—— (1998). Altruism and prosocial behavior. In D. T. Gilbert, S. T. Fiske, & G. Lindzey (Eds.), *The handbook of social psychology*. Boston, MA: McGraw-Hill.

Batson, C. D., Bolen, M. H., Cross, J. A., & Neuringer-Benefiel, H. E. (1986). Where is the altruism in the altruistic personality? *Journal of Personality and Social Psychology, 50*, 212–220.

Berkowitz, L., & Lutterman, K. G. (1968). The traditional socially responsible personality. *Public Opinion Quarterly, 32*, 169–185.

Bierhoff, H.-W., Klein, R., & Kramp, P. (1991). Evidence for the altruistic personality from data on accident research. *Journal of Personality, 59*, 263–280.

Blasi, A. (2004). Moral functioning: Moral understanding and personality. In D. K. Lapsley & D. Narvaez (Eds.), *Moral development, self, and identity* (pp. 335–347). Mahwah, NJ: Lawrence Erlbaum Associates.

Bolger, N., Davis, A., & Rafaeli, E. (2003). Diary methods: Capturing life as it is lived. *Annual Review of Psychology, 54*, 579–616.

Carlo, G. (2006). Care-based and altruistically-based morality. In M. Killen & J. G. Smetana (Eds.), *Handbook of moral development* (pp. 551–579). Mahwah, NJ: Lawrence Erlbaum.

Carlo, G., Allen, J. B., & Buhman, D. C. (1999). Facilitating and disinhibiting prosocial behaviors: The nonlinear interaction of trait perspective taking and trait personal distress on volunteering. *Basic and Applied Social Psychology, 21*, 189–197.

Carlo, G., Crockett, L. J., Randall, B. A., & Roesch, S. C. (2007). Parent and peer correlates of prosocial development in rural adolescents: A longitudinal study. *Journal of Research on Adolescence, 17*, 301–324.

Carlo, G., Eisenberg, N., Troyer, D., Switzer, G., & Speer, A. L. (1991). The altruistic personality: In what contexts is it apparent? *Journal of Personality and Social Psychology, 61*, 450–458.

Carlo, G., Okun, M., Knight, G. P., & de Guzman, M. R. T. (2005). Prosocial value motivation as a mediator and moderator of the relations between agreeableness, extraversion and volunteering. *Personality and Individual Differences, 38*, 1293–1305.

Carlo, G., & Randall, B. (2001). Are all prosocial behaviors equal? A socioecological developmental conception of prosocial behavior. In F. Columbus (Ed.), *Advances in psychology research* (Vol. II, pp. 151–170). Huntington, NY: Nova Science Publishers.

Carlson, M., & Miller, N. (1987). Explanation of the relation between negative mood and helping. *Psychological Bulletin, 102*, 91–108.

Carter, C. (1998). Neuroendocrine perspectives on social attachment and love. *Psychoneuroendocrinology, 23*, 779–818.

Cialdini, R. B., Brown, S. L., Lewis, B. P., Luce, C., & Neuberg, S. L. (1997). Reinterpreting the empathy-altruism relationship: When one into one equals oneness. *Journal of Personality and Social Psychology, 73*, 481–494.

Costa, P. T., Jr., & McCrae, R. R. (1992). *Revised NEO personality inventory (NEO-PI-R) and NEO five-factor inventory (NEO-FFI) professional manual.* Odessa, FL: Psychological Assessment Resources.

Crowne, D. P., & Marlowe, D. (1964). *The appraisal motive.* New York: Wiley.

Csikszentmihalyi, M., & Larson, R. (1992). Validity and reliability of the experience sampling method. In M. W. de Vries (Ed.), *The experience of psychopathology: Investigating mental disorders in their natural settings* (pp. 43–57). New York: Cambridge University Press.

Davis, M. H. (1983). Measuring individual differences in empathy: Evidence for a multidimensional approach. *Journal of Personality and Social Psychology, 44,* 113–126.

Davis, M. H., & Franzoi, S. (1991). Stability and change in adolescent self-consciousness and empathy. *Journal of Research in Personality, 25,* 70–87.

de Waal, F. (1996). *Good natured: The origins of right and wrong in humans and other animals.* Cambridge, MA: Harvard University Press.

Dovidio, J. F., Piliavin, J. A., Schroeder, D. A., & Penner, L. A. (2006). *The social psychology of prosocial behavior.* Mahwah, NJ: Lawrence Erlbaum Associates.

Eagly, A. H., & Crowley, M. (1986). Gender and helping behavior: A meta-analytic review of the social psychological literature. *Psychological Bulletin, 100,* 283–308.

Eisenberg, N. (2005). The development of empathy-related responding. In G. Carlo & C. P. Edwards (Eds.), *Moral motivation through the life span* (Vol. 51, pp. 73–117). Lincoln, NE: University of Nebraska Press.

Eisenberg, N., & Fabes, R. A. (1992). *Emotion and its regulation in early development.* San Francisco, CA: Jossey-Bass.

(1998). Prosocial development. In N. Eisenberg (Ed.), *Handbook of child psychology: Social, emotional, and personality development* (5th ed., Vol. 3, pp. 701–778). New York: Wiley.

Eisenberg, N., Guthrie, I. K., Murphy, B. C., Shepard, S. A., Cumberland, A., & Carlo, G. (1999). Consistency and development of prosocial dispositions: A longitudinal study. *Child Development, 70,* 1360–1372.

Eisenberg, N., Miller, G. E., Schaller, M., Fabes, R. A., Fultz, J., Shell, R. et al. (1989). The role of sympathy and altruistic personality traits in helping: A reexamination. *Journal of Personality, 57,* 41–67.

Emde, R. N., Plomin, R., Robinson, J., Corley, R., DeFries, J., Fulker, D. W. et al. (1992). Temperament, emotion, and cognition at fourteen months: The MacArthur Longitudinal Twin Study. *Child Development, 63,* 1437–1455.

Fleeson, W., & Leicht, C. (2006). On delineating and integrating the study of variability in personality psychology: Interpersonal trust as an illustration. *Journal of Research in Personality, 40,* 5–20.

Graziano, W. G. (1994). The development of agreeableness as a dimension of personality. In C. P. Halverson, Jr., G. A. Kohnstamm, & R. P. Martin (Eds.), *The developing structure of temperament and personality from infancy to adulthood* (pp. 339–354). Hillsdale, NJ: Lawrence Erlbaum Associates.

Greene, J. D., Sommerville, R. B., Nystrom, L. E., Darley, J. M., & Cohen, J. D. (2001). An fMRI investigation of emotional engagement in moral judgement. *Science, 293,* 2105–2108.

Hardy, S. A., & Carlo, G. (2005). Identity as a source of moral motivation. *Human Development*, 48, 232–256.

Hart, D., & Fegley, S. (1995). Altruism and caring in adolescence: Relations to self-understanding and social judgment. *Child Development*, 66, 1346–1359.

Hawley, P. H., Little, T. D., & Pasupathi, M. (2002). Winning friends and influencing peers: Strategies of peer influence in late childhood. *International Journal of Behavioral Development*, 26, 466–474.

Hoffman, M. L. (1982). Development of prosocial motivation: Empathy and guilt. In N. Eisenberg-Berg (Ed.), *Development of prosocial behavior* (pp. 281–313). New York: Academic Press.

  (1991). Empathy, social cognition, and moral action. In W. M. Kurtines & J. L. Gewirtz (Eds.), *Handbook of moral behavior and development: Theory* (Vol. 1, pp. 275–301). Hillsdale, NJ: Lawrence Erlbaum Associates.

Huston, A. C. (1983). Sex-typing. In P. H. Mussen (Ed.), *Handbook of child psychology: Socialization, personality, and social development* (Vol. 4, pp. 387–467). New York: Wiley.

Knight, G. P., Johnson, L. G., Carlo, G., & Eisenberg, N. (1994). A multiplicative model of the dispositional antecedents of a prosocial behavior: Predicting more of the people more of the time. *Journal of Personality and Social Psychology*, 66, 178–183.

Kochanska, G., Padavich, D. L., & Koenig, A. L. (1996). Children's narratives about hypothetical moral dilemmas and objective measures of their conscience: Mutual relations and socialization antecedents. *Child Development*, 67, 1420–1436.

Koenigs, M., Young, L., Adolphs, R., Tranel, D., Cushman, F., Haurser, M., et al. (2007). Damage to the prefrontal cortex increases utilitarian moral judgements. *Nature*, 446, 908–911.

Laible, D., Eye, J., & Carlo, G. (in press). Dimensions of conscience in mid-adolescence: Links with social behavior, parenting, and temperament. *Journal of Youth and Adolescence* 37, 875–887.

Lamm, C., Batson, C. D., & Decety, J. (2007). The neural substrate of human empathy: Effects of perspective-taking and cognitive appraisal. *Journal of Cognitive Neuroscience*, 19, 42–58.

Lapsley, D. K., & Lasky, B. (2001). Prototypic moral character. *Identity: An International Journal of Theory and Research*, 1, 345–363.

Latané, B., & Darley, J. M. (1970). *The unresponsive bystander: Why doesn't he help?* New York: Appleton-Century-Crofts.

Liu, D., Diorio, J., Tannanbaum, B., Caldji, C., Francis, D., Freedman, A. et al. (1997). Maternal care, hippocampal, glucocorticoid receptors, and hypothalamic-pituitary-adrenal responses to stress. *Science*, 277, 1659–1662.

Macaulay, J. R., & Berkowitz, L. (Eds.). (1970). *Altruism and helping behavior*. New York: Academic Press.

Matsuba, M. K., & Walker, L. J. (2004). Extraordinary moral commitment: Young adults involved in social organizations. *Journal of Personality*, 72, 413–436.

  (2005). Exemplars: The making of self through stories. *Journal of Research on Adolescence*, 15, 275–297.

Matthews, K. A., Batson, C. D., Horn, J., & Rosenman, R. H. (1981). "Principles in his nature which interest him in the fortune of others ...": The heritability of empathic concern for others. *Journal of Personality, 49*, 237–247.

Mischel, W. (2004). Toward an integrative science of the person. *Annual Review of Psychology, 55*, 1–22.

Moll, J., Eslinger, P. J., & de Oliveira-Souza, R. (2001). Frontpolar and anterior temporal cortex activation in a moral judgment task. *Arq Neuropisquiatr, 59*, 657–664.

Narvaez, D. (2005). The neo-Kohlbergian tradition and beyond: Schemas, expertise, and character. In G. Carlo (Ed.), *Moral motivation through the life span* (Vol. 51, pp. 119–163). Lincoln, NE: University of Nebraska Press.

(2008). Triune ethics: The neurobiological roots of our multiple moralities. *New Ideas in Psychology, 26*, 95–119.

Narvaez, D., Lapsley, D. K., & Hagele, S. (2006). Moral chronicity and social information processing: Tests of a social cognitive approach to the moral personality. *Journal of Resarch in Personality, 40*, 966–985.

Oliner, S. P., & Oliner, P. M. (1988). *The altruistic personality: Rescuers of Jews in Nazi Europe.* New York: The Free Press.

Penner, L. A., Brannick, M. T., Webb, S., & Connell, P. (2005). Effects on volunteering of the September 11, 2001, attacks: An archival analysis. *Journal of Applied Social Psychology, 35*, 1333–1360.

Penner, L. A., Dovidio, J. F., Piliavin, J. A., & Schroeder, D. A. (2005). Prosocial behavior: Multilevel perspectives. *Annual Review of Psychology, 56*, 365–392.

Penner, L. A., & Finkelstein, M. A. (1998). Dispositional and structural determinants of volunteerism. *Journal of Personality and Social Psychology, 74*, 525–537.

Penner, L. A., Fritzche, B. A., Craiger, J. P., & Freifeld, T. S. (1995). Measuring the prosocial personality. In J. Butcher & C. D. Spielberger (Eds.), *Advances in personality assessment* (Vol. 10, pp. 147–163). Hillsdale, NJ: Lawrence Erlbaum Associates.

Preston, S. D., & de Waal, F. B. M. (2002). Empathy: Its ultimate and proximate bases. *Behavioral and Brain Sciences, 25*, 1–20.

Quartz, S. R., & Sejnowski, T. J. (2003). *Liars, lovers, and heroes: What the new brain science reveals about how we become who we are.* New York: Quill.

Romer, D., Gruder, C. L., & Lizzadro, T. (1986). A person-situation approach to altruistic behavior. *Journal of Personality and Social Psychology, 51*, 1001–1012.

Rothbart, M., Ahadi, S., & Hershey, K. (1994). Temperament and social behavior in childhood. *Merrill-Palmer Quarterly, 40*, 21–39.

Schwartz, S. H., & Howard, J. A. (1984). Internalized value as motivators of altruism. In E. Staub, D. Bar-Tal, J. Karylowski, & J. Reykowski (Eds.), *The development and maintenance of prosocial behavior: International perspectives on positive development* (pp. 229–255). New York: Plenum Press.

Sober, E., & Wilson, D. S. (1998). *Unto others.* Cambridge, MA: Harvard University Press.

Staub, E. (1974). Helping a distressed person: Social personality, and stimulus determinants. In L. Berkowitz (Ed.), *Advances in experimental social psychology* (Vol. 7, pp. 293–341). New York: Academic Press.

(1978). *Positive social behavior and morality: Social and personal influences* (Vol. 1). New York: Academic Press.

(2005). The roots of goodness: The fulfillment of basic human needs and the development of caring, helping and nonagression, inclusive caring, moral courage, active bystandership, and altruism born of suffering. In G. Carlo & C. P. Edwards (Eds.), *Moral motivation through the lifespan* (Vol. 51, pp. 33–72). Lincoln, NE: University of Nebraska Press.

Tomkins, S. S. (1970). Affect as the primary motivation system. In M. B. Arnold (Ed.), *Feelings and emotions: The Loyola Symposium*. New York: Academic Press.

Trapnell, P. D., & Wiggins, J. S. (1990). Extension of the interpersonal adjective scales to include the Big Five dimensions of personality. *Journal of Personality and Social Psychology, 59*, 781–790.

Walker, L. J., & Pitts, R. C. (1998). Naturalistic conceptions of moral maturity. *Developmental Psychology, 34*, 403–419.

Wilson, E. O. (1978). *On human nature*. Cambridge, MA: Harvard University Press.

Young, L., Lim, M., Gingrich, B., & Insel, T. (2001). Cellular mechanisms of social attachment. *Hormones and Behavior, 40*, 133–138.

Zahn-Waxler, C., Robinson, J., & Emde, R. N. (1992). The development of empathy in twins. *Developmental Psychology, 28*, 1038–1047.

13

Growing Toward Care: A Narrative Approach to Prosocial Moral Identity and Generativity of Personality in Emerging Adulthood

MICHAEL W. PRATT, MARY LOUISE ARNOLD, AND HEATHER LAWFORD

In this chapter, we describe a program of research on the relation between moral identity and generativity development in late adolescence and emerging adulthood. Both constructs share a central concern, with the well-being of others as a core focus, leading us to expect that they will show considerable overlap in development. In examining moral identity, we draw on the framework of McAdams (2006a) specifically regarding the development of narrative identity.

We concentrate here on two complementary questions – first, how do the patterns in personal moral narratives relate to standard measures of moral values, moral behavior, and moral identity in emerging adulthood; and second, how do narratives of moral commitment assessed in late adolescence predict to generativity of personality? We begin by describing the construct of generativity in the personality literature, and then discuss the idea of moral identity and its development, focusing on a narrative approach. Following this, we examine the rationale for studying the interrelations between these two constructs of moral identity and generativity, summarize the results of two recent studies from our research, and finally consider the potential for a narrative approach to moral identity development.

GENERATIVITY OF PERSONALITY

Generativity was originally conceived by Erik Erikson (1963) as the hallmark of the period of midlife in the human life cycle, the seventh of eight life stages in his model of ego development (generativity versus stagnation).

Preparation of this chapter was supported by a Social Sciences and Humanities Research Council of Canada grant to the first author. The authors thank Darcia Narvaez and Dan Lapsley for their helpful comments on earlier versions of the manuscript.

Erikson saw parenthood as the prototype of generativity, the commitment to caring for future generations as a legacy of the self into the future. However, he argued that one might be generative as an adult in many other ways than simply parenting. For example, teaching, mentoring, and guiding youth in various life domains can be generative, whether these are biological offspring or not. Acting to improve the prospects of youth and the future of the species as a whole, for example by enhancing the health and quality of the environment, is a generative act. When directed to the future and as an expression of the self's concern for legacy, many kinds of prosocial acts qualify as generative in nature.

Erikson's is an epigenetic theory: each stage's key challenge is present in some way at every period of the life cycle. Erikson (1968) indicated this most clearly in the instance of identity, articulating the growth of self as a theme in relation to each of the key life-course turning points. Generativity may also be present across the life course. In particular, we contend that generativity should have its developmental roots earlier in the life course and demonstrate some sort of continuity, possibly complex in its form, over time. We focus on the beginning development of generativity in late adolescence and emerging adulthood.

McAdams (2001a) extended Erikson's theorizing on generativity in recent years, articulating a broader model of how generativity is expressed in personality (McAdams & de St. Aubin, 1992; McAdams, 2006a). McAdams's model focuses on the construct of generative *concern*, representing the individual's level of commitment to generative roles and activities. Generative concern is viewed as a conscious expression of the combination of inner generative desire (a "need to be needed" and to leave a lasting legacy of the self) and cultural expectations of intergenerational caring that foster and condition this expression. In turn, generative concern encourages generative *attitudes* (i.e., "belief in the species"), *goals* and *actions*, and ultimately, generative *narration* of a personal life story (McAdams & de St. Aubin, 1992). Interest in narration as the mature expression of generativity reflects McAdams's (2006a) emphasis on narrative as the core element of human meaning-making and identity (McAdams, 2006a). In this, he follows Bruner (1986, 1990) and others in arguing that the narrative mode of thinking is central to human reasoning about the social world (McAdams, 2001b).

McAdams and colleagues (1992) have led the exploration of generativity by developing a range of personality measures (Loyola Generativity Scale [LGS]; McAdams, 2006a), and by examining life stories narrated by adults who were independently judged higher or lower in generativity. In one study

(McAdams, Diamond, de St. Aubin, & Mansfield, 1997), they found distinctive features of a characteristic life story "script" that generative midlife adults tend to recount, a commitment script. In comparison to the life stories of less generative adults, the generative life story emphasized the important dimensions of an early concern for the suffering of others and a strong commitment to prosocial goals for the future. They also demonstrated a sense of "moral steadfastness" over time in the life course ("a commitment to a clear and detailed personal ideology," ibid, p. 684), which was coded based on depth, clarity, and continuity of ideology over time. (Two other elements of a generative life story – a sense of early blessing and a pattern of articulating redemptive themes that turn bad events into good outcomes – seem less clearly moral in nature.) In sum, these retrospective life-story accounts by generative midlife adults strongly emphasized the continuity of their moral and ideological commitments across the life course, and differed considerably from the life stories of less generative adults'.

The distinctive moral thematic material in the life stories of mature generative adults raises questions regarding the relations between generativity and morality as domains of personal concern, as well as the topic of how these domains may be developmentally linked. The origins of personal moral steadfastness and sustained concern may well be closely linked to identity growth and articulation during the period of late adolescence and emerging adulthood, as Erikson (1968) claimed. Thus, we have been exploring the possible roots and correlates of the generative personality in adolescence and emerging adulthood (Allen & Pratt, 2008; Frensch, Norris, & Pratt, 2007; Hasford, Rathwell, & Pratt, 2008; Lawford, Pratt, Hunsberger, & Pancer, 2005; Lawford, Davis, Dumas, & Pratt, 2008). Generative concern may be manifested in earlier life, at least as a precursor to its more mature midlife version (Stewart & Vandewater, 1998). Such early generativity would be consistent with Erikson's (1963) original epigenetic framework, which stressed the continuities as well as changes over time for each of the major ego strengths of his eight-stage sequence.

In fact, adolescents and emerging adults demonstrate quite consistent individual differences in generative concern, as assessed by the LGS across emerging adulthood (Lawford et al., 2005), validating the LGS for younger age groups. Furthermore, these patterns of individual differences have some degree of predictive power with respect to variations in prosocial community involvement (Hasford et al., 2008; Lawford et al., 2005), the use of generative thematic material in personal life stories in adolescence (Frensch et al., 2007), and patterns of responding regarding a sense of anticipations of parenting as part of the future self (Allen & Pratt, 2008).

MORAL IDENTITY

Erikson's (1968) framework emphasizes the sense of identity that emerges in later adolescence or early adulthood, which in modern cultures, at least, involves grappling with a range of ideological choices. Erikson considered identity and the moral self to be closely intertwined (Lapsley & Lasky, 2001), noting for example that "identity and fidelity are necessary for ethical strength" (Erikson, 1968, p. 26), but also that a moral or ethical sense is the "true criterion of identity" (ibid, p. 39). Moral and ethical concerns closely track the development of a sense of identity. As Lapsley and Lasky (2001, p. 358) put it, "This suggests that the formation of a moral identity is the clear goal of both moral and identity development and that these two developmental tracks are ideally conjoined in the moral personality."

Several recent researchers have suggested that those who are regarded as moral exemplars often exhibit a stronger sense of moral self and moral identity than do others (Hardy & Carlo, 2005; Hart, 2005; Hart & Fegley, 1995). This invocation of the identity construct in moral personality is meant to illuminate the issues of moral motivation – why do people actually choose to behave in a moral fashion, given their understanding of what is the morally right course of action in a situation (Rest, 1983)? Blasi (2004) pointed out that when adolescents develop a stronger sense of personal identity, their ideological values become more central to their self-understanding. As the self ultimately becomes more sophisticated and organized in later adolescence and young adulthood, self-consistency motives then may become more important in shaping moral behavior choices (Hardy & Carlo, 2005).

Recent authors have highlighted the need for a clearer definition and account of the moral identity construct. Both Hardy and Carlo (2005) and Hart (2005) argue that moral identity should be understood as the *intersection* of the self's growing commitment to a moral ideology on the one hand, and a developing sense of personal identity on the other (Kroger, 2007; Moshman, 2005). The interpenetration of moral ideology and personal identity provides the motivational grounds to pursue moral action (Hardy & Carlo, 2005), as suggested in the Erikson quotes above.

The relation between moral identity and moral action has been examined through the study of the lives and in-depth self-understandings of moral exemplars, individuals who exhibit uncommon moral commitment (Colby & Damon, 1992; Hart & Fegley, 1995; Walker & Frimer, 2007). Colby and Damon reported that their sample of mature adult moral exemplars showed little sense of conflict regarding moral choices, feeling that such choices flowed "naturally" as a product of their own core commitments.

Hart and Fegley (1995) found that a nominated group of highly engaged minority adolescents, compared with a matched comparison sample, showed both higher mentions of moral qualities and values in their self descriptions, and a more sophisticated sense of self on a standard interview about self-understanding (Damon & Hart, 1988). Interestingly, however, exemplars and nonexemplars did not differ on a standard measure of moral development; both groups scored at the conventional level on Kohlberg's standard assessment measure of moral reasoning (Hart & Fegley, 1995). Matsuba and Walker (2005) assessed differences between young adult exemplars of community engagement and a comparison sample. The exemplars showed clearer prosocial goals in life with respect to society in their story interviews, though the two groups did not differ with respect to prosocial goals for the self or the family. The young adult exemplars also showed greater "depth of understanding" in their personal moral ideology, in contrast to the comparison group, paralleling this aspect of McAdams's findings for midlife adults (Matsuba & Walker, 2005). In a recent study, Walker and Frimer (2007, this volume) reported that Canadian adults who received national awards for caring (sustained prosocial activities) or brave (specific act of heroism) activity differed in terms of a number of features of personality. Caring adults showed higher levels of communal aspects of personality, including generative strivings, care for others, nurturance, communion motives, and positive affective tone in analyses of their life stories, compared with the brave exemplars. Generally no differences were revealed on more agentic aspects of personality between the two samples, however. These findings suggest that there may be somewhat distinctive prototypes for moral personality in adulthood, which are captured to some extent by the different contexts of the actions that led to these awards.

A NARRATIVE PERSPECTIVE ON MORAL IDENTITY

Most of the exemplar studies just noted used narrative approaches to elicit a person's self constructs and identify the self's core commitments. Such an approach is likely to be useful even within nonexemplar samples. Following McAdams's (2001b, 2006b) theory of the narrative life story as the basic form of identity, we examined the development of the capacity for telling the personal life story during the period of adolescence and young adulthood (Habermas & Bluck, 2000). Because this is the period in the life cycle when identity concerns clearly come to the fore (Erikson, 1963), we have focused specifically on narratives of moral experiences in the life story as a way of assessing how a moral identity begins to take shape in late adolescence and into early adulthood (Lawford et al., 2008; Pratt et al., 2006).

MORAL NARRATIVES OF PERSONAL LIFE IN YOUNG ADULTHOOD

The Futures Study is an ongoing investigation of individual social, personal, and moral development, begun when several hundred Canadian youth were age 17 on average, and continued through age 26 (Jackson, Pratt, Pancer, & Hunsberger, 2005; Lawford et al., 2005). We obtained questionnaire measures of generativity, prosocial behavior, and moral values at several ages in this research program (19, 23, and 26). At age 26, 104 participants were asked to tell five stories of moral issues from their lives, including (1) a morally ambiguous situation or dilemma ("when you didn't know the right thing to do"); (2) a story of moral goodness or success; (3) a story of moral weakness or failure; (4) a story of moral courage; and (5) a story of moral cowardice. This task was adapted from earlier work by Colby and Damon with a midlife sample (Colby et al., 2001). Based on the narrative identity framework, we conceived of these five stories as providing at least an initial mapping of variations in moral identity during emerging adulthood.

In the Futures sample interview, then, individuals had the opportunity to tell five stories drawn from distinctive elicitations focused on moral topics. Stories were defined broadly as coherent texts that could be understood as referring to events or classes of events from the person's own experience. Despite the fact that a story might not seem clearly moral to an observer, we treated their responses to our elicitations as examples of morally relevant stories for the interviewee. Each of the five elicitation contexts was then rated on two basic dimensions, including presence/absence of any story at all, and the perceived seriousness of the issue recounted (Lawford et al., 2008). When we look across the five story elicitation contexts (see Table 13.3), between 58%–89% of the participants in our sample were able to tell a story for each topic, with the morally ambiguous dilemma eliciting a story the most reliably, and moral cowardice the least reliably. The capacity to recall an example for each of the five particular story types here was viewed from the narrative identity framework as indicative of greater elaboration of the moral identity domain for the self, whereas a failure to produce one or more of these story types was interpreted as reflecting less development of moral valuing as a central dimension of the self. Perceived seriousness was rated by the coders (on a 1–5 scale) as a reflection of the meaningfulness of this type of issue to the participant, again conceived as

TABLE 13.1. *Scoring levels for the global narrative moral commitment coding system*

Level	Characteristics
1	No evidence of moral commitment, or evidence of immoral acts without remorse
2	Minimal, ambivalent, and inconsistent expression of moral commitment
3	Moderate expression of moral commitment, but with sense of ambivalence or compliance, rather than direct personal investment
4	Clearly expressed moral commitment, showing personal investment in needs and rights of others as part of one's self-ideals
5	Strong and sustained evidence of moral commitment, with investment in the needs and rights of others as part of self-ideals, often at personal sacrifice or risk

an index of investment in the moral domain. Reliabilities for these two ratings across story types were generally adequate (all correlations or percentage agreements between independent raters were above .70).

In addition to specific judgments of raters about each story told, overall ratings of the individual's narrative moral identity (NMI) were made by independent raters. The five stories were rated globally for salience of moral identity, represented by higher levels of concern for the needs or rights of another, often at some cost to the self. Global ratings ranged from 1 (low) to 5 (high) (Mean = 3.08), with good interrater reliability (correlations in the .80s; Davis, 2007). Table 13.1 shows the levels in this coding scheme. Here are two example narratives, and their associated ratings, to provide a sense of the coding:

EXAMPLE 1: MORAL GOODNESS

In elementary school, we had a dance once, it was grade eight I think, and I don't know, it was, you know, everybody wants to be cool then, and I remember there was one boy who was not so cool, not that I was cool, but I had my group of friends and I was comfortable in there and the one boy was just standing all by himself at the side of the room, and I remember thinking, you know, I wanted to go over and get him and just bring him over, but I was thinking oh, you know, what are my friends gonna think, and then I said you know what, forget it, who cares, and I just went and got him, I said you know, you want to come and dance with us, and he came over to dance with us and you know, I could see just that little grin on his face and I remember that, and I remember just thinking okay, that's, I don't care what they think, you know, that just, seeing his smile was enough that I didn't care, you know, if my friends thought I was whatever, a loser for it, I don't know.

This story was coded as moderately serious (3, on a 1–5 scale) and this individual was coded as showing relatively strong moral identity commitment (3.5 overall on a 1–5 scale). By itself this story would rate a 4, reflecting a relatively transient commitment to the needs of another, but certainly at a clear cost to the self.

EXAMPLE 2: MORAL DILEMMA

I guess it was recently. I ended up getting pregnant. I was deciding what school I wanted to go to and what I was going to do. I ended up getting pregnant and I ended up getting an abortion. I was torn between what was right and wrong. I had been in a relationship. I love my partner, I want to marry him, I want to have his children. I was very distraught about that. I actually still am. At the time when it happened, I felt I was in a dead-end situation. I wanted to figure out what I wanted to do with my life. Like it was a now or never situation. I had that opportunity to go to school at that time, and if I didn't I would be stuck in a bad job and that I would really hate my life and really regret everything. When I am in school (this was just a year ago), I look back and I think it was stupid. Life happens, things happen. At the time, it really felt like it was a life and death situation. I felt terrible about myself. I felt very ashamed of myself and I still feel feelings that I made the wrong decision. Just because, I don't know that it was the right decision. I feel really bad. It just goes to show that I don't feel I am responsible enough. I was torn between the two things but if I was real mature and responsible would I have made the right decisions.

This story was coded as very serious (5, on a 1–5 scale) and this individual was coded as showing a relatively low level of narrative moral identity overall (2, on a 1–5 scale). This story itself would be rated a 2, showing considerable ambivalence about the self's moral capabilities.

We also used three other measures. The Loyola Generativity Scale measured generative concern (LGS; McAdams and de St. Aubin, 1992, at ages 23 and 26), a focus on caring for youth and leaving a legacy of the self (e.g., "I think I would like the work of a teacher."). Prosocial moral valuing (Schwartz & Bilsky, 1990, at ages 19 and 23) is organized as a universal circumplex model, with one domain of valuing represented by the prosocial dimension, which was administered here. This prosocial dimension consists of universalism and benevolence values, which share a motivational orientation toward the enhancement of others and the transcendence of selfish interests (Schwartz, 1994; Schwartz & Bilsky, 1990). Universalism values reflect a concern with the welfare of all people and nature (e.g., "a world at peace"), while benevolence values reflect a concern with the welfare of people with whom one is in frequent personal contact (e.g., "caring"). We developed a measure of prosocial behavior in which a person engages (Youth Involvement Inventory or YII, Pancer, Pratt, Hunsberger, & Alisat, 2007, at ages 17, 19, 23, and 26), regarding the frequency of involvement in community, political, and prosocial activities over the past year (e.g., "visited the sick in hospital"). These measures had Cronbach alphas above .80 in this sample.

To examine the validity of a narrative approach to moral identity development, we calculated correlations across time points and among measures of moral values and motivation (benevolence and universalism), and prosocial behavior, and the overall moral narrative identity rating of the set of moral stories collected at age 26 in our sample. The global moral identity rating was fairly consistently correlated with these moral motivational and behavioral measures (see Table 13.2), suggesting that a pattern of personal moral narratives reflecting moral identity at age 26 is at least moderately correlated with more traditional moral value and prosocial behavioral indices assessed across the period of emerging adulthood.

Next, we examined the more detailed descriptive coding of the five types of moral narratives provided separately at age 26 in relation to the global moral identity rating (Table 13.3). As shown in the first column of this table, most people (89%) told a story of a moral dilemma, but other types of story recall were more variably present. As shown on the bottom row of Table 13.2, the average scores for number of moral dilemmas told and ratings of dilemma seriousness were correlated positively with the narrative moral identity index (rs = .24 and .37, ps < .05). In addition, the presence of a story for each type of narrative elicitation, as well as its rated level of seriousness, were also analyzed in relation to the global narrative moral identity measure (as rated by another independent coder from the entire story set). As Table 13.3 indicates, this global rating of narrative moral identity was particularly associated with telling stories about moral goodness and moral courage. Interestingly, the ratings of moral seriousness showed

TABLE 13.2. *Correlations of narrative moral identity (NMI) ratings at age 26, and various value and behavioral moral indices (Futures Study)*

Measure	NMI rating age 26	Number of stories (1–5)	Mean story seriousness rating
Benevolence-Universalism Values (Age 19)	.23*	.18*	.06
Benevolence-Universalism Values (Age 23)	.32**	.15	.24*
Community Involvement (Age 17)	.25*	.05	.01
Community Involvement (Age 19)	.13	.22*	.05
Community Involvement (Age 23)	.11	.18	.08
Community Involvement (Age 26)	.28*	.13	.20*
LGS (Age 23)	.29*	.31*	.16
LGS (Age 26)	.27*	.13	.25*
NMI Rating (Age 26)	1.00	.24*	.37*

*$p < .05$
**$p < .01$

relatively consistent positive correlations with overall narrative moral identity across each of the five story types. Overall, then, the tendency to tell stories for each elicitation context was associated with a stronger sense of commitment to moral ideals as judged by the global coder, and this was particularly so for stories about moral goodness and moral courage, which typically involved "standing up" for others at some cost to the self. Second, the rated seriousness of all types of stories was quite consistently positively related to global narrative moral identity, as shown in Table 13.3, probably reflecting the participant's tendency to treat the task of moral narration in general with a greater (or lesser) sense of gravitas.

Finally, we explored associations between generativity and our moral narrative measures. Table 13.2 shows the correlations between the LGS as a measure of generative concern and the various moral narrative indices from our sample at age 26. While the pattern of correlations here was modest,

TABLE 13.3. *Correlations of narrative moral identity (NMI) ratings and generativity at age 26, and specific moral dilemma type story ratings (Futures Study)*

Moral story type:	Story present (%)	NMI × Told	NMI × Serious	LGS × Told	LGS × Serious
Dilemma	89	.09	.46**	−.13	.41*
Goodness	62	.19*	.31*	.08	.04
Failure	65	.02	.21	.03	−.10
Courage	65	.19*	.17	.25*	.09
Cowardice	58	.16	.32*	.14	.01

*$p < .05$
**$p < .01$

the overall indices were generally related as predicted, with narrative moral identity associated with higher generativity on the LGS at both ages 23 and 26. When we considered the particular types of moral dilemmas recalled (Table 13.3), there was a clear relation between generativity and moral courage examples, such that individuals high on the LGS at age 26 were particularly likely to tell moral courage stories compared to other types. These findings suggest that positive instances of this particular quality are especially salient in the sense of self being constructed by those who respond more generatively in early adulthood. An example story will help to illustrate this story type further:

EXAMPLE 3: MORAL COURAGE

When I was working for the [social work organisation]. There was a family that I worked with that was very, very poverty stricken and very in need of services and material items, everything and my moral dilemma basically was their microwave had broken and the autistic boy was so violent that um, the mother did not want to use the stove. This is a child who was the extreme of extreme. I've never seen an autistic child like that.

Um ... and ... throughout working for this organization, we were always told, do not buy anything for clients, do not put yourself in a position where there is any kind of, um, personal giving, but, um, I bought them a microwave because the kid would not eat otherwise, and I saw it as, you know, life versus a couple hundred bucks, you know, so, um, that ultimately led to me quitting. Because it became common knowledge around the office and my supervisor found out, and she threatened to, to fire me, and so I said alright, I went back to the office, I wrote out my letter of resignation and I said goodbye. I'm not, I don't want to be part of an organization that ... is that rigid in their social work belief that they are not able to see that this was quite possibly a life or death situation, so.

This story was coded as very serious (5, on a 1–5 scale). This individual's stories were also coded as showing strong moral identity commitment (4.5, on a 1–5 scale) overall. This particular story would be a 5 on our scale, reflecting sustained commitment to considering the needs of another at considerable personal sacrifice.

Interestingly, the recounting of more serious moral dilemmas, in which the individual reported not knowing what to do in a specific situation, was particularly associated with higher levels of generative concern (see Table 13.3). More generative individuals were especially likely to perceive and recall personally difficult choices for this story elicitation, and these challenging issues evidently remain with them as they remember their past life experiences. Some examples of responses to this type of dilemma in our data set included dealing with issues of abortion or infidelity, reporting an abusive parental figure, or confronting a friend or family member who had a drug and alcohol problem. Of course, generative individuals may selectively seek out such challenging life decisions, but it seems also plausible that these individuals may continue to wrestle with these concerns in a more complex and extended way than others do, given their focus on concern for others as a legacy of the moral self. Generative adults may thus be more sensitive to the ambiguities and complexities of moral experience; this may also reflect an increased sophistication of cognitive complexity in these adults (see Pratt & Norris, 1999).

LONGITUDINAL EXAMINATION OF EARLY MORAL NARRATIVE IDENTITY AND GENERATIVITY DEVELOPMENT IN EMERGING ADULTHOOD

Our second interest was to examine the possible moral identity roots of developing generative concern in emerging adulthood. The longitudinal data set for this question (the Teen-Parent Study) is a smaller, family-based study of 40 Canadian families, focusing on the process of value socialization in families (Arnold, Pratt, & Hicks, 2004; Pratt, Skoe, & Arnold, 2004). The data for these participants were collected by interviews and questionnaires, starting at age 14, then at ages 16, 20, and 24 for the target adolescent.

Included were standard questionnaire measures of prosocial behaviors, generativity, moral value endorsement, and adjustment measures. We also collected extensive narrative data in these interviews. In particular, we drew on specific life stories to characterize levels of narrative moral identity at ages 16 and 20, using the system described above. However, the types of autobiographical stories elicited in this study were somewhat different than those of the Futures sample interviews, and less targeted specifically to the moral domain.

As noted above, we expected that there would be significant relations between moral components of personality and generativity development. Study 1 above also suggested some concurrent links between these two constructs. In order to explore a more longitudinal framework in the Teen-Parent data set, we used our measure of narrative moral identity described above. As noted previously, this measure focused on level of caring for the needs and rights of others, even at some cost to the self. However, the types of stories available in this data set were more general in nature than the moral stories elicited in Study 1. Instead, participants in Study 2 at ages 16 and 20 told specific stories about (1) a turning point in their lives; (2) a situation of moral uncertainty ("not knowing the right thing to do"); (3) a time when they were taught a value by parents; and (4) a time when they were proud of themselves. Here are two example stories from the data set with their ratings:

> 21-year-old male's proud story: *"OK, I got kicked out of my parents' house. And that was probably the biggest life-turning thing that has happened to me. And now I have my own house, I have my own tenants. I get paid for a living. I think I'm stronger, more independent. I can hold my head high because I'm very proud of what I've accomplished. And this is only the start. I want a lot more... I'm zealous for money, sometimes overzealous. Having the house gave me a new drive for money, that it's achievable. It gave me more maturity. It gave me a different outlook on life... just knowing that I'm controlling people's lives. Like at the drop of a hat I can walk upstairs and get all three of these people out of my house, you know, and say, 'Come pick up your stuff next week at this time ...'"*

This individual's overall story set was rated very low (1, on a 1–5 scale) on moral identity; this dilemma would also be rated as a 1.

> Turning point story of a 16-year-old girl: *"You know in school I was always part of the little cool crowd... And then S came into my class, and she was Indian, and she was made fun of so much. I believe it was a real racial issue. I felt so badly for her because she did not stand up for her rights at*

all, she would smile or brush it off as if everything was OK. But I knew it wasn't OK. I thought 'Look, if she couldn't stand up for herself, she needs someone else to stand up for her, because what is happening here is not right.' So I started becoming her friend, and then all the members of the cool group totally ditched me... I remember one specific time...I just stood up and burst out and I started yelling. I don't even remember what I said, but I remember after that I just felt so good, and all the cool girls just stood around us in a circle and it was totally silent. It was like such a moment. It was a day I'll never forget."

This individual's story set was rated as high (5, on a 1–5 scale) on moral identity commitment to caring for others at a cost to the self. This dilemma rated a 5 as well.

To establish construct validity, we predicted that moral identity ratings would be related to endorsement of moral values as ideals for the self in adolescence. For the latter, we used a values task adapted from Arnold (1993), involving choices from a list of ten values, half of which were moral (e.g., "kind and caring"), and half of which were positive, but nonmoral ("ambitious") in nature. Table 13.4 shows correlational results. The longitudinal correlations between narrative moral identity ratings at 16 and 20, and moral value endorsements for the self at ages 14 and 16, were fairly consistently positive. Interestingly, Kohlberg stage level of moral reasoning, which we also measured in this study using standard procedures (Colby & Kohlberg, 1987), did not predict to these identity commitment ratings, as shown.

TABLE 13.4. *Correlations of narrative moral identity (NMI) measures with moral values, behavioral, and generativity indices (Teen-Parent Study)*

Measure	NMI rating at 16	NMI rating at 20
Self's Moral Value Choices (14)	.40*	.17
Self's Moral Value Choices (16)	.59**	.52**
Kohlberg WAS Scores (16)	.12	.15
Kohlberg WAS Scores (20)	.12	.16
Community Involvement (24)	.57**	.60**
LGS – Generative Concern (24)	.44*	.53**
Generative Story Themes (24)	.25	.41*

* $p < .05$
** $p < .01$

A second analysis explored whether the narrative ratings would predict to prosocial behavior in the community at age 24. We used the self-report questionnaire from Study 1 (Pancer et al., 2007), reasoning that such a prospective finding would support the construct validity of this narrative measure as an index of prosocial motivation. NMI ratings from stories told at ages 16 and 20 were strong predictors of the level of youth involvement in the community at ages 20 and 24 (see Table 13.4). Indeed, they predicted unique variance in prosocial behavior beyond moral values at these ages in simultaneous regression analyses (not shown here, see Pratt et al., 2006).

Finally, our third longitudinal question addressed whether a stronger narrative moral identity rating in late adolescence (ages 16 and 20) would be a precursor of a more generative self in young adulthood. We used the Loyola Generativity Scale to measure generative concern at age 24, and also obtained coding of turning-point and proud-story personal narratives at age 24 for use of generative themes (Frensch et al., 2007). The use of these themes was summed across the various narratives to provide an overall index. The data indicated that, as hypothesized, moral identity commitment ratings at ages 16 and 20 were positive predictors of generative concern on the LGS at age 24, as well as of the narrative use of generative themes in life stories at age 24 (see Table 13.4).

Thus, the results of Study 2 were generally quite consistent with those of Study 1. Ratings of narrative moral identity produced patterns of correlations with measures of moral value ideals and prosocial behaviors that were similar, albeit somewhat stronger in effect size, than in Study 1. Most interesting of all, the simultaneous correlations between generativity and moral identity in the first study were replicated and extended to a longitudinal pattern of prediction from the salience of narrative moral identity at 16 and 20 to subsequent generativity of personality in Study 2.

NARRATIVE APPROACHES TO MORAL IDENTITY: UNDERSTANDING THE MORAL SELF THROUGH STORIES

The developmental pattern of acquisition of the life story in late adolescence (Habermas & Bluck, 2000) suggests that this narrative transition overlaps closely with the traditional period of identity development as formulated by Erikson (1963). This convergence itself suggests potential evidence for the utility of the life story as an index of identity attainment (McAdams, 2001). Indeed, McLean and Pratt (2006) found some indications that traditional status measures of identity development may parallel indices of narrative identity development during this period (cf. Dumas, Lawford, Tieu, & Pratt, 2008).

Past research and theorizing have also indicated that the moral self is closely linked to moral motivation and its development (Hart & Fegley, 1995; Hardy & Carlo, 2005). Study 1 showed that young adults were generally able to recall a range of personal stories focused around moral themes, and established that the fluency of recall and rated seriousness of these stories were modestly positively linked to moral motivation levels, as well as (somewhat less clearly) to prosocial moral behaviors. In turn, the global rating of narrative moral identity, generated across the whole set of stories, was more consistently related to moral motivation and prosocial moral behaviors within this data set. These results were replicated and extended in Study 2, suggesting that a narrative approach to describing moral identity deserves further exploration. More extensive research followed by a broader description and taxonomy of the narratives of moral life may be a next step.

The seriousness of the moral narratives was an important element in coders' impressions of moral identity commitment, and this was especially reflected in the gravity of the "most difficult choice" described by participants. These difficult personal dilemmas may in fact reflect best the centrality of moral considerations for these youth within their developing self-concepts. Further research on this particular story type would be welcome in this exploration. In contrast, however, whether or not a particular type of story was told at all was most clearly related to positive instances of moral goodness, as well as instances of moral courage (see Table 13.2). A capacity to remember positive instances when the self was both good and courageous would seem like an important hallmark of a developing positive sense of narrative moral identity, as illustrated in the example stories provided earlier. The rich description of the various types of moral narratives of Study 1 and their links to the self-concept through separate consideration of each story type (see Table 13.3) offers a starting point for further study.

RELATIONS BETWEEN MORAL IDENTITY AND GENERATIVITY IN EMERGING ADULTHOOD

Narrative assessments of moral identity were consistently linked with measures of generativity in both studies. Those individuals judged to have exhibited a stronger sense of commitment to moral ideals were also more likely to report higher levels of generative concern on the LGS (Studies

1 and 2), and more generative theme usage in their personal stories (Study 2). The consistency of these results is noteworthy because the types of stories elicited were somewhat different across the two studies. The results in Study 2 were especially interesting because they supported the thematic findings of the McAdams et al. (1997) retrospective life-story research in midlife, but in this case, using a prospective longitudinal design following individuals from adolescence into emerging adulthood. Narrative moral identity development thus seemed to reflect, at least in part, a motivational commitment to moral values and action ("moral steadfastness") that may be gradually translated into a story of the self's moral life (Blasi, 2004; Hardy & Carlo, 2005). Narrative moral identity also serves as a key foundation for generativity development. The present results also extend the findings of earlier exemplar studies by examining an unselected sample of youth.

We also examined the links between specific types of personal moral stories and generativity in Study 1. They suggested two things: that those who were more generative on the LGS at 26 were more likely than others to tell stories of moral courage (Lawford et al., 2008), and that those who were generative were more likely to include dilemmas or "difficult choices" that were more serious than those of other youth. The first of these findings suggests that the prototype for moral courage stories (standing up for others at some risk to the self, as illustrated in the turning point dilemma of the adolescent in Study 2 presented above) is particularly salient in the narrative moral identities of generative individuals in our samples. A clear and salient story of the self's courage under difficult circumstances may serve to support future commitment to prosocial caring for disadvantaged others (Hasford et al., 2008; Lawford et al., 2008). Walker and Frimer's (2007) results suggested that generativity was less salient in adult exemplars of specific acts of physical bravery than in their caring exemplars, whose laudatory actions were commonly much more sustained over time. Nevertheless, our findings (e.g., story example 3 from the Futures sample earlier) suggest that young adults' life stories of moral courage and bravery often include complex aspects of both sustained caring and interpersonal courage over time. More exploration of this specific type of prosocial scene or story, and its implications for identity, generativity, and the moral domain, is needed.

The finding that generative young adults were especially likely to recall more serious moral dilemmas or choices may reflect again that these individuals devote the most extensive level of cognitive processing and reflection to such difficult choices of moral life. Generative young adults' way of constructing these dilemmas appeared to strike our coders as more even-handed and complex, with considerations on each side of the choice more elaborated than in the stories of less generative adults. Pratt and Norris (1999) reported a similar finding for more generative mature adults. These findings on dilemma seriousness and complexity may also parallel the narrative life-story evidence that generative midlife adults grapple more seriously with their own moral ideologies and show more depth of thinking about such complex moral choices (McAdams et al., 1997).

CONCLUSIONS

The present findings generally point to the consistent and sustained nature of individual variations in the sense of moral identity over time during the period of emerging adulthood, as revealed through personal narratives. They also give evidence of the strong intertwining of moral identity and generativity during this critical preliminary phase of adulthood, and thus provide further support for the integrity of generativity as a construct with relevance during this late adolescent/emerging adult time period (Frensch et al., 2007; Lawford et al., 2005).

How, then, does the present program of research address the central questions of this volume regarding the construct of moral personality? We think that the moral personality is best understood within a lifespan developmental framework, and we suggest that Erikson's (1963) ubiquitous model is a promising foundation for such a project. Following Erikson (1968), we foreground the notion of identity as the key element in his description of the life course, and further, we see moral identity as a core motivational element in the emerging self of young adulthood. This line of argument relies on the notion, explicit in Erikson's writings, that moral and identity development are mutually sustaining (Lapsley & Lasky, 2001). In some sense, each of the Erikson personality strengths across the life course may be understood as making claims about the good and moral life, but this is particularly true of the commitments and stances of identity and its manifestation in personal stories (McAdams, 2001). Indeed, simply authoring a narrative about one's life experiences in the construction of an identity may be seen in some respects as inherently taking moral responsibility for one's actions (Tappan & Brown, 1989).

Furthermore, we take seriously the idea of epigenesis that was explicit from the beginning within Erikson's (1963) iconic developmental chart or scheme of life "crises." We argue that the eight elements and strengths of the ego across the life span that characterize the predominant concerns of each of the stages in turn are also woven throughout the life span in various manifestations in both earlier and later periods of the life course, as Erikson suggests. Our longitudinal empirical results suggest close relations between an early sense of "moral steadfastness," or integrity, in moral identity and the subsequent growth of generative potential in young adulthood. These results are quite consistent with the retrospective life stories told by generative midlife adults about their own development (McAdams et al., 1997). While we do not claim that generativity is the identical construct in emerging adulthood that it is to become in midlife, we also resist the simplistic, if popular, notion that the various components of ego development in the Eriksonian scheme should be understood as isolated elements that emerge only at particular periods in the life course (and we believe that Erikson's epigenetic model clearly indicates that he understood these processes in the way we do as well). Given the host of issues raised by these admittedly preliminary findings, we want to pursue work on narrative measures of commitment to moral and generative purposes in the future, as a particularly promising way to study aspects of the formation of moral identity and the manifestation of adult moral personality in thought and action.

REFERENCES

Allen, J. W., & Pratt, M. W. (2008). *Emerging adults' expectations of a future parenting self: Differences by gender and level of Eriksonian generativity.* Poster presented at the Society for Research in Adolescence Meetings, Chicago, March.

Arnold, M. L. (1993). *The place of morality in the adolescent self.* Unpublished doctoral dissertation, Harvard University, Cambridge, MA.

Arnold, M. L., Pratt, M. W., & Hicks, C. (2004). Adolescents' representations of parents' voices in family stories: Value lessons, personal adjustment and identity development. In M. W. Pratt & B. H. Fiese (Eds.), *Family stories and the life course: Across time and generations.* (pp. 163–186). Mahwah, NJ: Lawrence Erlbaum Associates.

Blasi, A. (2004). Moral functioning: Moral understanding and personality. In D. K Lapsley & D. Narvaez (Eds.), *Moral development, self, and identity* (pp. 189–212). Mahwah, NJ: Lawrence Erlbaum.

Colby, A., & Damon, W. (1992). *Some do care: Contemporary lives of moral commitment.* New York: Free Press.

Colby, A., & Kohlberg, L. (1987). *The measurement of moral judgment. Volume 1.* New York: Cambridge University Press.

Colby, A., Sippola, L., & Phelps, E. (2001). Social responsibility and paid work in contemporary American life. In A. S. Rossi (Ed). *Caring and doing for other: Social responsibility in the domains of family, work, and community* (pp. 463–501). Chicago: University of Chicago Press.

Damon, W., & Hart, D. (1988). *Self-understanding in childhood and adolescence.* New York: Cambridge University Press.

Davis, N. (2007). *Moral identity in the life stories of young adults: Adolescent moral values, behaviour and generativity as predictors.* Unpublished honours thesis, Wilfrid Laurier University.

Dumas, T., Lawford, H., Tieu, T., & Pratt, M. W. (2008, submitted ms.). *Positive parenting in adolescence and its relation to low point narration and identity status in emerging adulthood: A longitudinal analysis.*

Erikson, E. (1963). *Childhood and society* (2nd Ed.). New York: Norton.

Frensch, K. M., Pratt, M. W., & Norris, J. E. (2007). Foundations of generativity: Personal and family correlates of adolescents' generative life story themes. *Journal of Research in Personality, 41,* 45–62.

Habermas, T., & Bluck, S. (2000). Getting a life: The emergence of the life story in adolescence. *Psychological Bulletin, 126,* 248–269.

Hardy, S., & Carlo, G. (2005). Identity as a source of moral motivation. *Human Development, 48,* 232–256.

Hart, D. (2005). The development of moral identity. In G. Carlo & C. P. Edwards (Eds.), *Nebraska symposium on motivation: Moral development through the lifespan: Theory, research, and application.* Vol. 51. Lincoln, NE: University of Nebraska Press.

Hart, D., & Fegley, S. (1995). Prosocial behavior and caring in adolescence: Relations to self-understanding and social judgment. *Child Development, 66,* 1346–1359.

Hasford, J., Rathwell, J., & Pratt, M. W. (2008). *Generativity, identity and emerging adults' narratives of community involvement/experiences.* Poster presented at the Society for Research in Adolescence Meetings, Chicago, March.

Jackson, L., Pratt, M. W., Hunsberger, B., & Pancer, S. M. (2005). Optimism as a mediator of relations between perceived parental authoritativeness and adjustment among adolescents: Finding the sunny side of the street. *Social Development, 14,* 273–304.

Kroger, J. (2007). *Identity development: Adolescence through adulthood* (2nd Ed.). Thousand Oaks, CA: Sage.

Lapsley, D., & Lasky, B. (2001). Prototypic moral character. *Identity, 1,* 345–363.

Lawford, H., Davis, N., Dumas, T., & Pratt, M. W. (2008). *Stories of morality and moral courage and their association with concern for future generations in emerging adulthood.* Poster presented at the Society for Research in Adolescence Meetings, Chicago, March.

Lawford, H., Pratt, M. W., Hunsberger, B., & Pancer, S. M. (2005). Adolescent generativity: A longitudinal study of two possible contexts for learning concern for future generations. *Journal of Research on Adolescence, 15,* 261–273.

Matsuba, K., & Walker, L. J. (2005). Young adult moral exemplars: The making of self through stories. *Journal of Research on Adolescence, 15,* 275–297.

McAdams, D. P. (2001a). Generativity in midlife. In M. Lachman (Ed.), *Handbook of midlife development* (pp. 395–443). New York: Wiley.

(2001b). The psychology of life stories. *Review of General Psychology, 5,* 100–122.

(2006a). *The person* (4th Ed.). New York: Wiley.

(2006b). *The redemptive self: Stories Americans live by.* New York: Oxford.

McAdams, D. P., & de St. Aubin, E. (1992). A theory of generativity and its assessment through self-report, behavioral acts, and narrative themes in autobiography. *Journal of Personality and Social Psychology, 62,* 1003–1015.

McAdams, D. P., Diamond, A., de St. Aubin, E., & Mansfield, E. (1997). Stories of commitment: The psychosocial construction of generative lives. *Journal of Personality and Social Psychology, 72,* 678–694.

McLean, K. C., & Pratt, M. W. (2006). Life's little (and big) lessons: Identity development and the construction of meaning in the turning point narratives of emerging adulthood. *Developmental Psychology, 42*, 714–722.

Moshman, D. (2005). *Adolescent psychological development: Rationality, morality and identity.* Mahwah, NJ: Lawrence Erlbaum.

Pancer, S. M., Pratt, M. W., Hunsberger, B., & Alisat, S. (2007). Community and political involvement in adolescence: What distinguishes the activists from the uninvolved? *Journal of Community Psychology, 35*, 741–759.

Pratt, M. W., Arnold, M. L., & Allard, E. (2006). *Themes of social responsibility in adolescent life stories as predictors of a young adult moral and generative self: Staying the course?* Paper presented at the Society for Research on Adolescence Meetings, San Francisco, March.

Pratt, M. W., & Norris, J. (1999). Moral development in maturity: Lifespan perspectives on the processes of successful aging. In T. Hess & F. Blanchard-Fields (Eds.), *Social cognition and aging* (pp. 291–317). New York: Academic Press.

Pratt, M. W., Norris, J. E., Hebblethwaite, S., & Arnold, M. L. (2008). Intergenerational transmission of values: Family generativity and adolescents' narratives of parent and grandparent value teaching. *Journal of Personality, 76*, 171–198.

Pratt, M. W., Skoe, E. E., & Arnold, M. L. (2004). The development of care reasoning in later adolescence: A longitudinal analysis. *International Journal of Behavioral Development, 28*, 139–147.

Schwartz, S. H. (1994). Are there universal aspects in the structure and contents of human values? *Journal of Social Issues, 50*, 19–45.

Schwartz, S. H., & Bilsky, W. (1990). Toward a theory of the universal content and structure of values: Extensions and cross-cultural replications. *Journal of Personality and Social Psychology, 58*(5), 878–891.

Soucie, K., Rathwell, J., & Pratt, M. W. (2008). *Factors influencing the development of empathy for a disadvantaged group in late adolescence: A narrative and longitudinal analysis.* Poster presented at the Biennial Conference on Human Development, Indianapolis, April.

Stewart, A. J., & Vandewater, E. A. (1998). The course of generativity. In E. de St. Aubin & D. P. McAdams (Eds.), *Generativity and adult development: How and why we care for the next generation* (pp. 75–100). Washington, DC: American Psychological Association.

Tappan, M., & Brown, L. (1989). Stories told and lessons learned: Toward a narrative approach to moral development. *Harvard Educational Review, 59*, 182–205.

Walker, L. J., & Frimer, J. A. (2007). Moral personality of brave and caring exemplars. *Journal of Personality and Social Psychology, 93*, 845–860.

14

Moral Identity, Integrity, and Personal Responsibility

BARRY R. SCHLENKER, MARISA L. MILLER,
AND RYAN M. JOHNSON

Most people think of themselves as being principled. College students regard themselves as more principled than the typical person and believe they behave consistently with their principles most of the time (Miller & Schlenker, 2009). Yet data document an increasingly prevalent "culture of cheating" and breakdown of traditional ethical behavior (Callahan, 2004), with dramatic increases in cheating over the last 30 years in the United States (Kleiner & Lord, 1999; McCabe, Treviño, & Butterfield, 2001). In one recent study, 75% of college students admitted to cheating on exams and papers, 70% admitted to stealing, and 89% said they broke promises (Schlenker, 2008). Principled conduct is admirable in the abstract, but the temptations and pressures of daily life often encourage expediency.

It is the thesis of this chapter that personal commitment to a principled ethical ideology, as opposed to a more expedient ideology, determines the strength of the relationship between moral beliefs and behavior. Personal commitment links the self-system to moral principles, producing a sense of obligation to perform consistently with those principles, a sense of responsibility for relevant conduct, and an unwillingness to condone and rationalize ethical failures and transgressions. With high personal commitment, a principled ethical ideology becomes a dominant schema for interpreting events and for guiding conduct. As such, the strength of commitment to a principled ideology has implications for a wide range of social activities. The remainder of this chapter will elaborate these ideas.

PRINCIPLED AND EXPEDIENT ETHICAL IDEOLOGIES

An *ethical ideology* is an integrated system of beliefs, values, standards, and self-assessments that define an individual's orientation toward matters of right and wrong (Schlenker, 2008). Such an ideology provides a *moral schema* for interpreting and evaluating events, and a *moral identity* that describes one's ethical character and provides a basis for self-regulation. In this view, ethical beliefs and identity are not separate systems but are intertwined, each having implications for the other.

A key dimension that distinguishes ethical ideologies is the strength of personal commitment to moral principles. The endpoints of this dimension can be labeled principled versus expedient. *Principled ideologies* involve the ideas that moral principles exist and should guide conduct; principles have a transsituational quality and should be followed regardless of personal consequences or self-serving rationalizations; and integrity, in the sense of a steadfast commitment to principles, is a vital, defining quality of one's identity. In contrast, although no one claims to be unprincipled, some people endorse greater ethical adaptability. *Expedient ideologies* involve the ideas that moral principles can be flexible: it is important to take advantage of opportunities and foolish not to do so; deviations from principles are often justifiable; and integrity, while important, is not a vital component of one's identity.[1]

We regard the principled-expedient continuum as one of the more important moral dimensions, both because of its recurring centrality in moral philosophy and because of its implications for moral identity and ethical conduct. First, from earliest recorded writings to the present, philosophers (e.g., Socrates, Plato, Aristotle, Marcus Aurelius, Aquinas, Hobbes, Locke, Kant, J. S. Mill, Adam Smith, and many more) discussed tensions between duty and desire, or between principled conduct and self-indulgence. Mortimer Adler (1952) described the tension as a "constant theme in the great poems," as "pivotal to the plot of most great love stories," and as an enduring "theme of tragedy" (p. 364).

Second, these ideologies carry implications for identity, self-regulation, and moral behavior. A principled ideology symbolizes personal *integrity*. The first dictionary meaning of integrity is the "steadfast adherence to a strict moral or ethical code," while other meanings reflect a state of being whole or undivided (*American Heritage Dictionary*, 2000). Integrity involves honesty, trustworthiness, fidelity in keeping one's word and obligations, and incorruptibility, or an unwillingness to violate principles, regardless of the temptations, costs, and preferences of others. When people endorse principled conduct and describe themselves as steadfastly

---

[1] Whether this ideology can be best described as expediency, which concerns self-serving means of dealing with problems, or pragmatism, which concerns practical, matter-of-fact ways of dealing with problems, will be discussed later in this chapter, after we have reviewed relevant data.

adhering to principles, they are asserting high integrity. They are making claims, to themselves and others, that describe important features of who they are, what they believe, how they should be treated by others, and how they should act in order to be the type of person they claim to be. In contrast, an expedient ideology permits people to compromise, allowing ethical flexibility and an identity that includes being somewhat principled, but also pragmatic.

THE COMMITMENT TO PRINCIPLES

The psychological impact of the commitment to principles should be similar to the impact of commitment to other attitudes or courses of action. Commitment crystallizes and strengthens corresponding attitudes, making them more accessible in memory, more resistant to subsequent change, and more likely to guide future behavior (Kiesler, 1971; Schlenker, Dlogolecki, & Doherty, 1994; Scholl, 1981; Tice, 1992).

Applied broadly, commitment reflects a pledging or binding of the self to something else, such as a goal (e.g., to earn a college degree), a set of ideas (e.g., a political policy, ethical position), another person (e.g., a marriage partner), or an organization (e.g., a social group or place of employment). Having a commitment means that people have selected a particular set of prescriptions that they agree to follow and that can be used to evaluate and sanction their conduct (see Schlenker, 1997; Schlenker, Britt, Pennington, Murphy, & Doherty, 1994). Concomitantly, they have downgraded alternative prescriptions that accomplish different goals, contain different paths, and offer different justifications for their conduct. Although commitments have associated advantages (the rewards to be gained via the commitment), they also have the disadvantages of limiting one's options, making it more difficult to explain one's prohibited conduct, and inviting greater condemnation for deviations.

Once people claim to "be" a particular type of person with specific beliefs, they have obligated themselves to behave commensurately with that identity and those beliefs. The socialization process emphasizes that people must be who they claim to be or risk serious interpersonal repercussions. After publicly taking a position, people even shift their attitudes to justify that position. Research indicates that publicly proclaiming oneself to have particular traits produces corresponding shifts in self-beliefs in the direction of the public commitment, but merely thinking about oneself privately as having those traits produces relatively little shift in self-beliefs (Schlenker, Dlugolecki, & Doherty, 1994; Tice, 1992).

In our view, moral behavior does not follow merely from the knowledge or understanding of moral prescriptions, or from the reasoning used to explain and justify moral decisions. Moral behavior follows from the psychological commitment to those prescriptions, which interlocks self and moral principles. The motivational force of moral convictions flows from this linkage. The spirit of the linkage is expressed in the words, "Here I stand, I can do no other," which were supposedly uttered by Martin Luther when he reaffirmed his convictions and refused to retract his condemnation of abuses of the Catholic Church (Diet of Worms, 1521). When there is a strong linkage between self and principles, represented by feelings of duty or personal obligation to follow the principles, the principles have been both internalized and appropriated as part of one's identity. They are no longer regarded as external rules that constrain behavior but as moral convictions that are "owned" by the self and that guide behavior. In their studies of people who served as moral exemplars, Colby and Damon (1992) observed that self-goals and moral goals become fused during the development of their moral identities, such that these moral exemplars regarded ethical conduct as expressing identity rather than following external rules.

Our analysis was developed in the context of research on identity, self-presentation, and how the self-system becomes engaged with (and disengaged from) various activities as a function of personal responsibility (Schlenker, 1997, 2003; Schlenker, Weigold, & Doherty, 1991; Schlenker, Pontari, & Christopher, 2001). Our conclusions are quite consistent, though, with approaches that emphasize the important self-regulatory role that moral identity plays in linking moral attitudes and behaviors (Aquino & Reed, 2002; Blasi, 1980, 1983, 2004, this volume; Colby & Damon, 1992; Hardy & Carlo, 2005; Lapsley & Lasky, 2001; Narvaez, Lapsley, Hagele, & Lasky, 2006; Peterson & Seligman, 2004). Beginning with Blasi's (1980, 1983) pioneering work, these approaches discuss the internalization of moral goals, codes, and traits into the self-concept, and they contrast with earlier models that focused on moral reasoning as a determinant of moral behavior (Kohlberg, 1969). Damon and Hart (1992) proposed that, "there are both theoretical and empirical reasons to believe that the centrality of morality to self may be the single most powerful determiner of concordance between moral judgment and conduct" (p. 455). Hardy and Carlo (2005) reviewed evidence suggesting that people who are highly committed to moral causes are more likely to describe themselves in moral terms, to regard moral values as more important to their sense of self, to have greater alignment between their personal goals and moral goals, and to engage in moral behavior. People who place greater importance on their moral identity as a central and defining feature of self seem to be more likely to access moral concepts in memory (Lapsley & Lasky, 2001; Narvaez et al., 2006); to mention moral themes when describing themselves (Aquino & Reed, 2002); and to engage in more volunteering to help needy others (Aquino & Reed, 2002).

How do people become committed to moral principles? Much of the literature on psychological commitment has focused on the impact of self-generated changes in beliefs, that is, changes produced by the individual's own actions. Research (Kiesler, 1971; Schlenker, Dlugolecki, & Doherty, 1994; Scholl, 1981) has shown that commitment to a course of action, which produces subsequent belief strengthening, is greater when (a) the action appears to have been done intentionally and with freedom of choice; (b) the action is prominent by virtue of being publicly known, vivid (memorable), and unambiguously interpretable; (c) the action and its consequences are more difficult to revoke or undo; (d) the actor has consistently acted in a similar fashion; and (e) the action is more important because of its consequences or the prescriptions that are involved. These factors all strengthen and make more conspicuous the linkage between the individual's identity and the type of action. Other possible sources for developing moral commitment include (a) enactive mastery (e.g., successfully engaging in moral behavior, with possible social reinforcement); (b) vicarious experience (e.g., observing and then modeling the actions of admired exemplars); (c) verbal persuasion (e.g., receiving consensual feedback indicating others believe one has moral qualities such as compassion; being persuaded that principled conduct is superior to alternatives); and (d) feedback from physiological and affective states (e.g., feeling happy after helpful behavior and guilty after transgressions) (Bandura, 1997). In any case, it is fair to conclude that we currently know relatively little about how people develop a moral identity (Hardy & Carlo, 2005; but see Thompson, this volume). We know more about the implications for behavior once a moral identity has developed.

INTEGRITY AS A VIRTUE

Integrity is universally admired because of its value to social relationships and, as many philosophers proclaim, its association with personal happiness. For groups to function effectively, their members must rely on one another to be honest, to keep their promises, to be the type of people they claim to be, and to follow their group's prescriptions for social well-being (Schlenker et al., 2001). Those with reputations for integrity are seen as reliable, valued group members. In contrast, behaviors associated with low integrity diminish trust, undermine reliability, delegitimize accomplishments (e.g., the cheater who wins), promote selfishness, and put others at risk. In addition, integrity is regarded as a virtue that is inherently valuable, regardless of its consequences (Peterson & Seligman, 2004; Schlenker, 2008).

Integrity-related constructs are among the most socially desirable of all traits. In Anderson's (1968) ratings of the desirability of 555 personality-trait words, the two highest rated were *sincere* and *honest*, with *loyal, truthful, trustworthy*, and *dependable* all in the top 10. Conversely, *liar* and *phony* are the two least desirable traits in the list, with *dishonest, untruthful, dishonorable*, and *deceitful* all in the bottom 10 and *untrustworthy* and *insincere* following closely behind in the bottom 11th and 13th places. Thus, integrity dominates the extremes, with fully 60% of the top and bottom 10 traits reflecting integrity and its opposite.

The social desirability of integrity is appreciated in everyday life. Most attributes, such as intelligence and physical attractiveness, are more relevant in some situations than others. Research shows that people want to act differently (Swann, Bosson, & Pelham, 2002), and actually do act differently, with different audiences (Leary, 1995; Schlenker, 1980, 2003), projecting qualities that help create desirable impressions given the circumstances. Yet integrity is uniquely important across situations as a lynchpin for social transactions. The self-presentational goal of appearing honest varies less across a variety of everyday interactions as compared to other interpersonal goals, including appearing likable, competent, friendly, intelligent, interesting, and attractive (Nezlek, Schütz, & Sellin, 2007). Further, people's evaluations of a group are more highly influenced by the group's morality than by its competence or sociability, traits which had been thought to be primary determinants of group attractiveness (Leach, Ellemers, & Barreto, 2007). Honesty can even affect perceptions of physical appearance. Targets who are described as honest rather than dishonest are later evaluated as more attractive and kind when judging their facial photographs, and this effect holds regardless of gender of the targets or evaluators (Paunonen, 2006). Honesty also has been suggested as a sixth factor of personality, distinct from the Big Five (Ashton, Lee, & Son, 2000). Integrity is thus a highly desirable quality. Yet, integrity can have a downside.

ATTRACTIONS OF EXPEDIENCY

Integrity can involve personal costs and sacrifices, as when standing up for convictions in the face of condemnation and threats. Just as situational pressures can override weaker attitudes, profitable opportunities and fears of disapproval can counteract personal principles, especially if those principles reflect weaker beliefs that are not anchored as a central component of identity. Surveys show that unprincipled behavior is more frequent today than in years past, and that people believe that lying, cheating, and infidelity are common and often justifiable (Kleiner & Lord, 1999). Research indicates that one of the better predictors of antisocial behavior (e.g., cheating, lying, stealing) is the tendency to rationalize or otherwise disengage psychologically from the behavior, and this includes the normative assertion that "everybody does it" (Bandura, Barbaranelli, Caprara, & Pastorelli, 1996; Bersoff, 1999; McCabe et al., 2001). Extreme expediency is illustrated by the Machiavellian approach of doing whatever is necessary to accomplish self-serving goals, while trying to foster the public appearance of one's integrity.

Expediency can also be packaged to create an image that appeals to many. There are popular images of attractive rogues who have the "street smarts" to accomplish their goals in unconventional, even morally questionable, ways. There is an admirable effectiveness associated with being savvy enough to bend, break, or ignore rules in ways that lead to victory. These images of crafty, wise, adaptable, and successful scoundrels are often contrasted with the images of a "goody two-shoes," who is nice but ineffective (reminiscent of the famous Leo Durocher quip, "Nice guys finish last"). Principles can also be seen as acting like straitjackets, limiting options and producing inflexibility and rigidity. Thus, not everyone sees the steadfast commitment to principles as unequivocally appealing. For many, being principled and being expedient are both desirable images, albeit in different ways.

ASSESSING PRINCIPLED VERSUS EXPEDIENT IDEOLOGIES

Given our conceptual analysis, we would expect to find systematic differences in the self-conceptions, values, social judgments, and interpersonal behaviors of people who endorse principled versus expedient ideologies, and these differences will have implications for psychological well-being and for relationships with others. To examine these relationships, an 18-item measure, called the Integrity Scale, was developed to assess the strength of people's claims of being principled as compared to expedient (Schlenker, 2008; Schlenker, Weigold, & Schlenker, 2008). Items assess the inherent value of principled conduct (e.g., "Integrity is more important than financial gain"), the steadfast commitment to principles despite temptations or costs (e.g., "The true test of character is a willingness to stand by one's principles, no matter what price one has to pay"), and the unwillingness to rationalize unprincipled behavior (e.g., "Some actions are wrong no matter what the consequences or justification"). The scale has good internal-consistency reliability (alphas ranged from .84 to .90 across 6 samples) and test-retest reliability (r = .82 and .72 over 2- to 5-week and 5- to 12-week periods). It appears to contain a single latent integrity dimension, reflecting the principled-expedient continuum, along with measurement effects reflecting positively and negatively (reverse-scored) worded items, as determined by confirmatory factor analysis (Johnson & Schlenker, 2009). The distribution is roughly normal, with an average score above the scale neutral point, indicating some agreement with principled statements. Only 8.4% of respondents fell below the neutral point to show average disagreement with principled statements, supporting the view that being principled is a valued quality and variation lies primarily in terms of the extent of one's commitment.

Scale scores display relatively little social desirability bias (rs ranged from .05 to .17 in 5 samples), as attempts were made to select items that balanced the advantages and disadvantages of principled and expedient conduct (Schlenker, 2008). Although social desirability bias probably can never be eliminated in self-report measures dealing with integrity, the small amount of shared variance (usually less than 3%) suggests this attempt to minimize such bias was at least somewhat successful. Integrity scores also are unrelated to measures of dogmatism and the need for closure, indicating that scores do not represent cognitive inflexibility, rigidity, or a closed belief system (Schlenker, 2008).

It is worth keeping in mind that the scale assesses people's integrity-related claims, not "true" integrity in a quintessential sense. When we talk about those with high or low integrity, we are describing scale scores and not describing intrinsic character. It can be empirically determined how much professed commitment corresponds with conduct.

INTEGRITY, MORAL IDENTITY, AND RELATIONSHIPS

Identity is a theory of self that is formed and maintained through actual or imagined interpersonal agreement about what the self is like (see Schlenker, 1985). For those who are committed to principles, integrity should be a central, important component of their identities. If our analysis is correct, they should think of themselves as having integrity, project integrity in their relationships with others, and prefer to receive feedback from others that affirms their high integrity. Indeed, they should be dissatisfied if they discover they are regarded as less than principled. In contrast, those who are less committed to principles should place less importance on moral aspects of their identities and show greater appreciation for expedient qualities, admiring success, savvy, adaptability, and getting things done, even if ethical shortcuts are taken. As such, those lower in integrity will be less likely to be seen by those who know them as being a moral person, and show less of a preference for evaluative feedback, indicating that others see them as principled or expedient (provided that expedient qualities are given a positive spin).

Research supports these hypotheses (Miller & Schlenker, 2009). People with higher as compared to lower integrity scores attach greater importance to being principled as part of their self-concepts and describe themselves as behaving more consistently with their principles, both absolutely and relative to typical others. They also have higher standards for moral conduct than those lower in integrity, reporting that both the average person and a highly principled person evidence greater integrity in their lives. If asked to evaluate prototypic others, they more strongly prefer principled characters to expedient ones. In contrast, expedient people display mixed evaluations of the prototypes, in that they see the principled character as more moral but the expedient character as more successful, happy, well adjusted, and wise.

Importantly, their friends accurately identified people's levels of integrity. Miller and Schlenker (2009, Study 3) asked pairs of friends to rate themselves, their friend, and their relationship. They found significant correlations between respondents' own integrity scores and their friends' appraisals of their integrity. Thus, integrity is not simply in the mind of the actor but comes across to friends in everyday behavior. In addition, those with higher integrity paired up with friends who were themselves more principled (a matching effect), and were more satisfied with friends who saw them as more principled. In contrast, those with lower integrity paired up with more expedient friends and were equally satisfied in their relationships, regardless of whether their friends saw them as principled or expedient.

In a laboratory experiment (Miller & Schlenker, 2009), people with higher integrity scores more strongly preferred evaluators who regarded them as principled rather than expedient. They regarded an evaluator who supposedly thought they were principled as a better judge of character and as more likable, and selected that evaluator as a partner for an upcoming task. In contrast, those with lower integrity scores saw merit in being regarded as either principled or expedient, judging both evaluators as equally capable and likable, and selecting each as a task partner with comparable frequency.

The results across the studies indicate that the commitment to principles is an important component of the identities of those with high integrity. It is firmly rooted in the self-concept and can influence interpersonal relationships by guiding how people perceive and respond to feedback, evaluate others, and select task partners and friends.

INTEGRITY, ADMIRATION, AND SOCIAL JUDGMENT

People's ethical ideologies come into play when thinking about and judging others. Those with high integrity should have a more stringent set of standards for right and wrong, chronically access this information in memory and use it in their decision making, and believe that these standards are binding, so that excuses and justifications become unacceptable ways to avoid the negative repercussions of transgressions. As such, we would expect that those higher in integrity would more strongly admire others who make an ethical choice over an unethical one, and this preference would be less influenced by the consequences of the decision (e.g., whether the decision produced success or failure).

Integrity and Social Judgment. To test these ideas, Schlenker et al. (2008) had participants evaluate central characters who behaved ethically or unethically while trying to advance their careers. More principled people strongly preferred characters who made ethical career decisions over those who made unethical ones, and this preference was largely unaffected by whether the character was successful or unsuccessful in the career moves. In contrast, more expedient people displayed a weaker preference for the ethical character and also preferred the successful to the unsuccessful character, thereby allowing the consequences of the character's behavior to influence their judgments. Once again, expedient people saw merit in the successful scoundrel.

In two other studies (Schlenker, Miller, & Johnson, 2009), participants read about a character who was part of a group's success or failure, and who later claimed either high or low personal responsibility for the performance. Overall, participants preferred successful targets who modestly minimized their responsibility, and unsuccessful targets who took responsibility over their egoistic (successful, responsibility-claiming) and excuse-making (unsuccessful, responsibility-denying) counterparts. As expected, this tendency was significantly more pronounced for participants who were higher rather than lower in integrity. A second study found the same patterns when a central character worked alone, so that claims of responsibility did not blame others or steal glory from them. People generally prefer humble winners and gracious losers, and this tendency is significantly stronger for those higher in integrity.

Integrity and Heroes. In another study, Schlenker et al. (2008) asked participants to list their heroes and describe the qualities that made those heroes special. Those higher in integrity spontaneously described their heroes as more principled, honest, benevolent (caring, kind, compassionate, as opposed to self-absorbed or egoistic), and spiritual. Later, when asked to rate their primary hero on closed-ended scales, they displayed the same patterns. Those higher in integrity rated their primary hero as more principled and honest, authentic (true to self), spiritual (as compared to materialistic), and benevolent (as compared to selfish and egotistical). On qualities such as likableness and intelligence, which could be associated with any hero regardless of morality, there were no integrity differences.

Ethical ideologies and heroes go hand in hand, and probably influence each other reciprocally. The heroes people admire can affect their own ethical ideologies, as people identify with their heroes' perceived personal qualities and values, and try to emulate them. And, once ethical ideologies are formed, people rely on their principles to think about and evaluate others, including the important figures in their lives. David Wong (this volume) similarly argues that character ideals have a normative impact that influences self-regulation.

Everyday Conceptualizations of Morality. The qualities that people of high integrity used to describe their heroes are precisely the types of qualities that are associated with people's everyday conceptions of moral exemplars. Research indicates that the attributes associated with a prototypical moral person or someone of good character, at least in Western society, include being seen as *principled* (concerned about doing right, having clear values and convictions), *honest* (truthful, genuine, sincere, trustworthy), *benevolent* (caring about others, respectful, kind, compassionate, cooperative, unselfish), and *dependable* (reliable, responsible, hardworking) (Aquino & Reed, 2002; Lapsley & Lasky, 2001; Walker & Hennig, 2004; Walker & Pitts, 1998). Many moral exemplars are also seen as being highly *religious* or *spiritual* (Aquino & Reed, 2002; Walker & Pitts, 1998). Although this is not to say that all moral exemplars have these qualities – and different types of exemplars can be distinguished (Walker & Hennig, 2004) – these qualities consistently emerge as representing a collectively shared, core notion of morality. We next turn to research indicating that these qualities are also those possessed by people who actually score higher in integrity.

INTEGRITY, PERSONALITY, AND WELL-BEING

Philosophers and psychologists have regarded integrity as a character strength and virtue that contributes to mental health, psychological well-being, and interpersonal effectiveness (Mowrer, 1976; Peterson & Seligman, 2004). In four samples, Schlenker (2008) examined personality correlates of integrity and found empirical support for the association between integrity and admirable personality qualities. The major findings can be summarized as follows.

Integrity is associated with a positive outlook toward life. When people are committed to ethical principles, they have a set of goals, rules, and standards about right and wrong, and these give directions for how they should behave and why they should do so. As such, it was expected and found that higher integrity was associated with a greater sense of purpose and meaning in life, with less alienation and anomie. These results are consistent with Colby and Damon's (1992) conclusions, based on interviews with moral exemplars, that in the face of challenges and problems the exemplars exhibited positivity and principled certainty – that is, certainty in the rightness of their principles and actions.

Integrity is associated with more beneficial beliefs about oneself. Consistent with the idea that principled conduct is associated with mental health and self-acceptance, integrity scores are positively related to self-esteem and internal control, but negatively related to narcissism. Further, principled conduct involves honor, and not merely social acceptance, so it was expected and found that higher integrity scores would be more strongly related to the preference to be respected rather than liked by others. Thus, a more principled ideology is related to greater self-worth, internal control, and desire for respect, and less self-absorption and grandiosity.

Integrity is associated with greater authenticity and a stronger inner orientation. One of the everyday meanings of integrity is being whole and undivided, which reflects being authentic or true to self. High authenticity is exhibited through a stronger integration of one's social roles into one's self-concept, consistency between internal states and actions, and consistency in behavior across audiences and situations. Schlenker (2008) found support for each of these relationships. Higher integrity was related to greater authenticity, greater role satisfaction, lower role strain, greater private self-consciousness, stronger preference for consistency, greater importance of personal (inner) identity, and lower self-monitoring. Integrity scores were unrelated to measures of outer orientation (public self-consciousness, importance of social identity) and social trepidations (e.g., social anxiety, fear of negative evaluation).

Our research also indicates that principled people are more likely than expedient ones to behave consistently with their principles in the face of social influence to do otherwise (Schlenker, Johnson, & Miller, 2009). In a decision-making experiment, expedient participants were more quickly and easily convinced by others to make what most consider an unethical decision.

Integrity is associated with greater spirituality and less materialism. There is no inherent reason why principled ideologies must be rooted in religion, but there does seem to be an association in most societies between a moral prototype and spirituality or religiosity, as well as a disassociation between morals and materialism. In discussing integrity, Carter (1996) noted that themes of devotion to an undivided life, based on principles of right and wrong, are found in Christianity, Judaism, and Islam, along with virtually all other religions. Moral exemplars, selected for study because of their national reputation or sustained contributions to organizations, have been found to exhibit faith (Colby & Damon, 1992) and to be more advanced in their religious beliefs (Matsuba & Walker, 2004).

Consistent with these ideas, integrity scores are positively related to intrinsic religiosity (believing in the inherent truth and value of religious tenets), and negatively related to both extrinsic religiosity (believing because of the personal and social rewards that religion can bring) and materialism (Schlenker, 2008). Similarly, integrity scores are positively related to the value that is attached to "salvation," and negatively related to the value attached to "a comfortable life" (Schlenker et al., 2008).

INTEGRITY AND PROSOCIAL BEHAVIOR

It was hypothesized that integrity would be positively related to prosocial orientations and behaviors. To test these hypotheses, Schlenker (2008) included measures of orientations toward others, as well as self-reports of a variety of helping and volunteering activities.

Integrity is associated with more positive orientations toward others. Moral philosophy has emphasized the theme of benevolence toward others, characterized by caring, respect, empathy, and compassion. In his doctrine of virtues, Kant argued that moral duties entail respect for others, and believed that it is a categorical imperative to treat others as ends in themselves, never as means to ends. Graham (2001) argued that integrity requires a "genuine regard" for the worth and well-being of others (p. 247). In these and many other cases, greater commitment to moral principles suggests greater caring and concern for others.

The theme of benevolence is also found in lay descriptions of moral prototypes and people of good character, which include qualities such as being kind, compassionate, respectful, considerate, generous, helpful, and supportive (Aquino & Reed, 2002; Lapsley & Lasky, 2001). It is also found in studies of the behavior of moral exemplars who display caring, compassion, agreeableness, and sustained helpfulness toward others (Colby & Damon, 1992; Hart & Fegley, 1995; Matsuba & Walker, 2004).

Consistent with this theme, Schlenker (2008) found that integrity scores are positively related to empathy, agreeableness (on the Big Five), and trust, but negatively related to cynicism and Machiavellianism (which is itself related to antisocial behavior, treating other people as means to one's own ends, and psychopathy). Of course, people who endorse an expedient ideology may be effective in the short run in accomplishing limited objectives. However, in the long run, expedient ideologies are associated with cynicism, an exploitative orientation toward others, and a lower sense of purpose and self-worth.

Integrity is related to more helping and volunteering. The benevolent orientation associated with high integrity also extends to helping and volunteering activities. Moral exemplars are distinguished in part by help to others (Colby & Damon, 1992; Hart & Fegley, 1995; Matsuba & Walker, 2004), and people for whom moral identity is a more important self-component are more likely to volunteer to help others (Aquino & Reed, 2002). Schlenker (2008) asked participants to report their frequencies of various types of helping and volunteering, and also had them complete an inventory that assessed various functions or purposes of volunteering. Integrity was positively related to overall helping and volunteering. Integrity also displayed predictive specificity in being related only to certain types of prosocial behavior. Integrity was positively related to helping for principled reasons (those focused on helping as a matter of principle or the right thing to do) and altruistic reasons (those focused on the welfare of others), and was negatively related to helping for egoistic reasons (to gain personal rewards or avoid costs). Similarly, integrity was positively related to both the importance and frequency of volunteering for value expressive reasons (because it typifies important values) and understanding (because it facilitates understanding of the world), and was unrelated to helping for more egoistic reasons – such as to facilitate one's career, gain social recognition or rewards, or to feel better about oneself. These relationships hold even after controlling for social desirability bias. The patterns indicate that people who are higher in integrity are more likely to help and volunteer for more noble reasons involving matters of principle, values, and concerns for others.

Western intellectual and religious traditions affirm a relationship between moral principles and concerns for other people (e.g., caring, empathy, helping). However, definitions of which "other people" are deemed worthy of moral concern (e.g., all of humanity or only ingroup members, such as those who share certain tribal or religious similarities?), and the type of treatment considered moral (e.g., does respecting others permit human sacrifice?), vary considerably across time and cultures, and there are individual differences within cultures. Different standards of morality are applied to ingroup and outgroup members, and ingroup morality often encourages violence toward outgroups (Cohen, Montoya, & Insko, 2006). Research indicates that higher integrity is related to greater benevolence and helping overall. We expect that it is also positively related to the size of the circle of people who are deemed worthy of inherent respect and benevolence. Speculating, the difference between principled people who are regarded as moral exemplars versus fanatics who will kill innocents in the service of their "cause" may be traced to the extent to which their moral principles include a wider circle of benevolence. Both the moral person and the fanatic may express high commitment, but those higher in integrity may have a higher overall level of benevolence and a larger circle of others who are included as part of the group that merits benevolence.

INTEGRITY AND ANTISOCIAL BEHAVIOR

Integrity should be highly predictive of antisocial tendencies and behaviors. To examine these relationships, Schlenker (2008) included measures of moral disengagement, rationalization, and self-reports of a wide range of antisocial activities.

Integrity is associated with less rationalization of illegal and immoral behavior. People who more readily rationalize or otherwise psychologically disengage from antisocial behavior are more likely to act in antisocial ways (Bandura et al., 1996; Bersoff, 1999; Haines, Diekoff, LaBeff, & Clark, 1986; Harding & Phillips, 1986; McCabe, 1992). When people can justify or excuse antisocial behavior, they become less concerned about moral condemnation, both from others and from themselves (Schlenker et al., 2001). Consistent with our conceptualization of the commitment to principles, higher integrity has been found to be related to lower scores on measures of (a) moral disengagement, which assesses people's tendencies to distance themselves from morally objectionable acts by constructing rationalizations; and (b) moral justification, which assesses the ease of justifying illegal and immoral behaviors (Schlenker, 2008).

Integrity is associated with fewer antisocial activities. For those higher in integrity, moral prescriptions create a stronger sense of personal responsibility for doing the right thing, with less tolerance of self-serving rationalizations of transgressions. In contrast, those lower in integrity should think less about the moral implications of their conduct, perceive greater flexibility in their moral options, and be more willing to rationalize intended or past moral violations. To examine the relationship between integrity and antisocial activities, Schlenker (2008) asked participants to complete an antisocial behavior survey. Integrity was negatively related to reports of telling self-serving lies, cheating in high school and college, stealing, breaking promises, infidelity, and alcohol and drug use. These relationships remained equally strong even after controlling for social desirability bias.

Machiavellianism was also assessed in the study, and found to be positively related to the same antisocial behaviors. However, when integrity, Machiavellianism, and social desirability were entered into regressions as simultaneous predictors, integrity still predicted all of these antisocial activities, whereas Machiavellianism no longer significantly predicted any of them. Machiavellianism apparently predicts a wide range of antisocial behaviors in part because it reflects an expedient ethical ideology and the willingness to admit to socially undesirable behavior.

Similarly, the relationships between integrity and antisocial behavior remained, even when the tendency to rationalize, as assessed by measures of moral disengagement and moral justification, was controlled. Although an unwillingness to rationalize transgressions is an important component of integrity, other aspects of the commitment to principles, such as self-definition as a principled person, the elevation of moral principles above other values, and the resistance to temptation, play significant roles in predicting antisocial conduct.

This research suggests that, although saintly behavior is rare, a principled ideology equips people with qualities that guide them toward beneficial conduct and away from detrimental conduct. Just as stronger attitudes are more likely to predict behavior, greater integrity is more likely to predict behavior that reflects moral principles.

INTEGRITY, ACCOUNTABILITY, AND PERSONAL RESPONSIBILITY

Why does the commitment to moral principles engage the self-system, guide conduct along clearer paths, deter wrong turns and detours, reduce the tendency to disengage via rationalization, and make people feel responsible for what they do? Some theorists answer by focusing on intrapsychic motivations, such as cognitive consistency. Our answer starts with interpersonal processes and focuses on the nature of accountability, because to be responsible means to be accountable, or answerable, for one's conduct.

To live and work in social groups requires that conduct be regulated to permit coordination and mutual benefit. The group's welfare depends on members being able to count on one another to do what they say they will do, to be what they claim to be, and to follow the group's prescriptions. Accountability is a mechanism of social control to enforce the prescriptions. Group members watch and judge one another, administering sanctions for violations and rewards for laudatory conduct, thereby promoting adherence and deterring violations of prescriptions (for further discussion, see Schlenker, 1997; Schlenker et al., 1991).

Socialization reflects in part the internalization of accountability, in which people become both actors and judging observers of their own conduct. People learn the prescriptions and then monitor and control their own behavior accordingly, observing, judging, and sanctioning (self-reward and self-punishment) their conduct in light of the prescriptions. When appraising possible courses of action, people take into consideration how their actions will look in relation to the prescriptions, and how those actions might be explained if questions or indictments arise. Courses of action can then be selected accordingly. As C. W. Mills (1940, p. 906) observed, "Often anticipations of acceptable justifications will control conduct ('If I did this, what could I say? What would they say?'). Decisions may be wholly or in part, delimited by answers to such queries." As part of this process, people acquire internal "problem detectors," such as social anxiety, guilt, and embarrassment, which warn of possible problems; and internal "accomplishment signals," such as pride, that express and reward laudatory behavior.

Ultimately, people become accountable to themselves as well as to others. Internalizing prescriptions means not only learning them and knowing how others will respond to violations, but also feeling obligated for behaving consistently with them and responsible for relevant conduct. When moral principles are internalized, the nexus of control shifts from simply a concern with being accountable to others (social responsibility and control), to being accountable to oneself as the primary audience for one's actions (personal responsibility and control). In our view, the pressure to be consistent flows from personal and social accountability.

The dynamics of self-regulation in the moral arena differ for those with different ethical ideologies. Those with a principled ideology have internalized moral prescriptions. They believe the principles are inherently right, a principled ideology is an important component of their identities, and they are responsible for following those principles with no equivocation and excuses. In contrast, those with expedient ideologies usually know the appropriate principles, but they have not made a personal commitment to them that obliges them to behave consistently and take responsibility for relevant conduct. Expedient ideologies are analogous to having a lenient and supportive internal judge who is usually willing to accept one's excuses and minimize one's responsibility for violations. Expedient individuals will follow prescriptions when social controls are salient (e.g., others are watching and can sanction violations), but cannot be counted on otherwise.

THE TRIANGLE MODEL OF RESPONSIBILITY

This view of accountability and commitment can be placed in the context of the triangle model of responsibility, which was developed to explain (a) when and why the self-system becomes engaged by tasks, and (b) how it can be disengaged from undesired events through a variety of strategic activities and accounts, such as excuses and justifications (Schlenker, 1997; Schlenker, Britt, et al., 1994; Schlenker et al., 1991, 2001). According to the model, the self-system becomes engaged when (a) a clear, well-defined set of prescriptions is seen as applicable in the situation (*prescription clarity*); (b) the actor is perceived to be bound by the prescriptions (*personal obligation, duty, or commitment*); and (c) the actor appears to have control over relevant events (*personal control*). (When visualized as connections between prescriptions, actor, and event, these three antecedents of responsibility form a triangle, hence the name of the model.) These are the conditions under which people are regarded as more personally responsible, by others and by themselves.

Research confirms that people are judged to be more responsible by others when prescriptions clearly indicate what should be done in the situation, when they are seen as obligated to follow the prescriptions, and they appear to have personal control over the outcomes (Christopher & Schlenker, 2001; Schlenker, Britt, et al., 1994; Tyler & Feldman, 2007). People also feel more personally responsible under these conditions. People's beliefs about prescription clarity, personal obligation, and personal control are directly related to their psychological engagement and behavioral performance in a variety of settings, including academic achievement (Schlenker, 1997), pharmaceutical care by professional pharmacists (Planas et al., 2005), voting behavior and involvement in the 2000 presidential election (Britt, 2003), and responsibility by soldiers on peacekeeping missions (Britt, 1999). For example, college students receive higher grades at the end of a semester if, earlier in the year, they expressed greater engagement in academics by stating that the prescriptions for academic success are clearer, they have greater control over the grades they receive, and they feel an obligation to be academically successful (Schlenker, 1997).

Conversely, when people fail to live up to prescribed levels of performance or commit transgressions, they attempt to disengage the self by weakening these linkages (Schlenker, 1997; Schlenker et al., 1991, 2001). The linkages can be weakened via excuses, which try to reduce the strengths of the linkages and thereby reduce responsibility. People can try to reduce prescription clarity (e.g., claiming moral principles were unclear or conflicting), personal control (e.g., claiming that external events had a large impact on the outcome), and personal obligation (e.g., claiming that one is not always obligated to follow the prescription). People can also try to rationalize transgressions via justifications. Justifications attempt to change assessments of the prescriptions (e.g., other prescriptions are also important), the event (e.g., not much harm was done), or aspects of the actor's identity (e.g., given who the actor claims to be, a rule violation is not important). Space does not permit a fuller discussion of disengagement (see Schlenker et al., 1991, 2001).[2] However, our research clearly indicates that moral disengagement is an option that seems to be more cognitively available and likely to be used by those with expedient rather than principled ideologies.

---

[2] The work of Bandura and colleagues (e.g., Bandura et al., 1996) on moral disengagement identifies eight mechanisms that permit people to protect themselves from the implications of detrimental conduct and reduce self-sanctioning. These mechanisms all reflect subcategories of excuses and justifications, in that they involve reducing personal responsibility (excuses) or transforming or minimizing the negativity of conduct and its consequences (justifications). Bandura's approach focuses on actions that harm others, whereas Schlenker's approach deals more broadly with any failure to fulfill prescriptions, regardless of the moral implications (e.g., failures in achievement situations, violations of social norms). Despite differences in terminology and overarching theoretical positions (Bandura's ideas are rooted in social learning theory; Schlenker's ideas are rooted in a transactional perspective), the two approaches share an interest in how people's accounts for undesirable conduct try to reduce negative repercussions.

The research we reviewed suggests that higher integrity increases the strengths of all three linkages in moral situations. A strengthening of the personal obligation or commitment link is obvious, in that, by definition, those with higher integrity are claiming a greater commitment to moral principles. In addition, those with higher integrity express greater purpose in life, less normlessness, and less alienation (Schlenker, 2008), suggesting that moral prescriptions are clearer for them than for those with lower integrity. Finally, those with higher integrity express greater internal control (Schlenker, 2008), suggesting that they have higher feelings of personal control overall, and probably when they confront moral situations. Although the triangle model of responsibility seems to have the potential for increasing an understanding of self-engagement and moral conduct, research on the topic is just beginning and more data are needed.

PRAGMATISM, EXPEDIENCY, AND PRINCIPLED COMMITMENT

A reasonable question is whether principled commitment often produces intransigence, which disrupts group functioning and generates detrimental effects, not beneficial social change. An example is an ideologue whose unwillingness to compromise blocks democratic solutions. Conversely, does the flexibility of expediency often serve beneficial objectives? An example may be a politician whose willingness to compromise makes democratic governance possible.

Based on the results of our research, these examples reflect, at best, exceptions to the general patterns. Those who are on the principled end of the distribution seem to be the more socially responsible, in that they are more agreeable, empathic, trusting, spiritual, and helpful. They also are no more or less closed-minded and dogmatic, so they do not seem to be inflexible as a general orientation. The combination of commitment to moral principles, respect and concern for others, and lack of closed-mindedness would usually seem to promote working effectively with others. In contrast, those who are on the expedient end of the distribution are more self-absorbed, in that they are more narcissistic, materialistic, cynical, Machiavellian, likely to rationalize and morally disengage, and likely to commit antisocial acts like lying, stealing, and cheating. At least for college students in the Southeastern United States, from whom our data were gathered, the commitment to moral principles seems to have far reaching social (as well as personal) advantages.

Speculating, the qualities associated with high versus low integrity suggest that the former are more socially responsible group members and are willing to work with others to accommodate different positions *provided* those positions do not violate their own core moral principles. They may stand firm on core ethical positions (democracy should not involve compromise on any and all principles), but show flexibility in most matters, including ways to accomplish their moral objectives. Going further, it may be that, when those high and low in integrity are willing to compromise in groups, it is for different reasons. Those high in integrity may compromise in the interests of the group, whereas those low in integrity may compromise to promote their own personal agendas. Research on these topics is needed.

Both pragmatism and expediency have similarities in that they deal with ways of working out solutions to problems. However, the empirical patterns suggest that the end of the continuum opposite principled commitment better reflects the concept of expediency, which concerns self-serving means of dealing with problems, than pragmatism, which concerns practical, matter-of-fact ways of dealing with problems.

CONCLUSIONS

Integrity is a personally and socially important character strength and virtue. The present theory holds that integrity, defined as the strength of personal commitment to a principled ethical ideology, determines the strength of the relationship between ethical beliefs and behavior. Personal commitment links the self-system to the ethical principles, producing greater accessibility of relevant moral constructs in memory, a sense of obligation to perform consistently with those principles, a sense of responsibility for the consequences of relevant actions, and less rationalization of deviations from principles. Lower integrity reflects an expedient ideology in which commitment to principles is lower, self-absorption is greater, and rationalization of violations is easier.

Popular author John D. MacDonald said, "Integrity is not a conditional word. It doesn't blow in the wind or change with the weather. It is your image of yourself, and if you look in there and see a man who won't cheat, then you know he never will" (in *The Turquoise Lament*). Although "never" may overstate the case, research supports the proposition that integrity plays an important role in self-regulation. Different ethical ideologies take people down different moral paths. Higher integrity equips people with personal qualities that are associated with psychological well-being and interpersonal success, guides them down prosocial paths, and deters them from antisocial ones.

REFERENCES

Adler, M. J. (Ed.) (1952). *The great ideas: A synopticon of great books of the Western world*. Chicago: Encyclopaedia Britannica.

American Heritage Dictionary (4th ed.) (2000). Boston: Houghton Mifflin.

Anderson, N. (1968). Likableness ratings of 555 personality-trait words. *Journal of Personality and Social Psychology, 9*, 272–279.

Aquino, K. F., & Reed, A., II (2002). The self-importance of moral identity. *Journal of Personality and Social Psychology, 83*, 1423–1440.

Ashton, M. C., Lee, K., & Son, C. (2000). Honesty as the sixth factor of personality: Correlations with Machiavellianism, primary psychopathy, and social adroitness. *European Journal of Personality, 14*, 359–368.

Bandura, A. (1997). *Self-efficacy: The exercise of control*. New York: W. H. Freeman.

Bandura, A., Barbaranelli, C., Caprara, G. V., & Pastorelli, C. (1996). Mechanisms of moral disengagement in the exercise of moral agency. *Journal of Personality and Social Psychology, 71*, 364–374.

Bersoff, D. M. (1999). Why good people sometimes do bad things: Motivated reasoning and unethical behavior. *Personality & Social Psychology Bulletin, 25*, 28–39.

Blasi, A. (1980). Building moral conviction and moral action: A critical review of the literature. *Psychological Bulletin, 88*, 1–45.

(1983). Moral cognition and moral action: A theoretic perspective. *Developmental Review, 3*, 179–210.

(2004). Moral functioning: Moral understanding and personality. In D. K. Lapsley, & D. Narvaez (Eds.), *Moral development, self, and identity* (pp. 335–347). Mahwah, NJ: Lawrence Erlbaum Associates Publisher.

Britt, T. W. (1999). Engaging the self in the field: Testing the triangle model of responsibility. *Personality and Social Psychology Bulletin, 25*, 696–706.

(2003). Self-engagement: Voting in the 2000 U.S. presidential election. *Motivation and Emotion, 27*, 339–358.

Callahan, D. (2004). *The cheating culture*. Orlando, FL: Harcourt.

Carter, S. L. (1996). *Integrity*. New York: Basic Books.

Christopher, A. N., & Schlenker, B. R. (2005). The Protestant work ethic and the assignment of responsibility: Applications of the triangle model. *Journal of Applied Social Psychology, 35*, 1502–1518.

Cohen, T. R., Montoya, R. M., & Insko, C. A. (2006). Group morality and intergroup relations: Cross-cultural and experimental evidence. *Personality and Social Psychology Bulletin, 32*, 1559–1572.

Colby, A., & Damon, W. (1992). *Some do care: Contemporary lives of moral commitment*. New York: Free Press.

Damon, W., & Hart, D. (1992). Self-understanding and its role in social and moral development. In M. Bornstein & M. E. Lamb (Eds.), *Developmental psychology: An advanced textbook* (3rd ed., pp. 421–464). Hillsdale, NJ: Erlbaum.

Graham, J. L. (2001). Does integrity require moral goodness? *Ratio, 14*, 234–251.

Haines, V. J., Diekoff, G. M., LaBeff, E. E., & Clark, R. E. (1986). College cheating: Immaturity, lack of commitment, and the neutralizing attitude. *Research in Higher Education, 25*, 342–354.

Hardy, S. A., & Carlo, G. (2005). Identity as a source of moral motivation. *Human Development, 48*, 232–256.

Harding, S., & Phillips, D. (1986). *Contrasting values in Western Europe: Unity, diversity and change.* London: Macmillan.

Hart, D., & Fegley, S. (1995). Prosocial behavior and caring in adolescence: Relations to moral judgment and self-understanding. *Child Development, 66*, 1346–1359.

Johnson, R. M., & Schlenker, B. R. (2009). *Assessing the commitment to ethical principles: Psychometric properties of the integrity scale.* Manuscript under review, University of Florida.

Kiesler, C. A. (1971). *The psychology of commitment.* New York: Academic Press.

Kleiner, C., & Lord, M. (1999, Nov. 22). The cheating game: 'Everyone's doing it,' from grade school to graduate school. *US News & World Report.* Retrieved from http://www.usnews.com/usnews/culture/articles/991122/archive_002427.htm.

Kohlberg, L. (1969). Stage and sequence: The cognitive-developmental approach to socialization. In D. A. Goslin (Ed.), *Handbook of socialization theory and research* (pp. 347–480). Chicago: Rand McNally.

Lapsley, D. K., & Lasky, B. (2001). Prototypic moral character. *Identity, 1*, 345–363.

Leach, C. W., Ellemers, N., & Barreto, M. (2007). Group virtue: The importance of morality (vs. competence and sociability) in the positive evaluation of ingroups. *Journal of Personality and Social Psychology, 93*, 234–249.

Leary, M. R. (1995). *Self-presentation: Impression management and interpersonal behavior.* Madison, WI: Brown & Benchmark Publishers.

Matsuba, M. K., & Walker, L. J. (2004). Extraordinary moral commitment: Young adults involved in social organizations. *Journal of Personality, 72*, 413–436.

McCabe, D. L. (1992). The influence of situational ethics on cheating among college students. *Sociological Inquiry, 62*, 365–374.

McCabe, D. L., Treviño, L. K., & Butterfield, K. D. (2001). Cheating in academic institutions: A decade of research. *Ethics & Behavior, 11*, 219–232.

Miller, M. L., & Schlenker, B. R. (2009). *Integrity and identity: Triangulating private and public perceptions of moral identity.* Manuscript under review, University of Florida.

Mills, C. W. (1940). Situated actions and vocabularies of motives. *American Sociological Review, 5*, 904–913.

Mowrer, O. H. (1976). Changing conceptions of neurosis and the small-groups movement. *Education, 97*, 24–62.

Narvaez, D., Lapsley, D. K., Hagele, S., & Lasky, B. (2006). Moral chronicity and social information processing: Tests of a social cognitive approach to the moral personality. *Journal of Research in Personality, 40*, 966–985.

Nezlek, J. B., Schütz, A., & Sellin, I. (2007). Self-presentational success in daily social interaction. *Self and Identity, 6*, 361–379.

Paunonen, S. V. (2006). You are honest, therefore I like you and find you attractive. *Journal of Research in Personality, 40,* 237–249.

Peterson, C., & Seligman, M. E. P. (2004). *Character strengths and virtues: A handbook and classification.* New York: Oxford University Press.

Planas, L. G., Kimberlin, C. L., Segal, R., Hepler, C. D., Brushwood, D. B., & Schlenker, B. R. (2005). A pharmacist model of perceived responsibility for drug therapy outcomes. *Social Science & Medicine, 60,* 2393–2403.

Schlenker, B. R. (1980). *Impression management: The self-concept, social identity, and interpersonal relations.* Monterey, CA: Brooks/Cole.

— (1985). Identity and self-identification. In B. R. Schlenker (Ed.), *The self and social life* (pp. 65–99). New York: McGraw-Hill.

— (1997). Personal responsibility: Applications of the triangle model. In L. L. Cummings & B. Staw (Eds.), *Research in Organizational Behavior* (Vol. 19, pp. 241–301). Greenwich, CT: JAI Press.

— (2003). Self-presentation. In M. R. Leary and J. P. Tangney (Eds.), *Handbook of self and identity* (pp. 492–518). New York: Guilford.

— (2008). Integrity and character: Implications of principled and expedient ethical ideologies. *Journal of Social and Clinical Psychology, 27,* 1078–1125.

Schlenker, B. R., Britt, T. W., Pennington, J. W., Murphy, R., & Doherty, K. J. (1994). The triangle model of responsibility. *Psychological Review, 101,* 632–652.

Schlenker, B. R., Dlugolecki, D. W., & Doherty, K. J. (1994). The impact of self-presentations on self-appraisals and behaviors: The power of public commitment. *Personality and Social Psychology Bulletin, 20,* 20–33.

Schlenker, B. R., Johnson, R. M., & Miller, M. L. (2009). *Integrity and social influence: Balancing public protection and corporate profit.* Manuscript submitted for publication, University of Florida.

Schlenker, B. R., Miller, M. L., & Johnson, R. J. (2009). *Integrity, responsibility, and excuse-making: Impressions of humble winners, gracious losers, and their egoistic counterparts.* Manuscript in preparation, University of Florida.

Schlenker, B. R., Pontari, B. A., & Christopher, A. N. (2001). Excuses and character: Personal and social implications of excuses. *Personality and Social Psychology Review, 5,* 15–32.

Schlenker, B. R., Weigold, M. F., & Doherty, K. (1991). Coping with accountability: Self-identification and evaluative reckonings. In C. R. Snyder & D. R. Forsyth (Eds.), *Handbook of social and clinical psychology* (pp. 96–115). New York: Pergamon.

Schlenker, B. R., Weigold, M. F., & Schlenker, K. A. (2008). What makes a hero? The impact of integrity on admiration and interpersonal judgment. *Journal of Personality, 76,* 323–355.

Scholl, R. W. (1981). Differentiating organizational commitment from expectancy as a motivating force. *Academy of Management Journal, 6,* 589–599.

Swann, W. B., Jr., Bosson, J. K., & Pelham, B. W. (2002). Different partners, different selves: Strategic verification of circumscribed identities. *Personality and Social Psychology Bulletin, 28,* 1215–1228.

Tice, D. M. (1992). Self-concept change and self-presentation: The looking glass self is also a magnifying glass. *Journal of Personality and Social Psychology, 63,* 435–451.

Tyler, J. M., & Feldman, R. S. (2007). The double-edged sword of excuses: When do they help, when do they hurt. *Journal of Social and Clinical Psychology, 26*, 659–688.

Walker, L. J., & Hennig, K. H. (2004). Differing conceptions of moral exemplarity: Just, brave, and caring. *Journal of Personality and Social Psychology, 86*, 629–647.

Walker, L. J., & Pitts, R. C. (1998). Naturalistic conceptions of moral maturity. *Developmental Psychology, 34*, 403–419.

15

The Dynamic Moral Self: A Social Psychological Perspective

BENOÎT MONIN AND ALEXANDER H. JORDAN

When psychologists explore the role of the self in moral motivation and behavior, they typically take a personological approach. Some seek to describe a general personality structure shared by widely recognized moral exemplars, whereas others examine individual differences in the centrality of mortality to one's personal goals. A social-psychological approach to the moral self complements these personological perspectives by taking into account the situational malleability of moral self-regard, or one's self-perceived moral standing at any given moment. Recent research reviewed in this chapter demonstrates the value added by this perspective: First, when people are made secure about their morality, they sometimes act less morally (moral credentials); second, moral exemplars are disliked rather than admired when their behavior is seen as an indictment of people's own choices (moral resentment); and third, people sometimes boost their moral self-regard to compensate for failures in other domains (moral compensation). These phenomena underscore the importance of understanding moral self-regard as just one aspect of a highly dynamic self-concept.

THE SELF IN MORAL PSYCHOLOGY

For decades, moral psychology mostly left the self out of its analyses. It focused instead on moral reasoning and on the cognitive underpinnings of decisions about right and wrong (Kohlberg, 1969). The neglect of the self and emphasis

---

Benoît Monin, Graduate School of Business and Department of Psychology, Stanford University, and Alexander H. Jordan, Department of Psychology, Stanford University. The authors wish to thank Elizabeth Mullen and the Stanford Moral Psychology Reading Group, as well as the editors of this volume, for their very helpful feedback on a previous version of this manuscript.

on the mechanics of moral reasoning was a reaction against the perceived murkiness of psychodynamic theories influential at the time, and the dearth of empirical support for concepts such as "superego strength" to explain moral learning (see Kohlberg, 1963). In addition, psychologists in the moral reasoning tradition wanted to isolate what was unique to moral thought and behavior, thus excluding general psychological elements (e.g., "ego controls") that were shared with nonmoral behavior and cognition (see Kohlberg & Candee, 1984). Whatever its causes, the choice to ignore the self paid off at first, leading to a rigorously narrow focus and making possible intensive research programs on the foundation of moral reasoning and its development.

Recently, however, moral psychology has begun to move beyond moral reasoning and to pay more attention to the moral self. Seminal work by Augusto Blasi (1983, 2004) suggested that the centrality of morality to one's self-identity might be a major factor influencing the strength of the link between moral judgment and moral action, and thus a major influence on the production of moral behavior. Moral psychologists have eagerly embraced the project of investigating the moral self, but in the enthusiasm typical of nascent research areas, agreeing on a precise definition of the moral self took a back seat to establishing the value of this new approach. Exciting new discoveries have shown that moral psychology can be enriched by adding the self to its models (as this volume demonstrates), but a closer look reveals that investigators vary greatly in their definition of this construct. In the first half of this chapter we describe and distinguish among the different approaches to moral self, identity, and character prevalent in the existing literature, and argue that these approaches have emphasized stable personality structures; in the second half, we propose a new, more social psychological understanding of the moral self that further enhances our understanding of moral thought and behavior.

PERSONOLOGICAL APPROACHES TO THE MORAL SELF

The approaches to moral self and identity prevalent in the existing moral psychology literature are for the most part personological, focusing on stable individual differences between adults – even if these differences are assumed to result from differences in developmental changes over the formative years. We group these approaches into two main categories: in the *moral personality* tradition, researchers aim to identify the general personality structure shared by individuals widely recognized as moral; in the *moral centrality* tradition, researchers focus on measures indexing how much one cares about being moral or the extent to which one moralizes life.

The Moral Personality Approach

One influential approach to the moral self seeks to map out the personality structure (the nonmoral substrate) that gives rise to extraordinary moral commitments or achievements. Just as one may talk about the personality type associated with politicians or with artists, so there is, according to this approach, a moral personality type associated with morally accomplished individuals. Identifying the signature personality profile of the moral individual could, in turn, guide moral education by determining which traits should be fostered in the general population to promote moral behavior. Two research methods have dominated this approach to moral identity: the exemplar method and the prototype method. The exemplar method seeks to identify the personality traits shared by real-life moral leaders; the prototype method consists in asking individuals which traits they associate with morality. We discuss each of these in turn.

The Moral Exemplar Method

The exemplar method begins by identifying individuals who are recognized by their community as moral, and then consists in investigating whether these individuals differ from the rest of the population on personality variables, including nonmoral ones. For example, Walker and Frimer (2007; this volume) found that moral exemplars (50 Canadians who had received medals for exceptional bravery or caring) were both more agentic and more communal, and had more secure attachments, compared to matched controls, supporting their proposal that the moral self is associated with what they call a "personological core" (2007, p. 845).

Colby and Damon's (1992) intensive study of 23 moral exemplars reported in *Some Do Care* shares elements of this approach. Through in-depth interviews, Colby and Damon identified distinctive nonmoral personality features shared by individuals considered moral exemplars by their communities, such as a singular disregard of risk, positivity in the face of discouraging circumstances, open-mindedness to the ideas of those around them, and a desire for personal growth. Furthermore, some of the exemplars' good deeds are described as habitual and nonreflective, as if they arose ineluctably from a personality structure rather than from self-conscious, deliberative moral reasoning. However, because Colby and Damon interpret these habitual moral choices as resulting from the merging of moral goals and personal goals, rather than as the nonmoral expression of a given personality structure, we return to them later when we discuss another understanding of moral identity, to wit, moral self-importance.

A personality approach also characterizes Hart and colleagues' studies of "care exemplars" among inner-city youths, selected through nomination by church groups, schools, or social agencies for their community work or civic engagement (Hart, Yates, Fegley, & Wilson, 1995). Hart and colleagues found that care exemplars described themselves using slightly more moral personality traits (e.g., honest, moral, trustworthy) than individuals in a matched control group, but sharper differences emerged in the way the exemplars structured their self-concept. They were more likely to incorporate parents and ideals in their self-concept, to include systematic beliefs and life plans, and to connect it to past and future selves, thus giving their self-concept a greater sense of continuity through time. Typical of the moral personality approach, Hart and colleagues identified nonmoral components of the self-concept associated with exemplary moral behavior. Thus the exemplar approach need not rely exclusively on a trait approach to personality, but can involve, as this example demonstrates, investigating more complex elements of the self-concept of recognized exemplars.

The Moral Prototype Method
Rather than tapping into the personality structure of actual individuals, as in the exemplar method, the prototype method involves identifying which traits or attributes are included in people's mental representations of a prototypically moral individual, or, in other words, their "naturalistic conceptions of moral maturity" (Walker & Pitts, 1998). Research using this method has identified a set of personality traits (e.g., caring, friendly, honest) generally seen as constitutive of moral individuals (Aquino & Reed, 2002, Pilot Studies 1 and 2; Lapsley & Lasky, 2001, Studies 1 and 2), and has shown that this prototype serves to organize new information, leading, for example, to false recognition of novel words associated with the activated prototype (Lapsley & Lasky, 2001, Studies 3 and 4). Walker and Hennig (2002) further documented the existence of multiple, distinct prototypes of a moral person (e.g., brave, just, caring), corresponding to different personality patterns. This plurality of prototypes resonates with the diversity of actual moral icons, be they historical, religious, or contemporary (e.g., George Washington, Martin Luther King Jr., or the Dalai Lama).

Whereas the exemplar method focuses on the unique personality features of actual exemplars, the prototype method documents the many facets of the moral ideal in a given culture. These two methods address related questions, insofar as individuals are probably recognized by their community as moral leaders (and thus studied by students of the exemplar approach) when they match the templates associated with the moral

The Dynamic Moral Self

ideal in their culture (as documented by proponents of the prototype approach).

The Moral Centrality Approach

Besides the moral personality approach, a second personological approach to the moral self focuses on the degree to which people think of themselves, or the world more generally, in moral terms. This *moral centrality* approach comes in two shades: moral self-importance, or the extent to which individuals care about being moral, and moral chronicity, or the extent to which individuals encode the social world in moral terms.

Moral Self-importance
Moral self-importance refers to how much one wants to be moral. One can place great importance on being moral without necessarily feeling moral (which is instead the hallmark of the moral self-regard approach that we propose later), or being recognized by the community as a moral leader (as in the moral exemplar approach earlier). For individuals high in moral self-importance, morality is a critical life goal and an important yardstick for measuring how well they are doing in the world. According to Colby and Damon (1992), moral exemplars stand out in the extent to which they are committed to moral values, so much so that their personal and moral goals have become indistinguishable: satisfying moral goals has gained a primary status as a basic need, explaining why exemplars happily ignore other typical basic needs, such as security or comfort, if this gives them a chance to move toward their more central moral goals.

If moral exemplars' exceptionally high level of moral self-importance is one factor helping to produce their moral behavior, might more ordinary individuals' differing levels of moral self-importance be an important predictor of the translation of moral judgment into moral action? Blasi (1983) argued exactly this, using the term "moral identity" (p. 201) to refer to the extent to which being moral and acting morally are parts of one's essential self, and explicitly discussing this as a dimension of interindividual difference.

More recently, Aquino and Reed (2002), following Blasi's lead, developed a self-report scale to measure the "self-importance of moral identity" – commonly abbreviated to "moral identity" by the authors themselves (Reed & Aquino, 2003; Reed, Aquino, & Levy, 2007). This scale comprises two subscales, one that taps into whether it is personally important for the individual to possess moral qualities (*internalization*), and one that measures the degree to which the individual believes that his or her day-to-day activities communicate morality to others (*symbolization*). Of note, given our prior discussion of the moral personality, Aquino and Reed's scales do not ask people explicitly whether they want to be moral, but instead whether they want to possess a set of characteristics associated with the moral prototype (caring, compassionate, fair, friendly, generous, helpful, hardworking, honest, and kind).

Parallel to this work, the virtue component of the Contingencies of Self-Worth scale developed by Crocker and Wolfe (2001) captures how much, for any given individual, virtuous behavior contributes to a general sense of self-worth, alongside other nonmoral sources, such as physical appearance, academic performance, and God's love. Indeed, one way to think of the self-importance approach to the moral self is that it conceives of morality as a contingency, something that individuals aspire to and depend on to feel good about themselves.

Moral Chronicity
An individual whose self-image depends on being moral must be attuned to opportunities in the environment for achieving morality, or at least have a clear sense that some actions make oneself more moral than others. Moral chronicity (Lapsley & Narvaez, 2004; Narvaez, Lapsley, Hagele, & Lasky, 2006) refers to the extent to which one encodes the world in moral terms, or how schematic (Markus, 1977) one is about morality. Narvaez and colleagues (2006), for example, identified moral chronics by asking respondents to list traits of someone they like, someone they dislike, someone they seek out, someone they avoid, and individuals they frequently encounter, and then coding how many of the first traits volunteered related to morality, as defined by prior moral prototype research (Lapsley & Lasky, 2001). Individuals who spontaneously employ more moral categories when describing important others, according to this logic, generally use morality to make sense of their social world, and are considered moral chronics. Using an experimental paradigms from cognitive psychology, Narvaez and colleagues (2006, Study 1) showed, for example, that moral chronics reading the sentence – "The accountant assists others with no expectation of a reward" – performed better in a later cued recall task if the cue was a moral trait (e.g., kind), rather than a semantic associate (e.g., numbers), but not if the trait invoked by the sentence was not moral. This effect, not exhibited by nonchronics, demonstrates that moral chronics spontaneously infer more moral traits when encountering morally relevant behavior. The world they perceive is more richly moral than that of nonchronics.

A SOCIAL PSYCHOLOGICAL APPROACH TO THE MORAL SELF: DYNAMIC MORAL SELF-REGARD

In contrast to the personological approaches presented so far, we propose a view of the self that is more reflective and more labile – one's moment-to-moment answer to the question "How moral am I?" This dimension of the self-concept we call *moral self-regard*. This construct is related to the personological approaches to the moral self reviewed above: individuals feel secure in their moral self-regard, for example, when they feel confident that they possess the traits identified in the moral prototype approach; furthermore, individuals high in moral self-importance probably attend more chronically to their moral self-regard, and this brand of self-regard may have a greater impact on their global self-worth than it does for individuals who place less general importance on being moral. Individuals may also show stable differences in their average moral self-regard. But we contend that, as with the self-concept more generally (see Markus & Nurius, 1987), people's thoughts and behavior are often guided by a "working" level of moral self-regard that fluctuates from moment to moment according to situational influences. Note that instead of just saying, in line with social-cognitive approaches, that the interaction between one's self-concept and the situation needs to be taken into account to best predict behavior, we contend that situations actually can affect aspects of the self-concept, and can therefore influence behavior through this mediator, rather than just moderate the link between self and behavior.

Social psychology can complement the stable individual differences approaches documented above by examining precisely the ways in which one's moral self-regard is sensitive to current circumstances, recent feedback, social comparison, or other situational factors. Whereas some authors have pitted situational forces against moral character (e.g., Doris, 2002), we see the two as intricately related: moral self-regard is by definition sensitive to situational demands, and when situations do influence behavior, they often do so by affecting moral self-regard. Moral self-regard is one part of a multifaceted and dynamic self-concept that is deeply motivational. People strive to preserve and enhance a positive self-concept. In the moral domain, they may do so behaviorally by actually acting like a good person, or cognitively by biasing their construal of the world, favoring self-flattering information, or putting down threatening others. Moreover, since moral self-regard is just one aspect of a self that is artful in compensating for deficiencies, feelings of moral inadequacy may sometimes be remedied by dwelling on another valued dimension, and, conversely, feeling morally superior may sometimes serve to make up for more practical failings.

We now turn to three sets of findings that illustrate the value of this social psychological approach to the moral self. This work documents the role of moral self-regard in everyday morality, and demonstrates how adding this dynamic self-concept to the study of moral experience broadens the scope of phenomena that can be studied. The first line of research (*moral credentials*) shows that bolstering people's moral self-regard can license them to act in more morally problematic ways in the future. The second (*moral resentment*) shows that when one's moral self-regard is threatened by the behavior of heroes or saints, one may come to resent these superior others, even though, by all accounts, their behavior is exemplary. The third (*moral compensation*) goes beyond securing or threatening individuals' moral self-regard, and shows instead that individuals may boost their own moral self-regard (and put down others' morality) to compensate for a threat to their self-concept in a nonmoral domain.

Moral Credentials: The Licensing Effect of Secure Moral Self-Regard

One consequence of considering the role of moral self-regard in moral behavior is that it forces one to think of moral choices as a sequence, rather than in temporal isolation. Moral and immoral actions occur in the context of prior moral and immoral actions, and moral self-regard provides a connecting thread between these instances. For instance, if what stops someone from engaging in immoral behavior is the fear of feeling immoral, then having engaged in unambiguously moral behavior beforehand could put that fear to rest, and, paradoxically, license later immoral behavior. Along these lines, Mordecai Nisan's (1991) moral balance model proposed that when individuals decide whether to engage in a morally relevant action, they do so in the context of previous such actions, keeping track of a moral balance that can incur credits (good deeds) and debits (bad deeds). Their goal is not to attain moral perfection, but merely to retain a reasonable level of moral self-regard, allowing for fluctuations as long as one remains above an unacceptable level that would clearly denote immorality. Individuals might thus feel that they can "afford" to engage in morally problematic behaviors given their accumulated moral credit – or they may feel less compelled to engage in moral behavior if they feel they have already done their good deed for the day. In support of this model, Nisan showed, for example, that participants encouraged to imagine that they had returned a found wallet in a first instance declared that they might be less likely to do so in a second instance.

Monin and Miller's (2001) work on moral credentials documented a related phenomenon by actually providing participants with the opportunity to engage in moral behavior on one relevant dimension (prejudice), and then showing that this token demonstration liberated participants to display an otherwise problematic response later on. For example, participants given the opportunity to select a stellar African American applicant in a first job-selection task (establishing nonracist credentials) were more likely than participants in a control condition (who picked from an all-White applicant pool) to express that a second, unrelated job in a racist police force would be "better suited" for a White person. This second task was crafted to make it attractive for participants to favor a White person, but given discomfort about engaging in a behavior that feels unethical in a prejudice-conscious society, participants did not express this preference unless they had been secured in their nonracist self-image by the first, liberating choice – a *moral credential*. Note that the effect was obtained even when the experiment was set up so that its two parts allegedly went to two different experimenters, suggesting that the effect is driven by internal concerns about retaining an egalitarian moral self-regard and not just by a desire for effective self-presentation to others.

Thus, consistent with Nisan's moral balance model, Monin and Miller's social psychological experiments show that a prior moral act (even a token one) can license later ethically questionable behavior. An important theoretical point of contrast, however, is that in the moral balance model, the actor fully recognizes the immorality of the second act (but feels that he or she can afford the debit), whereas the moral credentials model proposes that the first behavior serves as a cue with which to disambiguate the second behavior. In Monin and Miller's situations, the second decision is ambiguous in that both legitimate and illegitimate motives could explain the same behavior (favoring a White police officer because a Black officer would be uncomfortable [vs. incompetent] in a racist police force), and the role of credentials is to disambiguate the behavior in a positive way. A resolution of the apparent tension between the two models may be that the moral balance model best applies in unambiguous cases – in which the meaning of the behavior is unaffected by prior action, but one's moral self-image is debited – whereas moral credentials might be at work in more ambiguous cases, where the later behavior is interpreted as harmless because of one's history, and moral self-image is unaffected. The predictions for behavior, however, are the same: in both cases, these two models support the importance of considering a dynamic self-concept by arguing that one's moral self-regard based on recent past behavior affects future morally-relevant actions.

Moral Resentment: When Others Threaten Moral Self-Regard

A counterintuitive prediction that arises from incorporating a dynamic view of the self-concept into the study of morality is that highly moral others may not always receive the respect and appreciation that they deserve. In particular, individuals whose superior moral choices call into question the morality of others are likely to draw hostility. Moral rebels – individuals who take a principled stand against a morally problematic situation – may, for example, be respected and liked by uninvolved observers, but resented by individuals who were in the same situation but did not rebel, because the rebel's stance implies that it was wrong to remain passive. The reflexive defense of one's fragile moral self-regard can sometimes block people from learning from, and being inspired by, the behavior of morally exemplary peers (Monin, 2007).

In one experiment, a target individual who refused to complete a racist task was appreciated by neutral judges, but disliked by participants who had been asked to complete the racist task prior to the target – and who overwhelmingly did so without complaining (Monin, Sawyer, & Marquez, 2008). To participants who had willingly gone along with the problematic behavior, the otherwise exemplary stance of the rebel apparently represented a threat, which they addressed by putting him or her down, and reporting less respect for, and attraction to, the rebel. Demonstrating the role of the self-concept, participants whose self-concept had been secured before seeing the rebel (by reflecting on an important quality or value, and how they had recently demonstrated it) did not show the same backlash, even if they had done the racist task first. In fact, participants thus "self-affirmed" (Sherman & Cohen, 2006; Steele, 1988) were able to learn from the rebel's gesture. They admitted having had more freedom at the time of the task, and reported less comfort with their own choice.

This work directly supports the dynamic view of moral self-regard that we introduce in this chapter. First, a threat to individuals' moral self-regard motivates them to derogate others. Second, the fact that this effect can be eliminated by affirming one's general (typically nonmoral) skills or values demonstrates the connection between moral self-regard and other aspects of the self-concept that contribute to self-worth, allowing for cross-domain compensatory processes. Being reminded that one is a great tennis player may offset the discomfort of having just acted in an ethically dubious way, and prevent a knee-jerk backlash against others who acted better, allowing personal growth.

Moral Compensation: Moralization to Protect the Self

The fungibility of sources of self-worth, with nonmoral fixes addressing moral threats, raises the possibility that moral fixes can also serve to address nonmoral threats. If moral self-regard is just one component of a multifaceted self-concept, and one of the many sources that contribute to feeling like an adequate person, then feeling moral may sometimes serve to compensate for feeling less adequate in other, nonmoral domains. In particular, we propose that if you demonstrate to individuals that their choices may not have been as expedient as they could have been (e.g., when they have helped with a tedious task, followed a silly procedure, or respected an absurd rule, and then witness you avoid this inconvenience without incurring a cost), they may retrospectively justify what they did by attributing it to their greater morality, and put you down as less moral for choosing shortcuts.

In a recent study of this phenomenon (Jordan & Monin, 2008), participants who completed a boring task as a favor to the experimenter – repetitive number-writing – and then saw a confederate quit the same task, without any negative consequence befalling him, elevated their ratings of their own morality and castigated the morality of the confederate, compared to participants who simply completed the boring task (without seeing the confederate quit it) or who simply observed the confederate quit the task (without first having completed it themselves). Furthermore, self-affirming an important value or trait, as above, wiped out the phenomenon, suggesting once more that the effect was a response to self-threat. The conjunction of completing an exceedingly tedious task for no good reason and seeing another person effortlessly avoid that same task apparently constituted a threat to participants' general sense of self-worth as rational, efficacious agents, and they compensated by boosting their moral self-regard and dimming their view of the other's morality. In this case, feeling moral served mostly to feel a little less foolish. We see once more the considerable interplay between moral self-regard and other aspects of the dynamic self-concept.

CONCLUSION

This chapter had two main goals: in the first half, we outlined and provided a taxonomy of the existing personological approaches to the study of the moral self. This rapidly expanding area of research is richly textured, offering varied perspectives on moral self and identify. By sketching some broad distinctions between the *moral personality* and *moral centrality* approaches, our hope was not to further compartmentalize the field, but instead to dispel potential misunderstandings when similar terms are used to refer to different concepts, and thus to facilitate future discussion and collaborations by clarifying useful distinctions and complementarities. The second half of the chapter focused on developing a social psychological approach to the moral self – what we called *moral self-regard* – incorporating a view of the self-concept as dynamic, influenced by subtle situational cues and sometimes seemingly trivial behavior, and part of a global sense of self-worth (including non-moral sources) that individuals are strongly motivated to preserve. We presented three lines of research (moral credentials, moral resentment, and moral compensation) that we believe contribute to our understanding of the moral self, but do not fit within models that conceptualize the moral self as a personality structure or as moral centrality. All three lines of research speak to the moment-to-moment malleability (and behavior-generating power) of moral self-regard, even in response to minimal manipulations, supporting our claim that dynamic moral self-regard is an important construct to explore further if we wish to understand the moral self.

As the work in this volume demonstrates, the study of the moral self is rife with fascinating questions likely to keep researchers busy for years to come, and holds the promise of casting light on some of the thorniest issues in moral psychology. By carving out some of the emerging directions, and staking a claim for social psychologists in one of these promising avenues, we hope to foster continuing dialogue between the various areas of psychology eager to study moral phenomena. Rather than wanting to appropriate for social psychology one dimension of the endeavor, we hope that the proposal expressed in this chapter will be perceived for what it is, to wit, a commitment by social psychologists to do their share and contribute their expertise in the collective effort to better understand the role of the moral self in explaining everyday morality.

REFERENCES

Aquino, K., & Reed, A. II. (2002). The self-importance of moral identity. *Journal of Personality and Social Psychology*, 83, 1423–1440.

Blasi, A. (1983). Moral development and moral action: A theoretical perspective. *Developmental Review*, 3, 178–210.

(2004). Moral functioning: Moral understanding and personality. In D. K. Lapsley & D. Narvaez (Eds.), *Moral development, self and identity: Essays in honor of Augusto Blasi*. Mahwah, NJ: Lawrence Erlbaum & Associates.

Colby, A., & Damon, W. (1992). *Some do care: Contemporary lives of moral commitment.* New York: Free Press.
Crocker, J., & Wolfe, C. T. (2001). Contingencies of self-worth. *Psychological Review, 108,* 593–623.
Doris, J. M. (2002). *Lack of character: Personality and moral behavior.* New York: Cambridge University Press.
Hart, D., Yates, M., Fegley, S., & Wilson, G. (1995). Moral commitment in inner-city adolescents. In M. Killen & D. Hart (Eds.), *Morality in everyday life: Developmental perspectives* (pp. 317–341). New York: Cambridge University Press.
Jordan, A. H., & Monin, B. (2008). From sucker to saint: Moralization in response to self-threat. *Psychological Science, 19,* 683–689.
Kohlberg, L. (1963). Moral development and identification. In H. Stevenson (Ed.), *Child psychology: 62nd yearbook of the national society for the study of education* (pp. 277–332). Chicago: University of Chicago Press.
  (1969). Stage and sequence: The cognitive-developmental approach to socialization. In D. A. Goslin (Ed.), *Handbook of socialization theory and research* (pp. 347–480). Chicago: Rand McNally.
Kohlberg, L., & Candee, D. (1984). The relationship of moral judgment to moral action. In W. M. Kurtines & J. L. Gerwitz (Eds.), *Morality, moral behavior, and moral development* (pp. 52–73). New York: Wiley.
Lapsley, D. K., & Lasky, B. (2001). Prototypic moral character. *Identity, 1*(4), 345–363.
Lapsley, D. K., & Narvaez, D. (2004). A social-cognitive approach to the moral personality. In D. K. Lapsley & D. Narvaez (Eds.), *Moral development, self, and identity* (pp. 189–212). Mahwah, NJ: Lawrence Erlbaum.
Markus, H. (1977). Self-schemata and processing information about the self. *Journal of Personality and Social Psychology, 35,* 63–78.
Markus, H., & Nurius, E. (1987). The dynamic self-concept: A social psychological perspective. *Annual Review of Psychology, 38,* 299–337.
Monin, B. (2007). Holier than me? Threatening social comparison in the moral domain. *International Review of Social Psychology, 20,* 53–68.
Monin, B., Sawyer, P., & Marquez, M. (2008). The rejection of moral rebels: Resenting those who do the right thing. *Journal of Personality and Social Psychology, 95,* 76–93.
Narvaez, D., Lapsley, D. K., Hagele, S., & Lasky, B. (2006). Moral chronicity and social information processing: Tests of a social cognitive approach to the moral personality. *Journal of Research in Personality, 40,* 966–985.
Nisan, M. (1991). The moral balance model: Theory and research extending our understanding of moral choice and deviation. In W. M. Kurtines & J. L. Gerwitz (Eds.), *Handbook of moral behavior and development, Vol. 3* (pp. 213–249). Hillsdale, NJ: Lawrence Erlbaum.
Reed, A. II, & Aquino, K. (2003). Moral identity and the circle of moral regard toward out-groups. *Journal of Personality and Social Psychology, 84,* 1270–1286.
Reed, A. II, Aquino, K., & Levy, E. (2007). Moral identity and judgments of charitable behaviors. *Journal of Marketing, 71,* 178–193.
Sherman, D. K., & Cohen, G. L. (2006). The psychology of self-defense: Self-affirmation theory. In M. P. Zanna (Ed.), *Advances in Experimental Social Psychology* (Vol. 38, pp. 183–242). New York: Academic Press.

Steele, C.M. (1988). The psychology of self-affirmation: Sustaining the integrity of the self. In L. Berkowitz (Ed.), *Advances in experimental social psychology* (Vol. 21, pp. 261–302). New York: Academic Press.

Walker, L.J., & Frimer, J.A. (2007). Moral personality of brave and caring exemplars. *Journal of Personality and Social Psychology, 93*, 845–860.

Walker, L.J., & Hennig, K.H. (2004). Differing conceptions of moral exemplarity: Just, brave, and caring. *Journal of Personality and Social Psychology, 86*, 629–647.

Walker, L.J., & Pitts, R.C. (1998). Naturalistic conceptions of moral maturity. *Developmental Psychology, 34*, 403–419.

16

The Double-Edged Sword of a Moral State of Mind

LINDA J. SKITKA AND G. SCOTT MORGAN

> History is replete with atrocities that were justified by invoking the highest principles and that were perpetrated upon victims who were equally convinced of their own moral principles. In the name of justice, of the common welfare, of universal ethics, and of God, millions of people have been killed and whole cultures destroyed. In recent history, concepts of universal rights, equality, freedom, and social equity have been used to justify every variety of murder including genocide. (Mischel & Mischel, 1976, p. 107)

The word "morality" generally refers to conceptions of right and wrong, good and bad, and the principles that define propriety and vice. Moral behavior is therefore motivated by conceptions of right and wrong, and seems to be tied to promoting one's conception of the good, and preventing or punishing perceived moral transgressions. Nevertheless, behavior and actions that some perceive as the height of moral virtue or sacrifice, others might see as an apex of depravity and evil. For example, most Americans were horrified by the September 11, 2001, terrorist attacks on the World Trade Center and the Pentagon. More than 78% of Americans surveyed shortly after the attacks believed the attackers were "evil to the core" (Skitka, Bauman, & Mullen, 2004). In contrast, a Gallup poll of nine Muslim countries (December 2001–January 2002) found that 67% percent of the respondents felt that the 9/11 attacks were morally justified (George, 2002). In short, morality can sometimes be a double-edged sword: depending on

---

Preparation of this chapter was facilitated by grant support from the National Science Foundation (NSF-0518084, NSF-0530380). Correspondence about this article should be directed to Linda J. Skitka, University of Illinois at Chicago, Department of Psychology, m/c 285, 1007 W. Harrison St., Chicago, IL, 60607–7137, lskitka@uic.edu.

one's point of view, morally motivated behavior can be seen as the epitome of virtue or of evil.

One goal of morality research has been to gain a better understanding of the factors that make some people seemingly more moral, or more likely to act on their moral beliefs and principles, than others. Some researchers approach this problem by studying lay people's conceptions of moral excellence and the actual characteristics of people who might reasonably be called moral exemplars (e.g., people honored for exceptional bravery or caring, Walker & Frimer, 2007; Walker & Hennig, 2004). Other researchers study individual differences in morality by measuring the degree to which people rate normatively moral traits – such as fairness, friendliness, generosity, helpfulness, honesty, and kindness – as self-descriptive and desirable (Aquino & Reed, 2002; Reed & Aquino, 2003). Others take a less trait-based approach and argue that variation in moral behavior is primarily shaped by individual differences in the relative cognitive accessibility of moral constructs. Moral schemas, episodes, scripts, and prototypes may be more salient and "off the top of the head" for some people relative to others (i.e., some people may be high in moral chronicity); these differences, in turn, could shape the probability that people will act based on their moral beliefs (Lapsley & Narvaez, 2004; Narvaez, Lapsley, Hagele, & Lasky, 2006). Regardless of their differences, the moral exemplar, identity, and chronicity approaches to understanding the role of morality in human affairs typically assume that people with stronger or more central moral identities should be more likely to act on their moral standards than those whose moral identities are less central and important to them (see also Blasi, 1983; 2004). Furthermore, each of these approaches is based on a number of implicit or explicit assumptions about the nature of morality. Specifically, these approaches typically assume that (a) there are stable individual differences in the tendency for one's thoughts, feelings, and behavior to be shaped by, or related to, moral impulses; (b) moral motivations primarily stem from a desire to behave consistently with one's sense of self or identity; and (c) moral identity and motivations primarily have prosocial and virtuous implications.

Our approach to the study of morality has stemmed from an interest in a different set of issues. Specifically, our research has grown from the notion that people's positions on abortion, gay marriage, physician-assisted suicide, and a host of other controversial issues of the day are sometimes imbued with concerns about first and basic principles of what is right and wrong, moral and immoral. Public discourse about these issues often revolves around heated debates about whether policymakers should be involved in "legislating morality," and authors have written tomes about a basic divide in public life, best described in terms of "moral politics" (Frank, 2004; Lakoff, 2002; Mooney, 2001). Moreover, there is a long list of examples of people feeling compelled to take extreme actions to promote their conceptions of morality, or to take a stand against perceived moral violations. For example, the terrorist attacks on September 11, 2001, the Weatherman bombings in protest of the Vietnam War, ethnic cleansing in Bosnia, the assassination of abortion providers in the United States, and the Chicago man who recently self-immolated to protest the Iraq War, are each examples of extreme actions that were based on very different ideological beliefs. Nonetheless, all of these examples are united by a common theme: the people who did these things appeared to be motivated by strong moral convictions.

These basic observations beg the question of whether there might be an important psychological difference between attitudes held with strong moral conviction and equally strong but nonmoral attitudes. By focusing on a different starting position – that is, whether moral conviction might be a special property of attitudes in general, and perhaps some political attitudes in particular – we have also worked from different implicit and explicit assumptions than those who have taken a more moral exemplar, identity, or chronicity approach to studying morality. In contrast to these other approaches, our research and theorizing has been guided by the following assumptions: (a) people experience moral convictions about attitude objects, but the attitude objects that trigger moral convictions vary idiosyncratically across persons and contexts; (b) although a desire to live up to internalized moral standards may form one foundation for morally motivated thoughts, feelings, and behavior, there are other theoretical possibilities worth exploring as well; and (c) although not *de facto* inconsistent with the notion that morality can have prosocial consequences, the moral conviction approach suggests that seeing issues in a moral light can have normatively antisocial consequences as well. For the purposes of this chapter, we will focus primarily on this last point. We first review an integrated theory of moral conviction that leads to predictions that morally motivated behavior will not always be associated with most people's understanding of virtue. In fact, morality sometimes serves as the foundation for behavior (e.g., intolerance, vigilantism, violent political protests, or even terrorism) that third-party observers are likely to normatively perceive as antisocial, if not patently immoral. We will then review specific empirical examples that support the predictions that moral convictions can have what seems to be a "dark side." Finally, we end by discussing some of the practical and theoretical implications of our work for current theory and research on morality.

AN INTEGRATED THEORY OF MORAL CONVICTION

Building on theories of moral philosophy and development, Skitka, Bauman, and Sargis (2005) recently proposed an integrated theory of moral conviction (ITMC) to explain why attitudes experienced as strong moral convictions (what we have called "moral mandates") differ from otherwise strong but nonmoral attitudes. Among other things, Skitka and colleagues argued that people experience moral mandates as distinct from other types of attitudes. That is, people perceive moral mandates as *sui generis* – as immediately recognizable and being in a class of their own (Boyd, 1988; McDowell, 1979; Moore, 1903; Sturgeon, 1985). Moreover, people experience attitudes held with moral conviction as absolutes, or universal standards of truth, that others (if they too are moral) should also share. In other words, moral mandates appear often to have what the political satirist Colbert (2005) referred to as "truthiness," that is, something one knows intuitively, instinctively, or "from the gut," without reference to evidence, logic, intellectual examination, or actual facts (see also Haidt, 2001). Although one could presumably arrive at moral convictions through either intuitive or reasoned processes, the "truthiness" characteristic of moral convictions seems to be a common experience, and suggestive that moral convictions more often reflect moral intuitions than careful reasoning (Hauser, Cushman, Young, Jin, & Mikhail, 2007). Furthermore, the "truthiness" of a position seems to be something one expects others to immediately recognize and share, or to be easily persuaded to share as well, simply because one is so certain one is right.

Moreover, people experience moral mandates as beliefs about the world, or recognitions of fact, and at the same time as motivational guides. However, recognition of fact is generally independent of motivational force (Hume, 1888; see also Mackie, 1977; Smith, 1994, for detailed discussions). For example, recognition that 2 + 2 = 4 has no motivational corollary or mandate. In contrast, the recognition or judgment that physician-assisted suicide, gay marriage, or abortion is fundamentally moral or immoral has a motivational component and an action potential. In addition to the paradoxical feature of being simultaneously factual and motivational, moral convictions also provide their own inherent justification for responses or actions. Why must one act? – Because X is wrong! Because doing X is the right thing to do!

Furthermore, philosophical definitions of morality often include universality and generalizability as distinguishing features of moral as compared to nonmoral beliefs (Hare, 1981; Kant, 1947), and as part of what distinguishes moral convictions from personal tastes or normative conventions

(Nucci & Turiel, 1978; Turiel, 1983; 1998). Personal tastes, such as a simple preference that physician-assisted suicide be allowed or not be allowed, are by definition subjective. Other people are free to disagree or have alternative tastes or preferences. Other attitudes reflect normative conventions. For example, people might see physician-assisted suicide as wrong because it is against the law where they happen to live, but see it as perfectly acceptable in Oregon or Norway, where it is legally permissible. In contrast, a moral stance on physician-assisted suicide is one that is rooted in beliefs about moral truth – an absolute sense of right and wrong that transcends normative conventions, common practice, law, or cultural context. Because this feeling is a universal one, people are likely to think the practice is not only wrong in their own state, country, or cultural context, but is also wrong in other states, countries, or cultural contexts as well. For example, some Western activists vehemently object to the practice of female circumcision in Middle Eastern and African nations, where the practice is normative and culturally valued (Dorkenoo, 1994). Likewise, some consumers will boycott foreign goods when they learn that these goods are produced by child labor, even when there is no legal sanction against child labor in the countries where the goods are produced (Chowdhry & Beeman, 2001).

The ITMC also predicts that moral attitudes are likely to have different affective signatures than otherwise strong, but nonmoral, attitudes. What people experience when they think about issues that arouse a sense of moral conviction (e.g., female circumcision or child labor) has ties to different and potentially stronger emotions than people's equally strong, but nonmoral, attitudes (e.g., one's preference for Macintosh versus Windows operating systems) regardless of how strong their preferences may be. Although preferences may be equally strong, important, certain, and central to perceivers as their moral mandates, attitudes tied to moral conviction arouse quite different – and we think usually stronger – emotions than nonmorally mandated attitudes. Therefore, moral mandate effects might be a consequence of the emotions that are elicited when thinking about moral mandates relative to thinking about one's strong, but nonmoral attitudes.

Another distinction between moral and equally strong, but nonmoral, attitudes is that people perceive their moral convictions as authority independent (cf. Nucci, 2001; Nucci & Turiel, 1978; Turiel, 1983, 1998). People may sometimes behave in ways that are perceived as "moral" because they respect and adhere to the rules in a given context, rather than because they have any real moral commitment to those rules. For example, someone's belief that it is wrong for a twenty-year-old to consume alcohol would be authority dependent if it were based on a desire to adhere to the rules and legal norms of what constitutes underage drinking, or by a desire to avoid authority sanctions for breaking these rules. However, if the rules changed, so too would this person's view about the behavior. Someone whose view about this behavior was based on a sense of morality, however, would maintain their belief that the behavior was wrong even if the rules changed (e.g., if the legal drinking age changed to eighteen). In short, attitudes rooted in moral conviction are theoretically more authority independent than otherwise strong, but nonmoral attitudes (cf. Nucci, 2001; Nucci & Turiel, 1978; Turiel, 1983, 1998).

The ITMC leads to a number of predictions, including ones that suggest that morally motivated behavior is not always likely to be perceived in terms of moral virtues. For example, the ITMC proposition that people experience moral convictions as absolutes suggests that people should be more intolerant of differences of opinion when their attitudes about a given issue are high, rather than low, in moral conviction. In a similar vein, the ITMC prediction that people are less willing to compromise their moral convictions than their otherwise strong but nonmoral attitudes suggests, that people should find it more difficult to accept procedural solutions when they have moral mandates about decision outcomes (e.g., whether abortion should be legalized). Finally, when people have moral mandates about decision outcomes, they are likely to care more about whether the "correct" outcome is achieved, than whether it is achieved through fair procedures. Finally, when authorities make decisions inconsistent with perceivers' moral mandates, people's trust in authority, and therefore their willingness to obey other unrelated rules or laws, may erode. We briefly review research in support of each of these predictions of the ITMC below.

Intolerance

One implication of the ITMC is that tolerance of differing points of view has little or no room at the table when moral convictions are at stake: right is right and wrong is wrong. Consistent with this idea, some of our research indicates that people do not want to work with, live near, or even shop at a store owned by someone who does not share their morally mandated opinions. For example, we asked a community sample of adults ($N = 91$, who ranged in age from 19 to 81) to nominate what they thought was the most pressing problem facing the nation (Skitka et al., 2005, Study 1). Participants then rated how strongly they felt about their nominated issue, using traditional indices of attitude strength (i.e., attitude extremity, importance, and certainty, see Petty & Krosnick, 1995, for a more detailed discussion of attitude strength), and indicated the degree to which their feelings about the issue were held as a moral conviction.[1] Finally, participants indicated how happy they would feel to have someone who did not share their view on their nominated issue as a neighbor, as someone who might marry into their family, someone they might work with, or other possible social relationships (a measure of social distance and prejudice; see Byrnes & Kiger, 1988; Crandall, 1991).

Our results indicated that the strength of moral conviction people felt about their nominated issue explained unique variance in their preferred social distance from attitudinally dissimilar others. This result held even when controlling for indices of attitude strength. Specifically, when moral conviction was high, participants were equally likely to be intolerant of attitudinally dissimilar others, regardless of whether the prospective role was intimate (e.g., friend) or more distant (e.g., the owner of a store one might frequent). In contrast, when moral conviction was low, people were quite tolerant of attitude dissimilarity, especially in more distant than intimate relationships (Skitka et al., 2005, Study 1). Moreover, these same findings emerged in a second study that tested the same hypotheses using researcher nominated issues in another community sample of adults ($N = 82$, age ranged from 18 to 77; e.g., legalization of marijuana, abortion, capital punishment, and building new nuclear power plants in the United States), and when controlling for the tendency to see all issues – not just a specific issue – as related to moral convictions.

To further test the ties between moral conviction and intolerance, we used a behavioral measure to test whether participants (a college student sample, $N = 80$) were more likely to physically distance themselves from attitudinally dissimilar others when dissimilarity was associated with high moral conviction (Skitka et al., 2005, Study 3). Before the experimental session, we assessed participants' degree of attitude strength and moral conviction

---

[1] We conceive of moral mandates as attitudes held with strong moral conviction. To avoid potentially confounding moral conviction measures with structural indices of attitude strength, we generally operationalize moral conviction in terms of responses to a single face-valid item, "To what extent are your feelings about X a reflection of your core moral values and convictions?" (on a 5-point scale ranging from *not at all* to *very much*) or responses to a 7-point agree-disagree item, "My feelings about X are deeply rooted in my core moral values and convictions." We have also used these items in conjunction with another face-valid item, "To what extent are your feelings about X deeply connected to your beliefs about 'right' and 'wrong'?" A discussion of the construct and discriminant validity of this operationalization of moral conviction is provided in Skitka and Bauman (2008).

associated with their position on abortion. Later, participants came to the lab for a study that was ostensibly about how people get to know each other and whether this process unfolds differently when one person has "inside knowledge" about an unfamiliar counterpart. All research participants learned that they would be meeting another research participant and would engage in a brief get-to-know-you exercise. Participants also learned that they had been randomly selected to be the informed discussion partner and that the person they were about to meet was strongly pro-choice on the issue of abortion. After this introduction, the experimenter escorted the participant to another room. A variety of personal effects implied that someone else had taken the one available chair but had stepped out of the room. The experimenter feigned surprise at the missing "other participant," suggested that the real participant grab another chair from a stack against the wall, and then left the room to ostensibly look for the other participant. After waiting enough time for the real participant to be settled, the experimenter returned and measured how far the real participant had placed his or her chair from the chair that would ostensibly be occupied by the pro-choice student.

As in the social distance studies described earlier, results indicated that people's strength of moral conviction associated with the issue of abortion explained unique variance in the physical distance people maintained between themselves and a pro-choice target, an effect that was significant even when we controlled for a variety of other indices of attitude strength. People who morally opposed abortion maintained greater distance from the other chair than those whose opposition was not as strongly morally mandated. In contrast, people who morally supported legalized abortion sat closer to the other chair than those who were not as morally mandated. Other results indicated that people were more repulsed by moral dissimilarity than they were attracted to moral similarity.

Another way to test the intolerance hypothesis is to explore whether people are more intolerant of moral than other kinds of diversity. Although few studies have explored people's tolerance of moral diversity, there is scattered evidence consistent with the prediction that people respond more negatively to moral than nonmoral forms of diversity. For example, Rokeach and Mezei (1966) found that White and Black participants preferred to spend their coffee breaks with discussion group members (confederates) who shared their beliefs but not their race, more than with members who shared their race but not their beliefs. Interestingly, this result emerged during a period when race relations presumably were much more tense than they are today (see also Anderson & Cote, 1966). Recent research arrives at similar conclusions. Fraternity members, for example, valued diversity in socioeconomic status, ethnicity, and religion in their membership more than diversity of opinion on moral politics (Haidt et al., 2003, Study 1). Additional comparisons of men, women, Whites, Blacks, and Asian students each revealed a similar order of preferences for working with diverse others: all groups were happy to interact with demographically diverse others, but were reluctant to work with morally dissimilar others (Haidt et al., 2003, Studies 2 and 3). Taken together, moral diversity appears to be a more difficult interpersonal challenge than various forms of demographic diversity.

In summary, research indicates that as people's moral convictions in a given attitude domain increases, so too does their intolerance for attitudinal dissimilarity in that domain. People do not want to live near, be friends with, or even shop at a store owned by someone who does not share their moral point of view. People also act on their feelings of intolerance: strength of moral conviction associated with a given issue uniquely predicts increased distance in how far people will sit from someone with an opposing position on that issue. Finally, although people see value in many kinds of diversity, they explicitly dislike diversity of moral opinion.

Conflict Management

In addition to evidence that people dislike or are intolerant of people whose moral convictions differ from their own, moral diversity is also associated with greater personal and intraorganizational conflict than other kinds of diversity. For example, a study by Jehn, Northcraft, and Neale (1999) provided evidence consistent with the notion that value diversity presents unique interpersonal challenges. Jehn et al. found that value diversity correlated more strongly than social category (e.g., ethnicity or gender) or informational diversity of workgroups (e.g., the degree to which people had varying levels of information or expertise) with all forms of conflict at work. These conflicts ranged from personality differences to task-related difficulties, such as disagreements about who should do what, or the best way to accomplish work-related tasks. In other words, as value diversity in a given workgroup increased, so did levels of all forms of workplace conflict. In addition to associations with greater conflict, higher levels of value diversity in workgroups were associated with lower levels of performance and efficiency (Jehn et al., 1999).

Although the Jehn et al. (1999) study is consistent with the notion that moral diversity presents challenges to conflict resolution, not all values are connected to people's conceptions of morality. Recent research directly tested whether the Jehn et al.'s (1999) findings were really due to something specific about, and unique to, moral diversity. Specifically, Skitka et al. (2005, Study 4) examined people's behavior in small, attitudinally heterogeneous groups. In a pre-screening process, participants (college students, $N = 242$ individuals and 86 groups) indicated whether their attitudes on the issues of abortion or capital punishment were held with strong moral conviction. To be eligible to participate in the study, prospective participants had to have strong moral convictions about one, but not both, of these issues. In an additional condition of the experiment, participants had to have an extreme attitude, but low moral conviction about whether there should be mandatory testing as a graduation requirement.[2] Based on their responses on the pre-screening measure, we invited four participants with heterogeneous[3] attitudes to come to the lab, that is, we invited two participants who held beliefs on one side of an issue and two participants who held beliefs on the other side of that issue. Participants were not aware of anything about the other group members' attitudes, nor about the criteria used for group composition.

Upon arrival at the lab, groups were charged with the task of developing a procedure that could be used to resolve their assigned issue. Some groups were assigned to develop a procedure to resolve a morally mandated issue (e.g., group members who had moral mandates about abortion were asked to discuss procedures to decide once and for all whether abortion should be legal in the United States). Other groups were asked to develop a procedure to resolve a nonmorally mandated issue (e.g., group members with moral mandates about abortion were asked to discuss procedures to decide once and for all whether capital punishment should be legal in the United States). Still other groups were asked to develop procedures to resolve an issue about which they had strong but nonmoral attitudes (e.g., group members had moral convictions about either abortion or capital punishment and were asked to discuss procedures to decide once and for all whether there should be mandatory testing as a graduation requirement). Groups learned that discussion could end when they either (a) came to unanimous agreement

---

[2] These issues were selected based on pilot testing that indicated that the abortion and capital punishment attitudes were sufficiently uncorrelated, so that we could identify people with a moral mandate on one but not the other issue, and because about equal proportions of our subject pool supported or opposed these issues. Similar pilot testing indicated that mandatory testing as a graduation requirement was an issue that students in our subject pool felt strongly about on both sides, but was not an issue they tended to see in a moral light.

[3] Other conditions of the study also investigated problem solving in groups that were homogeneous in attitude composition. See Skitka et al. (2005, Study 4) for more detail.

about a procedure to resolve their assigned issue, (b) came to unanimous agreement that they would never agree on a procedure to resolve their assigned issue, or (c) they timed out before coming to unanimous consensus. This admittedly very complicated experiment allowed us to test several important nuances, including whether there was something special about the effects of diversity of moral beliefs about a specific issue that could not be reduced to something about the kinds of people who have moral convictions, or something about attitude strength rather than moral conviction.

Results indicated that group processes and climate were different in morally convicted heterogeneous groups that discussed procedures to resolve their morally convicted issue, than they were in all of the other group discussion conditions. Compared to other group configurations, heterogeneous groups that discussed procedures to resolve their morally convicted issue were (a) least likely to unanimously agree to a procedural solution to their assigned problem, (b) lowest in reported goodwill and cooperativeness toward their fellow group members, and (c) seen as more defensive and tense by third-party observers who were blind to the experimental conditions. By way of contrast, the groups who discussed procedures to resolve something they felt strongly but not morally about reported the greatest degree of cooperation and goodwill, and were also seen by third-party observers as the least tense and defensive of all the groups. In summary, trying to develop procedural solutions to resolve diversity of moral opinions was difficult, awkward, and painful, whereas trying to develop procedural solutions to resolve diversity of strong but nonmoral opinions was experienced as interesting and even fun (Skitka et al., 2005, Study 4). The contrast between the moral mandate and strong attitude conditions therefore provides quite persuasive evidence that there is something uniquely challenging about trying to resolve moral conflict.

Importantly, the results of the group study indicated that conflict and difficulty in developing procedural solutions for issues emerged even when participants were blind to one another's attitudes and strength of moral convictions. In addition, moral diversity in groups did not impede developing procedures to resolve nonmoral problems or disagreements, at least in the one-time group encounter studied by Skitka et al. (2005, Study 4). Future research is needed, however, to explore what happens when people are aware of the diversity of moral opinions in their workgroup when they are working to resolve nonmoral conflicts. For example, people who work together for longer periods are likely to be aware of areas of moral disagreement. In turn, this knowledge could affect how they perceive one another as well as their expectations about whether they can effectively resolve unrelated conflicts. In short, a remaining empirical question is whether people who disagree about fundamental issues of right and wrong assume that they are unlikely to agree about nonmoral issues or questions as well.

One might also hope that older adults might do better than the student sample did in the Skitka et al. (2005) conflict resolution exercise, and that life experience and interpersonal skills may provide people with greater skill at managing moral conflicts. That said, the Jehn et al. (1999) study found similar results with samples of adult workers, and much of our other research has been conducted with nationally representative samples of adults. We have found considerable evidence that adults – regardless of age – distrust and reject procedural solutions to conflict when they have a strong moral stake in decision outcomes (Skitka, Bauman, & Lytle, in press; Skitka & Mullen, 2002), research we will describe in further detail shortly.

In summary, research indicates that people have more difficulty resolving conflicts about issues when their feelings about the conflict are based on strong, rather than weak, moral convictions. Moreover, these effects appear to be something special about moral conviction, rather than simply how strongly people feel about the issue, individual differences in the tendency to have strong moral convictions about issues, or the age of those studied.

Authority Independence

Another frequently used strategy to resolve differences is appealing to legitimate authorities for resolving conflict. Previous research suggests that people obey and accept the decisions made by procedurally fair and legitimate authorities (see Tyler, 2006, for a review). However, few if any studies until recently tested whether this finding was true when authorities made decisions that were explicitly at odds with people's moral convictions. In other words, few studies had explored whether people have distinct psychological experiences when they believe that authorities have made immoral decisions. It is one thing to accept nonpreferred outcomes, but may be an entirely different thing to accept and comply with decisions that one sees as fundamentally wrong or immoral.

A number of recent studies have explored whether moral conviction about decision outcomes acted as a boundary condition on the general effects of authority legitimacy and procedural fairness on people's willingness to accept nonpreferred decision outcomes, something predicted by the authority independence hypothesis. For example, Skitka et al. (in press) used a longitudinal panel design to test the effects of people's moral convictions about decision outcomes in the context of the U.S. Supreme

Court decision in *Gonzales v. Oregon* (a Bush administration challenge to Oregon's Death with Dignity Act, a state law that legalized physician-assisted suicide under some circumstances in Oregon). Judgments of procedural fairness, trust, and legitimacy of the U.S. Supreme Court, as well as people's moral convictions about the issue of physician-assisted suicide, were collected from a large nationally representative sample of adults before the Supreme Court heard arguments about this case. Months later, when the Court announced its decision in the case (it ruled against the Bush administration, and upheld the Oregon law), the same people were surveyed again. A total of $N=731$ adults completed both surveys (whose ages ranged from 19 to 90, $M=45.94$, $SD=16.24$) and therefore constituted the analytic sample for hypothesis testing.

Even when controlling for a host of other variables (e.g., age, political orientation, religiosity), results indicated that the vast proportion of variance in perceptions of outcome fairness and decision acceptance of the Court ruling was explained by the joint effects of decision valence and moral conviction. Compared to those with weak moral convictions about physician-assisted suicide, people with morally mandated outcome preferences were more likely to reject the decision and see it as unfair if it was inconsistent with their outcome preferences. Surprisingly, people's pre-decision perceptions of the Court's procedural fairness, trustworthiness, and legitimacy explained no variance in post-decision perceptions of fairness and decision acceptance.

Moreover, the degree to which perceivers felt stronger moral convictions about their preferred outcome of the case also affected post-decision perceptions of the procedural fairness, trust, and legitimacy of the Court. People with stronger moral convictions against physician-assisted suicide perceived the Supreme Court to be less procedurally fair, trustworthy, and legitimate after the ruling than before its decision. In contrast, people with stronger moral convictions in support of physician-assisted suicide perceived the Supreme Court to be more procedurally fair, trustworthy, and legitimate than before (Skitka, 2006). Both of these latter effects held regardless of whether participants' perception of the Supreme Court was positive or negative before the *Gonzales v. Oregon* decision. In summary, perceptions of procedural fairness, institutional legitimacy, and related variables assessed before the Court ruling did not protect authorities from backlash when people morally disagreed with the authority's decision; instead, people's reactions to both the Court's decision and the Court itself were shaped primarily by whether the decision was consistent with their *a priori* moral preferences.

Similar support for the ITMC's authority independence proposition comes from a longitudinal study of people's perceptions of the widely publicized Elián González custody battle (Skitka & Mullen, 2002). In November 1999, five-year-old Elián González, his mother, and 12 others unsuccessfully attempted to cross from Cuba to the United States. Their boat capsized, and Elián's mother and most of the others drowned. Elián was rescued and placed in the temporary care of Miami relatives who in turn filed a petition to grant Elián political asylum in the U.S., despite Elián's father's request that Elián be returned to him to Cuba. After months of court decisions and appeals, armed Federal agents took Elián by force from his Miami relatives' home and returned Elián to his father in Cuba.

Skitka and Mullen (2002) conducted a natural experiment by collecting data from a nationally representative sample of U.S. adults ($N=626$, whose ages ranged from 18 to 86, $M=41.33$, $SD=14.96$) to assess public reactions as the case unfolded. Judgments were collected several weeks before the Federal raid, immediately after the raid, and immediately after Elián returned to Cuba. Results of the study were consistent with the notion that when people have moral convictions about decision outcomes, they care more about whether these outcomes are achieved than they do about cooperating with legitimate and procedurally fair authorities. For example, 83% percent of people with a moral mandate made at least one critical comment about the U.S. government, compared with only 12% of those without a moral mandate about how the case should be resolved. Analyses of open-ended comments about the case indicated that people who morally supported Elián's U.S. asylum criticized specific authorities (e.g., the INS, U.S. Attorney General Janet Reno) and the decision to use force to remove Elián from his relatives' home. In contrast, people who thought the only moral solution was to return Elián to Cuba and his father criticized authorities for taking too long to act, even though they accepted the final decision and perceived it to be fair in the end.

Analysis of closed-ended questions about people's reactions to the case also supported the prediction that perceptions of fairness and outcome acceptance would depend on whether outcomes were consistent with perceivers' *a priori* moral convictions about the case. Specifically, decision acceptance and perceptions of fairness were primarily predicted by whether authorities acted in ways that supported people's moral mandates about whether Elián should stay in the United States or be returned to Cuba. Pre-resolution perceptions of the procedural fairness of involved authorities, by comparison, had no effects on people's post-resolution fairness judgments or willingness to accept the resolution as the final word on the issue. In summary, the Elián study supported the hypothesis that when people have morally mandated outcome preferences, their judgments are shaped more by whether authorities yield the "correct" outcome, than by anything about the authorities' legitimacy or fairness.

Controlled laboratory studies also support the authority independence hypothesis. For example, Skitka and Houston (2001, Study 2) presented student participants ($N = 123$) with hypothetical news reports that indicated whether a defendant in a capital murder case appeared to be truly guilty or innocent, and whether the defendant was executed by the state following a fair trial or killed by a vigilante before the trial began. Results indicated that people perceived the death of a guilty defendant to be equally fair, regardless of whether it was the product of a full trial and meted by the state or was an act of vigilantism. Consistent with the authority independence hypothesis, what mattered most to people's perceptions of outcome fairness was whether they perceived the outcome in the case – i.e., that the defendant was punished – was morally right if he was thought to be guilty, or morally wrong if he was thought to be innocent. In contrast, when defendant guilt was ambiguous (in short, when people did not have a moral mandate about whether the defendant should be punished or set free), perceptions of outcome fairness were consistent with the predictions of procedural justice theories: punishment of the ambiguously guilty defendant was seen as unfair if it was a consequence of vigilantism, and fair if it was a consequence of due process (Skitka & Houston, 2001, Study 1b).

Finally, other research has found behavioral support for the prediction that people reject authorities and the rule of law when outcomes violated their moral convictions. Specifically, when people were exposed to unjust laws, they were more likely to report intentions to flout other unrelated laws in the future (Nadler, 2005), presumably because their faith in the system had been eroded. Mullen and Nadler (2008) further tested the flouting hypothesis in an experiment that involved exposing people to legal decisions that supported, opposed, or were unrelated to participants' moral convictions. The experimenters distributed a pen with a post-exposure questionnaire, and asked participants to return the questionnaire and pen at end of the experimental session. Consistent with the notion that decisions, rules, and laws that violate people's moral convictions erode perceptions of the legitimacy of authority systems, participants were more likely to steal the pen after exposure to a legal decision that violated rather than supported their personal moral convictions. In summary, people's reactions to laws that violated their moral convictions generalized and affected their willingness to comply with completely unrelated laws and norms of moral conduct.

Conclusions and Implications

Most morality research has focused on the psychological antecedents and consequences of virtue. However, the ways in which people's moral concerns play out in everyday social interaction may not always have implications that are normatively perceived as virtuous. For example, the research reviewed in this chapter reveals that stronger moral convictions about specific issues are associated with (a) intolerance of differences in opinion about those issues; (b) difficulties resolving conflict about these issues; (c) acceptance and endorsement of any means that yield morally "correct" ends, including vigilantism; (d) active disobedience of laws and authority dictates if they conflict with one's position on these issues; and (e) increased flouting of even unrelated laws or codes of conduct when moral mandates have been violated. Although morality research has commonly focused on virtue, each of these findings suggest that morality is a double-edged sword, capable of contributing to behavior that can easily be construed as anything but moral. Although primarily associated with prosocial and positive consequences, people's moral convictions, motives, and sentiments are sometimes associated with negative and antisocial consequences as well.

Moreover, we can be relatively confident about the generalizability of the phenomena reviewed here. Results in support of the conclusions made here have replicated across a variety of different methodological approaches (laboratory experiments and field studies), samples (students, community, and nationally representative samples of adults), and across a host of issues. Furthermore, the effects of moral conviction on various judgments, decisions, and behaviors emerges even when controlling for a host of alternative explanations for effects, including demographics (e.g., age, political orientation); various measures of attitude strength (e.g., attitude extremity, importance, and certainty); as well as measures that attempt to capture potential individual differences in moral rigidity (e.g., dogmatism, or various measures of a tendency to see all issues as moralized).

Although the moral mandate program of research has demonstrated the value of studying moral conviction as a unique characteristic of attitudes, there is considerable room for additional research. To a considerable degree, research to date has focused primarily on (a) the question of whether moral convictions yield new insights and variance explained in behavior that could not be accounted for by other well-known aspects of attitudes, such as their strength, importance, and so on; and (b) ruling out a number of other alternative explanations for findings associated with moral conviction (see Skitka et al., 2005; Skitka & Bauman, 2008). There is no end, in principle, to the search for nonmoral properties of attitudes that could explain away the effects of morality. For example, one could argue that perhaps moral conviction effects reduce to the absence of ambivalence, or are due instead to various forms of moral immaturity. Like all researchers, we can make only limited claims based on the research conducted thus far. That said, existing research suggests that moral mandates do not reduce to some combination of nonmoral content and structural attributes of attitudes (such as extremity, importance, etc.), or to various individual difference variables (e.g., a tendency to see all issues in a moral light). It will be interesting to test hypotheses about how and why moral mandates have the effects they do; however, further attempts at reductionism would seem to be relatively low on the list of interesting possible avenues for future research. Much more interesting areas for future research will be to explore not only the consequences of having strong moral convictions, but the antecedents of moral conviction as well. For example, how do people recognize when their feelings about an attitude says something about their moral convictions, rather than something about their strong, but nonmoral, preferences or senses of convention? Perhaps surprisingly, people who take very different sides on issues of the day are often equally likely to report that their positions on these issues are held with strong moral convictions (Skitka & Bauman, 2008). How is it that people tend to identify the same issues as ones they hold with strong moral convictions (e.g., abortion, gay marriage, and the Iraq War), but they nonetheless take very different sides or positions on these same issues? How easy or difficult is it to get people to moralize their position on a given issue, and how does one go about moralizing it? Of equal importance, how easy or difficult is it to get people to demoralize their position on an issue, and how does one go about accomplishing this end?

In conclusion, in addition to revealing that morality has potentially negative in addition to positive implications for interpersonal interaction, conflict resolution, deference to authorities, and social cohesion, the moral mandate program of research also points to psychological factors that may be important to study to gain a full understanding of when and why morality motivates human behavior. Specifically, in addition to studying individual differences in moral identity or character, our theory suggests it is also important to study the psychology that leads people to identify some attitudes and feelings as morally motivated. Although our theory tends to emphasize studying the antecedents and consequences of attitudes held with strong versus weak moral conviction (i.e., an emphasis on attitudinal differences, rather than on individual differences), to the extent that theorists or researchers remain primarily interested in individual differences in moral identity and character, our theory and research also suggests that it is as important to study the possibility that increasing the strength of moral identity, character, or chronicity may have negative, in addition to positive, consequences.

REFERENCES

Anderson, C., & Cote, A. (1966). Belief dissonance as a source of disaffection between ethnic groups. *Journal of Personality and Social Psychology, 4*, 447–453.

Aquino, K., & Reed, A., II. (2002). The self-importance of moral identity. *Journal of Personality and Social Psychology, 83*, 1423–1440.

Blasi, A. (1983). Moral cognition and moral action: A theoretical perspective. *Developmental Review, 3*, 178–210.

(2004). Moral functioning: Moral understanding and personality. In D. Lapsley & D. Narvaez (Eds.), *Moral development, self, and identity* (pp. 335–348). Mahwah, NJ: Lawrence Erlbaum.

Boyd, R. (1988). How to be a moral realist. In G. Sayre-McCord (Ed.), *Essays in moral realism* (pp. 181–228). Ithaca, NY: Cornell University Press.

Byrnes, D. A., & Kiger, G. (1988). Contemporary measures of attitudes toward blacks. *Educational and Psychological Measurement, 48*, 107–118.

Chowdhry, G., & Beeman, M. (2001). Challenging child labor: Transnational activism and India's carpet industry. *The Annals of the American Academy of Political and Social Science, 575*, 158–175.

Colbert, S. (2005). *The Colbert report.* October 17, 2005.

Crandall, C. S. (1991). Multiple stigma and AIDS: Medical stigma and attitudes toward homosexuals and IV-drug uses in AIDS-related stigmatization. *Journal of Community and Applied Psychology, 1*, 165–172.

Dorkenoo, E. (1994). *Cutting the rose: Female genitalia mutilation: The practice and its prevention.* London: Minority Rights Publications.

Frank, T. (2004). *What's the matter with Kansas? How conservatives won the heart of America.* New York: Metropolitan Books.

George, L. (2002). Muslims skeptical on terror war. Retrieved July 14, 2003, from http://www.cnn.com/2002/WORLD/europe/03/03/gallup.reaction.

Haidt, J. (2001). The emotional dog and its rational tail: A social intuitionist approach to moral judgment. *Psychological Review, 108*, 814–834.

Haidt, J., Rosenberg, E., & Hom, H. (2003). Differentiating diversities: Moral diversity is not like other kinds. *Journal of Applied Social Psychology, 33*, 1–36.

Hare, R. M. (1981). *Moral thinking.* Oxford: Oxford University Press.

Hauser, M., Cushman, F., Young, L., Kang-Xing, R., & Mikhail, J. (2007). A dissociation between moral judgments and justifications. *Mind and Language, 22*, 1–21.

Hume, D. (1888). *A treatise on human nature.* Oxford: Clarendon Press, 1968.

Jehn, K. A., Northcraft, G. B., & Neale, M. A. (1999). Why differences make a difference: A field study of diversity, conflict, and performance in workgroups. *Administrative Science Quarterly, 44*, 741–763.

Kant, I. (1947). *Fundamentals of the metaphysics of morals.* New York: Longmans. (Original work published 1786.)

Lakoff, G. (2002). *Moral politics: How liberals and conservatives think.* Chicago: University of Chicago Press.

Lapsley, D., & Narvaez, D. (2004). A social-cognitive approach to the moral personality. In D. Lapsley & D. Narvaez (Eds.), *Moral development, self, and identity* (pp. 189–212). Mahwah, NJ: Lawrence Erlbaum.

Mackie, J. L. (1977). *Ethics: Inventing right and wrong.* New York: Penguin.

McDowell, J. (1979). Virtue and reason. *The Monist, 62,* 331–350.

Mischel, W., & Mischel, H. N. (1976). A cognitive-social learning approach to socialization and self-regulation. In T. Likona (Ed.), *Moral development and behavior: Theory, research, and social issues* (pp. 84–107). New York: Holt, Rinehart & Winston.

Mooney, C. Z. (2001). The public clash of private values: The politics of morality policy. In C. Z. Mooney (Ed.), *The public clash of private values: The politics of morality policy* (pp. 3–20). New York: Seven Bridges Press.

Moore, G. E. (1903). *Principia ethica.* New York: Cambridge University Press.

Mullen, E., & Nadler, J. (2008). Moral spillovers: The effect of moral mandate violations on deviant behavior. *Journal of Experimental Social Psychology, 44,* 1239–1245.

Nadler, J. (2005). Flouting the law. *Texas Law Review, 83,* 1440–1441.

Narvaez, D., Lapsley, D., Hagele, S., & Lasky, B. (2006). Moral chronicity and social information processing: Tests of a social-cognitive approach to the moral personality. *Journal of Research in Personality, 40,* 966–985.

Nucci, L. (2001). *Education in the moral domain.* Cambridge: Cambridge University Press.

Nucci, L. P., & Turiel, E. (1978). Social interactions and the development of social concepts in pre-school children. *Child Development, 49,* 400–407.

Petty, R. E., & Krosnick, J. A. (1995). *Attitude strength: Antecedents and consequences.* Mahwah, NJ: Lawrence Erlbaum.

Reed, A. II, Aquino, K. (2003). Moral identity and the expanding circle of moral regard toward out-groups. *Journal of Personality and Social Psychology, 84,* 1270–1286.

Rokeach, M., & Mezei, L. (1966), Race and shared belief as factors in social choice. *Science, 151,* 167–172.

Skitka, L. J., & Bauman, C. W., (2008). Moral conviction and political engagement. *Political Psychology, 29,* 29–54.

Skitka, L. J., Bauman, C. W., & Lytle, B. L. (in press). The limits of legitimacy: Moral and religious convictions as constraints on deference to authority. *Journal of Personality and Social Psychology.*

Skitka, L. J., Bauman, C. W., & Mullen, E. (2004). Political tolerance and coming to psychological closure following September 11, 2001: An integrative approach. *Personality and Social Psychology Bulletin, 30,* 743–756.

Skitka, L. J., Bauman, C. W., & Sargis, E. G. (2005). Moral conviction: Another contributor to attitude strength or something more? *Journal of Personality and Social Psychology, 88,* 895–917.

Skitka, L. J., & Houston, D. (2001). When due process is of no consequence: Moral mandates and presumed defendant guilt or innocence. *Social Justice Research, 14*, 305–326.

Skitka, L. J., & Mullen, E. (2002). Understanding judgments of fairness in a real-world political context: A test of the value protection model of justice reasoning. *Personality and Social Psychology Bulletin, 28*, 1419–1429.

Smith, M. (1994). *The moral problem*. Oxford: Blackwell.

Sturgeon, N. (1985). Moral explanations. In D. Copp & D. Zimmerman (Eds.), *Morality, reason, and truth* (pp. 49–78). Totowa, NJ: Rowman & Allanheld.

Turiel, E. (1983). *The development of social knowledge: Morality and convention*. Cambridge: Cambridge University Press.

(1998). The development of morality. In W. Damon (Series Ed.) & N. Eisenberg (Vol. Ed.), *Handbook of child psychology: Vol. 3. Social emotional and personality development* (5th ed., pp. 863–932). New York: Academic Press.

Tyler, T. (2006). Psychological perspectives on legitimacy and legitimation. *Annual Review of Psychology, 57*, 375–400.

Walker, L. J., & Frimer, J. A. (2007). Moral personality of brave and caring exemplars. *Journal of Personality and Social Psychology, 93*, 845–860.

Walker, L. J., & Hennig, K. H. (2004). Differing conceptions of moral exemplarity: Just, brave, and caring. *Journal of Personality and Social Psychology, 86*, 629–647.

17

Moral Identity in Business Situations: A Social-Cognitive Framework for Understanding Moral Functioning

KARL AQUINO AND DAN FREEMAN

The concept of moral identity has gained considerable theoretical and empirical traction since Augusto Blasi (1983) used the term in his Self Model of Moral Functioning over 20 years ago. Since then, a number of scholars (Aquino & Reed, 2002; Colby & Damon, 1992; Hoffman, 2000; Lapsley & Narvaez, 2004) have expanded on Blasi's ideas, and the collected papers in this volume testify to the variety and richness of these perspectives. In this chapter, we contribute to the ongoing conversation about the role of moral identity in guiding moral action by presenting a social-cognitive model that we apply to the domain of business. As researchers whose areas of study are organizational behavior and marketing, we are convinced that the concept of moral identity holds enormous promise for broadening our understanding of how moral constructs and concerns influence business activities, ranging from negotiations, leadership, and teamwork, to strategic decision making, advertising, and consumer behavior. Our aim is to take moral identity from its roots in developmental psychology and apply it to a new arena where moral decisions – questions about right and wrong – are unavoidable, and where people often have to make difficult tradeoffs among competing and equally compelling moral values.

The outline of our chapter is as follows. First, we briefly review the social-cognitive perspective on moral identity, highlighting a conception proposed by Aquino and Reed (2002) that defines moral identity in terms of its *self-importance*. Second, we present a model that situates moral identity within a network of other constructs that have been shown by prior theory and research to be related to moral behavior. Third, we review existing empirical research supporting both the conception of moral identity

---

Preparation of this chapter was facilitated by a Social Sciences and Humanities Research Council of Canada grant awarded to Karl Aquino.

described by Aquino and Reed (2002) as well as the relationships in our proposed model. Fourth, we illustrate the application of moral identity in business contexts, focusing on ethical workplace behavior by managers and in the practice of advertising and marketing. Finally, we lay out an agenda for future research.

A SOCIAL-COGNITIVE DEFINITION OF MORAL IDENTITY

Blasi (1983) described the construct of moral identity as an individual difference reflecting the degree to which being moral is central or characteristic of a person's sense of self. Other scholars (Bergman, 2004; Colby & Damon, 1992; Damon, 1984) have adopted a similar conception and have equated having a moral identity with a sustained commitment to moral action in line with the demands of one's moral beliefs or values. According to Blasi (1983), the felt obligation to engage in a moral action is directly related to moral identity through the desire to maintain self-consistency. Blasi (2005) recently proposed a three-component model that lays out the theoretical requirements for *having* a moral identity. These requirements include willpower, moral desires, and integrity (Blasi, 2005).

Hardy and Carlo (2005) reviewed the theoretical and empirical literature on moral identity and suggested two limitations of Blasi's conception of moral identity. First, Blasi's model does not apply as well to explaining moral behaviors that are to some degree automatic and less deliberate (Hardy & Carlo, 2005). In fact, Blasi (1983, 1993, 2005) conceives of moral behavior as a consequence of volition – conscious deliberation about alternative actions that are driven by the strength of a person's moral desires. But limiting the study of moral behavior to acts that are the result of deliberate and conscious processes downplays the possibility that most of what constitutes the practice of everyday morality is tacit and automatic (Lapsley & Narvaez, 2004). Second, Blasi's model does not say much about *when* and under *what situations* a particular identity will be experienced as part of the sense of self. For example, when faced with a decision about whether to voluntarily disclose a product limitation that a would-be customer could not observe prior to purchase, would a salesperson always experience his or her moral self as providing the impetus for disclosure? Or could other aspects of the salesperson's self – such as an achievement-oriented or professional, role-based identity – be experienced instead? We believe that a model of moral identity based on social-cognitive theory fills these gaps in Blasi's definition, because it allows us to model moral functioning as being influenced by individual differences in the *chronic accessibility* of mental constructs, such as moral identity and its *temporary* activation (or deactivation) by situational cues and contingencies.

According to social-cognitive theory, moral functioning consists of the reciprocal influence of cognition and other personal variables, environmental factors, and an individual's behaviors (Bandura, 2001). A key contribution of social-cognitive theory to moral psychology is to introduce mechanisms from social cognition, memory, identity, and information processing to explain both the situational variability of moral behavior, and the intra-individual stability and coherence of the moral personality (Lapsley & Narvaez, 2004). Knowledge accessibility is a general principle of cognitive functioning in social-cognitive theory. The theory assumes that more readily accessible mental constructs should exert a stronger influence on behavior than those that are less accessible (Higgins, 1996). As there appear to be individual differences in the accessibility of knowledge structures (Higgins, 1996; Higgins, King, & Mavin, 1982), it is reasonable to treat the chronic accessibility of moral identity as a dispositional variable (Higgins, 1996).

Aquino and Reed (2002) proposed and tested a conception of moral identity that is consistent with the tenets of social-cognitive theory and that permits direct measurement of its centrality to the self, which they refer to as moral identity's *self-importance*. They defined moral identity as a self-schema organized around a set of moral *trait associations*. Explicit in this conceptualization is the idea that moral trait associations should be closely linked in memory for any given individual. Therefore, the activation of any trait that may be central to an individual's moral self-schema should spread to other closely linked traits. This conceptualization of moral identity is advantageous in two important ways. First, it does not require the specification of an exhaustive set of moral traits because activation of a subset of moral traits should increase the accessibility of the entire network of associations. Second, it allows for considerable variability in terms of which trait associations comprise a given individual's moral self-schema (see the chapters by Wong and Walker & Frimer in this volume for extended discussions relating to why this aspect of Aquino and Reed's [2002] conceptualization is vital to further understanding of moral identity). In other words, as long as an individual's moral self-schema includes at least *some* of the trait associations Aquino and Reed (2002) incorporated into their instrument for measuring of the self-importance of moral identity – traits like being caring, compassionate, fair, friendly, generous, helpful, hardworking, honest, and kind, which are consistent with lay construals of a moral prototype[1] – then they assume that the centrality of morality to the self can be validly assessed.

Aquino and Reed (2002) argued that making people aware of a moral prototype and its associated traits produces a distinct mental image of what a moral person is likely to think, feel, and do (Kihlstrom & Klein, 1994). Drawing from Erikson's (1964) assertion that an authentically experienced identity is rooted in the very core of one's being and involves being true to oneself in action, Aquino and Reed (2002) theorized that moral identity has a private as well as a public aspect (Hart, Atkins, & Ford, 1998). In other words, the cognitive representation of the moral self resides in memory, but it can also be projected symbolically to others through the person's actions in the world. They labeled the private aspect of moral identity *Internalization* and the public aspect *Symbolization*. Like Damon (1984) and Blasi (1983), Aquino and Reed (2002) proposed that a person's moral identity can occupy different levels of importance within a person's overall self-definition. Consequently, it is the self-importance of this identity, or the relatively enduring association between a person's sense of self and the mental representation of his or her moral character, that links the construct directly to moral action.

Aquino and Reed's (2002) conceptualization of moral identity is similar to Lapsley and Narvaez's (2004), since both emphasize the chronic accessibility of moral identity across different individuals and contexts. A person whose moral identity is self-important is someone for whom the moral self-schema is generally available, readily primed, and easily *activated* for processing social information (Aquino & Reed, 2002; Lapsley & Lasky, 2001). Hence, we use the terms self-importance and chronic accessibility synonymously in this chapter. Once moral identity is activated, it would align an individual's behaviors with the demands and standards prescribed by his or her particular understanding of morality. But even though moral identity may have higher self-importance for some people than others, situational cues may activate (or deactivate) knowledge structures – including the moral self-concept – that influence social information processing (Bargh, Bond, Lombardi, & Tota, 1986). We use the term moral identity *salience* to refer to the temporary activation of moral identity in consciousness by situational factors (Higgins, 1996), and we distinguish it from the

---

[1] This set of traits was empirically derived from a sample of 228 undergraduate business students who were asked to think about personal traits, characteristics, or qualities that a moral person possesses, and then to list as many as they could in an open-ended response format. The nine traits selected by Aquino and Reed (2002) were mentioned by at least 30% of participants.

self-importance of moral identity, which we treat as an individual difference variable that demonstrates greater cross-situational stability.

Aquino and Reed (2002) argued that moral identity is a self-regulatory mechanism that motivates choices and actions that demonstrate social responsiveness to the needs of others, an orientation that many psychologists and moral philosophers consider to be the defining feature of morality. The motivational potency of moral identity arises from the human desire for self-consistency (Blasi, 1983, 2005; Festinger, 1957). But because people must balance multiple and sometimes competing identities, of which only a subset – known as the working self-concept – is activated at any given time (Markus & Kunda, 1986), the influence of any one of these identities on moral functioning is likely to be strongest when that particular identity is more, rather than less, available for processing and reacting to information in any given situation (Carver & Scheier, 1998; Skitka, 2003). We treat the salience of moral identity as distinct from its self-importance, but both high salience and high self-importance refer to a moral identity that is available in the working self for processing social information relative to other possible identities that a person might use as a basis for self-definition.

MORAL IDENTITY IN A SOCIAL-COGNITIVE FRAMEWORK

The model in Figure 17.1 shows how moral identity as both an individual difference and a temporarily activated mental construct fits within a broader social-cognitive framework that predicts moral behavior.

The model begins with three constructs – moral reasoning, moral disengagement, and moral judgment – that prior research has shown to be related to moral behavior. *Moral reasoning* is a key element of the cognitive developmental model proposed by Kohlberg (1969), and later extended by Rest and others (Rest, Narvaez, Bebeau, & Thoma, 1999; Rest, Narvaez, Thoma, & Bebeau, 2000) that has dominated the field of moral psychology for many years. Central to the cognitive developmental model is the idea that moral reasoning is the strongest determinant of moral behavior. Moral identity theorists (Blasi, 1995; Colby & Damon, 1993; Damon, 1984; Hart & Fegely, 1995) have been among the most persistent critics of the cognitive developmental approach. Indeed, the concept of moral identity was introduced into the literature partly to account for why the empirical relationship between moral reasoning and moral behavior is not as strong as one might expect if moral judgment were the primary determinant of moral behavior. Our model shows that the relationship between moral reasoning and moral behavior partly depends on the self-importance or temporary salience of

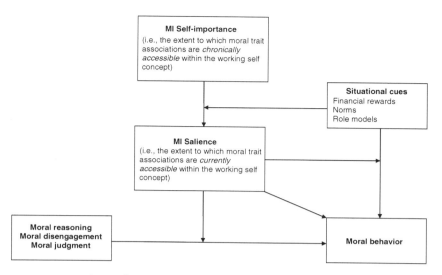

FIGURE 17.1. A social-cognitive model of the role of moral identity (MI) in moral functioning.

moral identity. Our hypothesis follows Blasi's (1983) assertion that moral reasoning in the absence of moral motivation, which moral identity provides, is insufficient for guiding moral action.

The concept of *moral disengagement* has received increasing attention as a predictor of moral behavior. Moral disengagement refers to a set of psychological mechanisms involving various types of cognitive rationalizations that people use to maintain a favorable view of the self when they contemplate or engage in immoral action (Bandura, Barbaranelli, Caprara, & Pastorelli, 1996). One basic prediction deriving from the application of social-cognitive theory to the moral domain is that most people *expect* to feel badly about themselves if they violate moral self-standards (Bandura et al., 1996). However, people are flexible in their definition of what is moral and what is immoral. By using moral disengagement mechanisms, people can take an action they would normally consider immoral and transform it so that it is seen in a neutral or even positive light (Bandura et al., 1996). By doing so, they are able to shield the self from personal condemnation and minimize cognitive dissonance.

Bandura and his colleagues (Bandura et al., 1996) have identified a number of moral disengagement mechanisms that people can execute to avoid self-sanctions against acting immorally. We propose that moral identity can influence the relationship between these mechanisms and moral behavior.

Our argument is based on Reed and Aquino's (2003) assertion that one of the consequences of having a self-important moral identity is that it enlarges the group of people toward whom a person feels obligated to show moral concern. When people care about those who lie outside their most intimate social groups (i.e., family, friends), they are said to have an "expansive circle of moral regard" (Reed & Aquino, 2003, 1270). Being concerned about the needs and interests of socially distant others is characteristic of a person whose moral identity is self-important, but uncharacteristic of those who are morally disengaged (Aquino, Reed, Thau, & Freeman, 2007). Thus, our model predicts that when moral identity is either self-important or made temporarily salient, it should minimize the "effectiveness" of moral disengagement mechanisms and the ability of cognitive rationalizations to weaken self-sanctions against harming others (Aquino et al., 2007).

Moral judgment refers to the determination of what is right and wrong. Researchers have typically measured judgment as a stage of moral development (Kohlberg, 1969), but other approaches have also been used (Forsyth, 1985). One alternative is to measure moral judgment as an ethical predisposition (Reynolds & Ceranic, 2007). Ethical predisposition refers to the cognitive frameworks people use when facing moral decisions (Brady & Wheeler, 1996). Consequentialism and formalism are two common frameworks. Consequentialism refers to ends-based decision making and contends that the moral act is one that leads to the greatest good or benefit (Brady, 1985). Formalism represents deontological or obligation-based approaches to morality (Kant, 1994). Reynolds and Ceranic (2007) argued, and showed empirically, that both ethical predispositions and moral identity directly predicted moral behavior (cheating, charitable giving); however, they also showed that the relationship between ethical predispositions and these behaviors was moderated by moral identity. Similarly, our model shows that the relationship between moral judgment and moral behavior is influenced by the self-importance or salience of moral identity.

In sum, our model suggests that the influences of moral reasoning, moral disengagement, and moral judgment on behavior are contingent on the salience of moral identity. For individuals with highly self-important moral identities, the moral self-schema should be chronically salient and provide motivational potency to regulate moral action as a result of the desire to maintain self-consistency (Blasi, 1984). In contrast, for individuals who do not place a high level of self-importance on their moral self-conceptions, moral identity should have little regulatory potency. However, because we adopt a social-cognitive perspective, the salience of moral identity, and its subsequent impact on moral functioning, can be influenced by situational factors.

Situational Influences on the Salience of Moral Identity

The salience of moral identity in any given situation depends on two conditions: whether moral identity is self-important for a particular person across situations, meaning it generally exists at a high level of activation relative to other constructs in a person's working memory (Bargh, Lombardi, & Higgins, 1988), and whether features of the situation evoke knowledge structures associated with moral concerns or the moral self. Research on implicit priming shows that subtle environmental stimuli, semantic primes, and primes involving names and images of other people can affect social perception (Higgins, 1996), construals of the normative demands of situations (Baldwin & Holmes, 1987; Kay & Ross, 2003), and interpersonal processes (Fitzsimons & Bargh, 2003). Studies also show that situational primes can influence which identities people use as a basis for self-definition (Forehand & Deshpandé, 2001; Forehand, Deshpandé, & Reed, 2002; Shih, Pittinsky, & Ambady, 1999). These findings suggest that the salience of moral identity, or any identity for that matter, in any particular situation might vary depending on the presence or absence of certain contextual cues. For example, situations that make people aware of notions about how they should or ought to act or that cause them to reflect on principles of fairness and moral virtues are more likely to activate knowledge structures associated with moral identity (Aquino, Reed, Stewart, & Shapiro, 2005; Weaver, 2006).

The preceding account of the role that situational factors play in making a particular identity salient is consistent with the tenets of social cognitive theory. Some situations may reinforce an already accessible moral identity and others might not. Our model shows three situational factors that might influence the salience of moral identity: financial rewards, norms, and role models. This set of situational factors displayed in our model is certainly not exhaustive, but we believe it represents a reasonable starting point for thinking about how situations interact with moral identity to influence moral behavior in business settings.

Financial rewards. The use of financial rewards to motivate behavior is a fundamental principle of running a business. The power of rewards to influence behavior is undisputed, and so any model of moral functioning in business settings must reckon with the fact that people do many things for money, including violate self-standards of moral behavior. In our model, we propose that one of the consequences of using financial rewards in organizations is that it can sometimes influence the relationship between the self-importance of moral identity and its temporary salience. Specifically, we theorize that the presence of financial incentives may, under certain conditions, activate alternative identities that might weaken the self-regulatory power of a self-important moral identity (Aquino, Freeman, Reed, Lim, & Felps, in press).

One identity that might be made salient by the presence of financial incentives is a *material identity*. Material identity refers to how people's possessions and relative wealth form one aspect of their sense of self (Belk, 1988). People's material identity is shaped and expressed by the clothes they wear, the car they drive, and their property, goods, and material financial holdings (Skitka, 2003). According to Skitka (2003), when a material identity is made highly salient, people focus on the most normatively self-interested or selfish aspects of the self-concept. Studies support this prediction. For example, Vohs, Mead, and Goode (2006) showed that participants tended to behave in more self-sufficient ways, preferring to play alone, work alone, and put physical distance between themselves and a new acquaintance, when they were reminded of money. In another study, Kay and his colleagues (Kay, Wheeler, Bargh, & Ross, 2004) showed that presenting people with material objects common to the domain of business (e.g., boardroom, tables, briefcases) increased the cognitive accessibility of the construct of competition and led people to behave less cooperatively when dividing resources, and also to interpret ambiguous social interactions as competitive (Kay et al., 2004). This latter perception could conceivably influence people's moral behavior by making them less cooperative, less trusting of others, and more likely to violate norms of honesty and fairness in their business relationships.

The studies described above suggest when people are asked to think about money, or primed to focus on material objects, they are more likely to think about acting in ways that advance their own interests, even if it comes at the expense of others. We hypothesize that one reason this can occur is because material identity becomes highly salient in conscious awareness which, in turn, can diminish or neutralize the salience of moral identity, because only a limited number of identities can be stored in a person's working memory and used for processing and acting on information. Hence, we theorize a possible weakening of the link between the self-importance of moral identity and its salience in situations where financial incentives, as opposed to normative (i.e., moral) ones, are used to motivate behavior.

Norms. Our model shows that the salience of moral identity can also be influenced by norms. Here we refer to behavioral norms displayed by group members. To illustrate the influence of norms, imagine a group of employees that regularly expresses their commitment to moral ideals by hanging posters in their offices that endorse virtues like honesty, peacefulness, purity, or modesty. Imagine that this group of employees also speaks openly about their moral beliefs or frequently wear clothes that show their commitment to moral causes or organizations that benefit the common good. Through these self-symbolizing acts, we contend that these employees can signal to their coworkers the importance they place on morally relevant issues, while also affirming to themselves that their moral identity is an important part of their overall self-definition. If such behaviors are exhibited by enough people in the workplace, they can establish a normative climate that is partly defined by moral constructs and concerns.

People exposed to this type of normative climate learn which identity or identities their fellow group members use as a basis for self-definition, through mechanisms of social information processing (Salancik & Pfeffer, 1978) and social learning (Bandura, 1977). According to social information processing theory (Salancik & Pfeffer, 1978), behavioral displays can convey information about how group members should think and feel about their work environments. From a social learning perspective (Bandura, 1977), people who express their identities symbolically may come to be viewed by other group members as role models worthy of emulation.

We theorize that normative expressions of morality at the group level can influence the salience of moral identity at the individual level through mechanisms of social information processing and social learning. If a person's moral identity has high self-importance, then the presence of others who express their morality symbolically merely reinforces what is already a salient moral identity. But for people whose moral identity is not chronically accessible (i.e., it has low self-importance), a normative climate that expresses morality and moral concerns may temporarily activate moral identity, which can influence how a person is likely to behave when faced with a moral decision.

Role models. The proposed effect of role models on the relationship between the self-importance of moral identity and its salience draws from theory and research on the construct of moral elevation (Haidt, 2000). Elevation is the opposite of social disgust (Haidt, 2000). Haidt (2000, 2003) describes the subjective experience of moral elevation as consisting of a distinctive feeling in the chest of warmth and expansion, which is accompanied by admiration, affection, and even love for a person who exhibits exemplary moral behavior. Saints, social activists, honorable and honest leaders, and ordinary people who exhibit great courage can all evoke the experience of moral elevation among those who witness their actions. We propose that from time to time people observe role models in organizations who display extraordinary virtue, and that these experiences can make moral identity salient.

Among the consequences of elevation is that it causes a desire to become a better person, and to open one's heart not just to the person or persons who triggered the feeling, but to others as well (Keltner & Haidt, 2003). Haidt (2003) also suggests that the state of elevation is associated with certain action tendencies that include the desire to emulate the moral exemplar and act prosocially. Algoe and Haidt (2006) provide empirical support for this hypothesis by showing that people who experience elevation are more likely to want to help others, give money to charity, and list prosocial actions when asked to write about their life goals. These findings suggest that the experience of elevation that follows from witnessing acts of extraordinary moral goodness can function as a kind of "moral reset button" in the human mind, creating a virtuous ripple effect that can lead to changes in behavior. We propose that one of the mechanisms through which moral elevation transforms behavior is by making moral identity more salient relative to other identities that people might use as a basis for self-definition.

Summary of the socio-cognitive model. Our model is built around a theoretical distinction between the chronic self-importance and the salience of moral identity. According to the model, the presence of financial incentives, norms, and role models may increase or decrease the salience of moral identity within the working self-concept. When the salience of moral identity increases (decreases), its self-regulatory potency should also increase (decrease). When situational influences are absent, salience, and by extension motivational potency, should be largely determined by the chronic self-importance of moral identity. The next two sections present empirical evidence relating to these basic tenets of the model.

EVIDENCE FOR A SOCIAL-COGNITIVE MODEL OF MORAL FUNCTIONING

The social-cognitive model presented above reflects several hypotheses regarding the role of moral identity in everyday moral functioning. An emerging body of research supports many of the model's predictions. The next two sections of our chapter describe this work as it relates to everyday moral behaviors and business-related behaviors, respectively. Since the relationship between moral identity and moral behavior is central to the model, both sections begin by reviewing evidence supporting the notion that the self-importance of moral identity is positively associated with the enactment of moral behaviors. We then consider evidence relating to the influence of situational factors on the self-regulatory potency of moral identity. Both sections end with discussions of extant research pertaining to the moderating influence of moral identity on the relationship between moral antecedents and moral behaviors.

Moral identity and behavior. Two studies from Aquino and Reed (2002) provide evidence for a positive relationship between the self-importance of moral identity and moral behavior. The first of these studies (study 5, p. 1433) found that greater self-importance of moral identity was associated with an increased probability that participants reported "volunteering at a local homeless shelter, organizing a food drive, mentoring troubled youth, or visiting patients at a nursing home" at some time during the preceding two years. The second study (study 6) examined actual donation behavior. Specifically, it examined the link between moral identity and whether, and how much, participants donated to a food drive. Results show that the self-importance of moral identity was positively associated with participants' likelihood of donating, as well as the amount of food they decided to give.

Further evidence for a positive relationship between the self-importance of moral identity and moral behavior comes from Reed and Aquino's (2003) examination of a person's moral regard for outgroups. Most notable in this series of studies was an examination of American participants' willingness to donate money to the New York Police and Fire Widows and Children's Benefit Fund (ingroup) and the United Nations Children's Fund (UNICEF) Emergency Effort for Afghan Children and Families (outgroup). Consistent with the notion that moral identity is associated with an expanded "circle of moral regard" toward outgroups, greater self-importance of moral identity was associated with an increase in the amount donated to UNICEF. Additional findings from Reed and Aquino (2003) show a positive relationship between moral identity and judgments of the worthiness of relief efforts to aid outgroups (study 2), a positive association between moral identity and participants' willingness to forgive the perpetrators of the September 11 terrorist attacks (study 3), and a negative association between moral identity and participants' perceptions of the appropriateness of killing those responsible for the attacks using any means necessary (study 4).

In addition to demonstrations of a positive relationship between moral identity and everyday prosocial behaviors, like charitable giving (Aquino & Reed, 2002; Reed & Aquino, 2003), there is evidence that the increased self-importance of moral identity is negatively related to antisocial behaviors. Sage, Kavussanu, and Duda (2006) utilized a sample of adult male footballers from the United Kingdom to examine the influence of goal orientations and moral identity on behaviors enacted while playing football.

Results show a negative relationship between moral identity and antisocial behaviors, like trying to get an opponent injured, diving to fool the referee, and elbowing an opposition player.

Evidence for the influence of situational factors on moral identity salience. Reed, Aquino, and Levy (2007) examined the relationship between moral identity and individuals' preference for donating time or money to a charitable organization. After first establishing that donations of time were considered to be a more moral act than donating money (study 1a), the authors proceeded to conduct an additional study that is pertinent to the notion that the relative salience of moral identity determines its self-regulatory potency. Rather than measure the self-importance of moral identity, the authors manipulated its salience by asking participants to complete a handwriting task. In the moral identity-priming version of the task, participants were asked to write each of the nine trait adjectives (e.g., caring, trustworthy, honest, kind) that are used to evoke contemplation of the moral self in Aquino and Reed's (2002) measure of moral identity, five times each. They were then asked to write a story about themselves that incorporated the nine adjectives. In the control condition, participants were asked to complete an analogous writing task (i.e., write the words and compose a story) using nine words that were devoid of moral content (e.g., book, car, chair, computer). After finishing the priming task, participants were informed that they would also be completing an unrelated donation request study in which they would be asked to make a decision about donating time, money, or neither time nor money. They were then asked to make this decision for one of two organizations that varied in terms of their responsiveness to the needs of others (i.e., the American Marketing Association or the American Red Cross). Results show that completing the moral identity priming task significantly increased participants' willingness to donate time as compared to money when the recipient organization was responsive to the needs of others. Although Reed et al. (2007) did not measure the salience of moral identity per se, this finding is consistent with the notion that the moral identity-priming task temporarily heightened the salience of moral identity, thereby strengthening its self-regulatory influence on moral behavior.

Additional evidence for the influence of situational factors on moral identity salience comes from a study by Aquino, Freeman, Reed, Lim, and Felps (in press). Using two distinct situational cues – recall and review of a list of the Ten Commandments (study 1), and the presence of a financial incentive for lying during a negotiation (study 2) – the researchers were able to influence the salience of participants' moral self-construals vis-à-vis other possible identities. Specifically, recalling and reviewing a list of the Ten

Commandments was found to increase the salience of moral identity, especially for those who placed relatively low self-importance on their moral self-conceptions. In contrast, the presence of a financial incentive reduced the salience of moral identity, especially for those who placed relatively high self-importance on their moral self-conceptions. Aquino et al. (in press) also showed that the salience of moral identity influenced participants' behavioral intentions in a predictable manner – higher salience resulted in higher (lower) intentions to engage in moral (immoral) behavior.

The moderating effect of moral identity. Moral identity is posited to moderate the relationship between antecedents like moral disengagement and moral judgments and moral behavior. The studies reported by Aquino et al. (2007) provide some support for this prediction, although they did not measure actual behavior. Of interest in these studies was the manner in which moral identity affected relationships between moral disengagement and thoughts and emotions pertaining to war. Study results revealed that moral disengagement: (1) enhanced the perceived morality of a highly punitive response to the perpetrators of the September 11 attacks on the United States, and (2) reduced the participants' reported negative emotions in reaction to abuses of Iraqi detainees by American soldiers. However, both effects were moderated by the self-importance of moral identity. Whereas moral disengagement was positively correlated with the perceived morality of killing the perpetrators of the attacks for participants who rated their moral identities as being relatively low in self-importance, this effect was not observed for participants with more highly self-important moral identities. Similarly, whereas moral disengagement was associated with reduction in the experience of negative emotions pertaining to the abuse of Iraqi detainees for relatively low moral identifiers, this effect was not observed for relatively high moral identifiers. This pattern of findings led Aquino et al. (2007) to conclude that moral disengagement mechanisms become less effective in justifying people's support of war-related activities as the self-importance of moral identity increases.

Reynolds and Ceranic (2007) examined the role of moral identity (symbolization and internalization) and moral judgments (consequentialism and formalism) in predicting charitable giving and cheating among students (study 1), and investigated the role of moral identity and moral judgments in predicting ethical behavior among managers (study 2). Data revealed that one of the sub-dimensions of moral identity – symbolization – was positively related to charitable behaviors, even after controlling for the impact of moral judgments. In addition, they found interactive effects of internalization and moral judgments on cheating behavior. Specifically, results showed a negative relationship between internalization and cheating behavior for people with low consequentialism, and a positive relationship between internalization and cheating behavior for people with high consequentialism. Results also showed a negative relationship between internalization and cheating for people with high formalism, and a positive relationship between internalization and cheating behavior for people with low formalism.

For the managers, data supported the interactive effect of internalization and formalism, as well as the interactive effect of symbolization and formalism on their ethical behaviors. Specifically, there was a negative relationship between internalization/symbolization and ethical behavior for people with high formalism, and a positive relationship between internalization/symbolization and ethical behavior for people with low formalism. Reynolds and Ceranic (2007) concluded that when the social consensus concerning a moral issue is high (charitable behavior), moral identity is positively associated with moral behaviors; whereas when the social consensus concerning a moral issue is low (cheating, managerial ethical behavior), moral identity interacts with moral judgments in predicting moral behaviors.

MORAL IDENTITY IN THE DOMAIN OF BUSINESS

A wide range of business decisions involve choosing from a set of options that may be deemed right or wrong. For example, a manager who has entered into salary negotiations with a prospective employee may need to decide whether to reveal information about the compensation of other employees, the financial health of the organization, or the likelihood that the prospective employee's position will be eliminated after the completion of a large project. Similarly, a marketing manager may need to decide how aggressively he or she wants to promote a new food product to a vulnerable population, or whether to advise a prospective customer that a competitor's product would be better suited to meeting his or her needs. To complicate matters, the actions that an individual deems to be morally right in a given business context may not always be the most profitable for the individual or the firm, at least in the short run. And some actions may be morally ambiguous (see Cervone & Tripathi's chapter in this volume for an interesting discussion of ambiguity in the moral domain).

Given that business contexts are likely to be fraught with conflict between what is right for others and what is best for oneself, they should prove to be fertile ground for observing person-by-situation effects pertaining to moral identity. Research on the self-regulatory influence of moral identity in business contexts is just beginning to emerge. This section of the chapter examines findings to date.

Moral identity and business behaviors. Aquino, Ray, and Reed (2003) examined the association between moral identity and lying behavior in business negotiations. They found that individuals' moral identity was negatively associated with their lying behaviors in business negotiations.

Evidence for the influence of situational factors on moral identity salience. Aquino and Becker (2005) examined the role of situational factors (ethical vs. nonethical climate, low vs. high negative consequences) and individual factors (lying, psychological distress, and self-perceived moral attributes) on the use of neutralization strategies (minimizing the lie, denigration of the target, and denial) after lying in negotiations among a sample of 192 MBA students. They argued that individuals with high self-perceived moral attributes might be more likely to use neutralization strategies after lying in negotiations than individuals with low self-perceived moral attributes, because they want to reduce the psychological distress associated with acting inconsistently with their moral identities. Data supported this prediction for concealers. Data also revealed an interactive effect of self-perceived moral attributes and ethical climate on the use of the denigration strategy. Specifically, in an ethical climate, there was a negative association between self-perceived moral attributes and use of denigration, whereas in a nonethical climate, no such trend was identified.

Caldwell and Moberg (2007) examined the moderating role of moral identity in the association between organizational ethical culture and moral imagination, defined as "a process that involves a thorough consideration of the ethical elements of a decision" (Caldwell & Moberg, 2007, p. 193). Data revealed an interactive effect of moral identity and organizational ethical culture on individuals' moral imagination. Specifically, the association between ethical culture and moral imagination was found to be stronger for individuals with low moral identity than it was for individuals with high moral identity.

FUTURE DIRECTIONS FOR RESEARCH

As the preceding sections illustrate, extant research provides considerable support for many of the linkages we have specified in our social-cognitive model of the role of moral identity in moral functioning. However, two aspects of the model appear to present fruitful opportunities for future research. First, as we have noted, most research to date has neglected to examine the relationship between the chronic self-importance of moral identity and its situational salience. Second, contextualizing the notion of situational variability in moral identity salience within the domain of business suggests a wealth of factors that warrant investigation.

As our model illustrates, the main and interactive effects of moral identity are mediated by the salience of moral identity, but there is minimal empirical evidence thus far to support this proposition. Future studies are needed to firmly establish this proposition. Nevertheless, the studies summarized above tell a coherent story about when moral identity will be related to morally laden choices and behaviors. They suggest that the relative strength of accessibility of an individual's moral self-concept vis-à-vis alternative identities will largely determine the regulatory potency of moral identity. Regulatory potency is strongest when situational factors increase the relative strength of moral identity accessibility, or its chronic level of accessibility is greater than relevant alternative identities. In contrast, regulatory potency is likely to be weakest when situational factors induce a strong shift toward a relevant alternative identity with different behavioral prescriptions.

Common experience tells us that in the presence of sufficient inducements (e.g., financial incentives), even those who hold morality as a central part of their self-concept may behave unethically. This observation indicates that in order to reduce unethical or immoral behavior in organizations, we must first remove or minimize the incentives to act unethically. It is only then that individual differences in moral identity can be fully expressed to effectively regulate ethical behavior.

Of course, financial incentives are just one type of situational cue that may influence the salience of moral identity in business situations. As we have argued, norms and role models also have the potential to increase or decrease the salience of moral identity within the working self-concept, thereby influencing moral behavior. Certainly, a wealth of additional factors may also affect the relative salience of moral identity (see Monin & Jordan's chapter in this volume for an interesting discussion of moral self-regard as a moderator of moral behavior). The challenge for researchers interested in advancing collective welfare is to produce an exhaustive accounting of such factors and fully articulate relationships between the person and the situation so that we can move toward a better world together. Hopefully, the social-cognitive model of moral identity offered herein will provide a strong theoretical foundation for advancing current understandings regarding how personality variables (such as moral dispositions or moral habits) interact with environmental variables (such as the presence of monetary incentives or cues about the appropriateness of self-sacrifice) to produce moral behavior.

REFERENCES

Algoe, S., & Haidt, J. (2006). Witnessing excellence in action: The "other-praising" emotions of elevation, gratitude, and admiration. Manuscript under review.

Aquino, K., & Becker, T. E. (2005). Lying in negotiations: How individual and situational factors influence the use of neutralization strategies. *Journal of Organizational Behavior, 26*, 661–679.

Aquino, K., Freeman, D., Reed, A., II, Lim, V., & Felps, W. (in press). Testing a social-cognitive model of moral behavior: The interactive influence of situations and moral identity centrality. *Journal of Personality and Social Psychology*.

Aquino, K., Ray, S., & Reed, A., II (2003). *Moral identity as a predictor of lying in negotiations*. Paper presented at the August, 2003, Academy of Management Meetings, Seattle, WA, USA.

Aquino, K., & Reed, A., II (2002). The self-importance of moral identity. *Journal of Personality and Social Psychology, 83*(6), 1423–1440.

Aquino, K., Reed, A., II, Stewart, M., & Shapiro, D. (2005). Self-regulatory identity theory and reactions toward fairness enhancing organizational policies. In S. W. Gilliland, D. D. Steiner, D. P. Skarlicki, & K. Van den Bos (Eds.), *What motivates fairness in organizations? Research in social issues in management* (pp. 129–148). Charlotte, NC: Information Age Publishing.

Aquino, K., Reed, A., II, Thau, S., & Freeman, D. (2007). A grotesque and dark beauty: How moral identity and mechanisms of moral disengagement influence cognitive and emotional reactions to war. *Journal of Experimental Social Psychology, 43*, 385–392.

Baldwin, M. W., & Holmes, J. G. (1987). Salient private audiences and awareness of the self. *Journal of Personality and Social Psychology, 52*(6), 1087–1098.

Bandura, A. (1977). *Social learning theory*. Orville, OH: Prentice Hall.

(2001). Social cognitive theory: An agentic perspective. *Annual Review of Psychology, 52*, 1–26.

Bandura, A., Barbaranelli, C., Caprara, G. V., & Pastorelli, C. (1996). Mechanisms of moral disengagement in the exercise of moral agency. *Journal of Personality and Social Psychology, 71*(2), 364–374.

Bargh, J. A., Bond, R. N., Lombardi, W. J., & Tota, M. E. (1986). The additive nature of chronic and temporary sources of construct accessibility. *Journal of Personality and Social Psychology, 50*(5), 869–878.

Bargh, J. A., Lombardi, W. J., & Higgins, E. T. (1988). Automaticity of chronically accessible constructs in person × situation effects on person perception: It's just a matter of time. *Journal of Personality and Social Psychology, 55*(4), 599–605.

Belk, R. W. (1988). Possessions and the extended self. *Journal of Consumer Research, 15*(2), 139–168.

Bergman, R. (2004). Identity as motivation: Toward a theory of the moral self. In D. K. Lapsley & D. Narvaez (Eds.), *Moral development, self, and identity* (pp. 21–46). Mahwah, NJ: Erlbaum.

Blasi, A. (1983). Moral cognition and moral action: A theoretical perspective. *Developmental Review, 3*, 178–210.

(1984). Moral identity: Its role in moral functioning. In W. M. Kurtines & J. L. Gewirtz (Eds.), *Morality, moral behavior, and moral development* (pp. 128–139). New York: John Wiley & Sons.

(1993). The development of identity: Some implications for moral functioning. In G. Noam & T. Wren (Eds.), *The moral self* (pp. 93–122). Cambridge, MA: MIT Press.

(1995). Moral understanding and the moral personality: The process of moral integration. In W. M. Kurtines & J. L. Gewirtz (Eds.), *Moral development: An introduction* (pp. 229–253). Boston: Allyn & Bacon.

(2005). Moral character: A psychological approach. In D. K. Lapsley & F. C. Power (Eds.), *Character psychology and character education* (pp. 67–100). Notre Dame, IN: University of Notre Dame Press.

Brady, F. N. (1985). A Janus-headed model of ethical theory: Looking two ways at business-society issues. *Academy of Management Review, 10*, 568–577.

Brady, F. N., & Wheeler, G. E. (1996). An empirical study of ethical predispositions. *Journal of Business Ethics, 15*, 927–941.

Caldwell, D. F., & Moberg, D. (2007). An exploratory investigation of the effect of ethical culture in activating moral imagination. *Journal of Business Ethics, 73*, 193–204.

Carver, C. S., & Scheier, M. F. (1998). *On the self-regulation of behavior.* New York: Cambridge University Press.

Colby, A., & Damon, W. (1992). *Some do care: Contemporary lives of moral commitment.* New York: The Free Press.

(1993). The uniting of self and morality in the development of extraordinary moral commitment. In G. G. Noam & T. E. Wren (Eds.), *The moral self* (pp. 149–174). Cambridge, MA: MIT Press.

Damon, W. (1984). Self-understanding and moral development from childhood to adolescence. In W. M. Kurtines & J. L. Gewirtz (Eds.), *Morality, moral behavior, and moral development* (pp. 109–127). New York: Wiley.

Erikson, E. H. (1964). *Insight and responsibility.* New York: Norton.

Festinger, L. (1957). *A theory of cognitive dissonance.* Oxford, England: Row, Peterson.

Fitzsimons, G. M., & Bargh, J. A. (2003) Thinking of you: Nonconscious pursuit of interpersonal goals associated with relationship partners. *Journal of Personality and Social Psychology, 84*(1), 148–163.

Forehand, M. R., & Deshpandé, R. (2001). What we see makes us who we are: Priming ethnic self-awareness and advertising response. *Journal of Marketing Research, 38*, 336–348.

Forehand, M. R., Deshpandé, R., & Reed, A., II (2002). Identity salience and the influence of differential activation of the social self-schema on advertising response. *Journal of Applied Psychology, 87*, 1086–1099.

Forsyth, D. R. (1985) Individual differences in information integration during moral judgment. *Journal of Personality and Social Psychology, 49*, 264–272.

Haidt, J. (2000). The positive emotion of elevation. *Prevention and Treatment, 3*, 3 (article C).

(2003). The moral emotions. In R. J. Davidson, K. R. Scherer, & H. H. Goldsmith (Eds.), *Handbook of affective sciences* (pp. 852–870). New York: Oxford University Press.

Hardy, S. A., & Carlo, G. (2005). Identity as a source of moral motivation. *Human Development, 48*(4), 232–256.

Hart, D., Atkins, R., & Ford, D. (1998). Urban America as a context for the development of moral identity in adolescence. *Journal of Social Issues, 54*, 513–530.

Hart, D., & Fegley, S. (1995). Prosocial behavior and caring in adolescence: Relations to self-understanding and social judgment. *Child Development, 66*, 1346–1359.

Higgins, E. T. (1996). The "self-digest": Self-knowledge serving self-regulatory functions. *Journal of Personality and Social Psychology, 71*(6), 1062–1083.

Higgins, E. T., King, G. A., & Mavin, G. H. (1982). Individual construct accessibility and subjective impressions and recall. *Journal of Personality and Social Psychology, 43*(1), 35–47.

Hoffman, M. L. (2000). *Empathy and moral development: Implications for caring and justice*. New York: Cambridge University Press.

Kant, I. (1994). *Ethical philosophy* (2nd ed: J.W. Ellington, Trans.). Indianapolis, IN: Hackett Publishing. (Original work published 1785.)

Kay, A. C., & Ross, L. (2003). The perceptual push: The interplay of implicit cues and explicit situational construals on behavioral intentions in the prisoner's dilemma. *Journal of Experimental Social Psychology, 39*(6), 634–643.

Kay, A. C., Wheeler, C. S., Bargh, J. A., & Ross, L. (2004). Material priming: The influence of mundane physical objects on situational construal and competitive behavioral choice. *Organizational Behavior and Human Decision Processes, 95*, 83–96.

Keltner, D., & Haidt, J. (2003). Approaching awe, a moral, spiritual, and aesthetic emotion. *Cognition and Emotion, 17*, 297–314.

Kihlstrom, J. F., & Klein, S. B. (1994). The self as a knowledge structure. In R. S. Wyer, Jr. & T. K. Srull (Eds.), *Handbook of social cognition* (pp. 153–208). Hillsdale, NJ: Lawrence Erlbaum Associates, Inc.

Kohlberg, L. (1969). Stage and sequence: The cognitive developmental approach to socialization. In D. A. Goslin (Ed.), *Handbook of socialization theory and research* (pp. 347–480). Chicago: Rand McNally.

Lapsley, D. K., & Lasky, B. (2001, April). *Chronic accessibility of virtue-trait inferences: A social-cognitive approach to the moral personality*. Paper presented at the biennial meeting of the Society for Research in Child Development, Minneapolis, MN.

Lapsley, D. K., & Narvaez, D. (2004) A social-cognitive approach to the moral personality. In D. K. Lapsley & D. Narvaez (Eds.), *Moral development, self, and identity* (pp. 189–212). Mahwah, NJ: Lawrence Erlbaum.

Markus, H., & Kunda, Z. (1986). Stability and malleability of the self-concept. *Journal of Personality and Social Psychology, 51*(4), 858–866.

Reed, A., II, & Aquino, K. (2003). Moral identity and the expanding circles of moral regard toward out-groups. *Journal of Personality and Social Psychology, 84*(6), 1270–1286.

Reed, A, II, Aquino, K., & Levy, E. (2007). Moral identity and judgments of charitable behaviors. *Journal of Marketing, 71*, 178–193.

Rest, J. R., Narvaez, D., Bebeau, M. J., & Thoma, S. J. (1999). A neo-Kohlbergian approach: The DIT and schema theory. *Educational Psychology Review, 11*, 291–324.

Rest, J. R., Narvaez, D., Thoma, S. J., & Bebeau, M. J. (2000). A neo-Kohlbergian approach to morality research. *Journal of Moral Education, 29*, 381–395.

Reynolds, S. J., & Ceranic, T. (2007). The effects of moral judgment and moral identity on moral behavior: An empirical examination of the moral individual. *Journal of Applied Psychology, 92,* 1610–1624.

Sage, L., Kavussanu, M., & Duda, J. (2006). Goal orientations and moral identity as predictors of prosocial and antisocial functioning in male association football players. *Journal of Sports Sciences, 24*(5), 455–466.

Salancik, G. R., & Pfeffer, J. (1978). Social information processing approach to job attitiudes and task design. *Administrative Science Quarterly, 23,* 224–253.

Shih, M., Pittinsky, T. L., & Ambady, N. (1999). Stereotype susceptibility: Identity salience and shifts in quantitative performance. *Psychological Science, 10,* 80–83.

Skitka, L. J. (2003). Of different minds: An accessible identity model of justice reasoning. *Personality and Social Psychology Review, 7*(4), 286–297.

Vohs, K. D., Mead, N. L., & Goode, M. R. (2006). The psychological consequences of money. *Science, 314,* 1154–1156.

Weaver, G. R. (2006). Virtue in organizations: Moral identity as a foundation for moral agency. *Organization Studies, 27*(3), 341–368.

18

The Moral Functioning of Mature Adults and the Possibility of Fair Moral Reasoning

AUGUSTO BLASI

"I should really free my slaves, all two hundred of them. How could I not do that, when I deeply believe, and wrote, that slavery is the worst offence against human nature? Am I really such a hypocrite, as the British accuse all of us of being? But how can I take this step by myself, on my own, individually? Perhaps black slaves are not inferior to us Whites, I'm not sure. But certainly they are not ready to independently manage their own life. Don't we need, first, to set up institutions to educate them, and to support them in the life of free people? Who will take care of them? And, then, more seriously, what would be the consequences of my decision for the other legitimate owners, for my Commonwealth and for the new Republic? It's bound to create dissension, animosity, among us, and instability in our still fragile Union. There will be discontent among the other slaves, and perhaps rebellions. And what about the health of our economy? No, the abolition of slavery is a decision that no individual can take on his own; it needs to be discussed, legislated, and regulated by each state… Is this really what's stopping me from taking what I consider to be a morally necessary step? Are my real motives the welfare of the slaves themselves, and the harmony and stability of our republic? Or isn't, rather, my own interest, the value of my property and my precarious financial situation, the fear of being unable to repay my heavy debts? What are my deeper concerns behind my hesitation and the guilt that I am enduring? I try to be fair, even kind and generous to my slaves. But is this enough? What else can I do?"

This interior monologue – attributed here to Thomas Jefferson – though fictional, is based on historical evidence. It is presented here as a concrete example of the way morally mature adults ought to confront moral situations and moral decisions, which is the central subject of this chapter. We know that the only slaves Jefferson freed before dying were the five children he had with Sally Hemings; the others were sold after his death to repay his debts, with sorry consequences for the slaves and their families. It may be relatively easy for us, looking at the events from outside, two centuries later, to decide what Jefferson should have done. Perhaps his decision, or lack of decision, concerning his slaves was morally wrong; perhaps he was indeed a moral hypocrite. What should matter to us as psychologists is not to judge, but to understand the kind of processes Jefferson went through – painstaking in analysing the various issues, honest in attempting to uncover hidden motives, critical and self-critical, thoughtful and reflective. From my perspective, it would be centrally important to know whether or not the self is in charge, using all the available skills, gathering the relevant material, confronting and weighing the various elements, and the imagined consequences of each alternative; in sum, whether or not the self takes possession of the process and becomes responsible for the decision.

This chapter originates in two converging concerns. The first comes from the perception, I think accurate, that one can find a reasonable level of decency in daily human interaction: frequent kindness within the family and with friends; courtesy with strangers; charity toward the beggar; mutual help, honesty, and trust. The examples of committed moral dedication are not so rare. And yet there seems to be widespread indifference for, or inattention to, the moral implications of the ways society at large and social institutions operate, and of the ways each of us functions in society. We seem to have difficulties in understanding that the public sphere – the world of work, of social, legal, and political institutions – involves important moral issues that demand attention from each of us. Perhaps we tend to define too narrowly the moral domain; perhaps the preoccupations that family and career bring to the adult years lead to a self-protective restriction of one's concerns; perhaps by the time the broad social issues become relevant to the adult, one's formal and informal moral education has already terminated, and many adults are unprepared to see the new moral responsibilities. Probably all these factors have a role. Whatever its explanation, it seems undeniable that there is an excessive restriction of morality to one's private world.

The second is about a conception of moral functioning that is being advanced through the converging work of several scientific disciplines – evolutionary anthropology and psychology, neurosciences, and the cognitive sciences (in the course of this chapter, I refer to this group of disciplines in their approach to moral functioning as "the biological and cognitive sciences"). According to this conception, morality would be a result of quick, emotionally based, intuitions, while careful reasoning and reflection are presented as rare, or as useless, and, in any event, invincibly biased.

These theories have been very effective in anchoring the academic discourse about morality, and also in influencing the culture at large. There are two aspects to my concern: theoretically, these positions offer a partial, truncated, and distorted view of moral functioning, in which moral responsibility would become essentially meaningless. Practically, if it were scientifically shown that reasoning and reflection are superfluous at best for morality, and at worst a source of distortion, it would be senseless to encourage people to engage in moral reflection, and for moral educators to prepare the younger generations for careful moral reasoning.

I should add that this dismissive view of moral reflection finds a receptive ground in several psychological disciplines: for instance, in social psychology there has been, for many years, a dominant scepticism concerning people's capacity for self-awareness, the rationality of reasons, or the possibility of disinterested altruism and of objective responsibility. Even in developmental psychology, after the fall from favor of the Piagetian and Kohlbergian approaches to morality, there has been a returning of social learning principles of socialization, a renewed emphasis on genetic and temperamental explanations of moral development, a great increase of interest in "early morality" – that is, in the moral manifestations among preschoolers and even infants, when, of course, emotional and intuitive processes are dominant if not exclusive; and lastly there is a new emphasis on "moral automaticity" (cf. Lapsley & Narvaez, 2004, Narvaez & Lapsley, 2005). Briefly, the present intellectual environment is not the most favorable for a serious study of the role of reasoned reflection among mature adults, or for urging moral educators to prepare the younger generations to approach moral decisions in a thoughtfully rational and critical manner.

This paper, then, attempts to tackle two different themes, each of which would require a long essay of its own. There is, however, a single underlying argument, which I hope will come through, in spite of the necessary brevity of the considerations. In essence, I claim that there is no scientific evidence that a reflective approach to moral judgment and functioning is something strange, almost unnatural, for people; that such a reflective approach, perhaps infrequently, is resorted to by many of us, and that, in fact, the normal tasks of adult morality need it very badly; finally that the distance between what is needed and what is observed can only be overcome through broad educational interventions that are guided by what is known about mature adult moral functioning. (A third theme can only be hinted at, and concerns the need of a methodological shift in the study of moral functioning, particularly among adults, from the present focus on individual or multiple variables to an emphasis on the organizing processes of the responsible self.) In elaborating the thesis that objective moral reflection may be infrequent, but is possible and, in fact, necessary, I proceed in two steps. First, I very briefly introduce the general ideas and empirical practices of the biological and cognitive sciences concerning morality, and discuss in greater detail their dismissal of reasoning and reflection. Then, I try to draw what I call the moral landscape of adulthood. From this picture, finally, I try to outline what I consider to be the essential capacities of morally mature adults.

THE APPROACH TO HUMAN MORALITY OF THE BIOLOGICAL AND COGNITIVE SCIENCES

The Program

The observation that various animal species behave in ways that recall aspects of human morality, and that can be looked at as its precursors in the evolutionary history of our species, is at least as old as Darwin, even though it was later reformulated and supported with new evidence (cf. Wilson, 1979; Wright, 1994). Also, that certain brain lesions can seriously impair specific aspects of human moral functioning was known already for close to a century (cf. Luria, 2005). However, in the past thirty years or so, there has been what seems to be a concerted effort to systematically tackle the issues concerning human morality from the perspective of scientific positive knowledge. Three main disciplines contributed to this effort: evolutionary anthropology, with its study of animal behavior; neuroscience, relying on various neuroimaging techniques, in addition to the study of brain lesions, to uncover the underpinnings of various aspects of moral functioning; and cognitive science, particularly with its study of the rules determining human choices and decisions. Even though, in a sort of division of labor within a common enterprise, they raise different questions and rely on different methods, these disciplines share the most basic assumptions. These assumptions can be summarized as follows: morally relevant tendencies exercise a crucial function for the survival of the human and other animal species; this function, like other necessary ones, is best protected, in fact guaranteed, through relatively simple, automatic, mechanisms; these mechanisms are then regulated by brain modules or other neural programs; these are a part of the species' genetic endowment, and ultimately are a result of evolutionary pressures and selections.

A great amount of energy has been invested in empirically investigating, from this perspective, different aspects of moral functioning; and the results, all fascinating and important, are accumulating at an increasingly rapid rate. Many questions are still unanswered, and many findings are vague and uncertain; and yet, when the findings are interpreted and organized through the starting assumptions, they lead many – scientists and laypeople – to a still sketchy formulation of a general conception of human morality. This approach, ambitiously or arrogantly, is presented as a new paradigm that should, and will, replace the traditional philosophical foundations of morality.

One aspect of this conception concerns the role of moral reasoning and reflection, the topic that interests me here. These processes are seen as being indeed a part of our moral phenomenology; but they are frequently considered to be largely irrelevant to moral functioning, and in any event flawed and even counterproductive. This idea too is not new. Nietzsche (1886) and Freud (1923/1961) had warned us that our reasons are in reality irrational rationalizations, especially when it comes to morality. This time, however, such a skeptical view comes to us with the cachet of scientific solidity. In what follows, I present briefly the empirical findings of these disciplines, and then enter the discussion concerning moral reasoned reflection.

The Theories and Some Findings

Starting with the reports of *ethologists, evolutionary anthropologists*, and *primatologists*, a range of emotions and behaviors have been observed among nonhuman primates, and also in other mammalian species, that have striking similarities with human moral emotions and behaviors. For instance, the great apes can express empathy and caring, engage in mourning, and attempt to console the loser in a fight; they can cooperate, help, and nurture. They have a sense of social order, and follow rules of expected behaviors; are concerned with the harmony within their group, can control aggression, and at times act as mediators to restore peace. They also have a sense of reciprocity and fairness: in one experiment, for instance, some chimps expressed dissatisfaction when they were given a different reward than what was given to their partners for the same task (cf. Cheney and Seyfarth, 2007; Sapolsky, 2001; particularly important are the reports of Frans de Waal [1989, 1996, 2006] covering over 30 years of systematic observations).

The similarities with human behavior are impressive. But there are differences. As one would expect, some of the differences have to do with the complexity of human behavior, and the distinctions that humans make, for instance, concerning whom and when to help. More important, humans value, and are capable of, impartiality; apes, by contrast, do not treat equally groups that are different from their own. In general, as several commentators to de Waal's work noted (Singer, 2006; Wright, 2006), superficially similar behaviors may be mediated by different proximate strategies: Wright (2006) suggests that while apes' behavior is most likely guided by emotions, similar behaviors in humans may be a result of conscious strategies. In this context, there is no evidence that moral behavior in apes is preceded, or for that matter followed, by judgment and reasoning, as is frequently the case in humans. We know expressions of moral tendencies in animals exclusively from observing what they actually do to each other.

Are these differences important from the perspective of moral functioning? The answer to this question differs also from scientist to scientist, and most likely depends on the conception of morality one starts with. Some have no doubts that the essence of morality, a result of biological evolution, is indeed expressed in primate societies, and they proclaim that biological considerations should replace philosophical arguments in discussing moral issues (Gazzaniga, 2005, and de Waal, 2006, seem to be in this group); others are more cautious in drawing from their observations conclusions about the nature of morality, and speak of "precursors" or "antecedents" in characterizing animal morality.

It seems to me that a key feature in understanding the differences between human beings and other animals lies in the presence among the former as a group, and in the absence in the latter, of judgments and reasons that are separate or separable from the actual behaviors. The distance between the impulse – be it emotional or not – and the decision to act provides the agent with the psychological space that is necessary to question the impulse, and to ask, for instance, whether the tendencies he or she factually experiences ought also to be followed; it stimulates the agent to discover criteria for answering this question, and to find reasons to justify the criteria. Briefly, it allows the agent to distinguish between physical necessity and moral necessity. As Sharon Street (quoted in Wade, 2007) wrote, "You can identify some value we hold and tell an evolutionary story about why we hold it, but there is always that radically different question of whether we ought to hold it." Answering this question requires judgment, as judgment is required to decide whether we ought to be impartial.

Of course, there is another side to the separation of judgment and action: even when the final judgment is formulated, it becomes then possible for a person not to follow one's judgment in action, and to be split and inconsistent within oneself. Moreover, reasoning brings rationalizations: we could distort morality as we see it, and find reasons to justify to ourselves and others our inconsistency, and ultimately to deceive ourselves with our reasoning. Frans de Waal (2006), commenting on Peter Singer's (2006) observation that primate morality does not know impartiality, noted that impartiality is fragile. Indeed. All of human morality is fragile, and must find uncertain strategies to achieve its goals, whereas nonhuman primates can safely rely on the workings of biological mechanisms. Sometimes one has the impression that many scientists, wishing to apply the standards of technology or, most likely, concerned with human welfare, are seeking also for humans a morality with guaranteed results. As should be obvious, this option is not available to us, and not because we have relied on philosophy rather than on biology. Human morality requires a minimum of freedom, and freedom implies the real possibility of opposite alternatives. For many of us, moral purposes have to be achieved through small steps and the alternation of progressions and regressions, in spite of our vulnerability to internal and external pressures and the vagaries and the strength of our nonmoral motives, through a painstaking search of what is right, struggling against distortion and self-deception, and finally aiming at personal responsibility rather than the safety of built-in mechanisms.

Coming now to *neuroscience research*, whether based on the study of lesions or on neuroimaging techniques with normally functioning people, one finds immediately a very important result, one that challenges our conscious perceptions: that is, even a relatively simple activity is not neurologically simple, but involves several areas and circuits in the brain; in other words, at the neurological level there seems to be a fragmentation of functions. For instance, the response to a picture of a violent act, and the task of evaluating a charitable donation are represented in the brain by different maps of activation that share some specialized units but differ in the stimulation of other units.

Neuroscientists begin to understand that different sections of the prefrontal cortex correspond to different kinds of cognitive activities: for instance, that the left hemisphere is related to the formation of hypotheses and the generation of beliefs, or, more generally, to what Gazzaniga (2005) calls "the interpreter"; that various aspects of social cognition – such as the understanding of others' intentions, the ability to take other people's perspective and to empathize, and the recognition of concrete and abstract social terms – are reflected in the activation of the anterior temporal lobe; that moral emotions and motivation are related to the activity of the limbic and paralimbic systems, or other subcortical areas; and finally, that the activated map differs depending on whether the moral judgment one engages is impersonal and abstract or socially concrete and emotional, on whether it is stereotypical and routine or difficult, or on whether more sophisticated moral emotions or more primitive emotions, such as fear and disgust, are involved (cf. Farah, 2004; Gazzaniga, 2005; Glannon, 2007; Greene, 2008; Hauser, 2006; Moll et al., 2005; Schulkin, 2000).

Many more are the important findings; they continue to be produced at a progressively rapid pace. And yet, in spite of occasional optimistic and even arrogant announcements, we are still far from having a reasonable understanding of the "ethical brain." In a recent interview, Hauser, in comparing our present neurological knowledge of moral functioning to that of language structures, declared: "There is somewhat of an illusion in the neurosciences, that we have really begun to understand how the brain works... It's a delusion that we are going to get close any time soon" (published in the *Edge* website, December 4, 2001). It is not surprising, therefore, that neuroscientists have proposed different frameworks or models to bring together the scattered islands of knowledge. In their review, Moll, Zahn, de Oliveira-Souza, Krueger, and Grafman (2005) point out the limitations of each model, and, more important, the many aspects of moral functioning for which the neurological counterparts are largely unknown. Some of these areas are the subtler variations of moral emotions; the concrete contents of moral judgment and behavior; the contextual situations; the cultural specific determinations, and the processes by which they are internalised. To these one should add the ways moral judgments, emotions, and attitudes are translated into action. Moll and colleagues (2005) offer their own architecture: in it they attempt to integrate, through different kinds of "binding mechanisms," three main components of moral functioning, which they label (1) the "structured event knowledge," or the content aspect of morality; (2) the "social perceptual and functional features," referring to the general procedural aspects; and (3) the "central motive and emotional states." Considering that each component is seen as involving a number of subordinate aspects, the model is quite complex. What I find striking, however, is the amount of information that would be needed for a relatively complete picture, and that is almost entirely missing, or only vaguely assumed from a general knowledge of the way the brain functions.

What can one learn from neuroscience research concerning the psychology of moral functioning, and, in particular, the possibility and the role of moral reflection? The terms "neuroethics" or "ethical brain" conjure up robotic images, in which the mechanical devices of the seventeenth- and eighteenth-century reconstructions are replaced by electrical impulses, chemical transformations, computer circuits, buttons, and clicks. These associations are facilitated by the liberal use, in these writings, of expressions like "triggering," "driving," "stimulating." In reality, neuroscientists openly recognize, and make use of, areas in the brain that correspond to processes of thinking, judging, reflecting, reasoning, etc. While insisting that the moral core is a result of evolution, and is shared by humans and other animal species, they try to make room for cultural variations and processes of learning, to which, of course, also correspond brain structures; they allow for the representations of past experiences, frequently in cognitive-emotional complexes, and for the use of this information in responding to a moral situation and for arriving at a judgment.

But the question still remains: What are the relations between the events that occur in the brain and the perception that we, as a group, have of ourselves as we go through the steps of evaluating a moral situation and making a moral decision? It is clear that the two representations of moral functioning, the neurological and the personal-subjective, differ in important ways: in the former, objective framework, there is a multitude of events that occur impersonally in more or less temporary structures; in the latter, subjective framework, what dominates is the unity of the agent, who considers the relevant informational elements, and makes a decision, for which he or she feels – and is – responsible. One problem is that, for many of us, the objective representation is scientific, while the subjective representation is, well, only subjective, that is, no more than a story we tell ourselves. For many, there is no question that, should the two representations be contradictory, the former corresponds to the truth. In reality, what neuroscientists find and describe are correspondences, relations, between the two series of events; they have no information concerning the direction of causality. Many scientists tend to slide over this issue. But it is quite plausible to maintain that moral functioning is the active, agentic, and responsible working of *an agent using brain structures as necessary tools*. Since the tools are necessary, if they are missing or defective, then moral functioning would also be defective; at the extreme, agency itself and personhood would be missing, at least operationally. From this perspective, it would be inappropriate and imprecise to look at the events in the brain simply as representations of what the agent does consciously. In fact, as a hammer in a sculptor's hand, neurological events do influence what the agent does, not as triggers but as tools to be used.

In sum, contrary to some neuroscientists' statements, there is no evidence from their research that, as we engage in moral reflection, as many of us do, our beliefs that we debate the various options, look for reasons, and question our motives in order to arrive at more rational and better moral decisions are illusory; that all this activity is useless to function morally, but aims at providing ourselves with fictional stories about our behavior, only after the decision has been made. This skeptical idea, to which several evolutionary anthropologists and neuroscientists subscribe (e.g., de Waal, Gazzaniga, and Hauser), does not derive from research in these fields, but was elaborated more systematically by their colleagues in the cognitive sciences, with the help, I would say, of traditional social psychological research.

In the *cognitive sciences* one can distinguish several approaches to human moral functioning: though different in important respects, they all adopt the methods of behavioral psychology, focus on certain emotions, sensitivities, and discriminations that are relevant to human morality, and assume that these manifestations are regulated, if not triggered, by mental programs in the brain, themselves a product of genetic evolutionary selections.

Moral heuristics. One such approach relies on the concept of heuristics, as is understood within the framework of bounded rationality in decision theory (cf. Baron, 1993, 1995; Cosmides & Tooby, 2004; Gigerenzer, 2008a; Gigerenzer & Todd, 1999; Sunstein, 2005, 2008). The basic idea is simple: many problems in real life are exceedingly complex for the limited cognitive human capacities, particularly when a decision has to be made in circumstances of inadequate information, or of external or internal pressures. In these instances it is impossible, or too costly in time and energy, to pursue the standards of optimal rationality; instead, people pay attention to a small portion of the information and tend to rely on relatively simple and stereotypical decision strategies, or heuristics. Heuristics are presented as rules of thumb, decision rules, or mind programs; as operating rapidly and economically ("fast and frugal") in response to environmental cues, to produce judgments and decisions; and as operating at a nonconscious level; that is, while we are aware of the intuitions we have or the judgments we make, typically we would not be aware of the rules that led us to the intuition or the judgment.[1]

---

[1] Cosmides and Tooby (2006) present the work of heuristics, as it is understood in cognitive science, as follows: "Evolved programs – many of them content-specialized – organize our experiences, generate our inferences, inject certain recurrent concepts and motivations into our mental life, give us our passions and provide cross-culturally universal interpretive frameworks that allow us to understand the actions and intentions of others. They invite us to think certain content-inflected thoughts; they make certain ideas, feelings, and reactions seem persuasive, interesting and memorable. Consequently, they play a key role in determining which ideas and customs will easily spread from mind to mind, and which will not – that is, they play a crucial role in shaping human culture and in stabilizing certain social forms" (p. 122).

Many cognitive scientists, in particular Gigerenzer and his colleagues (2000, 2001), insist on the rationality of many of our heuristics, in spite of the fact that they depart from the rules of rational decision, according to microeconomic criteria of utility maximization; their rationality, however, is ecological: that is, they are adapted to the specific environmental conditions – those of the evolutionary selection – for which they were originally designed. When their structure matches the structure of this specific environment, the judgment or decision that they determine can be as appropriate and adaptive to the real world as the decision one could have made through lengthy and costly analytic procedures. In fact, in some cases, they would be even more efficient and appropriate than if one were to consider all the relevant information. These investigators believe that such is the case not only for decisions in the economic, administrative, legal, or medical areas, but also in the domain of morality. Here too, they observe, heuristics are used frequently and effectively.

Moral heuristics discussed in the literature are many and varied: they concern issues of inbreeding and sexuality; of cooperation, sharing, and altruism; of fairness and justice; of obedience and conformity. They include rules for collective actions, rules concerning responsibility and punishment, trust and interpersonal relationships. Sometimes they are tied to emotional reactions, like outrage or disgust. Regardless of their nature, they typically can be formulated as rules to be followed. Examples that can be found in these writings are: don't break ranks; don't change the status quo; follow the majority of your peers; betrayal has to be avoided and punished; punishment should be proportional to the outrage elicited by an action; when you feel good, take more risks; do not tamper with nature.

Faced with such multiplicity and heterogeneity, a reader coming to this area of research from outside the field may wonder whether any rule of thumb leading to a moral judgment counts as a moral heuristic, or which, if any, "fast and frugal" direction would *not* be considered a heuristic. The important question, I think, can be formulated as follows: The set of characteristics that are typically attributed to heuristics – that they operate fast, on minimal information, and unconsciously; are a product of evolutionary processes; are represented in one's neural circuitry; and are adapted to a specific environment – are these, as a set, defining characteristics of the concept? Or are they, instead, empirical hypotheses to be tested; and if so, which ones? In the former case, in my view, it is unclear which among those discussed in the literature are true heuristics; in the latter, it is unclear to what extent the theory has empirical support. Some of the heuristics discussed in these works are plausible results of evolutionary selection; others seem to be no more than emotional-linguistic condensations of the experiential history of a culture, or even of the experience of a group during a specific time of history (think, for instance, of "don't trust people over thirty," that used to be popular among the youth in the late 1960s); some may simply be the outcome of the peculiar unconscious dynamics of a specific individual. In sum, it is clear that most of us, on occasion or frequently, use quick rules of thumb to arrive at moral decisions. It is not clear what is the theoretical status of these psychological processes. It seems to me that the heuristics approach to morality, if it wishes to compete as a viable explanation of moral functioning, would want to insist on what I consider to be the "hard" aspects of the theory – evolutionary and neurological foundation, plus adaptiveness; but these aspects are the most difficult to validate empirically, beyond a plausible story.

Universal Moral Grammar (UMG). The next cognitive science approach to morality to be considered does not present similar diffusion of meanings, or indeterminacy of the concepts' extension. This approach does not address itself directly to the multiplicity of moral intuitions, but attempts to uncover the higher source from which intuitions derive; in this view, moral intuitions, heuristics, and judgments should be understood by postulating a universal moral grammar, on the analogy of Chomsky's universal language grammar. Several authors, in particular Hauser, Mikhail, and their colleagues (Hauser, 2006; Hauser, Young, & Cushman, 2008; Mikhail, 2007) are impressed by the fact that morality, like language, is based on a limited number of universal ideas (e.g., intention, obligation, responsibility), the permutations of which can recursively generate an infinite number of moral judgments. They believe, then, that human beings are innately endowed with a "moral faculty," a computational system based on a coherent set of neural structures, a result of our species' evolutionary history. Its functions are to recognize which problems are morally relevant, to constrain the construction of culturally specific moral systems, and also to guide each person's moral intuitions and judgments, according to the principles of generative grammars. In sum, moral knowledge would be a result of the UMG, while moral action would be determined by the anchoring of intuitions to emotions. The moral grammar itself would not be accessible to consciousness; its principles, however, could be uncovered through the methods of scientific inference.

This is not the place to engage in a detailed critique of the UMG theory. In the following section I discuss its views concerning moral reasoning and reflection. For now I limit myself to simply list a number of problems that have been remarked by various commentators (Mallon, 2008; Prinz,

2008; Rorty, 2006). On one hand, there is a degree of underspecification at several nodal points: they concern, for instance, the mechanisms leading from the basic principles to concrete intuitions; whether the basic processes are understood as causally determining its effects, or as simply constraining them, thus setting the limits for cultural and individual constructions; also, the theory does not clarify the differences, or the relations, between the grammar's basic principles and local everyday norms, or even philosophically constructed moral systems. On the other hand, the empirical support for the theory is, as their authors acknowledge, neither univocal nor conclusive (Mikhail, 2007, p. 143). It is true that moral judgments are also a result of combining certain basic concepts – action, intention, permissible, forbidden, etc. – in a grammatically generative way, and that these concepts seem to be present in all natural languages; it is also true that perceptual stimuli do not provide adequate information to arrive at these concepts ("poverty of the stimulus" argument). But these facts could have other explanations in addition to a brain-based, causally determining computational system.

I should add that these writers, in relying on the findings of developmental psychology concerning the understanding of intention and the distinction between morality and conventionality, are rather selective and naïve – as selective and naïve as can be one who approaches a complex field of research from outside and with a thesis to prove. It is indeed the case that children begin to understand intentions by 18 months of age, but only much later do they reliably use intention as a criterion in moral judgment. Concerning the distinction between morality and conventionality, a lot depends on the empirical criteria investigators rely on; in any event, it is rare that children can reliably make such a distinction before the age of four (cf. Blasi, 2005), at an age, that is, when social-structural learning is quite possible, without having to resort to built-in computational mechanisms.

One central limitation of this theory, relevant also to the issue of moral reasoning, should be noted. The aspect of moral knowledge for which the UMG theory is most plausible concerns the grasp of the general characteristics of action (the praxeological aspect of moral judgments) – its causality, intention, responsibility, and the use of very general normative concepts, such as right, wrong, permissible, forbidden, etc. Most of the studies generated by this approach rely on various versions of the "trolley problem" (cf. Foot, 1978; Thomson, 1985), frequently requiring the grasp of the role of intention and of the notion of double effect, and focusing on people's use of "right," "wrong," "permissible," or "forbidden" in making their discriminations. Now, some of these concepts are not specifically moral, but are required for the understanding of any action, whether moral or morally neutral; others are normative, but vague and abstract. That is, each of them is very general, and acquires a moral meaning only by being inserted in a specifically moral framework. One example may clarify the issue: Hauser et al. (2008) mention two events, couched in the following statements: "The mother gratuitously hits 3-year-old son," to which he attaches the term, "wrong"; and "3-year-old son gratuitously hits mother," to which he attaches the phrase, "not wrong." The two are indeed different combinations of the same elements, and, in this respect, seem to point to a generative grammar. Hauser, however, or this grammar, does not explain why "wrong" is attached to the former, and "not wrong" to the latter. In other words, the theory has nothing to say about how and why the general normative concepts we possess are connected to one concrete action rather than to another. Incidentally, this is the same kind of limitation that characterizes Chomsky's generative grammar; in his case, though, it is the conceptual grasp of the factually occurring events that determines which is subject and which is predicate. When it comes to the grasp of morality, by contrast, no factual event carries with it its moral evaluation. This aspect must come from elsewhere, even though it may need the general concepts of right and wrong, permissible and forbidden.

In sum, the UMG theory, so far, has nothing to say about people's knowledge of prescriptivity – that is, how we go about determining what is morally right or wrong, permissible or forbidden. Hauser (2006) does acknowledge that the UMG does not determine the content of moral judgments. However, if, as it seems, this content is coextensive with moral prescriptivity, then his theory, plausible otherwise, has nothing to say about morality.[2]

Haidt's Social Intuitionism. The third approach to be considered (Haidt, 2001, 2007; Haidt & Bjorklund, 2008; Haidt & Graham, 2007; Haidt & Joseph, 2008), as the name suggests, more than the two previous theories, takes intuitions to be the basic elements of conscious moral functioning. Intuitions are said to occur rapidly and without awareness of their sources, conveying immediately and without the help of conscious reasons or reasoning the moral rightness or wrongness of certain human behaviors. Gigerenzer (2008) believes that heuristics are the sources of intuitions; in my view, however, these two concepts are not so rigorously defined or consistently used as to inform us of the precise relationships between moral

---

[2] In cognitive-developmental theory, the distinction between content and structure has a different meaning; here, the content of moral judgments is understood as the application to concrete events of criteria that are already moral.

heuristics and moral intuitions, or between both of these concepts and moral judgments.

Haidt agrees with the two previous approaches, that heuristics, intuitions, and judgments are causally derived from a set of computational modules, themselves a result of the evolutionary history of the human species. More concerned than his colleagues with the contents of morality, Haidt postulates five moral categories, anchored in brain structures, and generating what could be called five sets of moral sensitivities: to harm, suffering, and care; to reciprocity, fairness, and justice; to ingroup affiliation and loyalty; to hierarchy, authority, and obedience; and finally to the purity and sanctity of the human body. He places in this last category those emotional responses and evaluations that we observe for behaviors like incest and homosexuality, or for the choice of certain foods. Each of these five categories was selected as having been adapted to the species' evolutionary niche, and as favoring the success of our genetic pool. Together they form the innate source of all our moral intuitions.

Cultures, however, are not simply passive recipients of our evolutionary inheritance; rather, they have the power of affecting their members' moral intuitions by selecting which of the core sensitivities to emphasize; and by guiding their interpretation, perhaps in a direction that distorts, or runs counter to, the original meanings of the core categories. As one example of this process, Haidt points to the important difference in moral outlook between the liberal and the conservative American subcultures: in his view, the former would almost exclusively focus on harm and justice, while the latter would retain all five categories, including the purity of the human body, as valid contents of morality. Haidt's attempt to explicate the interaction, in the moral domain, of the innate and of the sociocultural factors is notable. But one crucial question remains unanswered: At what level does a culture exercise its influence, at the neural level or at the level of cognitive-emotional processes? How should one understand the influence of core moral modules, when they are ignored or radically distorted by a culture? If the culture is so powerful as to effectively bypass or deform the innate core sensitivities, shouldn't we say that, for all intents and purposes, morality is culturally determined, within certain broad biological constraints? And, finally, does the individual person have any role in determining the moral significance of his or her moral life?

This is, schematically, the theory. The evidence listed by Haidt and colleagues (2008) as supporting the theory is of three kinds: first, neurological evidence, showing that moral cognitive activity and moral emotional responses correspond to the activity of specific areas of the brain; second, moral judgment interviews, showing that most judgments are intuitive in nature, and that moral reasons most frequently are only given after the intuitive judgment, and mainly to provide biased justifications for one's decisions; finally, an analysis of five works about morality – two philosophical, two psychological, and de Waal's (1996) survey of animal behavior: from this analysis, he concludes that practically all instances of moral behavior can be clustered in the three core categories of harm, reciprocity, and harmony; to which, on the basis of cross-cultural observations, Haidt and colleagues added the other two categories of ingroup loyalty and body purity. I come back, below, to the definition of the moral domain and the ways such a definition depends on processes of reasoning and reflection.

MORAL REASONING AND REFLECTION ACCORDING TO BIOLOGICAL-COGNITIVE SCIENTISTS

The work concerning morality of evolutionary anthropologists, neuroscientists, and cognitive scientists that was sketched above is complex and involves a variety of theoretical and empirical aspects. My discussion here is limited to only one, admittedly central, issue: How do these authors understand the role of reasons and reasoning in moral functioning? Can their views be accepted from a psychological perspective? Even though I try to conduct my discussion from the perspective of empirical psychology, it is impossible to avoid normative issues, in that at least some people in fact ask, wonder, and worry about the legitimacy, and the moral adequacy, of what they feel, think, and do. It is, therefore, possible to ask whether the theories I reviewed earlier reflect people's behavior in all its complexity – what they tend to do, what they think they should do, and what they are capable of doing under favorable circumstances.

Concerning the role of reasoning and reflection in moral functioning, all these theorists seem to agree that these processes are unimportant, and even useless, in determining moral choices. However, for empirical support and theoretical details, they seem to rely on the work of cognitive scientists, in particular of Haidt and his colleagues. In the following discussion, therefore, I too focus on the ideas of these investigators. When one carefully reads their works, one realizes that their position on this issue is neither simple nor undifferentiated; in fact, it is useful to distinguish a general claim – what could be called a "default position" – from the exceptions and the qualifications. The default position is what, in Haidt and Bjorklund's (2008) words, is "intended to capture the great majority of moral judgments made by the great majority of people," and what these theorists emphasize. Incidentally, this position is also what is most easily communicated, and what readers most easily remember.

Haidt's default position can be stated as follows:

1. Normally moral judgments are caused by intuitions, whether the intuitions are themselves caused by heuristics, or the heuristics are intuitions; whether they are intrinsically based on emotions, or depend on grammar type of rules and externally related to emotions.
2. Intuitions occur rapidly and appear as unquestionably evident; either the intuitions themselves or their sources are unconscious.
3. Intuitions are responses to minimal information, are not a result of analyses or reasoning; neither do they require reasoning to appear solid and true.
4. Reasoning may occur but infrequently. In any event, its purpose, and the purpose of reasons, is not to lead to, and support, a valid judgment, but to justify the judgment after the fact, either to other people or to oneself. Reasons in sum do not have a moral function.
5. Because such are the empirical facts, the "rationalistic" theories and methods of Piaget and Kohlberg are rejected.

What is the evidence supporting the above statements? The studies on the frequency and cognitive validity of moral reasoning that have been conducted by cognitive scientists are few, and the findings are spotty and scattered (Cushman, Young, & Hauser, 2006; Greene, Sommerville, Nystrom, Darley, & Cohen, 2001; cf. Haidt & Bjorklund, 2008). The findings that gave the original impulse to this area of research, and that are frequently referred to in this literature, concern what Haidt (2001) labeled "moral dumbfounding." In this study, participants were presented with selected instances of sexual behavior – including masturbation, homosexuality, and consensual expressions of sexuality between brother and sister – and were asked to judge whether the actions were right or wrong, and to give reasons for their judgments. In these instances, many subjects quickly decided that the actions in question were wrong, and attempted to give reasons for their judgment (e.g., that incest may lead to genetic malformations); but, when their reasons were effectively neutralized (e.g., in the case of incest, it was explained that no child would be conceived), they maintained the original judgment, could not give any reason for it, and, in many instances, expressed perplexity and confusion. But, as the investigators noted, not all participants behaved in the same way: some, particularly among the culturally liberal, were able to rely on reasons. In a second unpublished study (the results are reported in Haidt and Bjorklund, 2008), the participants were given five moral judgment tasks: Kohlberg's Heinz dilemma; two harmless taboo violations (incest among siblings, and cannibalism); drinking apple juice with a sterilized cockroach in it; and selling one's soul for $2.00. Here there was a sharp difference between the Heinz dilemma and the others: for the former, participants did rely on reasoning, and were responsive to counterarguments; for the latter, the usual "moral dumbfounding" was frequently observed.

Cushman et al. (2006), and Greene et al. (2001), relying on indirect evidence of reflection, found that subjects' behavior depends on the content of the dilemma. The former investigators presented dilemmas involving three discriminative criteria – the presence or absence of intention, the action vs. omission distinction, and whether harm was inflicted through physical contact or by indirect means – and checked whether the principle suggested by the judgment was also used in its justification. They found that approximately 80% of the subjects consciously relied on the commission-omission criterion, and 60% on the physical contact criterion. Thus, people are frequently conscious of the relevant reason, whether or not it is explicitly used to arrive at the judgment.[3] Greene et al. (2001) presented their participants with two sets of moral actions, and asked them to decide whether the action was appropriate or inappropriate. In each set, in one case the harm was inflicted personally and directly; in the contrasting case, the same harm was an indirect result of the agent attempting to achieve a better result.[4] During the judgment process, the investigators could study the pattern of brain activation through imaging techniques. The two kinds of judgments were accompanied by a different activation pattern: for the former, there was a greater activation of the "emotional areas" and a lower activation of the "cognitive areas"; the pattern was reversed for the "impersonal" judgments. At the same time, there was a different reaction time for the two sets of judgments, more rapid for the former, and slower for the latter. The implication

---

[3] Strangely, these authors interpret their findings as supporting the intuitionist hypothesis, mainly because several subjects, in a forced-choice task, did not unambiguously support the principle that the investigators believed was the correct one, but which in reality is rather controversial when applied to the specific instances.

[4] The experimental task, a variation of the trolley dilemma, is difficult to grasp without the help of concrete details. In the typical case, subjects are told that a runaway trolley would kill five people, unless this is deviated from its course; in one alternative, the observer could manuever a switch to deviate the trolley, which then would kill one person; in another alternative, the observer could throw from above a fat person, who then would stop the trolley. In the second instance, the killing is said to be direct and personal, in the first, indirect and impersonal.

is that some, but not all, moral dilemmas are accompanied by reflection (cognitive areas and slow reaction time), and, presumably, reasoning.

Haidt and colleagues also engaged in a series of laboratory studies, aimed at demonstrating that moral judgments could be affected by manipulating irrelevant emotional processes, or by overloading cognitive processes, and that therefore moral judgment is not a result of objective reasoning (Haidt & Bjorklund, 2008). As one would expect, also from other social psychological studies, these manipulations tend to affect people's judgment. But it is not clear what conclusion one could draw from these studies; we don't need laboratory demonstrations to know that judgment and reasoning can be influenced by all sorts of factors, including strong emotional arousal, distraction, and fatigue. Investigators who were genuinely interested to find out about people's capacity to reason in connection with moral judgment would want to find out also about the resilience of their cognitive processes; for instance, they could ask the same subjects of Haidt's experiments, this time under normal cognitive and emotional conditions, whether they would still agree with the moral judgments that they had previously made under conditions of impaired cognitive processes, and would want to look for individual differences in this respect. In sum, there is no guarantee that reason would function under any psychological condition; we may have to learn how to facilitate the appropriate conditions, if we care to arrive at moral judgments that we can reflectively accept and approve.

The studies reviewed here did not always address both sides of the hypothesis in question – that moral reasoning is infrequent, and that, when it occurs, it does so after the judgment, not to rationally support it, but to rationalize it. The second part of the hypothesis is important; however, with the exception of confabulatory responses in many instances of "moral dumbfounding," the studies summarized by Haidt and colleagues did not present any evidence, nor was such evidence sought. Concerning the first part of the hypothesis, the evidence is mixed. Many people, on some tasks, seemed indeed not to rely on reasons for their judgments, but a good number did; the actual frequencies seem to depend on the type of dilemma, and perhaps on the type of people. Intuitive judgments were given most frequently on dilemmas concerning sexual taboos and disgusting food – those, in sum, that correspond to Haidt's "body purity" category. I think this difference is theoretically important.

In reality, as Narvaez (2008), Pizarro and Bloom (2003), and Saltzstein and Kasachkoff (2004) have pointed out in careful reviews, the evidence concerning the use of moral reasons and reasoning is far broader and stronger than what was reported above leads one to believe, and much of it cannot be assimilated by social intuitionism. This evidence, almost completely ignored by investigators in the cognitive science tradition, comes from two different sources. First, there is the informal experience each one of us has in dealing with moral choices and in observing the ways people around us confront moral issues – the doubts, the struggles to arrive at choices that we find reasonable, the attempts to deal with contradictions and inconsistencies, and so on. Second, there are literally hundreds, and perhaps thousands, of studies conducted within the cognitive-developmental tradition broadly understood; these studies were done on a large variety of subjects of various ages and cultures, and with a very wide sample of moral dilemmas ("body purity" dilemmas were an exception), including "real life" dilemmas. Many of these studies were carefully conducted, attempting to get at what people actually believed, mindful to differentiate personal beliefs from stereotypical answers, or from responses motivated by social conformity. In fact, this was one of the purposes of asking for reasons, and of challenging the reasons people would initially offer. Overall, these studies show that, starting at least from the end of the preschool years, people are not surprised when they are asked to support their moral judgments, can engage in moral reasoning for all moral dilemmas proposed to them, and can provide coherent reasons. Of course, it could be claimed that these studies, or those conducted by cognitive scientists, did not elicit objective reasons, but mostly ad hoc rationalizations. There is no evidence that such is the case. In fact, it is surprising that little or no effort was spent by cognitive scientists to empirically validate this important aspect of their intuitionist claim, probably because it is very difficult to distinguish empirically genuine reasons from rationalizing justifications. In many studies, there is evidence that several participants changed their judgments when effective counterarguments were proposed by the interviewers, which could be interpreted minimally as indicating that they were following the logic of the discussion around the moral situation. In conclusion, what I called Haidt's "default position" does not have the kind of broad empirical support that is claimed by cognitive scientists. Is the qualified position any stronger?

Haidt's qualified position. Partially as an attempt to take into account his and other people's common experience, partially in response to his critics' objections, Haidt and Bjorklund (2008) recognized that people do resort to moral reasons, also in order to support their judgments. He still considers this reflective approach to be rare, and more likely to occur:

1. among certain professional groups ("highly specialized subcultures," ibid.), e.g., philosophers or judges, trained to approach their tasks with "unnatural modes of thought" (ibid.);

2. in the course of dialogues and discussions, when people's typical difficulty to reflect is overcome through social interaction, and their intuitive judgments can be challenged (presumably many instances of moral reasoning that were obtained in interviews, according to cognitive-developmental methodology, fall in this category);
3. when the initial intuition is weak, when a dilemma is well balanced, or when intuitions are in conflict; then people may be able to pursue a process of reasoning by "sheer force of logic," that causally leads to an objective, impassioned, judgment (ibid.);
4. when, in thinking about a situation, other intuitions are elicited that contradict the initial one – for instance, this may occur in role taking, when empathic and other emotional responses are stimulated;
5. when one is attempting to make a moral decision (rather than a simple moral judgment); then there are real consequences for oneself and other people, and a person is likely to reflect on them.

At first sight, this list of exceptions seems to be reasonable enough. What strikes the attentive reader, however, is that the exceptions are many, are stated vaguely and, therefore, are difficult to test empirically. For instance, concerning the first exception, the issue is not whether philosophers, or lawyers, would come up with more and more complex reasons than matching samples, but whether, in supporting their judgments, those of the former groups exclusively (the "reasoning professionals") would resort to reasons. To my knowledge, the above hypothetical statements were not formally tested. This is unfortunate, because, for instance, we have no idea of how frequently intuitions are missing, or are too weak, or contradict each other; we don't know how frequently our moral judgments have real consequences of one kind or another for ourselves or others; we don't know how frequently we engage in moral reasoning in the context of a conversation, or whether we have internalized the dialogical context of moral reasoning, and rely on it systematically. One could argue that the cases listed as exceptions are not exceptional at all, but are normal in moral reasoning.

Haidt and his colleagues, however, treat the exceptions without departing much from the default position: "good reasoning," as they call it, still is very rare; intuition still is the "natural" cause of judgment; social conformity processes are widespread, and the tendency to rationalize is still seen as overwhelming. Thus, in addressing Narvaez's (2008) suggestion that there is a difference between formulating a moral judgment and deciding what action to engage in, and that the latter requires more thoughtful reasoning and deliberation, Haidt accepts the distinction and the suggestion, but still concludes that (a) for most morally relevant actions there is no deliberation;

(b) when deliberation does occur, it is often biased by desire and an uneven search for evidence; and (c) the phenomenology of moral choice blends intuition and conscious deliberation (Haidt & Bjorklund, 2008b). In sum, these authors do not deny that genuine moral reasoning – one that is unaffected by personal wishes, biases, or unreflected automatic processes – is possible; but they also think that, for such a process to occur, there would have to be an almost impossible conjunction of psychological and environmental events.

It must be acknowledged that some research findings seem to confirm the skepticism of cognitive scientists, also in a case that Haidt would have included among the exceptions. One study by Dhami and Ayton (2001) (reported in Gigerenzer, 2008), partially speaks to the expectation that certain professional categories of people would pursue their professional tasks, at least, in a more reflective way. This study looked at the way magistrates in two London courts approach bail decisions (in England this kind of magistrate does not have legal training), and found that the large majority of the decisions were made by applying two or three simple rules, without considering the specific circumstances of each person, and that the magistrates were unaware of having followed such a routinely, unreflective procedure.

In addition to the somewhat vague formulation, one problem in attempting to test Haidt's hypotheses is the difficulty of determining whether a reasoning process is a self-serving rationalization, or in any event a fictional story, unrelated to the rational purpose of reasoning. Based on his insistence on the timing of reasons as occurring "after the fact" of judgment, Haidt seems to think that, if reasons are given after the judgment was made, then they are irrelevant justifications to satisfy the audience, and thus probably rationalizations. This idea makes sense within a very abstract and unreal conception of moral thinking and reasoning, namely, that good rational reasoning is a linear top-down process, starting from first principles, and then, step by step, deductively going down the ladder, arrives at the concrete judgment. But this is a fantasy, in morality as in science. I don't know anyone, including Kohlbergian "rationalists," who would defend it or even believe it. As many have pointed out (Narvaez, 2008; Saltzstein & Bloom, 2004), reasoning is a recursive, iterative process, that can begin anywhere, and can resort, in any order, to a variety of psychological material, including perceptions, memories, emotions, intuitions, simple moral criteria, and abstract moral principles. The real question, from this perspective, is whether moral reasons have a determining influence in the final judgment adopted by the person. When Haidt concedes that sometimes, in judgment, intuition and conscious deliberation blend, thus reassuring us that the intuition is always there, he does not quite grasp the different logical role that intuitions and reasons play in moral judgment. One does not quite calculate the portion of influence that various psychological elements have in arriving at moral judgment. Perception, memory, intuition, may always be present, but each has a different function to exercise. If convincing, reasons are supposed to have the final word. If one replaces the temporal relation of *before* and *after* with the determining relation, then it is possible to find careful collected data showing that reasons do have a determining role in people's *changing* their moral judgment. The evidence comes from several studies attempting to test the role of interpersonal exchanges, discussions, or of conflicts in general, within the framework of Piaget's equilibration theory (cf. Berkowitz, Gibbs, & Broughton, 1980; Turiel, 1974; Walker, 1983; for a review, see Walker, 1986).

If I were to draw a conclusion concerning the use of objective moral reasons and reasoning in support of moral judgments from all the evidence available, from formal studies and informal observation, I would say that such a reflective approach occurs more frequently than cognitive science theorists are willing to concede, but much less frequently than we would wish. Cognitive scientists may not be far off the mark when they claim that a large number of moral judgments and even decisions, *arrived at outside of the laboratory or the interview room*, are made rapidly, inattentively, unreflectedly; that frequently reasons offered for one's judgments, when they are offered, do not represent what one actually thinks about the issue, but are ad hoc constructions, perhaps even self-serving stories, and rationalizations. This skeptical conclusion is not based on empirical data – we do know that the large majority of people are capable of carefully considering abstract moral issues, and to give appropriate reasons for their judgments – but on everyday observation of many people's casual relationship with moral issues in their everyday life.

This conclusion seems to be superficially similar to the claims of cognitive scientists concerning moral reasons and reasoning. In fact, it reflects a stance that is radically different from theirs. The core of the difference is that, for cognitive scientists, what is described as factually occurring reflects the way things should be theoretically. As they believe, we are endowed with intuitive capacities, a result of the way our evolutionary history determined our brain, and therefore naturally adaptive to human needs. In this framework, relying on reasons and reasoning is largely unnecessary, and is, as Haidt and Bjorklund (2008) put it, an effortful, unnatural activity. From my perspective, by contrast, what we observe so frequently is a departure from the way things should be, in a sense reflecting a breakdown of ideal moral functioning. I do not believe that many of us refrain from reflectively considering moral reasons because we are pushed by ready-made intuitions, which render reasoning unnecessary. We all have intuitions and rely on heuristics, the theoretical status of which is, at this point, purely hypothetical. But we are not compulsively controlled by either process, at least when we wish to be responsible for our moral judgments. From my perspective, the major problem of cognitive scientists, and other psychologists, in taking a factual representation of human functioning as the basis for a theoretically normative view, is that it leads to a distorted, truncated conception of human nature and of moral functioning. These authors – perhaps because they are not sensitive to the span of individual differences, or to developmental observations – tend to reduce human capacities to their statistical means; in sum, they tend to minimize the scope of human possibilities, of what people can do morally, if they are prepared, through development and education, to approach life's important issues in a thoughtful way.

THE NEED FOR MORAL REASONS, REASONING, AND REFLECTION

Most, if not all, of the authors discussed here point to unfortunate – and on occasion morally repulsive – consequences of actions regulated by heuristics and intuitions. Gigerenzer (2008) recounts a WWII event, in which the large majority of the soldiers of a German company volunteered to kill the women and children of a Jewish community in a Polish village; he explains their choice as determined by a "don't break rank" heuristic. Striking examples of systematic errors produced by intuitions and heuristics are reported also by Cosmides and Tooby (2006) and by Sunstein (2005, 2008): they concern, for instance, a vindictive and useless approach to punishment; a restricted, tribal attitude toward sharing resources; or the intuitive rule that nature should not be tampered with, which may prevent us from exploring and adopting agricultural and medical programs that would be beneficial to human welfare.

While accepting that morally relevant heuristics and intuitions were selected through evolutionary mechanisms and are adaptive in the ancestral environmental niche, these theorists observe that they could fail miserably in an environment like ours, which is very different from the ancestral one. As Cosmides and Tooby (2006) write: "Because our moral heuristics are now operative outside the envelope of environments for which they were designed, laws that satisfy the moral intuitions they generate may regularly fail to produce the outcomes we desire and anticipate" (p. 207). They continue with a text that is worth quoting in full:

> it is worth reflecting on where our conceptions of right, justice, and morality come from. Some of these conceptions spring from evolved moral heuristics. But these did not evolve because they produce objective justice (whatever that may be), even when operating in the ancestral environments that selected for their design. They evolved only because they advanced the fitness of their own genetic basis under ancestral conditions. These bizarre events of ancestral DNA editing are a strange foundation on which to confidently erect moral principles or modern legal systems. (p. 208)

The crucial question to ask is: In searching for moral solutions, how does one decide which heuristics, or which intuitions, one ought to follow, and when to follow them? Similar questions should be raised in many other instances: for example, when heuristics or intuitions are in conflict with each other, should one go with the stronger, or the emotionally more powerful? And what should one do when an intuition or an emotion contradicts one's judgment or one's friends' judgments? Or when the intuition is weak, barely audible? Or when there is no intuition at all? Could intuitions offer us a solution for the moral problems that occur, on occasion, when people rely on them? All the above instances of doubt were listed by Haidt and Bjorklund (2008), who admit that in these instances moral reasons are needed. Also many of the other authors acknowledge that, as Gigerenzer put it, "the study of heuristics will never replace the need for moral deliberation and individual responsibility" (p. 15). However, there is a problem. Having dismissed what they call the "rationalistic" approach of Piaget and Kohlberg, having emphasized the natural adaptiveness of intuitive judgments, and the distorted, self-serving character of much human reasoning, these authors are at a loss to explain how objective deliberation and reflection are possible, and how the latter ought to work in a moral psychological system, and are unwilling to attribute to these processes a central role in people's moral life, even when they should perform a monitoring job.

Moreover, it is worth noting that intuitions or heuristics are not immune from the distorting and deceptive mechanisms that so frequently mar our reasoning. It is an illusion, perhaps a result of some sort of romantic trust of nature, that intuitions, because they feel spontaneous and may be a part of our inherited nature, are as nakedly pure as they appear to us. Self-serving, defensive processes run deeply and corrupt widely, always more deeply and widely than we are prepared to recognize. In fact, we can unconsciously select those intuitions that fit our needs best, and can interpret those that arise in us in a direction that is convenient to our individual or group advantages. Haidt et al. (2008) think that cultures have the power to manipulate in this manner our core natural intuitions, and explain through this mechanism cultural differences in intuitive judgments. But what cultures can do, individuals can too. From a moral perspective, cultural manipulations of moral intuitions are not necessarily better than those performed by individuals. One important difference between intuition and reasoned reflection is that, whereas the latter has the capacity to correct itself, intuitions do not, since by definition they cannot go over themselves and examine what they are according to evaluative criteria.

In addition to examining and correcting intuitions, reasoned reflection is also needed, more fundamentally, to determine the criteria that should be adopted for moral evaluations. When various authors discuss the consequences of heuristics and intuitions, they use terms like "satisfactory," "unsatisfactory," "good," "bad," etc. What criteria do they use to arrive at their evaluations? Are their criteria meant to be moral? Do they differ from prudential, or economic criteria? Is the morally good the same as what we desire, individually or as a group? More generally, how de we construct criteria, and decide which to use in evaluating our intuitions? These are terribly complicated questions that have exercised moral philosophers, religious people, and common folk for millennia. In fact, they concern the very definition of the moral domain. For instance, Haidt and colleagues courageously tackled the issue of universal moral contents, not on the basis of theory, but from below, on the basis of empirical observation. In doing so they set aside any concern about the well-known ambiguity of terms such as "good," and "bad," "right" and "wrong," and even "moral," and ignored that even "harm" and "harmful" are subject to widely divergent interpretations. Is there any instance of human behavior, which, when seen from the perspective of one or another ideology, could not be included in the harmful category? Considering these authors' largesse, one wonders why certain issues were not included in their moral system, since they clearly are, for many people, objects of moral intuition and judgment. I am thinking, for example, of concern for freedom, concern for equal rights and for impartiality, universal respect, the nonnegotiable primacy of the individual person, issues concerning truth and truthfulness, etc. One suspects that these issues were left out because they do not elicit the type of strong emotions associated with physical harm, or with sexual and other taboos, that social intuitionists believe to form the core of moral intuitions.

The important point here, one that is related to my concern with reasoning and reflection, is not the completeness of the list or the number of moral categories, but the procedure for defining the moral domain. It is clear – Haidt and his colleagues from neuroscience and evolutionary anthropology would agree – that neural processes don't come with the label *moral* attached to them; neither do human or animal emotions and behaviors. Therefore morality must be a human construction, of course not an arbitrary one, but based on what we think human beings are, and what we know are the consequences of what we do. We are aware that there is more than one such construction, and that those that exist are not so readily compatible with each other. Because the multiplicity of moral constructions is a fact; because there seems to be something to be gained for us to arrive at a reasonable concordance of moralities; and because, most probably, polls and statistics will not provide it, we ought to ask whether reason, reasons, and reasoning, in spite of everything, may not provide us the only hope for finding a solution. It is difficult to imagine that we could reach even a partial agreement concerning lower-level principles without a careful, dispassionate analysis of human needs, in general and in the concrete circumstances of our lives. Philosophers too start from intuitions and use intuitions in the battles they have with each other; but they understand and accept the requirement of using reasons and critical reflection to objectively justify the intuitions they hold on to.[5]

---

[5] Haidt seems to avoid these questions, by arguing that the system of the five core moral sensitivities does not need to be justified from outside itself. Morality, he acknowledges, requires justifications, but the only justifications we can have and need lie in the evolutionary-selected, brain-inscribed, five basic intuitions. In the same way, he adds that we don't need to justify the kind of human nature we have, beyond the fact that it is our human nature; in fact, human nature is the ground for our justifications: as if it were obvious what belongs to human nature and what does not; as if we agreed on what human nature is, and how we can recognize it. A particular problem with Haidt's position is that (a) at least some people seem to have moral intuitions that don't fit his set of five; (b) some people do not seem to have intuitions that correspond to one or another of his categories; and (c) these basic intuitions can be changed, and oriented in different directions by different people. Haidt recognizes points (b) and (c), and explains them through the selective and interpretive power that cultures have. However, with this move, his biological intuitionism slides over to sociocultural intuitionism, and reliance on "natural" ethical ideas becomes reliance on sociocultural ethical views, with all the attendant problems of ethical relativism, acritical conformity, etc. For instance, what can Haidt tell American liberals, who are no longer sensitive to the moral validity of "body purity," and argue that what they don't feel cannot belong to "natural morality"? Could this debate be pursued without reasoning, reflection, rational objective justifications? Or is each of us stuck with our factual, unjustified intuitions, whether they come from our culture or not?

Another need for reasoned reflection is related to the exercise of moral responsibility, a term that one encounters only rarely in the literature about morality from the fields of brain and cognitive sciences, perhaps because this work mostly deals with judgment and not with action. It is clear, however, that one ought to be responsible not only for one's actions, but also for one's judgments, whether they are general and abstract, or concern the concrete actions of other people or of oneself. The fact is that the theories I presented and discussed here – from neuroethics and evolutionary anthropology and psychology to cognitive science – attempt explanations of moral judgments and moral actions as if these events were occurring in an impersonal field. The processes brought into their explanatory models, whether biological or psychological in nature, conscious or unconscious, are understood in causal terms: factors a and b determine event c, which determines y and z. There is no room, in these models, for an agentic self.

To take responsibility for a judgment or an action, and to feel responsible for it, means to own it and take possession of it. This involves, as a first step, creating between oneself and the judgment some space in which to operate, distancing oneself from the judgment and relating to it as an object of consideration and reflection. Here, I think, in this capacity to distance oneself from one's processes and products, lies the significance of the fact that in animals, including the great apes, there is no judgment that is psychologically separate from the action, at least none that is observed. The animal's actions of sharing or nurturing proceed directly from the impulses and are driven by them; the animal cannot distance itself from the action, possess it, and be responsible for it.

In practical terms, in order to assume ownership of a judgment, a second step is needed, namely, to exercise control over it. This is done, perhaps partially, through a reasoned analysis of its origin, of the elements, including emotions and intuitions, by which it was constructed, and of the personal motives that might distort its meaning and corrupt its validity. The quickly formulated judgment – as also the intuitions and the emotions, or the stereotyped automatic associations that led to it – may already be there; but one has the power to go back to it, and accept it or reject it according to one's criteria of validity and truth. One could even exercise some control over one's spontaneous emotions and intuitions, perhaps not to the extent of eliminating them or preventing them from occurring, but in the sense of evaluating them, concluding that they are undesirable, and wanting not to have them. All this implies that in moral functioning, as in all human conscious functioning, there is a unity of the self, in the sense that the self experiences and grasps that processes occurring in him are his to take possession of; the self is a self, if the emotions, the desires, the memories, the thoughts that occur in him, and the actions of which he is the agentic source, potentially are all under him to organize, control, and own. When Haidt and Bjorklund (2008b), in reply to their commentators, claim that moral judgment and moral decision making "are not closely related, functionally speaking," that, from an evolutionary perspective, "judging others and choosing actions for oneself are very different processes," they view the issue from the perspective of the fragmentation of neural processes, not from the perspective of the self.

THE MORAL LANDSCAPE OF THE MATURE ADULT

That human beings have the capacity to support their moral judgments with reasons, implicitly or explicitly, is recognized by most authors within the biological-cognitive approach to morality. As mentioned earlier, these same authors also acknowledge that in some instances moral heuristics and intuitions are insufficient, and that we may need moral reflection and deliberation to avoid the undesirable consequences that may derive from a blind reliance on intuitive judgments. At the same time they argue that heuristics and intuitions are generally adaptive, at least in the ancestral environment; that people, including adults, rarely rely on reasons in formulating moral judgments, and, when they do, their reasons tend to be biased, divorced from objective reality and truth. If, trusting these authors' empirical claims, we accept the above statements, we are then left with two important questions: First, how frequent are the undesirable consequences of intuitive moral judgments, and how seriously do they affect the well-being of individuals and societies? Second, what can be done by individuals and societies to make their moral functioning more adequately responsive to moral needs? On these questions, the theorists I reviewed earlier tend to be silent. In what follows, I assume that the consequences of a widespread failure on the part of adults to engage in reflected moral judgment may be serious, but that they could be mitigated by preparing people to responsibly assume their adult roles.

The purpose of this section is to show that the daily life of ordinary mature adults is filled with situations and encounters that present opportunities, and sometimes the necessity, to make moral judgments and engage in moral choices; that many such situations, from a moral perspective, are complex, ambiguous, cognitively and motivationally difficult; and that this sort of complexity ought to be approached by focusing on the role of the responsible self. The people I have in mind are not moral exemplars or moral heroes, but ordinary people, who, while caring about morality, also care about many other dimensions of human living; and who, in addition to the domain of family and friends, are also engaged in the world of work, and in the public issues of their communities and of the entire planet. As I use the concepts here, to be a mature adult means to take one's adult roles seriously, also in the public spheres; and to be a morally mature adult means to be able to approach these roles also from one's moral concerns. Here, therefore, I focus on broad social issues. The strategy I follow is to mention several such issues that seem to have the potential to raise moral questions for the attentive adult. The examples I use – no more than items on a list – are a tiny portion of morally relevant situations. The hope is that they stimulate the reader's imagination, his or her ability to generate details and variations, to grasp the intricacies involved in each case, and, most important, to sense the mass of people whose lives are touched, morally, by these and similar events around us. What matters for my argument is to produce a sense of the normality, and also of the complexity and moral urgency, of much that occurs in our world. To show that many situations encountered by adults are morally complex, and that moral solutions may be far from obvious, is to show that quick intuitions, "fast and frugal" heuristics, or automatic and habitual rules are inadequate, and that, therefore, thinking, reflection, and reasoning are needed. This, of course, does not suggest that these processes are readily available, and normally carried out; but minimally it points to the necessity of educational interventions, broadly conceived, in order to prepare people for adequately responding to the moral demands of their public life.

Starting with the world of work – that area of activities and concerns that, together with the family, intimately touches the life of practically every adult – one finds there at least three aspects that present questions for moral judgment.[6] There is, first, the context of horizontal and vertical relations in which work activities occur: at one extreme, the encouragement among the employees of a sense of ownership of the company and of responsible participation in it; at the opposite extreme, rigidly hierarchical and authoritarian forms of communication and controlling micromanagement. The moral implications of this aspect clearly appears, when one considers

[6] Work is not frequently seen through moral psychological lenses. One exception is professional ethics, which has been the object of a large number of studies (cf. e.g., Bandman, 2003; Pritchard, 1999; Rest & Narvaez, 1994). Though very valuable in themselves, from my present perspective these studies are of limited interest. In particular, they tend not to raise the question that is central in this essay: How do professionals respond to, evaluate, and attempt to resolve the moral issues that arise in the context of work?

two examples of micromanagement: the recent attempts to closely control the decisions of professional medical staff by managed care organizations (MCOs), and the serious consequences that ensued for the well-being of both patients and medical personnel; and the step-by-step control to which millions of people working for the innumerable call centers are subjected to every day (Sennett, 1998, 2007, has written incisively about the human aspect of micromanagement).

A second aspect of work that frequently carries moral implications is related to the tasks that have to be exercised in certain roles. For instance, the role of manager or of corporate leader involves a number of morally sensitive decisions: investing and borrowing of money; dealing with government officials at the federal and state level in order to obtain conditions that are most favorable for business; the setting of salaries, benefits, and rewards of various kinds; and the task of hiring and firing. Perhaps more than any other, this last task touches human needs and human emotions, and is most directly relevant to morality, because it affects not only the economic life of the workers and their families, and sometimes of entire communities, but also the workers' sense of self-worth.

Not infrequently moral questions arise from a third aspect of work, namely, from what a company, an industry, or a corporation produce. Sometimes, if they reflect on it, workers cannot take pride, as they should, in the products of their minds and hands, not because they are made incompetently, but because of their questionable ethical value. Ethical questions may have to do with the strategies by which the product is researched, obtained, and marketed. Certain companies and entire industries (e.g., financial investment companies and the banking industry; chemical and pharmaceutical industries) have acquired a less than shiny reputation in this respect (cf. Angell, 2004; Healy, 2006; Rothman, 2000; Stephens, 2000). Other companies and industries are organized around products that themselves raise moral questions. One example is the very powerful arms industry, which employs close to nine million people worldwide. A second example is the tobacco industry, with its history of deception and manipulation (cf. Brandt, 2007; Epstein, 2007). Both these sectors of the industrial world demand a serious moral attention, not only on the part of managers and executive officers, but also on the part of the huge number of people that they employ, and on the part of the population at large.

Outside of the areas of one's closest and most personal involvements with family and work there are the widening spaces of communities, from one's neighborhood to the more distant, frequently anonymous, social and administrative areas of the town, to the abstract institutional and legalized space of one's country. These public spaces are filled with events, entrenched attitudes and practices, situations so constantly present that they are no longer noticed by us, long-standing traditions, political arrangements, and so on, all presenting issues that call for moral judgment, or problems that require morally satisfying solutions. There is the widespread poverty, in all its dirty and shameful details; there is the worldwide phenomenon of migration – masses of people running away from oppression, unemployment, and hunger; there is the related phenomenon of ghettoization at the margin of most large cities. A huge global problem has to do with prisons and prisoners. Linked with the issues of poverty and employment is the issue of medical care, with all its myriad questions, many with serious moral implications. Closely related, there is the question of how society should manage the care of the old, and also the divisive issues of birth control, abortion, and euthanasia.

And then there are wars. In spite of the fact that we are made increasingly aware of the terrible disasters that they unleash upon us, wars have become a constant presence in our landscape. Since the end of WWII, one can count over 70 wars and civil wars; for the same time period, the number of military and civilian casualties was estimated at between 40 and over 90 million (cf. Leitenberg, 2006). These estimates leave out the destruction of cities, fields, and factories; the breakup of families; the loss of stabilizing values and traditions; and the large number of people that are rendered physically and psychologically damaged. The question of war brings up two more general issues that certainly have moral implications, and demand reflective judgment. One has to do with that complex set of emotions and attitudes that we call patriotism, the other with truthfulness and transparency in communication. Patriotism, particularly in certain contexts, easily slides into nationalism, with its irrational feelings of superiority and arrogance, contempt and hostility for people of other nations, and a tendency to blindness and cognitive distortions, especially when distance and objectivity become more necessary. Truthfulness is one of the most multifaceted and complex moral issues. In the context of war, when citizens are called on to take a personal stance, and also to sacrifice their lives and the lives of family and friends, truthfulness by the authorities and by the media is as necessary as it is universally abused.

All of the issues mentioned above – a small sample among the many that confront us – reflect important moral concerns. In addition, all of them are difficult, complex, and sometimes ambiguous: in each instance, the relevant considerations are many, frequently conflicting with each other; in practically every case, one could invoke contrary moral ideas and values.

For instance, in decisions related to work, besides looking at the welfare of workers and their families, managers should also consider efficiency, productivity, the cost of products, responsibility to shareholders, and the general state of the economy. In some instances, to keep everyone on the payroll may mean a delayed closing of factories and the loss of the entire work force. Even in the case of the tobacco industry, the moral issue is not as simple and straightforward as it may seem: representatives of these companies, correctly or incorrectly, were able to argue their case in terms of civil liberties and the rights of smokers, the importance of their industry in the overall economy, the number of jobs, and the tax revenues that are generated. A similar case is frequently made for the arms industry. Even wars – certainly the greatest intentionally created disasters – may not be so simple to judge morally: we know how difficult it is to distinguish between just and unjust, defensive and aggressive wars, or to evaluate the seriousness of the situations that are said to require armed intervention, or the positive and negative consequences of such interventions.

One aspect of the difficulty in formulating dispassionate moral judgments is the well-known human ability to hide egocentric motives and personal biases behind moral considerations, and the fact that frequently such motives and biases are unconscious and operate unconsciously (cf. Bandura, 2002; and particularly Odier, 1943). Precisely because of the difficulty of formulating moral judgments, I tried to refrain from imposing my moral views; only the moral subject, from his or her perspective, can decide to what extent morality is relevant, and what would be the morally correct evaluations and choices. What matters – this is one central point here – is that personal judgments be arrived at responsibly, that is, thoughtfully, reflectively, and with the support of reasons one can vouch for. Personally, I find it puzzling that, while such corruptive human tendencies ought to call for moral reflection, analysis, and self-examination, they are used to argue for a nonreflective intuitionism.

How do people respond to the situations listed above and many similar ones? How did the business leaders who opted for micromanaging their workers, or decided to lay people off and to close factories, or aggressively pursued the selling of arms and tobacco; the shareholders who approved these strategies; the medical personnel in MCOs and the employees of call centers; the leaders who decided to enter a war, perhaps preemptively; the citizens who supported this decision with their votes, or those who protested against it, and so on – how did all of these people judge the situations they were confronted with? The witnesses and outside observers, those who, from nearby or from afar, were aware of the same situations, how did they evaluate them? What were their immediate feelings, intuitions, and concerns? How did they manage, and organize together, the information and their several personal reactions to arrive at a judgment? Did morality enter at all in the equation? Did they question their own feelings, intuitions, or values? Did they ever doubt, morally, their own line of defense, the story they were telling themselves, the criteria guiding the decisions, the correctness of their moral justifications and of their reconstructions? Most important, did they feel in charge of the judging process, or vice versa, did they feel carried away by a hazy atmosphere of emotionality, or trapped in the system, by "the way things are done," or by "what everybody thinks"; pushed by their needs, or the desire to avoid complications, and perhaps satisfied with a superficial sincerity. In sum, did they feel fully responsible for the judgment and the decision, accountable for their moral correctness, validity, and objectivity?

Ideally, what is needed by a morally mature adult is a stance that rejects inattention, distraction, and avoidance; one that examines the issues, the information, the possible alternative actions and the consequences of each; weighs the relative importance of different values and criteria, and responsibly decides what is right or wrong, knowing that he or she is accountable for the judgment. The information may be insufficient; the many aspects may be too complicated to sort out; the conclusions, therefore, can be uncertain. And yet this judgment would be responsibly one's own. I suspect that such a clear moral stance is not assumed frequently enough by adults, even when they have the required cognitive capacities, and even when they care about morality. There may be several explanations for this situation: it is possible that we were not prepared to fully assume the moral responsibilities of adulthood; or that we follow categorical distinctions whereby the moral is too sharply separated from the economic, or the political. In addition, there are several common difficulties in adopting and maintaining such a stance: one is a tendency to mind one's own business, and to restrict one's moral concerns to one's own private world; a second is a desire to "think positively," that is, to protect a reasonable level of serenity in one's life by diverting one's attention from what is ugly and corrupt; a third has to do with a sense of hopelessness and helplessness whenever one enters the realm of public moral concerns.

This last response, widespread among those who are morally more thoughtful and aware, requires a brief comment. Frequently it is not a result of laziness or of a paranoid vision of the world, nor an excuse for inaction, but it seems to derive from a realistic appraisal of the near impossibility to become independently and critically engaged in the world of public morality: many public issues are too complicated, too "technical" to be grasped by the common person (we may be encouraged to accept such a belief, and therefore, to simply trust the authorities, the "grown-ups"); the necessary information is not made available. In fact, we are intentionally lied to, even by those whom we had learned to trust; and the stark reality is distorted by a corrupted language. And then, when we engage in whatever protest is possible, we frequently realize that it makes no difference, except as an expression of personal frustration. In sum, we realize that our moral world is being restricted to decency in personal interactions; that, for what concerns the world in which the big moral events take place (poverty, systematic injustices, discriminations, wars, etc.), we are reduced to the role of trusting participants, of loyal supporters. No moral judgment is required from us, but only identification, with our company, our group, or our country.

And yet, it is precisely in these cases, when adult agency seems to be taken away from us, when we are pushed into a child's attitude, that a clear stance as a moral judge is needed. Such a stance is, at the same time, an affirmation of the moral perspective, and a reestablishment of one's presence and relevance in the world. In asserting one's right to judge and to express indignation and contempt, one bears witness to morality, when all other intervention seems to fail. Most important, it is an attempt to resist being used as unaware, "innocent" cogs by systems – whether it be one's company, or one's country – for goals one does not know or understand, and being made complicit in the immoral consequences of their projects. In those instances, when one unwittingly and unknowingly participates in destructive results, trusting sincerity and good intention are not reliable guides of the morality of one's actions, particularly when one has not questioned one's ideas, or doubted one's information, or one's trusting acceptance of others' goals, and therefore are not morally valid justifications for a mature adult. What counts is a judgment for which one assumes full responsibility (for a clear discussion of these points, see Neiman, 2002, particularly pp. 267–288).

THE CHARACTERISTICS AND STUDY OF THE MORALLY MATURE ADULT

This is not the appropriate place to attempt a relatively complete catalogue of the mature adult's moral characteristics. My intention is simply to provide a sketch of those competencies and attitudes that seem to be required to function morally in a context of normal adulthood, emphasizing in particular the central role of the responsible self in utilizing its resources to arrive at a fair moral judgment, and to then sustain the corresponding action.

There is, first, the awareness of the moral implications of one's adult roles – in one's family, as spouse and parent, including the issues related to sexuality; in one's employment and profession, including issues of professional ethics; in one's community, as a citizen in one's society and in the world. One aspect of mature adulthood is to view oneself as a member of the whole of humanity and, at some level, a participant in the events that occur in a planet that has now become a village.

Overlapping this knowledge, and articulated with it, there should be a clear grasp of four sets of more abstract, structural issues. One has to do with the understanding of the common good, and of its primacy relative to individual interests. From such an understanding derive the sense of citizenship and of one's civic obligations; and also such competencies as the ability to abstract social roles and their functions from the individual characteristics (including the moral views) of those who occupy the roles, and from the personal relationships one has with them; the ability to evaluate, and be critical of, leaders and authorities from the perspective of an organization's nature and purpose, and not on the basis of one's own private interests and preferences. Not all the judgments that a person can formulate within this framework are moral – many would follow economic, political, or simply functional criteria – but some are. Among the latter, one should count judgments concerning discriminations, invidious and arbitrary preferences, the abuse of one's authority, or of one's role in general, for personal advantages, and so on. The evaluation of one's own organization for the possible immoral consequences of one's activity (as, e.g., in the cases of pharmaceutical and tobacco companies) will have to be done from the perspective of the legal and moral norms of the wider system to which one's organization is subordinated. It is possible to recognize in this set of cognitive competencies many of the elements of Kohlberg's stage 4, but without its structural and developmental assumptions.

The second set of cognitive competencies is related to what Kohlberg (1984) and Rest et al. (1999) called postconventional moral thinking, emphasizing its descriptive aspects, and bracketing out the more controversial theoretical ideas. Whether there is, or can be, a type of moral understanding that relies on universal principles and goes beyond the laws and moral expectations of any concrete society, are questions that have been debated in philosophy and the social sciences. However this debate is resolved theoretically, it seems clear to me that some version of such a moral perspective is needed and can be observed in many people. The organizational framework discussed earlier does not offer the necessary tools for a moral judgment of the overarching organization. The history of the twentieth century has taught us this much: one needs to take a moral stance vis-à-vis the unjust laws of one's society, its cruel practices, its slavery, its wars of aggression and conquest, its colonial adventures, the exploitation of foreign populations, and the destruction of their cultures – projects frequently pursued in the name of a national morality or of a religious good. This kind of moral stance requires a degree of distancing from, and sometimes opposition to, the laws and the accepted morality of one's society, and the ideological presuppositions of one's culture as a whole – distancing and opposition that could take different forms (provided one does not confuse one's conscious or unconscious needs with the moral perspective), and that could be variously nurtured by empathic emotions and the vivid images of the suffering and humiliation of other people, or by a clear grasp of humanity and human dignity, or by a religious sense of universal brotherhood.

A third set of characteristics includes cognitive habits and attitudes that are not specifically moral, but have the general purpose of monitoring one's beliefs, and the processes by which they were acquired and accepted. Among them, there is the ability and habit to reflect on, and examine, the rules, moral norms, and implicit assumptions of one's society, looking at their consequences and their validity; but also to reflect on, and examine oneself: those moral norms and ideas that one has acquired in childhood and adolescence, and tends to accept as unquestionably true; the affective tendencies, such as one's response to civic or religious authorities, one's patriotism or national identity that one built around them; the more or less unconscious reactions – of admiration or suspicion, of approval or rejection – that one has toward specific moral beliefs and expressions.

As already suggested, particularly important in certain situations is the ability to bracket one's trusting attitude, or a mindset of lazy acceptance, and to assume instead a critical, wary, even a skeptical attitude; to be alert for signs of cover-ups, disinformation, and lies, particularly when a vaguely enthusiastic language is being used, one that appeals to loyalty, faith, and self-sacrifice. An individual has to have, at the same time, such a respect for the truth that wariness is not transformed into a paranoid search for plots. However, the mature adult should be equally critical and skeptical toward oneself: being concerned with self-deception, one would have acquired the habit of routinely questioning one's motives, one's moral intuitions, and the accounts and justifications one gives for one's behavior. This brings us to a fourth set of characteristics, related to the relationship one has with oneself: the abilities to control fear and anxiety, to resist social pressure, to be autonomous in thinking and action, to be courageous when courage is needed.

Central among these characteristics is responsibility, in both of its components, the sense of personal obligation to act according to the norms and ideals that one has appropriated and made one's own, and the attitude of accountability to oneself and to others, this too based on the ownership of one's actions. Ultimately it is responsibility that generates the monitoring of one's mental processes and the organized use of all of one's resources to arrive at moral judgments and decisions that would match as faithfully as possible one's standards and ideals.

What do we know, empirically, about these characteristics, their development, and their variations among adults? After many years of research, we have learned a great deal about several central moral aspects – particularly the cognitive ones (moral knowledge, and different aspects of moral understanding), but also about moral emotions and motivation. However, it is fair to say that we still know very little about moral functioning, that is, about the ways all these aspects come together in specific situations to generate morally relevant decisions and actions. The central idea in the concept of the moral personality is that moral functioning is the work of a subject self, and not of any specific component, including cognitive components; that the self manages the tasks of arriving at moral judgments and at the corresponding actions, by relying on the person's various resources; and that the moral self feels responsible for the process and the outcome, that is, for the use of the conscious elements, and, to some extent, also for the unconscious ones, once their positive or negative effects become known. To study the moral personality, then, would mean to study the work of the moral self, and the developmental and individual differences in the way it operates.

The issue of moral functioning has not been raised, at least not in precisely these terms. The central reason for this state of affairs, I think, is that most of psychology, across its various disciplines, thinks in terms of variables and combination of variables, sometimes in the hope of finding that central variable that would offer the complete, or almost complete, explanation of even complex behaviors. It is not surprising, therefore, to realize that the recent shifts of attention to the moral personality consist of attempts to explain moral behavior by adding emotional and motivational variables to cognitive variables. Moreover, the combined effect of multiple variables is automatically understood in correlational and factorial language, using as a major evaluative criterion the amount of variance that each variable and their combinations contribute to the effects. This approach is conceptually and methodologically incapable of capturing the systemic and agentic work of the self: in fact, in any analysis of variance approach, the specific function of each aspect is lost, responsibility becomes a variable like any other, different from the others exclusively by the amount of variance that it explains; while the agentic role of the self is irretrievably hidden behind the causal interactions among the variables.

This conceptual and methodological impasse is probably more debilitating than we imagine. One way out could be an approach that might be called systematic clinical study of moral functioning. Here, the unit of analysis would be the individual person, and not the psychological variable; the primary source of data would be descriptive accounts, given by the agents themselves, of the processes, as they are consciously experienced, in confronting moral dilemmas – misperceptions, attempted diversions, doubts, fluctuations, choices, decisions, and actions. The descriptions could focus on a single decision; or on a protracted engagement in a project; or on a period of one's life in all its richness and complexity. The methods of data collection can vary: from confronting real personal issues, in the present or in the past, to dealing with hypothetical issues in imagined roles; from diaries to conversations and systematic interviews; to dramatic play from the perspective of those characters with whom subjects identify. It is readily granted that the typical moral decision is not taken in full awareness of its components; that after-the-fact reflection and reconstructions can introduce guesses and distortions; and that self-deception is always possible. However, the material thus obtained is too precious to give it up, particularly if investigators resort to appropriate corrective strategies. For example, subjects' accounts could be followed by questions aimed at opening their awareness to aspects they might have missed; encouraging more detailed and articulated descriptions; questioning the correctness or the objectivity of the accounts – by pointing out possible contradictions, or, more generally, by making subjects aware of the distorting effect of self-presentation or of other self-deceptive strategies.

This sort of clinical approach is not incompatible with quantitative analyses, if one resorts to categories – ideal types of moral responses that summarize complexly organized processes. In any event, it would be a first step that hopefully would open up a more careful study of individual variables, or particularly meaningful combinations of variables, according to standard procedures; this time, however, we would have some background knowledge of the role of the variables in the overall moral process.

SUMMARY AND CONCLUDING REFLECTIONS

The central point of this essay is the importance, for society and for each individual, that adults be morally concerned about public social issues, not only in their immediate environment, but everywhere else in the world, when events, decisions, and policies carry moral consequences. Related points were that, reflected moral judgment, in spite of contrary claims by biological-cognitive sciences, is in fact possible; that moral judgment may not occur as frequently as would be desirable; that one explanation of this state of affairs may lie in the ways children's and adolescents' moral education is approached, both in the family and in the schools – an education that frequently follows a too restrictive definition of morality as limited to interpersonal issues; that tends not to take into account the complexities that characterize adult roles; and that, while emphasizing sincerity, tends to neglect the skills of careful social criticism, self-criticism, and the attention to self-deceptive strategies.

In discussing adult moral functioning, emphasis was placed on moral judgment, not because this is the end or the apex of human morality, but because it is its essential starting point; and, more immediately, because moral judgment is the focus of the conception proposed by the cognitive sciences. Of course, whatever its origins and explanations, moral judgment is, and cannot be but, cognitive in nature, immediately a result of cognitive processes. However, it would be a mistake to interpret the present emphasis on moral judgment as indicating a limited and reductive view of moral functioning. In fact, moral judgment, or any judgment, has certain essential characteristics, is of such a nature that it necessarily brings into the picture the subjective self, and with it, the rest of the individual's personality. A judgment is not the passive product of causal processes impersonally running in the psyche. A judgment – whether factual, scientific, aesthetic, or moral – is not an association, a categorization, the automatic application of a label or a tag to a perception or a phrase; but it is the assertion of a person that X is true or untrue, wrong or correct, ugly or beautiful, good or bad. Therefore a judgment expresses the stance of a person on one aspect of the world. For these reasons, moral judgments cannot really be assimilated either into the cognitive-developmentalism of Piaget or Kohlberg, or into the various information processes approaches, including those of the cognitive sciences, nor can they be fully understood within any of these viewpoints. Ultimately it is a self that produces a judgment, using cognitive processes and skills as tools; it is a self that owns it, and is responsible for it. In other words, a moral judgment is one episode within a project, the project of responding to certain specific aspects of reality; it is preceded by other episodes (including the perception and interpretation of reality, the recognition, the acceptance or rejection, of one's emotions, etc.), and is naturally followed by other episodes (including the recognition of other emotions, the management of other motives and defences, the decision on how to act).

It is this complex of the self that moral psychology has not yet succeeded in capturing and studying. There certainly is a need for fresh perspectives. It seems to me, however, that the revolution proposed by the biological-cognitive sciences – involving a fragmentation of the components, the assumption of passivity and impersonality of processes – departs at the start from the right direction.

REFERENCES

Angell, M. (2004). *The truth about the drug companies: How they deceive us and what to do about it.* New York: Random House.

Bandman, B. (2003). *The moral development of health care professionals.* Westport, CT: Praeger.

Bandura, A. (2002). Selective moral disengagement in the exercise of moral agency. *Journal of Moral Education*, 31, 101–119.

Baron, J. (1993). *Morality and rational choice.* Dordrecht, The Netherlands: Kluwer.
  (1995). A psychological view of moral intuition. *The Harvard Review of Philosophy*, 5, 36–40.

Berkowitz, M, Gibbs, J., & Broughton, J.M. (1980). The relation of moral judgment stage disparity to developmental effects of peer dialogue. *Merrill-Palmer Quarterly*, 26, 341–357.

Blasi, A. (2005). What should count as moral behavior? The nature of "early morality" in children's development. In W. Edelstein & G. Nunner-Winkler (Eds.), *Morality in context* (pp. 119–140). Oxford, UK: Elsevier.

Brandt, A.M. (2007). *The cigarette century: The rise, fall, and deadly persistence of the product that defined America.* New York: Basic Books.

Cheney, D.L., & Seyfarth, R.M. (2007). *Baboon metaphysics: The evolution of a social mind.* Chicago: University of Chicago Press.

Cosmides, L., & Tooby, J. (2004). Knowing thyself: The evolutionary psychology of moral reasoning and moral sentiments. In R.E. Freeman & P. Werhane (Eds.), *Business, Science, and Ethics. The Ruffin Series in Business Ethics, Vol. 4* (pp. 93–128). Charlottesville, VA: Society for Business Ethics.
  (2006). Evolutionary psychology, moral heuristics and the law. In G. Gigerenzer & C. Engel (Eds.), *Heuristics and the law* (pp. 181–212). Cambridge, MA: MIT Press.

Cushman, F., Young, L., & Hauser, M.D. (2006). The role of conscious reasoning and intuition in moral judgment. Testing three principles of harm. *Psychological Science*, 17, 1082–1089.

Dhami, M.K., & Ayton, P. (2001). Bailing and jailing the fast and frugal way. *Journal of Behavioral Decision Making*, 14, 141–168.

Epstein, H. (2007). Getting away with murder. *The New York Review of Books, 54,* No. 12 (July 19), 38–40.
Farah, M. J. (2005). Neuroethics: the practical and the philosophical. *Trends in Cognitive Sciences, 9,* 34–40.
Foot, P. (1978), The problem of abortion and the doctrine of the double effect. In *Virtues and Vices.* Oxford, UK: Basil Blackwell, (2005).
Freud, S. (1923/1961). *The ego and the id.* In J. Strachey (Ed.), *The standard edition of the complete psychological works of Sigmund Freud, Vol. 19* (pp. 1–66). New York: Basic Books.
Gazzaniga, M. (2005). *The ethical brain.* New York: The Dana Press.
Gigerenzer, G. (2000). *Adaptive thinking: Rationality in the real world.* New York: Oxford University Press.
 (2008). Moral Intuition = Fast and Frugal Heuristics? In W. Sinnott-Armstrong (Ed.), *Moral Psychology. Vol. 2: The cognitive science of morality: Intuition and diversity* (pp. 1–26). Cambridge, MA: MIT Press.
Gigerenzer, G., & Selten, R. (Eds.). (2001). *Bounded rationality: The adaptive toolbox.* Cambridge, MA: MIT Press.
Gigerenzer, G., & Todd, P. M. (1999). *Simple heuristics that make us smart.* New York: Oxford University Press.
Glannon, W. (Ed.) (2007). *Defining right and wrong in brain science: Essential readings in neuroethics.* New York: The Dana Press.
Greene, J. D. (2008). The secret joke of Kant's soul. In W. Sinnott-Armstrong (Ed.), *Moral psychology. Vol. 3, The neuroscience of morality: Emotions, brain disorders, and development* (pp. 35–79). Cambridge, MA: MIT Press.
Greene, J. D., Sommerville, R. B., Nystrom, L. E., Darley, J. M., & Cohen, J. D. (2001). An fMRI investigation of emotional engagement in moral judgment. *Science, 293,* 2105–2108.
Haidt, J. (2001). The emotional dog and its rational tail: A social intuitionist approach to moral judgment. *Psychological Review, 108,* 814–834.
 (2007). The new synthesis in moral psychology. *Science, 316,* 998–1002.
Haidt, J., & Bjorklund, F. (2008). Social intuitionists answer six questions about moral psychology. In W. Sinnott-Armstrong (Ed.), *Moral psychology. Vol. 2: The cognitive science of morality: Intuition and diversity* (pp. 181–218). Cambridge, MA: MIT Press.
 (2008b). Social intuitionists reason, in conversation. In W. Sinnott-Armstrong (Ed.), *Moral psychology. Vol. 2: The cognitive science of morality: Intuition and diversity* (pp. 241–254). Cambridge, MA: MIT Press.
Haidt, J., & Graham, J. (2007). When morality opposes justice: Conservatives have moral intuitions that liberals may not recognize. *Social Justice Research, 20,* 98–116.
Haidt, J., & Joseph, C. (2008). The moral mind: How five sets of innate intuitions guide the development of many culture-specific virtues, and perhaps even modules. In P. Carruthers, S. Laurence, & S. Stich (Eds.) *The innate mind. Vol. 3. Foundations and the future* (pp. 367–391). Oxford, UK: Oxford University Press.
Hauser, M. D. (2006). *Moral minds: How nature designed our universal sense of right and wrong.* New York: Ecco Press.

Hauser, M. D., Young, L., & Cushman, F. (2008). Reviving Rawls's linguistic analogy. Operative principles and the causal structure of moral actions. In W. Sinnott-Armstrong (Ed.), *Moral psychology. Vol. 2: The cognitive science of morality: Intuition and diversity* (pp. 107–144). Cambridge, MA: MIT Press.

Healy, D. (2006). *The unhealthy relationship between the pharmaceutical industry and depression.* New York: New York University Press.

Kohlberg, L. (1984). *Essays on moral development. Vol. 2, The psychology of moral development: The nature and validity of moral stages.* San Francisco: Harper & Row.

Lapsley, D. K., & Narvaez, D. (2005). The psychological foundations of everyday morality and moral expertise. In D. K. Lapsley & F. C. Power (Eds.), *Character psychology and character education* (pp. 140–165). Notre Dame, IN: University of Notre Dame Press.

Leitenberg, M. (2006). *Deaths in wars and conflicts in the 20th century.* Ithaca, NY: Cornell University, Peace Studies Program, Occasional Paper No. 29.

Luria, A. R. (2005). *The autobiography of Alexander Luria: A dialogue with the making of mind.* Mahwah, NJ: Lawrence Erlbaum Associates.

Mallon, R. (2008). Reviving Rawls's linguistic analogy inside and out. In W. Sinnott-Armstrong (Ed.), *Moral psychology. Vol. 2: The cognitive science of morality: Intuition and diversity* (pp. 145–156). Cambridge, MA: MIT Press.

Mikhail, J. (2007). Universal moral grammar: Theory, evidence, and the future. *Trends in cognitive sciences, 11,* 143–152.

Moll, J., Zahn, R., de Oliveira-Souza, R., Krueger, F., & Grafman, J. (2005). The neural basis of human moral cognition. *Nature Reviews Neuroscience, 6,* 799–809.

Narvaez, D. (2008). The social intuitionist model and some counter-intuitions. In W. Sinnott-Armstrong (Ed.), *Moral psychology. Vol. 2: The cognitive science of morality: Intuition and diversity* (pp. 233–240). Cambridge, MA: MIT Press.

Narvaez, D., & Lapsley, D. K. (2004). A social-cognitive approach to the moral personality. In D. K. Lapsley & D. Narvaez (Eds.), *Moral development, self, and identity* (pp. 189–212). Mahwah, NJ: Lawrence Erlbaum Associates.

Neiman, S. (2002). *Evil in modern thought. An alternative history of philosophy.* Princeton, NJ: Princeton University Press.

Nietzsche, F. (1886/1966). *Beyond good and evil,* translated by Walter Kaufmann, New York: Random House.

Odier, C. (1943). *Les deux sources consciente et inconsciente de la vie morale.* Neuchâtel, Switzerland: Éditions de la Baconnière.

Pizarro, D. A., & Bloom, P. (2003). The intelligence of the moral intuitions: Comments on Haidt (2001). *Psychological Review, 110,* 193–196.

Prinz, J. J. (2008). Resisting the linguistic analogy. A commentary on Hauser, Young, and Cushman. In W. Sinnott-Armstrong (Ed.), *Moral psychology. Vol. 2: The cognitive science of morality: Intuition and diversity* (pp. 157–170). Cambridge, MA: MIT Press.

Pritchard, M. S. (1999). Kohlbergian contributions to educational programs for the moral development of professionals. *Educational Psychology Review, 11,* 395–409.

Rest, J., & Narvaez, D. (Eds.). (1994). *Moral development in the profession: Psychology and applied ethics*. Hillsdale, NJ: Lawrence Erlbaum Associates.

Rest, J., Narvaez, D., Bebeau, M. J., & Thoma S. J. (1999). *Postconventional moral thinking. A neo-Kohlbergian approach*. Mahwah, NJ: Lawrence Erlbaum Associates.

Rorty, R. (2006). Born to be good. Review of Marc Hauser "Moral Minds." *The New York Times, Science Section* (August 27).

Rothman, D. J. (2000). The shame of medical research. *The New York Review of Books, 47*, No. 19 (November 30).

Saltzstein, H. D., & Kasachkoff, T. (2004). Haidt's moral intuitionist theory: A psychological and philosophical critique. *Review of General Psychology, 8*, 273–282.

Sapolsky, R. M. (2001). *A primate's memoir: A neuroscientist's unconventional life among the baboons*. New York: Simon & Schuster.

Schulkin, J. (2000). *Roots of social sensibility*. Cambridge, MA: MIT Press.

Sennett, R. (1998). *The corrosion of character: The personal consequences of work in the new capitalism*. New York: Norton.

——— (2007). *The culture of the new capitalism*. Yale University Press.

Singer, P. (2006). Morality, reason, and the rights of animals. In F. de Waal, S. Macedo, & J. Ober (Eds.), *Primates and philosophers:: How morality evolved* (pp. 140–160). Princeton, NJ: Princeton University Press.

Stephens, J. (2000). The body hunters. Where profits and lives hang in balance (A six-part series). *The Washington Post* (December 17).

Sunstein, C. R. (2005). Moral heuristics. *Behavioral and Brain Sciences, 28*, 531–543.

——— (2008). Fast, frugal, and (sometimes) wrong. In W. Sinnott-Armstrong (Ed.), *Moral psychology. Vol. 2: The cognitive science of morality: Intuition and diversity* (pp. 27–30). Cambridge, MA: MIT Press.

Thomson, J. J. (1985). The Trolley Problem, *Yale Law Journal, 94*, 1395–1415.

Turiel, E. (1974). Conflict and transition in adolescent moral development. *Child Development, 45*, 14–29.

Waal, F. B. M. de (1989). *Peacemaking among primates*. Cambridge, MA: Harvard University Press.

——— (1996). *Good natured:: The origins of right and wrong in humans and other animals*. Cambridge, MA: Harvard University Press.

——— (2006). *Primates and philosophers: How morality evolved*. Princeton, NJ: Princeton University Press.

Wade, N. (2007). Scientist finds the beginnings of morality in primate behavior. *The New York Times, 139* (March 20).

Walker, L. J. (1983). Sources of cognitive conflicts for stage transitions in moral development. *Developmental Psychology, 19*, 103–110.

——— (1986). Cognitive processes in moral development. In G. L. Sapp (Ed.), *Handbook of moral development: Models, processes, techniques, and research* (pp. 109–145). Birmingham, AL: Religious Education Press.

Wilson, E. O. (1979). *On human nature*. Cambridge, MA: Harvard University Press.

Wright, R. (1994). *The moral animal. Evolutionary psychology and everyday life.* New York: Pantheon Books.
   (2006). The uses of anthropomorphism. In F. de Waal, S. Macedo, & J. Ober (Eds.), *Primates and philosophers: How morality evolved* (pp. 83–97). Princeton, NJ: Princeton University Press.

19

Moral Personality: Themes, Questions, Futures

DARCIA NARVAEZ AND DANIEL K. LAPSLEY

In this final chapter we reflect on some of the themes that resonate throughout the volume, but also raise some enduring questions for the field of moral personality, and some possible future lines of research.

THEMES

A primary theme of the volume is that traditional ways of carving up the disciplines is no longer a productive way to investigate moral personality. There is something about the rhythm of science that seeks integrative frameworks, and there is now a palpable movement toward engaging broader perspectives that cross traditional disciplinary boundaries. The disjunction between trait dispositional and social-cognitive approaches to personality, for example, no longer seems forbidding. A second example is McAdams' new Big Five framework that was designed to provide a unifying framework to personality science, but ends up rich with implications for lifespan development research as well, as several chapters attest in the present volume. There is a convergence of meta-theoretical perspectives on person-context transactions that unify the work of personality, social, and developmental researchers. And within developmental science there is a blueprint for merging social and cognitive developmental research in a way that makes contact with the study of social cognition in adults. The study of moral personality, then, is a topic that is inherently interdisciplinary, much in the way that cognitive science necessarily brings together scholars from many fields of study.

A second theme is that the foundations of the moral self are laid early in development. By the second birthday, and certainly as toddlers, an increasing dispositional stability emerges that has significance for prosocial behavior and moral development. With this stability comes an increasing appreciation of perspectives, an awareness of behavioral norms, a sense of obligation, duty, and conscience that imbue the personality with its moral qualities. Much of this was missed, or dismissed, when developmental science was preoccupied with reasoning and dilemma solving. But developmental research across a wide front of topics illustrates just how richly moral is the fabric of early childhood.

The third theme is that the study of moral personality development requires a more expansive view of the moral domain. For example, the vast literatures on temperament, attachment, the development of self-regulation and of event representations – to name four examples – are now revealing how these acquisitions have implications for moral and prosocial functioning. Research on trait dispositions have charted long-term relationships with numerous outcome variables, but often those that reflect adaptation in the breech – with conduct problems or psychopathology, or with broad indices of adaptation, are only rarely linked with distinctly prosocial outcomes.

The fourth theme is that context and culture matter in any account of moral personality. The display of dispositional tendencies is moderated by environmental contexts, from childrearing practices to neighborhood effects to work setting demands. The dispositional view of traits as if-then contingencies is a useful heuristic for conceptualizing the dynamic transaction between personal and contextual variables, and calls as much attention to the structure of settings and situations for influencing moral behavior as to the structure of personality. What's more, the present volume highlights broader cultural factors, too, as crucial for understanding moral personalities. Moralities are part of cultures, and cultures provide different narrative options for making sense of our moral vision, and for framing our moral conversations.

QUESTIONS

Of course, a volume that is intended to serve as a seedbed of ideas for an emergent, interdisciplinary field of study cannot wrap things up too neatly. Progressive research programs anticipate novel facts, and generate new hypotheses and questions. And certainly the present volume raises questions. One question concerns just what neuroscience and evolutionary perspectives will tell us about moral personality. Neuroscience and evolutionary psychology are themselves "young and provisional" sciences, and much of the extant research has focused on localizing brain regions during moral decision-making tasks using exotic moral dilemmas. The chapters by Moll and his colleagues, and by Narvaez, point us in promising directions insofar as they alert the field to how deeply integrative are our cognitive and emotional moral response systems, and how varied moral responses are linked to evolved structures of the brain.

A second question concerns how to think about the defining attributes of moral identity. Is moral identity a matter of the self-importance of moral commitments? Does it mean that morality is central, essential, and important to self-understanding? Or does it mean that such notions are chronically accessible? A related question concerns the role of self-consistency as a motivational force for moral action. Some theorists in the present volume endorse such a view, but others wonder if self-consistency is empirically credible or is strictly necessary. Several authors point out the shifting nature of moral identities in their studies. Others postulate multiple identities that vary by context.

This raises several questions. How inclusive is the notion of moral identity? Do only some people have moral identities, based on the centrality of moral concerns to the self? Exemplar research supports such a view when it finds differences in moral concerns between exemplars and controls. But the research on adult moral functioning in social psychology experiments is shaking up the standard account of moral identity. Although the standard account is deontological, the adult studies suggest that individuals are situational utilitarians, modifying their behavior according to a balance sheet or according to what is morally mandated by their convictions in the moment. These findings raise many questions: How stable is a moral identity? Does it shift, as some find, based on priming or other conditions? How many identities does a person have? Or, does moral identity involve a broader swath of what a good life entails, incorporating notions of purity or ingroup security? Does everyone have a moral identity, or only one that varies based on context or "ideo-affective posture" (Tomkins, 1965)?

Related to the question of defining features is the question of whether moral identity invariably cashes out in ways that "pay off" – that is, are adaptive, salutary, morally praiseworthy, and the like. Most researchers agree that a committed moral identity provides one a schematic way of appraising the interpersonal landscape. Yet we have seen evidence in this volume that morally committed ways of viewing the world can harden into ideology, be a double-edged sword, or be trumped by situational variables. That the work of moral identity interacts with situational variables is not itself a theoretical embarrassment of any kind. Indeed, it is expected, given the orienting frameworks noted earlier. Yet it does invite reflection as to when one should be credited with having a moral identity, in what areas of one's life, and under what conditions.

A further question concerns whether it makes sense to study particular virtues in isolation. Kohlberg's research team focused on justice as a kind of master virtue, so there is certainly precedent for investigating how particular dispositions – gratitude, say, or altruism – play out in the moral life of persons. How particular virtues cohere within the structure of personality as a dimension of individual differences is an interesting empirical question, one that points up the fact that there could be many kinds and varieties of moral personality; that there are many virtues around which to organize dispositional tendencies; and that how these develop, cohere, and relate to the world suggests productive lines of research.

How much consciousness is required of a moral personality? Does moral identity entail an approach to the moral life that is reflective, effortful, and deliberative – as something consuming attentional resources? Or is there automaticity to the work of moral identity? Is it intuitive or prereflective in any way? The traditional view of moral identity, following foundational sources in ethical theory (e.g., Harry Frankfurt and Charles Taylor), hold out for reflectiveness as the defining hallmark of the mature moral person. Others are not so sure if this is strictly required. Perspectives guided by findings in the cognitive and social-cognitive literatures are open to dual processing models that allow for the possibility of intuitive, heuristic, automatic behavior, as well as the more deliberative kind. But the question of how much and what kind of cognitive resources are required for moral self-identity, character, and personality is one that is not going away any time soon.

Perhaps the most fundamental question begged by the entire volume, and one that will take some time to answer, is whether it is even sensible to talk about moral personality, or moral traits, or moral character, or moral self-identity. What does "moral" add to our understanding of psychological processes? Of decision making? Of personality structure? What does *moral* character add to our understanding of character? Are there traits, and then another class of things called *moral* traits? When is a personality a *moral* personality? If it is said that one has a moral identity when moral notions are central to one's self-definition, is it clear just what the notion of centrality points to? Our hunch is that even deeply motivated moral action – or pervasively moral ways of being-in-the-world – is driven by clusters of dispositional tendencies that could just as well drive other ways of being-in-the-world. Questions of this sort will require robust collaboration with philosophers of moral psychology.

FUTURES

We close by considering some possible future lines of research for the field of moral personality. The juxtaposition of different research paradigms often shakes out in many new research ideas. It is not always possible to see the future clearly, and it would be presumptuous to articulate a research agenda that is too detailed and too prescriptive. In our view, what is needed is theoretical and methodological pluralism. Still, the present volume suggests some fruitful new lines of research.

One suggestion is to attend to initial life conditions, developmental constraints, and opportunities as these are experienced in sensitive periods. A moral identity presumably has work to do in the way the personality is organized and functions. It is assumed to influence the negotiation and construction of experiences across the life course. Attachment and its neurobiological imprints appear to influence moral personality in terms of fostering agreeableness and conscience. Other elements of the environment of evolutionary adaptedness may also be relevant to cultivating moral personality. At the very least, there appear to be sensitive periods in development (e.g., first year of life for emotion regulation and motivation; first five years for social functioning; early adolescence for social functioning; late adolescence for executive functions). Conscience development is related to responsive parenting in the early years whereas community service during adolescence fosters moral identity and civic engagement in adolescence. Mapping the sensitive periods for different elements of the moral personality, and how these are influenced by contextual factors, may help guide family, school-based, and community interventions.

Erikson's lifespan theory of development proved useful in framing research on the role of moral identity and the life tasks of generativity in middle adulthood. Indeed, Pratt and his colleagues make the interesting point that perhaps generativity itself is a nascent developmental variable that has manifestations in earlier periods of the lifespan, and otherwise resonates throughout the lifespan much the way self-identity issues do. We might push this idea further and ask: What then about other psychosocial tasks, such as trust, autonomy, and initiative? How are these tasks experienced across the lifespan, and how does their articulation influence one's moral orientation? For example, built from caregiver responsiveness, trust appears to have a strong influence on early conscience development, supporting compliance with adult directives and prosocial behavior in childhood. How does this extend across the lifespan? Similar research questions attend other psychosocial tasks.

There is one Eriksonian viewpoint that has never been tested. This concerns his claim that each successful resolution of developmental challenges in the psychosocial stage sequence entails the cultivation of a characteristic virtue. One does not have to buy the whole Eriksonian meta-theory in order to wonder if there is structure and sequence to the acquisition of virtues; or if, and how, such developmentally crucial virtues can be assessed. Wedding positive psychology's emphasis on strengths and virtues (Peterson & Seligman, 2003) with a developmental perspective generally seems highly promising.

In recent writings, William Damon (2008) has written on "youth purpose" as an organizing construct in the study of positive youth development. Youth purpose is understood as a stable and generalized intention to accomplish something that is meaningful to the self, and that leads to productive engagement with some aspect of the world beyond the self. The search for self-meaning that is also self-transcendent is a strongly ethical enterprise that goes to the heart of what it means to live well the life that is good for one to live. Indeed, for Aristotle, the highest of human purposes involves *eudaimonia*, where flourishing has a pronounced ethical dimension. How does purpose organize self-identity and the moral dimensions of personality? This invites broader investigations about how moral personality maps into the emerging field of positive youth development, positive psychology, and the nature of well-being in adulthood.

Personality research, and moral personality research more so, has hardly begun to examine the effects of mediated technology on personality development. Youth are spending an increasing amount of time interacting through technological (e.g., text messaging) and virtual means (e.g., Second Life), and not necessarily to their intellectual benefit (Bauerlein, 2008). How do these experiences, and the lack of the face-to-face experiences they replace, influence identity? We know that young people take up different identities online and in electronic role games. Are there measurable effects of these activities on moral identity?

Augusto Blasi's chapter advocates an expansion of the parameters for research into moral functioning to include the public sphere, more specifically, the challenges adults face in the workplace. He reflects on the narrowness of everyday adult moral functioning, which is typically focused on family and private issues, and less thoughtful about broader social issues. He urges researchers to broaden their views of moral functioning to emphasize the self's coordination of multiple elements critical for citizenship and adult responsibilities. Adults need skills of reflection; intuition will not do (and he has much to say against the "intuitions as normal" perspective; also see Narvaez, 2009). Examining the landscape of adult functioning and how to foster it is an area ripe for study.

Allied with Blasi's suggestion to examine mature moral functioning is a plea to expand the study of moral personality beyond moral exemplars in highly restricted domains of social life (e.g., volunteer behavior). What about "moral collapse"? What about moral functioning in the breech? Or research on the structure and malleability of vices? Moreover, it may be useful to study the elements of moral personality in such domains as moral sensitivity, focus, and action skills.

Although Casebeer (2005) and Churchland (1998) have argued that moral personality understood in terms of virtue ethics is the most neurobiologically plausible moral theory, none of our authors directly incorporated virtue theory into their work. Virtues are cultivated by particular life experiences. What are they? How do people transform themselves into virtuous agents? How do ordinary people become morally focused, if not moral exemplars? Elsewhere, Bill Puka (2006 Symposium talk) suggested that the acquisition of virtues is a practical affair – they are "experiments in truth," that can be scientifically studied, and for whose impediments interventions can be designed.

Progress on social phenomena will also require theoretical innovation in understanding the brain's distinctly biological form of functioning, which is anchored by emotions, needs, drives, and the instinct for survival. As of yet, the basic neural principles governing the relation of these basic functions to planning, judgment, and moral decision making are barely understood. Moll et al. and Narvaez make suggestions for how to bridge the gaps between general biological aspects of human functioning and moral functioning. More recent research on the epigenome (environmental effects on gene expression) indicates that the environment plays a leading role in determining how genes function in physiology and personality. For example, during gestation the fetus interprets "environmental information to predict aspects of its future environment and thus resets its developmental trajectories to optimise its future performance ... in adult life" (Gluckman & Hanson, 2004, p. 23). No doubt there are social and morally relevant impacts to be examined.

Last but perhaps most important, the question of assessment, particularly developmental assessment, will play a crucial role in developing a field of moral personality. We generally lack well-attested assessments of many core constructs in the field. One reason that Kohlberg's stage theory was so productive and so influential was because highly regarded assessments of moral reasoning were available to generate research. Nothing like that exists with respect to moral personality constructs, and nothing can stop the momentum of research more surely than the absence of adequate measurement strategies.

REFERENCES

Bauerlein, M. (2008). *The dumbest generation: How the digital age stupefies young Americans and jeopardizes our future.* New York: Tarcher/Penguin.

Blasi, A. (this volume). Moral reasoning and the moral functioning of mature adults. In D. Narvaez & D. K. Lapsley. (Eds.) *Personality, identity, and character explorations in moral psychology* (pp. 396–440). New York: Cambridge University Press.

Casebeer (2005). *Natural ethical facts.* Cambridge, MA: MIT Press.

Churchland, P. (1998). Toward a cognitive neurobiology of the emotions. *Topoi, 17,* 83–96.

Damon, W. (2008) *The path to purpose: Helping our children find the calling in life.* New York: The Free Press.

Gluckman, P. D., & Hanson, M. A. (2004). Living with the past: Evolution, development, and patterns of disease. *Science, 305,* 1733–1736.

McAdams, D. (this volume). The moral personality. In D. Narvaez & D. K. Lapsley. (Eds.) *Personality, identity, and character explorations in moral psychology* (pp. 11–29). New York: Cambridge University Press.

Moll, J., de Oliveira-Souza, R., & Zahn, R. (this volume). Neuroscience and morality: Moral judgments, sentiments and values. In D. Narvaez & D. K. Lapsley. (Eds.) *Personality, identity, and character explorations in moral psychology* (pp. 106–135). New York: Cambridge University Press.

Narvaez, D. (this volume). Triune ethics theory and moral personality. In D. Narvaez & D. Lapsley (Eds.), *Personality, identity, and character explorations in moral psychology* (pp. 136–158). New York: Cambridge University Press.

(2009). The fatal attraction of truthiness and the importance of mature moral functioning. Manuscript under review.

Peterson, C., & Seligman, M. (2004). *Character strengths and virtues: A handbook and classification.* New York: American Psychological Association and Oxford University Press.

Tomkins, S. (1965). Affect and the psychology of knowledge. In S. S. Tomkins & C. E. Izard (Eds.), *Affect, cognition, and personality* (pp. 72–97). New York: Springer.

AUTHOR INDEX

Adler, M., 317
Alger, H., 68
Allport, G., 11–12
Anscombe, E., 56–57
Aristotle, 52, 58, 446

Bandura, A., 35, 149
Bartlett, M., 261
Batson, C. D., 277
Blasi, A., 31, 39–45, 197, 202, 319, 375, 376, 380, 446
Block, J., 191
Bloom, P., 414
Blum, L., 59
Boyd, R., 83

Camus, A., 96
Carlo, G., 319
Casebeer, W., 447
Chomsky, N., 407
Churchland, P., 447
Cialdini, R., 278
Cicero, 257
Colby, A., 21, 298, 319
Confucius, 59
Cosmides, L., 419
Cotterill, R., 147

Damon, W., 21, 298, 319, 446
Darwin, C., 145, 399
DeSteno, D., 261
de Waal, F., 259, 401, 402, 411

Dewey, J., 56
Doris, J., 55

Eisenberg, N., 194, 198
Erikson, E., 18–19, 214, 295, 297, 298, 312–313, 445

Foucault, M., 87
Freud, S., 400
Fry, D., 141

Gazzaniga, M., 402
Gigerenzer, G., 405–406, 409, 419
Greene, J., 115

Haidt, J., 14, 409–419
Hardy, S., 319
Harman, G., 55
Hart, D., 298–299, 319
Hartshorne, H., 34
Hauser, M., 403, 407–409
Heine, S., 41

Jefferson, T., 396

Kant, I., 59, 257, 328
Kagan, J., 168
Killen, M., 170
Kochanska, G., 174–176, 199–200
Koenigs, M., 116
Kohlberg, L., 34, 161, 185, 232, 281, 299, 308, 420, 431

449

Konner, M., 146
Kuhl, J., 44–45
Kymlicka, W., 89

Lakoff, G., 23, 357
Lapsley, D., 18, 201, 203, 346, 356, 377, 378, 391
Lewin, K., 188
Locke, J., 71, 73, 74
Loevinger, J., 15
Luther, M., 319

MacIntyre, A., 20
MacLean, P., 136, 145, 146
Mahmood, S., 87
May, M., 34
McAdams, D., 146, 148, 194, 198, 206, 216, 237, 238, 241, 242, 246, 247, 296, 299, 313
McCullough, M., 262, 264
Mencius, 59
Mill, J. S., 59
Miller, J., 41
Mischel, W., 34
Moll, J., 403
Mozi, 59
Murdoch, I., 57, 59

Narvaez, D., 18, 201, 203, 346, 356, 377, 378, 391, 414, 416, 417
Nicholas, C., 86
Nietzsche, F., 400
Nisan, M., 348
Nucci, L., 34

Panksepp, J., 136–137
Piaget, J., 161, 162, 418, 420
Pizarro, D., 414
Puka, B., 447

Rawls, J., 99
Rest, J., 30, 379, 431
Richerson, P., 83

Saltzstein, H., 414
Sandel, M., 99
Schore, A., 137, 144, 145
Seneca, 257
Simmel, G.
Singer, P., 402
Skitka, L., 31
Sperber, D., 86
Stich, S., 55

Taylor, C., 99
Tomasello, M., 173
Tompkins, S., 141
Tooby, J., 419
Tsang, J., 261–262

Walker, L., 15, 21, 146, 198, 215, 281, 299, 343, 356
Warneken, F., 173
Watkins, P. C., 262, 264
Weil, S., 59, 144
Whitehead, A. N., 57
Wittgenstein, L., 90
Wong, D., 59
Worthman, C., 92

SUBJECT INDEX

Abortion, 356, 362, 364, 371
Adaptation, 11, 13, 120, 123, 145
Adolescents, 146, 151, 191, 193, 195, 198, 214, 217–220, 220–228
Adults, 424–436
Agency, 430, 434
   Moral, 404, 423
   Rational moral, 185
Agreeableness, 15, 16, 18, 23–24, 25, 192, 193, 194, 195, 196, 198, 264, 265, 282, 283, 285
Altruism, 173, 257, 262, 271–289
   Evolutionary basis, 275–277
Antisocial behavior, 331, 335
Aretaic judgments, 185
Attachment, 118, 119–122
   Extended attachment, 121, 145
   Relation to moral exemplarity, 244, 249
   Security, 238
Authenticity, 327
Authority independence, 359, 360, 366–370
Autobiographical reasoning, 20

Bag of virtues, 232
Benevolence, 328, 330
Biology, *see* Neurobiology
Brain, 106–127
   Cortical, 119
   Limbic system, 115–116
   Orbitofrontal cortex (OFC), 123, 148

Prefrontal cortex (PFC) and related structures, 114–115, 116, 117–118, 120–121, 125, 147, 148, 276
   Central executive, 114
   R-complex (extrapyramidal action nervous system), 143
Buddhism, 102

Camden Sports Teaching Adolescents Responsibility and Resiliency (STARR), 227–228
Capital punishment, 361, 364
Categorical imperative, 328
Character, *see* Personality, Dispositional traits
Character strength, 327
Characteristic adaptations, *see* Personality, Characteristic adaptations
Charitable behavior, 389
Cheating, 316, 389
Child labor, 359
Child saturation, 222, 224, 225
Childhood distress, 144
Childrearing, 140, 145–146, 152
Circumcision, female, 359
Cognitive science, 399–419
Communitarianism, 80
Community service, 228
   see also Volunteering
Compassion, *see* Empathy
Conflict management, 363–366
Confucianism, 94, 102

Conscience, 174–178, 288–289
Conscientiousness, 15, 199–200
Contingencies of Self-Worth scale, 346
Cosmopolitanism, 88–89, 95
Culture, 13, 79, 85–99, 121, 124, 125, 148, 442
  As conversation, 96–101
  Hybridity, 95
  Morality as cultural invention, 82–85
  Organizational, 390
  Resistance, 87–88
  Thick concept, 86–87
  Thin concept, 86
Cultural norms, *see* Norms
Cultural transmission, 98

Daoism, 94, 102
Deliberation, *see* Moral reasoning
Development
  of conscience, 199–200
  of obligation, 169–171
  of understanding intention, 169–171
  social cognitive, 200–205
Disgust, 123, 384
Disposition, 60–64, 192–197, 198–200
  Grateful, 263
  Prosocial, 285, 287
  Traits, *see* Personality, Dispositional traits
Diversity, 79–104
Dogmatism, 323
Duty, 81

Early childhood, 137, 142, 145–146, 148, 160–179, 442, 445
Ego resiliency, 191–192
Elian Gonzalez case, 368–369
Emotions, 136–137, 163–164
  Moral emotions, 216–217
Empathy, 172, 260, 278–279
Environment of evolutionary adaptedness, 12, 138–140, 145, 152
Epigenetics, 296, 312, 447
Ethic, 94, 100
  Engagement, 138, 139, 142, 145–146, 149
  Imagination, 138, 139, 142, 146–149
  Security, 137, 139, 142, 143–145, 149, 150
Ethical brain, 403
Ethology, 400–405
Eudaimonia, 52–53
Evil, 144
Evolution, 14, 82–83, 136–137, 274–277, 400–405
Executive function
Exemplar, moral, 202, 215, 232–253, 271, 280, 298–299, 319, 326, 329, 341, 343–344, 356, 447
  Brave, 236
  Caring, 236
  Folk conceptions, 235
Expertise, moral, 203, 204

Faith, 328
Fight-or-flight response, 143
  Also see Stress hormones
Free will, Free won't, 147

Gay marriage, 356, 371
Generativity, 17, 295–313, 445
Generosity, 258
Genes, 13, 137
Genetic similarity hypothesis, 275
Gratitude, 256–269
Gratitude Questionnaire, 264
Gratitude, Resentment, and Appreciation Test, 264
Gratitude Toward God scale, 264
Guilt, 172, 260

Honor, 327
Hormones, *see* Neurobiology

Identity, 18–19, 42–45, 296
  Development, 298
  Material, 383
  Moral, 186, 205–207, 214–228, 274, 279–282, 298–313, 317, 319, 320, 323, 329, 345, 356, 375–391, 443, 445
  Business, 389–390
  Internalization, 345, 378, 388
  Moderation, 388

Subject Index   453

Narrative, 19–23, 295, 301
   Personal fable, 20
   Practical identity, 85
   Salience, 387
   Self-importance, see Moral self, importance
   Self-perception, 390
   Sources, 215–218
   Symbolization, 346, 378, 388
Ideology
   Ethical, 316–337
   Expedient, 316–337
   Principled ethical, 316–321, 322–337
Imitation, 161, 162
Impartiality, 401–402
Individualism, 80–81
Information processing, 195, 205, 377–379, 384
Ingroup, 137–138, 139, 142, 143
Institutions, 220
Integrity, 197, 317–318, 320–322, 376
Integrity Scale, 322
Intention, 169–171
Intolerance, 360–363
Intuition, see Moral intuition

Judgment-action gap, 233

Knowledge accessibility, see Schema, Accessibility

Liberalism, 99–100
Life review narrative, 238, 239
Limbic resonance, 145
Loyola Generativity Scale (LGS), 296, 302, 309

Machiavellianism, 329, 331
Mature moral functioning, see Personality, Moral, Maturity
Memory, 203–204
Metaphysics, see Narrative, Metaphysic thesis
Moral action, see Moral components
Moral affect, 171–172
   Also see Empathy, Shame, Guilt
Moral ambivalence, 80–82, 150

Moral balance model, 348–349
Moral barometer, 260
Moral centrality, 342, 345
Moral chronicity, see Schema, Moral Chronicity
Moral cognition, 137, 250, 251
   Cortico-limbic integration model, 115
Moral condemnation, 330
Moral commitment, 320
Moral compensation, 341, 348
Moral components
   Action, 250–251
      Opportunities, 216–218
   Judgment, see Moral reasoning
   Motivation, 118–119, 260, 261, 262, 298, 310, 341
   Sensitivity, 21, 112, 143, 144, 162, 164, 246, 277
Moral conviction, 357, 358–363
   Integrated theory of moral conviction (ITMC), 358–360
Moral courage, 304, 305–306, 310
Moral credentials, 341, 348–350
Moral desert, 54, 66, 69–71
Moral desire, 376
Moral dialect, 99
Moral dilemma, 115
Moral disengagement, 331, 334, 380, 381, 388
Moral diversity, 363
Moral dumbfounding, 412–413, 414
Moral education, 152
Moral exemplar, see Exemplar, moral
Moral faculty, 407
Moral heuristics, 405–407, 419, 425
Moral ideal, 344
Moral identity, see Identity, Moral
Moral internalization, 199
Moral integrity, 313
Moral intuition, 397, 407, 408, 409–419, 425
Moral judgment, see Moral reasoning
Moral luck, 71–72
Moral mandate, 358, 365, 370–371
Moral motivation, see Moral components
Moral necessity, 401
Moral norms, 83

Moral personality, *see* Personality, Moral
Moral point of view, 185
Moral principles, 332
Moral prototype, *see* Prototype theory
Moral reasoning, 250, 299, 308, 379, 411–436
  Conventional, 162
  Postconventional, 15, 431
  Preconventional, 162
Moral reflection, 398, 411–436
Moral relativism, 80
Moral resentment, 341–348, 350
Moral responsibility, 398, 423, 433
Moral schema, *see* Schema, moral
Moral self, 172–174, 298, 310, 341, 441–442
  Moral self-importance, 345–346, 347, 375, 377, 378, 387, 443
  Moral self-regard, 347, 348, 351
  Moral self-schema, 377
  Self model of moral functioning, 375
Moral sense, 145
  Emerging, 168, 169
Moral sensitivity, *see* Moral Components
Moral sentiments, 67, 106–127
Moral steadfastness, 311
Moral values, 89, 97, 123, 124–126
Motivated cognition, 137
Mutually responsive orientation, 199

Narcissism, 327, 335
Narrative, 65–76
  Accomplishment and desert, 69–72, 73
  Contamination, 238, 247
  Free agency, 72–73
  Generative, 297
  Identity, 19, *see also* Identity
  Life, 12, 19, 147–148, 299, 309–310
  Master narratives, 54, 67–76
  Metaphysic thesis, 54, 65
  Redemption, 21, 238, 247–248, 249
  Self, 238
National Educational Longitudinal Study (NELS:88), 224
National Household Educational Survey of 1999 (NHES-99), 223
National Longitudinal Study of Adolescent Health (ADD Health), 220

National Longitudinal Survey of Youth (NLSY), 219
Naturalism, 79, 82
Negative state relief model, 278
Neurobiology, 399–405
  Hypothalamic pituitary adrenal axis, 275
  Mirror neurons, 276
  Hormones
    Neuropeptides (e.g., Oxytocin), 119–120, 122, 140, 275
    Stress, 138
Neuroethics, 403
Neuroscience, *see* Brain
Nichomachean Ethics (see also Aristotle), 52
Norms, 383, *also see* Moral nomis
Nurturant caregiver morality, 23

Obligation, 169–171
Ontology, 53
Openness to experience, 15
Optimism, 242–243
Outgroups, 386

Parent-child relationships, 174–176
Parental practices, 176–177
  Socialization, 175, 176
Personal fable, 20
Personality, 11–13, 32–34
  Aristotelian, 187
  Characteristic adaptations, 12, 16–18, 24, 237
  Consistency, 34, 36–37
  Dispositional traits (*also see* Disposition, Trait), 12–16, 23, 141, 237
  Dominance, 237
  Five-factor theory (*also see* Agreeableness, Conscientiousness, Openness to experience), 13–16, 32–33, 188, 189–191, 193, 282, 321, 329
  Galilean, 188–189, 190–191
  Knowledge-and-Appraisal Personality Architecture (KAPA), 35–39
  Life narratives, 24–25, 237, 240–245, 246, *also see* Narratives

Mentor, influence of, 249
Moral, 13–25, 141, 215, 232–253, 342–345
    Maturity, 151, 396–436
    Typology, 237
    New Big-Five (McAdams), 12, 441
    Nurturance, 237
    Personal Strivings, 237, 239
    Social cognitive theory, 37–45, 186, 188, 201–207, 375–390
    Structure, 32
    Trauma, 243
    Two disciplines, 187–189
    Types, 191, 206, 219–220
Personality-Systems Interaction Theory (PSI), 44
Positive youth development, 446
Postconventional thinking, *see* Moral reasoning
Poverty, 218–228
Preschoolers, 160–163, 169–171, 172–173, 174–177
Primatology, 400–405
Prosocial behavior, 198–199, 260, 262, 267–268, 272–274, 300, 309
Prototype theory, 90–91
    Moral, 343, 344–345, 346, 347, 378
Psychological realism, 57
Public sphere, 426–428, 431–433
Purpose, 446

Rationalism, 420
Reasoning, 147, *also see* Moral reasoning
    Autobiographical, 20
Reciprocal altruism hypothesis, 275
Reciprocity, 259–260, 263
Redemption narrative, *see* Narrative, Redemption
Religiosity, 328
    Extrinsic, 328
    Intrinsic, 328
Role models, 384–385

Schema
    Accessibility, 201, 377
    Moral, 316–317, 356
    Automaticity, 398
    Chronicity, 18, 201, 203, 346, 356, 377, 378, 391
Self
    Moral, *see* Moral self
    Self-concept
        Moral, 344, 347
        Working self concept, 379, 385
    Self-consistency, 40–42, 376, 381, 443
    Self-criticism, 41
    Self-evaluation, 216
    Self-identity, 42, 186
    Self-regulation, 193, 317, 333, 336, 342, 379, 385
    Self-schemas, 35, 377
    Self-system, 319, 332
    Self-worth, 267
Shame, 171, 172, 260
Situation, power of, 141, 149, 150, 382
    Person-situation debate, 189
Social capital, 221
Social cognitive, *see* Personality, Social cognitive theory
Social cooperation, 83–85
Social desirability, 330
Social information processing, 384
Social intuitionism, 202, 409–411
Social referencing, 164–165
Spirituality, 328
Spontaneous trait inferences, 203
Standards, 165–169
Stoics, 60
Stress
    Hormones, *see* Neurobiology
    Poverty, 218–220
Strict-father morality, 23
Subjective well-being, 265–267
Suicide
    Physician-assisted, 356, 359, 367

Temperament, 13, 193–196, 200, 216, 219–220, 276
    Elaboration of, 194
Ten Commandments, 387–388
Theory of mind (ToM), 164
Thoughts and Feelings Questionnaire, 284

Trait, 187, 189, 198–200, *also see* Disposition
Dysregulation, 195
Triangle model of responsibility, 333
Tribalism, 143
Trolley problem, 111, 113, 116, 117, 408
Triune Ethics Theory (TET), *see* Ethic, Engagement/Imagination/Security

Ultimatum game, 117
Universal moral grammar, 407–409
Universalism, 81
Utilitarianism, 117

Values, 11, 18, 23, 24, 30, 39, 44, 106, 107, 137, 143, 145, 146, 160, 161, 163, 174, 175, 176, 199, 217, 220, 224, 225, 280, 345, 350, 363, 427, 429
  Value conflict, 80, 81, 100–103
Varieties of Moral Personality, 55–57
Virtue, 57–65, 257, 268, 320–321, 382
Volition, *see* Willpower
Volunteering, 223, 225, 282–287, 329

War, 427
Willpower, 197, 376
Workplace, 425–426, 427–430

Youth Involvement Inventory (YII), 303

Printed in the United States
By Bookmasters